2013
Year C-I

THE ALMANAC FOR PASTORAL LITURGY

SOURCEBOOK

FOR SUNDAYS, SEASONS, AND WEEKDAYS

Kathy Coffey	Corinna Laughlin	S. Anne Elizabeth Sweet, OCSO
Peggy Eckerdt	Graziano Marcheschi	Paul Turner
J. Philip Horrigan	Biagio Mazza	Denise Simeone
Maureen A. Kelly	Jill Maria Murdy	Vivian E. Williams
John Thomas Lane, SSS	Kristopher W. Seaman	Daniella Zsupan-Jerome

LTP
LITURGY
TRAINING
PUBLICATIONS

Nihil Obstat
Very Reverend Daniel A. Smilanic, JCD
Vicar for Canonical Services
Archdiocese of Chicago
January 12, 2012

Imprimatur
Reverend John F. Canary, STL, DMIN
Vicar General
Archdiocese of Chicago
January 12, 2012

LTP is grateful to the many authors and publishers who have given permission to include their work. LTP is especially grateful for authors of Celebrating *the Lectionary, Foundations for Teaching and Preaching,* and *The Word to Go.* Every effort has been made to determine the ownership of all texts to make proper arrangements for their use. Any oversight that may have occurred, if brought to our attention, will gladly be corrected in future editions.

The introduction for this book includes texts from previous editions of *Sourcebook.* The editor wishes to thank previous authors and editors whose contributions to this book have enabled the compilation of an introduction that best serves our customers.

As a publisher, LTP works toward responsible stewardship of the environment. We printed the text of *Sourcebook for Sundays, Seasons, and Weekdays 2013: The Almanac for Pastoral Liturgy* with soy-based ink on paper that contains 50% less wood fiber than traditional paper in its category. This reduced quantity of wood pulp content benefits the environment by using fewer trees. The wood pulp that was required in the making of this paper was sourced from certified forests, meaning that it was harvested from a managed and re-planted forest. Additionally, this paper was processed using ECF (Elementally Chlorine Free) technologies in order to reduce the release of elemental chlorine (Cl) into the environment.

The printing process used to manufacture this book uses a non-heatset process that significantly reduces emission of volatile organic compounds (VOCs) into the atmosphere.

SOURCEBOOK FOR SUNDAYS, SEASONS, AND WEEKDAYS 2013: THE ALMANAC FOR PASTORAL LITURGY © 2012 Archdiocese of Chicago: Liturgy Training Publications, 3949 South Racine Avenue, Chicago IL 60609; 1-800-933-1800, fax 1-800-933-7094, e-mail: orders@ltp.org. All rights reserved. See our website at www.LTP.org.

Printed in the United States of America.

ISBN 978-1-61671-023-1

SSS13

CONTENTS

INTRODUCTION

Overview of Sourcebook

SOURCEBOOK *for Sundays, Seasons, and Weekdays 2013: The Almanac for Pastoral Liturgy* helps those in parishes, schools, institutions, religious communities, and other Catholic faith communities understand the liturgy and how it transforms our lives. Through the unpacking of liturgical time, the sanctoral cycle, and the various rites, *Sourcebook* provides a context for a Catholic community's life of worship.

Sourcebook provides guidance regarding the various liturgical elements (music, environment, prayers, readings, etc.) so that communities can prepare liturgies rooted in the vision of the Second Vatican Council. The practical suggestions are oriented to assist parishes and other communities to celebrate the liturgy in the best possible way—thoughtfully, deliberately, and with confidence and faith in the God who has claimed us in Baptism and who desires us to worship him in spirit and in truth (see John 4:24).

Sourcebook is organized to help you follow liturgical time in sequence. It begins with Advent, which is the start of the liturgical year, and it continues with Christmas Time. Next begins Ordinary Time, so-named because the Sundays are designated by their ordinal (counted) numbers. *Sourcebook* tags the Sundays in Ordinary Time after Christmas Time and up until Lent as "Ordinary Time during Winter." This is not an official description or designation, but merely a chapter heading *Sourcebook* uses to differentiate between the two parts of Ordinary Time.

Next you will find Lent, followed by the Sacred Paschal Triduum, and then Easter Time. After the Solemnity of Pentecost, Ordinary Time resumes. *Sourcebook* refers to this longer stretch as "Ordinary Time during Summer and Fall." When Ordinary Time concludes, the next liturgical year begins, so this chapter takes us right up to the end of the liturgical year. A supplemental liturgical music preparation sheet and a checklist for those who serve during the Triduum are available online at www.ltp.org/resources. These sheets may be reproduced and distributed to your ministers for free.

Within each of the chapters of *Sourcebook*, you will find two sections: "The Liturgical Time" and "The Calendar." "The Liturgical Time" was formerly called "The Seasons." It is organized into several parts:

◆ *The Meaning:* the theological meaning and history of liturgical time

◆ *The Saints:* how the living witness of the saints can deepen and enrich liturgical time

◆ *The Liturgical Books:* what the *Lectionary for Mass*, *The Roman Missal*, and other ritual texts tell us about liturgical time; information particular to the third edition of *The Roman Missal* is under this same category

◆ *The Liturgical Environment*: ideas for the appearance of worship spaces

◆ *The Liturgical Music*: the musical expression of liturgical time and how to enhance it

◆ *Devotions and Sacramentals*: ideas to foster the parish's devotional life while emphasizing the primacy of the liturgy

◆ *Liturgical Ministers*: tips and formational notes for all liturgical ministers

◆ *Children, Youth, and Ritual*: how to form children for liturgies, and additional preparation tips for school Masses

◆ *The Parish and the Home*: how to carry liturgical time from the parish to the domestic Church (at home)

◆ *Mass Texts*: original prayers for the Order of Mass (where options are permitted)

"The Calendar" is a straightforward almanac for each day of the liturgical year. You can look up any day of the year and find basic liturgical information as well as ideas for how to celebrate it. The primary purpose of *Sourcebook*, however, is to help you celebrate Sundays, solemnities, feasts, and all of liturgical time. For this reason, you will find most of the material in "The Calendar" devoted to Sundays, solemnities, and feasts, which include the following four sections:

◆ *Orientation*: what the Church is celebrating on this day and why

◆ *Lectionary for Mass*: an explanation of how the scriptures of the day relate to what is being celebrated

◆ *The Roman Missal*: insights into the prayers and suggestions about options; particular notes are provided for the third edition of the Missal

◆ *Other Ideas*: additional pastoral notes for parishes and families to celebrate the liturgical themes beyond the liturgy itself

About the Authors

◆ Kathy Coffey has won 13 awards from the Catholic Press Association for books such as *Hidden Women of the Gospels* and *Women of Mercy*. Her articles and poetry have appeared in *America*, *U.S. Catholic*, *St. Anthony Messenger*, and *National Catholic Reporter*. She is the mother of four and lives in Denver, Colorado. She conducts retreats and workshops nationally and internationally. She wrote this year's "The Parish and the Home."

◆ Peggy Eckerdt is currently a Pastoral Associate at Visitation Catholic Church in Kansas City, Missouri. She is responsible for the parish religious education program, including adult faith formation, along with pastoral care and marriage preparation. She holds an MA in Pastoral Ministry from Boston College and a certificate in spiritual direction from the Souljourner Program at Mount St. Scholastica in Atchison, Kansas. Her work, previously published by LTP, has been compiled for many of the seasonal sections regarding "The Meaning" and the Scripture commentaries for the Third, Fourth, and Fifth Sundays of Lent.

◆ J. Philip (Phil) Horrigan is a presbyter of the Archdiocese of Kingston Ontario. He has a BA in Theology (STB) from St. Paul University, Ottawa; a masters degree in Education (MED) from Queens University, Kingston, Ontario; and a graduate degree in Theology (MTH, 1994–95) from the Institute for Spirituality and Worship at the Jesuit School of Theology at Berkeley CA. In June 1997 he received his Doctorate of Ministry (DMIN, liturgical studies) at Catholic Theological Union in Chicago, and was appointed the director of the newly formed Department for Art and Architecture in the Office for Divine Worship, Archdiocese of Chicago, a position he held for 12½ years. In this capacity he acted as a liturgical consultant/resource person for all the new church building and renovation projects for the Archdiocese, and chaired the Diocesan Commission on Church Art and Architecture. He is an adjunct faculty member in the Word and Worship department at Catholic Theological Union, Chicago. Since 2009 he has developed his ministry as a liturgical design consultant and maintains a number of consulting projects in Canada and the United States, both with Roman Catholic and Lutheran congregations. He is a frequent presenter at conferences and workshops on various topics related to the building and renovation of worship spaces, as well as issues on the liturgical environment, the history and components of liturgical design, sacramental theology, the spiritual and ecclesial dimensions of liturgical ministries, and the pastoral implications of liturgical rituals, documents and praxis. He has written a number of articles for liturgical publications and his particular interest is understanding and exploring the relationship between ritual space and ritual event. He has provided the commentaries on "The Liturgical Environment."

◆ MAUREEN A. KELLY is a well known catechist and lecturer in the field of religious education of adults and children. She has an MA in theology from the University of Louvain in Belgium and has held parish, diocesan and national positions in catechesis. Maureen has done extensive work with the Rite of Christian Initiation of Adults (RCIA); has worked in various positions with publishers of Catholic catechetical materials. She has also written numerous articles for catechetical magazines and newsletters and authored *Children's Liturgy of the Word* (LTP); *Call to Celebrate: Eucharist, Reconciliation and Confirmation* (Harcourt Religion Publishers); *Christian Initiation of Children: Hope for the Future* (Paulist Press). Maureen's contributions to this year's *Sourcebook* include "The Rite of Christian Initiation of Adults," "Children's Liturgy of the Word," and some of the "Orientations."

◆ JOHN THOMAS LANE, SSS, is a Blessed Sacrament priest. He is pastor of Saint Paschal Baylon Roman Catholic Church in Highland Heights, Ohio. He writes a column for *Emmanuel* magazine on pastoral liturgy, contributes to BlessedSacrament.com, and has served on two national liturgical boards. Besides giving workshops on and writing about the liturgy, he serves as his religious order's vocation minister. Father Lane has provided the Ordinary Time during Summer and Fall commentary for "Devotions and Sacramentals."

◆ CORINNA LAUGHLIN is the director of liturgy for Saint James Cathedral in Seattle. She is also serves on the Liturgical Commission for the Archdiocese of Seattle. She is the co-author of LTP's *The Liturgical Ministry Series: Guide for Sacristans* and *The Liturgical Ministry Series:* *Guide for Servers*, and a frequent contributor to *Sourcebook for Sundays, Seasons, and Weekdays: The Almanac for Parish Liturgy*. Corinna has also written articles for *Pastoral Liturgy*, Today's Liturgy, *Ministry and Liturgy*, and *AIM*. She holds a doctorate in English from the University of Washington and a BA in English from Mount Holyoke College. Corinna has provided the commentaries on "The Roman Missal" and "The Saints."

◆ GRAZIANO MARCHESCHI is the Director of Ministerial Resource Development in the Archdiocese of Chicago and recently completed 18 years as the Archdiocesan Director of Lay Ministry Formation. He is a former Advisor to the Subcommittee on Lay Ecclesial Ministry of the US Conference of Catholic Bishops and speaks frequently at national gatherings on ministry and catechesis. Among Graziano's publications are several editions of LTP's *Workbook for Lectors*, *Scripture at Weddings*, and commentaries on the books of the Pentateuch and Gospels *The Catholic Bible, Personal Study Edition* (Oxford University Press). He has also created several audio and video products. Graziano hosts a local cable TV program entitled *The Church, the Cardinal, and You* and is a frequent co-host on the Archdiocese of Chicago's radio programming. He holds an MA in Theater from the University of Minnesota, a Master of Divinity from Loyola University in Chicago, and a Doctor of Ministry from the University of St. Mary of the Lake in Mundelein, IL. Graziano has provided many of the commentaries for "Other Ideas."

◆ BIAGIO MAZZA is currently a Pastoral Associate at St. Sabina Parish in Belton, Missouri. He has over thirty years of experience in parish and diocesan ministry. Biagio received his MA in Theology and Religious Education from Fordham University and has done post-graduate work in Scripture and theology. His work, preivously published by LTP, has been compiled for many of the seasonal sections regarding "The Meaning" and the Scripture commentaries for the Gospel for the Procession with the Palms on Palm Sunday.

◆ JILL MARIA MURDY has a passion for all things liturgical. She has been Director of Liturgy and Music at St. Frances Cabrini Parish, West Bend, Wisconsin for over a decade. Her background includes working with small rural parishes, monastic communities, and very large parishes. She is a member of the Archdiocesan Liturgical

Commission, the Archbishop's Community Advisory Board for Sexual Abuse, the Archdiocesan Liturgical Musicians Association, and her local Ecumenical Ministerial Association. She holds a BS in Composite Music from Dickinson State University, and an MA in Liturgical Theology from the University of Notre Dame, South Bend. She is also a busy author and speaker, and has written for RevisedRomanMissal.org, and was part of the DVD *Preparing for the New Roman Missal.* Her credits include *Sourcebook, Daily Prayer Book, The Benedictine Handbook, Liturgy 90, Rite, Modern Liturgy, Celebrations, AIM, NCR,* and has a weekly column in *Connect.* Her article on a "Healing Prayer Service for Sexual Abuse" won her an award from the American and Canadian Catholic Press Associations. Her website is www.jillmaria.com. Jill has contributed to the commentaries for "The Liturgical Music," "Liturgical Ministers," and "Devotions and Sacramentals."

◆ KRISTOPHER W. SEAMAN is the director of the Office of Worship for the Diocese of Gary as well as an adjunct instructor in theology and philosophy at Calumet College of Saint Joseph, Whiting, Indiana. Before going to the Diocese of Gary in 2002, Kristopher was director of the Office for Liturgy of the Diocese of Juneau (Alaska). He earned masters degrees from Saint John's University (Collegeville, Minnesota) and Catholic Theological Union (Chicago), as well as a Doctor of Ministry from Catholic Theological Union. Currently, he is a PHD student at King's College, University of London (United Kingdom). Kristopher provided the commentaries on "The Liturgy of the Hours."

◆ S. ANNE ELIZABETH SWEET, OCSO, PHD, is a Cistercian nun at the monastery of Tautra Mariakloster in Norway, who writes regularly on Scripture and Liturgy in both the US and in Norway, including a weekly blog (reflection) on the Sunday readings at www.klosterliv-monastic life.org. She has provided the majority of the Scripture commentaries for this year's edition.

◆ PAUL TURNER is the pastor of St. Munchin parish in Cameron, Missouri, and its mission, St. Aloysius in Maysville. A priest of the diocese of Kansas City–St. Joseph, he holds a doctorate in sacred theology from Sant' Anselmo in Rome. He is the author of many pastoral resources about sacraments and the liturgy. He has provided the Scripture commentaries for the days of the Triduum and Pentecost.

◆ DENISE SIMEONE is a consultant for staff development, long-range planning, and group facilitation for churches, non-profit organizations, and small businesses. She writes a monthly column on issues relating to parish staffs and committees for *Celebration* magazine. She has past experience in educational development on both the parish and diocesan levels in New York and Missouri. She holds an MA in Pastoral Studies from Loyola University in Chicago.

◆ VIVIAN E. WILLIAMS serves as the liturgy director for the St. Giles Family Mass Community in Oak Park, Illinois and frequently speaks and writes on topics related to liturgy, ministry and catechesis. She holds her MA in Pastoral Studies with a concentration in Word and Worship from Catholic Theological Union in Chicago. She is a presenter in the Chicago Archdiocesan "Fundamentals of Catholic Theology Program" for Catholic school teachers and "Fostering Faith Program" for catechists. Her experience includes 25 years as a Catholic school teacher and ten years as a parish catechist.

Vivian is the author of *Classroom Prayer Basics* (Oregon Catholic Press), and co-author of the *When Children Gather* liturgy series (GIA Publications, Inc.) and has contributed to the *Sourcebook for Sundays, Seasons and Weekdays* (LTP) and OCP's online newsletter *Today's Liturgy With Children.* Vivian contributed to "Other Ideas," "Book of Blessings," Rite of Marriage," Pastoral Care of the Sick," "Rite of Penance," and the "Order of Christian Funerals."

◆ DANIELLA ZSUPAN-JEROME, PHD is currently Assistant Professor of Liturgy, Catechesis, and Evangelization at the Loyola Institute for Ministry at Loyola University New Orleans. Her bachelor's degree is in theology from the University of Notre Dame, and she holds two master's degrees: one in liturgy from St. John's in Collegeville, and one in religion and the arts from Yale Divinity School. She earned her doctoral degree in the field of theology and education at Boston College's School of Theology and Ministry. Her dissertation is entitled "Digital Media at the Service of the Word: What Does Internet-mediated Communication Offer the Theology of Revelation and the Practice of Catechesis?" Her research continues to explore how Internet-mediated communication is shaping our culture, a culture where

Christians are also called by Baptism to proclaim the Good News of Jesus Christ to all the world.

Overview of the Third Edition of The Roman Missal

THE Roman Missal is a new edition, and a new translation, of the book we formerly called *The Sacramentary*. For the most part, the book is organized in the same way, but just enough has changed to keep us on our toes! The following outline will help you to navigate your way through this freshly translated edition of our most important collection of liturgical prayers.

At the beginning of *The Roman Missal*, you will find a series of official documents, including the *Apostolic Constitution* of Pope Paul VI, published with first edition of the renewed Roman Missal in 1969. Next in the volume is the *General Instruction of the Roman Missal* (GIRM), which is often printed and referred to as if it were a separate document. In fact, it is an introduction to *The Roman Missal*, and provides detailed rubrics and explanations of the "hows" and "whys" of the Roman Catholic liturgy.

After the *General Instruction*, you will find the *Universal Norms on the Liturgical Year and the General Roman Calendar*, which offers an outline of the liturgical year. You might take special note of the "Table of Liturgical Days," which provides a ranking of all the observances of the liturgical year.

Then you will find the *General Roman Calendar*, which includes saints' days, holy days, and their rank (optional memorial, memorial, feast, solemnity). While your local Ordo will provide you with the most complete information on observances, it's useful to have this calendar at your fingertips as well.

The *General Roman Calendar* concludes the introductory matter in *The Roman Missal*. Following this document, the primary content of *The Roman Missal* (the liturgical texts for the celebration of the Eucharist throughout the year) begins, with the Proper of Time (formerly called the Proper of Seasons). "Proper" refers to prayers that are specific to a particular occasion; here, to the "Time" of the year. In the Proper of Time you

find the prayers for the Sundays and weekdays of Advent, Christmas Time, Lent, the Sacred Paschal Triduum, Easter Time, and Ordinary Time. The Proper of Time ends with the "Solemnities of the Lord during the Ordinary Time," which include the Most Holy Trinity, the Most Holy Body and Blood of Christ (*Corpus Christi*), the Most Sacred Heart of Jesus, and Our Lord Jesus Christ, King of the Universe.

One change is to be noted in the Proper of Time. Formerly, all the Prefaces were located together, following the Order of Mass. Now, proper Prefaces can be found with the prayers of the day. This includes the Prefaces for the Feast of the Baptism of the Lord, the Sundays of Lent, Palm Sunday of the Passion of the Lord, the Chrism Mass, Pentecost, and the Solemnities of the Lord during Ordinary Time. The other Prefaces are still found after the Order of Mass. Notice that the prayers for the Evening Mass of the Lord's Supper on Holy Thursday include not only the Preface but the entire Roman Canon (Eucharistic Prayer I), with the special insertions proper to that day.

After the Proper of Time comes the Order of Mass, the section of *The Roman Missal* used at all times of the year. This section is set apart by tabs, to make it easy for the priest to find his way from the Order of Mass to the Prefaces and Eucharistic Prayers.

This section of *The Roman Missal* is organized in the order that the different elements appear at Mass. The Order of Mass begins with the Introductory Rites: the Greeting, the Penitential Act, the Gloria, the dialogues and prayers for the Liturgy of the Word, and the Creed. Then comes the Preface Dialogue, followed by 50 Prefaces for the feasts and particular times of the year. Note that the six Prefaces for weekdays have not disappeared: they are now called "Common Prefaces."

Following the Prefaces come the Eucharistic Prayers, marked by tabs. The new translation of *The Roman Missal* collects in one place several texts which were formerly published as appendices, or in separate volumes. These include the "Order of Mass with the Participation of a Single Minister" (when the priest celebrates Mass by himself), the two Eucharistic Prayers for Reconciliation, which formerly appeared at the end of the book, and the four Eucharistic Prayers for Use in Masses for Various Needs. This new arrangement makes these Eucharistic Prayers much more

accessible than before, making the resources of *The Roman Missal* more readily available to the priest.

Following the Eucharistic Prayers, the Order of the Mass continues with the prayers of the Communion Rite, and a wide range of Solemn Blessings and Prayers over the People.

While some appendices have been incorporated into the main body of the book, some other elements that we are used to seeing in the Order of Mass are now found in appendices. These include the Rite for the Blessing and Sprinkling of Water, which is used especially during Easter Time. These texts are now found in Appendix II. The sample invocations for the Penitential Act, which can still be composed for the local community, are now found in Appendix VI. These texts are now in the Appendix simply because that is where they are in the Latin edition of *The Roman Missal*. Their placement does not mean that they are not recommended for use. Mark them with a ribbon and use them just as you did before.

After the conclusion of the Order of Mass comes the next major section, the Proper of Saints. This includes Collects, and sometimes also Prayers over the Offerings and Prayers after Communion, for the saints of the liturgical year, from January through December. (As a general rule of thumb, you'll find "fixed feasts," those which always occur on the same day of the calendar, in the Proper of Saints, while "movable feasts" such as Easter are found in the Proper of Time. This is not always the case, Christmas being the most notable exception. Though it always occurs on December 25, it is found in the Proper of Time.)

The next four sections in *The Roman Missal* provide prayers for a variety of different occasions. Commons are prayers for memorials that have no "proper" prayers. This section includes the Common of the Dedication of a Church (including prayers used on the anniversary of dedication), Common of the Blessed Virgin Mary, Common of Martyrs, of Pastors, of Doctors of the Church, of Virgins, and of Holy Men and Women. These are regularly used for the memorials of saints, which often have only a proper Collect.

The Ritual Masses are prayers for Masses at which a special rite is celebrated, whether a rite from the Rite of Christian Initiation of Adults, Baptism, Confirmation, conferral of Holy Orders (Ordination), or Viaticum. In this section you will also find the prayers for the wedding Mass, wedding anniversaries, and religious profession.

Many of the Prefaces for the ritual Masses are now found with the other prayers for the Mass, so when using these Masses, be sure you know where the Preface is.

The Masses and Prayers for Various Needs and Occasions are a wonderful resource. As the name of this section suggests, it includes a wide variety of prayers for many different circumstances. There are prayers for the Church, for the pope, for the unity of Christians, for vocations, for peace and justice, for productive land, for rain, for prisoners, and for many other "needs and occasions." The third edition of *The Roman Missal* includes a new Mass for use in the United States, "For Giving Thanks to God for the Gift of Human Life." These prayers can be used on January 22, the anniversary of the Supreme Court decision *Roe v. Wade*, or at other times of the year, as permitted.

In the next section are the Votive Masses. "Votive Masses of the mysteries of the Lord or in honor of the Blessed Virgin Mary or of the Angels or of any given Saint or of all the Saints may be said in response to the devotion of the faithful on weekdays in Ordinary Time, even if an optional memorial occurs" (GIRM, 375). Votive Masses differ from Masses for Various Needs and Occasions in that they are not directed toward a specific need; rather, they honor a mystery, like the Holy Trinity, the Holy Cross, the Holy Eucharist, or a person, like Mary, Joseph, the Apostles, Peter or Paul.

Toward the end of *The Roman Missal* we find the prayers for Masses for the Dead, including the prayers used at Funeral Masses, prayers for the anniversary of death, and prayers for all the dead and for specific needs.

The appendices are not to be overlooked, either. They include Various Chants for the Order of Mass, including chant settings for the Greeting, the Penitential Act, and the Blessing, as well as Presidential Tones for the chanting of the Collects and the Readings. Credo III, the most familiar Gregorian setting of the Creed, can be found here as well, along with the musical setting of the Easter Proclamation and the Christmas Proclamation, the Nativity of Our Lord Jesus Christ. As mentioned above, the Rite for the Blessing and Sprinkling of Water is now found in Appendix II, and the Invocations for the Penitential Act are found in Appendix VI. Appendix III is a new addition to the third edition of *The Roman Missal*, a Rite of Deputing a Minister to Distribute Holy

Communion on a Single Occasion, for those times when insufficient priests and commissioned ministers are available. Appendix IV includes the Rite of Blessing a Chalice and a Paten within Mass, which is also found in the *Book of Blessings*. Examples of Formularies for the Prayer of the Faithful are found in Appendix IV. These examples may be used as they are; they can also serve as models for those entrusted with the task of writing the petitions for the parish. There are several general formulas, plus examples for every time of the liturgical year.

The Roman Missal: Treasure of Catholic Tradition

Eucharistic Prayer I is also called the Roman Canon. Parts of this prayer are mentioned by Saint Ambrose in a treatise on the sacraments dating from 378. The Latin text was fixed by the seventh century, and in the Middle Ages it became the only Eucharistic Prayer in the Roman Rite. That continued until 1969, when the new Missal was published following the Second Vatican Council.

Eucharistic Prayer II, added to the Missal in 1969, is actually the most ancient Eucharistic Prayer, based on a prayer of Hippolytus of Rome dating from 215! Eucharistic Prayer III is a new composition from the years following the Council. Eucharistic Prayer IV also dates from the reforms of the Council, but it has deep roots: it is based on the Anaphora of Saint Basil (330–379), and brings into the Roman liturgy some of the richness of Eastern liturgical texts. The Eucharistic Prayers for Reconciliation (1975) and the Eucharistic Prayer for Various Needs and Occasions (1991) were composed well after the revised Missal appeared in 1969.

The Prefaces are some of the most beautiful texts in the Missal. The Preface is a prayer of praise addressed to God the Father, thanking him—in nearly ninety different ways—for what he has done for us. Each Preface answers the same question of why "it is truly right and just, our duty and our salvation, / always and everywhere to give you thanks." This prayer is not called a "Preface" because it comes before the Eucharistic Prayer, like the Preface of a book; rather, it is a Preface (from the Latin *praefari*, to speak before) because it is said in the presence of God (Soubigou, 3) and of God's people (Johnson, 79). Before the reforms of the Second Vatican Council, *The Roman Missal* included just 15 Prefaces (including three added in the twentieth century for Saint Joseph, the

Sacred Heart, and Christ the King). The reforms brought back many ancient Prefaces, and added a number of new ones. For example, the two Prefaces for Advent are new additions from 1969 (before that, *The Roman Missal* had no Preface specifically for Advent), but based on ancient Prefaces in the Verona Sacramentary (dating from the sixth century).

In addition to the Eucharistic Prayers, *The Roman Missal* contains more than fifteen hundred prayers: Collects, Prayers over the Offerings, Prayers after Communion, Prayers over the People, and Solemn Blessings. The Collect, prayed at the beginning of the Mass, "collects" or gathers the prayers of the assembly into one. The Prayer over the Offerings, prayed at the altar at the beginning of the Liturgy of the Eucharist, asks God to receive the bread and wine we bring and to transform them and us as well. The Prayer after Communion, prayed just before the Blessing and Dismissal, asks for the fruits of the Eucharist we have celebrated and received.

The sources of the prayers are as varied and complex as those of the Eucharistic Prayers. Many of them are found in ancient Sacramentaries, reaching as far back as the sixth century—and some probably had venerable histories already when they were written down long ago. Some, however, are quite recent, especially the proper Collects for contemporary saints.

All of our liturgical texts are full of scriptural echoes. This is most evident, perhaps, in the Eucharistic Prayers, where the Institution narrative at the heart of the prayer closely follows the accounts given in the synoptic Gospels and in the writings of Saint Paul. But there are countless echoes in the Collects and other prayers as well. Some of these echoes are pointed out in the commentaries in the "Calendar" section of this book.

—Corinna Laughlin

Overview of the Lectionary for Mass

IN the *Lectionary for Mass*, the proclamation of the Gospel is truly the anchor of all three readings. The **First Readings** for Masses on Sundays were chosen to connect in some way to the theme of the Gospel that is proclaimed or to fit the liturgical time or observance celebrated. Because of this, the First Reading rarely comes from the same book of the Bible two weeks in a row. For all liturgies, except throughout Easter Time, the First Reading is from the Old Testament.

The **Responsorial Psalms** were chosen, for the most part, to follow the story, narrative, theme, or theology of the First Reading. However, sometimes the Psalm corresponds to the liturgical time or to the observance of the saint. The Lectionary does provide suggestions for "seasonal Psalms" suitable for the liturgical time. Parishes may choose to use the "seasonal Psalm" rather than the song of the day. These are grouped together, following the section for "Solemnities of the Lord during Ordinary Time."

The response may also be from an Old or New Testament canticle rather than a Psalm. Canticles are songs of praise, and some are rather ancient. For example, on a feast of the Blessed Virgin Mary, the response may be the Canticle of Mary (the Magnificat), her song of praise (see Luke 1:46–55).

During Advent, Christmas Time, Lent, and Easter Time, the **Second Readings** were chosen, like the First Readings, to connect to the seasonal theme emphasized in the Gospel. During Ordinary Time, the Second Readings are semicontinuous proclamations from various epistles over several Sundays.

The translation of Scripture approved for liturgical proclamation in the United States of America is the *New American Bible.* In the early 1990s, the Lectionary readings were revised. The revised translation was published in the Lectionary for Sundays, solemnities, and feasts of the Lord in 1998. These readings constitute Volume I of the revised Lectionary. In 2000 the revised *Book of the Gospels* was approved, and in 2001 the complete revised Lectionary was approved and published in three remaining volumes:

◆ Volume II: Weekday Masses for Year I and Readings for Saints Days

◆ Volume III: Weekday Masses for Year II and Readings for Saints Days

◆ Volume IV: Readings from the Commons of Saints, Ritual Masses, and Masses for Various Needs and Occasions.

The Book of the Gospels

Using this ritual book is actually a very ancient tradition. This specially designated and decorated book contains all the readings of the Gospel for the Sundays and special liturgical observances throughout the year. It fell out of use in some parishes once the Lectionary was developed (which contained all the readings, including the Gospel). However, the revised *General Instruction of the Roman Missal* limits the use of the Lectionary and calls for a more widespread use of the *Book of the Gospels* (see GIRM, 120.D).

Lectionary for Masses with Children

In 1992, the United States received approval from Rome to use *Lectionary for Masses with Children*, a collection of Scripture readings for Masses with an assembly primarily of children (e.g., school liturgies). This Lectionary may also be used for a Liturgy of the Word for children during Sunday Mass. The translation of these readings "adheres as closely as possible to the selection and arrangement of readings for Sundays, solemnities, and feasts of the Lord in the *Lectionary for Mass*, while adapting them to the needs and capacities of children" ("Introduction," *Lectionary for Masses with Children*, 11).

In November 2005 a revised translation of the *Lectionary for Masses with Children* was approved by the United States Bishops. The translation is based on the *New American Bible.*At the time of this book's publication, this translation is awaiting the *recognitio* (approval) from Rome. See page XIV for an overview of Children's Liturgy of the Word.

The Gospel for Year C: Luke

The Gospel according to Luke is perhaps the favorite of many contemporary believers. As we know, each of the four Gospel accounts has its own particular flavor and focus, its own Christology and themes, its own way of presenting the challenges of Christian discipleship. Luke, perhaps more than any other evangelist, touches the hearts of believers with his emphases on prayer, mercy, and forgiveness, with his prominent concern for the poor and the outcasts of society, and with his way of giving equal time to women and men among the believers and disciples of Jesus.

Luke actually authored two New Testament books. His second work, the Acts of the Apostles, might be seen to pick up where his Gospel account ends, with a bit of overlap for the sake of continuity: the Gospel ends with the Ascension of Jesus and Acts of the Apostles begins with it. Both of these works are dedicated to a man named Theophilus, whose name means "friend of God." Perhaps he was Luke's benefactor, the one who had commissioned and supported his writing. Luke is careful to set out his purpose: "to write it [a narrative of the events that have been fulfilled among us] down in an orderly sequence" (Luke 1:3).

In addition to the Gospel according to Mark, Luke had two other sources at his disposal in composing his account of the Gospel: a collection of sayings of Jesus (we find these in various contexts in Luke and in Matthew) and his own unique source with information on the events preceding the births of Jesus and John the Baptist as well as the infancy and childhood of Jesus. Luke also records narratives about the appearances of the Risen Christ to his disciples, one of which is unique to his Gospel. His sources, as Luke himself says, can be traced back to "those who were eyewitnesses from the beginning and ministers of the word" (Luke 1:2). Luke in turn hands on to Theophilus and readers of every time and age, including our own, what has been "handed on" to him.

Luke writes for a Gentile (non-Jewish) audience. He traces Jesus's ancestry back to Adam, the first human creature (Luke 3:38). When the child Jesus is presented in the Temple he is called "a light for revelation to the Gentiles" as well as "glory for . . . Israel" (2:32). At the end of the Gospel, Jesus "opened (his disciples') minds to understand the scriptures" including "that repentance, for the forgiveness of sins would be preached . . . to all the nations" (Luke 24:45, 47).

Although he writes for Gentiles, Luke nonetheless portrays Jesus as the fulfillment of all that was promised in the Old Testament (see, for example, Luke 4:21 and 24:44). He, his parents, and his disciples are all faithful Jews, observing the precepts and rituals of the Law. Luke's account of the Gospel begins and ends in the Temple in Jerusalem.

As in all the Gospel accounts, John the Baptist has a unique role as the one who prepares the way for Jesus. Luke tells about the content of John's preaching and what was required of those who came forward for baptism. His role is given added emphasis with Luke's story of the announcement to the elderly Zechariah, as he performed his priestly duties in the Temple, that he would be the father of a son named John (Luke 1:5–23). Elizabeth, John's mother, also belonged to a priestly family. Both she and Zechariah were "righteous in the eyes of God" (Luke 1:5–6). It is Elizabeth who proclaims Mary as the mother of the Lord when John leapt in her womb at the sound of Mary's voice (Luke 1:43–44). It is

Elizabeth who insists that her child be named as instructed by the angel even before this is confirmed by her mute husband (Luke 1:60–64).

It is Luke who tells of the angelic annunciation to Mary of Jesus's birth (1:26–38). It is Luke who tells of Jesus's birth in a barn or stable in Bethlehem and of the visit of the shepherds (2:1–20), and of the 12-year-old Jesus in the Temple (2:41–52).

Following the basic structure of the Gospel according to Mark, Luke depicts Jesus beginning his ministry of preaching and healing in Galilee after his baptism by John and time of testing in the desert. God's Holy Spirit is upon him in all that he does (Luke 4:18). One of Jesus's first acts is to call disciples, and in Luke, the first to be called follow Jesus because they experienced his extraordinary knowledge and powerful words (5:1–11). Luke also mentions the women disciples who follow Jesus from Galilee to Jerusalem (8:1–3), witness his death (23:48), and are at the empty tomb on Sunday morning (24:1–10).

In his proclamation of the kingdom of God, Luke's Jesus preaches a God who is above all compassionate and merciful. Believers are to be merciful like their heavenly Father (6:36), showing compassion for those in need (10:29–42).

Luke gives Jesus's journey from Galilee to Jerusalem a definite starting point in 9:51. His wording is most significant: "When the days for his being taken up were fulfilled, he resolutely determined to journey to Jerusalem." The Greek word used with reference to "being taken up" is the same word used for Jesus's Ascension in Acts of the Apostles (1:2, 11–22). This suggests that the Ascension, the return to his heavenly Father, is the real or ultimate goal of Jesus's journey, or "exodus" as it is called in 9:31. Along the way, we see Jesus engaged in teaching his disciples and often in controversy with his opponents. Much of the material in this section of the Gospel is unique to Luke and it is here that his special themes are developed: prayer (11:1–13), forgiveness (15:1–32), attitudes toward and use of wealth and riches (12:13–21, 33–34; 16:19–31), and concern for the poor and needy (10:29–37; 14:12–14).

At his birth, Jesus as acclaimed as "Savior" by the angels (2:11) and throughout the Gospel we witness the many ways this salvation is experienced in healings (4:38–41; 6:6–10; 13:10–17; 14:1–6; 17:11–19), exorcisms (4:31–37; 8:26–39), restoration to life (7:11–17), and forgiveness (5:20; 7:36–50; 15:11–32). Often, we see Jesus sharing a meal, a deeply symbolic gesture, a sign of welcome, acceptance, and fellowship with disciples (22:14–20), friends (10:38–42), and with sinners (15:1–2; 19:1–10). His table fellowship with sinners led to much conflict with the self-righteous Pharisees.

Jesus's salvific ministry continues and culminates in his Passion, Death, Resurrection, and Ascension. At his Last Supper with his disciples, Jesus not only gives the bread and wine, his body and blood, as the meal of the new covenant, he teaches his disciples about service and mission (22:14–38). Even in the midst of his own passion, Jesus heals (22:51) and forgives (23:34). It is Luke who tells of the two criminals crucified with Jesus and his promise that the one who believed would be with him that day in Paradise (23:43).

The much-loved story of the Risen Christ's appearance to the two disciples on the road to Emmaus (24:13–35) is also unique to Luke, as is his appearance to the disciples in Jerusalem on Easter night when he asked them for something to eat (24:36–49). On both occasions, he interpreted the Scriptures for them. The disciples en route to Emmaus recognized him in the breaking of the bread. We, too, recognize the Risen Lord in our midst in the Scriptures and in the breaking of the bread.

Throughout his Gospel account, Luke repeatedly emphasizes the theme of today as the moment of salvation: at Jesus's birth (2:11), in the synagogue in Nazareth (4:21), in the house of a sinner and outcast (19:9), to the condemned criminal on the cross who believed in him (23:43). As we move through this year of Luke, let us bear in mind that today is the time of salvation for us as well. Let us open ourselves to the healing and deep peace, the joy of forgiveness and the communion with God and with others that is salvation's gift.

— Anne Elizabeth Sweet, ocso

Overview of Children's Liturgy of the Word

CHILDREN's Liturgy of the Word is liturgy. It is ritual! This rite enables children to encounter the Word of God at a cognitive level. What transpires in this ritual should resemble what is going on in the adult assembly. After the Collect, the priest celebrant invites the prayer leader to come forward to receive the children's Lectionary. It is also customary to have the children come forward to hear the words of dismissal (see the optional dismissal prayers in this *Sourcebook*). The prayer leader then takes the Lectionary and processes, with the children following, to the space where the Liturgy of the Word is to be celebrated.

◆ PASTORAL IDEAS: When all have reached the location of where this liturgy will be celebrated, invite the children to sit on the floor, perhaps in a circle. The prayer leader should sit with them, but not at too dominating or overpowering a height.

Those involved in preparing children's Liturgy of the Word should create a liturgical environment for the space where it is to be celebrated. This liturgical environment should reflect what has been prepared in the main worship space. This may be achieved simply by covering a table with a cloth of the same color as the liturgical time. You might place sanctuary candles on the table as well.

Once the children have settled, the prayer leader may put into context the readings of the day, giving the children a sense of time and place in the continuum of salvation history. The *Directory for Masses with Children* indicates that you only have to proclaim the Gospel; however, some communities will add the First or Second Reading followed by a sung Responsorial Psalm (use the same musical setting that will be used in the main assembly). After the Responsorial Psalm, invite the children to stand while an Alleluia is sung (or alternate Acclamation during Lent). Incorporate a procession for the reading of the Gospel. You could invite two young people to carry candles in front of the leader of prayer who is holding the Lectionary. Again, what happens in the general assembly should be reflected here in this space. After the proclamation of the Gospel, the prayer leader may give a brief reflection. The prayer leader should connect his or her reflection to what the priest or deacon will be saying in his Homily. The prayer leader should speak with the priest or deacon prior to the celebration of the Liturgy of the Word to share ideas to better connect the reflection to the Homily. You may use a question and answer format in order to better engage the children.

At the end of the reflection, invite the children to stand. It would be appropriate to recite the Creed. It is suggested that the Apostles' Creed be used for liturgies with children. The Prayer of the Faithful follows the Apostles' Creed. After the intercessions, the leader says the closing prayer and invites everyone to return to the main worship space. Coordinating this movement is important, so you might ask the ushers and greeters to help.

Other things to note:

Children's Liturgy of the Word is not a catechetical session. Although the ritual is full of liturgical catechesis, it should not become another religious education class. If you follow the principle that children's Liturgy of the Word should reflect what is going on in the main liturgical assembly, then those who prepare and lead this ritual should strive to be prayer leaders, not catechists.

Children's Liturgy of the Word does not distinguish age groups. It is for children of all ages (pre-school through those who have not yet received first Eucharist) to gather together, with younger children learning from older children.

Craft activities and handouts shouldn't be used at children's Liturgy of the Word. There are some great activity sheets on the market, but consider adding them to the bulletin or distributing them during catechetical sessions or religious education meetings. You might have those who prepare children's Liturgy of the Word write a column for the parish bulletin or post to the parish website. These writers could simply cite the readings that will be used and summarize a few points they will be making in their reflection. Add questions that the family can discuss on their way home from Mass or at mealtime that day or in the coming week.

A good resource to help you prepare liturgies with children is *Children's Liturgy of the Word 2012–2013: A Weekly Resource* (LTP). Formerly a part of the *Celebrating the Lectionary* series, this resource provides liturgy preparation pages and liturgy guides for every Sunday and Holyday of Obligation. Prayer leaders are provided with everything they need to effectively guide children in a prayerful and fruitful celebration of the Word.
— Robert W. Piercy, Jr.

Overview of the Saints

WINDING throughout the liturgical year is the observance of the sanctoral cycle. This is the cycle of solemnities, feasts, and memorials in which we remember and honor God's holy ones—the Blessed Virgin Mary and the saints. These are the Apostles and martyrs, the evangelists, and the fathers of the Church. They are popes and religious founders, peasants and statesmen. They are men and woman, clerics and married people, the elderly and the young. All of them have lived some aspect of Christ's Paschal Mystery in a unique and powerful way.

These holy men and women, the heroes of our faith upon whose shoulders we stand (the pillars of the Church), are revered and memorialized as members of the "great multitude, which no one could count, from every nation, race, people, and tongue," who stand now before the throne of the Lamb, dressed in white and waving palm branches (Revelation 7:9). In this, they also stand with us each and every time we gather around the banquet table of the Lamb. As we praise and thank God through the complete praise and thanksgiving of Christ in Eucharist, we join the saints in their eternal praise of God through Christ.

This is the cloud of witnesses that each of us, we pray, will one day join in the halls of the heavenly banquet. It is the company we hope to keep for all eternity. It is the end of our journey of faith, the end of our pilgrimage here on earth. The sanctoral cycle offers yet another level throughout the year for observing and celebrating the "whole mystery of Christ" (*Constitution on the Sacred Liturgy* [CSL], 102).

Overview of the Liturgy of the Hours

THE Liturgy of the Hours, the Divine Office, the Breviary are all terms that refer to what the *General Instruction of the Liturgy of the Hours* (GILOH) calls the official, daily prayer of the Church with Christ and to Christ (see GILOH, 2). The Hours are principally a prayer of praise, and secondly of petition. As the prayer of the Church, the Hours are the very prayer of Christ, since Christ's prayer is *always* a prayer of praise to the Father and petition for the salvation of the world. In the praying of the Hours, the Church fulfills her baptismal obligation to do as Christ commanded—to pray. The GILOH notes that in praying the Hours, the baptized members of Christ's Body (the Church), through the Holy Spirit, are united with the perfect prayer of Christ to the Father.

The full celebration of the Liturgy of the Hours covers the passing of the day and includes the Office of Readings, Morning Prayer (Lauds), Daytime Prayer (midmorning, midday, and mid-afternoon), Evening Prayer (Vespers), and Night Prayer (Compline). Over the course of these celebrations, the whole day is sanctified and offered to God in praise and thanksgiving. In this day-to-day prayer all time is made holy.

Although the Liturgy of the Hours is the official daily prayer of the Church, few communities celebrate it as part of the regular liturgical life of the parish. It is thought to be the prayer of the clergy rather than the prayer of everyone. Many, however, do celebrate some portion of the Hours at various liturgical times of the year. During the "high seasons" (for example, Advent/ Christmas Time, Lent/Triduum/Easter) many parishes will offer Morning Prayer or Evening Prayer on one day of the week.

Morning and Evening Prayer are the two hours that are the "hinges" upon which the whole liturgy moves through the day. In the morning the community, ideally, gathers to commend the day to God, to ask God to bless it and lead them through it. In the evening the community again comes together to give God praise for blessings received throughout the day and to ask him for protection through the coming night.

Overview of the Sacraments

THE whole liturgical life of the Roman Catholic Church revolves around the celebration of Eucharist and the other sacraments. There are seven sacraments in the Church: Baptism, Confirmation, Eucharist, Reconciliation, Anointing of the Sick, Marriage, and Holy Orders.

The sacraments are communal celebrations of the Church, grace-giving encounters with Christ that articulate what God is doing in our lives now. Sacraments mark the peak moments of our lives. They celebrate the grace of God that calls us to conversion and membership in the Church and gifts us with the Holy Spirit, that offers us reconciliation and healing, that calls some to leadership in the Church community and others to the vocation of Christian Marriage, and invites us into the mystery of Christ's suffering, Death, and Resurrection.

In Christ, God became visible and tangible. In the Church, Christ, and hence God, remains visible and tangible among us. The Church in turn becomes visible and tangible in the seven signs. They are Christ's hands that now touch us and Christ's words that now ring in our ears. Those who prepare sacramental celebrations have the sacred and serious responsibility of doing these well, of familiarizing themselves with the rites and understanding them fully. Read the introductory notes of the ritual text (the *praenotanda*); know the signs and symbols, the rubrics and prayers, and the shape of the ritual well. Invite collaboration, encourage ministries, and allow grace to flow.

Overview of the Order of Christian Funerals

THE Order of Christian Funerals is an event that unfolds over time, in stations. Beginning with the first moment that the family encounters the deceased, all the way to the moment when that person's mortal remains reach their final resting place, the Church honors the one who has died and walks with those who mourn.

Some people prepare their funerals in advance. Parish ministers should be ready to prepare the funeral liturgy efficiently, on short notice, with good collaboration among clergy, musicians, sacristan, funeral director, parish bereavement committee, and members of the family. It is a difficult time for those in mourning to prepare the liturgy, although some families will welcome the chance to be involved in the liturgical preparations. The parish should have a reliable process already in place that conforms to liturgical norms and standards. This is often a powerful moment of evangelization.

In 1997, the National Conference of Catholic Bishops approved an appendix to the *Order of Christian Funerals* in light of pastoral circumstances concerning the cremated remains of a body. The text *Appendix: Cremation with Reflections on the Body, Cremation, and Catholic Funeral Rites by the Committee on the Liturgy* is exceptionally helpful in explaining how the funeral liturgy is celebrated with cremated remains. One liturgical difference, for example, is that no pall is used, since this represents the clothing of the body with the baptismal garment.

Sensitive ministry to the bereaved calls upon the gifts of a variety of people, including clergy, pastoral ministers, musicians, and bereavement counselors. Not all of these ministries are strictly liturgical, but all will ultimately have an impact on liturgy as they shepherd people through this passage in life.

Overview of the Book of Blessings

THE *Book of Blessings* (BB) provides multiple orders of blessing for various needs and occasions. The book for use in the dioceses of the United States of America contains those from the Roman volume (*De Benedictionibus*) as well as blessings proper to the United States of America.

It would be helpful to review the *Book of Blessings* periodically to see how the parish calendar can incorporate blessings during the year. Blessings are liturgical prayers that flow from the Word of God. In addition to the usual blessings for people, buildings, objects, and special occasions, there are some entries that might surprise you, such as blessings for victims of crime, for sick children, or for those suffering from addiction. People who need such blessings will not usually ask for them; therefore, the parish staff ought to be attentive to these orders of blessings and the needs of the faithful. In the right setting, such prayers can be wonderful. A blessing is an event of worship, and so calls for a variety of ministries. Be attentive to musical selections, scheduling liturgical ministers, and encourage parishioners or a small community to attend.

For this new liturgical year, note the Order for the Blessing of Articles for Liturgical Use (chapter 39). This would be most appropriate for the blessing of the new edition of *The Roman Missal*.

Overview of the Liturgical Environment

THE liturgical environment must be in balance with the religious and devotional art of a community. The signs, symbols, and elements of the environment must be dignified and beautiful. They need not be expensive, and because of the transitory nature of liturgical time, prudence should be used in expenditures. At the same time, a budget that appreciates the importance of the liturgical environment to the community's prayer is essential. Dignity and beauty is inherent in the natural world: the variety of grasses and herbs; the textures of stone, wood, and glass; the multiplicity of fruits and vegetables; the grandeur of rivers, lakes, and oceans; the majesty of the stars, the moon, and the sun. Care should be taken to use natural materials whenever possible and practical. The climate of your region will produce natural symbols that speak to you. Harvest in your community may mean pumpkins and wheat, or it may mean oranges and grapefruits. Coral and seashells will suggest water in coastal communities, while cattails and native gravel will remind inlanders of rivers and lakes. Using local resources limits the need for artificial symbols, but when these are chosen, care must be taken to assure that beauty is preserved.

During liturgy, symbols take four forms: action, word, images, and music. The postures we assume show our relationship to God and community; the words we pray and music we sing communicate beliefs, emotions, and tone. As ministers of the liturgical environment, you are concerned primarily with images. Attending to the other forms of symbols, and consulting with music ministers in particular, can reinforce the symbols' power. Whatever symbols are selected for the liturgical environment, they must speak for themselves.

Overview of Liturgical Music

The Church earnestly desires that all the faithful should be led to that full, conscious, and active participation in liturgical celebrations, called for by the very nature of the liturgy; . . . In the reform and promotion of the liturgy, this full and active participation by all the people is the aim to be considered before all else. For it is the primary and indispensable source from which the faithful are to derive the true Christian spirit. . . .

— *Constitution on the Sacred Liturgy*, 14

FOR music ministers, these lines from the first document of the Second Vatican Council should resonate strongly. Within our day-to-day secular existence, singing is increasingly viewed as something best "left to the professionals." The very act of standing and singing together is countercultural. However, our ministerial mission is to help shape the sung prayer of the People of God. Whether we serve in a large parish with thousands of families and multiple choirs or a tiny congregation with only a few cantors; whether our primary instrument of worship is a pipe organ or a rhythm ensemble or a single piano; whether our repertoire is built mostly of hymns and chant or consists primarily of contemporary-styled music, our fundamental purpose and mission remains the same. We are here to enable, empower, and sing with our assemblies, to guide their sung prayer through the peaks, valleys, and level ground of the Year of Grace.

The musical sections of this *Sourcebook* are intended to build upon the liturgical commentary and address some of the concerns, both practical and theoretical, particular to music ministry. Musicians will still want to (and should) examine the sections of *Sourcebook* not specifically addressing the musical issues of shaping sung worship. Remember that part of what we do as music ministers is to shape an aural environment for worship that enhances and harmonizes with the visual and tactile environment already present. The liturgical music sections provide some concrete suggestions for songs, hymns, chants, and/or service music appropriate for particular liturgical times.

Overview of Devotions and Sacramentals

Worship of the Eucharist Outside Mass

Devotion to Christ present in the Blessed Sacrament should flow from the liturgy and lead the people back to the liturgy. It is best celebrated in the context of liturgical time. This worship may take the form of personal visits or of collective adoration in formal rites such as exposition, or exposition and benediction. The *Order for Solemn Exposition* is clear and careful to subordinate these events to the celebration of the Mass.

Eucharistic adoration, in its various forms, should be a regular part of the parish's life of worship. For solid, profound reflections on this aspect of Catholic worship, see Pope John Paul II's *Mane Nobiscum Domine* (MND), a wonderfully poetic and personal reflection on the centrality of the Eucharist. Opportunities for people to make visits to the Blessed Sacrament should, if possible, be offered by providing easy access to the place of reservation. Note the difference between adoration and exposition. Adoration of the Blessed Sacrament in the tabernacle may take place at any time, while exposition (the adoration of the Blessed Sacrament in a monstrance or ciborium) is a liturgical rite regulated by *Holy Communion and Worship of the Eucharist Outside Mass* (HCWEOM). The Order for the Solemn Exposition of the Holy Eucharist (1992) is based on HCWEOM and is an excellent resource. On the other hand, it is the same Christ present in the tabernacle or in the monstrance; reverence to the Blessed Sacrament in the monstrance or in the tabernacle is made by a genuflection on one knee in both instances.

Processions with Eucharist are a "public witness to the people's devotion, especially on or near the solemnity of the Most Holy Body and Blood of Christ" (HCWEOM, 102). Such events are subject to the discretion of the bishop, however, who discerns whether they are suitable in local circumstances.

Other Devotions and Sacramentals

One of the paths setting Catholics apart from many other Christians is the principle of sacramentality. Sacramentals are associated with the Church's official rituals. They include public and private devotions, religious signs, symbols, gestures, prayers, rituals, images, music, and natural or synthetic objects. While not always inherently religious (e.g., water, a color, or a posture), they become sacramentals, or sacred, in their religious use. They are not part of the Church's official liturgy of sacraments and prayer, but are used to worship God, honor the saints, or seek divine favor. Sacramentals allow us to touch the invisible mystery of God in a physical way.

The reverent use of sacramentals, such as keeping holy water or blessed palms in the home, can also be devotional. The list could go on. Usually devotions spring up as popular piety and are later sanctioned and regulated by the Church if they are judged to be particularly beneficial and foster a very personal love for the mysteries celebrated in the liturgy. They are to always be viewed in relation to the liturgy. The *Constitution on the Sacred Liturgy* (CSL) highly endorses devotion; however, it notes that they should always "be so fashioned that they harmonize with the liturgical seasons, accord with the sacred liturgy, are in some way derived from it, and lead the people to it, since, in fact, the liturgy, by its very nature far surpasses any of them" (CSL, 13). The Stations of the Cross, for example, allow us to meditate on the Passion of the Lord while walking in a "pilgrim way," and the Rosary reflects on the mysteries of Christ through the experience of Mary. Novenas can strengthen our appreciation for the intercession of the saints, and call us to holiness of life.

The *Directory on Popular Piety and the Liturgy* (DPPL), issued in 2001 by the Congregation for Divine Worship and Discipline of the Sacraments, can be a helpful resource. It reminds us that "the history of the Western Church is marked by the flowering among the Christian people of multiple and varied expressions of simple and fervent faith in God, of love for Christ the Redeemer, of invocations of the Holy Spirit, of devotion to the Blessed Virgin Mary, of the veneration of the Saints, of commitment to conversion and of fraternal charity" (DPPL, 6).

Devotions should lead us to a more active and intentional liturgical participation as the Church proceeds through the liturgical year, and not to the creation of a parallel structure or alternative rituals. As we know from pastoral experience, popular devotions can easily present their own challenges, pushing us toward a variety of alternative themes. Thus the *Directory* states clearly that whether we are gathered for liturgical prayer or exercising some form of popular piety, it is the Paschal Mystery that must remain at the very center, and Sunday as the primordial feast.

Abbreviations for Common Liturgical and Catechetical Documents

ADVENT

The Meaning

As we begin the new liturgical year with Advent, we are once again reminded of the joyful expectation to which we are called as members of Christ's Body, the Church. Celebrating Advent well helps us to understand and celebrate Christmas Time more profoundly. Although separate periods of liturgical time, they are best appreciated together. During Advent, the time of expectation, we are reminded of the coming of Christ not only at Christmas, but of his Second Coming in glory at the end of time. This is a time of grace, a time for a new advent of Christ into our lives. Our attention is drawn to the light that brings brightness to the darkest places of our lives. Christ will come again in glory, lead us from darkness, and make us his own. The liturgical celebrations echo that feeling of hope and expectation about Christ's return and the reality that our preparation for his return is now. Toward the end of Advent, we prepare more specifically for the celebration of Christmas—the celebration of the dawn of our salvation. The joy of Christmas lies in the realization of the great dignity that is ours because Christ became human. How great is the hope to which we are called!

In our Advent celebrations, we find a strong emphasis on issues of justice and peace. On the First Sunday of Advent, we are called to prepare for the Second Coming of the Lord (in Greek, *parousia*; in Latin, *adventus*) and to celebrate Christ's entry into our lives by living as men, women, and children of justice who work for a more peaceful world. And yet, we know that the commercial world has come to dominate our Advent preparations, causing us at times to miss the real wealth that Advent holds forth for those who immerse themselves in its unfolding celebrations.

For many, Advent is not that time when we pause to reflect on the promise of Christ's return at what is called the "end times." In our day-to-day lives, we find ourselves running around doing all those Christmas things before Christmas—Christmas shopping, Christmas parties, Christmas decorating, general Christmas frenzy. Then Christmas arrives and we find ourselves somewhat ready, usually tired, but not prepared. The expectation, the waiting, which is the posture of the Christian during Advent, seems lost in the shuffle of pre-Christmas hysteria. Yet the great figures that we meet in the Advent liturgies (the prophets Jeremiah, Baruch, Zephaniah, and Micah, along with John the Baptist and Mary, the Holy Mother of God) remind us of the importance of listening, paying attention, patient waiting, and hope-filled living.

The Roman Missal

T HE theme that comes up again and again in the rubrics for Advent is moderation. Music, especially the use of the organ, is subdued, full of hope and longing, but not anticipating the "full joy of the Nativity of the Lord" (GIRM, 313). Flowers are not forbidden, as in Lent, but they are to be "marked by a moderation suited to the character of this time of year" (GIRM, 305). The Gloria is omitted, except on the Solemnity of the Immaculate Conception of the Blessed Virgin Mary and on the Feast of Our Lady of Guadalupe, so that it can ring out with greater joy at the Vigil Mass for the Nativity of the Lord. Advent is subdued, but it is not somber: the liturgies of this holy time express hope, trepidation, anticipation, joy, fear, and, above all, the longing of the Church for the presence of Christ.

◆ TEXTS FOR THE PRIEST CELEBRANT: Each Sunday of Advent has its own set of prayers, and there is a wide variety of texts for the Advent weekdays as well: each weekday has a proper Collect, while the Prayer over the Offerings and the Prayer after Communion on weekdays follow a weekly cycle (i.e., the same prayers are said on the Mondays of Advent, Tuesdays of Advent, etc.).

Like the readings, the Missal texts shift in meaning as Advent progresses. During the first weeks of Advent, the focus is on waiting for the second coming of Christ. We ask God to "prepare our hearts" (Wednesday of the First Week of Advent, Collect) for Christ's coming, and to "keep us alert" (Monday of the First Week of Advent, Collect) and full of eager "resolve" (First Sunday of Advent, Collect). The prayers express a strong awareness of our sin and weakness, and a yearning for freedom: we recall the "ancient enslavement" of the human race (Saturday of the First Week of Advent, Collect), and recognize that we are surrounded by "the pressing dangers of our sins" (Friday of the First Week of Advent, Collect). Images of light are frequent: we want to "hasten, alert and with lighted lamps" to meet Christ when he comes (Friday of the Second Week of Advent, Collect). We ask God to cast "light on the darkness of our hearts" (Monday of the Third Week of Advent, Collect) and we look forward to the day when "all shadows of the night" are "scattered" by "the splendor of [God's] glory" (Saturday of the Second Week of Advent, Collect).

Christ's birth becomes the primary focus of the prayers of the last week of Advent, which, on weekdays beginning December 17, are proper to each day. The mystery of the Incarnation changes everything for us: now that Christ has "taken to himself our humanity," we have "a share in his divinity" (December 17, Collect). That is why it is so important that we "venerate with integrity of faith" the great mystery of Christmas (December 19, Collect).

The Prefaces of Advent reflect the same movement. Preface I of Advent, subtitled "The two comings of Christ," expresses the watchfulness and hope of Advent, awaiting Christ's second coming. In taking on our flesh, Christ "opened for us the way to eternal salvation." And now we "watch for that day," longing for the fulfillment of "the great promise / in which now we dare to hope." Preface II of Advent, called "The twofold expectation of Christ," is used from December 17 through December 24, on Sundays as well as weekdays. It recalls the great longing of all the ages for the coming of Christ—"the oracles of the prophets foretold him," Mary "longed for him / with love beyond all telling," and "John the Baptist sang of his coming." We stand in the line of these holy ones of God, and in celebrating Christ's Nativity, we prepare for his coming among us, "that he may find us watchful in prayer / and exultant in his praise."

The Roman Missal also includes a special Solemn Blessing for Advent. It is a prayer for the Advent virtues of faith, hope, and charity.

The Lectionary for Mass

ADVENT, perhaps more than any other time of the year, is preparatory. Getting ready for Christmas Time is the focus of our thoughts and activities throughout these four weeks. In fact, many will have already begun preparations, perhaps weeks ago. Others are now in a state of panic in the face of all that needs to be done in such a short time. For the most part, our preparations focus on the gift-giving, the card-sending, and the party-attending that characterize these weeks.

Sadly, the spiritual dimension of preparation for the real meaning of Christmas is all too often neglected or, worse yet, completely absent. This latter point was powerfully brought home to me recently when I was in a bookstore a few weeks before Christmas. Not one Christmas card in the shop had a religious theme, not one!

Preparing, being prepared, is a striking theme in the Sunday readings for Year C. The Gospels for the first week and the Second Reading for the First, Second, and Third Sundays of Advent look to the final coming of Christ at the end of time. What is more, they speak of how we should think and live in light of that coming. In other words, we must consciously prepare ourselves and be ready to meet the Lord.

In two of the three Eucharistic acclamations, we profess our belief that the Lord will come again and pray for his coming. Are we really aware of what we are saying? Do we really mean it? The first Christians could hardly wait for it. In fact, they expected it in their own lifetimes. I suspect that we today are not too anxious for the Lord to come again, at least not at the end of time, or even at the end of our own lives. That, however, is not the spirit of the writers of the New Testament!

John the Baptist is center stage on the second and third Sundays, as he goes about preparing the way for the immediate manifestation of the coming of the Lord Jesus in his public ministry. John also heralded the presence of Jesus when both were still in the wombs of their mothers as we hear in the Gospel for the Fourth Sunday of Advent. Even then, John leapt with joy in the presence of the Lord.

The adult John is likewise filled with joy in the presence of the Lord (John 3:29). Are we? When he comes to us in the Eucharist? In prayer? In other people? Making ready the way of the Lord and being joyful in his presence are both good Advent practices!

The weekday readings for the Second and Third Weeks of Advent offer us an interfacing of texts which emphasize the Lord's coming to us and the necessity of our coming to him and being receptive to him. This can only happen if we are ready and prepared!

Returning to the Gospel for the fourth Sunday, we can note how the scene of the meeting of Mary and Elizabeth reflects their own receptivity to the coming of the Lord and his message and mission in their lives. It is a beautiful trait for us all to strive to imitate! How fitting that two of Advent's special days celebrate Mary's life. In the Solemnity of the Immaculate Conception, we remember how God poured out his grace upon Mary from the beginning of her existence so that she might be ready to receive his Word and give flesh to his Son. The Feast of Our Lady of Guadalupe celebrates Mary's special care and motherly presence not only for Mexican and Hispanic peoples, but for all peoples of the Americas.

The last week of Advent focuses on how God accomplishes his plan of salvation in and through the life not only of Mary but of others as well, people who are open to God's call and obedient to God's Word. We, too, must be prepared and ready to receive him. We must come before him with the "gift" of receptivity and obedience, the gift of ourselves.

During Advent, in the midst of all the preparations, the selection and giving of gifts, the Christmas cards and e-mails, the celebrations of the season, what "gift" will be ours to the Lord? What greeting will the One who comes receive from us? May the closing days of Advent truly find us prepared and ready to welcome the One who comes with the gift of ourselves.

Children's Liturgy of the Word

A T this time of year young children embody anticipation, waiting, and joy. These are feelings that contemporary consumer culture taps into, readily supports, and calls forth. However, Advent also promises special family times and rituals which are important to children and enhance their sense of celebration and belonging. At the same time that modern day "visions of sugar plums dance in their heads" (*The Night Before Christmas*) children are fascinated by the Advent Gospel stories, people, and seasonal rituals. They have a wholesome sense of preparing their hearts for Jesus.

Advent Readings

Unlike other years, this year's (Year C) Gospel readings, with the exception of the first week, do not focus on the Second Coming of Jesus but rather on the coming of Jesus, the Son of God, into history. The Advent readings for Year C call for joyful reflection. They remind the hearer of God's faithfulness in fulfilling his promises. The First Readings for each of the four Sundays are especially hopeful and foresee great celebration and happiness when God's promises are fulfilled. They emphasize that the coming of Jesus is good news—Good News to hope in and to believe in.

It is helpful to remember that the Second Readings were written for an audience who were more aware of the Second Coming of Jesus than we are today. Many of those early churches had a belief that Jesus's Second Coming was imminent. There is more stress in these readings on the behavior of the believers in preparation for Jesus' Second Coming.

The Gospel readings for the Second, Third and Fourth Sundays present the Advent people: John the Baptizer, Elizabeth, and Mary. They model the spirit of hope, preparation, and joy that we are called to. They are readings that lend themselves to drama and dramatic narrative which young children enter into easily. If you choose this option be sure to prepare and practice with those who will do the dramatization.

During the reflection/Homily for Liturgy of the Word focus on children preparing their hearts for the coming of Jesus. Whatever reading(s) you choose to reflect on, weave into your remarks and questions concrete suggestions and images for children. You cannot be too concrete in suggestions and images with younger children. It is how they learn. For example, using the image of their hearts being like a manger that they are preparing with soft straws of acts of kindness or generosity to others is helpful for them to make connections to Jesus coming into their own hearts

Advent Environment

Violet is the traditional color for Advent (with the exception of rose, which may be used on the Third Sunday of Advent). Violet was the most costly dye in ancient times and was therefore used by kings to indicate their royal status. Violet also signifies the repentance of God's people as they patiently await the celebration of Christmas, the feast of the Prince of Peace. Use violet banners and cloths to decorate the worship space.

Place an Advent wreath in a central location. If children have not been present at an Advent wreath-lighting with the assembly, do the lighting with the group at the beginning of the session.

Music

Children love to sing, and music plays an important part in liturgical celebration. Use suggestions given in *Children's Liturgy of the Word: A Weekly Resource* from LTP or make music selections from your parish repertoire.

Younger children may be unfamiliar with some of the hymns. Take a few minutes to go over them with the children. If this is the case you may want to use the same songs and refrains throughout the season. Live music is preferable. Ask the parish music or choir director if it is possible to get a parish musician. If you are not comfortable leading song, use a recording to assist the children.

The Saints

A DVENT is a time for saints. Our celebrations include one solemnity (Immaculate Conception of the Blessed Virgin Mary), one feast (Our Lady of Guadalupe), four obligatory memorials (Saint Francis Xavier, Saint Ambrose, Saint Lucy, and Saint John of the Cross), and four optional memorials (Saint John Damascene, Saint Nicholas, Saint Damasus I, and Saint Peter Canisius)—all in four short weeks! Given the importance of Advent, and the richness of the prayers for each day, you may choose to omit the optional memorials. Here are some ideas for celebrating the saints in the light of Advent:

The Solemnity of the Immaculate Conception of the Blessed Virgin Mary is celebrated on December 8. (Please note that even though the solemnity falls on a Saturday, it is still a Holyday of Obligation because this is the Patronal Feastday of the United States of America.) This solemnity, in which the Gloria briefly reappears, should not feel like an interruption to Advent, but like an intensified expression of it. "There can be no doubt that the feast of the pure and sinless Conception of the Virgin Mary, which is a fundamental preparation for the Lord's coming into the world, harmonizes perfectly with many of the salient themes of Advent. This feast also makes reference to the long messianic waiting for the Saviours's birth and recalls events and prophecies from the Old Testament, which are also used in the Liturgy of Advent" (*Directory on Popular Piety and the Liturgy* [DPPL], 102). This solemnity should look and sound like your other Advent liturgies. If the Immaculate Conception novena is observed in your parish, make sure it focuses on Christ.

Saint Nicholas (December 6) was the holy bishop of Myra. A major figure of devotion in the East, in the West he gradually metamorphosed into "Santa Claus," and for us the saint can be difficult to see through the legend. The real Saint Nicholas was a holy and compassionate shepherd, a wonder-worker, and a very generous man. Since Saint Nicolas is the patron saint of children, parishes might mark his optional memorial with a blessing of children. The *Book of Blessings* includes an order for the blessing of children (Chapter I, IV), which takes the form of a simple Liturgy of the Word. The petitions provided could easily be adapted for use during the celebration of the Eucharist. Please refer to page 19 in this *Sourcebook* for a more thorough treatment of this saint's biography.

Our Lady of Guadalupe (December 12), patroness of the Americas, is observed as a feast in the United States. The miraculous image of Our Lady of Guadalupe is very appropriate for Advent. The image is full of symbolic details. The black sash tied around Mary's waist was worn by pregnant women, indicating that Mary is carrying the infant Jesus in her womb. Other details—the rays of light behind Mary, the angels at her feet, even the stars on her gown—have cosmic symbolism, appropriate to this season of meditation on the end times.

Saint Lucy (December 13), like Saint Nicolas, is an Advent saint whose story has been overshadowed by the popular traditions that have sprung up around her. All we really know about her is that she was a virgin martyr of the early Church. The name Lucy means "light," and she is honored in the darkest days of winter (in fact, in the Julian calendar, December 13 marked the winter solstice, the shortest day of the entire year). Devotion to Lucy took root throughout Europe, but especially in Scandinavia, where it survived the Reformation. In Scandinavian countries, "Saint Lucy's Day" is still observed with great festivity, in homes, churches, and in the broader community. Traditionally, the eldest daughter in the family wears a crown of candles (an echo of the legend of the saint, whom, it is said, flames refused to burn) and carries a special breakfast of saffron buns to her parents. Schools and towns elect a "Lucia" who sings traditional carols and gives out treats. And in Lutheran churches in both Scandinavia and the United States, the Sunday closest to December 13 is set aside for a special observance of this beloved saint, who is an image of light shining in darkness.

The Liturgy of the Hours

ADVENT begins a new liturgical year. In this time of new beginnings, the parish could introduce Evening Prayer. Perhaps Evening Prayer could simply be scheduled on Sunday evenings or Friday evenings or Wednesdays of Advent. Afraid no one will show? One parish began their generational formation program each week with Evening Prayer, and even included the Liturgy of the Hours as part of their formation so that "people are invited, and prepared by suitable instruction, to celebrate the principal hours in common, especially on Sundays and holydays" (*General Instruction of the Liturgy of the Hours* [GILOH], 23).

The Office of Readings for Advent provides deep spiritual formation. The readings from Athanasius, Augustine, Basil the Great, and Cyril of Jerusalem connect Advent to Christ's two natures: human from Mary and divine as the second member of the Trinity. Thus, the Liturgy of the Hours provides a contemplative way to reflect on Christ's Incarnation. A beautiful and eloquent example is from Ephrem: Christ's "final coming is like his first. As holy men and prophets waited for him, thinking that he would reveal himself in their own day, so today each of the faithful longs to welcome him in his own day, because Christ has not made plain the day of his coming" (p. 177). Or another example, from Irenaeus: "From the beginning the word of God prophesied that God would be seen by men and would live among them on earth; he would speak with his own creation and be present to it, bringing it salvation and being visible to it. He would *free us from the hands of all who hate us*, that is, from the universal spirit of sin, and enable us *to serve him in holiness and justice all our days*" (p. 287). The Liturgy of the Hours for Advent provides valuable reflection and prayer on the Christ who became human so that we might grow in holiness.

Most of the Advent hymns are well known by many people: "O Come, O Come Emmanuel," "On Jordan's Bank," "The King of Glory," or the traditionally chanted "Creator of the Stars of Night." Thus, beginning the Liturgy of the Hours during Advent does facilitate the participation of the lay faithful. Keeping progressive solemnity in mind, the opening hymn could be a cappella or even simply accompanied by a flute playing the melody. Even hymns like "The King of Glory" or "The King Shall Come when Morning Dawns" connect Advent to the eschatological theme. The *Universal Norms on the Liturgical Year and the Calendar* (UNLYC) notes the "two-fold character" of Advent when it states that Advent "is a time of preparation for the Solemnities of Christmas, in which the First Coming of the Son of God to humanity is remembered, and likewise a time when, by remembrance of this, minds and hearts are led to look forward to Christ's Second Coming at the end of time" (UNLYC, 39). In particular, December 17–24 prepare for Christ's birth (see UNLYC, 42). These days are associated with the O Antiphons that mark immediate preparation for the celebration of Christ's Incarnation. However, in the busy rush for Christmas it must be noted that Advent is also about Christ's final coming to us. This coming we await in hope and joy, for we shall be united with Christ forever.

The Rite of Christian Initiation of Adults

"The children's progress in the formation they receive depends on the help and example of the companions and on the influence of their parents" (RCIA, 254).

No matter how you feel about the Harry Potter books and movies, they have a lot to say about the significant impact a peer community has on the education and formation of young people. In the final film, *Harry Potter and the Deathly Hallows,* Harry and his friends have the ultimate confrontation with the Dark Lord, Voldemort, and his wicked allies. It's a brutal battle in which Harry and his friends fight fearlessly alongside their adult companions to defeat evil. In the end, goodness overcomes evil. Harry, with the mentoring of the Headmaster and others, teaches his friends that if they are loyal and true and stand united they can overcome even the evil Lord Voldemort. And they do. Good triumphs.

The *Rite of Christian Initiation of Adults* describes very directly the importance of peer companions in the child's journey of faith. Just as Harry's classmates learn from him, young catechumens learn faith in Jesus Christ and the ways of discipleship from their Catholic peers, from dialogue with their parents and other adults, and from being present in the liturgical assembly.

We can push the comparison a little further. Harry has a mission to make his world a better place, and with the help of his community and "catechists" he succeeds. Isn't that the message of the Gospel and the mission of all the baptized as we live out our baptismal callings? What can we learn from Harry's journey that helps us with the liturgical catechesis and prominence of the community so central to ministry with children in the RCIA?

Liturgical Catechesis

There are three different starting points for liturgical catechesis: the preparation, the experience of the liturgical celebration, and reflection back on the experience. No matter what stage of the initiation process a child is in during Advent, the liturgical time presents many opportunities for liturgical catechesis.

The liturgical decorations in the church, in the space for the Liturgy of the Word for children, and in the formational environment, are wonderful "catechists" in themselves when they are prominent and explained. Children respond to color. Deep violet decorations and evergreens alert them to the fact that something different is happening. The ritual of lighting the Advent wreath while singing of "O Come O Come Emmanuel" forms them in the sense of waiting and anticipation.

◆ The celebration of the Liturgy of the Word with children from the parish makes them aware of Catholic reverence for the Word of God and its liturgical significance. Young catechumens also hear the opinions and thoughts of their peers as dialogue happens during the Homily/reflection.

◆ In the follow-up catechetical session to the Sunday liturgy, have the children reflect on and talk about what they saw, heard, and felt during their experience with the assembly and with the Liturgy of the Word. Probe for any questions they may have.

◆ Besides the Liturgy of the Word there are different ways of involving the baptized peers and families in the Rite of Christian Initiation of Adults during Advent. Many parish religious education programs have special family activities during Advent, such as making Advent wreaths or Jesse trees for homes or getting involved in outreach projects for the poor and homeless. Ask those who are in charge of these activities to invite, welcome, and include families of young catechumens.

◆ If parish activities are not provided, invite catechumen families (families of adult and child catechumens) to come together to make Advent wreaths or become involved in an outreach project.

◆ If there are children of catechetical age or adults who have been baptized, or who have participated in a separate ecclesial community, or who are seeking full communion with the Roman Catholic Church (see RCIA, 473) before Easter, this is a good time to prepare them to celebrate the Rite of Penance with the parish community.

The Sacraments of Initiation

THE practices for preparing and celebrating the Sacraments of Initiation with infants and baptized children are diverse and varied throughout the Catholic Church today. In these pages you will find information and resources for infant Baptism, Confirmation, and first Holy Communion. Baptized children who are celebrating

first Holy Communion will also be preparing for their first celebration of Reconciliation, and suggestions are also given for that. Although practice may be diverse there are elements common to most of these practices (see *National Directory for Catechesis* [NDC], 36):

◆ The involvement of children and parents in some type of immediate preparation for the celebration of these sacraments

◆ A catechetical model that gradually and systematically introduces the child and parent to the meaning of the rites and symbols of the sacrament the child will be celebrating (NDC, 35)

◆ A preparation and celebration of Reconciliation separate in time from the preparation of first Holy Communion (see NDC, section 36 B,2)

◆ A text distinct from the basic religious education text which is based on the principles of liturgical catechesis and includes rituals introducing each aspect of the respective sacrament and/or rites to be celebrated with family groups or those involved in lifelong intergenerational programs in the parish.

Both the *General Directory for Catechesis* and the *National Directory for Catechesis* call for models of formation inspired by the baptismal catechumenate. This means involving the liturgical assembly more in the initiation of the children. Involvement may include the actual participation in their preparation, praying for the children and their families, or participating with them in intergenerational gatherings of liturgical and doctrinal catechesis.

Most parishes have communal celebrations of Reconciliation during Advent. Children preparing for their first Reconciliation may participate in these celebrations. Confer with the director of liturgy and director of music on ways to include some of the elements from the rituals the children celebrate during their catechetical sessions. Also ask them to acquaint children with music and hymns which will be used during the celebration.

Use the lighting of the candles as an opportunity to review the giving of a candle at Baptism and being called to be a "child of the light" (*Rite of Baptism for Children*, 180).

A part of the catechumenal model is a sense of apprenticeship for those preparing for initiation. Often during Advent the assembly is called to do acts of service and charity for those in need. Encourage children to participate in those activities.

Advent marks the beginning of the new liturgical year. Make it a point to spend time reflecting on the Sunday readings with children. Be attentive to the First Reading for each of the Sundays and absorb the hope that is there. Advent is a time to "take stock." Help children experience the power of John the Baptizer's "Prepare the way of the Lord, / make straight his paths" (Luke3:4b–5a) proclaimed on the Second Sunday of Advent. Use this as an opportunity for all children to review how to do an examination of conscience in preparation for celebrating the Sacrament of Reconciliation during this liturgical time.

The Rite of Penance

ADVENT is not a specifically penitential time but rather a time of "devout and expectant delight" (UNLYGRC, 39). However, when we expect visitors at home we often prepare to welcome them by organizing and cleaning up. Celebrating the Sacrament of Reconciliation or a prayer service with reconciliation themes (see Appendix II, part II in the *Rite of Penance* for a variety of non-sacramental penance services) is one way for us to prepare and clean up spiritually, for our coming celebration of the Incarnation of Jesus Christ.

Invite parishioners to take advantage of individual reconciliation opportunities offered each week. Encourage parents to bring their children to the Sacrament of Reconciliation. Make it clear that the parish priests will welcome people to contact them if there is anything separating them from the Church.

The whole parish could be gathered for a Rite of Reconciliation of Several Penitents with Individual Confession and Absolution (Form II), of course. But also consider a parish penitential prayer service without individual reconciliation. There is a good sample penitential prayer service for Advent in Appendix II, Part II of the *Rite of Penance* (RP). This penitential service without individual confession gives the parish great flexibility. Everyone can fully participate, even those who have not celebrated first Reconciliation, like very young children and the catechumens. The parish can choose Scriptures that express its own Advent longings and hopes. It is interesting to note that the Introduction to the rite invites us to choose readings from sources other than the Scriptures for these services. These may come from the Doctors (Latin, *docere* = "to teach") of

the Church like Saint Teresa of Avila or Saint Thomas Aquinas or from other inspirational writers and theologians (see RP, 36). Liturgy Training Publications has an excellent resource called *A Lent Sourcebook* that contains many texts from these writers. Be sure to remind people that a penitential prayer service is not the Sacrament of Reconciliation because it does not include individual confession and absolution.

In the Rite of Reconciliation with individual confession we tend, rightly, to focus on our individual growth. But the penitential non-sacramental prayer service suggested in Appendix II can help the parish see itself as a reconciling body for the whole world. It can help us see the more systemic or "social" sin that interferes with the establishment of God's justice and peace. There is an Examination of Conscience (found in the Appendix of the rite) and an Act of Repentance (see RP, Appendix II, 29, E) that can be adapted to the circumstances and needs of the community and the world at this particular moment in time.

The candles on the Advent wreath should be lit near the ambo for the proclamation of the Scriptures. Invite people to light a candle after their confession and place it in a pot of sand before returning to their seat to begin their penance. Watching the candles can help people stay together until the very important Proclamation of Praise for God's Mercy and the Concluding Prayer of Thanksgiving, which are integral parts of the rite.

Candles can also be used during the non-sacramental service. A connection can be made with our longing for the Light of the World to break down the darkness of sin. The light from the Advent wreath could be shared, and candles held during the Examination of Conscience. The examination might be constructed as a kind of litany of lament. For example:

Leader: When people starve, we pray.

All: Come Jesus, come!

The candles should be extinguished after the Act of Repentance (see Appendix II, 29, E).

The Pastoral Care of the Sick

THE Church encourages those who are dangerously ill to ask for anointing at any time (*Pastoral Care of the Sick*, 13) in full faith that they will be strengthened by Christ. The rest of the Church, the family or the liturgical assembly bears witness to that same faith and supports the sick with their prayers. It makes sense that the parish offer communal celebrations of the Anointing of the Sick more than once a year, and Sunday is often a good time because the congregation is present.

However, for the Sundays of Advent, the ritual Mass of anointing is excluded. This means the prayers and readings of the Advent Sunday must be used rather than those from the Mass of Anointing. Nonetheless, the Anointing itself can still be celebrated.

The texts and readings for the Anointing Within Mass (see *Pastoral Care of the Sick*, 131–148) may be used if the parish chooses to anoint at a weekday Mass. The parish may also use the form of Anointing Outside of Mass (111–130) and choose more pertinent texts and readings.

Is there a place in the bulletin that talks about how to ask for Anointing of the Sick and Viaticum? Consider creating a permanent place for this information.

The Rite of Marriage

THE Church sets great store by liturgical time, which forms the faithful. For this reason there are limits to what we may do on Sunday or at the Saturday Mass of anticipation. If Marriage is celebrated on Sunday or at the Mass of anticipation, only the Advent Scriptures and prayers may be used. On other days the Scriptures and prayers may be taken from the *Rite of Marriage*. This is only true for the *Rite of Marriage* in the context of a Mass (Form I). Form II and III (Liturgies of the Word) may use the usual Scripture readings and prayers for Marriage.

There are some other considerations, too. It is Advent—a joyful, but still reflective, time. We have certain colors and symbols during this liturgical time that help us enter into its spirit. The couple should be made aware of the implications of this in regard to the parish environment. The parish should not feel compelled to make changes for the wedding. However, the couple might appreciate some assistance in choosing floral arrangements. In northern climates, for example, the parish might suggest small, unadorned evergreen trees or sprays of evergreen and other foliage.

The Order of Christian Funerals

THE same exclusions we saw for Marriage and Anointing of the Sick apply to ritual Masses of the Dead on Sundays in Advent and on the Solemnity of the Immaculate Conception of the Blessed Virgin Mary. However, a funeral Mass from the *Order of Christian Funerals* may be celebrated on any other day. The other rites, i.e., the vigil and committal service, may be celebrated as usual throughout Advent.

Experiencing the death of a loved one is never easy, but this time of year can be particularly stressful for those who grieve. It may be a good time to examine how the parish ministers to families. Does everyone get the same help from the parish in preparing the funeral? How does the parish deal with sensitive issues of music choices and eulogies? Is much of the pastoral care done by the funeral directors in the neighborhood?

Consider establishing a funeral ministry of people who know the parish conventions as well as the theology of the *Order of Christian Funerals*. Proper formation will allow the minister to answer questions with compassion and pastoral sensitivity. These ministers can meet with the families about music and scripture choices, serve as leaders at the wake service if necessary, and serve as a coordinator for the funeral Mass.

The Book of Blessings

IF the parish uses an Advent Wreath it may be blessed on the First Sunday of Advent. It can also be blessed the evening before at Evening Prayer or in a Liturgy of the Word. The *Book of*

Blessings has good models for both circumstances. Interestingly, the wreath may be blessed by a priest, deacon, or a lay minister (see *Book of Blessings* [BB], 1516).

Perhaps the parish can encourage each household to have an Advent wreath by making them available for purchase in early November. (Children are particularly engaged by lighting and blowing out candles—with adult supervision). Include the blessing from *Catholic Household Blessings & Prayers* or one composed by the parish.

The parish might consider inviting parents and their young children to join in the Blessing of the Christmas Manger or Nativity Scene (BB, chapter 48) when it is put up. Note that the *Book of Blessings* states the manger should not be placed in the sanctuary but in a place "suitable for prayer and devotion and easily accessible by the faithful" (BB, 1544). If very young children are included the language of the prayers may have to be adapted to their sensibilities and the scripture abridged. A lay minister can lead this blessing.

A Christmas tree can be seen as a kind of connection between heaven and earth, with its star or angel at the top and its train or village at the bottom. Chapter 49 of the *Book of Blessings* has a blessing for the tree that can be led by a lay minister. So, too, does *Catholic Household Blessings & Prayers*. Encourage parishioners to bless their trees.

The Liturgical Environment

The Nature of the Liturgical Time

We spend a lot of time waiting: for guests to arrive, for events to unfold, for responses to e-mails, for appointments and vacations, for celebrations to start, and long journeys to end. We all wait. Waiting is a part of life itself, and a part of whatever we wait for. We anticipate the event itself, entering into what has yet to happen with feelings of wonder and curiosity, and with a sense that it's worth waiting for. The event is already part of our consciousness before it happens.

Advent is a time of spiritual waiting; a time that unfolds both on the calendar and in the hearts of believers. Like all waiting it is an active experience in which we consciously enter into the images

and stories of Advent, into its tradition and its profound message for today. Advent is a time of transition as a new liturgical year arrives, a time to pause and contemplate the preparations needed to enter into the profound mystery that we will celebrate at Christmas Time. Each year we renew the images, retell the stories, rejoin the biblical companions, and refresh our memories and our embrace of the astonishing gift of God who takes up a dwelling in our world and in our lives.

Although there is something wonderful about all the expectation that consumes our thoughts and energy during Advent, we can get caught up in the busyness of the time and fail to enter more deeply into the mystery of what and for whom we are waiting. Advent comes from the Latin, *adventus*, which means "the arrival." The word referred to the arrival of a king on an official visit to a town or area of his empire, or to his return from a victorious battle. The citizens would greet him with feasting and exaltation. We will get to Christmas Time, but will we be ready for the arrival of the Lord?

A Pastoral Insight

It is often noted that the liturgy of the Church is countercultural, challenging and critiquing the current ideology of society around us. This may be especially true at this time of year. As the Church celebrates the beginning of a new liturgical year with Advent waiting and reflection, the world around us is "in a hurry" with shopping, parties, and year-end gatherings—all good things in themselves, but they can distract us from entering into the wonder and rich spirituality of Advent. The parish can help by creating places and opportunities that allow people to pause and contemplate the true beauty and spirit of the season.

Practical Suggestions

The beginning of any new year is always a good time to revisit the past and do a personal inventory of what should stay, what should change, what should be discarded, and what can be refreshed and given a new face. The environment and art committee could do the same concerning the liturgical environment. Of course the preparations for Advent and Christmas Time should start two or three months before the First Sunday of Advent. Maybe the time has come to replace that old Advent wreath, to relocate the crèche scene to a more appropriate place (see notes below), to consider a less extravagant display of Christmas plants, trees, swags, or other decorations, and to give more prominence to the principal liturgical furnishings and ritual areas.

The *General Instruction of the Roman Missal* notes that any floral decoration of the sanctuary should be marked by moderation that is suited to the season. The following suggestions might be helpful in respecting this principle:

◆ It is important to realize that the Advent wreath is a secondary liturgical item and does not need to be in a prominent location—it is best if it is not in the sanctuary area.

◆ The Advent wreath has become the most recognizable sign of the liturgical time so it is appropriate that it receive some attention—both by its location and design.

◆ The gathering area, a space adjacent to the sanctuary, a niche or devotional space on the side of the nave, or suspended over the assembly are all suitable places for the Advent wreath.

◆ The wreath should be made of real evergreen boughs; other items that can give the wreath some beauty include white birch twigs, dried flowers like hydrangea blossoms, and winter berries. Adding branches of eucalyptus and incense cedar can add to the aroma of the season. The four candles should be violet, not blue; one of the candles may be rose colored, but that is not required. It is not necessary to place a white candle in the center to represent Christ; this gives a mixed message. The candles can be changed to white at Christmas and the wreath renewed with fresh boughs and other festive items for Christmas Time.

◆ The blessing and lighting of the wreath is not a liturgical rite and should not replace the Penitential Act.

◆ It is appropriate to add plants and flower arrangements for feast days during Advent, e.g. the Feast of Our Lady of Guadalupe, but these should not be lavish and should be left in place only for the day itself.

◆ The use of fabrics can also call attention to Advent; for example, swags over the entrance doorways, simple accents in the sanctuary, and the vesture for the liturgical ministers that reflect the liturgical color tones.

◆ The liturgical color for Advent is violet.

The Liturgical Music

Advent has a rich tradition of hymns. "O Come, O Come Emmanuel" is the all-time favorite, but there are numerous variations of this theme available, including "Wake, Arise" (WACHET AUF), "The King Shall Come," "Wait for the Lord," and other hymns telling us to prepare the way. So for this Advent portion we are not going to provide you with a long list of musical choices; rather, we will review the past year to see what sort of an advent (small "a") it was for your congregation.

For those involved in liturgical music, the past year has been a whirlwind of activities involving the implementation and integration of the third edition of *The Roman Missal*. Now is a good time to evaluate how the first year has been, to take an honest look at the liturgies and programs and ask a few questions. What has gone well? Where are we still on shaky ground? What work remains to be done? How can we continue to grow? How did our initial Mass setting work? Is it a "keeper" or one that simply got us through the transitions? Do we need to move on to another musical setting, and is now the time to do so?

Ideally, you will develop a repertoire over time with several Mass settings that the congregation can begin to associate with different seasons of the year. This is more than a "nifty idea"; it is good, solid liturgical theology. Because your congregation is still experimenting, it is an ideal time to continue to implement changes related to the *General Instruction of the Roman Missal* (GIRM) and the music document from the United States Conference of Catholic Bishops, *Sing to the Lord: Music in Divine Worship* (STL). Take a few moments to read paragraphs 110–119. They provide some very good food for thought on the concept of progressive solemnity and how and why we choose our music.

As STL, 113 reminds us, "The most solemn musical expressions retain their primary responsibility of engaging human hearts in the mystery of Christ that is being celebrated on a particular occasion by the Church." When we recite prayers, it is easy to do so by rote, and move along in "autopilot" mode. That is the double-edged sword of ritual. Familiarity is its gift and its curse. For many many of us this was a year for learning new responses, but as that old comfort level returns, we may become less conscious of what we are saying and praying. When we engage music in our prayer, it reaches another level.

GIRM, 40 reminds us that: "Great importance should therefore be attached to the use of singing in the celebration of the Mass. . . . In the choosing of the parts actually to be sung, however, preference should be given to those that are of greater importance and especially to those to be sung by the priest or the deacon or a lector, with the people responding, or by the priest and people together."

Paragraph 115 of the STL fleshes that out for us and creates a hierarchy:

◆ Dialogues and Acclamations, e.g., "The Lord be with you." Anyone can sing one or two notes. Learn them by heart, and be able to sing a cappella.

◆ Antiphons and Psalms

◆ Responsorial Psalm, Entrance, and Communion chants (Introits)

◆ Refrains anquiet d Repeated Response (Kyrie, Lamb of God, the response to the Prayer of the Faithful and the Litany of the Saints)

◆ Hymns

This includes the Gloria and a few hymns suggested by *The Roman Missal*, as well as the common custom of Entrance Chant, Preparation of the Gifts, Communion Song, and Recessional (the latter is custom, and not required in the ritual). STL notes that hymns must fill their proper liturgical role and may be drawn from other faith traditions as long as they do not contradict Catholic theology.

Now would be an ideal time to begin singing the dialogue chants, and to encourage your priest to sing the Eucharistic Prayers. National Pastoral Musicians (NPM) has created free online rehearsal resources to help us learn the musical parts. The chant notation itself is also online in PDF format through the International Commission on English in the Liturgy (ICEL) and the NPM websites, and could easily be incorporated into your orders of worship. By singing these simple dialogues now, we also create building blocks for other seasons. Indeed, you will be preparing the way. J. Michael Joncas also recorded a series of a cappella chants published by LTP, *Learning the Chants of the Missal, Parts I and II*. These CDs include the complete Order of Mass and the presidential prayers for Sundays, solemnities, and feasts of the Lord. This collection is a fine way for priests to continue to learn the chants included in the third edition of *The Roman Missal*.

Liturgical Ministers

WE commonly associate Advent with John the Baptist and his admonition to "Prepare the way." For the liturgical minister, the cry "Prepare the day" is also most appropriate. All involved in this ministry, whether as readers, choir members, musicians and cantors should do their homework and be well prepared before the assigned Mass time.

Knowing the readings and music is more than just pronouncing the words right, or playing the notes on the page correctly. One must understand the history and context of the Scriptures in order to be a true harbinger like John the Baptist, proclaiming the coming Christ in word and song.

For other ministries, being prepared means getting to church early to find out if there is anything you ought to know about, such as a second collection or a visiting priest who may not be familiar with the Communion distribution plans. Many unexpected things can happen in the daily life of a parish. Do not show up two minutes before and then have a pile of questions for the priest or liturgist. Those moments before Mass begins can be hectic, so don't add to the chaos by arriving unprepared. Most importantly, don't forget to pray before you begin.

For those of you who coordinate liturgical ministries, make sure all involved receive their schedules and preparation materials well in advance. They will thank you. This will give them time to practice or to find replacements for themselves should this be required for some reason.

Devotions and Sacramentals

LITURGY is the source and summit of our worship, but there is a whole other element of personal, devotional prayer in our lives. Historically, there have been times when Church leaders and the people of God have been miles apart in their beliefs, experiences, and educational backgrounds. When the liturgy was unavailable to the people, devotional practices flourished.

For example, the Liturgy of the Hours is a popular prayer of the Church, but when the Psalms were recited in Latin, only the clerics had access to them. This exclusion led to the development of the Rosary, its fifteen decades being a substitute for the one hundred and fifty Psalms. It continues to be a popular devotion, accessible to anyone, anywhere, and at any time.

Devotional prayers often have ethnic and regional cultural considerations, and are centered around the Holy Trinity, Jesus, Mary, or the sanctoral calendar. The *Constitution on the Sacred Liturgy* (CSL) spoke eloquently about this prayer: "Popular devotions of the Christian people are to be highly endorsed, provided they accord with the laws and norms of the Church, above all when they are ordered by the Apostolic See" (CSL, 13) and in 2001, the Congregation for Divine Worship promulgated a wonderful guideline for devotional practice, the *Directory on Popular Piety and the Liturgy* (DPPL). As stated in DPPL (96), "Advent is a time of waiting, conversion and of hope." And it is often popular piety that has sustained the faith of the people through many generations and liturgical periods.

The Advent wreath is a devotion that hails from the Germanic cultures and is widespread. Often because it is so popular, parishes can get carried away liturgically and overwhelm the simplicity of Advent in the process. The *Book of Blessings* (BB, chapter 47) has a simple service, and there are also numerous musical settings available. *Built of Living Stones* (BLS, 128) reminds us to keep the wreath in perspective to the church itself.

Latino cultures bring us two different Advent devotions and traditions. *Las Posadas* is a celebration where the faithful act out the scene of Joseph and Mary trying to find room at the inn. (This devotional activity is carried out in the neighborhood.) People gather inside the church, in the narthex, or outside of the worship space. Two groups of people sing back and forth to each other. Often parishes may combine this celebration with an Advent party with piñatas. While the tradition may have begun with Saint Ignatius, it is celebrated by many Protestants and Catholics alike.

The second celebration centers around Our Lady of Guadalupe. *Las Mañanitas* is a procession to wake the Virgin early on the morning of December 12. Again, the music is accessible from each of the major publishers and several independent locations on the Internet. GIA Publications

offers "Diciembre en México" by Donna Peña, a good resource for both celebrations.

The Filipino Church has a Marian devotion which is very similar to *Los Posadas*. The novena, *Simbang Gabi*, often begins on December 16. This novena also reenacts Mary and Joseph looking for a place in the inn, but a very significant element in this celebration is the use of star-shaped lanterns, or paróls. The star shape is a sign of the Magi. After the early morning Mass, the people would feast on special treats like queso de bola, biblinga, and hot chocolate.

The Jesse Tree is a variation on an Advent calendar, and is a wonderful parish or family activity. It is a scripturally based tradition which explains the genealogy of Jesus: "But a shoot shall sprout from the stump of Jesse, / and from his roots a bud shall blossom" (Isaiah 11:1). The tree has symbolic ornaments and a scripture passage for each day of Advent.

In many parishes, the Christmas pageant is an annual event in which the children take on various roles to act out the story of Jesus's birth. Watching the children retell the sacred story in this way can be very touching. And role playing is a great way for children to enter into the meaning of Christmas. Nonetheless, it would be a good idea to remember the difference between reenactment and remembering. To use acting as a teaching tool for children is a good thing, but not during the liturgy itself. Scripture is to be proclaimed in the usual way, and this type of dramatization would not be acceptable.

DPPL (105) understands this and human nature well as it says, "Popular piety intuitively understands that it is not possible coherently to celebrate the birth of him 'who saves his people from their sins' without some effort to overcome sin in one's own life, while waiting vigilantly for Him who will return at the end of time."

The Parish and the Home

FOLLOWING the Catholic calendar through the year can enrich a parish and its families with the varying sounds, sights, textures, tastes, and smells of different seasons. Children, with their highly attuned sensitivity, should respond easily and quickly to the changes that occur—especially if the seasons are presented in concrete, tangible ways.

Advent is a time when people naturally draw together, indoors. The weather in most parts of the country is colder, the days shorter, and nights longer. It's instinctive to light a candle or a fire, cook hot soup, and be grateful for warm shelter. We still harbor deep fears of winter. To us it often brings illness; to our ancestors it could mean life-threatening blizzards. Starting with that natural impulse, it becomes easier to build an appreciation for Advent.

Families with microwaves and instant communications can also teach the importance of waiting. It may feel unusual, but seems a necessary preparation for anything worthwhile. The Church does not leap immediately into Christmas joy or its vibrant red, gold, and green colors. Instead, Advent is characterized by muted, reflective colors: violet and rose.

Lighting the candle(s) on the Advent wreath nightly, opening a window on the Advent calendar, reading a Scripture passage, singing a song, or making a craft: all these regular practices convey, sometimes without words, a sense of order and ritual to children. If they see that other family members make time for these important traditions, they too will value them.

Advent songs and the scriptures express a longing for Christ to come. Historically, he has already come, into a small Judean town during the reign of the Roman emperor Augustus. We yearn now for the world to change, becoming soaked in the Gospel, permeated with Christ's presence, and for us to become more compassionate, Christ-like people. We ask for justice to reach the most vulnerable and oppressed, and for conflict to end peacefully.

Such an attitude begins at home, where we work to disarm our hearts. Isaiah's vision of the lion and lamb lying down together doesn't mean that the lion sprouts fur or the lamb begins to roar. Each remains unique and individual, distinct and harmonious. One way to practice this in the home is the ancient custom of placing a piece of straw in a manger to soften the bed of the coming Christ child. The manger can be one from the crèche set, or one made from cardboard. Family members place their straws there every time they avoid a nasty comment or argument, each time they compliment or encourage each other.

Advent is also rich in feasts which enliven home celebrations. For the optional Memorial of Saint Nicholas (December 6), some families put their shoes outside their bedroom doors; then one member fills them with tiny gifts or candies. Another custom is to do anonymous good deeds for each other: sewing on a missing button, washing a car, emptying the trash. For the Solemnity of the Immaculate Conception (December 8), two children (or two people with puppets) could act out the story of the angel Gabriel's announcement to Mary (Luke 1:26–38). The Feast of Our Lady of Guadalupe is on December 12. Prepare for it by telling the story of Juan Diego, then making crepe paper flowers in bright colors to honor the way his cloak miraculously filled with roses in December to prove that his vision of Mary was true. On December 13, Scandinavian families honor Saint Lucy whose name means "light." The oldest daughter prepares rolls and coffee or hot chocolate. Wearing a crown of lit candles, she then brings breakfast to family members.

Las Posadas begins December 16. For nine days, Mexican families walk through their neighborhoods singing and looking for a place to shelter Mary and Joseph. They are turned away from many doors. Finally, on the last night (Christmas Eve), they are welcomed. The Nativity figures are enshrined in this home, and a party follows. It's a way to remember the strangers in our midst, through whom we welcome Christ. Just as children's anticipation for Christmas grows, so does the Church's. On December 17, the world-wide Church begins to sing the O Antiphons. The prayers use many of Christ's titles. Families could try to find concrete representations for some of these: for instance, a flower, a key, a picture of dawn.

Mass Texts

◆ Sample Text for the Prayer of the Faithful

Additional texts are found in Appendix V of The Roman Missal

Celebrant:

As we begin this holy time of Advent,
let us ask the Lord Jesus
to come again to our world,
bringing salvation to all who stand in need.

Our response is:

Come, Lord Jesus!

Deacon/Lector/Reader:

For the Church,
that she may joyfully welcome the Savior,
Jesus Christ,
in the poor and lowly of this world.
We pray:

For all nations,
that in this time of hope
they may let go of old grievances,
and walk the way of peace together.
We pray:

For the homeless,
that by God's grace and our help
they may know the comfort of a hot meal
and a safe place to sleep
during these winter months.
We pray:

For our beloved dead,
especially N._____,
that they may be brought into the peace
of God's presence,
with all their sins forgiven.
We pray:

For this parish community
at the beginning of a new liturgical year,
that the coming months may be a time of grace
for each of us, and for all whose lives touch ours.
We pray:

Celebrant:

Come, Lord, and do not delay!
Open our hearts in love, our hands in sharing,
and make us ready for the coming of that
    kingdom where you live and reign with the
Father in the unity of the Holy Spirit,
one God, for ever and ever.
Amen.

◆ **Dismissal Text for Catechumens**

Nourished by the Word of God,
go forth from this assembly now
to ponder deeply the meaning of God's word
for you and for the Church.
Our prayers and encouragement go with you
as together we await the coming of our Savior,
    Jesus Christ.

◆ **Dismissal Text for Children's Liturgy of the Word**

Dear children, God speaks to all our hearts;
and his message has a special meaning for you
as well as for the rest of us.
Go now with your leader who will help you
    listen and respond to God's word.
When you return to us here,
we will join together in giving God praise and
    thanks for all his goodness.

◆ **Dismissal Text for Extraordinary Ministers of Holy Communion**

Go now to undertake your sacred ministry of
    bringing the Bread of Life
to those whose illness keeps them from our table.
Speak to them God's healing word and share
    with them Christ's body,
which is kneaded with our love and supplication.
Be as Christ to them,
reminding them their absence from our midst
makes them no less a member of our community,
and that their suffering is rich soil
in which God's mercy and salvation take
    deep root.

December
Month of the Divine Infancy

2 #3   violet
First Sunday of Advent

Orientation

As we enter into Advent and begin another liturgical year, the Gospel account reorients us to our ultimate hope in the second coming of the Son of Man, our Lord Jesus Christ. Hope in Christ's return at the end of the age is indeed what fills us with profound joy and anticipation, as we await the power and glory of Christ that will put an end to all sorrow, suffering, and pain, and bring the reign of God into fullness. As Christians, this truth underlies the way we make sense of our world in the here and now, and makes us into a People of Hope, who are in constant preparation to stand erect before Christ in Majesty at the end of time.

Lectionary for Mass

◆ FIRST READING: The prophet's words are set in the context of the Babylonian conquest of Jerusalem. Just as all seems lost, God reiterates his promise of a Davidic heir on the throne in Jerusalem (see 2 Samuel 7:16). What is more, the future king will be a righteous king whose reign shall bring peace and security to a troubled land. Christians see this promise as ultimately fulfilled in Jesus, the Son of David (see Luke 1:32).

◆ RESPONSORIAL PSALM 25 is a confident hymn for guidance in the ways of the Lord, who is Savior.

◆ SECOND READING: Paul prays for his readers and exhorts them to be faithful to the manner of life learned from him as they await the coming of the Lord Jesus—an event they expected to happen within their own lifetimes.

◆ GOSPEL: Using the language of apocalyptic literature, Luke speaks of the cosmic signs that will herald the coming of the Lord, here called by the title Son of Man. While many fear the day as one of judgment, Luke's audience has every reason to see it as a day of redemption if they have been faithful. As they await that great day, they must be careful to live with expectation and fidelity.

The Roman Missal

Advent involves waiting. We wait with joy for the celebration of Christmas, and we wait with hope for the second coming of Christ. This hope can often be tinged with fear, because the second coming will be a time of judgment; Jesus's words about the second coming in the Gospel accounts are full of this uncertainty. The Entrance Antiphon for the First Sunday of Advent, taken from Psalm 25:1–3, is a prayer for confidence. "To you, I lift up my soul, O my God . . . / let me not be put to shame . . . / let none who hope in you be put to shame." In the words of the old hymn, "'twas grace that taught my heart to fear, and grace my fears relieved."

The Collect for the first Mass of Advent echoes the Last Judgment parables of Matthew 25. The first part of the prayer recalls the wise virgins (Matthew 25:1–13). We pray for the resolve to be among those who "run forth" with eagerness to meet Christ at his coming, carrying, not lamps, but "righteous deeds." The second part echoes the parable of the sheep and the goats (Matthew 25:31–46). We hope to be gathered with the sheep at his right hand, and "possess the heavenly Kingdom."

Today's Prayer over the Offerings is also prayed on Mondays and Thursdays during the first three weeks of Advent. It expresses the divine exchange that takes place in the celebration of the Eucharist. We can only offer to God what God has already given to us; we pray that our devout celebration of the Eucharist "here below" will gain for us the eternal life of heaven.

Preface I of Advent is used today.

The Prayer after Communion (also prayed on Mondays and Thursdays during the first three weeks of Advent) contrasts earth with heaven. In our celebration of the Eucharist, the "mysteries . . . / in which we have participated," we bridge the space between the two. We "walk amid passing things," but the Eucharist teaches us to cling to what lasts forever, "the things of heaven."

Other Ideas

Place an Advent wreath in your home. Its circular shape and greenery symbolize eternity and everlasting life. The candles celebrate Jesus, the Light of the World. Violet is the liturgical color of preparation, reminding us to turn our hearts to God, and the rose-colored candle exhorts us to rejoice, for we are assured of our Lord's faithfulness. As you light the candles, pray together, read a passage from the Gospel for that Sunday, and sing an Advent hymn.

M O N **3** #175 white
Memorial of Saint Francis Xavier, Priest

Lectionary for Mass

◆ FIRST READING: "In days to come . . ." (Isaiah 2:2). We hear all that the Lord will accomplish as teacher of the nations, as judge, as the one who proclaims and makes peace. Come . . . let us listen to the voice of the Lord. "Come, / let us walk in the light of the Lord!" (Isaiah 2:5).

◆ RESPONSORIAL PSALM 122 is a pilgrimage Psalm, sung as pilgrims made their way to the Temple. Notice how themes from the First Reading are echoed here: the Lord's house, judgment, peace.

◆ GOSPEL: "Comings" are likewise mentioned throughout today's Gospel. (This is not evident in the English translation, but both Jesus's entry into Capernaum and the centurion's approach to Jesus are forms of the Greek verb meaning "to come.") Jesus the healer offers to come to the centurion's house to heal his servant. Protesting his unworthiness and knowing the authority his own word carries, the centurion asks only for a healing word from Jesus because he believes in its power. In the Gospel, as is foretold in the First Reading, the days *have* come . . . when Gentiles as well as Jews come to the Lord. And on the last day, Gentiles from all nations will come with Jews to the banquet of the Lord.

The Roman Missal

The prayers today are found in the Proper of Saints. If desired, the seasonal Collect for Monday of the First Week of Advent may be used at the conclusion of the Prayer of the Faithful.

With Saint Thérèse of the Child Jesus, Saint Francis Xavier is the patron of the missions. The Collect reflects his missionary zeal, and the preaching through which God "won many peoples." We pray that the same zeal for the faith may burn in us, so that the Church may rejoice "in an abundance of offspring." We, too, are called to spread the Gospel.

The Prayer over the Offerings makes the same point: Saint Francis "journeyed to distant lands / out of longing for the salvation of souls." We pray that we may also bear witness to the Gospel, and "hasten" toward God with a great company of our brothers and sisters.

In the Prayer after Communion, we pray that the mysteries we have celebrated may kindle in us the fire that burned in Saint Francis Xavier, so that we may do as he did, and share his reward.

Today's Saint

Saint Francis Xavier (1506–1552), a native Spaniard, was one of the founding members of the Society of Jesus (the Jesuits). Francis Xavier felt called to be a "spiritual soldier" through missionary endeavors to Christianize foreign lands and convert the hearts of unbelievers. One of the many honors Francis received in his life was his appointment by the pope as apostolic nuncio (an ambassador of the Church) to the East. He traveled to many places, including India, the Philippines, and Japan. In his travels, Francis tended to the needs of the sick and infirm, revitalized the liturgical and sacramental life of already existing Christian populations, and drew people to faith in Jesus Christ.

T U E **4** #176 violet
Advent Weekday

Optional Memorial of Saint John Damascene, Priest and Doctor of the Church / white

Lectionary for Mass

◆ FIRST READING: Today's text begins and ends looking to "that day" of the Lord when his messianic promise will be realized. Jesse, the father of King David, his longed-for descendant who would reestablish the nations and restore peace is likewise mentioned in both of these places. The first half of the reading describes the qualities of this anointed one; in particular, his endowment with the Spirit of the Lord and the gifts the Spirit brings. His reign will be marked by harmony among people, within nature, and between humankind and nature. The glory of this messianic era will be recognized not only by Jews, but also by Gentiles.

◆ RESPONSORIAL PSALM 72: Today's Psalm response reiterates the qualities of the messianic king's reign. Indeed, these qualities are characteristics of God: justice, concern for the poor and the afflicted. Note also the reference to the Gentiles. All tribes of the earth shall be blessed, all nations shall praise him.

◆ GOSPEL: Luke portrays Jesus as the Spirit-endowed Messiah spoken of in today's First Reading. Today's text focuses on the depth of the relationship between Father and Son and the communication between them, all of which Jesus shares with those who follow him. Thus, his disciples are truly blessed, for they see and hear the fullness of what the prophets and kings of old longed for.

The Roman Missal

If the optional Memorial of Saint John Damascene is observed, the Collect may be taken from the Proper of Saints, with the remaining prayers and Preface of the Advent weekday.

In the Collect, we ask God's "compassionate help" to meet the challenges of life, so that in all our trials we may be consoled by Christ's presence, and freed from "the corruption of former ways." Even as we are consoled by Christ's presence, we await his coming.

See Second Sunday of Advent for the Prayer over the Offerings and the Prayer after Communion.

Today's Saint

Monk, Doctor of the Church, theologian, scholar, poet, hymnologist, liturgist—these are just a few of the roles Saint John (657–749) fulfilled as a faithful son of the Church. Most notably, he is remembered for his avid defense of the use of sacred art in churches, monasteries, and homes. Born only five years after the death of Muhammad, John was thrust into conflict, particularly regarding a heresy called iconoclasm. The iconoclastic heresy, which sought to destroy all images of devotion, resulted from the misinterpretation on the part of the emperor and many others that Christians were using sacred art as a means of idol worship. Saint John composed three treatises with the goal of lifting up images of Christ, the saints, and Mary as a doorway to the mystery of God's saving work.

WED 5 #177 violet
Advent Weekday

Lectionary for Mass

◆ FIRST READING: God's words, addressed to a people enshrouded in the darkness of sorrow and death, bring a message of hope: the God for whom they wait will come, bringing salvation and providing an abundant feast for his people on his holy mountain. What joy will be theirs!

◆ RESPONSORIAL PSALM 23 is a beautiful song of confidence and trust in the Lord who shepherds us through the valley of darkness and death to an abundant feast. Truly we can know that we will live in the house of the Lord all the days of our life.

◆ GOSPEL: On a mountain in Galilee, Jesus removes the darkness and sorrow of those with physical afflictions and provides a meal for the hungry crowd that has followed him. What joy was theirs as they glorified God for the salvation they experienced in Jesus. Do we allow him to remove the darkness and sorrow that enshroud us and to provide for our needs as well?

The Roman Missal

We know that only God's power can "prepare our hearts" for the coming of the Lord. In the Collect, we pray that we may be found worthy to come to the banquet of life, where we will receive "heavenly nourishment" from the Lord's own hands. In the Eucharist, we have the foretaste of that heavenly banquet.

THU 6 #178 violet
Advent Weekday

Optional Memorial of Saint Nicholas, Bishop / white

Lectionary for Mass

◆ FIRST READING: "On that day"— the phrase is a repeated refrain in our readings thus far this week. On that day the Lord comes with power to save his people, a song will be sung throughout the land. The people of Israel, a just and faithful people, enter the holy city. It is a time of freedom for the oppressed and downtrodden, the destruction of the high and lofty, and the lifting up of the poor and needy.

◆ RESPONSORIAL PSALM 118 is a song of thanksgiving for the merciful deeds of God. The theme of trust (heard two times in the First Reading) pervades the first stanza. The second speaks of opening the gates so God's people can enter. The third focuses on the salvation that accompanies the arrival of the one who comes in the name of the Lord.

◆ GOSPEL: Entering the kingdom is the focus of today's Gospel. The requirements are doing the will of the Father and acting on the words of the Lord that one has heard. Does not building on the rock evoke the firm purpose of the First Reading? What is our house or "where we're at," as the expression goes, built on?

The Roman Missal

If the optional Memorial of Saint Nicholas is observed, the Collect may be taken from the Proper of Saints, with the remaining prayers and preface of the Advent weekday.

The Collect (Proper of Time), which echoes Psalm 80:3, is full of urgency: "Stir up your power, O Lord, / and come to our help with mighty strength." Our sins hold us back, but God's mercy can overcome these obstacles and speed us on our way.

Today's Saint

Little is known about Nicholas, the "wonderworker," other than the fact that he lived sometime during the fourth century and was bishop of the city of Myra in Asia Minor. There is some evidence that he was imprisoned during the Diocletian persecutions, and later condemned Arianism, a heresy that denied the Son was co-eternal with the Father. Many stories exist about Saint Nicholas, but the best known is the one about a poor man who could not feed or clothe his three daughters. Upon hearing of this man's dire situation, Saint Nicholas tossed three bags of gold through his window one evening so the man could tend to his daughters' needs. Modern folklore about Santa Claus, Kris Kringle, and Father Christmas are based on the stories of Saint Nicholas and his great love for and generosity toward children.

#179 white
FRI 7 Memorial of Saint Ambrose, Bishop and Doctor of the Church

Lectionary for Mass

◆ FIRST READING: "On that day . . . the deaf shall hear . . . the blind shall see . . ." (Isaiah 29:18). Earlier in chapter 29, verse 9, not included in today's reading, the blind are those who have blinded themselves in a metaphorical rather than physical way. That longed-for day of the Lord will be a day of healing and insight, of rejoicing in the Lord, of freedom from oppression. This is the saving work of the Lord in our midst.

◆ RESPONSORIAL PSALM: The Lord is light for those unable to see, the salvation of all who are oppressed and afflicted. Psalm 27 speaks of deep confidence in the Lord. Note the three "seeing" words in the last two stanzas. The Psalm ends with the very fitting Advent exhortation to "wait for the Lord."

◆ GOSPEL: Today's account of the healing of the blind men is a nice complement to both the First Reading and the Responsorial Psalm. Note that the blind men "followed" (an image of discipleship) Jesus into the house. By seeking the presence and touch of the Lord they receive sight. This experience of salvation was too much to contain, and they spread this Good News throughout the land.

The Roman Missal

The prayers today are found in the Proper of Saints. If desired, the Collect for Monday of the First Week of Advent may be used at the conclusion of the Prayer of the Faithful.

The Collect for this Memorial of Saint Ambrose is a prayer for vocations. We ask God to "raise up . . . / men after your own heart," who will govern the Church with courage and wisdom as Saint Ambrose did.

In the Prayer over the Offerings, we pray that the Holy Spirit, who enlightened Saint Ambrose with such great wisdom for the spreading of the Gospel, may fill us with light as well.

In the Prayer after Communion, we pray that we may learn from Saint Ambrose, and walk "fearlessly" in the Lord's ways, so that we may be prepared for the eternal banquet of heaven.

Today's Saint

Saint Ambrose (339—397) was esteemed as a man of ardent faith with a flair for diplomacy. He was unanimously chosen as bishop of Milan at a time when the Church was in upheaval over the Arian controversy. He was an unlikely choice: although a professed Christian, he had not yet been baptized. Throughout his life he boldly rebuked emperors such as Theodosius and Valentinian, warriors like the ruthless Maximus, and unfaithful Christians. He prevented wars and invasions, demanded repentance on the part of sinful leaders, and brought people and nations together when reconciliation seemed impossible. Saint Ambrose, a prodigious writer of homiletics, is counted as one of the four original Doctors of the Church, along with Saint Augustine, Saint Jerome, and Saint Gregory.

#689 white
SAT 8 Solemnity of the Immaculate Conception of the Blessed Virgin Mary, Patronal Feastday of the United States of America
HOLYDAY OF OBLIGATION

Orientation

Although our Gospel reading narrates the story of Jesus' conception, today's solemnity celebrates the Immaculate Conception of Mary, as she was conceived in her mother's womb. Prepared by God from the very first moment of her life to receive Jesus Christ, God's grace preserved Mary from sin from the womb to the end of her life, because of her role in the mystery of salvation as the mother of Jesus Christ. Today's solemnity praises God for the hope and possibility that Mary embodies, as we turn to our Blessed Mother to learn from the first and most important relationship Jesus Christ experienced among us.

Lectionary for Mass

◆ FIRST READING: A stark contrast can be drawn between the responses of Adam and Eve to God in today's First Reading and that of Mary in today's Gospel. Adam and Eve had reason to fear God because of their disobedience; Mary, who had found favor with God, had no reason to fear. Adam and Eve's disobedience led to punishment; Mary's receptivity and obedience, to salvation. Adam and Eve's sin resulted in enmity between the woman and the serpent (the evil one); Mary's offspring was to be holy. Eve became the mother of all the living; Mary became the mother of the Son of God—and of all who would be reborn in him.

◆ RESPONSORIAL PSALM 98 is a hymn of praise to God the King. He has done, and is doing, marvelous deeds. Ever faithful to his covenant of old, he brings salvation not only to Israel but to all nations.

◆ SECOND READING: This is yet another contrast with today's First Reading given Paul's emphasis on the blessings believers have received in Christ. We were chosen (mentioned two times) even before the foundation of the world (and the fall of the first human creatures) to receive God's salvation and to be a people of praise.

◆ GOSPEL: Mary is "full of grace" and "found favor with God" when she received the angel's message that she was to be the mother of Jesus, the Son of the Most High (Luke 1:28). Mary is perplexed, "greatly troubled" the text says, at what this means, at how it could be (Luke 1:29). It can be, and is, through the power of God. In contrast with Adam and Eve, who asserted their own will over and against God, Mary humbly acquiesces in the face of the mystery: I am God's servant.

The Roman Missal

The Gloria and the Creed are said or sung on this Solemnity.

God preserved Mary from the stain of original sin that she might be "a worthy dwelling" (Collect) for his Son. There is a great mystery here: Mary was kept sinless "by virtue of the Death" of Christ (Collect). Even before the Word became flesh in Mary's womb, she was a sharer in Christ's Paschal Mystery. We pray that through her intercession, we too may be

"cleansed" and come into God's presence (Collect).

In the Pryaer over the Offerings, we praise the "prevenient grace" of God, which preserved the Virgin from "any stain of sin." We pray that through her prayers, we may know God's forgiveness.

The Preface points to Mary as the "beginning of the Church, / his beautiful Bride without spot or wrinkle" (echoing Ephesians 5:27). In her innocence, Mary gives birth to "the innocent Lamb" who will take away the sins of the world. For us, God's people, the Virgin is both "advocate of grace" and "model of holiness."

Only Mary is preserved from original sin from the moment of her conception. But, in the Prayer after Communion, we pray that by the power of the sacrament we receive, "the wounds of that fault" may be healed in us.

Solemn Blessing #15, "The Blessed Virgin Mary," may be used.

Other Ideas

Visit the statue of Mary in your parish church. Light a candle, thank God for Mary saying yes to God's marvelous plan, and say a prayer together for all expectant mothers and for all those entrusted with leading children to Jesus.

Place a statue of Mary near your Advent wreath or in another prominent place in your home. Say the Rosary together, using the Joyful Mysteries, or say one decade if your child is young. Point out that the first part of the Hail Mary is taken from the angel's greeting. Tuck a pink rose into your Advent wreath in honor of Mary, the Mystical Rose, or weave a white ribbon through the greenery to celebrate the pure-heartedness of our Blessed Mother. Sing a Marian hymn together, or play a recording of the "Ave Maria."

☀9 #6   violet
Second Sunday of Advent

Orientation

John the Baptist's proclamation to prepare the way of the Lord is urgent, full of joy and excitement, as well as concern about readiness to face the glory of God. this busy season of preparation, when our calendars fill with social engagements and so much needs to be done before Christmas arrives, we can identify somewhat with John's joyful urgency. At the same time, John's cry in the desert offers us a moment of transcendence: what we are really preparing for is the coming of the Lord, who brings justice, wholeness, and right relationship with God. As we approach Christmas, the coming of the Lord grounds our hearts in the joy of preparing his way, even amidst the busyness of our lives.

Lectionary for Mass

◆ FIRST READING: Baruch's words stem from the time of the Babylonian conquest of Jerusalem, when many of its leading citizens were led into Exile, and its Temple destroyed. It was indeed a time of mourning. The prophet calls for an end to this, promising a new era to be inaugurated by God: a time of peace and glory, a time of restoration and return. God will lead his people into this new period of their history with joy, guiding them by his own light.

◆ RESPONSORIAL PSALM 126 is a joyful hymn of praise celebrating the return of God's people from exile to their own land.

◆ SECOND READING: Paul prays with thanksgiving for his beloved community at Philippi, that has supported, indeed shared in, his ministry on behalf of the Gospel. Note the two references to the day of Christ. All of Paul's work, all of Christian life, keeps this day in view. It is the day of the coming of the Lord who will reward his faithful people for their fidelity.

◆ GOSPEL: Luke situates the prophetic ministry of John the Baptist within its historical context. Yes, the Lord will come into human history, visible to human eyes, bringing God's salvation. His way must be prepared.

The Roman Missal

"O people of Sion, behold, / the Lord will come . . . ." The Entrance Antiphon for the Second Sunday of Advent is a good summary of Advent. Again and again, the Advent liturgy calls us to sit up and take notice, to "behold"! And what are we to take notice of? The Lord's coming! The signs of his presence and action are all around us; we just need to open our eyes.

The intricate Collect reminds us that we are on a journey to meet Christ. We pray that "no earthly undertaking" may distract us from our pilgrim progress, so that, taught by divine wisdom, we may be welcomed into Christ's presence.

Saint Thérèse of the Child Jesus famously said that she would come before God with empty hands. In the Prayer over the Offerings, the Church expresses the same awareness that "we have no merits to plead our cause," and so we ask God to

save us not because we deserve it, but because of his mercy.

In the Prayer after Communion, we pray that our sharing in the Eucharist may lead us to greater discernment, that we may "judge wisely the things of earth / and hold firm to the things of heaven."

Other Ideas

John the Baptist fed on locusts and wild honey. Enjoy a special snack of apple slices dipped in honey as a reminder of the sweetness of God's love and goodness. As you eat, make a game of counting your family's blessings, and see who can think of the most.

Like voices crying out, "Prepare the way of the Lord" (Isaiah 40:3), go caroling in your neighborhood or a nursing home, singing not Christmas carols, but the Advent carols and hymns your parish is singing at this liturgical time. If you don't know the words by heart, ask to borrow a couple of hymnals for the week. For added fun, dress in the colors of Advent, pass out inexpensive violet ornaments, and wish everyone a happy Advent!

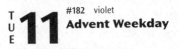

#181 violet
Advent Weekday

Lectionary for Mass

◆ FIRST READING: Here is your God; he comes with vindication. He comes to save you. The coming of the Lord will be a time of full blossoming of the earth and total healing of human infirmities. God makes a way for his people to walk as they journey to the holy city Jerusalem—for Isaiah, an exiled people; for us, a people exiled from our heavenly Jerusalem.

◆ RESPONSORIAL PSALM: The antiphon is from the First Reading: "our God will come to save us."

Psalm 85 speaks of the characteristics of the time of salvation: kindness, truth, justice, peace, prosperity.

◆ GOSPEL: The Lord has come, bringing salvation in the person of Jesus of Nazareth. Note that Jesus heals by the "power of the Lord" (Luke 5:17). What tremendous faith the paralyzed man's friends had! What lengths (or rather heights) they went to in order to bring their friend to Jesus! In Jesus' day it was thought that physical infirmities were punishment for sin. The salvation Jesus came to bring included not only physical healing, but forgiveness of sin.

The Roman Missal

The Collect echoes Psalm 141, with its image of prayer rising to God like incense: "May our prayer of petition / rise before you, we pray, O Lord." This is a prayer for purification, that we may be worthy to celebrate the Incarnation of God's only Son at Christmas.

Prayer over the Offerings and Prayer after Communion: See First Sunday of Advent.

11 **#182** violet
Advent Weekday
T U E

Optional Memorial of Saint Damasus I, Pope / white

Lectionary for Mass

◆ FIRST READING: The same reading as on Sunday, with the inclusion of verses 5–8 (omitted on Sunday). These verses invite us to reflect on the transitory nature of human existence and the enduring power of the Lord.

◆ RESPONSORIAL PSALM 96, a joyful hymn of praise, celebrates the kingship of God. The reference in the third stanza to nature as fully alive stands in contrast with what we heard in today's First Reading. The last stanza picks up on the theme of the Lord's coming.

◆ Gospel: The image of shepherd at the end of today's Gospel is fulfilled in Jesus, the Good Shepherd.

Today's text emphasizes in particular Jesus' seeking out, and finding, the lost sheep.

The Roman Missal

God has shown his salvation to the very ends of the earth! In the Collect, we pray that we may "look forward in joy" to the coming feast of Christmas.

See Second Sunday of Advent for the Prayer over the Offerings and the Prayer after Communion.

Today's Saint

Saint Damasus I (+ 384): Two significant historical events formed the backdrop of this saint's life: the witness of courageous martyrs during the Diocletian persecutions and the granting of religious freedom to Christians by Emperor Constantine. Saint Damasus I reigned as pope for 24 years, He is remembered for revitalizing devotion to the relics of martyrs by adorning catacombs, building churches, making shrines more accessible, and marking the resting places of the martyrs with unique inscriptions and epigrams. He is also remembered for his innate ability to bring about uniformity and peace in an empire recently characterized by persecution and infiltrated with paganism. Among his many other accomplishments, Saint Damasus is credited with encouraging Saint Jerome to produce a new translation of the Latin Bible, called the Vulgate.

WED 12   #690A or #707–712   white
Feast of Our Lady of Guadalupe
PATRONESS OF THE AMERICAS

Orientation

Behind the miraculous appearance and icon that define Our Lady of Guadalupe is a story of persistence and courage. When Our Lady appeared to Juan Diego, she sent him to the bishop to request that a church be built. Juan Diego, an indigenous peasant farmer, had no status, power, or influence with which to impress the bishop, yet he followed Our Lady's request. Risking rejection or even ridicule, he returned twice with his amazing story of the vision. With the blooming flowers packed in his tilma (poncho), and the miraculous icon that emerged beneath them, Our Lady helped Juan Diego make his point. The story teaches us trust, and the certainty that when God calls us to proclaim his kingdom, we are surrounded by the grace we need to see our mission through. May we persist in sharing the Good News, even in the face of great challenges.

Lectionary for Mass

◆ First Reading: Today's reading from Zechariah takes on new meaning in light of today's feast of Our Lady of Guadalupe and her appearance to the humble peasant, Juan Diego. This visitation of God's mother was an occasion of deep joy, as nations of Hispanic peoples join themselves to the Lord through her, celebrating his presence among them.

◆ Canticle: A hymn from the book of Judith, the Jewish woman who saved her people from destruction at the hands of the foreign enemies. Christians see her as prefiguring Mary, the mother of God, who had a preeminent role in saving humanity from eternal destruction.

◆ Second Reading: We hear of the vision of the Christian prophet John about a woman in the heavens, traditionally interpreted as Mary, the Mother of God. Her child, rescued from the devil's fury, is ruler of the nations and enthroned with God. The woman is led to a place God has prepared for her.

◆ Gospel: Two choices are given, both from Luke 1: the Annunciation to Mary or the visitation of Mary and Elizabeth. Both focus on the marvelous deed of Mary, the mother of Jesus, in her "yes" to be the mother of the Lord, thus saving her people from eternal destruction.

The Roman Missal

The Gloria is said or sung.

God has placed us under the protection of the Mother of Christ. In the Collect, we pray that all who invoke the Virgin of Guadalupe may "seek . . . / the progress of peoples in the ways of justice and peace." Our Lady of Guadalupe came not to the rich and powerful, but to the poor and humble; we are to do the same.

When the Virgin appeared to Saint Juan Diego, she called him her "dear son." In the Prayer over the Offerings, we ask that the sacrifice we offer may strengthen us to live "as true children of the Virgin Mary."

One of the two Prefaces of the Blessed Virgin Mary is used. The second option, with its echoes of Mary's Magnificat, might be especially fitting today.

In the Prayer after Communion, we pray that the Eucharist may "reconcile us," and that all who rejoice in Our Lady of Guadalupe may live in unity and peace.

Other Ideas

If the parish has a devotion to Our Lady of Guadalupe, a good-sized image—a picture, statue or window—can be reverenced during the Introductory Rites with incense, flowers, and candles.

13 #184   red
Memorial of Saint Lucy, Virgin and Martyr

Lectionary for Mass

◆ FIRST READING: How much lower could Israel, addressed as maggot and worm, go? How much more fearful could they become? What words of assurance—and indeed of promise—are spoken to them! God is their helper and redeemer, the one who delivers them from their oppression. Their lot will be completely overturned. Joy and flourishing new life, a new creation accomplished by the hand of the Lord, await them.

◆ RESPONSORIAL PSALM 145: This hymn of praise and thanksgiving to God the King is a fitting response to today's reading. Note the reference to God's might (last line, second stanza), echoing the motif of the power of "the hand of the Lord" in today's First Reading. Note also the references to God's goodness and compassion to his creatures (first stanza), the major theme of today's First Reading.

◆ GOSPEL: Jewish tradition, drawing on Malachi 3:23–24, expected the return of the prophet Elijah before the coming of the Messiah. This prophecy, fulfilled in the presence of John the Baptist, affirms Jesus in today's Gospel. Jesus's words to the crowds contain a haunting warning: "If you are willing to accept it. . . . Whoever has ears ought to hear" (Matthew 11:14–15). They, and we, must be receptive to Jesus and his teaching.

The Roman Missal

The Collect is from the Proper of Saints. The other prayers may be drawn from the Common of Martyrs: For a Virgin Martyr, or from the Common of Virgins: For One Virgin, or from the Advent weekday.

Saint Lucy was blinded by the cruelty of her persecutors, but saw heavenly things with great clarity. In the Collect, we ask for "new heart" through her intercession, so that we may "behold things eternal" as she did.

Today's Saint

Even from a young age, Saint Lucy (c. + 304) had a burning desire to serve God and an infinite love for the poor. Living in Syracuse, a city in Sicily, she fell prey to the Diocletian persecutions, which eventually resulted in her martyrdom. She resisted a man, believed to be a Roman soldier, who tried to rape her. He, in turn, denounced her as a Christian and had her tortured and killed. Numerous legends revolve around her death. One well-known legend is that she tore out her eyes to resist her attacker. Her name comes from the Latin *lux / Lucia*, meaning light; therefore, many northern countries honor her at this time of year when darkness is pervasive. Sweden celebrates the virginity and martyrdom of Saint Lucy during a festival of light with a sacred procession of young girls clothed in white dresses with red sashes, and crowned with lit candles.

14 #185   white
Memorial of Saint John of the Cross, Priest and Doctor of the Church

Lectionary for Mass

◆ FIRST READING: Isaiah must have written these words after spending some time on the seashore, where nature spoke to him of Israel's relationship with God. Today's text emphasizes God's role as "Teacher," and the commandments are what is taught. If Israel obeyed, their prosperity would be like a flowing river with its abundant harvest of fish. Israel's descendants would be as numerous as the sands on the seashore (as God had earlier told Abraham in Genesis 22:17); their vindication, like the waves of the sea—at times powerful, at times gentle—rolling over and washing all that they encounter.

◆ RESPONSORIAL PSALM 1: We hear a continuation of the theme of the Lord as teacher, and the happiness and prosperity of those who obey him. Note that we also have more images from nature: the flourishing tree and the chaff.

◆ GOSPEL: There is a sad irony in today's text. No matter who the messenger or what the message, the generation of Jesus's contemporaries failed to respond. God's wisdom, personified in Jesus, will ultimately be made known.

The Roman Missal

Today's prayers are found in the Proper of Saints. If you wish, you may use the Collect for Friday of the Second Week of Advent (Proper of Time) at the conclusion of the Prayer of the Faithful.

In the Collect, we pray that through imitation of Saint John, especially his "perfect self-denial / and love of the Cross," we may come, as he did, to the eternal contemplation of the glory of God.

◆ PRAYER OVER THE OFFERINGS: In the Liturgy of the Eucharist, we "celebrate / the mysteries of the Lord's Passion." We pray that we may "imitate what we . . . enact," as Saint John of the Cross did. The Cross is to be the model for our lives.

The Preface of Pastors, of Holy Men and Women, or Preface I of Advent may be used.

In the Prayer after Communion, we pray that we may "cling faithfully to Christ" and work for the salvation of all people.

Today's Saint

Saint John of the Cross (1542–1591), a Carmelite priest and Doctor of the Church, is hailed as one of the greatest mystical theologians in Church history. Along with his spiritual friend, Saint Teresa of Avila, he set out to reform the Carmelite Order to its original spirit—a life of simplicity centered on interior prayer. Saint John was persecuted by his Carmelite brothers, eventually imprisoned because his reforms challenged their comfortable lives of opulence and indulgence. During his imprisonment he composed a beautiful poem, known as *The Dark Night*, which expressed his intense desire for God. Saint John composed other well-known mystical texts, including *The Ascent of Mount Carmel* and *The Living Flame of Love*. Saints John and Teresa founded a new branch of the Carmelites, known as the Discalced (meaning "without shoes") Carmelites.

S A T 15 #186 violet
Advent Weekday

Lectionary for Mass

◆ FIRST READING: The focus in both readings today is Elijah. His brief but powerful prophetic ministry is recounted in 1 Kings 17–19, 21 and 2 Kings 1–2. The Lectionary text omits Sirach's summary of Elijah's miracles in verses 5–7. The focus is not so much on his ministry as on his mysterious translation (being taken up) into heaven via a fiery chariot (see 2 Kings 2:11), which gave rise to an expectation that he would return before the coming of the Messiah. Sirach alludes to this expectation in verse 10 of today's reading. The "it is written" can be found in Malachi 3:23–24, the last words of the Old Testament.

◆ RESPONSORIAL PSALM 80: Three images for Israel are found in today's Psalm: the "flock" of the Lord, who is shepherd (see verse 2); the vine (see verse 15, see Isaiah 5:1–7); and the "son of man," referring to Israel as a nation of people here. The Psalm is a prayer for help and protection. Both the antiphon and the closing stanza speak of Israel's distance from the Lord. The psalmist knows that God's help is needed even to turn back to him.

◆ GOSPEL: Today's text opens on the note of the expectation of Elijah's return before the coming of the Messiah. Jesus proclaims John the Baptist as the Elijah figure who came preaching repentance before his coming, but whose message was not heeded.

The Roman Missal

The Collect is full of imagery of light. We pray that God's glory may "dawn in our hearts," and that when the "shadows of the night" are scattered by the advent of Christ, we may be revealed as "children of light."

☀ 16 #9 violet/rose
Third Sunday of Advent
GAUDETE SUNDAY

Orientation

The Advent readings of Year C, the current Lectionary cycle, call for a joyful celebration of this liturgical time. They remind the hearer of God's faithfulness in fulfilling his promises. They emphasize that the coming of Jesus is Good News to hope and believe in. God is really the source of joy and we can pass on that joy to others.

In the excerpt from the letter to the Philippians that we hear today, Paul encourages the people to look past their conflicts and troubles and rejoice because the Lord is near. Help the assembly to understand this nearness by stressing that God will never abandon them. They cannot see God, but he is always with them.

Lectionary for Mass

◆ FIRST READING: Joy resounds. The Lord, the King of Israel, the Savior, is in your midst. Note that the people experience joy at the Lord's presence, and the Lord rejoices in his people.

◆ CANTICLE: Today's response is actually a hymn taken from the prophet Isaiah. Our antiphon is the last line of the third stanza and echoes the joyful realization of God's presence in the midst of Israel as heard in the First Reading. The stanzas are a confident and joyful hymn of praise to the Lord who is and has been experienced as Savior.

◆ SECOND READING: The theme of joy continues in this reading from the last chapter of Paul's letter to the Philippians. The nearness of the Lord that Paul speaks of is actually a reference to his Second Coming, which the first Christians believed would happen in their own lifetimes. Once again, Paul speaks of the attitudes and practices which should characterize the lives of believers as they prepare for this day.

◆ GOSPEL: John the Baptist has very practical things in mind when he speaks of the behaviors that should characterize those who repent in expectation of the coming of the Lord. His words could well speak to our own manner of life. For the Baptist, for Luke, the coming of Jesus will be Good News for the faithful people who receive him. His coming will bring not only judgment, but the Holy Spirit, into the lives of believers.

The Roman Missal

The special name for this Third Sunday of Advent, *Gaudete Sunday,* comes from the Entrance Antiphon. Rejoicing is the theme of the day: "Rejoice in the Lord always; again I say, rejoice. / Indeed, the Lord is near" (Philippians 4:4–5). The Collect is a prayer for joy: we ask that we may reach the "joys of so great a salvation" and celebrate that salvation with "glad rejoicing" at Christmas.

Today's Prayer over the Offerings frequently reoccurs during Advent. In this prayer, we ask that the unceasing celebration of "the sacrifice of our worship," the celebration of the Eucharist, may accomplish God's saving work among us.

The simple Prayer after Communion asks that the heavenly food we receive in the Eucharist may "cleanse us of our faults" and prepare us for Christmas.

Other Ideas

If you are a teacher or a parent, point out to your children the rose-colored candle on the Advent wreath at church and in your home. Explain that this color symbolizes rejoicing. This Sunday has a special name: *Gaudete Sunday. Gaudete* is the Latin word for "rejoice." We remember today that God is faithful and that Jesus will come again as he promised. On that day, every tear will be wiped away, and there will be no more pain or death. Invite your children to listen closely to today's readings for words like "glad," "rejoice," and "joy."

Go for a walk in your neighborhood this evening and enjoy the Christmas lights at the homes of your neighbors. Point out to your children that Christmas lights remind us that Jesus is the Light of the World. He came to help us see how we should live according to God's plan. Like John the Baptist, Christmas lights proclaim the Good News of Jesus. If you have no lights on your home, consider putting at least one electric candle in a window to share the joy of Christ.

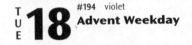

MON 17 #193 violet
Advent Weekday

Lectionary for Mass

◆ FIRST READING: The setting of today's reading is Jacob's deathbed testament to his 12 sons. Jacob, whose name was changed to Israel, is the grandson of Abraham and Sarah. The descendants of his 12 sons comprise the 12 tribes of Israel. Here, the tribe of Judah is given priority. The references to the "scepter" and to the reception of the homage of the people's (nations) have led to a royal or messianic interpretation of the text.

◆ RESPONSORIAL PSALM 72 is a royal Psalm, a prayer for the king, for justice and peace, in and through his reign. How fully this is realized in the reign of God inaugurated by Jesus!

◆ GOSPEL: Today's Gospel is Matthew's account of the genealogy of Jesus. Note Judah's name, fourth in the list, after Abraham, Isaac, and Jacob. Note also that the first verse mentions David, to whom the promise of an everlasting throne was first made. The genealogy we hear today was of utmost importance for the Jewish Christians, and served as evidence of Jesus' messianic identity. Note also the names of the five women: Tamar, Rahab, the wife of Uriah, whose name was Bathsheba, Ruth, and Mary. Their stories all have some element of the exceptional about them.

The Roman Missal

The special prayers for the final days of Advent are used beginning today.

In the mystery of the Incarnation, the divine Word took on our human nature. In the Collect, we pray that in this marvelous exchange, we may share in Christ's divinity.

The Eucharist is a great mystery, worthy of veneration; here, God feeds us with "the bread of heaven" (Prayer over the Offerings).

Preface II of Advent is used beginning today.

In the Prayer after Communion, we ask God to set us on fire with his Spirit, so that we may burn "like bright torches" in Christ's sight when he comes again.

TUE 18 #194 violet
Advent Weekday

Lectionary for Mass

◆ FIRST READING: Jeremiah's words would have deeply touched the hearts of his exiled people, for he speaks of a coming day of salvation when the Exile would be over and the people would return to their land. It would be nothing less than deliverance from slavery, as was the Exodus from Egypt earlier in their history. And how do his words touch our hearts, what exile do we experience? For Israel of old, a future Davidic king would bring deliverance, and his reign would be characterized by wisdom, righteousness, fidelity to the Lord, security, and salvation. How do we, today, experience the reality of that kingdom? How do we still await it?

◆ RESPONSORIAL PSALM 72: Characteristics of this hoped-for king are further elaborated in today's Responsorial Psalm, a royal prayer for the king. The antiphon celebrates the justice and peace that all will experience during his reign.

◆ GOSPEL: Matthew's account of the events preceding Jesus's birth focuses on the angelic appearances to Joseph, of the house of David, assuring him that the child was conceived through the Holy Spirit. The child, whose birth is the fulfillment of Isaiah's prophecy about the soon-to-be-born Davidic heir, is Jesus the Savior, God-is-with-us.

The Roman Missal

The Collect contrasts old with new. We are weighed down by the old "yoke of sin." We pray that we may be freed from this burden "by the newness" of Christmas. The Incarnation is not past, but present; not old, but new.

In the Prayer over the Offerings, we ask that the sacrifice we offer may make us acceptable to God, so that we may live forever in Christ, whose death brings us eternal life.

The Prayer after Communion is another prayer for readiness for the coming solemnity of Christmas.

W E D 19 #195 violet
Advent Weekday

Lectionary for Mass

◆ FIRST READING: The reading recounts the appearance of an angel of the Lord to the barren wife of Manoah, promising the birth of a son. She is given special instructions regarding her pregnancy and the upbringing of her son. These instructions are in fact taken from Numbers 6:2–8, pertaining to the "Nazirite" (sacred, vowed) consecration to the Lord. When he grew up, Samson had a significant role to play in the deliverance of Israel from the power of its Philistine enemies.

◆ RESPONSORIAL PSALM 71 is both a prayer of confidence and a prayer for deliverance, prayed by one who is elderly. These themes are heard in the first two stanzas of the Psalm. Both the antiphon and the third stanza proclaim God's praise for his wondrous deeds.

◆ GOSPEL: Juxtaposed with the announcement of Samson's birth is that of John the Baptist. Elizabeth, like the wife of Manoah, was unable to conceive. Like Samson's parents, Zechariah and Elizabeth were righteous. Note how the description of John's future mission and behavior evoke the Nazirite prescription heard in today's First Reading. John, filled with the Spirit, will go before the Lord, preparing "a people fit" for him through their repentance. Note also that both Zechariah and Elizabeth are advanced in years, a nice link to today's Psalm. Zechariah's angelic messenger even gives a sign that his words are true: Zechariah will be made mute, unable to speak, until the silence is broken by the birth of his child.

The Roman Missal

The child born of Mary revealed God's glory to the world. In the Collect, we pray for right faith and due reverence as we prepare to celebrate the mystery of the Incarnation.

In the Prayer over the Offerings, it is evident that we can offer so little, but we know that God's power is greater than our weakness.

In the Eucharist, we receive a great gift from God, but the Eucharist is only a foretaste of the heavenly banquet. We ask God to "arouse in us . . . / the desire for those [gifts] yet to come" (Prayer after Communion).

T H U 20 #196 violet
Advent Weekday

Lectionary for Mass

◆ FIRST READING: God's presence with his people is nowhere more evident than in the promised child who will bear the name Emmanuel: God-with-us. God's promised sign comes in a time of great affliction, when the kingdom of Judah feared destruction at the hands of its enemies. The child is a sign that Jerusalem will be spared and its enemies destroyed.

◆ RESPONSORIAL PSALM 24: Today's Psalm juxtaposes the Creator's power and might with God's nearness to his people: "Let the Lord enter; he is the king of glory." We also hear of the closeness God wants his people to have to him. Conducting ourselves according to his teaching prepares his way. Gospel: Mary is the one who preeminently allowed the Lord to enter into the whole human race by her "yes" to God's call. Of her, Jesus, the Son of the Most High and the Savior of all people, would be born through the power of God's Holy Spirit.

The Roman Missal

The Collect extols Mary, who was filled with the Holy Spirit, and became "the dwelling-place of divinity" when the Word took flesh in her womb. We pray for the grace to imitate her by following her example of humble obedience to God's will.

The Prayer over the Offerings reveals that Advent is about waiting in hope. Participating in the Eucharist, we have a pledge that one day we will possess fully the gifts for which faith teaches us to hope.

In the Prayer after Communion, we ask for a share in the fruits of the Eucharist: "the joy of true peace."

F R I 21 #197 violet
Advent Weekday

Optional Memorial of Saint Peter Canisius, Priest and Doctor of the Church / violet

Lectionary for Mass

◆ FIRST READING (OPTION 1): Christian tradition, beginning with Origen of Alexandria in the third century, has loved to interpret the Song of Songs, a biblical love song, as pertaining to Christ (the lover) and the Church (the beloved). How fitting, then, to have this text about the "coming" of the Lover on this twenty-first day of December. Note that the Lover invites the Beloved to come and meet him.

◆ FIRST READING (OPTION 2): In Zephaniah, joy resounds. The Lord, the King of Israel, the Savior, is in your midst (mentioned two times). Note that Israel experiences joy at this presence, and the Lord rejoices in his people.

◆ RESPONSORIAL PSALM 33: The theme of joy continues in this song of praise. The themes of waiting for the Lord's coming and the joy of those who are the Lord's own are voiced in the third stanza.

◆ GOSPEL: The theme of joy resounds. Even the child in Elizabeth's womb leaps for joy at the presence of the Lord in Mary's womb. We must be a people of faith, believing that the Lord's promise will be fulfilled.

The Roman Missal

If the optional Memorial of Saint Peter Canisius is observed, the Collect may be taken from the Proper of Saints, with the remaining prayers and Preface of the Advent weekday.

Christmas is close at hand, and the Collect is full of love and joy. We ask God "in kindness" to hear our prayers, that we who rejoice at his coming in our flesh may attain eternal life when he comes in glory.

The Prayer over the Offerings reveals that the Eucharist is God's gift. God gives us what we offer, and transforms these gifts into the mystery of our salvation.

In the Prayer after Communion, we pray that our sharing in the sacred mysteries may give us protection, so that we may have health in mind and body as we dedicate ourselves to the service of God.

Today's Saint

The religious landscape during this saint's life (1521–1597) life was tumultuous due to the Protestant Reformation. In the midst of religious chaos he chose to solemnly profess vows as the eighth member of the newly founded Jesuits. Saint Peter, born in Holland and educated in Louvain, firmly believed in responding to the reformers in a non-threatening, compassionate manner. Pope Leo XIII called Saint Peter "the second apostle to Germany after Boniface" because of his ability to foster dialogue between opposing sides during the Reformation and enliven faith in the hearts of distressed Catholics. He published his *Catechism* in 1551, which is a series of three scholarly works that convey the tenets of the Catholic faith without ever referencing his opponents. As an avid believer in the power of the written word, Saint Peter wrote extensively and encouraged others to defend the truth with pen and paper as well.

S A T 22 #198 violet
Advent Weekday

Lectionary for Mass

◆ FIRST READING: Faithful to her earlier promise, Hannah brings her only son, Samuel, to the Temple to dedicate him to the Lord. It will be Samuel who will anoint King David. The focus of the reading is more on Hannah than on Samuel. She is one of the faithful women instrumental in the story of salvation.

◆ CANTICLE: Today's response is Hannah's hymn of praise after presenting her child to the Lord. Through the gift of a child in her barrenness, Hannah has been raised up and exalted by the Lord (see 1 Samuel 2:1, 4–5, 6–7, 8abcd).

◆ GOSPEL: Today's Gospel speaks of Mary as a deeply prayerful woman who meditated on the Jewish scriptures. Indeed, her prayer of praise is patterned closely on that of Hannah. The Word of Scripture is truly God's Word to us when it becomes the prayer of our lives. As Mary greets her cousin Elizabeth and they recount to one another what God has done in their lives, Mary proclaims God's greatness in a hymn of praise.

The Roman Missal

God redeemed the human race from death by the coming of Christ. In the Collect, we pray that we who believe in his Incarnation may know him as our Redeemer.

The Prayer over the Offerings is a prayer for purification, that the "mysteries we serve" at the altar may cleanse us through God's grace.

Strengthened by the sacrament we have received, we pray that we may meet the Savior "with worthy deeds" (Prayer after Communion) so as to be counted among the blessed.

☼23 #12 violet
Fourth Sunday of Advent

Orientation

Christmas is almost here. Most of us, children and adults alike, are engaged in last minute preparations on the externals of the Christmas celebrations. We live in an era when the preoccupation with material preparations can overshadow the call for spiritual preparation. Mary's example in today's Gospel helps us reflect on the importance of preparing for the feast through actions and attitudes of service and sharing.

Lectionary for Mass

◆ FIRST READING: The prophet looks to a future king from Bethlehem, the city of David. His birth, his kingship, will be in fulfilment of God's promise to David that his kingdom would last forever (2 Samuel 7:16). This text from Micah is quoted in the Gospel according to Matthew (2:5–6) with reference to the birth of Jesus in Bethlehem. Note the description of his kingship in the last lines of today's Gospel. Note also Micah's assertion that this future king would be peace. This is the same message that the heavenly choir of angels proclaimed to the shepherds when Jesus was born (Luke 2:14).

◆ RESPONSORIAL PSALM 80: The antiphon voices the need for God's help even to turn to him. Note in the stanzas of the Psalm, the images used for God (shepherd of Israel, Lord of hosts) and Israel (flock, vine). The "son of man" (verse 16) refers to the king who stood in special relationship to the Lord.

◆ SECOND READING: The reference to Christ's coming into the world has no doubt prompted the choice of this text as our second reading. Psalm 40—and the fulfillment of these words in and by Jesus—is at the heart of the reading. The Old Testament makes the point again and again: God desires obedience, not empty (heartless) rituals. Through Jesus's obedience, through the sacrifice of his life, we have been made holy.

◆ GOSPEL: While today's Gospel is most commonly interpreted in terms of the exchange between Mary and Elizabeth, let us focus today on John the Baptist, still within the womb of his mother. John has, after all, been the subject of the Gospels for the last two Sundays. As an adult, John prophesied the need for readiness and preparation for the coming of the Lord. In the womb of Elizabeth, he simply delights in being in the presence of the Lord, who is still in the womb of Mary. Preparing the way for the Lord and delighting in his presence—we must do and be both in Advent and Christmas Time.

The Roman Missal

◆ ENTRANCE ANTIPHON: As the birth of Jesus draws near, we hear this beautiful antiphon, based on Isaiah 45:8. "Let the clouds rain down the Just One," that the watered earth may "bring forth a Savior."

The Collect is familiar to all who pray the traditional Angelus of the Blessed Virgin Mary. We ask God to pour his grace into our hearts, so that we who have received the Good News of the Incarnation through the angel's word may be brought to the Resurrection by the power of Christ's "Passion and Cross."

The rich imagery of birth continues in the Prayer over the Offerings. We pray that the Holy Spirit may come upon the gifts we place on the altar, "just as he filled with his power the womb of the Blessed Virgin Mary." The same Christ who took flesh in Mary's womb comes to our altars in the Eucharistic sacrifice.

Beginning on December 17, the Preface of Advent II is used every day, including this Sunday. This Preface beautifully expresses that Christ is the desire of the nations from the time of the prophets to the present day. We who look with joyful expectation to the celebration of his Nativity also hope to be found ready when he comes again.

In the Eucharist, we receive the "pledge of eternal redemption," the foretaste of the heavenly banquet (Prayer after Communion). We pray that as Christmas draws near, we may come to the feast ready and eager.

Other Ideas

Begin setting up a crèche in your home by choosing a site but only put out a stable and an animal or two. Leave the crib empty. Don't add Mary and Joseph until Christmas Eve, and don't add the Christ child until Christmas morning. Make a ritual of gradually adding the rest of the figures throughout Christmas Time, with the Magi arriving on Epiphany. Say a prayer for those who are homeless when you add the Mary and Joseph figures, for suffering children as you add the baby Jesus, for those whose work is hard or lonely as you add shepherds, and for all who seek God when you add the Magi.

Make arrangements to share the hospitality of Christmas. Invite someone who will otherwise be alone to join you for Mass and Christmas dinner. Plan to pay a visit during Christmas Time to someone who is housebound and unable to come to you.

M O N 24 #200 violet
Advent Weekday

Lectionary for Mass

◆ FIRST READING: Today's reading was also the text for the Fourth Sunday of Advent. King David, at peace from all his enemies, and having built himself a magnificent palace, now wants to build a house (temple) for the Lord. Note the beautiful account of what God has done for David and Israel. And God will do even more: David's throne shall stand firm forever.

◆ RESPONSORIAL PSALM 89 is a hymn of praise and thanksgiving for the covenant God has made with David. The second and third stanzas speak directly of this.

◆ GOSPEL: Today's Gospel is Zechariah's hymn of praise at the birth of John the Baptist. Note the reference to the Davidic covenant and the recounting of God's promises to Israel. The child's mission is to prepare the way for him who is "dawn from on high" and mighty Savior.

The Roman Missal

The urgency of the Church's desire is unmistakable in the Collect, addressed directly to the Son: "Come quickly, we pray, Lord Jesus, and do not delay" (Collect). We trust in the compassion of Christ, and we long for the solace and relief his coming will bring.

In the Prayer over the Offerings, we ask God to receive and make his own the offerings we bring, and to give them back to us for our purification as we await the coming of Christ.

The Eucharist gives us "new vigor" to prepare Christmas and hope to "possess in gladness" the reward of eternal life (Prayer after Communion).

CHRISTMAS TIME

The Meaning

CHRISTMAS Time, like Advent, spreads over a period of liturgical time. The challenge for those who serve in the areas of liturgy or faith formation is to continue to celebrate Christmas Time beyond December 26. Christmas Time extends from the Vigil of the Solemnity of the Nativity of the Lord (Christmas Eve) until the celebration of the Feast of the Baptism of the Lord. Usually within the Octave of Christmas, we celebrate the *Comites Christi* or "Companions of Christ." We observe the Feast of Saint Stephen, the first martyr, and the Feast of the Holy Innocents. Both feasts show the cost of discipleship in witnessing for the Messiah.

The Feast of the Holy Family on the Sunday following Christmas was established by the Church early in the twentieth century for the encouragement of families, and its celebration situates Jesus's birth within the context of a human family. On the eighth day of the Octave of Christmas, the Church celebrates the Solemnity of Mary, the Holy Mother of God. This title is the oldest title given to Mary in the Church. She is the image of the Church and the model of discipleship and holiness. This is also the day on which the naming of Jesus is celebrated, hence its association with the circumcision which would traditionally be celebrated eight days after the birth of a male, Jewish child.

The Solemnity of the Epiphany of the Lord is associated with the visit of the Magi, but it also offers a deeper reflection on the mystery of the Incarnation. Epiphany (*epiphaneia*) means "manifestation." In ancient times, an epiphany could be twofold in nature: the appearance of God and the visit of an important person, such as a king. The visit of the Magi proclaims that Christ, the Light of the Nations, is the Savior of all, both Jew and Gentile. The Feast of the Baptism of the Lord, which formally concludes Christmas Time, is the second epiphany. The feast proclaims salvation to all peoples and its Gospel reading attests to Jesus as the beloved Son of God and the anointed Messiah. Jesus's baptism inaugurates his public ministry and leads us to ponder the mission to proclaim the Good News connected to our own baptismal promises. The third manifestation actually takes place this year on the Second Sunday in Ordinary Time, the Sunday after the Baptism of the Lord. On this Sunday, the Gospel according to John tells of the wedding feast at Cana, the first miracle Jesus performed, in which his identity as the Messiah, the Son of God, is manifest. The whole of Christmas Time, from the Infancy Narratives of Christmas Day to the epiphanies, unfolds for us the splendor of the Incarnation. When we come together to celebrate that mystery, we bring all our joys and sorrows, our successes and failures. In our own lowliness, we support one another and celebrate our joy. Christ is born into our lowliness and we, too, will be raised by his glory. It all points to Easter; it is all about the Paschal Mystery.

The Roman Missal

SOLEMNITY of the Nativity of the Lord: There are four Masses of Christmas—a Vigil, plus three Masses of Christmas Day. As early as 604, Saint Gregory the Great began a Homily by giving thanks to God for the privilege of celebrating Mass three times on Christmas Day, referring to the Mass during the night, Mass at dawn, and Mass during the day. The general struture of these liturgies took shape in the Holy Land, where the faithful would celebrate the Eucharist during the night of Christmas in Bethlehem. Then, returning to Jerusalem, they would gather at the church of the Resurrection at dawn for another liturgy, followed by a third in the same place later on Christmas Day. The practice in Rome reflected this pattern closely. The pope would celebrate Mass during the night at the Basilica of St. Mary Major, where the relics of the manger are venerated—Rome's Bethlehem. At dawn, he would proceed to the church of St. Anastasia (the name means "Resurrection"); and the third Mass, the Mass during the Day, would be celebrated at St. Peter's (in later centuries, the pope returned to St. Mary Major for this Mass).

These various Masses of Christmas, which we still celebrate today, are not repeats of the same liturgy, as we are used to on a busy Sunday morning in our parishes—that is, the same prayers, the same readings. Instead, each of them is a distinct liturgy, with its own prayers and Scriptures, and each of them opens up a new facet of the Christmas mystery. See below, in the Calendar pages 43–45, for a fuller exploration of the liturgical texts of each of the Christmas Masses.

Prayers of Christmas Time

Each day during Christmas Time has its own unique Collect. On weekdays, however (just as in Advent), there are just three Prayers over the Offerings and three Prayers after Communion which are repeated in a regular rotation. The light which was on its way in the prayers of Advent now shines out brightly in the Collects. "We are bathed in the radiance of your incarnate Word" (Mass at Dawn, Collect). God pours out "light on all the nations," "the newness of heavenly light," "brilliant light," "eternal light," "kindly light," "new light" (from the Collects for the Weekdays of Christmas Time). The Prayers over the Offerings emphasize the "glorious exchange" that happens in the celebration of the Eucharist: we give to God what he has given to us, and in return, we receive God's very Body and Blood.

The Roman Missal provides three Prefaces of Christmas which, not unlike the three Masses of Christmas Day, reveal different facets of the mystery we celebrate in Christmas Time. Preface I of the Nativity of the Lord, "Christ the Light," praises Christ as "a new light" of God's glory: by this light our invisible God has become visible. Preface II of the Nativity of the Lord, "The restoration of all things in the Incarnation," focuses on how Jesus has come to restore "unity" and right relationship with God, to "call straying humanity back to the heavenly Kingdom." It reminds us that Christmas, the feast of the Incarnation, is also a feast of our redemption. And Preface III of the Nativity of the Lord, "The exchange in the Incarnation of the Word," echoes the theme of "exchange" that comes up again and again in the prayers of Christmas Time—Jesus takes on "our frailty" that we may take on a share in his divine strength, and be "made eternal." The Preface of the Epiphany of the Lord echoes all these themes. Christ is "light for the nations," who "made us new" by sharing with us "the glory of his immortal nature."

Weekdays of Christmas Time (from January 2 to the Saturday before the Feast of the Baptism of the Lord)

The Roman Missal includes two Collects for each day of the week, one for use when the day falls before the Epiphany, one for after. The prayers used after Epiphany emphasize the spread of the Good News of the Gospel to the whole world.

Both before and after Epiphany, any of the Christmas Prefaces may be used. After Epiphany, the Preface for Epiphany may also be used at any Mass.

At all Masses of Christmas, the Gloria returns: the Church joins in the song of the angels. The Creed is said (or sung) as well, and all kneel at the words "and by the Holy Spirit was incarnate," to honor the great mystery of the Incarnation which we celebrate at Christmas.

The Gloria, with its echo of the Christmas song of the angels, is one of the most ancient hymns of the Christian people. It originated as a song for the office of Morning Prayer. Around the sixth century bishops began singing it at the Masses of Christmas. Though now the entire assembly joins in this song, it is still customary in some chant settings for the priest celebrant—whether priest, bishop, or pope—to intone the first words, "Gloria in excelsis Deo."

After the "fast" of Advent, the Gloria returns at the Vigil Mass of Christmas. Throughout Christmas Time, take special care with how the Gloria is prayed during the liturgy. It is a song, and ideally it should be sung.

Christmas Time gives us many opportunities to sing with the angels—the Gloria is prayed every day during the Octave of Christmas.

The Lectionary for Mass

OUR Christmas preparations have no doubt centered on giving gifts and sending greetings. Our hearts have been lifted by the greetings and gifts we received that conveyed the love and care of another. Do we recognize the greatest gift of all, the gift that changed our lives once and for all? Do we grasp that the love of our Heavenly Father for us is so great that he sent his only Son into the world that we—you, me, each one of us— might have eternal life? Are we really receptive to the gift of Jesus and a personal relationship with him in our lives?

The readings for the Vigil of Christmas stress the newness of what God is doing in the Incarnation of his Son—entering into a relationship so intimate with his people that it is described in terms of the love of a bridegroom for his bride. Extraordinarily new, yes—in a way far exceeding anything we could imagine, but at the same time fulfilling God's promises of old.

The readings for the Mass during the Night proclaim that in the birth of the child prophesied by Isaiah, the darkness and gloom enshrouding humanity are pierced by light. Similarly, the light of glory fills the night sky at the birth of Jesus the Savior. Both the First and the Second Readings for the Mass at Dawn speak of God our Savior, with the second actually ascribing the title to Jesus. Luke tells us that when the shepherds heard the news of the angels' revelation, they went in haste to find the child. Do we go in haste to his word? To prayer? To worship him at the Eucharistic assembly?

What a wonderful Word God has spoken to us in Jesus (see John's Prologue, the Gospel for the Mass during the day). Do we see the Word God speaks as glad tidings (see the First Reading for Christmas Day, Isaiah 52:7–10), as far exceeding any words God spoke in the past (see Hebrews 1:1–6, the Second Reading)? His Word, his coming, brings joy to human hearts and to all the earth as well (a point reflected in the Responsorial Psalms). This is a magnificent gift. Do we receive it as such?

On the Feast of Saint Stephen, December 26, we remember a person who received the Word, the gift of Jesus, and gave his own life for the sake of his name in return. In our own day as well there are Christians who, like Stephen, experience suffering, persecution, and even death because of the name of Jesus.

The Feast of Saint John, Apostle and Evangelist, sets before us the gift of a deeply personal experience, indeed relationship, with the Lord Jesus. Christian tradition identifies John with the beloved disciple of the Fourth Gospel.

The tragedy of the death of the Holy Innocents, cut off from life at such a young age, must not obscure the reality of the gift of fullness of life which would be theirs since they died in Jesus's name. As the Responsorial Psalm attests, the snare was broken and they were freed.

The gift of family life is highlighted on the Feast of the Holy Family of Jesus, Mary, and Joseph. In the First Reading we learn that Hannah's son Samuel was indeed a gift, an answer to her prayer. In turn, she presented him to the Lord as a gift for the rest of his life. To dwell in the house of the Lord is indeed gift as Responsorial Psalm 84 attests. The Holy Family of Mary, Joseph, and Jesus is the subject of Gospel reading for this feast. We see them journeying to Jerusalem on pilgrimage for Passover, where they will present gifts at the Temple in accordance with Jewish law. We recognize another gift in the attentiveness of Jesus to his Father's works, and still another in his submission to his parents—the gift of self, the gift of obedience. Our Second Reading reminds us of the gift of being God's child and having received his Spirit.

These words are echoed in the Second Reading for the Solemnity of Mary, the Holy Mother of God just two days later. This, too, can be thought of as a "family" feast, focusing as it does on Mary's motherhood. Mary held all of the words and events concerning her son in her heart, pondering their meaning. Mary's "mothering" of Jesus included forming him to be prayerful and open to the call of God.

The Solemnity of the Epiphany of the Lord immediately brings to mind the gifts of the Magi. But what a gift the proclamation of his birth is for them! God's salvation is for Gentiles as well as Jews, as the Second Reading from Ephesians emphasizes.

This year we have a full week between the Solemnity of the Epiphany of the Lord and the Feast of the Baptism of the Lord. The Epiphany theme is heard throughout the week in the repetition of Responsorial Psalm 72. The First Readings are a continuation of the First Letter of John begun during the octave. It is a beautiful letter to

read at this time, stemming as it does from the witness and conviction of one who knew the Lord when he walked on the earth and who heard his teaching and witnessed his marvelous deeds. All is handed on to new generations of believers that they—that we—might have life in Jesus's name. The letter likewise deals with the internal challenges and external threats facing the community. The Gospel readings for these feasts relate events of the first days of Jesus's public ministry. The glory, the light becomes visible. The promises of the prophets are fulfilled.

Christmas Time ends with the Feast of the Baptism of the Lord, the event that the Gospel accounts portray that heralds the start of Jesus's public ministry. In a sense, the feast recapitulates the readings we've heard: Jesus is the Beloved Son of God on whom God's Spirit rests. He is the fulfillment of God's promises of old: the revelation of God's power and glory, a Savior in their midst, bringing comfort and care, healing and wholeness to God's people. All is God's gift to us if we are willing to receive it.

Children's Liturgy of the Word

To a child Christmas is a day. To the Church, it is an entire period of liturgical time. Christmas Time begins with the celebration of Evening Prayer on Christmas Eve and ends with the celebration of Evening Prayer on the Feast of the Baptism of the Lord. The Christmas liturgy sings the glory of the night when the angels appeared to the shepherds in the region of Bethlehem and proclaimed the Good News that the Messiah is born. The glory and solemnity of Christmas Time are marked by external signs at liturgy. The brightly lit church and the beautiful decorations evoke a sense of the glory of God which we celebrate. The singing of the Gloria and the use of a variety of musical instruments help the assembly enter into the awesome mystery— that God has taken on human flesh and become one of us. The Sunday liturgies and feasts speak of the various ways the Son of God was shown to our world. During Christmas Time several feast days frame the brilliance of the Incarnation, namely Holy Family, Epiphany, and the Baptism of the Lord. January 1 fittingly celebrates the

Solemnity of Mary, the Holy Mother of God and the naming of Jesus.

The gathered assembly of children meets Christ in the Word of God proclaimed and reflected on. Nourished by that Word, encourage the children to go forth to spread the Good News that God became man. While on earth, Jesus taught that his Incarnation is embodied in the commandment of love, especially loving those who are poor or oppressed. The message for children is that Christ is incarnate in their lives and in the lives of those around them as they live out the law of loving God and neighbor.

Readings

The Gospel readings for Sundays and other feasts in Christmas Time give few details about Jesus's life between his birth and his baptism, a period sometimes known as his hidden life. Children are very interested in the human person of Jesus. They identify with him and his childhood circumstances. Be aware of this tendency as you prepare your Homily/ reflections. Any connections you can make between readings and situations in the children's lives will help make the message of the Gospel more real to them.

The Second Readings come from a variety of sources. They address issues of importance within the early Church, or, as in the case of the Acts of the Apostles, describe the events and challenges the early Christian community faced as it expanded into the world. These readings affirm that God became one of us and that this Good News is intended for all the world to hear, and believe. Finally, these readings also deal with the attitudes and behavior expected of Christans as members of the Church, the Body of Christ.

Environment

The environment for children's Liturgy of the Word should be rich and vibrant. The liturgical color is white. The banners and cloths on the lectern and prayer table should be white. You may wish to highlight this color with gold and silver cloths, beads, or ornaments. Place a crèche in a visible space in the worship area. Decorate with Christmas flowers or plants, such as poinsettias or Christmas cactus, and evergreens. However, the crèche should not be more prominent than the space where the readings are proclaimed.

Liturgy is a sensate experience. The sights and smells of evergreen and of burning incense in front of the lectern will stay with children and enrich their worship experience. If your parish permits the use of lighted candles or votives, place them strategically in the worship space. These rituals and symbols help children develop a sense of reverence for the Word of God and a sense of the sacredness of Christmas Time.

Music

As always, live music is most appropriate if it can be arranged. Ask your parish liturgy or music director if there is someone who can accompany children or be a cantor. Also check with the parish youth director. There may be teens with music ability or band experience willing to share their talents with the children during this period. Refrain from using popular secular Christmas music for worship. Use suggestions given in *Children's Liturgy of the Word: A Weekly Resource* from LTP or make music selections from your parish repertoire.

Children tend to be excited on Christmas day. Try to develop your Homily/reflection in such a way that you can intersperse it with a hymn or the Psalm refrain to help them participate more fully and to create an atmosphere for sung prayer.

The Saints

CHRISTMAS Time is full of observances of the saints. In just three weeks, we observe three solemnities, five feasts, three memorials, and four optional memorials. In the Middle Ages, the saints of Christmas were known as the *Comites Christi*, the "companions of Christ." They are martyrs, like Saint Stephen (December 26), the Holy Innocents (December 28), and Saint Thomas Becket (December 29). They are Evangelists, like Saint John (December 27); popes, like Saint Sylvester (December 31); bishops, like Saints Basil and Gregory (January 2) and Saint John Neumann (January 5); religious, like Saint Elizabeth Ann Seton (January 4); and priests, like Saint Raymond of Penyafort (January 7).

The Feasts of Saint John and the Holy Innocents have their own presidential prayers, found in the Proper of Saints. One of the Christmas Prefaces is used. For memorials falling within the Octave of Christmas (December 26–31), the

Collect for the saint may be used, while the remaining prayers are from the appropriate day in the Octave. For memorials and optional memorials during the rest of Christmas Time (i.e., between January 2 and January 12), the Collect may be taken from the Proper of Saints, while the rest of the prayers are taken from the ferial weekday, or from the appropriate Common. Readings from the Proper of Saints or from the Commons may be chosen for any memorial or optional memorial during Christmas Time (except during the Octave), but in general it is best to stick with the readings of the day.

The Liturgy of the Hours

CELEBRATING the Liturgy of the Hours during Christmas Time is always a challenge. But there are certain things you can do. For example, this is the period of the darkest evenings of the year, so you can take advantage of this to rely more on candles than artificial light to create a prayerful environment for the celebration. This would provide a strong connection to the many Psalm prayers that speak of Christ the light: "The darkness that covered the earth / has given way to the bright dawn of your Word / made flesh. Make us a people of this light" (p. 406). To respect the notion of progressive solemnity, use incense during the canticle and during the first Psalm to add solemnity. If Evening Prayer is celebrated on Epiphany, the use of incense would highlight one of the gifts of the Magi. Musically, instrumentation could be added. For example, playing a trumpet with and an organ for the opening hymn and the canticle offers a contrast to Advent.

Perhaps the parish liturgy committee could devise ways to interest parishioners in the Liturgy of the Hours. Or, they could discuss ways to expand their celebrations. So, if Evening Prayer was offered during Advent, perhaps it could continue during Christmas Time. Another way is to focus on the domestic Church—the household. To encourage household participation, a shortened form of the Liturgy of the Hours could be used for Advent and Christmas.

The opening hymns for Christmas from the Liturgy of the Hours are quite familiar and elicit strong participation from the people: "O Come, All Ye Faithful," "What Child Is This?" and "Unto Us a Child Is Given." On Christmas and on the Octave, the "Te Deum" may be chanted following the readings, but before the closing prayer (see p. 651, Volume I). If your parish has a history of celebrating Evening Prayer on major feasts and seasons, including the "Te Deum" adds solemnity to the celebration.

The readings from the Office of Readings provide an opportunity for a more contemplative participation in Christmas Time. Pope Paul VI's words eloquently illuminate the power of Christmas Time: "Here we can learn to realize who Christ really is. And here we can sense and take account of the conditions and circumstances that surrounded and affected his life on earth: the places, the tenor of the times, the culture, the language, religious customs, in brief everything which Jesus used to make himself known to the world. Here everything speaks to us, everything has meaning. Here we can learn the importance of spiritual discipline for all who wish to follow Christ and to live by the teachings of his Gospel" (pp. 426–427, Volume I). Christmas, therefore, is an entrance into the mystery of the Incarnation. The Liturgy of the Hours can help us contemplate even more the depth of this mystery of our faith. Christ lives and moves not as a child but as the Risen Lord, and he beckons us to participate in his life so that we might achieve greater holiness in ours.

The Rite of Christian Initiation of Adults

"The Christian initiation of these children requires a conversion that is personal and somewhat developed, in proportion to their age and the assistance of the education they need. The process of initiation thus must be adapted both to their spiritual progress, that is, to the children's growth in faith, and to the catechetical instruction they receive" (RCIA, 253).

"The period of initiation will also provide a good opportunity for the family to have contact with priests and catechists" (RCIA, 254.2).

THE whole Christmas cycle is a crescendo of Christ's manifesting himself as God and King—to the shepherds, to the Magi, at his baptism, to Simeon and the prophetess, Anna. The days from Christmas to Epiphany are popularly known as "The Twelve Days of Christmas." Liturgically, however, Christmas Time ends on January 13th with the celebration of the Feast of the Baptism of the Lord.

The weeks of Christmas Time are busy ones, not only for families, but also for the parish initiation team—the peer companions, sponsors, and catechumens. It is such a rich season of story and symbol that it would be a shame to "take a break." There are options to formal catechumenal or inquiry sessions at this point. One of the events we don't take a break from is the Sunday assembly. If young catechumens are usually involved in a Liturgy of the Word with children, make every effort to ensure this continues during Christmas Time. If this is not possible, do continue the dismissal and dismissal catechesis.

The visit of the Magi, the finding of Jesus in the Temple, and the baptism of Jesus are foundational stories for the doctrine of the Incarnation. Yes, God did become human and live among us. Those stories are important for children to break open and to hear over and over again.

Conversion, the heart of the catechumenate, is a movement from one set of values and ways of seeing things to another. Conversion is a deep change, an about-face, often initiated by attraction or involvement. Guilt rarely causes conversion. Conversion at this time of year might mean rejecting consumerism in favor of simplicity and spirituality. These few weeks of Christmas Time provide an excellent opportunity for catechetical instructions and celebrations with catechumen children and their families to help them think about the true meaning of Christmas by using familiar customs and traditions that they can see, hear, and touch.

Liturgical Catechesis

Plan an informal social family session celebrating the Feast of the Holy Family. During the session the catechist might simply explain the following using the decorations and symbols in Church or the gathering space. White is the liturgical color of Christmas Time, but green and red are also prominent. The green of the Christmas tree is unchanging and represents the hope of eternal life in Jesus. Red is deep, intense, vivid. It is the color of love. During Christmas Time we celebrate that God's love for us was so great he sent his Son to us as a gift.

The star is God's sign of promise. God promised a Savior for the world, and the star was the sign that God kept his promise when Jesus Christ was born. Remind children that God always keeps promises and that wise people still look for God's signs to guide them.

Christmas candles remind us of the light that the coming of Christ brought into the world. The soft glow from its one tiny flame can brighten a room. When we follow Jesus's example and do good, we carry his light into the world. One of the things to think about when we see Christmas lights is that they represent all of the people who bring Christ's light into the world.

A Christmas wreath is a circle, without beginning and without end, just like God's love for us.

Work with the liturgy or music director to adapt one of the Blessings of Catechumens (RCIA, 95–97) or one of the Blessings of Families from the *Book of Blessings* (Chapter 1).

The blessing for homes for the Solemnity of the Epiphany is found in the *Book of Blessings* (Chapter 50). Distribute it to the families of catechumens. Or ask volunteer families from the parish to invite a family from the catechumenate for their Epiphany blessing of the home. Be sure to secure copyright permission.

If there are children of catechetical age or adults who have been baptized, who have participated in a separate ecclesial community, or who are seeking full communion with the Roman Catholic Church (see RCIA, 473), the Solemnity of Epiphany and the Feast of the Baptism of the Lord are appropriate times to have them received into full communion. Consult with the pastor and liturgy director for decisions about planning and celebrating these rites. Entering into full communion at this time allows these candidates the opportunity to share more fully in the assembly's celebration of Ordinary Time, Lent, and Easter Time.

The Sacraments of Initiation

CHILDREN love Christmas Time and it is packed with symbols and signs and Scripture readings that proclaim the presence of God among us. This liturgical time provides opportunities to work with the liturgy and music directors to prepare liturgically appropriate celebrations for young people preparing for full initiation or the reception of Confirmation and/or first Holy Communion, or for youngsters who are learning about sacraments and liturgy. Involve their families also in preparation and execution.

Infant Baptisms often take place during the Sunday Masses of Christmas Time. Ask one of the couples who are having their child baptized to speak to the group about why baptizing their child is important to them. Invite children who are preparing for the Sacraments of Initiation and their families to the celebration. Encourage them to attend. At the conclusion of Mass, gather children around the baptismal font and have them talk about what they saw and heard. Show them the sacred objects that were used in the celebration.

The Feast of the Holy Family of Jesus, Mary, and Joseph is an occasion to gather all families involved in sacramental preparation, including those in the catechumenate, at a designated Sunday Mass. Plan ahead of time with the priest celebrant, liturgy director, and music director to incorporate a blessing of families at that liturgy. Following Mass, invite families to a simple meet-and-greet continental breakfast in the parish hall prepared by one of the parish groups or organizations.

Provide the blessing of homes (found in the *Book of Blessings*) to the families whose children are preparing for first Holy Communion. Encourage them to invite a family of one of the catechumens to join them for their house blessing.

The Rite of Penance

SINCE Christmas Time liturgies are often attended by many people who are otherwise disconnected from the parish, they provide an opportune moment to re-establish contact. Be sure to include a warm welcome in the opening remarks, in the bulletin, and on the parish website. You might include an invitation to consider "coming back home" by contacting one of the parish priests. List the times people may come for the Sacrament of Reconciliation, but make it clear they are welcome just to come and talk, too.

The Pastoral Care of the Sick

A ritual Mass of Anointing is not permitted on the Solemnities of the Nativity of the Lord; Mary, the Holy Mother of God; or Epiphany. Although this Mass could be celebrated on a weekday, it is probably not a good idea to schedule a communal service in Christmas Time. Do the parishioners know when and whom to call for individual Anointing of the Sick or Viaticum? Is it stated somewhere in the bulletin? Posted on the parish website?

Caring for the sick and homebound of the parish continues with home and hospital visits. Sometimes people are lonely or alone. Perhaps parishioners would contribute Christmas cards with handwritten notes of encouragement for the homebound when the minister of care visits. Maybe people could donate a small poinsettia.

Some churches have a year-round "prayer shawl" ministry. Those who knit and crochet make triangular shawls for the sick as a visible sign of being wrapped in the community's prayers.

The Rite of Marriage

WEDDINGS may take place during Christmas Time, but at Saturday Masses of anticipation or on Sunday during the day, the Mass of the day is used. However, the First or Second Reading may be replaced with a reading from the *Rite of Marriage*. If a Liturgy of the Word (*Rite of Marriage*, Form II or III) is celebrated, the Scripture readings and prayers for weddings may be used.

Be clear with the couple about how the worship space will look in Christmas and encourage them to harmonize with the environment. Since the space is usually lavishly decorated, suggest the money they would have spent on extra flowers might be given to a local soup kitchen or food pantry.

The Order of Christian Funerals

THIS is a very hard time of year to lose a loved one. More than ever people need parish ministers for the pastoral care that is beyond what the local funeral director can provide. In the midst of all the Christmas joy we Christians know that the wood of the manger and the wood of the Cross bracket Jesus's life. So we always proclaim that, while we will experience the Cross, Resurrection is on the other side.

We do not celebrate a Mass of Christian Burial on Christmas Day; Mary, the Holy Mother of God; or Epiphany.

The "prayer shawl" ministry mentioned under Pastoral Care of the Sick might be engaged in ministering to the grieving, too. This tangible sign of the Church's concern is often quite touching for those who mourn. It is probably most appropriate when a surviving spouse is a member of the parish.

The Book of Blessings

BOTH the *Book of Blessings* and *Catholic Household Blessings & Prayers* contain lovely models for the blessing of the manger or Christmas tree. There are also fine blessings for families and homes. Look at Chapter 1 of the *Book of Blessings*, "Order for Blessing of a Family for the Feast of the Holy Family." The introduction and first blessing speak specifically of Marriage. The second blessing does not and so may be more pastorally sensitive if a single parent is to be blessed. The parish might provide a blessing that families can take home. Part II of *Catholic Household Blessings & Prayers* has a Blessing of the Home and Household on the Epiphany. When reproducing texts from these resources, be sure to secure reprint permission from the copyright holder.

The Liturgical Environment

THE Church has always paid special attention to the liturgical celebration of Christmas, the Triduum, and Easter Time (including Pentecost). This means that liturgical ministers should prepare the liturgies with great care so that the whole assembly of worshippers can celebrate fully and actively the mysteries of faith. The liturgical environment needs to contribute to the beauty and the solemnity of these celebrations. Here are some suggestions to keep in mind:

◆ Resist the temptation to overdo the decorations for Christmas; sometimes the arrangements for Christmas reflect the principle that "too much is never enough." Lavish displays of Christmas flowers and trees, with hundreds of lights and ornaments give the appearance of a shopping mall display or a department store venue.

◆ The liturgical space is first and always a place for liturgical ritual and the principal furnishings have pride of place. The altar, ambo, priest celebrant's chair, font, tabernacle, and cross must never be seen as secondary to the decorations, or diminished by the scale and placement of the decorations.

◆ Do not place all the elements of the Christmas environment in or near the sanctuary. Utilize other spaces, such as entry areas, the gathering space, corners of the nave, and outdoor sites for various seasonal items.

◆ The location for the crèche can often pose a challenge for environment and art committees. The crèche and the practice of stopping to pray before it is a devotion, albeit a revered and longstanding one. However, as noted above, it does not deserve the same attention as the principal liturgical furnishings. Ordinarily, it should not be placed in the sanctuary. Since people like to view it, or pray before it, especially children, it should be placed in an accessible location: in the gathering area, in a side alcove, or even in a separate chapel. It is appropriate to place the Advent wreath close by, since the lighting of the four candles of the wreath is in anticipation of the birth of Christ, the Light of the World.

◆ The elements of the Christmas environment should be kept fresh and in place for the entirety of Christmas Time, which includes the Feast of the Holy Family, the Solemnity of Mary, the Holy Mother of God, the Solemnity of the Epiphany, and the Feast of the Baptism of the Lord.

◆ On Epiphany, it is customary to add the figures of the three Magi to the Nativity scene; some parishes place three wrapped "gifts" there as well to symbolize the gifts of the Magi. Children could be invited to bring a small wrapped "gift" to add to the scene as a symbol of their own gift to the Lord on this day.

◆ The liturgical color for Christmas is white. Gold and silver may also be used.

The Liturgical Music

IN the Advent section, we spoke much of progressive solemnity. Let us continue to reflect on this as it relates to Christmas Time. STL, 112 tells us:

> Progressive solemnity includes not only the nature and style of the music, but how many and which parts of the rite are to be sung. For example, greater feasts such as Easter Sunday or Pentecost might suggest a chanted Gospel, but a recited Gospel might be more appropriate for Ordinary Time. Musical selections and the use of additional instruments reflect the season of the liturgical year or feast that is being celebrated.

Imagine the beauty and solemnity of Mass during the Night with the incensation of the *Book of the Gospels* followed by a chanted proclamation of the Gospel reading. If your parish has never done so, now would be a good time to consider trying it. ICEL's (International Commission on English Language) website (http://www.icelweb.org/musicfolder/openmusic.php) offers the musical and theological principals for chanting the Gospel. CanticaNOVA has published a selection of 42 notated Gospels for chanting. This is a good and inexpensive resource.

Elsewhere STL says in 153–154:

> While the readings are ordinarily read in a clear, audible, and intelligent way (see *Lectionary for Mass* [LFM], no. 14), they may also be sung. "This singing, however, must serve to bring out the sense of the words, not obscure them" (see LFM, no. 14).

> Even if the First and Second Readings are not sung, the concluding acclamation *The Word of the Lord* may be sung, even by someone other than the reader; all respond with the acclamation *Thanks be to God*. "In this way the assembled congregation pays reverence to the word of God it has listened to in faith and gratitude" (see LFM, no. 18).

If your parish is not ready to chant the proclamation of the Gospel, the option of responding with "The Word of the Lord" and "Thanks be to God" might be a good place to start. Even if you choose to chant the readings at this solemn occasion, singing the response could be a regular part of the liturgy throughout the year. However, before introducing something like this, make sure that the congregation and the liturgical ministers receive solid catechesis, and that those who will do the intoning are properly trained.

Another text to chant at the Mass during the Night is the Christmas Proclamation (*The Nativity of Our Lord Jesus Christ*). It is from the *Roman Martyrology*, has been newly translated, and is included in the third edition of *The Roman Missal*. Note that the rubrics have changed: it is to be done during the Liturgy of the Hours or prior to the beginning of the Mass during the Night.

"Angels We Have Heard on High" is a popular carol with the Latin text of the Gloria as the refrain. Sometimes parishes replace the Gloria with this song of praise, but they should not: no other text is to replace the Gloria. However, three music publishers have creatively incorporated the refrain of "Angels We Have Heard on High" with the revised text of the Gloria. WLP revised the Hughes/Hommerding version of "Gloria for Christmas Time." GIA has done the same with Daniel Laginya's "Christmas Gloria." Finally, Paul Gibson has revised his setting based on the same tune to create a whole "Christmas Mass" available as a PDF download from OCP. It uses "God Rest Ye Merry Gentlemen" as the basis for the Holy, Holy and the Amen, and DIVINUM MYSTERIUM ("Of the Father's Love Begotten") for the Memorial Acclamations. While it is easy to follow, one may wonder if working in convenient melodies is enough.

I can't help but recall the words of my friend and professor, Michael Joncas, speaking of the need for "cohesive macro-units" within the liturgy. What does the use of two separate hymns (three if you count the Gloria) do to the Mass setting as a cohesive macro-unit when the settings in this case jump between decidedly major and minor keys? You have to weigh this criticism against the pastoral decision to have something very singable for those who may be guests at the Christmas liturgies.

If you are trying to work with a variety of instrumentalists during Christmas Time, Kevin Keil has a lovely collection entitled "See Amid the Winter's Snow" that works well with piano, flute, cello, oboe, and violin. Many of these pieces work beautifully for a Christmas wedding as well. These are truly duets between the piano and

other instruments, as opposed to a flute solo with piano accompaniment.

Liturgical Ministers

IF we were to use one word to remember Christmas Time it would be "hospitality." Sure, there are greeters and ushers who formally welcome and assist those attending services, but the truth is, there will be many who seldom come or will be attending your church for the first time. It is everyone's responsibility to make them feel welcome, and to help them enter into the liturgy.

This may mean simple things like pointing out a restroom or drinking fountain, or helping someone find the page in the songbook or follow the flow for the reception of Holy Communion. While long commentaries before the Mass are usually unecessary, it may be wise to have a more detailed script for the cantor or commentator to use before the Entrance Chant. For example:

> Welcome to Saint _____ Parish. Thank you for joining us for the Christmas liturgy. For your convenience, all the materials you need for this Mass have been printed in the worship aid [OR: All the music for the liturgy may be found in the brown hymnal. Thank you for returning them to the rack after the Mass.) Restrooms are located on the right hand side of the narthex. Please feel free to ask an usher or greeter if you need help.

This is an ideal time to thank all of your liturgical ministers and other volunteers. In this time of tight budgets, costly gifts are inappropriate, but a simple handwritten note, a basket of cookies, or an inexpensive present would be nice ways to say thank you. Most people simply want to know their efforts are appreciated.

Devotions and Sacramentals

DURING this rich liturgical time we recognize the "epiphanies," the "aha moments" in the manifestations of Christ to the shepherds, to the Magi, and to the wedding guests at Cana as well as the importance of the Holy Family, the Holy Innocents, and the Presentation of the Lord.

Because all these stories are so rich in imagery they bring out the childlike innocence or piety in all of us. The *Directory on Popular Piety and the Liturgy* (108) tells us that piety intuitively grasps:

- the spirituality of the gift: God gives his Son to us as an expression of his infinite love;
- solidarity with sinful man;
- the sacredness of human life in the birth of Jesus;
- messianic joy and peace;
- the spirit of simplicity, poverty, humility, and trust in God.

During Christmas Time every parish celebrates differently and some activities are celebrated both in the home and in the larger community. You would do well to create a handout with family blessings for the Christmas crèche, the Christmas tree, Christmas supper, and the blessing of homes. The *Book of Blessings* has many resources including BB 1551 and 1558.

Within the parish, a live crib could be a place to gather and sing carols before the Mass begins, or as a way of keeping vigil between late afternoon and midnight Mass. (Perhaps you could connect this with collecting food for the poor.) As stated earlier, these activities should not be part of the Mass itself, although the Christ child is often placed in the crèche scene at the beginning of the liturgy or as part of a procession. Similarly, in some traditions, people reverence the Christ child in the manger with a kiss after Christmas Mass.

A blessing for families is included in the *Book of Blessings*. It would be appropriate to include this blessing in the Mass on the Feast of the Holy Family on December 30. Consider hosting a holy hour following the Mass for all children who have died. Also focus ministerial efforts on mothers in need.

New Year's Eve and New Year's Day certainly cannot be overlooked. One can combine good fun and popular piety by creating a potluck/vigil service on New Year's Eve. Consider Exposition of the Blessed Sacrament followed by a social event, or hosting an ecumenical evening of Taizé prayer. As to New Year's Day, DPPL, 115 states: "The solemnity of the 1 January, an eminently Marian feast, presents an excellent opportunity for liturgical piety to encounter popular piety: the first celebrates this event in a manner proper to it; the second, when duly catechised, lends joy and happiness to the various expressions of praise offered to Our Lady on the birth of her divine Son, to deepen our understanding of many prayers, beginning with that which says: 'Holy Mary, Mother of God, pray for us, sinners.'"

This day is a liturgical celebration which shows the dual nature of Mary as Mother of God and Mother of Jesus, and the example of living faith. As a devotional activity, invite your congregation to pray the Rosary before the liturgy, or have a Mother of God novena from January 1–9.

The Parish and the Home

FAMILIES may already be so overloaded with Christmas activities that the role of the parish might be to help them slow down and simply enjoy their holidays together. The fact that Jesus became human in a family setting—not in a palace, a synagogue, or a military institution—blesses all human families. He entered the world in an ordinary, nurturing circle of affection—exactly what he calls us to create.

Especially with young children, the simpler, the better. They may be overly influenced by the advertising hype of the media, focused on acquiring more toys. To offset that, families could take time reading Christmas books from the library, preparing a gift for a poor child or family, gathering around the crèche or fireplace to snuggle and sing carols, and taking walks outdoors to admire the beauties of the liturgical time, like icicles, crisp temperatures, and shadows on the snow.

Parents who feel they must create the perfect decorations, gifts, parties, and meals should be reassured by the parish's message: Come as you are. Relax. Be yourself. The first Christmas was by no means carefully planned or perfect. (To be consistent, we must also let go of our expectations for the perfect Christmas pageant, choir performance, and liturgy!)

In the liturgical calendar, Christmas Time extends for several weeks, until the Baptism of the Lord, usually the second Sunday in January. This should allow time to try out different cultural customs, foods, and music, entertain guests, and savor the cards which may have arrived when people were too busy to appreciate them. If the Christmas tree starts growing dry and brittle, put it outdoors and hang it with food for the birds, such as suet, peanut butter and bird seed on pine cones.

There are also many saints' feasts to celebrate: Saint Stephen the first martyr; Saint John, Evangelist, fisherman, and Apostle (read the story of his calling in Matthew 4:18–22); and the Holy Innocents. The Holy Innocents presents a good time to read the story (Matthew 2:16–18); and pray for children who are still not safe: living in war-torn areas, poverty, or violence, and abusive families.

Major feasts to celebrate are New Year's Day/Mary, the Holy Mother of God/World Day of Peace, Epiphany, and Jesus's baptism. It's customary on Epiphany to bless the house, marking the year over the front door with chalk, with the initials of the three kings (according to legend, Caspar, Melchior, and Balthasar) in the middle: 20 C + M + B + 13. Decorate the home with stars made of aluminum foil or foam board hung from the ceiling or a light fixture with thread or fishing line. Bake a special cake in which a small plastic figure of the Christ child or a coin is hidden. Whoever finds it becomes queen or king and receives a crown made of construction paper or foil. On the feast of Jesus's baptism, talk about the Baptisms of family members. If possible, bring out photos, the baptismal candle, garment, or other mementos. Children love stories about themselves when they were smaller, and especially when they were at the center of the stage.

In the second century, people began to celebrate Jesus's birth on the Epiphany. Later, it was moved to coincide with the Winter Solstice, December 21. In the northern hemisphere, this marks the shortest day and longest night of the year. After this, the days begin to lengthen gradually. If we understand this natural cycle, it makes it easier to appreciate the birth soon afterward of Christ our Light, "who brings us out of darkness into his marvelous light" (1 Peter 2:9).

Mass Texts

◆ SAMPLE Text for the Prayer of the Faithful
Additional texts are found in Appendix V of The Roman Missal

Celebrant:

[On/During this holy night/day/liturgical time,] the heavens rejoice,
and the earth is glad, for the Word is made flesh; Christ is born of the Virgin Mary.
In confidence and love, let us pray.

Deacon/Lector/Reader:

For all Christians,
that the celebration of the birthday of our Savior
may renew us in faith, and unite us in love,
    we pray to the Lord.

For all who live in the shadow of death and war,
that the peace sung by the angels
on the first Christmas night may become
    a reality in our world, we pray to the Lord.

For children everywhere,
that the God who became a little child
may bless them with his gifts of wisdom, love,
and grace, we pray to the Lord.

For all who feel hopeless, lonely, or abandoned;
for those who have lost their faith;
that during these holy days of Christmas
they may be filled with Christ's own peace
and joy, we pray to the Lord.

For all our beloved dead,
especially N._____,
that they may know eternal light, rest, and peace,
    we pray to the Lord.

For all of us,
that we may welcome the Lord Jesus
every day of the year
in the poor, the homeless, and all those
whom we find it difficult to love,
    we pray to the Lord.

Celebrant:

God of everlasting love,
when you took flesh and were born
    of the Virgin Mary,
angels proclaimed peace on earth, good will
    to all.
Give us peace in our day.
May all your children work together
to build a more just and peaceful world.
Grant this through Christ our Lord.
Amen.

◆ DISMISSAL TEXT FOR CATECHUMENS

You who seek full membership in the Church
    of Christ
have experienced the joy of proclaiming
    Emmanuel, "God-with-us!"
Go forth to ponder this great mystery,
supported by our sincere prayer
that the one who was born in a stable
will lead you to eternal glory in his
    heavenly kingdom.

◆ DISMISSAL TEXT FOR CHILDREN'S LITURGY
OF THE WORD

At this time when we remember the Christ child
let us also remember that it was to the child-like
that Christ promised the kingdom of heaven.
Go now, children, to hear and understand God's
    wonderful Word
so that as you grow,
it can become the food that makes you
    spiritually strong.

◆ DISMISSAL TEXT FOR EXTRAORDINARY
MINISTERS OF HOLY COMMUNION

This holy time makes us mindful of the rich
    gifts that grace our lives.
Go forth, now, with the greatest gift of all,
Christ, the Bread of heaven, the healing Lord
who always made time for the sick and the needy.
The hay of the manger gave the Christ child
    a warm place of rest.
By sharing God's saving Word and the love
    of this community
become for our absent sisters and brothers
a place of comfort and security in God's love.
As you go forth, take with you our fervent
    prayers and earnest Christmas greetings.

December
Month of the Divine Infancy

Vigil #13, Night #14,
Dawn #15, Day #16   white

T U E 25
Solemnity of the Nativity of the Lord (Christmas)
HOLYDAY OF OBLIGATION

Orientation

The first people to hear about the birth of the Savior are shepherds, who not only encounter an angel but also witness a whole heavenly choir singing the glory of God. It is remarkable that the first recipients of the glorious news are rough and common folk who live on the outskirts of society, and spend most of their time in the hills with their animals. God's wisdom may have sought these shepherds out to foreshadow the image of his Son as Good Shepherd. Or, the angel's visit to the shepherds is a sign of the radical equality and availability of God's salvation to all people, starting with the most marginalized. Truly, the Savior is born for all people. He comes freely to share in our humanity out of love and grace, not in response to status, wealth, power or invitation.

Lectionary for Mass

Vigil Mass

◆ FIRST READING: Jerusalem, the city once desolate and forsaken, will shine with the glorious light of the Lord, and all nations will see it. Joy abounds as God renews his covenant of love with Jerusalem, his bride.

◆ RESPONSORIAL PSALM 89 is a song of praise, acclaiming the deeds of the Lord, celebrating God's covenant with David and the promise that his throne will last forever.

◆ SECOND READING: Our Second Reading consists of excerpts from Paul's proclamation of the Gospel to the Jews in Antioch. We hear the high points of Israel's history: the Exodus from Egypt, the anointing of David as king, the covenant made with him, and finally, the presentation of Jesus as this promised descendant whose coming John the Baptist heralded.

◆ GOSPEL: Matthew's genealogy of Jesus traces his ancestry back to Abraham, the father of the Jewish people. The second part of the Gospel (and the shorter option) consists of Matthew's account of the events preceding Jesus's birth, focusing on the angelic appearances to Joseph, assuring him that the child was conceived through the Holy Spirit. The child, whose birth is the fulfillment of the prophecy of Isaiah, is Jesus the Savior, God-with-us.

Mass During the Night

◆ FIRST READING: Isaiah describes the life situation of an oppressed people in time of war. In the midst of darkness, a shining light is seen, a light that brings joy. The light is associated with the birth of a child, an heir to the Davidic throne. Notice the names given to him: they point to the mission he is to accomplish and the role he will have on behalf of the people. All is the work of God. Christian tradition sees this fulfilled in Jesus of Nazareth, whose birth we celebrate today. In the midst of our winter darkness, we celebrate Jesus, the Light of the World.

◆ RESPONSORIAL PSALM 96: The antiphon is taken from Luke's account of the birth of Jesus and is the angel's proclamation to the shepherds: "Today is born our Savior . . . ." Psalm 96 is a song acclaiming God's kingship over all creation and all nations. Notice how all creation joins in this hymn of praise.

◆ SECOND READING: Two comings of the Lord are juxtaposed in this reading. The first coming of Jesus is mentioned in the first line (" the grace of God has appeared," Titus 2:11). Note also the reference to Jesus's work of redemption at the end of the reading. The focus of the reading, however, is on Jesus's Second Coming at the end of time, with particular reference to how believers are to live in anticipation of that coming.

◆ GOSPEL: In his account of the birth of Jesus, Luke stresses, first of all, Joseph's Davidic ancestry—thus the journey to Bethlehem. Luke also portrays Mary and Joseph as travelers lacking a room of their own, forced to take shelter in a stable where animals live. (Might we think of them as homeless or as street people?) Some simple shepherds living in a nearby field first receive news of his birth from the proclamation of the angels. The scene is far from comfortable and luxurious. The infant Jesus has a manger for a crib. How symbolic! He will come to be recognized in the breaking of the bread, in the food given in memory of him.

Mass at Dawn

◆ FIRST READING: Isaiah's words are first spoken to an exiled people, soon to return to their homeland as a result of the Lord's salvific work among them. Once considered by themselves, and others, as forsaken by the Lord, they are given a new identity as a holy and redeemed people. Today, we celebrate the coming of Jesus as Savior and the new identity we receive through participation in his life.

◆ RESPONSORIAL PSALM 97: The antiphon's mention of light evokes the second stanza of the Psalm as well as the image of the glory of the Lord shining around the shepherds in the field. To this light, the angelic proclamation "the Lord is born for us" is joined. The Psalm celebrates the kingship of the Lord over all creation. How appropriate in light of the birth of the newborn king of the Jews.

◆ SECOND READING: The appearance in the first line refers to the birth of Jesus. Paul emphasizes that God's salvific act on our behalf stems from his mercy, not our merit. Closely connected with the birth of Jesus is the theme of our rebirth in Baptism and our renewal through the gift of God's Spirit.

◆ GOSPEL: We see the shepherds receiving and acting upon the message of the angel. They are the first to seek Jesus in Luke's account of the Gospel. Finding him, they become bearers of the Good News to others—these early shepherd witnesses to Jesus. The shepherds praise and glorify God. Mary ponders the meaning of it all in her heart, something she will do repeatedly in Luke's account of Jesus's childhood.

Mass during the Day

◆ FIRST READING: The reading begins and ends on the note of salvation—that which is accomplished by the Lord—not just for Jerusalem, but for all nations. First, we have the announcement of salvation and the proclamation of the Lord's kingship. Then, there is the eye-witness of what God is doing and the jubilant response of praise.

◆ RESPONSORIAL PSALM 98: Our antiphon acclaims the salvation of our God, now seen by all nations. These themes are further elaborated in the stanzas of the Psalm. Note also the reference to God's covenant fidelity in accomplishing salvation and the joyful, musical response of praise.

◆ SECOND READING: This beginning of the Letter to the Hebrews takes us full circle: from God's promises to the prophets of old,

through its fulfilment in the coming of his Son into the world, to the heavenly exaltation of Jesus when he had accomplished his mission on earth. Note also the affirmations about the Son: his active part in creation and in sustaining the world; the glory he shares with the Father.

◆ GOSPEL: We hear the beginning of the fourth evangelist's account of the Gospel. Note the presence of themes we just heard in Hebrews: the Son's pre-existence, his active part in creation, the glory he shares with God. References to the ministry of John the Baptist are interspersed in today's text, as is the theme of the light and enlightenment that Jesus brings. The end of the reading speaks of the grace and glory we have received from him and our call to become more and more his children through the gift of his grace.

The Roman Missal

Vigil Mass

Christmas begins with the Vigil Mass, but the prayers still "look forward . . . / to the coming festivities" (Prayer over the Offerings). The Entrance Antiphon, based on Exodus 16:6–7, captures this sense of almost, but not yet: "Today you will know that the Lord will come, and he will save us, / and in the morning you will see his glory."

We who welcome Christmas with joy should not fear to welcome Christ when he comes as our judge. In the Collect, we pray that we may "merit to face him confidently."

The Prayer over the Offerings is a prayer for joy in service: we pray that we may serve God "all the more eagerly," recognizing that at Christmas we celebrate "the beginnings of our redemption." We have a stake in what's happening, so we should be especially eager to celebrate!

Any of the three Christmas Prefaces may be used. Preface II of the Nativity of the Lord speaks of Christ who at Christmas began to "exist in time." He came to restore unity, and to "call straying humanity back to the heavenly Kingdom." This Preface might appropriately be used at the Vigil Mass, when the Gospel of the genealogy of Christ is read.

If you choose Eucharistic Prayer I, be sure to include the special Christmas form of the *Communicantes* ("In communion with those whose memory we venerate").

The Prayer after Communion asks for "new vigor" from the sacrament we receive and the mystery we celebrate at Christmas.

The Solemn Blessing for the Nativity of the Lord (#2) can be used at this or any of the Masses of Christmas.

Mass During the Night

Darkness surrounds us, but the beautiful Collect speaks of light. God's power has made this "sacred night / radiant with the splendor of the true light." We pray that we who have seen this light may come to the joys of heaven.

The Prayer over the Offerings touches on one of the primary themes of Christmas: the "holy exchange" by which Christ takes on our human nature and grants us a share in his divine nature. We pray that by our sharing in the Eucharist, "we may be found in the likeness of Christ."

Any of the three Prefaces for the Nativity of the Lord may be used. Preface I of the Nativity of the Lord, with its focus on Christ the light, is especially appropriate.

If you choose Eucharistic Prayer I, be sure to include the special Christmas form of the *Communicantes* ("In communion with those memory we venerate").

In the Prayer after Communion, we ask that we may also live in a manner worthy of the Lord in whom we rejoice at the liturgy of Christmas.

You may use the Solemn Blessing for the Nativity of the Lord (#2) at this or any of the Masses of Christmas.

Mass at Dawn

The Collect is full of imagery of light. Today, "we are bathed in the new radiance of . . . [the] incarnate Word." We have received the "light of faith," but it is not enough to believe in Christ in our minds: we must let his light shine in our deeds as well.

Prayer over the Offerings: Christ became "true man, yet very God," as the carol has it. We pray that the "earthly gifts" of bread and wine we bring to the altar may become for us God's divine gift. Every celebration of the Eucharist recalls the mystery of the Incarnation, the Word made flesh.

Any of the three Christmas Prefaces may be used. Preface I of the Nativity of the Lord with its focus on Christ the light, is an appropriate choice.

If you use Eucharistic Prayer I, be sure to include the special Christmas form of the *Communicantes* ("In communion with those whose memory we venerate").

In the Prayer after Communion, we ask that as we celebrate Christmas, we may come to a greater knowledge and love of "the hidden depths of this mystery."

You may use the Solemn Blessing for the Nativity of the Lord (#2) at this or any of the Masses of Christmas.

Mass During the Day

The Collect reminds us of why it is so important that we gather to celebrate and wonder at the mystery of the Incarnation. When God's Word became flesh, the "dignity of human nature," lost in Eden, was "wonderfully restored." In the same way that Christ shares our humanity, God wants us to share his divinity.

The Prayer over the Offerings asks God to receive our gifts on "this solemn day," which marks our reconciliation with the Father.

Any of the three Christmas Prefaces may be used. Preface III of the Nativity of the Lord, with its focus on the "holy exchange" of divine and human, is especially appropriate.

If you use Eucharistic Prayer I, be sure to include the special Christmas form of the *Communicantes* ("In communion with those whose memory we venerate").

In the Prayer after Communion we ask that Christ, who was born this day to give us a share in the divine life, may also give us eternal life.

You may use the Solemn Blessing for the Nativity of the Lord (#2) at this or any of the Masses of Christmas.

The Nativity of Our Lord Jesus Christ from the *Roman Martyrology* (Christmas Proclamation)

This proclamation comes from the *Roman Martyrology*, the official listing of the saints honored by the Roman Rite of the Catholic Church. Traditionally, this proclamation has been read on Christmas Eve, before the celebration of the Mass during the Night. It situates the nativity of Christ within the context of salvation history, making reference not only to biblical events but also to the Greek and Roman worlds. The coming of Christ at Christmas, then, is seen as the summit of both sacred

and secular history. It begins with the creation of the world, mentions certain key events in the history of the people of Israel, and concludes with the birth of Jesus during the Roman Era.

In the 1980s, Pope John Paul II restored this proclamation to the papal celebration of the Mass at Night. Many parishes have followed the custom. A newly revised translation has been included in the third edition of *The Roman Missal*. It is found in Appendix I.

The *Christmas Proclamation* may be sung or proclaimed during the Liturgy of the Hours or before the beginning of the Mass During the Night. It may not replace any part of the Mass. According to circumstances, the proclamation may be sung or recited at the ambo by a deacon, cantor, or reader.

Other Ideas

The shepherds initiated the announcement of the Good News, yet two thousand years later, many still don't really know Jesus. Think of one person in your life who needs to hear the Good News of Jesus, and resolve to do something special for him or her.

#696 red

26
W E D

Feast of Saint Stephen, The First Martyr

Lectionary for Mass

◆ FIRST READING: Today's reading is excerpted from the two chapters of the Acts of the Apostles where we meet Stephen, the first person named among those chosen to assist the Apostles with the daily distribution to those in need. He is described as a man filled with faith and the Holy Spirit (see Acts of the Apostles 6:5). Today's reading jumps from Acts of the Apostles 6:10, which notes the wisdom with which Stephen spoke, to 7:54–59, which describes his martyrdom. Omitted are the accusations of blasphemy made by his opponents (named at the beginning of the reading) and his consequent trial before the Sanhedrin (Jewish council). The immediate reference to the "this" that so infuriated the Sanhedrin (v. 54) is his charge against the Jewish leaders for their obstinacy in refusing to believe in Jesus and putting him to death. Stephen is sustained by his vision of the glorified and exalted Christ at the right hand of God. This was blasphemy to the Jewish leaders and deserved punishment by death. Stephen's prayer as he dies is that of Jesus: into your hands, I "commend my spirit" (Luke 23:46).

◆ RESPONSORIAL PSALM: The antiphon is the prayer of Stephen (and Jesus) as they die. Psalm 31 is a song of confidence and a prayer for deliverance from enemies.

◆ GOSPEL: Stephen was among the first to experience severe opposition from his own people. Believers thus share in the suffering of Christ. The verb "hand over" is the same verb used in the Passion narratives. Jesus gives assurance of the Spirit's presence in such times and the promise of salvation to those who endure.

The Roman Missal

The Gloria is said or sung today and throughout the Octave of Christmas.

We are called to "imitate what we worship," that is, to imitate the self-sacrificing love of Christ (Collect). In so doing, we will learn to love our enemies, and to pray for our persecutors, as Stephen did

In the Prayer over the Offerings, we ask God to accept the offering we make on the Feast of Saint Stephen.

One of the Prefaces of the Nativity of the Lord is prayed on this feast.

The Prayer after Communion is a prayer of thanksgiving to the God who saves us through his Son and gives us this feast in honor of the "blessed Martyr Stephen."

Today's Saint

Saint Stephen (first century) is the protomartyr, the first martyr. When the Apostles chose deacons to help in their ministry, he was among the first seven. Stephen was arrested and tried by the Sanhedrin for blasphemy. His fate was sealed when he had a vision during his trial and cried out, "Behold, I see the heavens opened and the Son of Man standing at the right hand of God" (Acts of the Apostles 7:56). He was dragged out of the city and stoned to death by the mob, which included Saul of Tarsus. Stephen is shown in art with three stones and a martyr's palm, sometimes wearing a dalmatic, a deacon's vestment.

THU 27 #697 white
Feast of Saint John, Apostle and Evangelist

Lectionary for Mass

◆ FIRST READING: "We have heard . . . we have seen . . . and touched with our hands . . . " (1 John 1:1). John's proclamation of Jesus is rooted in the reality of a personal experience of the Lord. He has found life—eternal life—in fellowship with Jesus. His desire and hope is that others will receive the Word and have life. In this is his joy.

◆ RESPONSORIAL PSALM 97: The antiphon echoes the theme of joy (note also the references to "glad" in the last two stanzas). The Psalm celebrates the kingship of the Lord. All of creation joins in praise.

◆ GOSPEL: Today's Gospel takes us to the end of Jesus's life, to the tomb, in fact. Tradition holds that

John is the "other disciple" (John 20:2) and the one with whom Jesus had a special bond. It is he, the beloved disciple, who sees and believes.

The Roman Missal

The Gloria is said or sung today.

The prayers for this feast echo the words of the Gospel according to John. In the Collect, we praise God who through John "unlocked for us the secrets of your Word," and we pray for a deeper understanding of the Gospel. In the Prayer over the Offerings we echo that prayer, asking that the "supper" from which John drew heavenly wisdom may be for us as well the source of "the hidden wisdom of the eternal Word." In the Prayer after Communion we pray that "the Word made flesh" may "ever dwell among us."

One of the Christmas Prefaces is used.

Today's Saint

Saint John (first century), apostle and fourth Evangelist, is called the "beloved disciple" because of his close relationship with Jesus. Throughout his account of the Gospel, Saint John, named as the son of Zebedee and brother of Saint James the Greater, makes an appearance at significant moments in Jesus's life; specifically, at the Last Supper, the Garden of Gethsemane, the foot of the Cross, and the upper room. These appearances point to the intimate relationship he had with our Lord. His account of the Gospel is quite different from the synoptic accounts (Matthew, Mark, and Luke) due to his high Christology (divine emphasis), which is proclaimed through symbolic language and poetic form. The eagle is the chosen symbol for John's account, ultimately representing the depth and height to which the human spirit must soar in order to grasp the meaning of John's text. Among his many important contributions to the Church, other scriptural writings are attributed to his name, including three epistles and the Book of Revelation.

FRI 28 #698 red
Feast of the Holy Innocents, Martyrs

Lectionary for Mass

◆ FIRST READING: Having fellowship with the Lord means that his light and life are evident in our behavior. Only in this is there true fellowship with him. John calls all believers to honest self-appraisal and recognition of their sinfulness, and correspondingly, to appeal for forgiveness to Jesus, our Advocate with the heavenly Father. He lived, and died, that we might have the light of eternal life.

◆ RESPONSORIAL PSALM 124: Today's Psalm is one of thanksgiving for deliverance from the enemy. We can think of it as applying not only to our own deliverance, accomplished by Jesus, from the snares of the devil, but also to the deliverance of the Holy Innocents through death to life everlasting. In all ways and at all times, our help is in the Lord.

◆ GOSPEL: While there is no mention of the event described in today's Gospel in historical sources, such an action is entirely in keeping with the character of Herod the Great as it is described elsewhere. Herod is enraged at the possibility that his throne will be usurped and seeks immediately to wipe out any perceived opposition. Note how Matthew describes the events as fulfilling the scriptures, an important point for his Jewish Christian community. Note, too, how the history of the Jewish people is relived in Jesus: he is taken down to Egypt, that his life might be spared (as were the sons of Jacob), and is later called "out of Egypt" (Matthew 2:15).

The Roman Missal

The Gloria is said or sung today.

The Holy Innocents gave witness to God "not by speaking but by dying" (Collect). Our prayer is that we may confess our faith not just with our lips, but with our lives.

In his power and mercy, God grants "justification / even to those who lack understanding," like the Holy Innocents (Prayer over the Offerings).

One of the Christmas Prefaces is used.

We ask "abundant salvation" for all who receive "holy gifts" on this Feast of the Holy Innocents, who died for Christ though too young to speak (Prayer after Communion).

Today's Saints

◆ HOLY INNOCENTS: Herod the Great, fearing for his throne after the Magi told him about the birth of Jesus, ordered the execution of all male children in Bethlehem, hoping that Jesus would be among those killed (see Matthew 2:16–18). According to Matthew, this fulfilled the prophecy of Jeremiah (31:15): "In Ramah is heard the sound of sobbing, bitter weeping! Rachel mourns for her children." The haunting Coventry Carol refers to this episode as it asks, "O sisters too, how may we do, / For to preserve this day / This poor youngling for whom we sing / By, by, lully, lullay."

SAT 29 #202 white
Fifth Day within the Octave of the Nativity of the Lord

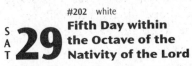

Optional Memorial of Saint Thomas Becket, Bishop and Martyr / white

Lectionary for Mass

◆ FIRST READING: Our reading opens on the theme of knowing Jesus, and not just on an intellectual level. It is, rather, a knowledge that is relationship, true discipleship, obedience to Jesus's teaching. In such a person, the love of God

(God's love for us? Our love for God? Both?) reaches maturity. Darkness and light are prominent motifs in the second part of the reading. Christmas is a feast of light—the Light of Christ. Are we in his light or still in darkness?

◆ RESPONSORIAL PSALM 96: All of creation rejoices in the salvation of the Lord. God's people sing his praise and recount his marvelous deeds to all the nations.

◆ GOSPEL: Mary and Joseph are presented as people who walk by the light of the Lord's teaching in the law and who fulfill the Lord's precepts. The Lord's promise to another righteous man, Simeon, is fulfilled when his eyes behold Jesus, the light of the nations.

The Roman Missal

If the optional Memorial of Saint Thomas Becket is observed today, the Collect is taken from the Proper of Saints. The remaining prayers may be drawn from the Common of Martyrs, the Common of Pastors, or the Christmas weekday. One of the Christmas Prefaces is used.

We cannot see the invisible God, but we can see his light in the coming of Christ among us. We ask that God may "look . . . with serene countenance upon us," so that we may fittingly praise the Nativity of Christ (Collect).

The Prayer over the Offerings is a simple expression of the "glorious exchange" that is the Mass: we offer to God what God has given, and in return, God gives us himself.

In the simple Prayer after Communion we pray that the mysteries we receive may sustain us.

Today's Saint

Heeding the Gospel call "to lay down one's life" (John 15:13) for the sake of the kingdom, Saint Thomas (1118–1170) shed his blood to declare that God's power far surpasses the authority of a monarch.

Saint Thomas was appointed chancellor and eventually archbishop of Canterbury by his close friend, King Henry II. He was hesitant to accept these appointments, for he was concerned about the king's motives in lifting him up the ranks, but Saint Thomas said yes in spite of his fears. It became quite evident that the king wanted to claim jurisdiction over Church matters, especially issues regarding the clergy. Saint Thomas stood on the side of Church independence and the absolute supremacy of God; therefore, he fled to a Cistercian monastery for a period of time. After many attempts at reconciliation, Saint Thomas was murdered in the cathedral of Canterbury while preparing for Evening Prayer. As he lay dying on the floor of the cathedral, he cried out, quoting Luke 23:46, "Father, into your hands I commend my spirit."

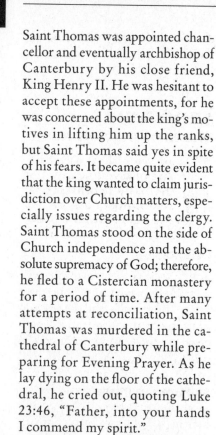

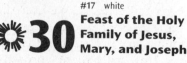

#17   white

30 Feast of the Holy Family of Jesus, Mary, and Joseph

Orientation

Between the Infancy Narratives and the beginning of his public ministry as an adult, Scripture is silent about the life of Jesus, except for today's Gospel passage about the 12-year-old Jesus who is lost and found in the Temple of Jerusalem. This story grants us a glimpse into the Holy Family, as Mary and Joseph search frantically for the missing Jesus, are astonished to find him teaching in the Temple, and then are puzzled by his justification that he must be in his Father's house. Yet, like his presentation to Simeon, this story foreshadows Jesus's ultimate mission and identity as Savior. In a few years' time, he will again head up to Jerusalem for the Passover, and give himself over to his Father's will and service completely as he takes up the cross. His obedience to his parents prepares his heart for the dark night spent in prayer at Gethsemane, when he gives his will over to his heavenly Father.

Lectionary for Mass

◆ FIRST READING: Today's First Reading is perhaps best understood by reading the first chapter of 1 Samuel in its entirety. Prior to the birth of her child, Hannah was a woman of deep suffering and shame. She had promised the Lord that she would dedicate her child to him ("nazirite," see Numbers 6:1–21) if he answered her prayer. We have the beautiful and tender scene of his dedication to the Lord in the second part of the reading. Samuel had an important role in the history of salvation: he was the prophet who anointed David to be king of Israel (1 Samuel 16).

◆ RESPONSORIAL PSALM: The beauty of God's dwelling place and the joy of those who dwell there is the focus of today's Psalm 84. The Psalm describes the Temple in Jerusalem. The Lord's dwelling place spoken of in the First Reading was the shrine of the Lord at Shiloh.

◆ SECOND READING: John's words bring home to us the reality of the family of God to which we belong through the loving gift of our Heavenly Father. We have life from the Father and share in the divine life through his love. John says that the world does not recognize us. Do we recognize this reality in ourselves? Note the importance given to keeping his commandments if we are to "remain," to live in this reality. Jesus "remains," dwells within us, through the gift of his Spirit.

◆ GOSPEL: Today's Gospel gives us a beautiful image of the Holy Family faithfully keeping the traditional practices and observances of Judaism. Today it is the pilgrimage to Jerusalem at the time of Passover. The mention of Jesus's 12 years also calls to mind the customary Bar Mitzvah that we know today. We witness Jesus's deep interest in the scriptures and his desire to know and understand them. Note how themes of his Passion are previewed in today's reading: the Passover, the three days, the business of the Father which he must be about.

The Roman Missal

The Holy Family is a "shining example" for us, a model of "the virtues of family life" and the bonds of love. By imitating the Holy Family on earth, we hope one day to come to eternal "joy" and "delight" in the Father's house (Collect).

In the Prayer over the Offerings we ask the intercession of Mary and Joseph for our families, that they may be grounded in God's grace and peace.

Any of the three Prefaces of the Nativity of the Lord may be used. Preface II of the Nativity of the Lord, with its reference to the reconciliation of "straying humanity," might be an appropriate choice.

The Prayer after Communion, like the Collect, is a prayer that we might imitate the example of Jesus, Mary, and Joseph, and come one day to "share their company for ever."

The *Book of Blessings* includes an "Order for the Blessing of a Family" (40ff). Either of the options for the Prayer of Blessing (65–66) could be used as a Prayer over the People at the end of Mass today.

Other Ideas

If older relatives join you for Christmas, ask them to share their childhood memories of Christmas and stories they heard from their parents and grandparents. Ask them to recount old family traditions, and look for ways to incorporate some of these into your future festivities. Ask if you can videotape them telling stories, and plan to show the tapes next year. Save your Christmas cards, reread one each day or week in the coming year, and pray for the sender.

#204   white

MON 31
Seventh Day within the Octave of the Nativity of the Lord

Optional Memorial of Saint Sylvester I, Pope / white

Lectionary for Mass

◆ FIRST READING: John and his community thought that they were living in the end time. We may well be without realizing it. People of Jewish and early Christian tradition believed that the end time would be characterized by the presence of false teachers. John's community has experienced this, and his words today are reassuring: you do have knowledge, knowledge of the truth, and you have the anointing of the Spirit. Do not waver in the face of those who would oppose you.

◆ RESPONSORIAL PSALM 96 recounts the joyful response of all creation to the Lord's coming. We think not only of his first coming, but also his last.

◆ GOSPEL: Today's reading is the same as for the Mass of Christmas Day. In light of today's First Reading, note the mention of opposition to the Word and the contrast between those who believe and those who do not. Truth comes through Jesus. Believers have received from his fullness. Because he became one

of us, we receive his grace to become as he is, a child of God.

The Roman Missal

If the optional Memorial of Saint Sylvester is observed today, the Collect is taken from the Proper of Saints. The remaining prayers may be drawn from the Common of Pastors: For a Pope or from the Christmas weekday. One of the Prefaces of the Nativity of the Lord is used.

With the birth of Christ, God established "the beginning and fulfillment of all religion" (Collect/Proper of Time). Christ is the alpha and the omega, the first and the last. We pray that we may be among those who belong to him.

God alone gives the gifts of "true prayer and of peace." We ask for these gifts, so that through our sharing in the mystery of the Eucharist, we may be one in "mind and heart" (Prayer over the Offerings/Proper of Time).

The Prayer after Communion is the perfect prayer to end Mass on the last day of the calendar year. We ask for God's continued guidance "now and in the future" and that, while making necessary use of passing things, we may "strive with ever deepened trust" for the things that do not pass away.

Today's Saint

Very little is known about Saint Sylvester I. He was pope from 314 to 335 during the era of Constantine, when the Church was able to come out of hiding after years of persecution. During his pontificate some of the great churches in Rome were built, such as the Lateran Basilica and the original Saint Peter's Basilica on the Vatican Hill (the present Saint Peter's Basilica was constructed between 1506 and 1626). The First Council of Nicea in 325, at which the Nicene Creed was

adopted, occurred during his papacy. Sylvester did not attend, but he sent two legates.

January
Month of the Holy Name

#18   white

TUE 1
The Octave Day of the Nativity of the Lord Solemnity of Mary, the Holy Mother of God
HOLYDAY OF OBLIGATION

Orientation

Today's solemnity celebrates the relationship between Mary and Jesus, a relationship full of hope and promise for all of us. In the fourth century, the Church granted the title "Theotokos," or "God-bearer," to Mary, clarifying that she was indeed the Mother of the Son of God, not just the mother of the human part of Jesus. Jesus's humanity and divinity cannot be separated, nor can the relationship he offers be dissected into human and divine components. As fully human and fully divine, Jesus embodies the unity of heaven and earth, and Mary as Mother of God is the first of us to exist in the midst of this blessed unity. In celebrating Mary, we offer our prayers in joyful hope to follow her in her relationship to her Son.

Lectionary for Mass

◆ FIRST READING: We hear the words the Lord gave to Aaron, his priest, to use in blessing the Israelites. How truly these words are fulfilled in the Christ event, as the face of the Lord shines upon us in and through Jesus. In his humanity, he possesses the fullness of the divine radiance. Peace, or *shalom* in the Hebrew connotes the fullness of well-being, God's preeminent gift in Christ. All who follow Christ now bear his name. Note that this is the text used for Solemn Blessing #10.

◆ RESPONSORIAL PSALM 67 is a prayer for God's blessing. Note the echoes of the First Reading in the first line. This joyful hymn of praise acclaims God's salvation for all the nations.

◆ SECOND READING: Jesus's birth happened in the fullness of time, ordained by God for the revelation of his salvation. The text emphasizes Jesus's humanity and his Jewish identity as well as his divine sonship. What is more, it proclaims our adoption as children of God through him. Jesus's Spirit dwells in our hearts, crying out *Abba*, the Aramaic word for "Daddy," to the Father.

◆ GOSPEL: The visit of the shepherds to the manger is center stage in today's Gospel. These people, so receptive to the Good News they received from the angels, in turn become bearers of the Good News themselves. What is significant on this solemnity is the Gospel's comment about how Mary reflected in her heart on all that was said. She is truly one who "listens" to God in all of life. There is also a brief reference to the eighth-day celebration of Jesus's circumcision according to the Law of Moses and the conferral of his name.

The Roman Missal

Through the Blessed Virgin Mary, humanity has received the grace of salvation. We pray that we may know the intercession of Mary, through whom "the author of life" has been given to us (Collect).

We rejoice today at the "beginnings" of grace by celebrating the motherhood of Mary; we hope to see its "completion" in eternal life (Prayer over the Offerings).

Preface I of the Blessed Virgin Mary is used.

In the Prayer after Communion, we pray that the Eucharist may "lead us to eternal life" as we proclaim Mary Mother of God, Mother of the Church.

Other Ideas

Shepherds were poor. They worked outdoors year round, regardless of the weather, and few people paid them any attention. Yet God sent his Good News angels to them, not to royalty or the wealthy. Think of the people in your community who work in harsh conditions with little recognition. Send a thank-you note to your trash collector, say a prayer for road workers while driving *slowly* past their orange barrels, or buy fair-trade products to assure just compensation for those who labor over the goods you purchase.

#205 white

WED 2

Memorial of Saints Basil the Great and Gregory Nazianzen, Bishops and Doctors of the Church

Lectionary for Mass

◆ FIRST READING: False teachers who would deceive believers and lead them away from the truth of Jesus are a major concern. Repeatedly we hear the word "remain" (mentioned six times), which can also be translated as "live," "dwell," or "continue." Remain true to Christ's teaching so as to live or dwell in him and the Father. Keep his word so that the Father and the Son are at home in you. Remain in the anointing of his Spirit.

◆ RESPONSORIAL PSALM 98: Our abiding with the Father and the Son is the result of the saving power of God at work in our lives. This Christmas Time we celebrate not only his coming to the earth, but his presence in our lives. All creation, all Israel, all the nations, and we ourselves, have seen the saving power of God. We sing his praise.

◆ GOSPEL: Today's Gospel sounds like Advent, with the centrality of John the Baptist. True teachers point to Christ, his coming, his presence, his teaching, and not to themselves.

The Roman Missal

The prayers are found in the Proper of Saints.

The Gloria is said or sung today.

Saints Basil and Gregory taught the faith, and lived it. We pray that we may learn the truth with humility and practice it with love (Collect).

In the Prayer over the Offerings, we ask for eternal salvation as we offer the sacrifice in honor of the saints.

In the Prayer after Communin, we ask for the strength that flows from the Eucharist, that we may preserve the faith "in integrity" and follow the path God has marked out for us.

Today's Saints

Saints Basil and Gregory became close friends as students in Athens. Together they fought against the Arian heresy, which denied the full divinity of Christ. Their writings also aided the Church's understanding of the Holy Spirit and the Trinity. With Basil's brothers, Gregory of Nyssa and Peter of Sebaste, they are among the Capadocian Fathers. Gregory is known as "the Theologian" by the Eastern Churches. Basil is known as the father of Eastern monasticism and had a great influence on the development of liturgy, East and West.

**T
H
U 3** #206 white
Christmas Weekday

Optional Memorial of the Most Holy Name of Jesus / white

Lectionary for Mass

◆ FIRST READING: The central section of today's text pertains to the great love God has bestowed upon us in making us his children (i.e., sharing something of his very own life with us). What is more, his will is that his children become as he is. Framing this central section is instruction on how to live and become like him: by being righteous (in right relationship with God) and keeping ourselves pure (unblemished by sin).

◆ RESPONSORIAL PSALM 98, a joyful hymn of praise, is used often in Christmas Time as a Responsorial Psalm. Not only have the Jews seen the fulfillment of God's promises, but all nations have seen his glory.

◆ GOSPEL: John the Baptist introduces Jesus as the Lamb of God. The attribution will be important in the fourth evangelist's account of the Gospel, where Jesus is crucified at the hour that the Passover lambs are sacrificed for the annual celebration of Israel's redemption from slavery. John further testifies that Jesus is endowed with the Holy Spirit and will baptize those who come to him with this same Holy Spirit. Note also the reference in the second line of the Gospel to Jesus's preexistence, which was already mentioned in the Prologue of this Gospel account. Finally, in the last line, there is yet another title, another confession of faith: Jesus is the Son of God.

The Roman Missal

If the optional memorial is observed, the Prayers are drawn from the Proper of Saints, while the Preface of Christmas is still used.

◆ COLLECT BEFORE EPIPHANY: We ask for "firmness of faith," that we may persevere in following Christ's guidance and come to the fullness of redemption.

Today's Optional Memorial

Names are important. They tell us something of who we are and where we come from, and they speak of our parents' hopes and dreams for us. The name of Jesus is especially important. It means "God saves." His family does not choose the name of Jesus; rather, God gives it to him before his birth: "You are to name him Jesus," the angel tells Joseph in a dream, "because he will save his people from their sins" (Matthew 1:21). Jesus's name is both his identity and his mission. Jesus's name is powerful: "Whatever you ask in my name, I will do," he tells his disciples (John 14:13). In the letter to the Philippians, Saint Paul sings a hymn to the power of Jesus's name: "God greatly exalted him and bestowed on him the name that is above every name, / that at the name of Jesus every knee should bend, of those in heaven and on earth and under the earth, / and every tongue confess that Jesus Christ is Lord, to the glory of God the Father" (Philippians 2:9–11).

In Jewish tradition, a boy was named and circumcised eight days after birth. That is why the Church celebrates this memorial so close to January 1, the octave day of Jesus's birth.

The Memorial of the Holy Name of Jesus is another "idea-feast" or "devotion-feast." The fifteenth-century Franciscan Saint Bernardine of Siena (May 20) popularized devotion to the holy name of Jesus, devising the monogram IHS, which represents the first three letters of Jesus's name in Greek.

Other Ideas

If the optional memorial is celebrated, the Litany of the Holy Name of Jesus might be prayed before or after Mass today. Here is a link to the prayer: http://www.ewtn.com/faith/teachings/incab3c.htm.

**F
R
I 4** #207 white
Memorial of Saint Elizabeth Ann Seton, Religious

Lectionary for Mass

◆ FIRST READING: Do we act in righteousness; that is, do our actions and decisions put us in a right relationship with God as the Law and the Gospel teach us? The one who lives in God commits no sin since God's life within that person becomes more fully alive. Note the specific behavior that is mentioned: love for the brother or sister.

◆ RESPONSORIAL PSALM: Today's verses from Psalm 98 call upon seas, rivers, and mountains to join the hymn of praise. Note the emphasis on judgment, literally God's righteous judgment, in the last stanza.

◆ GOSPEL: Today's Gospel is a continuation from yesterday's reading. In the first line we hear again, "Behold, the Lamb of God" (John 1:36) as John the Baptist shows his disciples the way to Jesus. They, in turn, become disciples of Jesus. How beautiful are these words: "Come, and you will see" where I live and stay with me (John 1:39). Like John the Baptist, Andrew shows his brother Simon the way to the Messiah, the Anointed One. Jesus then gives Simon a new name.

The Roman Missal

The Prayers are found in the Proper of Saints.

One of the Christmas Prefaces is used.

The prayers for today ask for a share in the "burning zeal" of Saint Elizabeth. We pray that, like her, we may seek God with love and find him in service (Collect), filled with "burning desire" for the Eucharist (Prayer after Communion). We believe that through "the power at work in this sacrifice," we can be ever more deeply incorporated into the mystery of Christ (Prayer over the Offerings).

Today's Saint

Saint Elizabeth Ann Seton (1774–1821), referred to as Mother Seton, was a heroic woman with an innovative and pioneering spirit. In every difficult situation she encountered, especially the death of her husband, Saint Elizabeth said that God continually "raise[d] her from the Dust" (*Butler's Lives of the Saints, January, New Full Edition*, p. 37) so that she might ardently demonstrate his love to the poor. Even though Mother Seton was raised in a faithful Episcopalian family, she felt drawn to the Catholic faith. Upon her conversion, which happened after the death of her husband, she wanted to give her life more fully to God and the education of the poor. She was a woman of many firsts: she is the foundress of the first group of women religious in the United States of America (Sisters of Charity); she started the first Catholic school, ultimately laying the foundation for the American parochial system; and she was the first American-born person to be canonized a saint.

S A T **5** #208   white
Memorial of Saint John Neumann, Bishop

Lectionary for Mass

◆ FIRST READING: We are confronted with the realities of jealousy and resentment, which can lead to violence, as in the story of Cain and Abel (Genesis 4). Do not be like Cain, John warns his community. Be like Jesus, who laid down his life. Love is to be unconditional. There is no room for hate, retaliation, or lack of compassion in Jesus's teaching. Love must be manifest in deed and truth, and not merely talked about. This is the litmus test for whether or not we belong to him.

◆ RESPONSORIAL PSALM 100 is a hymn of joyful praise. Note the reference to "serve" in the first stanza. We might think of this as the service of love in light of today's First Reading. We are the Lord's. We can enter his courts if we live according to his teaching.

◆ GOSPEL: A beautiful model for believers is found in the example of Andrew, and today, Philip, who, after they have found Jesus, now bring others to him. Nathanael is uncertain. How can he know if Jesus is the one promised in the Law and the prophets? Nathanael needs a sign and he gets one from Jesus. Immediately he confesses faith in Jesus, who in turn assures him that there will be even more signs.

The Roman Missal

The Prayers are found in the Proper of Saints.

As we observe the feast of the saintly bishop of Philadelphia, we pray in the Collect that we may foster the growth of the Church's family through education of youth and love of neighbor.

Saint John Neumann did more than celebrate the Mass—he imitated it in his self-sacrificing love and service. We pray that our lives, too, may "reflect / the image of Christ" (Prayer over the Offerings).

In the Prayer after Communion, we pray that we may know the power of the sacrament we have received, that the Church may be bound together in "unity and truth."

Today's Saint

With an intellectual capacity far surpassing his peers and a special talent for languages, Saint John Neumann (1811–1868) came to the United States from what is now called the Czech Republic with the dream of being a priest and missionary. Received with open arms by the bishop of New York, Saint John was ordained and immediately asked to help build churches and schools for German immigrants and Native Americans. Needing spiritual support and companionship, he eventually entered a religious order, the Redemptorists, where he was made novice-master and eventually vicar of all the Redemptorists in the United States. The larger Church recognized his holiness and affinity for leadership by appointing him bishop of Philadelphia, the largest diocese at the time. While bishop, he was an avid supporter of the work of religious orders, a proponent of Catholic education, and an advocate for the needs of immigrants.

☀ **6** #20   white
Solemnity of the Epiphany of the Lord

Orientation

Heaven and earth bow down to the newborn Jesus. A star leaves its celestial course to shine above the birthplace of the Lord, foreign sages come to do him homage with rare and expensive gifts, and even King Herod senses that Christ's true power outshines the importance of his royal throne. One of the first mysteries of our faith is that all this glory and power manifests itself in the simplicity of a stable, in a helpless infant born to two people without rank, traveling on their way to a national census. The glory of the Savior is found in the most common of places, in the most basic surroundings, among the simplest of people. This is Good News, revealing the radical pervasiveness of God's grace, present to us in the most ordinary and everyday circumstances of our lives. No part of the human experience is too mundane for the presence of God.

Lectionary for Mass

◆ First Reading: It was the shining star that led the three Magi from the east to Jerusalem, thus fulfilling the words of the prophet Isaiah heard in today's First Reading. In Isaiah's day, the shining light signified the dawn of a new period in the nation's history after the exile, a time of rebuilding and resettling the land. Joy abounds—so much that the human heart cannot contain it and the face glows. Jerusalem's glory is visible not only to herself, but to all the nations.

◆ Responsorial Psalm 72: Today's Psalm is a prayer for the king, most fitting on this day when we celebrate the manifestation of the newborn king to those from distant lands who come bearing gifts (see the third stanza). Indeed, they represent "every nation," the Gentile nations of today's antiphon. Note how the first, second, and fourth stanzas are apt descriptions of Jesus's future ministry.

◆ Second Reading: Throughout his letters, Paul attests to the transforming grace he has personally received. In today's reading, we hear of another dimension of this grace. It is not solely for himself; it is something with which he is entrusted, something to which he has

been given stewardship as he proclaims the Gospel in the world of his day. The fullness of this message is that Gentiles as well as Jews are offered salvation, coheirs and members of the same family of God.

◆ Gospel: It was a commonplace in antiquity that a new star signaled the birth of a new ruler. This shining light led the Magi (astrologers or wise men; no mention of them being kings) to seek the newborn king. King Herod, an easily threatened and insecure person, was far from overjoyed at the news. He deceitfully tries to ascertain the child's whereabouts, so that he might be killed. Herod typically did this with any would-be contenders to his throne. When the Magi find the child we again encounter the theme of joy, the same expansive joy we heard about in today's First Reading. As was the case with Joseph, a dream instructs the Magi, and the child's life is spared. Note also Matthew's inclusion of a citation from the Old Testament to demonstrate the fulfillment of the scriptural prophecy that the child was to be born in Bethlehem.

The Roman Missal

At the Vigil Mass

The beautiful entrance antiphon for this Vigil Mass, from the prophet Baruch (5:5), is also echoed at the beginning of Eucharistic Prayer III: "Arise, Jerusalem, and look to the East / and see your children gathered from the rising to the setting of the sun."

The Magi were led to Christ by the light of a star. We pray that God's light may shine in our hearts, to lead us "through the shadows of this world" to the light of heaven, "our eternal home" (Collect).

In the Prayer over the Offerings, we ask God to receive our gifts, that praise may be offered to him, and eternal salvation given to us.

The Preface for Epiphany expresses the marvelous exchange that we recall over and over again in the prayers of Christmas Time: God has become one of us, so that we might become like him. At Epiphany, Christ appears "in our mortal nature" and renews us "by the glory of his immortal nature."

If Eucharistic Prayer I is used, be sure to use the proper form of the *Communicantes*.

The Prayer after Communion alludes to the star that led the Magi to the infant Christ and to the precious gifts they brought him. We ask that "the star of [God's] justice" may shine in our minds, and that we may regard our faith as our greatest treasure.

At the Mass During the Day

The wise men were led to Christ by the light of a star; we are led to him by the light of faith. We pray that one day we may behold him clearly and see "the beauty of your sublime glory" (Collect).

The Prayer over the Offerings asks God to look upon the offering we make, "not gold or frankincense or myrrh," but the one those gifts proclaimed: Christ himself.

The Preface of the Epiphany is used today.

The lovely Prayer after Communion asks for the guidance of "heavenly light," so that we may clearly see, reverence, and love the great mystery in which we participate when we celebrate the Eucharist.

Other Ideas

Together, make a menu for the week, incorporating everyone's favorite foods from other countries. Children's favorites often include pizza, tacos, and French toast. Read a little about each country represented in your menu, learn a word or phrase in the language, listen to the nation's traditional music, and so on. When you say grace, pray for peace and blessings for the people of each land, remembering that Jesus is the Shepherd of all.

Bake a "king's cake." You'll find plenty of recipes online. Just as the Holy Family welcomed the world on the day of the Epiphany, invite your neighbors over for an impromptu desert. If it seems appropriate, suggest that whoever finds the bean (or baby) hosts the next impromptu neighborhood desert, at his or her convenience. Warm the winter with hospitality.

MON 7 #212 white
Christmas Weekday

Optional Memorial of Saint Raymond of Penyafort, Priest / white (U.S.A.) ◆ *Optional Memorial of Blessed André Bessette, Religious / white (Canada)*

Lectionary for Mass

◆ FIRST READING: The first part of today's reading echoes Jesus's words at the Last Supper in the Fourth Gospel about: prayer in his name (John 14:13; 16:23); the command to love one another (13:34; 15:12–17); remaining in him (15:4–10); and the Spirit he has given to believers (16:13–15). The second part of the reading deals with the necessity of discernment in recognizing whether or not a spirit (or a teacher) is of God, and John sets forth specific criteria. The community would seem to be threatened by the danger of these false teachers. John reminds them that they have received the Spirit of truth (16:13) and they belong to God.

◆ RESPONSORIAL PSALM: In its original context, Psalm 2 was about the Davidic king. At this time, it can readily be applied to Jesus, the Messiah. Juxtaposed with today's first reading, it can be applied to all who believe in the name of Jesus, who have received his Spirit, and belong to God. We are in the world,

but we belong to God and must live accordingly.

◆ GOSPEL: At the beginning of his public ministry, Jesus enters fully into the "world," all the while belonging to God and proclaiming the Good News of the kingdom of God. As he will do throughout his Gospel, Matthew cites texts from the Old Testament to demonstrate to his Jewish Christian community that Jesus is the fulfillment of all that was promised of old. Jesus's healing ministry goes hand in hand with his preaching. His light overcomes the darkness enshrouding both body and soul.

The Roman Missal

If the optional Memorial of Saint Raymond is observed, the Collect is taken from the Proper of Saints, while the other prayers are drawn from the Common of Pastors or from the Christmas weekday.

◆ COLLECT AFTER EPIPHANY: We pray that Christ, who "adorns the face of the heavens" yet became flesh in Mary's womb, may show himself to all for the salvation of the whole world.

Today's Saints

Saint Raymond (c. 1175) was born near Barcelona, Catalonia, into a prominent family. He received his education in Barcelona and at the University of Bologna, Italy, earning doctorates in both civil and canon law. While teaching canon law at Bologna, he heard the preaching of Blessed Reginald, the prior of the Dominicans there, and joined the order in 1222. By 1238, he was made General of the Dominicans, and during his term, he revised the order's constitutions. In 1230, Pope Gregory IX asked him to come to Rome to lend his legal expertise to the organization of the canon law. At that time, there was no systematic codification of canon law, which

was scattered among multiple sources. Raymond helped organize canon law into a collection known as the *Gregorian Decretals*, which replaced the *Decretals of Gratian* and was considered the standard collection of Church law until the promulgation of the first *Code of Canon Law* in 1917. When he returned to Spain, his focus shifted to the conversion of Jews and Muslims to Christianity, and he encouraged the Dominicans to study and teach Arabic and Hebrew. Legend has it that he prompted Saint Thomas Aquinas to write the *Summa contra Gentiles*, a work thought to have been composed as a response to the teachings of Islam and Judaism for use by Dominican missionaries. In an unfortunate footnote to history, Raymond was among those who established the Inquisition in Catalonia. Saint Raymond is patron of canon lawyers.

Saint André Bessette (1845–1937), known as Frère André, was born to an impoverished working-class French-Canadian family. His father worked at various trades, trying to make enough to support his family. Eventually he found work as a lumberjack but was tragically killed by a falling tree, leaving behind a widow and ten children. Three years later, André was orphaned at the age of 12 when his mother died of tuberculosis. He was taken in by his aunt and uncle. He tried his hand at several trades, but his poor health and lack of education made it difficult for him to hold a job, so he emigrated to the United States and spent time working in a textile mill in New England. André was always exceptionally pious, and he eventually returned to Canada and entered the Congregation of the Holy Cross in Montreal. He was made doorkeeper at Notre Dame College in Côte-des-Neiges, Quebec. He held this position for

40 years and developed a great following once his reputation for wisdom and holiness spread. In 1904 he began building a small chapel on Mount Royal, which later developed into Saint Joseph's Oratory. Thousands of miraculous healings were attributed to him during his lifetime, but he always gave credit to Saint Joseph, to whom he had a great devotion. When he died in 1937, aged ninety-one, a million people paid their respects. André Bessette was canonized by Pope Benedict XVI on October 17, 2010.

8 #213 white
Christmas Weekday
T U E

Optional Memorial of Saint Raymond of Penyafort, Priest / white (Canada)

Lectionary for Mass

◆ FIRST READING: Note how many times the word "love" occurs in the space of these four verses. God is love; God's love initiated and accomplished the plan of our salvation; God's love lives on in our love for one another.

◆ RESPONSORIAL PSALM 72 is a prayer for the Davidic king, that his reign will be marked by God's justice and peace. It is most appropriate for this season when we celebrate the birth of the Messiah and his manifestation as the Savior of all people. God's concern for the poor and afflicted is mentioned twice in the verses chosen for today. That concern was given flesh in Jesus, who came and lived among us, giving himself as an offering for sin, that we might live fully in God's love and life. Now it is up to us to live in such a way that his kingdom can be realized among us.

◆ GOSPEL: Today's Gospel recounts one incident when Jesus showed a special concern for those who were "needy" not only physically but in mind and soul, "like sheep without a shepherd." He feeds their hungry minds with his teaching and feeds their bodies with the meager provisions at hand to provide abundantly. Note the Eucharistic overtones in Jesus's blessing, breaking and distributing the bread.

The Roman Missal

◆ COLLECT AFTER EPIPHANY: Christ took on our flesh, and we recognize him as one like ourselves. We pray that "we may be inwardly transformed" to grow in likeness of him.

Today's Canadian Saint

Saint Raymond is celebrated on different days in Canada and the United States. Please see biography on January 7.

9 #214 white
Christmas Weekday
W E D

Lectionary for Mass

◆ FIRST READING: The theme of "remaining" in Jesus and in God is prominent in the Johannine literature (see, for example, John 15), and the word "remain" occurs four times in today's text. "Remaining" in Jesus and in God is the mark of discipleship. Today's reading elaborates on what this means. God is love, so if we wish to remain in God, we must remain in love—in God's love for us, in total love for God and faith in Jesus, and in love for one another. We must strive for this love to be brought to perfection, that is, to maturity, in us.

◆ RESPONSORIAL PSALM: Once again we hear echoes of the Epiphany in today's Responsorial Psalm (second stanza), which was also the Psalm for that feast. Notice the reference to the rescue of the poor who cry out (third stanza). This is what the disciples do in today's Gospel— they cried out and Jesus rescued them.

◆ GOSPEL: Today's reading is a continuation of yesterday's Gospel. After feeding the multitude, Jesus withdraws into solitude on the mountain for prayer. After praying, he came down to the shore and saw the distress of his disciples who were out on the lake in the midst of the storm. Walking on the sea, he comes to their aid. The ability to walk on the sea is an attribute of God in Job 9:8. Jesus's words "It is I" (*ego eimi*) echoes the divine self-revelation to Moses in Exodus 3:14. In other words, Mark is depicting Jesus manifesting his glory for those who have the ability to see and understand.

The Roman Missal

◆ COLLECT AFTER EPIPHANY: Through all the ages, God has poured his light into the hearts of those who believe. We pray that our own hearts may be filled with that same light that "purified the minds of our fathers in faith."

10 #215 white
Christmas Weekday
T H U

Lectionary for Mass

◆ FIRST READING: John's words are strong. If anyone says he loves God but hates his brother or sister, he is a liar (and that hate can be expressed in actions as well as in words). Simply put, the measure of our love for God is our love for one another. Loving one another is not an option, it is a commandment from God. We are not left to our own abilities in doing this: we have been begotten by God and his grace is operative within us. We need only believe.

◆ RESPONSORIAL PSALM: Our Epiphany Psalm is used once more. Note the reference to fraud and violence in the second stanza. Is this not the hate that Jesus has overcome and that we are to overcome through our love for one another? In mutual love, there is true blessing.

◆ GOSPEL: Today we hear from Luke about the beginning of Jesus's public ministry. After his baptism and his time in the desert enduring temptation, Jesus returned to Galilee where he had grown up and lived as an adult. Note the reference to his empowerment by the Spirit. Today we see him attending a synagogue service in Nazareth where he reads from the prophet Isaiah. The text is programmatic of what his whole mission would be. Indeed, Isaiah's prophecy was fulfilled in Jesus.

The Roman Missal

◆ COLLECT AFTER EPIPHANY: We pray that all people may come to know Christ and, "bathed ever more in his radiance," possess eternal life.

F
R 11 #216   white
I   **Christmas Weekday**

Lectionary for Mass

◆ FIRST READING: Throughout the Johannine writings, there is an inherent tension between the world, or the flesh (understood as anything opposed to Christ and the Spirit), and the way of truth and life inaugurated by Jesus. Thus, we find the word "victor" in the first line of the reading. The thrust of the reading, however, validates Jesus as truly the Christ, the one sent and attested to by God, who gives eternal life to all who believe. Perhaps we are hearing words intended to reassure believers who feel threatened by false teachers, who were a problem in the Johannine community. John's whole purpose in writing was to remind them that those who believe in Jesus have eternal life—now.

◆ RESPONSORIAL PSALM: 147 Today's Psalm is a hymn of praise. The reference to God's Word in the second and third stanzas echoes the theme of the "testimony of God" heard in the first reading. How privileged are God's people for the revelation they have received.

◆ GOSPEL: Today's text recounts a miracle that happens early in Jesus's ministry. At that time lepers were outcasts in society, as they still are in many places in our world today. His healing brought about not only a physical cure, but a restoration to human community. In this time after the Epiphany, note the reference to the man falling "prostrate" before Jesus in adoration and supplication.

The Roman Missal

◆ COLLECT AFTER EPIPHANY: We pray that the mystery of Christ's birth, first made known by "the guidance of a star," may be revealed ever more fully to us.

S
A 12 #217   white
T   **Christmas Weekday**

Memorial of Saint Marguerite Bourgeoys, Virgin / white (Canada)

Lectionary for Mass

◆ FIRST READING: Today's reading is the conclusion of the first letter of John, which provides a summary of the themes that we have heard this week: particularly the themes of belonging to God, prayer, discernment, and truth. Note also today the mention of prayer for a brother or sister whom we see sinning. The reading ends with a warning about idols. Asking ourselves if we have any idols is always worthwhile. What do we worship, or idolize, in our thoughts and actions, with our time, money, and energy?

◆ RESPONSORIAL PSALM 149: Today's Psalm is hymn of praise sung by the children of Jerusalem (Zion), the children of God. God delights in them! It's as if God says to each one of us: "You are mine. I take delight in you."

◆ GOSPEL: Today's Gospel contains the only reference to Jesus baptizing, a claim later refuted in John 4:2. It is a non-issue for John

the Baptist. He gladly defers to the presence and the ministry of the Christ whose way he prepared. In Christ's presence, John's joy has been made complete.

The Roman Missal

◆ COLLECT AFTER EPIPHANY: In the Incarnation, divine and human are united. God has become like us; we pray that we may grow in likeness to him.

Today's Saint

The first Canadian woman to be canonized, Marguerite Bourgeoys was born in France on April 17, 1620. When she was nineteen, her mother died, and Marguerite took on the responsibility of caring for her brothers and sisters. A year later, during a procession in honor of Our Lady of the Rosary, she felt inspired to consecrate herself to the service of God. She tried joining the Carmelites and the Poor Clares, but both communities refused her entrance. But once Marguerite learned about the French settlement at Ville Marie in Canada, later known as Montreal, she realized that her vocation was to missionary work. She started a school, but soon realized she would need help and returned to France to recruit other young women. These became the founders of the Congrégation de Notre-Dame. The Congregation of Notre Dame received approval from the Vatican in 1698, and by the late nineteenth century, the sisters had spread through Canada and into the United States. Marguerite Bourgeoys is considered the co-foundress of Montreal, where she died on January 12, 1700 after offering her life for the cure of a younger sister.

#21   white

13 Feast of the Baptism of the Lord

Orientation

As the baptized Jesus emerges from the waters of the Jordan, God's voice declares: "You are my beloved Son, with you I am well pleased," (Luke 3:22) revealing his true essence and identity. This is a remarkable reminder of the importance of our own Baptism as the sacrament that declares our own identity as members of the Body of Christ. Just as God declares the baptized Jesus to be his Son, in Baptism we become sons and daughters of God in Jesus Christ, and the Spirit of God descends on all of us to strengthen us in our Christian mission of love and service. Jesus Christ is baptized, not to receive forgiveness, but to reveal to us his identity and to show us the way to ours.

Lectionary for Mass

◆ FIRST READING: Isaiah's words, heard in Advent, take on new meaning on this Feast of the Baptism of the Lord. Our God comes in the person of Jesus, the Good Shepherd, speaking words of comfort and bringing salvation to the people. Today he comes to the one who has prepared the way for his coming.

◆ RESPONSORIAL PSALM 104: Note the references to water in this song of praise. Today the waters of the Jordan are sanctified by the presence of the Lord. What glory, majesty and light surround the Lord in the words of the Father. Truly all things will be sustained and created anew through the Beloved Son on whom the Spirit rests.

◆ SECOND READING: Paul's words about our cleansing and rebirth in Jesus our Savior are most fitting for this feast of the Baptism of the Lord. Believers must live justly and devoutly as they await his second coming in glory.

◆ GOSPEL: The Baptist proclaimed the coming of the Messiah, the One who would baptize with the Holy Spirit and with fire. (Note the reference to the Spirit in both the Second Reading and the Psalm.) Luke depicts Jesus praying after being baptized by John. This is when the Holy Spirit descended upon him, and the voice of the Father confirmed him in his mission to the people. Jesus is the Beloved Son with whom the Father is pleased as he commits himself to the work of the Father.

The Roman Missal

There are two options for the Collect. The first echoes the words of the Gospel accounts of Christ's baptism, when the voice of the Father was heard, declaring Christ the "beloved Son." We are God's adopted children by our Baptism. We pray that we "may always be well pleasing" to God the Father. The second option, which is also prayed on Tuesday after Epiphany, is a prayer for inward transformation in the likeness of Christ.

◆ PRAYER OVER THE OFFERINGS: We ask that our offerings may become the sacrifice of Christ, who came "to wash away the sins of the world."

The Preface of the Baptism of the Lord describes the "signs and wonders" at the Jordan. The Father speaks, that "we might come to believe" in the Word made flesh. The Spirit appears as a dove, that we might recognize Christ as the Messiah, "anointed with the oil of gladness and sent to bring the good news to the poor."

◆ PRAYER AFTER COMMUNION: "Listen to him": the Father's words echoed over the waters of the Jordan. We pray that we may faithfully listen to the Only-Begotten Son of God, and become God's children "in name and in truth."

Other Ideas

It is important to understand that John's baptism was a baptism of repentance. It was not the same as the Sacrament of Baptism the Church celebrates. Jesus did not need to repent since he was without sin, but he asked for baptism to fulfill the will of his Father. His baptism did mark the beginning of his public life.

ORDINARY TIME DURING WINTER

The Liturgical Time

The Calendar
January 14, 2013 to February 12, 2013

The Meaning

Besides the times of year that have their own distinctive character, there remain in the yearly cycle thirty-three or thirty-four weeks in which no particular aspect of the mystery of Christ is celebrated, but rather the mystery of Christ itself is honored in its fullness, especially on Sundays. This period is known as Ordinary Time (UNLYC, 43).

AFTER the Feast of the Baptism of the Lord, Ordinary Time begins. In these Sundays, we will witness the beginnings of Jesus's ministry. We will hear of the call to discipleship and the paradoxes and difficulties that will be encountered in the proclamation of the reign of God. There is a continuity between Christmas Time and these Sundays of Ordinary Time. That continuity is the call for a time of recommitment to our baptismal mission.

Ordinary Time could be called the "season of Sundays." Interspersed with a certain number of Holydays of Obligation, it allows us to celebrate fully the special character of our original feast day, Sunday, called the Lord's Day, the first day, the eighth day, and the day beyond our cycle of time.

Ordinary means "numbered," not "commonplace," but we do tend to think of Ordinary Time as the "nothing in particular" time of the year. But since the Resurrection of Jesus Christ from the dead, time itself is anything but ordinary. Not only on Easter, but every Sunday of the year, the Church relives the Paschal Mystery. And Ordinary Time, because it celebrates no particular mystery of Christ, gives us an opportunity to enter more deeply into the mystery of Sunday.

The Roman Missal

DURING Advent and Christmas Time, there are unique Collects for each day, which add a great deal of variety to the weekdays. In Ordinary Time, there is just one set of prayers for each week, to be used not only on Sunday, but on weekdays as well (although you can add as much variety as you like by judicious use of the many other options *The Roman Missal* provides, including the Masses for Various Needs and Votive Masses [see the Introduction to Ordinary Time in the Summer and Fall for more information about these]).

The Roman Missal provides eight Sunday Prefaces for Ordinary Time, any one of which may be used on any Sunday. There are also six Common Prefaces for use on ferial days, that is, weekdays in Ordinary Time without obligatory celebrations. Six different Solemn Blessings are provided specifically for use during Ordinary Time, and any of 26 Prayers over the People add even more range to the possibilities for both the Sundays and weekdays of Ordinary Time.

Sunday Prefaces

If Advent is about waiting for the Lord, and Christmas Time is about celebrating his nearness in the Incarnation, then Ordinary Time isn't really "about" anything! Although it's probably more accurate to say that it's about everything: it is about the unfolding of the Paschal Mystery, God's plan for us and for all of creation. Each of the Sunday Prefaces of Ordinary Time expresses,

in a different way, the sweep of God's plan for the human family. "Through his Paschal Mystery . . . he has freed us from the yoke of sin and death, / summoning us . . . to glory" (Preface I). "He humbled himself . . . he freed us . . . he gave us life eternal" (Preface II). Through Christ, "the cause of our downfall" has become "the means of our salvation" (Preface III). We are part of this great plan, chosen by God "to rule" in his name over all he has made, "and for ever praise" him through Christ (Preface V). Our daily lives are shaped by this mystery, for in him "we live and move and have our being," experiencing "the daily effects" of God's care for us, even as we are given "the pledge of life eternal" (Preface VI). Ordinary Time is about the extraordinary mystery of God's love for humanity, and the slow, patient unfolding of the divine plan in the lives of people like us.

Common Prefaces

The Prefaces for weekdays in Ordinary Time, called "Common Prefaces," continue this focus on the saving work of Christ in our midst. In Christ, God was "pleased to renew all things" (Common Preface I), re-creating his creation (Common Preface IV). Christ loved us so much that "he stretched out his hands as he endured his Passion" (Common Preface VI). To praise this great and saving work of Christ is itself God's gift to us (Common Preface V), and so in every liturgy, "His Death we celebrate in love, / his Resurrection we confess with living faith, / and his Coming in glory we await with unwavering hope" (Common Preface V).

The Lectionary for Mass

WE return to ordinary days, to the ordinary rhythms of life. The gifts that gave such joy and delight when they were received become a part of daily life, speaking to us of the giver's love whenever we see or use them. We might most appropriately then ask ourselves: What about the greatest gift of all—the Son of God, whose Incarnation we have just celebrated?

The daily readings for Mass at this time of year show us not only how great is the gift we have received in Jesus, but also the gifts he continually offers us. In the first four weeks of

Ordinary Time, we hear from the Letter to the Hebrews. As its name suggests, this letter was addressed to Jewish Christians. As we might expect, it draws upon the Scriptures and cult of Israel in its proclamation of the "Good News" of Jesus and the significance of his once and for all gift of himself given to us and offered for us. Jesus is the fulfillment of all that was promised in ages past, far superior to anyone or anything under the old covenant. He is God's Son, the Word God has spoken to us, the eternal high priest who continually intercedes on our behalf.

Jesus's life of fidelity and obedience to God is to be the model of our own lives. Hebrews stresses in several places that because Jesus experienced the same weakness and temptations that we do, he is a most compassionate helper and intercessor for us in our daily lives (see Hebrews 4:14–16; 5:7–10). The last two chapters of Hebrews offer a number of exhortations on living a Christian life in the day-to-day realities of our lives.

The Responsorial Psalms and antiphons, chosen on the basis of their relationship to the theme of the First Reading, invite us to enter prayerfully into the message we have heard and take its teaching to heart.

Our daily Gospels are from the first seven chapters of Saint Mark. We see the almost magnetic attraction Jesus has for the people. He is literally swarmed by crowds that desire to listen to his word. Do we hear his teaching as a gift to us, a gift to show us the way to life? We hear of the many who brought their loved ones to be healed. Do we recognize the gift of healing that he offers us? We also witness Jesus in major—and victorious—confrontation with the powers of evil. How does the power of evil impinge on our own lives? Jesus conquers this evil as well when his grace is at work within us. This, too, is a source of healing.

Yet, Jesus also meets with rejection and opposition in daily life, as is evident not only in his conflicts with the Pharisees and religious leaders (see, for example, the Gospel for Tuesday of the Fifth Week in Ordinary Time) but also from members of his own family (see Saturday of the Second Week in Ordinary Time). Even his disciples fail to believe in him (Saturday of the Third Week in Ordinary Time). Fidelity to his call was not easy, not without effort—as is also the case in our own lives.

On Sunday of the Second Week in Ordinary Time, we have the Gospel of the wedding at Cana where Jesus changed the water to wine. In the Gospel according to John, this is the first of the "signs" (miracles) that Jesus performed, manifesting his glory and power as the Son of God. In both the Old and the New Testaments, God's covenant with his people is described in terms of the marriage relationship (see, for example, today's first reading, Isaiah 62:4–5 and also 2 Corinthians 11:2 and Revelation 21:2).

On the Third through Fifth Sundays in Ordinary Time, we hear from chapters four and five of the Gospel according to Luke, the Gospel for this Year C in the Lectionary cycle. These texts deal with the beginning of Jesus's public ministry. We see Jesus as an "ordinary" Jew taking part in an "ordinary" synagogue service in the town where he grew up. We hear both of the opposition he meets from the people who cannot receive his message and the receptiveness of those who crowd in to hear him. The opening verses of the Gospel, also heard on the Third Sunday in Ordinary Time, state the author's purpose in writing (see also Acts of the Apostles 1:1–2, Luke's second volume in the New Testament).

The First Readings for these Sundays also deal with "ordinary" life. On the Third Sunday, there is the liturgical assembly with a reading from the law of the Lord led by Ezra, the priest and scribe, after the return from exile. On the Fourth and Fifth Sundays, we hear of the call of the prophets Jeremiah, a very young man when called, and Isaiah, who received his call while worshipping in the Temple.

The Second Readings for the Sundays of Ordinary Time are from Paul's First Letter to the Corinthians, a community graced with many spiritual gifts. On the Second through Fourth Sundays, we hear Paul's instructions concerning the proper use of, and attitude toward, these gifts. All have received gifts, and each gift is necessary for the proper functioning of the Body of Christ. These words challenge us to recognize and acknowledge the spiritual gifts we have received and to use them so that the Body of Christ, the Church, may function as the Lord intended!

The reading for the Fifth Sunday, from 1 Corinthians 15, is the earliest account of the Resurrection of Christ from the dead (the letters of Paul were written before the Gospels). This reading also mentions Paul's encounter with the Risen Christ on the road to Damascus (verse 11; see also Acts of the Apostles 9:1–22; 22:3–16), an event commemorated on January 25, the feast of his conversion. Paul was a man deeply rooted in his own religious tradition and he exhibited tremendous fervor in practicing it and unrelenting zeal in protecting it. Paul's unexpected encounter with the Risen Christ changed his life and reframed his values and beliefs. Paul the persecutor became Paul the believer as a result of his encounter with the Risen Christ, an event which can also be considered his call to Apostleship. What a gift for our lives is the corpus of writings Paul has left us in the New Testament.

The Feast of the Presentation of the Lord is likewise rooted in the ordinary of everyday life with its practice of prayer and fidelity to the Law. When Mary and Joseph presented Jesus in the Temple to consecrate him to the Lord, they were met by the righteous Simeon and the prophet Anna, for whom Temple worship was part of everyday life. What a gift they received when they took the child in their arms and recognized him as the fulfillment of God's promises.

Yes, God's promises are fulfilled in everyday, ordinary life. The Lord is encountered in everyday, ordinary life—at times in ways we least expect. And what a gift in our life he is; what gifts he continually offers us. As we move into winter Ordinary Time, let us listen each day for his voice (see Psalm 95 cited in Hebrews 3) and receive the gifts of salvation given not only on Christmas Day, but each day.

Children's Liturgy of the Word

Readings

Each year we focus on the teaching and ministry of Jesus, but we rotate the Gospel readings. This year (Year C) the majority of the texts are from the Gospel according to Luke. Remember that the First Reading and the Gospel usually follow the same theme or thread of meaning. During these four weeks we are immediately presented with the glory of God and with Jesus as a miracle worker. As the Sundays continue though, we are challenged by a recurrent theme in Luke's account of the Gospel: the call to follow, to be a disciple or prophet, is not without cost.

At the beginning of each of the three annual cycles of Ordinary Time, the Second Reading comes from Saint Paul's Letters to the Corinthians. Corinth was the best known of the early communities because a number of its members are named and described in Acts of the Apostles 18, 1 Corinthians 16, and Romans 16. Notice that this year's readings describe the Church community as the Body of Christ and call the Corinthians to use those gifts to build up the body. There is a responsibility to being a believer.

Environment

It is helpful during Ordinary Time to focus on some of the primary liturgical symbols. You may wish to have a prayer table where you place a glass bowl with holy water, a candle which, if your parish permits, you light when you enthrone the Lectionary or *Book of the Gospels.* The liturgical color for this liturgical time is green. The banners and cloths on the lectern and prayer table should be green. Use these four weeks to evaluate how reverent and prayerful your celebration environment is. Set up your celebration space ahead of time. Be sure there is room to process, form a circle if necessary, and do liturgical and other bodily prayer comfortably. Ask yourself if you have established guidance and structures for consistent and quiet procession from the narthex of the church to the celebration space. If not, consult others to help you do this.

Music

Keep in mind that the music is an integral part of the liturgical experience. It is also a source of learning for the child. Music is an important catechetical element since music forms, shapes, and gives voice to what we believe. If you are not confident in your musical abilities, do not let your lack of musical skill lead you to abandon music as part of the content. Ask a musician to help you and the children experience the fullness of the celebration or use a recording.

For music selections use suggestions given in *Children's Liturgy of the Word: A Weekly Resource* from LTP or make music choices from your parish repertoire.

The Saints

Ordinary Time during the winter has an abundance of sanctoral observances. We observe two feasts: The Conversion of Saint Paul the Apostle on January 25 and the Presentation of the Lord on February 2. There are memorials of many well-loved saints, including Saint Anthony (January 17), Saint Agnes (January 21), Saint Francis de Sales (January 24), Saints Timothy and Titus (January 26), Saint Thomas Aquinas (January 28), Saint John Bosco (January 31), Saint Agatha (February 5), Saint Paul Miki and Companions (February 6), and Saint Josephine Bakhita (February 8).

Because February 3 falls on a Sunday this year, the optional Memorial of Saint Blaise is not observed. If desired, the traditional blessing of throats that marks his feast could be offered outside of Mass, at a celebration of the Word, or during the Liturgy of the Hours.

On January 22, there is a commemoration unlike any other in the liturgical year. In the United States of America, this anniversary of the Supreme Court decision *Roe vs. Wade* is a Day of Prayer for the Legal Protection of Unborn Children.

February 11 is the optional Memorial of Our Lady of Lourdes, also the World Day of the Sick. Each year, the Holy Father issues a message to the Church on this occasion.

Some civil observances may also impact our liturgical life during the weeks of winter Ordinary Time. On January 18, we observe the birthday of Dr. Martin Luther King Jr., an opportunity to pray for reconciliation and peace. And the month of February is Black History Month. You might take this time to explore the legacy of great African American Catholics like Venerable Pierre Toussaint, a Catholic layman who worked and ministered in New York in the first half of the nineteenth century. Learn about Sister Thea Bowman, an inspired teacher, who famously addressed the United States bishops in 1989—and had them singing "We Shall Overcome" before she finished! (Her talk is available in the July 6, 1989 issue of *Origins*. You can read excerpts in *The United States Catholic Catechism for Adults*.) These holy people continue to inspire and challenge us today.

We also observe the Week of Prayer for Christian Unity, which traditionally begins on January 18, and concludes on January 25, the feast of the Conversion of Saint Paul the Apostle.

The Week of Prayer for Christian Unity began to take shape at the beginning of the twentieth century. In 1908, an American Episcopalian priest, Paul Wattson, proposed an octave of prayer between January 18 and January 25. For Wattson, the focus of prayer was the return of the separated Churches to Rome. (Wattson himself, with the monastic community he founded, entered the Catholic Church in 1909.)

In the 1930s, another pioneer for ecumenism, Catholic priest Paul Couturier of Lyons, France, realized that for the Week of Prayer to have a real impact, Catholics and non-Catholics needed to pray together for unity, and that meant a shift in focus. Father Couturier suggested that the prayer be for the "unity that Christ wills, as he wills, and when he wills." (http://www.weekofprayer2008.org/about-history.html) It was a controversial move at the time. But the movement caught on and received formal sanction from Pope John XXIII in 1959.

The Second Vatican Council gave a huge impetus to the ecumenical movement. In 1965, the year the Council closed, the Vatican's Secretariat for Christian Unity met with the World Council of Churches, and for the first time they prepared joint materials for the Week of Prayer for Christian Unity. Every year since then, Catholic and non-Catholic Christians prepare a document which includes suggestions for prayer services, Bible study, and discussion.

This year, ponder how your parish might observe the Week of Prayer for Christian Unity. You could invite local Christian communities to come together in a joint prayer service. If that's not possible, perhaps the various churches within your parish boundaries could commit to praying for each other's congregations on the Sunday within the Week of Prayer, January 24. The parish might also make a gift to the social service programs of a neighboring church.

The music and prayer of the ecumenical community of Taizé in France offers a starting-point for shared prayer with other Christians. Their website (www.taize.fr) has many materials, and their music and an abundance of other resources are available in the United States through GIA Publications.

The Liturgy of the Hours

THE movement from Christmas Time with tons of poinsettias, decorations, and lights to a more subdued Ordinary Time during winter can be a nice bridge in preparing for Lent. Therefore, in preparing the Liturgy of the Hours, a sense of the progression of liturgical time could provide a lens through which to prepare the Hours. The Church has a method.

Progressive solemnity is a method the Church has for preparing liturgies, particularly in terms of music (see also the Advent Introduction under "Liturgical Music"). The *General Instruction of the Liturgy of the Hours* defines progressive solemnity as a principle "that recognizes several intermediate stages between singing the office in full and just reciting all the parts. Its application offers the possibility of a rich and pleasing variety. The criteria are the particular day or hour being celebrated, the character of the individual elements comprising the office, the size and composition of the community, as well as the number of singers available in the circumstances" (273). Therefore, the particular liturgical time or feast day will affect the preparations for the liturgy. For instance, Evening Prayer for Easter ideally is prepared differently than Evening Prayer on a Wednesday during Ordinary Time. Perhaps more will be sung for Easter than Ordinary Time. Of course, the opening hymn, the Psalms, and the canticles should be sung. However, perhaps the opening invitatory, intercessions, and Psalm prayers will be chanted or sung based on the liturgical time or feast day. The use of instruments and singers will also be determined on the principle of progressive solemnity. Perhaps Evening Prayer on Pentecost (which closes Easter Time) will have a choir with a couple of trumpet players, a few stringed instruments, a cantor/psalmist and organist, whereas Evening Prayer on Wednesday of Ordinary Time may be prepared with a psalmist and a pianist. Even the use of incense and candles could be employed based on the feast and season. Christmas and Easter Times would have lavish use of candles and incense while Wednesday in Ordinary Time for a small assembly possibly would forgo their use.

If your parish has not begun celebrating the Liturgy of the Hours together as a community, perhaps the parish worship commission could begin thinking about preparing Evening Prayer for Lent, Holy Week, the Sacred Paschal Triduum, and Easter Time. Ideally, the Triduum should include Morning Prayer and Evening Prayer on Good Friday, Morning Prayer (with the Ephphatha rite for the elect seeking initiation at the Easter Vigil) and midday prayer for Holy Saturday, and Evening Prayer on Easter Sunday. The parish could be encouraged to make the Triduum a time of retreat. Granted, most people are no longer off work on Good Friday, but parishioners could still be encouraged and invited to gather for Morning Prayer on that day.

The Rite of Christian Initiation of Adults

CHILDREN catechumens and candidates have just been initiated into the extraordinary seasons of Advent and Christmas Time. These were liturgical times which carried a lot of drama, narrative, color, ritual, and Catholic devotion. They were also heightened by the emotion and values that contemporary society places on preparing, planning, and celebrating Christmas. Ordinary Time does not celebrate a specific aspect of the mystery of Christ as Advent and Christmas Time did and it does not have the pull from contemporary society. However, Ordinary Time is devoted to the mystery of the Risen Christ in all its aspects, especially his public life and ministry.

In our Catholic life no time is "ordinary." Every day is holy or sacred. No Sunday is really ordinary because every Sunday is a celebration of the Resurrection of the Lord. It is important to teach catechumens and candidates the reverence we have for every Sunday of the year and also to point out that ordinary does not mean less than other seasons but is called ordinary because it is ordered, or counted, time.

Liturgical Catechesis

If you have not yet celebrated the minor rites (celebrations of the Word, minor exorcisms, blessings, anointing, and presentations of the Our Father and Creed) as part of your catechesis, begin during this time. Familiarize yourself with paragraphs 81–105 of the RCIA. Consult with the liturgy director on different times and ways these

celebrations may be celebrated more robustly. Good ritual celebration forms the religious imagination of children. It is important to prepare them ahead of time.

Some of these rites may be presided by the catechist; others by a priest or deacon. Celebrations of the Word are different from dismissal catechesis. Notice that celebrations of the Word may be held in the context of instructional sessions to facilitate an environment of prayer (RCIA, 84). You might choose to have a minor exorcism celebrated in the context of a catechesis on sin or an anointing before or after a service project.

Now is the time to discern the readiness of those catechumens who will be initiated at the Easter Vigil for the Rite of Sending and the Rite of Election. The question is always "Are they ready and willing to take upon themselves the responsibilities of an active participating Disciple and Roman Catholic? Has the child experienced some change (conversion) according to his or her capacity?" One of the simplest ways to think about how to discern is to think about how they are exhibiting that behavior now. Discernment should involve conversations with the family, the child, the sponsor, and the catechists of the group. There are questions the sponsor/godparent are asked during the Rite of Election which make a good focus:

◆ Are the children sincere in their desire to receive the Sacraments of Initiation?

◆ Have they listened well to the Word of God?

◆ Have they tried to live as faithful followers?

◆ Do they take part in the community's life of prayer and service?

Parishes and dioceses have different customs as to how they celebrate and/or include catechumens in the Rite of Sending and the Rite of Election. Conversation needs to happen between the pastor, liturgy director, and catechumenate director and team to discern what will most benefit the faith of the child catechumens and the assembly. It is this writer's opinion that the ritual of bearing witness to the growth of faith of the catechumen children (as in the Rite of Sending), the actual signing of the *Book of the Elect*, and the participation of catechumen children being called to election by the bishop in the midst of an intergenerational diocesan Church are of far more value than is efficiency.

If there is a year-round catechumenate in your parish, some catechumens will not be ready for the Rite of Election and will remain in the catechumenate during Lent. In that case, some planning is necessary for the different type of catechesis for the elect preparing for Scrutinies and the Sacraments of Initiation.

The Sacraments of Initiation

As you prepare young people for the celebration of the Sacraments of Initiation it is important to keep in mind two principles:

◆ Liturgy is "the privileged place for catechizing the People of God" (*Catechism of the Catholic Church*, 1074).

◆ Preparation for sacraments involves gradually introducing young people to the meaning of the rites and symbols of the sacrament.

At this time of year many parishes begin immediate preparation for celebration of Confirmation and first Holy Communion in the spring. Sacramental preparation programs usually provide some type of ritual enrollment celebration for candidates. Sometime during these four weeks would be a good time to celebrate these rites within a Sunday Eucharist. Both Confirmation and first Holy Communion programs provide some kind of ritual that connects to call and renewal of baptismal promises. It is ideal to be able to do these rites of enrollment "in the midst" of the Sunday assembly where young people's commitment to prepare can be affirmed by the assembly. It is also for the benefit of the assembly to witness the ongoing faith journey of young people and to be made aware of ways to support them. It is possible to celebrate a combined rite for both groups by adapting the different rites to include candidates for Eucharist and Confirmation. Consult with the liturgy director and music director to adapt the rite, to design it so the symbols are robust and the whole community is involved.

This is a good time for directors or coordinators of parish preparation processes to meet together with priest celebrants, the liturgy director, and music director to discuss how sacraments are being celebrated in the parish. Some parishes are plagued by a kind of sacramental minimalism that shows a lack of trust in the power of our primal symbols. Sacraments certainly work *ex opere operato* (the sacraments are efficacious from the grace of the sacrament, not the work of the priest or other minister). But for the celebrations of the sacraments to be fruitful for all, more than technical correctness is required. Celebrations should be designed to engage the faith of those who participate in them. For example, the lifting and presentation of the infant to the community, or some ritual of affirmation or musical participation of the community as they renew their own baptismal promises, can be a transforming experience for members of the assembly. An intentional, full, and robust use of the primal symbols associated with this sacrament (water, oil, touch) is essential. For some communities, this is already the common experience of Baptism. For others, there will need to be a "conversion" of lesser or greater proportions for Baptism to be celebrated as it should be. Liturgy Training Publications offers numerous resources that will help communities improve the way they celebrate infant Baptism.

In catechetical settings, it is helpful for young people during Ordinary Time to focus on some of the primary liturgical symbols. These would include something as simple as a prayer table with a clear glass bowl of holy water and a branch you use to sprinkle and bless young people at the beginning or conclusion of a session, or large white candle which, if your parish permits, you light as you enthrone the Lectionary or *Book of the Gospels* at each session. The color for this liturgical time is green. The banners and cloths on the lectern and prayer table should be green. Use these four weeks to evaluate how reverent and prayerful your catechetical environment is.

Toward the end of Ordinary Time remind candidates for the Sacraments of Initiation that Lent is coming and that they will be joining the catechumens/elect in their final journey toward full initiation. Explain that Lent is the time the whole community prepares to renew baptismal promises. Explain that on Ash Wednesday, Catholics, and other Christians, attend services in which their foreheads are marked with ashes and we are reminded that we are beginning a season of turning back to God or deepening our relationship with him. The ashes come from the palms used in the previous year's Palm Sunday service. They are collected, burned, and then blessed by a priest. Being signed with ashes helps us develop a sense of humility and sacrifice. Encourage them to attend Eucharist on Ash Wednesday and receive ashes.

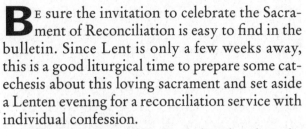

The Rite of Penance

BE sure the invitation to celebrate the Sacrament of Reconciliation is easy to find in the bulletin. Since Lent is only a few weeks away, this is a good liturgical time to prepare some catechesis about this loving sacrament and set aside a Lenten evening for a reconciliation service with individual confession.

The *Catechism of the Catholic Church* on the Sacrament of Reconciliation (Part II, chapter 2; article 4) is a rich resource.

The Pastoral Care of the Sick

WINTER can be a hard time for the elderly and those suffering illness, so this is a good time to schedule an Anointing of the Sick at Mass. Since it may be difficult for the elderly and ill to get to the worship space, gather volunteers to pick people up, drive them to the church, and assist them at Mass. Welcome people and give everyone name tags. After Mass hold a reception in an accessible place to extend the festivity.

We have no specific stories of healing in this short section of Ordinary Time, but we may choose other scripture readings and texts for a Sunday Anointing (PCS, 134). The scriptures do, however, have powerful testaments to Christ's power and teachings about the Church. On the second Sunday we hear about the wedding at Cana, and on the third Sunday Jesus announces that he is the Messiah. Also on the third Sunday, Saint Paul declares we are one body, affected by and dependent on one another. On the fourth Sunday, Saint Paul reminds us that love is the primary virtue. And on the fifth Sunday the prophet Isaiah asks us to consider what it means to be a disciple, i.e., one who is "sent." The Gospel for this same Sunday suggests that we are in the business of "catching" people for Christ.

The Rite of Marriage

CONSIDER how the parish catechizes and advises the couples who come seeking the Sacrament of Marriage. Most couples do not get much catechesis about the sacrament and truly do not understand that they, "as ministers of Christ's grace mutually confer upon each other the sacrament of Matrimony" (*Catechism of the Catholic Church*, 1623).

Many parishes offer the couple a chance to choose the scripture readings and music, but they might also be invited to consider the configuration of the Entrance Procession. The procession truly says something about the festivity or solemnity of a liturgy and, at a wedding, gives the couple a chance to express something about themselves. The *Rite of Marriage* (19–20) encourages us to offer various ways to form the procession at a wedding and encourages all ministers to be part of the procession. This includes the groom since he and the bride are the ministers of this sacrament. Including the groom in the procession also avoids the troublesome notion that the bride is more important than the groom, as well as the image of the father "giving away" the bride to the groom. Of course, young people are so accustomed to that model of procession they don't think to question what the action symbolizes or ask how their procession should reflect what they believe about themselves. (See some more suggestions under "The Rite of Marriage" in Ordinary Time during Summer and Fall.).

The Order of Christian Funerals

WE might continue looking at how we minister to grieving families. Funerals are catechetical moments, but they are fraught with "land mines" for the parish. This is especially true if the funeral comes to the parish only because the deceased was a member. Guidelines and understandings about what is appropriate vary from parish to parish. Families come with various expectations and ideas about what would be "nice." The staff need to know what the surrounding parishes allow and have conversations about their own guidelines. Our goal is always to give consolation "to those who have suffered the loss of one whom they love" (*Order of Christian Funerals* [OCF], 8).

Does anyone from the parish offer to go and sit with the family at the funeral home or in their home to prepare the liturgies? The minister could bring materials for choosing scripture readings and written guidelines about music and eulogies. The minister could also help the family formulate the intercessions. It would be wonderful if that minister led a short vigil service at the wake and was at the funeral Mass to assist those doing the proclamations and intercessions and presenting the gifts.

If the funeral is on a weekday, invite the family to consider having the Mass in the evening, when more people can attend and gather around the family. There can be a short visitation beforehand. In the case of visitation before Mass, the Rite of Reception of the Body (with sprinkling and placing of the pall) would take place when the body is brought to the church, and Mass would begin later in the usual way (see OCF, 158). If the coffin is to be open, some adaptation will have to be made.

The diocese will probably have specific guidelines about eulogies. It makes good sense to limit the number and time of eulogies. It is also a good idea to offer to listen to the eulogies ahead of time and give advice on the content. A short eulogy at the beginning of Mass may be a pastoral as well as practical thing to do since some members of the assembly may not know the deceased. A well-shaped eulogy can introduce the person, which may help the assembly's prayer.

The Book of Blessings

THE *Book of Blessings* is a rich resource at all liturgical times of the year. Blessing prayers basically praise God as the source of goodness and remind us, through people and objects, of the many signs of God's graciousness.

When people meet in the parish what kind of prayer is said? Does every parish meeting begin with prayer? The Orders for the Blessing of Those Gathered at a Meeting (chapter 6) is a very good model. Is there a Bible, candle, and cloth in liturgical color in these meeting places? Liturgy Training

Publications has many prayer resources, in both English and Spanish, that could be left in these meeting places, including one called *Daily Prayer 2013* (this resource is only available in English).

If you hold a prayer service during the Week of Prayer for Christian Unity, consider using the Order for the Blessing of Ecumenical Groups and Prayers for Interfaith Gatherings in chapter six of the *Book of Blessings*.

The Liturgical Environment

A Pastoral Insight

In these weeks of Ordinary Time the Church lives in the light of the birth of the Messiah, and enters a new calendar year with a renewed hope that the world will know that peace and justice are truly possible. The manifestations of the Lord and Savior recorded in the Scriptures include the visit of the Magi, the baptism of the Lord, the wedding feast t Cana, Jesus teaching in the Temple. These readings serve to announce that a new time of salvation has once again entered the lives of all the people of God. The time has come to leave the gentle comfort of Bethlehem and answer the call of discipleship with the Lord, who invites us into his mission to bring the kingdom of God to the ends of the earth.

Practical Suggestions

The liturgical space and the environment may not need a lot of attention in these weeks. This can be a time for the liturgical space to "breathe," to be somewhat less decorated than during Christmas Time, but still not as somber as it will be during Lent. The liturgical environment, as always, serves the ritual action of the Church, points toward the underlying nature of the season, and accents the primary places and furnishings of the liturgical space.

◆ The first order of business for the liturgical environment committee is to remove those elements that still have a Christmas "theme." The different seasons and times of the liturgical year have their own distinctive "texts"—the music, the liturgical colors, the scripture selections, the proper prayers of the Mass, the homilies, etc. This also applies to the liturgical environment. If the Christmas decorations are carried over into Ordinary Time, then the liturgical

environment is at odds with the rest of the elements that make up the overall unity and message of the liturgy.

◆ The liturgical color for Ordinary Time is green. During these winter days it would be appropriate to choose a darker, warmer tone of green. There is a wide variety of colors that coordinate well with darker green tones and these can be found in fabrics that can be used to accent the space.

◆ Arrangements that include birch branches mixed in with red willow branches and sprigs of winter berries can be simple and beautiful accents during this season. A variety of green plants (e.g., peace lilies) and others of this size work well in the liturgical space at this time and can be used to brighten entry areas and corners instead of fresh flower arrangements—leave the latter for Easter Time.

◆ It's good to remember that the scale of most churches dictates that these arrangements should be in large vases—though not a lot of them, and they can be placed in different locations throughout the space. If all the decorative items are in or near the sanctuary such that they can only be seen from the front half of the space, then they tend to make the sanctuary a stage setting for those who sit in the front pews. The assembly occupies the whole space—that should be a guide for how the whole space is included in any scheme for seasonal decorations.

◆ A note to liturgical environment committees: the environment for these weeks of Ordinary Time usually won't need much change, so a good amount of time can be spent planning for the Lenten environment—Ash Wednesday is not far off.

The Liturgical Music

CHANCES are that as we are moving into Ordinary Time, you are considering another Mass setting, or contemplating your options for later in the year. As you probably well know, searching through all the websites of publishers, listening to sound clips, and looking at sample PDFs is an arduous task. After a while it becomes hard to keep all the available resources straight.

Why not create a spreadsheet and keep track of your assessments of the various Mass settings? Include columns for parts (SAB/SATB), instrumentation, key, time signature, and general observations. If you do a lot of work with surrounding parishes, it may be also good to note other uses of the settings, i.e., "St. Therese's uses this setting." If your diocese did not suggest a set of common settings at the time of the Missal implementation, this may help you come closer to establishing a common repertoire. This is especially important for rituals like shared Confirmations, weddings, and funerals as people cross parish boundaries.

As you are learning new settings, make sure that all the liturgies within your parish and school are on the same page. If the contemporary Mass uses a setting different from the one used at another Mass, you may confuse members of your assembly who attend various Masses. By providing a common repertoire, you are giving your congregation the proper tools to worship well.

Michael Silhavy prepared a very copious list of new and revised Mass settings for NPM. See their website: www.npm.org/roman_missal/settings.html. As of writing this column, it is a directory representing every Mass published by CanticaNOVA, GIA Publications, Inc., Good for the Soul, Liturgical Press, MorningStar Music Publishers, Oregon Catholic Press, and World Library Publications.

A typical entry looks like this:

Collegeville Composer Group

Psallite Mass, The: At the Table of the Lord

Language: Includes Spanish

Publishing: Liturgical Press, Date:
NEW SETTING

Acclamations & Responses: Ky; PA; SR; Gl; GA(v); LGA(v); Holy; Acc 1; Acc 2; Acc 3; Amen; Lamb

Voicing: SATB and Keyboard with optional Guitar

The entries may be accessed in alphabetical order by the title of the Mass setting or by the name of the composer. This inventory of settings is extremely helpful for your own organization of titles, settings, and musical reviews.

Liturgical Ministers

WHILE the holidays are wonderful, everyone appreciates getting back into the rhythm of Ordinary Time. It is easy to pull out all the stops for Christmas Time and Easter Time, bring in extra musicians, and schedule your best readers. But does this really provide a true picture of your parish and its ministries? It is in the week-after-week, service-after-service schedule of Ordinary Time that you can tell the strength or weakness of the program.

Instead of evaluating only your big liturgies with the worship committee, consider evaluating a weekend of liturgies, inviting the congregation to participate in a poll, or bringing in an outsider to offer their insights.

One might ask these or similar questions:

◆ Does the liturgy support "full, conscious and active participation" (CSL, 14)?

◆ Are there worship aids or hymnals for all?

◆ Is there a common repertoire among all liturgies for music, Mass parts, Psalms?

◆ Do people feel welcome, and can they see and participate?

◆ Is musical accompaniment adequate?

◆ Do cantors and choirs support the liturgy or dominate the ritual?

◆ Are acoustics and microphones in good working order?

◆ Do parish ministers understand the structure of the liturgy and the meaning of the parts of the Mass?

◆ Does the congregation know the responses and the roles?

◆ Does the music serve its purpose at particular points in the liturgy?

◆ Is there adequate silence in the liturgy?

◆ Do ministers participate fully in the liturgy, singing and responding as needed, and demonstrating correct postures of prayer?

◆ Do the liturgical ministers know their responsibilities and perform them well?

◆ Does the reader have the Lectionary in place?

◆ Do servers know their role and function or do they need constant cues?

◆ Are those who come late assisted with finding seating?

◆ Do extraordinary ministers sanitize their hands before distribution of Communion? Do they know when to come forward during the liturgy?

◆ Are greeters present at all liturgies?

◆ Are rituals being carried out clearly?

◆ When do you start the Communion song? When do musicians and liturgical ministers receive Holy Communion?

◆ Is the Communion procession simple? Do Communion procedures follow the norms established in the GIRM?

◆ Is the liturgical environment neat, pleasing, and appropriate? Does it impede the ritual?

◆ Are music areas cluttered with cases, music sheets, and stands?

◆ Is the narthex neat or is it cluttered with pamphlets, handouts, and old bulletins?

Ask those involved within the ministries themselves to evaluate the programs. How long has it been since you've reviewed training procedures and methods of communication or looked at the ministries in light of Church documents? Some of the most dangerous words in a parish are, "We've always done it that way."

Devotions and Sacramentals

IF you do not have time to sit and read the *Directory of Popular Liturgy and Piety* (DPPL) but would like to refresh your basic knowledge and understanding of the nature of devotional prayer, the United States bishops have provided an excellent Q and A resource on their website:

http://www.usccb.org/prayer-and-worship/devotionals/popular-devotional-practices-basic-questions-and-answers.cfm.

Ordinary Time during the winter may be an opportune time to evaluate the devotional life of your parish or worshipping community. With your liturgy committee, for example, prepare ahead for Lent. People are often more open to communal prayer experiences during this penitential period. Invite different cultural groups to share their religious devotions and customs with the rest of the parish. Jointly schedule and prepare celebrations, inviting parish musicians, and follow this up with a dinner. Our cultural diversity should be recognized and honored as often as possible.

The Parish and the Home

FIRST make clear to the parish that "ordinary" in this sense means "counted," a way of ordering time—not dull drudgery or lifeless routine. Just as cocoa, sleds, skates, or skis enliven winter, so the Church enriches this time with feasts. Until Candlemas, February 2, it's appropriate to keep up some Christmas decorations such as the crèche or evergreen boughs—beauty and color when the weather is dreary!

During the time between Christmas Time and Lent, families could focus on studying one saint. There are several excellent possibilities. The widowed mother of five, Elizabeth Ann Seton, struggled to raise her family in an era when women didn't have jobs or careers. When two of her daughters died, she was heartbroken. Her sons managed to ruin every opportunity her friends provided them; in sadness, Seton said, "What's a parent to do but pray and dote, pray and dote?" Because her school in Emmitsburg, MD was the first Catholic school in the U.S., she is honored as the founder of the system. Her memorial is celebrated on January 4.

The story of Saint Paul's conversion, celebrated January 25, is a good one for children to dramatize or illustrate. The full story can be found in Acts of the Apostles 9. Two teachers' memorials—Saint Thomas Aquinas (January 28) and Saint John Bosco (January 31) offer an opportunity to praise and bless teachers. At home, families could talk about their best teachers—and not only those in schools. Sometimes an employer, friend, relative, or neighbor conveys profound lessons beyond textbooks. Voicing this appreciation might prompt thank-you notes or cards. And how teachers love being thanked by a former student they thought had probably forgotten!

The Week of Christian Unity, January 18–25, is an opportunity for various congregations in a neighborhood to come together for music, preaching, potlucks, and prayer. Introduce children to members of other Christian traditions through this respectful sharing, modeled by their parents and other adult members of their parish.

For Candlemas (February 2), read aloud or act out the story of Jesus's Presentation in the Temple, Luke 2:22–38. Because Anna and Simeon are elderly prophets, this is a good time to invite grandparents and other older parish members to participate in a celebration such as the blessing of candles, a procession, or the singing of Simeon's canticle.

Because the Gospel readings of Ordinary Time contain the stories of Jesus calling his first disciples, a prayer corner could be decorated with netting, shells, fish, and small boats made and decorated by family members. The liturgical color of Ordinary Time is green, so use that for a table cloth or backdrop.

The days commemorating Martin Luther King, Jr. and Presidents Lincoln and Washington provide opportunities to read children's stories about these heroes, to research them online, to find films or documentaries about them, or to attend local presentations in libraries or civic centers.

Before Lent begins, plan a Mardi Gras (Carnival) celebration. In medieval times, Lent meant fasting from meat and dairy products. So the traditional Shrove Tuesday foods are rich in these: donuts, fritters, and pancakes. Carnival is also a time for masks and costumes, jazz music, parades, dancing, and stories like Esther's in the Old Testament. The colors of this time are purple, gold, and green, signifying a spirit of fun before the Lenten fast.

The feasting might conclude with burying the Alleluia. Write the word in beautiful calligraphy on a banner or scroll, then place it in a box. If possible, bury it in the earth, to be dug up on Easter. This ritual symbolizes that we do not sing nor say Alleluia during Lent.

Mass Texts

◆ SAMPLE TEXT FOR THE PRAYER
 OF THE FAITHFUL

Additional texts are found in Appendix V of The Roman Missal

Celebrant:

To the Lord who changed the water into wine,
let us pray for the transformation
of our hearts and minds.

Deacon/Lector/Reader:

For the Church,
that she may recognize and nurture the gifts
of the Spirit in all her members,
young and old, ordained and lay, we pray:

For peace in our world,
that there may be an end to violence,
racial discrimination, and hate, we pray:

For married couples, that Christ,
who blessed the marriage feast at Cana.
may be with them in their joys and sorrows,
    we pray:

For all our beloved dead,
    especially N._____,
that they may come into God's kingdom of light,
        love, and peace,
    with all their sins forgiven, we pray:

Celebrant:

Lord Jesus Christ,
you give us to drink of your new wine
in this Eucharist.
May this food from heaven strengthen us
to build your kingdom of peace and love.
You live and reign for ever and ever.
Amen.

◆ DISMISSAL TEXT FOR THE CATECHUMENS

You continue your journey toward the font
    during these days of Ordinary Time.
Your presence nourishes our faith, reminds us
    of the commitments we have made,
and challenges us to learn, and know, and live
    our faith with ever greater zeal.
As you go now to let God's Word possess and
    penetrate your hearts,
we remain to rejoice in God's goodness in calling
    you to him
and to yearn with you for the day when you will
    join us at the banquet of the Lamb.

◆ DISMISSAL TEXT FOR CHILDREN'S LITURGY
 OF THE WORD

Each day you grow a little taller, a little smarter,
    a little more mature.
God keeps his watch over you,
gently guiding you to become the man or woman
    you were made to be.
Go listen now to God's special Word for you.
Drink it in and let it make you stronger
in your love of your family, your friends, and
    your community.
When you return, we'll sing together the praises
    of the God who made us all.

◆ DISMISSAL TEXT FOR EXTRAORDINARY
 MINISTERS OF HOLY COMMUNION

Need seldom diminishes;
hearts are ever aching and breaking and seeking
    the solace of God's love.
We have chosen you to go forth from here
to bring a message of salvation,
a word of hope.
a healing touch,
and, most importantly, the Bread of
    everlasting life.
Go forth aware of the privilege you've
    been granted,
and of the awesome gifts of Word and sacrament
    you have been given to share.

January
Month of the Holy Name

Except for the days of the First and Thirty-fourth Weeks in Ordinary Time, The Roman Missal *does not provide prayer texts for the weekdays in Ordinary Time. Instead, priest celebrants and those who prepare the liturgy may select from among the prayers provided for the Sundays in Ordinary Time. Your diocesan* Ordo *will provide suggestions for which prayers to use. On days celebrated as optional memorials, prayers may be from the Sundays of Ordinary Time, the Proper of Saints, or the Commons. On all Saturdays during Ordinary Time that do not have an obligatory memorial, a memorial to the Blessed Virgin Mary may be celebrated. The prayers may be selected from the* Common of the Blessed Virgin Mary.

MON 14 #305 green
Weekday / First Week in Ordinary Time

Lectionary for Mass

◆ FIRST READING: Today's reading, the beginning of the Letter to the Hebrews, reaches back into Israel's history, recalling all the ways God spoke to his people of his love and salvation. Hebrews points to the culmination of this revelation in the Incarnation of Jesus, himself the glory and fullness of God. Having accomplished our salvation during his life on earth, he now reigns in glory with his Father, exalted even over the angels.

◆ RESPONSORIAL PSALM 97: Today's acclamation echoes the closing lines of the First Reading, calling all angels to worship him. In its original context as a Psalm acclaiming God's kingship, the "him" of our acclamation is God. Juxtaposed with the text from Hebrews, it refers to Jesus. This is fitting, given the exaltation of Jesus at the end of

the reading. He now reigns with God in heavenly glory.

◆ GOSPEL: Jesus's public ministry begins after John's arrest. His proclamation of God's kingdom calls for repentance and a new manner of life from those who would receive it, one turned toward God. The immediacy of Simon and Andrew's response is not evident in the Lectionary translation of today's Gospel. Mark's text has the word "immediately" in verse 18. Jesus acts with an immediacy as well (again, not evident in the translation) as he "immediately" calls James and John when he sees them.

The Roman Missal

The prayers for today are those for the First Week in Ordinary Time, found in the Proper of Time. The Collect is a simple prayer that we may see what needs to be done — and do it! In the Prayer over the Offerings, we ask to be restored to holiness through the sacrifice we offer. Renewed by the sacraments, we pray that our lives may be pleasing to God (Prayer after Communion). Since there is only one set of prayers for the First Week in Ordinary Time, today's prayers are repeated each ferial weekday.

TUE 15 #306 green
Weekday

Lectionary for Mass

◆ FIRST READING: Psalm 8 is at the heart of today's First Reading, a Psalm which extols the dignity God has bestowed on the human creature. The author of Hebrews sees this Psalm preeminently fulfilled in Jesus. In particular, the author reflects on the death of Jesus as both the lowest point of his life and the highest, for through it he was crowned with glory and honor, exalted at God's right hand. By embracing death, Jesus demonstrated the full extent of his humanity.

Through it he was perfected (the Greek word means "fully matured"), and so will we be upon entering the fullness of the glory he has bestowed upon us.

◆ RESPONSORIAL PSALM: Most appropriately, Psalm 8. The Psalm speaks of the glory and dominion the human creature has over all other earthly creatures (so Genesis 1:28). The antiphon, echoing Hebrews, interprets the "son of man" (verse 5; human creature) of the Psalm as Jesus, Son of Man and Son of God.

◆ GOSPEL: The "followers" in the first line of today's Gospel are Simon and Andrew, James and John, whose response to Jesus's call was described in yesterday's reading. Jesus goes first to the synagogue, that gathering place for prayer and study of the scriptures. Note how Mark contrasts Jesus's teaching ability with that of the scribes. Jesus has an authority that they lack. The evil spirits know who Jesus is and rightly fear that he has come to destroy them. Nothing more is said of the man who was healed. The focus is on Jesus and his power over evil, something which led those who saw and heard him to ponder who he was.

The Roman Missal

See Monday of the First Week in Ordinary Time.

WED 16 #307 green
Weekday

Lectionary for Mass

◆ FIRST READING: Today's reading continues Hebrews' commentary on Jesus's death. Jesus destroyed the power of death through his resurrection from the dead. This promised reality of risen life serves to free all of us from our natural fear of death. Jesus knows well the temptations and the struggles of human life. He experienced them himself and can knowingly intercede for us.

◆ RESPONSORIAL PSALM 105: In Jesus, the fullness of God's covenant promises is realized. Could God have done anything more marvelous for us than to send his very own Son to live among us, to be one with us? Note the references to Abraham, mentioned in the First Reading, in the last two stanzas of the Psalm. Abraham was the ancestor of the Jewish people, the first one called by God (see Genesis 12). The Letter to the Hebrews was written for a Jewish Christian community.

◆ GOSPEL: Today's text recounts several events in one of the early days of Jesus's ministry. What warmth is conveyed in the picture of Jesus in the home of his disciples and friends, Simon and Andrew. What tenderness and compassion Jesus showed to Simon by healing his mother-in-law, and also to all who gathered at the door and found in him the way to healing and wholeness. (Notice that Jesus's power over demons and evil spirits is mentioned three times.) We glimpse the source of Jesus's healing power and teaching authority in his time alone in prayer. Note that he rises early and seeks solitude to prepare himself for what he was sent to do.

The Roman Missal

See Monday of the First Week in Ordinary Time.

THU **17** #308 white
Memorial of Saint Anthony, Abbot

Lectionary for Mass

◆ FIRST READING: The author of the Letter to the Hebrews continuously reinterprets the beloved Scriptures of old in light of the new covenant inaugurated by Jesus. Psalm 95 is the focus of today's First Reading, interpreted here as a call to open our ears and hearts to the

Good News of Jesus. We must hear and believe.

◆ RESPONSORIAL PSALM: Today's response, as we might expect, is Psalm 95. Our antiphon repeats the call not to harden our hearts in rebellion and lack of faith. The first stanza is a call to praise and worship. It also speaks of who God is for us, and who we are before him. The next two stanzas were quoted in the reading from Hebrews. We must live so as to be able to enter into the rest of God's heavenly kingdom.

◆ GOSPEL: We hear of a leper who kneels before Jesus, begging for deliverance from his affliction. What the scriptures call leprosy is much broader than what we now know as Hansen's disease. It included any number of skin afflictions. Fear of contagion was paramount and lepers were isolated. (Notice that Jesus's compassion for the man leads him to touch him.) The instruction to go to the priest accords with Leviticus 13–14, for the priest's declaration was necessary for the healed leper to be readmitted to the community. At the end of today's text Jesus's commands the leper to be silent. The nature of Jesus's messiahship would only be gradually revealed and understood.

The Roman Missal

It would be hard to imitate Saint Anthony's "wondrous way of life in the desert" (Collect), but we can imitate him by denying ourselves and loving God above all else. In the Prayer over the Offerings we ask to be "released from earthly attachments" and to find "riches" in God "alone." Saint Anthony suffered great temptations in the desert. Like him, we ask that we may "escape every snare of the enemy" (Prayer after Communion).

Today's Saint

Early in his life, Saint Anthony of Egypt (251–356) discovered the importance of solitude in knowing oneself in relationship to God. Solitude provides the vehicle through which one battles demons and removes worldly distractions that distance the heart from the will of God. Saint Anthony journeyed in the desert for nearly thirty years where he lived a life of solitary prayer, self-discipline, and utter dependence on God. After his time in the desert, he emerged as a man of balance, ready to share all he learned regarding the human thirst for God. Realizing that the spiritual life takes root within a community of believers, he founded a group of monks. While serving as abbot, or spiritual father to the monks, Saint Anthony mentored them in the ways of contemplative prayer and helped them overcome illusory thinking. His dynamic personality continued to attract individuals. As a result, he counseled a steady stream of pilgrims and laid the foundation for many monasteries.

FRI **18** #309 green
Weekday

Lectionary for Mass

◆ FIRST READING: The author of Hebrews compares the Christians of his day (and ours) to the Israel of old. We must not be like the Israelites in their failure to hear and obey. Let us hear God's Word and believe, that we might enter into the promised land of rest which God sets before us.

◆ RESPONSORIAL PSALM 78 recounts Israel's history in terms of God's fidelity and Israel's infidelity. Today's antiphon calls us to remember the works of the Lord and to tell them to subsequent generations. Remembering what God has done in the past creates trust in God's providence today and in the future. The last stanza of today's response focuses on the infidelity of Israel's ancestors, as does the text from Hebrews, and calls the current generation to steadfastness and fidelity.

◆ GOSPEL: Jesus's acclaim grows. As we heard yesterday, it was impossible for him to enter a town without drawing a crowd, and today that crowd is at the door of his home. The thatched grass roof of his house provided an alternative route for the paralyzed man and his friends who could not get as close as they wished. Today's text portrays Jesus not only as teacher of the Word, but as healer, as one who forgives sins, and as one who knows the thoughts of the human heart. How charismatic he must have been! What power and authority were manifest in his words and deeds! The people had never seen anything like it.

The Roman Missal

See Monday of the First Week in Ordinary Time.

S A T **19** #310 green
Weekday

Optional Memorial of the Blessed Virgin Mary / white

Lectionary for Mass

◆ FIRST READING: Today's passage, which follows upon the last line of yesterday's reading (Hebrews 4:11), speaks of judgment. The "word" spoken of would seem to be Jesus (see also the reference to the "word" God spoke in Hebrews 1:1). All creatures will be held accountable to his piercing judgment. At the same time, our Judge is a compassionate and merciful high priest who intercedes for us, knowing our weaknesses and struggles from his own experience.

◆ RESPONSORIAL PSALM 19: Today's antiphon is adapted from Jesus's testimony about the words of his teaching (John 6:63). The verses chosen from Psalm 19 bear witness to the attributes and supreme value of God's law, the Word of Torah, and to what it can do in our life. Let us make the prayer of verse 15, the last line of today's response, our own.

◆ GOSPEL: Again we have a large crowd gathering around Jesus, and again, he teaches them. We hear also of the call of Levi (Matthew). As agents of the Roman government, tax collectors were a despised lot, who also used their position to supplement their own income. This unlikely—and to some, unrighteous—man was called by Jesus. The official religious leaders strongly object to Jesus's table fellowship with Levi and his friends, since sharing a meal with them was a sign of acceptance and relationship. In the minds of the Pharisees and scribes, the righteous should separate themselves from sinners. Yet, Jesus welcomed sinners and entered into their company. At the end of today's text, he tells why.

The Roman Missal

See Monday of the First Week in Ordinary Time.

Saturday has traditionally been a day of devotion to the Blessed Virgin Mary. On all Saturdays during Ordinary Time that do not have an obligatory memorial, a memorial to the Blessed Virgin Mary may be celebrated. The prayers may be selected from the Common of the Blessed Virgin Mary.

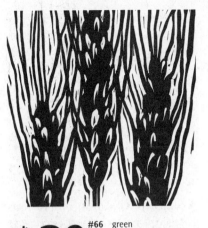

☀ **20** #66 green
Second Sunday in Ordinary Time

Orientation

In following Jesus Christ, there is always something better to come. Jesus's first miraculous sign at the wedding feast of Cana communicates to us the profound hope that underlies the Christian life. The better wine saved for the end of the festivities, like the joy of eternal salvation, is what we anticipate with hope in the here and now. Christ who is risen from the dead reveals to us that the best is yet to come, and this joyful outlook colors our experience of life. In Christ, we can always trust in ultimate triumph over our lacks, our needs, our problems, and our struggles. Let us let Christ surprise us with the bounty of God's grace.

Lectionary for Mass

◆ FIRST READING: Jerusalem, the city once desolate and forsaken at the time of the Babylonian destruction, will be restored and shine with the glorious light of the Lord. All nations will see it. The imagery of the Marriage relationship, the symbol of God's covenant with Israel, is the focus of verses 4 and 5. Joy abounds as God renews his covenant of love with Jerusalem his bride.

◆ RESPONSORIAL PSALM 96: The post-exilic restoration of Jerusalem, a result of the conquest of Cyrus of Persia, was indeed perceived as God's marvelous deed for his people (see Isaiah 44:28–45:25). Although the word "joy" does not occur in today's response, it certainly is implied. References to nations, lands, and all peoples occur in each stanza (see Isaiah 62:2).

◆ SECOND READING: The various gifts God bestows upon believers are yet another marvelous deed. Paul speaks of the variety of gifts. All are manifestations of God's spirit. They are distributed to various individuals, as God deems fit, to be used for the benefit of others. What is your gift?

◆ GOSPEL: Again, a wedding is the focus. In the New Testament, the heavenly banquet in the kingdom of God is sometimes depicted as a wedding feast (see Matthew 25:1–13; also Revelation 22:1–5). In this first sign (the Johannine word for miracle) performed by Jesus, water is changed into wine at a wedding banquet—another marvelous deed of God! In so doing, Jesus manifested his glory, a glory that would be fully revealed at the "hour" of his death, which is also, in the Gospel according to John, the hour of his exaltation.

The Roman Missal

In the Collect, we pray to God, the Lord of heaven and earth, for "peace in our times."

In the Prayer over the Offerings, we pray that we may "participate worthily" in the mysteries we celebrate, because whenever the sacrifice of the Mass is offered, "the work of our redemption" is being carried out.

In the Prayer after Communion, we pray that all who are fed with "one heavenly Bread" may be "one in mind and heart" as well.

Other Ideas

From the vestments of the priest and deacon, to the words of each reading, the call to change and newness of life resounds clearly in today's Mass. Invite your child to point out any differences he or she notices in your parish church's art and environment or the vestments worn by your priest and deacon. Explain that the Church has moved into another liturgical time, not one of preparation like Advent, or of solemn celebration like Christmas Time, but a time of growing and deepening in our relationship with God. This period is called Ordinary Time, and its color is green, the color of growing things.

In light of today's Gospel, look at your wedding album with your children, and talk about your call to married life and to parenthood. Let your child know that you see your commitment to your family as a sacred trust. Invite your child to help you write a prayer for your family, that God will strengthen your Marriage, guide you in all parenting decisions, and bless your child with faith and good character. Place your prayer where you will see it, and pray it together often.

Invite a priest, deacon, or religious sister or brother to have dinner with you one evening and to tell your family about his or her vocation. Ask how it was recognized as a call from God, whether or not the person responded right away. Ask who might have helped your guest discern or heed the call, and how he or she has felt the presence of the Holy Spirit in living out this vocation. Keep your guest in your family prayers.

It's in our parishes that we're taught, fed, and renewed for our task of building the kingdom of God in the world. If your parish has a welcoming ministry for new parishioners, ask how your family

can help. If not, offer to recruit help and begin one. A visit from parishioners with information about the faith community, and perhaps a freshly baked loaf of bread, is a great way to say to new members: "Welcome! We're glad you're here. Let's get acquainted and discover how we can work together for the glory of God."

#311   red

MON 21 Memorial of Saint Agnes, Virgin and Martyr

Lectionary for Mass

◆ FIRST READING: Hebrews highlights the fact that Jesus is called to his high priestly role by God his Father. The letter cites two Psalm verses, which originally referred to the Davidic king, Psalm 2:7 and Psalm 110:4, to refer to Jesus's royal priesthood. The latter links Jesus's priesthood with that of Melchizedek, king and priest of Salem or Jerusalem (see Genesis 14:18–20). Perhaps it is the last part of the reading that speaks to us the most: his intense prayer, his suffering, his obedience. Let us look to him as the source of our salvation. May his example be our model and strength.

◆ RESPONSORIAL PSALM 110: Today's responsorial antiphon is cited in the First Reading. Originally, the Psalm was associated with the day of the king's enthronement. We see its fulfillment in the heavenly exaltation of Jesus our high priest.

◆ GOSPEL: On the heels of the account of a meal shared with sinners, Mark turns to the issue of fasting, or more particularly, to the fact that Jesus's disciples do not. Fasting is a religious practice that signifies both repentance and self-denial, and receptivity for the coming of God. As noted earlier, Marriage was a biblical symbol of the covenant God had made with Israel. Wedding celebrations are neither the time nor the place for fasting. So it was for

Jesus's disciples: the Bridegroom was in their midst. What God was doing in Jesus was new, and this called for a new way of looking at traditional practices.

The Roman Missal

The Collect is from the Proper of Saints. The prayer alludes to Saint Paul (I Corinthians 1:27): God chooses "what is weak in the world to confound the strong." We pray that we may be like Saint Agnes, constant in faith.

The Prayer over the Offerings and the Prayer after Communion are drawn from the Common of Martyrs: For a Virgin Martyr or the Common of Virgins: For One Virgin. The Preface of Martyrs or of Virgins may be used.

Today's Saint

Saint Agnes (291–304) lived a very short life, but each and every moment was filled with inestimable worth. She felt called to consecrate her virginity to Christ in a culture that lived according to the flesh rather than the spirit. When Saint Agnes refused numerous marriage proposals because of her betrothal to Christ, she was tried and beheaded. Two words embody the whole of her life: faithfulness and purity. No human being or earthly promise could shatter Saint Agnes's commitment to her beloved God, nor could any hatred or vengeance taint her virginal heart. Devotion to Saint Agnes gained popularity in the Middle Ages, along with other virginal saints like Ursula, Dorothy, and Barbara. In religious art, she is often depicted with a lamb, symbolizing the spotless (pure) sacrifice she made for the Lord.

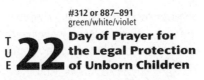

#312 or 887–891
green/white/violet

TUE 22 Day of Prayer for the Legal Protection of Unborn Children

Optional Memorial of Saint Vincent, Deacon and Martyr / red (Canada)

Orientation

On January 22, 1973, the United States Supreme Court handed down a decision known as *Roè vs. Wade*, which made abortion legal throughout the United States, and struck down many states' laws restricting abortion. Since that decision, more than 50 million abortions have been performed in the United States. In all dioceses of the United States, today is observed as a day of penance for violations to the dignity of the human person committed through acts of abortion, and for the full restoration of the legal guarantee to the right to life. We pray not only for the innocent children who will not be born, but for all mothers and fathers who are considering abortion. On this day, hundreds of thousands will participate in pro-life marches across the nation. The largest of these takes place in Washington, D.C., where some 400,000 gather on the Mall and march up Capitol Hill to witness to the Gospel of life. During this sensitive day, we should remember that there may be members of our parish who are still in the process of reconciling with God and the Church because they have had an abortion. If able, provide counselors to support those who have participated in an abortion. Using this day to condemn rather than to show mercy can cause pain. We are called to show compassion and God's mercy as we restore all and renew all in Christ's love and life. You might also host a Rosary for life.

Lectionary for Mass

◆ FIRST READING: Discouragement is, unfortunately, a common experience that most people have at one time or another. Today's text from Hebrews offers us an encouraging word of hope, not based on our own efforts or resources but on God's fidelity. We are to look to Abraham as an example, and even more, Jesus. Note the mention of the "anchor" of hope at the end of the reading. Perhaps this is the source of this popular Christian symbol.

◆ RESPONSORIAL PSALM 111: This heartfelt and public song of thanksgiving celebrates God's covenant fidelity in providing for the needs of his people. As a response to the reading from Hebrews, we pray it with a spirit of thanksgiving for the gift of deliverance and redemption we have received through Jesus, the inaugurator of a new and eternal covenant.

◆ GOSPEL: Controversy with the Pharisees, those strict interpreters of the Law, continues. At issue are Laws pertaining to the Sabbath and Jesus's disciples, presumed violation of them. Jesus shrewdly points out biblical precedent for exceptions to the Law. The Sabbath was made for the sake of humankind. Jesus, Son of Man, has authority over it.

The Roman Missal

On this special day of prayer, *The Roman Missal* provides two options, both drawn from the Masses and Prayers for Various Needs and Occasions. The Mass "For Giving Thanks to God for the Gift of Human Life" (No. 48/1) may be used, with white vestments, or the Mass "For the Preservation of Peace and Justice" (No. 30) may be used, with violet vestments.

The first of these options is a new addition to the third edition of *The Roman Missal*. The prayers all speak of the dignity of human life, which flows from God, "Lord of the living" (Prayer over the Offerings) and author of all life. God has made us "stewards of creation" (Collect); we pray that we may be good stewards "safeguarding the dignity of human life" (Collect).

Today's Canadian Saint

See below for a biography.

WED **23** #313 green
Weekday

Optional Memorial of Saint Vincent, Deacon and Martyr / red

Lectionary for Mass

◆ First Reading: Hebrews' focus on Melchizedek continues. Melchizedek's sudden and brief appearance in Genesis 14:18, without mention of ancestry, birth, or death gave rise to the Jewish tradition associating him with an eternal priesthood. In verses not included in today's Lectionary text (verses 4, 11–14), Hebrews emphasizes that Melchizedek's priesthood was superior to the levitical priesthood, just as Melchizedek was superior to Abraham. Jesus has been raised up through God's power as high priest according to the order of Melchizedek. He continually intercedes on our behalf.

◆ Responsorial Psalm: As on Monday, our response is from Psalm 110. See comments there.

◆ Gospel: Today's Gospel follows immediately after yesterday's text. Again, there is controversy with the Pharisees over observance of the Sabbath. We can only surmise how the man's physical disability impacted his everyday life. As Mark tells the story, one almost gets the sense of Jesus and the Pharisees aligned in battle opposite one another. Note that Jesus is angry. He realizes they were watching him, wanting to accuse him. Indeed, as the last line indicates, they sought

to put him to death. Like their ancestors, the Pharisees were hardened of heart. They were not open to the salvation Jesus came to bring.

Today's Saint

Saint Vincent was from Saragossa in third-century Spain. He is also known as Vincent the deacon and served under Saint Valerius, bishop of Saragossa. He was martyred in 304 during the persecution by the emperor Diocletian. Just before he was killed on a gridiron or grill, he was offered his freedom if he would throw a copy of the scriptures on the fire that was prepared for him, but he refused. After witnessing Vincent's faith and heroism, his executioner converted to Christianity.

Roman Missal Update

The United States Conference of Catholic Bishops have approved the inclusion of an optional Memorial of Blessed Marianne Cope. This memorial is pending approval from the Holy See. Check for updates on www.RevisedRomanMissal.org regarding the status of this memorial and prayer texts.

Blessed Marianne Cope (1838 – 1918) was born in West Germany, but a year after her birth the Cope family emigrated to the United States of America to seek work and educational opportunities. From a young age, she felt the call to enter religious life which led to her decision to enter the Sisters of Saint Francis in Syracuse, New York. She had a deep affection for the suffering and sick. Blessed Marianne was instrumental in the establishment of two of the first hospitals in the central New York area—hospitals that were open to all people regardless of ethnicity, religion, or race. While serving as superior general of her religious community, she accepted an invitation to care for the sick, especially those afflicted

with leprosy, in Hawaii. Blessed Marianne joined the mission to Hawaii where she helped establish homes for leprosy patients and cared for Saint Damien De Veuster of Molokai who contracted leprosy because of his ministry to the sick. Following the death of Saint Damien, Blessed Marianne continued his compassionate ministry of care for leprosy patients. Blessed Marianne lived the Franciscan call to serve the "crucified," the most vulnerable, in society. Normally, a saint's feast day is their death date, their *dies natales*, or birthday into heaven. However, Blessed Marianne died on August 9. This is the same date as the obligatory memorial for Saint Teresa Benedicta of the Cross (Edith Stein). Becuse of this, the American bishops have suggested this date, January 23, her birthday.

THU **24** #314 white
Memorial of Saint Francis de Sales, Bishop and Doctor of the Church

Lectionary for Mass

◆ First Reading: Hebrews' discussion of Jesus's high priesthood continues today with special emphasis on the uniqueness of his priesthood since he is also the Son. Having mediated the new covenant through the once-and-for-all offering of himself, and now exalted in the heavenly sanctuary, he lives to make intercession for us.

◆ Responsorial Psalm 40 is quoted in chapter 10 of the Letter to the Hebrews. Verses 7–10 can easily be seen as fulfilled in the ministry of Jesus. The last line is a prayer, addressed to our heavenly intercessor, that we can readily make our own.

◆ Gospel: Such large crowds continue to gather around Jesus that he asks that a boat be ready for him. There, at least, he would have some space. Today's Gospel is a bit of a summary statement of Jesus's healing ministry and of his power over evil spirits who know his true identity. The command to secrecy (last line) indicates that it is not yet time for Jesus's true identity to be revealed.

The Roman Missal

The Prayers are found in the Proper of Saints.

The Collect echoes the words Saint Paul, who "became all things to all, to save at least some" (I Corinthians 9:22). Saint Francis de Sales did the same, and through his preaching and writing helped people in every walk of life to find the way to holiness. We pray that we may follow his example, showing God's love through service to our neighbor. We ask that we may burn with the same "divine fire" that burned in Saint Francis (Prayer over the Offerings), and that we may imitate his "charity and meekness" (Prayer after Communion). The Preface of Pastors is used.

Today's Saint

Saint Francis de Sales (1567–1622), bishop of Geneva, contributed immensely to the development of spirituality through the publication of his book *An Introduction to the Devout Life*. Living at a time when manuals on spirituality were written primarily for clerics and members of religious orders, Saint Francis's book provided a practical path to holiness for people from all states of life. He challenged the prevailing belief that only a select few could obtain sanctity. Along with his accomplishments in the area of an everyday, or lay, spirituality, he cofounded with Saint Jane Frances de Chantal the Order of the Visitation of Holy Mary, a religious community of nuns that would move beyond traditional enclosure to a healthy blend of prayer and service to the poor. Together, Saints Francis and Jane, with their close friends Saints Vincent

de Paul and Louise de Marillac, transformed the face of the Church in France. Saint Francis has been named a Doctor of the Church.

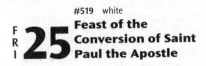

#519 white

FRI 25 Feast of the Conversion of Saint Paul the Apostle

Orientation/Today's Saint

Today's feast celebrates God's triumph, even in the most unlikely circumstances. Before Saint Paul meets the Risen Lord on the Road to Damascus, he is Saul, dedicated to viciously persecuting the followers of Jesus Christ. Imagine yourself among those early Christians, and hearing that Saul, one of the most feared enemies of your community, has encountered the Lord and changed his life entirely to serve him from then on. Although certainly astonishing, the conversion of Saint Paul is also deeply inspiring, for it tells us that God does not hold our mistakes against us, but rather calls us to turn our minds and hearts to follow his Son instead. The conversion of Saint Paul is proof that no one is too far beyond the call of the Lord to follow, and that in Christ, change for the better is always possible.

Lectionary for Mass

◆ FIRST READING: Two options are given for the First Reading. Both are Paul's account (as reported by Saint Luke) of his experience of the Risen Christ on the road to Damascus and the important identification of Jesus with believers. In the first option, we hear of Paul's Jewish heritage, particularly that of a Pharisee. The second option focuses on Ananias's, understandable fear and hesitancy about going to Saul. He is obedient, nonetheless. Both readings speak of Paul's experience of the bright light (identified with the Lord) and his hearing

the Lord's voice (note the discrepancy though, in Acts of the Apostles 22, where Paul's companions hear the voice as well). Both readings contrast Paul, the zealous and aggressive defender of Judaism, with the blinded man who needed to be led by the hand. Paul's blindness is the result of his experience of the Risen Christ manifest in light so bright that he was left unable to see. Paul is led by the hand literally by his companions and figuratively by Ananias whose word led Saul to Baptism and an understanding of his call and mission from Jesus.

◆ RESPONSORIAL PSALM: The response is from Mark's account of the Risen Jesus's commission of the his disciples. Psalm 117 is a song of praise, calling upon all peoples, Gentiles as well as Jews, to sing God's praise.

◆ GOSPEL: Jesus sends the Twelve to the whole world (Gentiles as well as Jews) to proclaim his Good News and to baptize those who believe. Their divine commission will be confirmed by signs and they will continue Jesus's work of healing and exorcism.

The Roman Missal

The Gloria is said or sung today.

The Prayers are found in the Proper of Saints.

Through Saint Paul, God has "taught the whole world." We pray that we may follow the example of the Apostle and become "witnesses to [God's] truth in the world" (Collect). We want to be filled with the "light of faith" (Prayer over the Offerings) and "fire of charity" (Prayer after Communion) which strengthened Saint Paul to spread the Gospel and to preach in the Christian communities.

S A T 26
#520, Gospel #316   white

Memorial of Saints Timothy and Titus, Bishops

Lectionary for Mass

◆ FIRST READING: Two options are given for this memorial honoring two prominent assistants to Saint Paul: Timothy and Titus. Both texts are taken from the beginning of the letters which, according to tradition, the Apostle wrote to them. Notice Paul's self-identification in each letter, presenting his ministry as a vocation from God. Note also that both Timothy and Titus are addressed as "my . . . child" (2 Timothy 1:2; Titus 1:4), thus pointing to Paul's role in enlivening and nurturing their faith. The text to Timothy stresses Paul's gratitude and prayer for him. The reference to Timothy's mother and grandmother and their role in Timothy's faith makes them models for our own day. Timothy is encouraged not to take for granted the grace received through Paul's laying hands on him—a gesture evoking the sacraments as we celebrate them today, and good advice for us as well. He is encouraged to fidelity despite the hardships involved, knowing that strength will be given him from God. Titus's mission is to complete the work Paul had begun and to appoint presbyters or local leaders of the Church in every town.

◆ RESPONSORIAL PSALM 96: The antiphon is most appropriate for today's memorial, given the ministry of Timothy and Titus. The reference to the nations points to the universal outreach (to Gentiles) of their mission. God's marvelous deed in sending his Son Jesus has truly brought salvation to all.

◆ GOSPEL: Today's text is not the most flattering regarding Jesus's family. Mark puts it simply—they think he is crazy. This is early in the Gospel. Jesus has been drawing huge crowds, healing people, naming disciples and Apostles, overcoming the power of evil. Even his family doesn't know what to make of all that is happening. Coming to faith in Jesus as God's Son was not so easy for those who thought they knew him well.

The Roman Missal

The prayers are found in the Proper of Saints.

Appropriately on this memorial, the Collect echoes the words of Saint Paul's letter to Timothy (2:12). We pray that we may live "justly and devoutly in this present age" and so come to our "heavenly homeland." In the Prayer over the Offerings, we ask for "sincerity of heart," that we may be acceptable to God. We pray that the sacrament we receive may nourish us in the faith which was taught and "kept safe" by Saints Timothy and Titus (Prayer after Communion).

The Preface of Pastors is used.

Today's Saints

These two missionaries, Saint Timothy and Saint Titus, were catalysts in the spread of early Christianity. As companions of Saint Paul, both were installed as bishops and received public acclaim for their charismatic leadership, but each had his own gifts. Saint Timothy was a powerful preacher who inspired faith, often without ever saying a word. Saint Titus, on the other hand, had a knack for peacemaking. Paul entrusted him with the difficult task of delivering letters of correction and reprimand because his demeanor fostered a spirit of reconciliation in even the most difficult of circumstances. They had diverse gifts, but were motivated by the same goal: to tell all people that the cross of Jesus Christ is the only path to salvation. Death befell them in two different ways. Saint Timothy was martyred for his opposition to polytheistic worship, and Saint Titus most likely died of old age.

☀ 27
#69   green

Third Sunday in Ordinary Time

Orientation

Luke reveals that after pondering the Good News of Jesus Christ, he too has decided to join the eyewitnesses and ministers and hand on the story of the Lord in his own way, by compiling a narrative of the events in an orderly sequence, and sharing them with his friend Theophilus. Theophilus, whose name means "God's beloved," is also a term that describes each of us. Luke's narrative is thus intended for a much wider audience than this one person. It shares the Good News of Jesus Christ with us, but it also inspires each of us to follow Luke's example in sharing the story of Jesus Christ in unique and personal ways. We may not write another Gospel, but we can share the Good News with those around us through our service, our relationships, our choices and convictions.

Lectionary for Mass

◆ FIRST READING: Today's reading is set in the historical context of the return to Jerusalem after the Babylonian Exile. Ezra the priest presides at a solemn assembly of all the people, including the children old enough to understand, and proclaims the Book of the Law of the Lord to them. (Note how the ritual described in today's text parallels our own celebrations of the Liturgy of the Word.) Were the people crying tears of joy because they realized they were God's people and that God had made a covenant with them? Or were these tears of sadness because of their failures?

◆ RESPONSORIAL PSALM: The antiphon is adapted from Jesus's words in John 6:63c. Psalm 19 acclaims the Law of the Lord as priceless treasure and as that which gives light to our eyes. We pray that our thoughts and words may be formed by the Word of God and be pleasing to God.

◆ SECOND READING: Just as the human body is one body with many different parts (members), each with unique and necessary functions, so too, the Church of God has many members, roles, and gifts, each with its own function necessary for the working of the One Body.

◆ GOSPEL: The first part of today's Gospel is the beginning of the Gospel according to Luke. We hear his purpose in writing the Gospel and its dedication to his Theophilus, whose name means friend of God. Theophilus was perhaps Luke's benefactor (see the similar introduction in Acts of the Apostles). The second part, from the fourth chapter of the Gospel, recounts the beginning of Jesus's ministry. Jesus returns to Galilee after his baptism and temptation. Today we see him attending a synagogue service in Nazareth where he does the reading (again, note the rituals). The text he reads is programmatic of his whole mission. Indeed, Isaiah's prophecy is fulfilled in Jesus.

The Roman Missal

In the Collect, we ask God to direct all our actions according to his "good pleasure," so that we may "abound in good works."

In the Prayer over the Offerings, we pray that the offerings we make may "profit us for salvation."

The sacrament we have received is the source of "new life." In the Prayer after Communion, we pray that we may always "glory" in this great gift.

Other Ideas

Show children your Bible and any holy cards, letters, or photos that you keep there. Point out the table of contents, explaining that there are many books within this book. Give your Bible a place of honor in your home in keeping with its authorship. If you don't have a children's picture Bible, purchase an age-appropriate one, and share stories from it often.

#317   white

28 MON
Memorial of Saint Thomas Aquinas, Priest and Doctor of the Church

Lectionary for Mass

◆ FIRST READING: The theme of Christ as the inaugurator of a new and eternal covenant is continued, with emphasis today on his once-and-for-all sacrifice. Through his death, Christ has entered into the true, heavenly sanctuary. Note the mention of his second coming at the end of time. Are we among those who eagerly await him?

◆ RESPONSORIAL PSALM 98: Our response is a hymn of joyful praise. God has done wonderful deeds, above all in the sacrificial Death, Resurrection, and Ascension of Jesus, the eternal high priest. All the earth sings joyful praise with orchestral accompaniment of harps, trumpets, and horns!

◆ GOSPEL: By manifesting power over demons, Jesus provokes controversy and confusion over his identity. The scribes accuse Jesus of being possessed and of being a tool of Satan. Jesus responds with a parable that invites them to recognize the illogic of their reasoning and subtly warns them about failing to recognize the power of the Holy Spirit.

The Roman Missal

The Prayers are found in the Proper of Saints.

The Collect highlights Saint Thomas's "zeal for holiness" and "study of sacred doctrine." We pray that we may understand his teaching and follow his example of holy living.

The Prayer over the Offerings and Prayer after Communion are drawn from the Common of Doctors of the Church or the Common of Pastors: For One Pastor. The Preface of Holy Pastors is used.

Today's Saint

Saint Thomas Aquinas (1225–1274), a Doctor of the Church, felt drawn to the charism of the Dominicans, even though his parents wanted him to become a Benedictine monk. As a young Dominican, his reserved demeanor led his classmates to believe he was unintelligent; therefore, they called him the "dumb ox." Little did they know Saint Thomas was a brilliant man who would write the *Summa Theologica*, a theological masterpiece that explicates the truths of the Catholic faith by demonstrating the intimate relationship between reason and revelation. His intellectual genius and method of theological inquiry were greatly influenced by his mentor and teacher, Saint Albert the Great. The person once thought to be a "dumb ox" became known as the "angelic doctor" due to his profound and far-reaching impact on theological thought.

T U E **29** #318 green
Weekday

Lectionary for Mass

◆ FIRST READING: Hebrews focuses on the annual day of atonement (Yom Kippur, as we know it), a day of sacrifice and repentance. The sacrifices of the old covenant could never perfect those who offered them; they were incapable of doing so. But Christ, whose sacrifice was once and for all, is the sacrifice of obedience that God desires. Through Jesus's offering of himself, we have been made holy.

◆ RESPONSORIAL PSALM: Most appropriately, our response is from Psalm 40, cited in today's First Reading. The antiphon is a beautiful summary of the life and Death of Jesus. The first stanza, with its mention of "waiting," evokes the centuries of waiting for Christ who would inaugurate a new covenant.

◆ GOSPEL: Our relationship with Jesus transcends the bonds of blood ties to members of our own family. We come into relationship with Jesus, an intimate relationship with close family ties, by doing the will of God.

W E D **30** #319 green
Weekday

Lectionary for Mass

◆ FIRST READING: A continuation of yesterday's reading, and a reiteration of its themes. The citation from Jeremiah 31, with its focus on the new covenant, prompts us to ask if we really grasp the newness of what God has done in Jesus. Do we really believe that God no longer remembers our sins? That we have been consecrated—made holy—to God? Are we living mindful of this "new" reality inaugurated by Jesus?

◆ RESPONSORIAL PSALM 110: Originally this Psalm was associated with the day of the king's enthronement. The king also had a priestly function. In the context of the liturgy and our readings from Hebrews, the focus is on Jesus's priesthood. With his conclusive offering he has entered the heavenly sanctuary and is enthroned there in glory forever.

◆ GOSPEL: The parable of the sower and the seed is a familiar one. As Jesus teaches the crowd, he himself is the sower of the seed of the Word, as are all who proclaim the Gospel after him. The parable's interpretation invites us to examine our own receptivity to the Word of God. What type of ground is our heart? Sandwiched between the parable and its interpretation is Jesus's private teaching to his disciples. Note their privileged, or rather, blessed status, as recipients of God's revelation. The text from Isaiah serves to explain why so many did not hear and take the Word to heart.

T H U **31** #320 white
Memorial of Saint John Bosco, Priest

Lectionary for Mass

◆ FIRST READING: Under the old covenant, only the high priest was allowed to enter the Holy of Holies, and then, only once a year. As a result of Jesus's sacrifice, all believers have access to that innermost sanctuary in the heavenly Temple if only we will follow his way. The reading ends with words of practical encouragement to believers to love, do good works, and regularly attend the Christian assemblies. The day of the Lord—when the promises will be realized—draws near.

◆ RESPONSORIAL PSALM 24: Since the First Reading speaks of the promise of coming into the presence of the Lord, our response is the prayer of longing to do so. Note

the practical behaviors set forth in the second stanza.

◆ GOSPEL: Two short parables and an enigmatic saying invite the listener to further reflection. Note the emphasis on hearing. Both images, the lamp and the measure, are familiar items from everyday life. What do we take in? What do we "put out" for others?

The Roman Missal

The Prayers are found in the Proper of Saints.

God raised up Saint John "as a father and teacher of the young." In the Collect, we ask that we may be "aflame with the same fire of love," seeking souls and serving God as he did.

The Prayer over the Offerings and the Prayer after Communion are taken from the Common of Pastors: For One Pastor or the Common of Holy Men and Women: For Educators. The Preface of Holy Pastors is used.

Today's Saint

God gifted Saint John Bosco (1815–1888) with the ability to read and interpret the signs of the times. Living during rapid industrialization and growing anti-clericalism, he became very concerned about the emotional and spiritual livelihood of people, especially the plight of the young. Saint John worked to provide positive and affirming environments, including orphanages and oratories, where the young could learn and recognize their infinite potential. In the spirit of his favorite hero, Saint Francis de Sales, he founded the Salesians, a religious congregation devoted to works of charity, with an emphasis on empowering young people to become strong pillars of faith in a culture of instability. His work among young men living in the slums proved to be a worthy endeavor. Whether he was presiding at Mass or playing games with children or carrying the sick to hospitals, it was obvious he lived until his "last breath . . . day and night, morning and evening" for the neglected and abandoned (as quoted in *Butler's Lives of the Saints, January, New Full Edition*, p. 229).

February
Month of the Passion of Our Lord

F R I **1** #321 green
Weekday

Lectionary for Mass

◆ FIRST READING: We hear more words of encouragement from Hebrews, addressed to a community that is perhaps wavering in their endurance and commitment after experiencing intense suffering. It's as if the author says: "Look at what you have been through! Why are you wavering now?" Perhaps the wavering results from the seeming delay in the fulfillment of the Lord's promises. The author conjoins words from the prophets Isaiah and Habakkuk as a way of building up their trust and readiness to endure.

◆ RESPONSORIAL PSALM 37: Fittingly, today's response is an exhortation to trust by reiterating the Lord's promises of salvation and deliverance.

◆ GOSPEL: Jesus appeals to his listeners' experience of nature to teach them the mystery of the growth of the kingdom of God. Signs of the growth of a seed are visible, and while scientists today may be able to explain the process of growth, the force underlying it remains mysterious. Jesus's parables teach people with images and invite them to ponder their meaning. Can we hear with these same ears today?

S A T **2** #524 white
Feast of the Presentation of the Lord

Orientation

The Feast of the Presentation of the Lord reminds us that respecting God's laws and commandments are part and parcel of following Jesus Christ. Through word and example, Christ teaches us to honor and respect the Law, but to view the Law always as an expression of the greatest commandment: the love of God and the love of neighbor as oneself. Our lives become more joyful when considering the laws and commandments of Christian life as expressions of love. By so doing, attending Mass on Sundays and Holydays of Obligation, for example, is not simply something we have to do; rather it becomes a joyful opportunity to grow in our relationship with God. May Christ, as the fulfillment of the Law, lead us to use God's commandments to structure our lives to grow in holiness and the love of God.

Lectionary for Mass

◆ FIRST READING: *Malachi* is not so much a proper name but rather a Hebrew word which means "my messenger." This very short prophetic book (only three chapters) targets the Temple priests in particular for their lack of fidelity to the Lord and their "unfit" sacrificial offerings. The messenger who will come to God's Temple will be like fire (light) refining and purifying the people so that Israel may offer worthy sacrifice to God. Today's feast celebrates Jesus as that messenger.

◆ RESPONSORIAL PSALM 24: Today's Psalm was most likely in its origins was likely a hymn used when the Ark of the Covenant, which signified God's presence with his people, was carried in procession in the Temple.

◆ SECOND READING: Jesus is portrayed as the "merciful and faithful high priest" (Hebrews 2:17) who offers fitting sacrifice to God. The reading stresses his oneness with his brothers and sisters when he embraced human life and death. Like his brothers and sisters, he knows temptation and, as a result, is a sure help for us in our own.

◆ GOSPEL: Repetitions of themes in today's other two readings are heard in the Gospel: purification, sacrifice, the Lord coming to the Temple, *light*. Simeon, echoing themes first voiced in the Old Testament, proclaims Jesus as a *light* for the Gentiles and glory (another *light* image) for Israel. There is also mention of purification and refining with reference to the child's destiny: "for the fall and rise of Israel" and the revelation of the thoughts of human hearts.

The Roman Missal

◆ BLESSING OF CANDLES AND PROCESSION: Mass today begins with the blessing of candles and the procession. The people gather in a separate place, such as a chapel or the main entrance of the church, for the blessing. All receive unlit tapers before Mass begins. The priest celebrant, wearing a white chasuble or cope, and ministers join the faithful in the designated place (the rubric says simply that the priest "approaches with the ministers"—there is no indication of a formal procession to the place where the people are gathered). The candles are lit before the introduction begins. *The Roman Missal* suggests singing a setting of "Behold, our Lord will come with power, to enlighten the eyes of his servants, alleluia," although another song with imagery of light could also be used.

After the people's candles are lit, the priest gives the greeting as usual, followed by the introduction. The priest celebrant is free to adapt this introduction; the only requirement is that the address encourage "the faithful to celebrate the rite of this feast day actively and consciously" (*The Roman Missal*). The text provided reminds us that 40 days have passed since Christmas and recalls that on this day Jesus came into the Temple, both "fulfilling the Law" and meeting "his believing people," Simeon and Anna. We are part of the story, for we, too, are led by the Spirit into the house of the Lord. And, like Simeon and Anna, we will recognize the Lord Jesus, but in the breaking of bread, until he comes in glory.

After the introduction, the priest celebrant blesses the candles. Two options are given. The language of the first is more closely tied to the readings of the feast; the second is full of wonderful imagery of light, which is to shine from the candles we carry, and within our hearts. After the blessing, the candles are sprinkled with holy water. The priest then adds incense to the thurible and receives his own lit candle from the deacon or another minister. Then the deacon or priest invites all to go forth in peace "to meet the Lord." The procession forms: thurifer, cross-bearer, other ministers, priest celebrant, and all the faithful. *The Roman Missal* suggests a setting of the *Nunc dimittis*, the Canticle of Simeon, to accompany the procession, with a simple refrain for the people. Another antiphon is provided: "Sion, adorn your bridal chamber," is full of rich poetic imagery, inviting the Church to "take Mary in your arms . . . for she herself is carrying the King of glory and new light."

Upon entering the church, the priest celebrant proceeds immediately to the altar, venerates it, and incenses it (if incense is used). Meanwhile, the people go to their places, still carrying their lit candles. The priest goes to the chair,

puts on his chasuble (if the cope has been used for the procession), and the Gloria begins. The Collect follows, the candles are extinguished, and Mass continues as usual.

If it is impossible for the people to join in the procession with candles, a second form, called the Solemn Entrance, is provided. The people gather in the church with their unlit tapers. The ministers enter and stand near the door or in another suitable place where the people can see them. The candles are lit—light will need to be brought to the people—and then the blessing of candles follows. The Entrance Procession forms and proceeds to the altar as usual.

◆ OTHER MISSAL PRAYERS: Christ was presented in the Temple "in the substance of our flesh." In the Collect, we pray that we may be presented to God "with minds made pure."

◆ THE joyful encounter with Simeon and Anna also has its note of impending sadness: Simeon's prophecy speaks of contradiction and the Cross, for Jesus and his Mother. The Prayer over the Offerings speaks of the Only Begotten Son, offered "for the life of the world / as the Lamb without blemish."

The proper Preface puts us in the place of Simeon and Anna, going forth "rejoicing to encounter your Salvation."

The Prayer after Communion expresses the hope that just as God granted Simeon's longing to behold the Messiah, so we also might receive the sum of our desires, the gift of eternal life, when we go forth to meet the Lord.

Notice that the Creed is said only when the feast falls on a Sunday.

Other Ideas

A clear message of today's readings is that Christ will make a difference in people's lives: he will refine and purify; he will cause "the fall and

rise of many." Today might be an excellent time to allow Christ to do some purifying within us. Think of a part of yourself that needs the fuller's lye or refiner's fire. Offer up that part of yourself to Chirst and pray for his purifying love to transform it. As an outward sign of your prayer and resolution, think of a neglected clean-up or fix-up chore and incorporate the doing of that task into your prayer.

☀ **3** #72　green
**Fourth Sunday
in Ordinary Time**

Orientation

Why does it seem like no prophet is accepted in his native place? Is it indeed easier to accept God's truth from a stranger than from a familiar face? Sometimes our idea of integrity gets in the way. We know a person too well to allow them to speak God's truth authoritatively, because we recall a time when they themselves made mistakes. Who are they then to preach? At the same time, God calls all of us to share the Good News of Jesus Christ, the joy and hope of which outshines the imperfections of those who proclaim it. The proclamation of the Good News, through our imperfect lives, words, and deeds, is a testimony to God's grace working in our lives. Familiar prophets, whose pasts make us wonder about their right to preach, are in fact witnesses of God's healing grace, transforming those among us with checkered pasts into witnesses of the Gospel.

Lectionary for Mass

◆ FIRST READING: We hear the call of Jeremiah, chosen by his Creator for a prophetic mission even before his birth (see verses 4–5). In the second part of the reading, God encourages Jeremiah to stand firm in his mission, telling him of the difficulties that he will encounter, but above all assuring Jeremiah that he will be with him and be his strength.

◆ RESPONSORIAL PSALM: The message that Jeremiah spoke was one of salvation for those who would heed God's Word. Psalm 71 is a prayer of confidence and trust in the Lord. Both the references to birth and mother's womb in the first stanza and the images of strength in the second stanza echo the First Reading. The last stanza speaks of being taught from youth—and indeed, Jeremiah was but a youth when called by God (see Jeremiah 1:6–7).

◆ SECOND READING: Two options are given for the reading. Chapter 13 of 1 Corinthians is the heart of chapters 12–14, which speak of spiritual gifts. The Corinthians particularly esteemed the gifts of prophecy and speaking in tongues, as we see in the first part of the longer form of the reading. Paul's message is clear: no matter how great the gifts and the talents, only the manifestations of love really matter. Love is a spiritual gift like prophecy and tongues whose source is the Holy Spirit of God. Is there a subtle call to the Corinthians to be like Paul and put aside "childish" (verse 11) ways so as to live as a mature person in Christ, gifted by the Spirit? There is a longer and shorter form of the reading.

◆ GOSPEL: Today's text is a continuation of last Sunday's Gospel where Jesus read from the prophet Isaiah during a synagogue service in Nazareth. We literally pick up where we left off with his words: "Today this Scripture is fulfilled . . ." (4:21). Like Jeremiah, Elijah, and Elisha before him, Jesus meets with opposition in his prophetic ministry. The people of Jesus's home town, who think they know him but really don't, are so enraged by his words that they try to kill him.

The Roman Missal

The simple Collect echoes the words of Christ to the scribe who asked him which commandment was most important: we are to "honor [God] with all our mind, / and love everyone in truth of heart."

In the Prayer over the Offerings, we ask God to transform the "offerings of our service" and make them "the Sacrament of our redemption."

In the Prayer after Communion, we pray that the "redeeming gifts" we receive may help the faith to spread. The sacrifice is offered not just for our own salvation, but for that of the whole world.

Other Ideas

Increase children's familiarity with the Gospel that we preach by inviting all family members to tell a favorite Gospel story in their own words. Provide drawing materials, and invite your child to draw a picture of his or her favorite Gospel story. If your child is old enough, play a game of Gospel or parable charades.

Think of someone who has been a modern prophet. Compile a profile of the person by gathering photos, articles, and biographical information.

M
O
N **4** #323   green
Weekday

Lectionary for Mass

◆ FIRST READING: Hebrews' account of the faithful witness of Israel's ancestors continues. Today's focus is the judges (Gideon, Barak, Samson, and Jephthah), those military leaders after Joshua, the successor of Moses, Samuel the prophet, and David, Israel's greatest king. The sufferings of countless unnamed others also receive mention. These persevered through faith. Only in Jesus is the fullness of their hope—and ours—realized.

◆ RESPONSORIAL PSALM 31 is a prayer during a time of distress. The verses chosen for today focus on the experience of the Lord's deliverance, truly an answer to the prayer! The reference to fearing the Lord in the first stanza aptly describes the reverence and faith that the people named in today's first reading manifested in their lives. The words of the psalmist are a fitting prayer in our times of distress, giving assurance of the Lord's protection.

◆ GOSPEL: Once again, Jesus demonstrates his power over the world of the demonic and restores to health a man described as wild and self-destructive. Note the change in the possessed man's demeanor and behavior as a result of his healing encounter with Jesus. Subsequently, the healed man went and proclaimed all that Jesus had done for him.

T
U
E **5** #324   red
Memorial of Saint Agatha, Virgin and Martyr

Lectionary for Mass

◆ FIRST READING: The great crowd of witnesses described in Hebrews 11 should serve as encouragement for all who lived after them, including us! The author of Hebrews speaks of our life's journey as a "race." Our victory is assured if our eyes are fixed on Jesus, our model in endurance, hope, and trust in God.

◆ RESPONSORIAL PSALM 22 is a most appropriate response to today's reading from Hebrews with its reference to the Cross. The Gospel accounts of Matthew and Mark depict Jesus praying Psalm 22 as he hung on the Cross. The verses chosen for today are from the latter part of the Psalm, a hymn of thanksgiving for God's deliverance in a time of distress. The second stanza, with its reference to bowing down before the Lord, ties in with Hebrews' reference to Jesus's exaltation.

◆ GOSPEL: There are two miracle accounts in today's Gospel, one framed by the other. Both are strong stories of faith and trust in the power of Jesus (despite the lack of faith shown by some at Jairus's house). Jesus's touch—and touching him—brings healing and life. How might we experience this touch in our day?

The Roman Missal

The Collect is found in the Proper of Saints. We ask the intercession of Agatha, whose courage and chastity found favor with God.

The Prayer over the Offerings and the Prayer after Communion are taken from the Common of Martyrs: For a Virgin Martyr or the Common of Virgins: For One Virgin.

Today's Saint

Agatha was born in Sicily, probably around the year 231, and is one of the women mentioned by name in Eucharistic Prayer I. According to legend, she was the daughter of a prominent family and was very beautiful. The Roman senator Quintianus wished to marry her, but when Agatha spurned him, he had her put in a brothel. In spite of this, Agatha held to her Christian

faith. Quintianus then had her tortured by having her breasts cut off. She eventually died in prison in 253. Saint Agatha is the patron of the city of her martyrdom, Catania, and is invoked against the fire, earthquakes, and eruptions of Mount Etna. In recent years, because her breasts were cut off as part of her torture, she is considered the patron saint of breast cancer patients.

#325   red

WED 6 Memorial of Saint Paul Miki and Companions, Martyrs

Lectionary for Mass

◆ FIRST READING: Today's reading opens with the repetition of the last line from Tuesday's reading. No matter how great their difficulties may seem to them, the Christians addressed by Hebrews have yet to shed their blood as Jesus did. What is more, they must see their struggles in a positive light, specifically as discipline, as training from the Lord who, like a good Father, teaches his children to endure difficult trials. What good advice are the last two lines of this reading for our daily lives!

◆ RESPONSORIAL PSALM 103: This song of praise reiterates the theme of God's merciful love for his sons and daughters. Note the reference to father and children in the second stanza, a nice link to the First Reading from Hebrews. When faced with struggles, we must not forget the blessings, the benefits of the Lord.

◆ GOSPEL: Jesus is at home in Nazareth, and his fellow citizens think they know all there is to know about him. Their assumptions and presumptions become a stumbling block to faith in Jesus and to the reception of his healing works. Faith elicits the divine power at work in Jesus.

The Roman Missal

The Collect is found in the Proper of Saints. As we remember these saints who suffered crucifixion for Christ, we pray that we may persevere in our faith until death.

The Prayer over the Offerings and the Prayer after Communion are found in the Common of Martyrs: For Several Martyrs.

Today's Saints

Saint Paul Miki (+1597), a Jesuit priest, was one of the 26 martyrs of Japan. Feeling threatened by the growing influence of the Jesuits, the local governor had members of the Christian community arrested and thrown in jail. They were forced to walk 600 miles from Kyoto to Nagasaki as a deterrent to other Christians, but they sang the *Te Deum* as they went. At Nagasaki they were crucified. When Christian missionaries returned to Japan in the 19th century, they found that a secret Christian community had survived by transmitting their beliefs and prayers from generation to generation.

#326   green

THU 7 Weekday

Lectionary for Mass

◆ FIRST READING: Hebrews loves to contrast the old and the new covenants. When God inaugurated the first covenant with Moses on the earthly Mount Sinai, the manifestation of his power and presence was terrifying (see Exodus 19:16–25). Now God's people journey to the heavenly Mount Zion, the heavenly Jerusalem, where there is the joyful assembly of those redeemed by the Lamb. The Book of Revelation develops this latter theme at length.

◆ RESPONSORIAL PSALM 48 originally acclaimed the earthly Jerusalem as the city of God. Juxtaposed with today's First Reading, our attention is on the heavenly Jerusalem where we hope to ponder God's mercy forever.

◆ GOSPEL: We hear Mark's account of Jesus's commissioning of his disciples. The disciples are to travel light, trusting in God's providence for all their needs, manifest in what they receive from others. The disciples' ministry includes first of all, the expulsion of demons, an important theme in the Gospel according to Mark and the subject of any number of Jesus's miracles. Lest we be too quick to dismiss this as irrelevant for our times, we might reflect on how a spirit of evil might be present in our own lives. Note also the mention of the disciples anointing the sick with oil and healing them, evoking the continuation of this ministry today in the Sacrament of the Anointing of the Sick.

F R I 8 #327 green
Weekday

Optional Memorials of Saint Jerome Emiliani / white; Saint Josephine Bakhita, Virgin / white

Lectionary for Mass

◆ FIRST READING: Hebrews addresses some practical implications of discipleship in terms of the conduct of believers. The admonitions are timeless, as is the Lord Jesus who is our model and our goal. The community addressed would have easily understood the implied references to various Old Testament events and teachings, such as Abraham's hospitality (see verse 2).

◆ RESPONSORIAL PSALM 27, a song of confidence, is quoted in today's First Reading. It is a most fitting prayer in times of difficulty, especially if we pray it with trust in the Lord who is indeed our salvation. Its words can easily move us beyond our fears and anxieties into a stance of trust if we open ourselves to their power.

◆ GOSPEL: Mark's account of Herod's musings on Jesus's identity provides an occasion for telling of John the Baptist's death. Today's text offers an interesting character study of Herod, son of Herod the Great. He is said to have feared John, recognizing his righteousness and holiness. Herod's weakness was his determination to uphold his own image before his guests, even at the cost of John's life, rather than act in accord with the truth he knew in his own heart.

Today's Saints

While being held as a political prisoner, Saint Jerome Emiliani (1481–1537) had a conversion experience in which he repented for his past sinful ways and devoted his life to Mary. After a miraculous escape he developed a special love for the unfortunates of society, concentrating on the needs of orphans and prostitutes. He founded a religious community, Clerks Regular of Somasca, with the intent of providing food, clothing, housing, and catechesis for the needy. Saint Jerome is credited with developing the question-and-answer format for teaching catechism.

Saint Josephine Bakhita (1869–1947), born in the Sudan, was enslaved at the age of ten and eventually sold to an Italian consul. Later in life she felt drawn to the Catholic faith through interaction with the Canossian Sisters. Following her conversion, she joined the sisters to live a life fully devoted to Jesus Christ and works of charity. She gained increasing popularity due to her exceptional spiritual practices, which led to her canonization.

S A T 9 #328 green
Weekday

Optional Memorial of the Blessed Virgin Mary / white

Lectionary for Mass

◆ FIRST READING: We hear the final words of Hebrews, which are a continuation of exhortations on the practicalities of daily life. The last lines of the reading are in fact a prayer, reminding the Hebrews that the Risen Christ, the maker of the new and eternal covenant, is their shepherd and will care for all their needs. It is God, at work in them, who accomplishes all the good that they do through Jesus.

◆ RESPONSORIAL PSALM: Hebrews' reference to Jesus as the Good Shepherd prompts the selection of Psalm 23 as today's response. As Hebrews points out, there is nothing we can need or want with the Risen Christ as our shepherd. Pray these words in light of your life.

◆ GOSPEL: Jesus's disciples had been hard at work faithfully carrying out the mission with which they had been entrusted: preaching, repentance, expelling demons, healing the sick. No doubt, they were physically and mentally tired. How welcome Jesus's invitation to go apart with him for some rest must have been! The urgency heard so often in Mark's account of the Gospel is evident in the description of the people as "hasten[ing]" (Mark 6:33) ahead of Jesus and his disciples to this deserted place. Instead of showing frustration or even annoyance on seeing them there, Jesus shows compassion. Sensing their hunger for his word, he began to teach them.

 **10** #75 green
Fifth Sunday in Ordinary Time

Orientation

Simon Peter's humble exclamation illustrates what is often referred to as the fear of God, one of the gifts of the Holy Spirit. The word "fear" gives us the impression of something dark, negative, and harmful, but the fear of God is better defined as a moment of clarity and light. When we experience the fear of God, the Holy Spirit illuminates for us God's holy presence in our lives. In the face of God's holiness, we can often recognize, like Peter, the long way we have to go in our own holiness. The moment of the fear of God is a moment of awe and humility, when we recognize God's amazing power, love, and grace, and become aware of our human weakness and limitations. It is an honest and inspiring moment of conversion, inviting us into God's holy presence, no matter the distance we find ourselves from it.

Lectionary for Mass

◆ FIRST READING: We hear of the call of the prophet Isaiah during a vision he had in the Temple in Jerusalem. Isaiah sees the splendor and grandeur of God enthroned in heaven, surrounded by choirs of angels singing his praise (the words we sing at the beginning of the Eucharistic prayer at every Mass). Isaiah's experience of the holiness of God makes him aware of his own sinfulness as well as that of his people. He—and we—are purified as a result of our encounter with God.

◆ RESPONSORIAL PSALM 138: The Israelites believed that their hymns of praise were joined with those of the angels, as is expressed in the first verse of today's Psalm (also the antiphon). Verse 3 (second stanza) evokes Isaiah's cry for help in the experience of his own unworthiness and God's cleansing of his lips. The "hear" of verse 4 evokes Isaiah's mission to speak the words of the Lord.

◆ SECOND READING: Paul "handed on" what he had first "received" (1 Corinthians 15:3) from the proclamation of the Apostles and teachers who preceded him. Some of the appearances mentioned are recounted only here. Note that Paul considers his own experience of the Risen Christ on the road to Damascus in the same category as these earlier appearances. Like Isaiah before him, Paul realizes his own unworthiness as a result of his encounter with the Lord.

◆ GOSPEL: This text might be entitled "The Call of Peter." Like Isaiah before him, Peter was willing to set aside his own objections to obey the Lord. Like Isaiah and Paul, Peter also became conscious of his own sinfulness through his encounter with the Lord and the miraculous catch of fish. The Lord has his ways of readying those he will send.

The Roman Missal

The Collect is a prayer for divine protection, that God may keep us safe and defend us, and that we may rely on our "hope of heavenly grace."

Prayer over the Offerings: Bread and wine are God's gifts "to sustain us in our frailty." In the Eucharist, he gives us an even greater gift— "the Sacrament of eternal life."

We have shared one Bread, one Chalice. In the Prayer after Communion, we pray that we may be "made one in Christ" and "bear fruit / for the salvation of the world." The work of the Gospel is our work.

Other Ideas

Discuss with family, friends, or parish staff what you can do to enter more fully into Lent, which begins in three days. If you will be fasting from favorite foods or forms of entertainment, calculate how much money you will save and donate it to charity. You might also try fasting from aggressive driving, interrupting others, being overly competitive, and other bad personal habits. Help one another discern what these habits are in a spirit of love and compassion, not criticism.

If your parish has a palm-burning event this week, bring last year's dry palms and participate.

Attend Mass with your family and receive ashes on Wednesday.

M O N 11 #329 green
Weekday

Optional Memorial of Our Lady of Lourdes / white

Lectionary for Mass

◆ FIRST READING: We begin a series of readings from the Book of Genesis, hearing today the first half of the account of the creation of the world (to be continued tomorrow). In the beginning, there was only darkness, emptiness, and the waters—the symbol of chaos. Creation comes into being at the mere word of the Lord, bringing forth life and setting all in order: light and darkness, heaven and earth, land and sea, vegetation, trees, sun, moon, stars. And God saw that all was good.

◆ RESPONSORIAL PSALM: May the Lord be glad in his works—and indeed God was when he declared that all was good. Psalm 104 is a hymn of praise. The first stanza praises God in heavenly splendor; the second and third focus on the created works of earth, sea, rivers, and birds; the fourth praises God for the marvels of creation, all of which manifests his wisdom! In the face of it all we can only sing God's praise.

◆ GOSPEL: Once again, we sense the urgency in Mark's account of the Gospel. People "immediately" (Mark 6:54) recognize Jesus and scurry to bring their sick to him. Jesus's reputation as healer has spread. Particularly interesting is the fact that people had only to touch the tassel of his cloak to be healed. This mention of touch is reminiscent of the woman with the hemorrhage in an earlier chapter who was healed after touching Jesus.

Today's Optional Memorial

Today's feast celebrates Mary's miraculous apparitions to Saint Bernadette Soubirous, a French peasant girl in Lourdes, France, in the middle of the 19th century. Saint Bernadette encountered Mary in a grotto outside of town a number of times, and shared with her

community that she had been seeing a vision of a beautiful lady who identified herself as the Immaculate Conception. After much scrutiny, the bishop confirmed that Saint Bernadette's visions were authentic, and the grotto of Lourdes soon became a place of pilgrimage and healing. People continue to visit Lourdes today, and many experience physical and spiritual renewal there. The proper Collect can be found in the Proper of Saints, with the remaining prayers drawn from the Common of the Blessed Virgin Mary.

T U E **12** #330   green
Weekday

Lectionary for Mass

◆ FIRST READING: Today's reading is a continuation from yesterday's account of creation in Genesis 1. We hear of the creation of all that lives in the sea, the birds of the air, animals of all kinds, and the culmination of God's creative work, the human creature, made in God's image, male and female. God provided for the needs of all and entrusted all creation to human beings. On the seventh day, God rested and

blessed the Sabbath day of rest, making it holy.

◆ RESPONSORIAL PSALM 8: All creation speaks of God to the psalmist, who is filled with awe in beholding it. Similarly, the psalmist, moved with awe and wonder, reflects on the miracle of his own existence and that all creation is entrusted to humankind. To care for the earth and its creatures is to give praise to our God.

◆ GOSPEL: The heart of today's Gospel is to be found in Jesus's citation of the words of the prophet Isaiah: "This people honors me with their lips [and their practices too, we might add], but their hearts are far from me" (see Isaiah 29:13). Rationalizing our thoughts and actions to justify ourselves is so easy. But God looks not at the appearances of external rituals in which the Pharisees, who set themselves apart, took such great delight, but into their hearts.

LENT AND HOLY WEEK

The Meaning

Sometimes time just flies! Here we are at Lent again and we may be wondering how another year has gone by. Maybe we get lulled into thinking we know what Lent is about and that we don't really need to spend any extra preparation time for Easter Time again. On the Third Sunday of Lent, Jesus talks with people who had gathered around him about repentance in order to be saved. He tells them a parable about a fig tree. This was an ordinary and real symbol for his listeners. Many lived off and cared for crops. They under-

stood times of good and bad harvest. In the parable, the owner of the fig tree had waited for three years for the tree to bear fruit. Nothing! So he tells the gardener it's time to cut the tree down because it's only exhausting the soil. But the gardener asks him to leave it for a year while he cultivates and fertilizes the ground around it. If nothing happens, then it can be cut down. Lent is our time to cultivate and fertilize the ground around us. As we do, God offers us his abundant care and mercy. The Church fills our time with Lenten possibilities and rich Scripture passages. The time is at hand. Are you ready?

Fire plays a part as we begin Lent on Ash Wednesday, marked by the ashes burned from last year's palms. Fire also culminates this liturgical time as we gather after the sun sets around the Holy Saturday bonfire and prepare ourselves to celebrate the Easter Vigil. Fire can be a destructive as well as a constructive force. Anyone who has helplessly watched a burning home or wild fires burning prairie land or Pacific acres knows its intensity. Yet new life springs from burned ground and desolate landscapes. Signs of green shoots, budding plants, and new animal life begin to appear after fire. The searing heat and destructive fire lead to resurrected life.

Lent may be the right time for us to allow the searing heat and fire of real conversion and repentance to envelop our lives so that new life might spring forth. We gather with our communities to pray. We fast so our bodies and spirits may understand this as sacred time. We give alms so we can recognize our solidarity with one another and all God's people. God promises life from death. Our call this Lent is to believe it is true.

The Roman Missal

IN Lent, most of us give up some good things, and in the liturgy we do the same. We give up the Gloria, our joyful song of praise, except on the Solemnities of Saint Joseph, Spouse of the Blessed Virgin Mary (March 19) and the Annunciation of the Lord (March 25; which is moved to Easter Time this year). And we give up the Alleluia without any exception at all: "From the beginning of Lent until the Paschal Vigil, 'Alleluia' is to be omitted in all celebrations, even on solemnities and feasts" (*Paschale Solemnitatis*, 18).

In Rome, the Alleluia (the word means "praise God") was at first sung only on Easter. And though eventually it became a regular part of the liturgy, it retained its Easter character, and was therefore omitted during Lent. A medieval liturgist by the name of Durandus found a strictly penitential meaning in the missing Alleluia: "We desist from saying Alleluia, the song chanted by the angels, because we have been excluded from the company of the angels on account of Adam's sin . . . . For as the children of Israel in an alien land hung their harps upon the willows, so we too must forget the Alleluia song in the season of sadness, of penance and bitterness of heart" (quoted in Pius Parsch, *Year of Grace*, volume 2,

p. 6). Others would argue that the Alleluia is omitted during Lent simply so that it may resound more powerfully at Easter. In any case, the omission of the Alleluia marks this liturgical time in a most powerful way. And the return of the Alleluia, this word that is a prayer all by itself, becomes an unmistakable sign of resurrection and joy at the Easter Vigil.

No specific texts are prescribed for the music accompanying the Gospel procession during Lent. Most often, parishes use an acclamation praising God's wisdom, revealed in Jesus Christ: for example, "Glory and praise to you, Lord Jesus Christ!" or "Glory to you, Word of God, Lord Jesus Christ." *By Flowing Waters: Chants for the Liturgy* provides modern English adaptations of the ancient "tracts" for Lent. The tracts, with texts drawn from the Psalms, powerfully express the Lenten themes of sorrow for sin and trust in God. A different tract is provided for each Sunday of Lent.

The Penitential Act

During Lent, the season of penance, the Penitential Act takes on a special significance. *The Roman Missal* provides three different forms for this rite with which our liturgy begins.

◆ The *Confiteor*, the "I confess," is a powerful communal confession of sin. When the *Confiteor* is prayed, the prayer of absolution follows, and then the Kyrie without invocations, which can be sung or spoken.

◆ The Penitential Act can also take the form of a litany, with invocations addressed to Christ, with the response "Lord, have mercy" or "Kyrie eleison." These invocations are not about us—our failures and shortcomings. They are about the incredible mercy of God in Jesus Christ. Seven different sets of invocations for the Penitential Act can be found in Appendix VI of *The Roman Missal*. These can be used as is, or as models for parishes to compose their own. When composing the invocations, follow the pattern of *The Roman Missal*—don't write a litany of human sins, but focus instead on God's loving action in our world.

◆ There is still another form of the Penitential Act, which is less often used. It consists of a dialogue between the priest and the people: "Have mercy on us, O Lord," to which the people respond, "For we have sinned against you." The priest says, "Show us, O Lord, your mercy," and the people add, "And grant us your salvation." The priest prays the absolution, and the Kyrie, sung or spoken, follows.

Lenten Prefaces

Nine Prefaces are provided for Lent. There are proper Prefaces for the First and Second Sundays of Lent. There are also proper Prefaces for the Third, Fourth, and Fifth Sundays of Lent, specific to the Gospel narratives of the woman of Samaria, the man born blind, and the raising of Lazarus. On weekdays, the priest celebrant may choose from among the four general Lenten Prefaces, which explore the meaning of the Lenten practices of fasting and self-denial. Notice that only the four general prefaces are found in the Order of Mass. In *The Roman Missal*, the proper Prefaces are found in the Proper of Time, along with the other Mass prayers for the day.

Prayer of the Faithful

Paschale Solemnitatis suggests that during Lent, the faithful be reminded of their responsibility to pray for sinners, and to include this intention in the Prayer of the Faithful (see article 14). Whether there are elect in the parish or not, it is also good to pray for those who, throughout the entire Church, are preparing for Baptism at the Easter Vigil.

In Appendix V, *The Roman Missal* provides two sample sets of intercessions for Lent and one for weekdays of Holy Week, which can be used as a model for the Prayers of the Faithful during this season. Notice that in the sample intercessions, the response of the people is varied—not only "Lord, hear our prayer," but also "Lord, have mercy," "Christ, hear us," "Kyrie, eleison," and "Grant this, almighty God." A distinctive response to the intercessions, whether sung or spoken, can be another way to mark Lent.

The Lectionary for Mass

HAVE you ever thought of Lent as a gift? Perhaps gift is not the first word we associate with a liturgical time characterized by the theme of repentance and marked by practices of sacrifice and self-denial. Many of us, perhaps, go into Lent with a sense of heaviness and dread, focusing on what we "can't do" or "can't have." The forty (plus) days that stretch out before us can seem an eternity. Lent becomes a "given" to be endured rather than a "gift" that is not only very useful but that can also lead to deep joy.

Lent is a gift from the Lord given through the Church, a sign of his love. Lent's gift is time— a long time—in which to focus on, to think over, and to make any changes that are needed in our lives—as is the meaning of the Greek word, *metanoia*. We are invited to "Repent, and believe in the Gospel" when we are marked with ashes. The two (repentance and conversion) go hand in hand.

Lent's "givenness"—once a year, every year— is also gift. Luke says that Jesus was "led" by the Holy Spirit that filled him at his baptism into the desert for forty days (see 4:1–2, Gospel for the First Sunday of Lent). He also says that this was "to be tempted by the devil" (4:2). The Greek word translated as tempted also has the meaning of being proven or tried, in the sense of proving authenticity, and that is exactly what it did and was for Jesus. Truly he was the Son of God, not in a self-serving, self-exalting way, not as one hungry for power and control, but as one who loved the Lord his God with all his heart and lived by his words.

Obviously Jesus had a deep knowledge of Scripture for he responds to each temptation from the devil with a word from Scripture. We, too, must strive for a deep knowledge of Scripture so that we, too, can live by the very Word that comes from the mouth of God. The Lectionary readings for Mass are an excellent place to begin. Can we hear "The word of the Lord" addressed to each one of us personally? It is.

"I will lead her into the wilderness / and speak persuasively to her," says God of Israel, of Jesus and of each one of us (Hosea 2:16) Lent is meant to be a sort of desert time. If you've ever been in a desert, you know its starkness and barrenness; you know the intensity of its silence. There is little distraction. It is a place where one easily comes face-to-face with oneself—and with God.

Lent is a time when God speaks to our hearts. "Come, now, let us set things right" (Isaiah 1:18, Tuesday of the Second Week in Lent). Let us set right not only the wrongs we have done but the good we have failed to do. Let us set right the things we have neglected. Our standard is always the Word of God, what God commands and calls us to be and do—above all in the Gospels.

On weekdays, the First Reading—always from the Old Testament during Lent—and the Gospel are closely connected. So, too, is the Responsorial Psalm, an often neglected part of the Liturgy of the Word. See yourself as the one called to conversion and repentance—you are. See yourself as the one in need of healing—you are. See yourself as the one who receives Jesus' healing touch—you can. See yourself as the one whom Jesus forgives—you are.

Beginning with the fourth week, the Gospel accounts are always from John, whose emphasis is very different from that found in Matthew, Mark, and Luke. We hear clearly how Jesus was sent from heaven to do the works of the Father; and of how the Father was at work in him. We hear of the healings Jesus performed; these are signs that manifest his glory and reveal his divinity. We hear of the growing controversy between Jesus and the Jewish religious leaders as we draw closer to the Triduum. Sadly, they were unable to hear and believe the words that Jesus spoke. They could not believe that this was God's chosen Son (Luke 9:35, Gospel for the Second Sunday of Lent).

The First Readings on the Sundays of Lent highlight key moments in salvation history. We hear a bit of an overview on the first Sunday, almost a summary of Israel's early history from the patriarchs to the exodus and settlement in the land. We backtrack a bit with the story of God's covenant with Abraham on the second Sunday, the call of Moses on the third, and the first celebration of Passover in the Promised Land on the fourth. On the fifth Sunday we hear God's promise of deliverance and a new creation to his people exiled in Babylon. The Second Reading—with themes of faith, repentance, and Baptism—is often related to the First Reading during Lent.

God's patience with his sinful people and his desire for their lives to bear good fruit comes to the fore in the Gospel for the Third Sunday of Lent this year. On the fourth, there is the beautiful story of the loving father who so joyfully welcomes his prodigal son home. On the fifth Sunday, we see Jesus confront the scribes and Pharisees with their own hypocrisy and his refusal to condemn the sinful woman. Jesus came to bring the message of God's loving forgiveness, not condemnation.

On the Third, Fourth, and Fifth Sundays of Lent, the readings for Year A may be used when there are catechumens present. These readings emphasize the baptismal themes of living water, light, and new life. The glory that Jesus revealed when he was transfigured before his disciples (Gospel for the second Sunday) is the glory for which we are destined as his beloved sons and daughters.

At the procession with palms (or greens from our own gardens and lawns!) on Palm Sunday, we hear the account of Jesus' entry into Jerusalem from the Gospel according to Luke. The people jubilantly proclaim Jesus' kingship. Note the objections of some of the Pharisees here as well. The Gospel during the Eucharist is the Passion narrative from Luke. Notice how Jesus' ministry of teaching, healing, and forgiving continues until the very end of his life and the trusting words he prays from Psalm 31 at the moment of his death—dying, as having lived, by the word of the Lord.

Our First Reading on Palm Sunday is one of the four "Suffering Servant" texts from the prophet Isaiah (Isaiah 50:4–7). In the course of the week, we will hear the other three (Isaiah 42:1–7; 49:1–6; 52:13–53:12). In Isaiah's day, these texts could have referred to the prophet himself or to the Israelite nation as a whole. Christians, however, understand them as fulfilled in Jesus, the Servant of God, whose suffering and Death brought healing and life to others.

Open yourself to this healing and new life this Lent. Believe that these are offered to you. They are. These are Lent's gifts. Listen with your heart. Open yourself to the joy of the experience of forgiveness—the forgiveness of God, forgiveness received from another person, forgiveness given to another person. All are experiences of the new creation God promises. All take us further along on the lifelong journey of conversion, of becoming who God has created us to be: beloved and chosen sons and daughters.

Children's Liturgy of the Word

LENT encourages us to examine our lives, to realize our shortcomings, and to change from within. The forty (plus) days of Lent extend from Ash Wednesday until the Evening Mass of the Lord's Supper on Holy Thursday. It has traditionally been recognized as a time of formation and renewal for Christians. Those already baptized are called to renew themselves in the image of Christ through prayer, fasting, penance, and acts of charity—to prepare to renew their baptismal promises at Easter. The elect, adults and children of catechetical age preparing for Baptism,

use this liturgical time of preparation as a time of purification and enlightenment, a time of retreat and prayer to make a strong commitment to full initiation, which is celebrated at the Easter Vigil.

Early in the history of the Church, Lent became the time of preparation for Baptism. The emphasis was on conversion. As the Sacrament of Penance developed in history, Lent also became a time of reconciliation for those who had sinned. The emphasis was on forgiveness. Today, both elements are present in the Church's observance. The liturgies of Lent invite us to conversion of heart. They call us to prepare for Baptism or the renewal of baptismal promises. They also proclaim God's forgiveness.

Readings

During Lent, parishes in which there is an active Catechumenate often use the readings from Year A, as suggested in the *Rite of Christian Initiation of Adults*. The elect, the unbaptized who will be celebrating the Sacraments of Initiation at the Easter Vigil, participate in the rites of scrutiny, usually celebrated on the Third, Fourth, and Fifth Sundays of Lent. In these rites, the elect are called to scrutinize their own lives through reflection on the Gospel stories of the Samaritan woman, the man born blind, and the raising of Lazarus. Through reflection and celebration, they and the assembly are called to look to the Risen Christ who promises living water, light for the world, and power over death to root out and exorcise anything that stands between them and their commitment to Jesus and the Church.

Other parishes will choose to proclaim the readings from Year C, which call us to listen and respond to God's voice, find our way back from sin, and ask God's forgiveness. Unlike other liturgical times, all three readings have been chosen to relate to each other with a common theme.

Be sure to check with the parish liturgy director to find out which readings are being used. The Gospel reading for Palm Sunday of the Passion of the Lord is very long, especially for younger children. Having several people narrate it or dramatize it is a good idea.

Environment

Lent is a time of retreat. Signs of festivity that are normally part of the Sunday liturgy, such as the Gloria and Alleluia, are set aside. The environment for worship is simple and sparse. During Lent, we rediscover the holy and place it at the center of our lives. The liturgical color for the season is violet, the color of repentance. Use violet banners and cloths to decorate the worship space. The primary symbol to highlight in the worship space is the crucifix. Another thing to add to your environment, since this is a time of reflection, is some periods of silence, for example, at the beginning of worship to center children on the meaning of Lent, before some of the prayers, or during the Homily/reflection.

Music

Check with the music or liturgy director to find out what music will be used during the Lenten liturgies. Do not forget that live music is preferable. Ask the parish music or choir director if it is possible to get a parish musician either to lead children or to teach them unfamiliar music. If you are uncomfortable leading song, use a recording to assist the children. Psalm refrains are good choices for children. They learn them quickly and tend to remember and repeat them later.

The Saints

"THE weekdays of Lent have precedence over obligatory memorials" (*Paschale Solemnitatis*, 11). This means that during Lent, memorials of the saints are, in general, observed as commemorations. The Collect for the saint's day may be used, but the other prayers and the readings are taken from the Lenten weekday; either the Lenten Preface or the appropriate Preface for the saint may be used. Still another option is to use the readings and prayers of the Lenten weekday, but to incorporate the Collect for the saint as the conclusion of the Prayer of the Faithful. The Saturday memorial of the Blessed Virgin Mary is not permitted during Lent.

The only exception to this rule comes with feasts and solemnities—there is one of each during Lent this year. On February 22, we observe the Feast of the Chair of Saint Peter the Apostle. And on March 19, we observe the Solemnity of Saint Joseph, Spouse of the Blessed Virgin Mary. The Solemnity of the Annunciation of the Lord on March 25 falls during Holy Week. That means that it is not observed until after the Octave of Easter—this year, the Annunciation will be celebrated on Monday, April 8.

In addition to these obligatory observances, Lent includes many optional memorials of the saints. You may choose to omit these observances entirely in order to focus on the readings and prayers of the Lenten weekdays, which are so rich in meaning. But you may also find that the observances of the saints enhance the meaning of Lent: they are the perfect guides for this spiritual journey.

The Liturgy of the Hours

DISCIPLESHIP is about relationship. In Baptism, Christians become disciples because they are marked with the Sign of the Cross—the sign of the triune God who is Father, Son, and Holy Spirit. Disciples enter communion with God and with the Church in Baptism. And Lent is the time when disciples focus on their relationship with God and with the Church. We turn away from all that is evil (renounce sin and Satan) in order to turn ever more closely to God. This is the path of discipleship, a path of growing in holiness that God calls us to.

Once again, progressive solemnity provides a good method for preparing the Liturgy of the Hours for Lent. Keep the music simple, perhaps setting the Psalms to chant. The liturgical assembly could chant the Psalms antiphonally, that is, with side one doing the first section of the Psalm and then side two doing the second section, alternating between the two sides to the end of the Psalm. If the chant is well known, if could even be done a cappella. If less well known, it might be advantageous to have the cantor chant the first section and the people chant the second section and so forth. Again, congregational size will affect the method.

The opening song could likewise be sung unaccompanied. Many well-known hymns for Lent are appropriate to engage the participation of the people. If the parish has been celebrating the Liturgy of the Hours for many years now, and the congregation is familiar with the celebration, consider having seasonal canticles. Perhaps Ruth Duck's text to for the Benedictus or Magnificat (GIA Publications) could be used during Lent since they are familiar tunes that can be sung unaccompanied. Whereas, Bernadette Farrell's

texts for the Benedictus and Magnificat (OCP) are better suited to Christmas Time and Easter Time since they lend themselves to accompaniment. Finally, Alan Hommerding's text for these same tunes (WLP) offers further versions for use at other times of the liturgical year.

Keep everything simple and reflective for Lent. Use incense on the penitential Psalms well as during the canticles. The cantor could chant the intercessions, and the assembly could respond with a simple refrain. This format could be seasonal. The elect have three scrutinies on the Third, Fourth, and Fifth Sundays of Lent. These scrutinies have separate litanies that mirror intercessions, which are themselves litanies. Chanting the same tune for both the litanies and the intercessions would strengthen the connection.

The Rite of Christian Initiation of Adults

LENT has traditionally been recognized as a time of formation and renewal for Christians. Since the restoration of the catechumenate after the Second Vatican Council, Lent has become the season of purification and enlightenment for the elect and the whole assembly. The faithful prepare to renew their baptismal promises at Easter. The elect, adults and children of catechetical age, prepare for full initiation. The RCIA refers to this period as a time of Purification and Enlightenment, a time "consisting more in interior reflection than in catechetical instruction" (RCIA, 139).

Liturgical Catechesis

If at all possible, celebrate all three scrutinies with the children who will be fully initiated at Easter. Encourage collaboration with the liturgy director, music director, and adult RCIA coordinator to celebrate the scrutinies in the midst of the Sunday assembly with the adult elect. It is a much more visible sign to the elect and the assembly that initiation is a communal, public experience.

As mentioned in Advent (see page 6), there are three different starting points for liturgical catechesis: the preparation, the experience of the liturgical celebration, and the reflection back on the experience. Here are some suggestions for preparing and reflecting with children on the scrutinies:

- Do all preparations for the scrutinies in the context of a celebration of the Word (see outline in the RCIA, 86–89)
- Use the First Readings from Year A for each preparation. It is helpful to include parents, sponsors, and godparents in the preparation session.
- For all preparations, give a short reflection followed by a conversation and discussion.

The Scrutinies

- BACKGROUND FOR PREPARATION: The scrutinies are not a public confession of sins. To *scrutinize* means "to take a hard look at." In some ways, the liturgical fullness of a scrutiny might be understood as a reflection on those evils or sins that are bigger than the individual and are expressed in certain behaviors of individuals or communities. For example, the pervasive evil of greed keeps millions of people in the world homeless while millions of others own more than one home or are living in homes that are far more spacious than they need. The same evil may cause a child to refuse to share. A preparation session helps children and their families identify what evils they are powerless over and that hold them back from living life as a follower of Jesus. The actual celebration of the scrutinies names those evils in the litany and then celebrates an exorcism in which the power of the Risen Christ to overcome those evils is prayed for with confidence.

- IF your parish adapts the litany from the rite, it is very helpful if the people involved in the adaptation can be present at the reflection or, if they cannot be, that what is discussed at the reflection is communicated to them for inclusion in the liturgy.

Questions for Preparation Sessions

- What does it feel like to be thirsty? What do you "long for" when you are thirsty? What might be some things besides water that people long for in their hearts? What keeps us and others from getting what we long for? What are some obstacles to attaining peace in our homes or in the world; to having friends; to sharing with others?

- Have you ever been in the dark? What is that like? What happens when the light goes on? What changed when you could see? What keeps us from seeing that we should be kind to others, or help those in need, or understand others when they disagree with us?

- What is it like to be really sick? What helps you feel better? What is it like to be sad, to be lonely? Can you think of some things that hold us back from helping people who are sick, sad, or lonely?

Reflection

Gather children after each scrutiny and ask them to share what they remember about the rite. What did they see or hear? Did they learn anything about Jesus or the Church? Using their responses, make connections to the promises and power of Jesus to overcome sin and evil.

The Sacraments of Initiation

FOR most parishes preparation for first Holy Communion and Confirmation is more intense during Lent. Often the celebration of these sacraments occurs during Easter Time. Previously, Lenten observances were rigorous, but tended to be individualistic, and lacked a meaningful context. Today the emphasis of Lent is more communal, liturgical, and contextual.

We have become more aware that Lent is a time of retreat. Signs of festivity that are normally part of the Sunday liturgy, such as the Gloria and the Alleluia, are set aside. The environment for worship is simple and spare. Lent is the time to rediscover the holy and place it at the center of our lives.

Parishes draw more attention to the Lenten Scripture readings, and often highlight the experience of the elect, who are preparing to celebrate the Sacraments of Initiation.

The following are suggestions to integrate the richness of Lent with the sacramental preparation:

- In all catechetical preparation sessions with children and adults, begin with a reflection on the previous Sunday's readings. Using one of the readings, do the following three steps:

(1.) Proclaim the Word.

(2.) Ask the question, "What word or image in the reading touched you or stood out for you?" Do a simple short exegesis of the reading.

(3.) Ask the question, "What does this reading say to you about what God may be calling you or the community of the Church to do or change?" Note that younger children will relate more with the personal than the communal.

- Together with the liturgy and music directors plan a Lenten retreat day for all young people preparing for sacramental initiation and parents preparing for infant Baptism. Invite parishioners and family members to attend. Use themes such as "Called to Change and Grow," "Forgiveness," or "The Lenten Journey." Pay attention to setting a prayerful environment with time for group interaction, individual reflection, and prayerful, reflective Lenten music.

◆ If there are elect, plan for the older Confirmation candidates to attend one of the scrutinies together and meet afterward to talk about their responses to it. Emphasize that the purpose of the scrutiny is to take a hard look at the evils, personal and communal, that affect the lives of people today and to proclaim that as a result of Jesus's dying and rising the power of evil is broken. Explain that through active membership in the Church, especially celebrating the sacraments, we claim that power.

◆ Infants are usually not baptized at the Easter Vigil, but the practice of infant Baptism at the Easter Sunday Masses is most appropriate and enhances the celebration. Invite parents who are preparing for their infant's Baptism to choose one of those Masses to celebrate the sacrament with the community.

The Rite of Penance

DURING Lent, it is common to prepare Form II of the *Rite of Penance*: Rite of Reconciliation of Several Penitents with Individual Confession and Absolution. Schedules for confessions and communal celebrations should be arranged in each parish and among parishes, and well publicized, so that all may be served adequately. Ideally, parishioners should celebrate the Sacrament of Penance before the Sacred Paschal Triduum begins. Although "it is fitting that the lenten season should be concluded, both for the individual Christian as well as for the whole Christian community, with a penitential celebration, . . . these celebrations, however, should take place before the Easter Triduum and should not immediately precede the evening Mass of the Lord's Supper" (*Paschale Solemnitatis*, 37). There are sample penitential services in Appendix II of the rite that are excellent. Some are non-sacramental and may help in the preparation for the celebration of the sacrament, for RCIA candidates, for example. They inculcate a penitential spirit and help form the conscience.

The Pastoral Care of the Sick

HIGHLY recommended is a visit to the sick and homebound on Ash Wednesday to share already blessed ashes. There is a simple order in the *Book of Blessings*, chapter 52. A priest, deacon, or lay minister may distribute ashes, but the lay minister excludes the prayer of blessing. The lay minister should bring already blessed ashes.

Because of Lent it seems especially appropriate to offer the Sacrament of Reconciliation to those who are ill or homebound. The ministers of care in the parish should ask those they visit if they'd like a priest to come and celebrate the sacrament with them. The non-sacramental penance service called "The Time of Sickness is a Time of Grace" (RP, Appendix II, VI) may be useful if there is no priest to offer sacramental absolution, since it can be led by a deacon or lay minister.

One of the signs that the reign of God is at hand was Jesus's many healings. Another sign often linked to healing was Jesus's forgiveness of sin. Our sacraments of Anointing and Reconciliation lovingly point to God's unlimited care for us and celebrate our belief in this love and mercy. So, this is a good time to celebrate the Sacrament of Anointing of the Sick, either at Mass or in a service outside of Mass.

If the sacrament is celebrated at Mass, the rite suggests the priest be sure those seeking anointing have the opportunity to celebrate the Sacrament of Reconciliation ahead of time (PCS, 133). If anointing takes place outside of Mass, and "if it is necessary for the sick person to confess, . . . this takes the place of the penitential rite" (PCS, 113).

This may be a good time to examine how our ministers of care are formed. Can they lead other prayer services (see below)? Do they know where to get resources to assist them? Do staff members know how to answer questions about suffering and death? Do they speak the Church's teachings clearly?

The Rite of Marriage

IF couples are seeking to be married at a Mass there are restrictions in Lent as in Advent. On Saturday evening, on Sunday, or on a solemnity (for example, March 19, the Solemnity of Saint Joseph), the Mass of the day is used, but one of the readings from the *Rite of Marriage* may be chosen. Even if the wedding is at another time, and the readings and prayers can be from the wedding Mass, the parish environment should be respected and the music should be in keeping with the liturgical time. Interestingly, even in Lent, white vestments are worn if a wedding is celebrated.

If the wedding is celebrated outside of Mass the usual prayers and readings may be taken from the *Rite of Marriage*. However, Catholic couples should be encouraged to celebrate their covenant at a Mass which is considered the norm for them.

The Order of Christian Funerals

A funeral Mass may not be celebrated on the Sundays of Lent (see OCF, 178). The liturgical color is usually white since we believe the funeral Mass or the service outside of Mass is an expression of our "Easter hope" (OCF, 177) in the Resurrection. The pall we lay is a reminder of the white garment received at Baptism. Violet or black vestments may also be worn (see OCF, 39).

Families may be comforted by the idea that their loved one's "Lent" is now over and we believe and pray that the promise of their Baptism is at hand for them.

The Book of Blessings

CHAPTER 52 of the *Book of Blessings* contains the Order for the Blessing and Distribution of Ashes (Ash Wednesday). You might integrate this blessing into a classroom prayer to highlight the blessing and give children a more intimate participation in the distribution of ashes. Each individual classroom could celebrate this service with the teacher or an older child leading. If a layperson leads the service, previously blessed ashes are used and the blessing prayer is omitted.

Saint Joseph (honored with a solemnity on March 19) is a beloved saint in many cultures, and the tradition of gathering food for or feeding the poor at a Saint Joseph's Table is appropriate for Lent. Some parishes schedule this blessing during the weekend so more people can participate. The tradition includes a blessing with the beautiful Litany of Saint Joseph. Some parishes use this as a community-building event and share some of the food, but the intent is to share most of the blessed food with the poor. The order of service for this blessing is found in chapter 53.

Catholic Household Blessings & Prayers has a blessing of a "Place of Prayer" in the home during Lent and a blessing for the "Placing of Palms in the Home." Lent might be a good time to encourage households to establish a permanent prayer space in the home. It could be a shelf or a table where the family can gather. The space can have a cloth of liturgical color, a Bible, a candle, and any other natural or religious items that seem appropriate.

The Liturgical Environment

The Nature of the Liturgical Time

Lent is a time of contrasts, opposites, and paradox. As we move through the days of Lent we encounter the biblical geographies of the Sunday Gospel, the images of the Church's traditions, and the spiritual exercises that engage our bodies and our hearts.

Consider the 'geography' of Lent: the desert, the mountain, the site of Jacob's well, the neighborhood of the man born blind, the tomb of Lazarus, the upper room, the entry into Jerusalem, Golgotha, the burial place of Jesus, and finally the empty tomb. All of these places have their unique story that in turn shapes the spirituality of those who, in this time, walk with the Lord. And consider the images of Lent: fasting and feasting, foreheads marked with ashes and feet washed with tenderness, thirst for water and immersion into water, blindness and new sight, darkness and the Light of the World, dying and rising.

These seeming opposites invite us into a an ever-deeper understanding of God's intervention in human life through Jesus Christ. And consider the postures and exercises of Lent: prayer, fasting, and almsgiving, "making the stations" and seeking forgiveness, looking within our hearts, and reaching out to others. These are the practices of those on the journey of conversion.

The geography of Lent, the images of our tradition, and the exercises of both our personal Lenten journey and that of the community of believers are the source of inspiration for those responsible for the liturgical environment for this liturgical time.

A Pastoral Insight

Lent could be called a retreat for the whole Church. It is a time of much reflection: on our personal response to the Lord's call to discipleship (which we have heard in the Sunday Gospel since Christmas Time); on our response as a community of believers to the needs of our brothers and sisters; on our acceptance or non-acceptance of the call to a new conversion; and for the elect, a serious reflection on their intent to celebrate the Sacraments of Initiation during the Easter Vigil. These are retreat-like activities: taken sincerely into our hearts and expressed in our actions, they will give us a contrite heart and a renewed spirit, ready to exalt in the joy and grace of the Resurrection.

Perhaps we could transfer this analogy to the liturgical environment by letting the worship space undergo a kind of retreat, a "fasting" from the usual decorations and arrangements that often tend to add a festive (but we hope not busy) atmosphere. This does not necessarily mean bare or boring spaces, but rather simpler elements that underline the "moderation" that is associated with the tone and tenor of Lent.

Practical Suggestions

◆ This is the time to make sure that any accumulated clutter is removed; liturgical "house-cleaning" is always a good idea at the beginning of Lent.

◆ The liturgical color for Lent is violet, usually understood to be a deeper color than the violet of Advent. One guide to the difference is to choose the violet for Lent that works with red; the violet for Advent is softer, with a blue undertone.

◆ There are of course many hues of violet that would be suitable. When using fabrics and vesture it's best if they coordinate, so think of using accent material

that is not always a solid color. Textile hangings and swags with patterns and other colors that go with the dominant violet tone are appropriate.

◆ Altar vesture: although the main altar cloth is always white, it is appropriate to use other colored fabric (in this case violet) as an accent piece. The white altar cloth need not cover the entire altar, as long as it covers the top portion.

◆ The covering of statues and crosses in the church with violet draping is a custom in some parishes. This is not required, but if it is done, there isn't any particular rubric on how it is done. There was a time when it was done for the last two weeks of Lent (Passiontide) or for all of Lent. If this is a custom in the parish, some catechesis (perhaps an explanation in the bulletin) would be helpful. The draping is removed from the crosses on Good Friday and then from the statues before the beginning of the Easter Vigil. In each case the removal of the draping is carried out apart from the liturgy.

◆ In many parishes there are scheduled devotions for the Stations of the Cross. This devotion is a journey from one station to the next, and it would be good to mark that journey with some environment pieces. The Stations don't need to be "decorated," but a small branch with a fabric swag could be placed at certain ones, special lighting could be arranged, or candles (floor standing ones if available) could be located at each station and lighted as the procession moves from one to the next.

◆ Since the celebration of the Sacrament of Reconciliation is a more common practice during Lent than other times of the year, consider placing some environment elements in or near these rooms. Such items as artwork that depicts a biblical scene of forgiveness; a significant cross placed on the interior wall of the room; an arrangement (in scale) that echoes the arrangements in the larger space. When the parish has a communal celebration of the Sacrament of Reconciliation, there are usually additional places for confession. These places can be "marked" by placing a large candle on a pedestal, draping a violet pendant over the pedestal, and a small table placed nearby with an open Bible on it.

◆ The cross is undoubtedly one of the main symbols of Lent. If the main sanctuary cross of the church cannot be removed, then consider placing a cross of significant size elsewhere in the church, for example, in the gathering area, or at a midway point of the center aisle. In these locations everyone encounters the cross as they enter and leave the space and are reminded of the central meaning of the Cross of Christ in our lives. If possible, this should be the cross that is carried in procession and used for the gesture of veneration on Good Friday.

◆ A recent custom in some parishes during Lent has been to empty the baptismal font and place sand, stones, or other objects (like cactus plants) in it. This simply should not be done. The baptismal font is a primary liturgical furnishing and is intended to hold the water for the Sacrament of Baptism. It is first and always a vessel for the waters of Baptism; it is never anything else, not even during Lent. Although the parish may not celebrate the Sacrament of Baptism during Lent (a practice recommended by the pastoral notes in the rites of initiation), the water should still be available for all those who bless themselves as they enter and leave the liturgical space, and for the gesture of blessing the body for the funeral liturgy. The font can be emptied during Holy Week for the necessary and practical purpose of cleaning, after which fresh water is immediately added for the celebration of Baptisms at the Easter Vigil.

◆ Lent is a good time to add some decorative items like banners and door swags to the exterior of the church; this calls attention to a new liturgical time, and even as the faithful move from the parking lot to the portals of the church they are reminded that the whole Church is embarking on a different part of its journey of faith, a time of metanoia.

◆ It is a given that the liturgies of Holy Week attract many visitors to our churches. One of the most important gestures from the parish is making sure that hospitality is extended to all. For the liturgical environment that means ensuring there are enough palms for everybody. If the parish prints worship aids for the liturgies of Holy Week, then there should be enough for everybody; nothing says "we're glad you have joined us" more than making sure everyone has whatever they need to participate.

◆ The liturgical color for Palm Sunday is red. Although most of the environment for Lent is still in place, red accents can be added with some fresh flower arrangements and fabric swags. These additions need not be very elaborate and can be left in place, and with careful planning, can be incorporated into the environment for Holy Thursday.

◆ If the blessing of the palms and the proclamation of the first Gospel take place in a space apart from the main body of the church (as the ritual suggests), then some items can be arranged in this space. The use of large urns to hold the palm branches for distribution looks better than cardboard boxes; some fabric hangings around the space work well; and the use of brightly colored streamers can be incorporated into the procession, especially if it begins outside the entrance of the church.

◆ For the proclamation of the Passion both today and for Good Friday, make sure that all the lectors and readers have suitable books for their script; avoid the use of office binders and file folders. It is important that the sound system be checked ahead of time; the solemn proclamation of the Passion account is intended (as with all Scripture readings) to be heard by everyone.

◆ In addition to a welcoming environment as people gather for the first liturgy of Palm Sunday, the liturgical environment committee could assist the ushers in making sure that the space is neat and ready for every liturgy.

For more information about Holy Week, refer to pages 25–30.

The Liturgical Music

THE Gloria is not said or sung (except on the Solemnity of Saint Joseph). We fast from the Alleluia and use alternative refrains. The playing of the organ and other musical instruments is allowed only to support the singing.

Do not be afraid to integrate more silence into your Lenten liturgies. Aside from the obvious parts of the liturgy, you might consider omitting the closing song during Lent. Liturgical theologian Anthony Ruff once made an interesting point about silence. There is a difference between easy and uneasy silence. Uneasy silence happens before something, like waiting for a reader to reach the ambo, or a musician to get to the right page. Easy silence is the reflective silence that takes place after something has happened.

For many parishes it is easy to fall into the "four hymn syndrome" and use common hymns for entrance, offertory, Communion, and recessional singing. But if one looks a little more closely at the documents, there is another form of music that is frequently overlooked. I am referring to the antiphon, or the Introit, as it is often called. Over the last few years, composers have been working with them more again, and now might be a good time to add them to your program. WLP is publishing Paul French's "Lenten Entrance Rite." It begins with a call and response version of the Introit, and then works into Alan Hommerding's text "From Ashes to the Living Font," but couples it with "Land of Rest" rather than "St. Flavian," as Hommerding did originally. In this day of tight budgets, and limited time, it is an octavo that will work well through all three years of the entire Lenten cycle.

GIA has published "To You My Eyes are Turned," a Lenten Introit by Delores Dufner and

Lynn Trapp, as well as a number of other individual Introit octavos for the year.

For the ultimate collection, WLP has "Introit Hymns for the Church Year" which features one hundred hymns compiled and written by Christoph Tieze. Each antiphon and Psalm is set to a common metrical hymn, and four-part harmony is provided.

If you are looking for other good multipurpose Lenten pieces, here are some suggestions. GIA has published "Merciful God: A Ritual Song for Lent," which offers the same melody to "Sign Us with Ashes," "Gather Your People," or "Feed us and Guide Us." Tony Alonso and Mary Louise Bringle teamed up for that project.

GIA is offering a beautiful collection entitled "Choral Essentials for Lent" that offers 15 octavos for about a dollar a piece, and would be a very economical way to gain a whole new library in one book. If your budget is tight, it is the type of tangible resource you could ask someone to donate money for, or encourage choral members to purchase their own copies.

If you are working with a Latino community, OCP's *De La Cruz a la Gloria* by Lourdes Montgomery offers Spanish-language music for Lent and Easter Time, from Ash Wednesday through Pentecost. And Cyprian Consiglio's "Awake At Last: Liturgical Songs for Dying and Rising" calls on elements of world music and multiple cultures as only Consiglio can do. As the description suggests, it offers 16 hymns, Psalms, Gospel Acclamations, and more for liturgies throughout Lent, Easter Time, and Pentecost. Intended for contemporary liturgical ensembles, many songs feature arrangements for piano, guitar, oboe, and percussion.

Liturgical Ministers

THERE are many "RCIA moments" in Lent. Be sure ministers know in advance what is happening when, and if anything different is expected of them. Similarly, provide ministers with information about Holy Week, ministry rehearsal times, and a ministry schedule early on. Your efforts will be appreciated.

Liturgists, priests, RCIA leaders, or those involved in liturgy preparation need to remember that not everybody lives in the world of liturgy full time. It is easy to assume your ministers know things that they don't. Or, just because you taught it to the community three years ago doesn't mean there haven't come many new ministers in that time.

Consider an evening with a short class or "Q and A" on the liturgical time, and a simple social or time of prayer. Sometimes ministers are so busy helping others pray that their own prayer lives suffer. Help them enter into the Lenten experience. It could be helpful for you as liturgical leader as well.

Create a road map or diagrams for any processions or rituals that may be taking place. People have many different learning styles. If you don't have a rehearsal scheduled, send out this information early as an e-mail with an attached PDF. If you have a video from another year, send it or attach a link to it as well.

This may be a good time of year to have a volunteer call and check in with all ministers and remove any who no longer wish to be involved in ministry. Similarly, one can update e-mail lists and phone numbers.

It would also be a good time to explore some of the newer social communication tools to reach your ministers.

Devotions and Sacramentals

FOR many, devotional prayer is a natural path for this journey. The traditional elements of prayer, fasting, and almsgiving could all be seen as spiritual exercises that take place in our daily lives—manifested when we attend liturgies and then take that message out into our community and the world. As DPPL 125 notes: "the Christian faithful, during Lent, are clearly conscious of the need to turn the mind toward those realities which really count, which require Gospel commitment and integrity of life which, through self-denial of those things which are superfluous, are translated into good works and solidarity with the poor and the needy."

Obviously, the Cross is a source of prayer throughout Lent. The Stations of the Cross is a powerful devotion that may be prayed privately or as a group. There are numerous versions. LTP publishes three: *The Way of the Cross: Traditional*

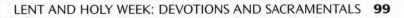

Jerusalem Stations, The Way of the Cross: Scriptural Version, and *The Way of the Cross: Women of the Gospels.* A leader's edition is available as well.

While speaking of the Advent crib, we noted the difference between remembering and reenacting. The Passion is another place where we need to keep this in mind. Within the liturgy, the Passion is to be proclaimed. But elsewhere it is acceptable to "dramatize" the Passion. Like children's "Living Stations," these dramatizations have a purpose and a place as long as they are outside the liturgy. This is an area you may need to educate your congregation about.

The palms blessed at the Palm Sunday liturgy are to be taken home, placed in the house, and displayed throughout the year. Sometimes people take extra palms and weave them, but it is important for them to realize these are not to be sold, or discarded rashly, as the palms have been blessed and are considered sacramental. Perhaps you may want to have a "palm party" at some point during the year and collect the old palms that are no longer in use. These palms will then be burned for next year's distribution of ashes.

The Parish and the Home

FAMILIES who attend Ash Wednesday services can talk afterward about the meaning of the mark on their foreheads. How do we turn from sin and trust the Good News? How are we specially claimed for Christ, with his symbol on our skins? What negative habits could we shed, to be reborn fresh at Easter Time? How can we enter fully into the springtime spirit of this time?

Families should decide together how to adapt to their own circumstances the traditional practices of prayer, fasting, and almsgiving. They might begin by setting aside more quiet time, perhaps an hour after dinner. Prayer then can include thoughtful reading of Scripture, a spiritual book or magazine, or children's stories about heroes like the saints. It's also a good time to try other prayer forms such as daily Mass, *lectio divina*, centering prayer, a litany or Rosary, Stations of the Cross, or listening to religious music.

A prayer corner could include a table covered with violet fabric. On it, place a Bible, crucifix, cactus plant or bare branch, and candle. Add other Lenten symbols such as stones, an ark (LTP makes one called *Forty Days and Forty Nights* from cardboard with windows to open each day), bowl of water, and during Holy Week, palm branches, a loaf of bread, cup of wine, hammer and nails, and a figure or picture of a rooster (who crowed at Peter's denial). The symbols speak loudly and clearly, not requiring much verbal explanation.

One Catholic custom for almsgiving is Operation Rice Bowl. See Catholic Relief Services, http://orb.crs.org, or call 1-800-608-5978. Families might also want to research the websites of causes they feel especially close to, such as: the Mercy Corps www.mercycorps.org; Catholic Charities, www.catholiccharitiesusa.org; Maryknoll, www.maryknoll.org; Pax Christi, www.paxchristiusa.org; Campaign for Human Development, www.usccb.org/cchd/; or Homeboy Industries, www.homeboy-industries.org, which helps Los Angeles gang members get jobs and leave the gangs. Or divide it up so that each family member researches one cause, then reports to the others, so that all can decide where to donate their Lenten alms.

Fasting is one way to contribute to almsgiving. By preparing simpler meals, such as soup and bread, or having frequent meatless meals, the savings can go into a special "pot," box, or envelope for the poor. Families should at the same time discuss how many people of the world are hungry, while North Americans often overeat. It's also heartening to fast from wasting time, negative comments, too much time on computer or TV. With children, it's important to make Lenten practices tangible and concrete. Spanish-speaking people make a scorpion from black paper, with eight legs to represent the six weeks of Lent, Ash Wednesday, and Holy Saturday. Each week, they tear off a leg which symbolizes another bad habit they've conquered. Finally, what's left is thrown into the Easter Vigil bonfire.

From the Scriptures of Lent, draw symbols on cardboard, foam core, or felt that can be hung onto a bare branch; for instance, a lion (for Daniel in the lion's den), an ark (for Noah, his family, and the animals), the rainbow, a crown (Queen Esther), a whale (Jonah), a burning bush (Moses), the father welcoming the prodigal son home, a mountain (Transfiguration), and a well (the Samaritan woman).

Mass Texts

- ◆ SAMPLE TEXT FOR THE PRAYER
  OF THE FAITHFUL

*Additional texts are found in Appendix V
of* The Roman Missal

Celebrant:

We have set out with Jesus, our King, on his
journey to Jerusalem. In confidence and love,
we pray.

Deacon/Lector/Reader:

That the Church throughout the world may be
renewed by the celebration of the Passion,
Death, and Resurrection of Christ, we pray:

That there may be peace in every nation, every
family, and every human heart, we pray:

That those preparing for Baptism may know the
peace of Christ in their hearts, we pray:

That those who are persecuted unjustly may be
filled with courage and hope, we pray:

That all the dead, [especially N._____
and N._____], may know the
mercy of Christ, crucified for our salvation,
we pray:

Celebrant:

Lord Jesus Christ,
by your holy Cross you have redeemed the world.
Help us to take up our Cross and follow
   after you,
who live and reign for ever and ever.
Amen.

- ◆ DISMISSAL TEXT FOR CATECHUMENS

Each day of Lent brings you closer to the waters
   of Baptism
that will claim you for Christ and incorporate
   you into his holy body, the Church.

God's Word becomes richer fare during these
   days of penitence
challenging us to consider our choices and renew
   our commitments.
May your reflection on God's holy Word
deepen your conviction to surrender your whole
   life to him
and strengthen you for the mission of discipleship
   you will undertake
at the great Vigil when we celebrate
   Christ's victory
and God's incomprehensible love.

- ◆ DISMISSAL TEXT FOR CHILDREN'S LITURGY
  OF THE WORD

With the rest of our community you understand
   that we are in a special time.
Lent asks us to try harder—
to give all we can give and receive all God has
   prepared for us.
Your special time of listening to God's Word
   will help you understand
what God is asking even of your young hearts.
Go ready to listen and return ready to respond.

- ◆ DISMISSAL TEXT FOR EXTRAORDINARY
  MINISTERS OF HOLY COMMUNION

Deprived of our communal worship,
the sick and homebound thirst for the waters
   of fellowship.
In our name, go forth to bring the solace of our
   steady affection
and the refreshing waters of our abiding prayers.
May the Eucharistic bread consecrated at
   this liturgy
bring comfort and healing to those whom illness
   has kept from our company;
and may the Lenten journey we all share
bring us and them to the shores of our
   eternal home.

February
Month of the Passion of Our Lord

WED 13 #219 violet
Ash Wednesday

Orientation

Fasting during Lent is a practice of intentional interruption of our everyday routine, a practice by which we embody our renewed commitment to grow in relationship with God. By taking less food, we symbolize our utter dependence on God, Source and Author of Life. We acknowledge that despite our own efforts to live safely and comfortably, we are not ultimately in control. For this day, we put aside our own efforts and re-orient ourselves to the true Source of Life, as we begin Lent.

Lectionary for Mass

♦ FIRST READING: It is not enough to perform external rituals of repentance unless the heart is pierced by sorrow. All of Israel, even its youngest members, are called to seek mercy from the Lord.

♦ RESPONSORIAL PSALM 51: Fully aware of sinfulness, the psalmist prays for God's help and for the clean heart, which alone can see God.

♦ SECOND READING: The Word of God calls out: Be reconciled to God. Now is the favorable time, the right time! Do not fail to receive God's grace. Today is the day of salvation.

♦ GOSPEL: Prayer, fasting, and works of mercy are the traditional acts of Lenten repentance. They are not to be performed for the acclaim of others but rather done in secret, that the heavenly Father may reward us.

The Roman Missal

♦ ENTRANCE ANTIPHON: Lent begins with words of mercy: "You are merciful to all, O Lord, / and despise nothing that you have made . . . " (Wisdom 11:24). This season of repentance is a gift from a merciful God.

Because of the Distribution of Ashes later in the Mass, the Penitential Act is omitted.

The Collect for Ash Wednesday uses imagery of warfare, but this is war turned on its head. Our "campaign" is "Christian service," our enemies are "spiritual evils," and our only "weapons" are those of "self-restraint." Fasting is about more than not eating! Fasting trains us in self-control, and helps us to become masters of our desires and not be mastered by them.

♦ BLESSING OF ASHES: Two options are provided. Both are prayers that all who are marked with the ashes may find forgiveness from a merciful God after a faithful observance of Lent. The second option, with its reference to "dust," would be especially appropriate when the second formula for the distribution of ashes is used: "Remember that you are dust . . . ." There are two formulas for the distribution of ashes, both drawn from the Scriptures. The first, "Repent, and believe in the Gospel," comes from the early preaching of Jesus (Mark 1:15). At the beginning of Lent, these words which Jesus spoke to the people of Galilee as he began his saving ministry are spoken again, to us. The second option is "Remember that you are dust, and to dust you shall return" (Genesis 3:19), God's words to Adam and Eve as they were banished from the garden of Eden. We are reminded of the first disobedience of humanity as we continue our struggle against the effects of original sin in our own lives.

♦ THE Prayer over the Offerings for this first day of Lent already looks to the celebration of the Paschal Mystery. We pray that the penance and love we offer may help us to "turn away from harmful pleasures," and enable us to celebrate with devotion the Passion of Christ.

♦ PREFACE III or IV of Lent is used. Preface III focuses on the need for abstinence: by it we give God thanks, we humble ourselves, and we help others by giving to "the feeding of the poor." Preface IV emphasizes fasting, through which God strengthens us in virtue and gives us the rewards of virtue.

♦ PRAYER AFTER COMMUNION: We ask that the sacrament we have received may sustain us through our Lenten fast, "and be for us a healing remedy." The Eucharist is not only the bread of angels, but medicine for sinners. In the words of Saint Thomas Aquinas, we come "sick to the physician of life" to receive the healing he offers us in his Body and Blood.

♦ PRAYER OVER THE PEOPLE: One of the distinctive features of Lent is the Prayer over the People for each day of the season. Following the greeting "The Lord be with you," the celebrant prays this prayer with hands extended over the people. On Ash Wednesday, the prayer is for the "spirit of compunction" for our sins. Only by doing penance can we "merit the rewards" God promises to the repentant sinner.

Other Ideas

Invite your child to look for signs of the new liturgical time of Lent in your parish church. Are the decorations fewer and simpler? Ask your child to tell you where he or she sees the color violet. Note that we don't sing or recite the Gloria. How is the Gospel Acclamation different? We simplify everything during Lent so there are fewer things to distract us from following the path of the Lord. The outward signs of the liturgical time remind us to look inward for thoughts, attitudes, and behaviors that we need to change.

THU 14 #220 violet
Thursday after Ash Wednesday

Optional Memorial of Saints Cyril, Monk, and Methodius, Bishop / violet

Lectionary for Mass

◆ FIRST READING: Like Israel of old, we have a choice: life or death, blessing or curse. Are we willing to take God's Word to heart and live accordingly?

◆ RESPONSORIAL PSALM 1: Fidelity to God's law is the source of true happiness and flourishing life. The one who is faithful thrives, like a beautiful tree with deep roots and leafy branches in abundance.

◆ GOSPEL: Jesus sets the paradox before us: true life comes only through death. It was the way for him, so must it be for us.

The Roman Missal

The Collect is the perfect prayer for the beginning of Lent. We ask that God may be with us in all we do: inspiring our actions, helping them along, and bringing them to completion.

In the Prayer over the Offerings, we ask God to give us his forgiveness, so that the offerings we make may give him honor.

In the Prayer after Communion, we ask that the "heavenly gifts" we have received may bring us both forgiveness and salvation.

The Prayer over the People is a prayer that God, who made known the "ways of eternal life," will also guide his people along those ways. If the optional Memorial is observed, the prayers are drawn from the Proper of Saints. Use the Preface of Holy Pastors. Another option is to use the Collect for today's saints at the conclusion of the Prayer of the Faithful.

Today's Saints

Saints Cyril (827–869) and Methodius (815–884) were brothers bound not only by biology, but by their longing to evangelize the unenlightened heart. Their missionary zeal led them to Slavic territories where the seeds of Western Christendom had yet to be planted. At the time, the Western Church only recognized the Hebrew, Greek, and Latin languages; therefore, they were charged with the task of translating the Bible and liturgical texts into Slavonic. Because Slavonic did not have a written language, the brothers had to develop a script, which later became known as the Cyrillic alphabet, named after Saint Cyril. Shortly after his brother died, Saint Methodius was consecrated a bishop. Because Saints Cyril and Methodius are venerated in both the East and West, they are considered the patrons of ecumenism.

FRI 15 #221 violet
Friday after Ash Wednesday

Lectionary for Mass

◆ FIRST READING: God calls the people to account for their meaningless rituals of fasting and acts of penance. Though performing the externals, they have failed to obey God's commandments. Fidelity to the law's demands for justice is the sign of true repentance.

◆ RESPONSORIAL PSALM 51: The repentance God desires is conversion of the heart.

◆ GOSPEL: Both the prophet Isaiah and the Book of Revelation describe God's covenant with Israel in terms of a bridegroom and bride. A question about fasting leads to Jesus's self-revelation: He is the Bridegroom, the fulfilment of God's covenant promises.

The Roman Missal

The Collect is a prayer for the strength to complete the "bodily observances" we have undertaken this Lent.

Our Lenten observance is a sacrifice that we offer to God. We pray that it will be acceptable to God, and strengthen "our powers of self-restraint" (Prayer over the Offerings). We do not fast from enjoyable things because they are inherently bad. We fast because it shows us the way to self-control.

In the Prayer after Communion, we pray for the fruits of the Eucharist, that we may be forgiven, and made ready for "the remedies of [God's] compassion."

We are a people on a "pilgrim journey," and the disciplines we undertake during Lent are "age-old." In the Prayer over the People, we pray that, always giving God thanks, we may deserve to come into God's presence forever.

SAT 16 #222 violet
Saturday after Ash Wednesday

Lectionary for Mass

◆ FIRST READING: God calls Israel to fast from evil deeds, especially those that violate the well-being of others. Israel must be a people who are faithful to God if they are to flourish and find life and rest, if they are to be restored and rebuild what has been destroyed.

◆ RESPONSORIAL PSALM 86: Of ourselves, we are poor and helpless. We need God, God's help and God's deliverance. We need to learn God's wisdom.

◆ GOSPEL: No one is rejected by Jesus, not even the scorned tax collector, hated because of his allegiance to the Romans and his self-serving practices. It is not because he is virtuous that he—and we—are called, but because Jesus knows our need. May we be open to the healing he offers us.

The Roman Missal

We are weak, but we ask God to look with compassion on us, and protect us with the "right hand" of his majesty (Collect).

In the Prayer over the Offerings, we ask God to receive the sacrifice we offer, which is a "sacrifice of conciliation and praise." The Eucharist we celebrate can cleanse us and make our minds "well pleasing" to God.

The Eucharist we receive is a mystery and will always remain a mystery "in this present life"; but it has power to help us toward eternity.

The Prayer over the People for today is a prayer for protection in affliction of all "who have touched the sacred mysteries" in the celebration of the Eucharist (Prayer after Communion).

☼ **17** #24 violet
First Sunday of Lent

Orientation

During the 40 days Jesus spends in the wilderness, he undergoes thorough temptation. As his body is craving food, he is tempted to create loaves of bread and escape the spiritual discipline of fasting. As his mind prepares for his public ministry, he is tempted to seize great power in a worldly way, instead of the simple life of preaching, teaching, service, and sacrifice ahead of him. Finally, his spirit is tempted to test God to ascertain if God will

really be there for him, even through Calvary. Like us in every way but sin, Jesus's temptations grew out of the fears he may have had about having to carry out his calling. Yet his trust in God was greater. What are your greatest fears? Take these in prayer to God as you entrust yourself to God's care.

Lectionary for Mass

◆ First Reading: Today's text is set within the context of a sacrificial offering to the Lord. The words, in effect, recount the early history of the Israelite people beginning with the patriarchs. Both Abraham, the father of the chosen people, and later Jacob, his grandson with his sons and their households, went down to the land of Egypt to escape the famine in their own land. Over time, the Hebrews were oppressed and enslaved by the Egyptians. When they cried out for deliverance, the Lord raised up Moses as their leader and spokesman, and brought them out of the land of Egypt into the freedom of a new life in the promised land (see the Book of Joshua). In this new land, we hear today that they are to offer the fruits of the harvest as a sacrifice of thanksgiving.

◆ Responsorial Psalm: The antiphon aptly expresses the plea of the Israelites in their distress. Psalm 91 is a prayer of confidence in the Lord's protection during times of danger.

◆ Second Reading: We hear the confession of the Christian faith: Jesus is Lord and God raised him from the dead. In the new covenant inaugurated by Christ, there is no distinction between Jew and Greek. All people are offered salvation through faith. (Note the repetition of the words "believe," "faith," and "saved.")

◆ Gospel: Today's Gospel follows upon Jesus's baptism and must be seen in connection with it. At his

baptism, the Holy Spirit of God descended upon him—and remained, directing all the subsequent events of his life. In today's Gospel, the Spirit leads Jesus out to the desert to be "tempted" (Luke 4:1–2). The Greek word used here can also be translated as "tested" or "proved." More than a test of endurance, this was a test of fidelity and commitment to who he was as the Son of God and to the use of the extraordinary powers God had bestowed upon him. Jesus is faithful. Note how the Scriptures were a support to him in this fidelity. But the devil had not given up. He only awaited another opportunity.

The Roman Missal

◆ Psalm 91 provides both the Entrance Antiphon and the Communion Antiphon for this First Sunday of Lent. These ancient words of prayer for deliverance and trust in God resonate with the meaning of Lent. This is also the Psalm the tempter cites when he urges Jesus to leap from the parapet of the Temple.

At the beginning of Lent, we pray in the Collect that through our observance "we may grow in understanding / of the riches hidden in Christ" and act upon them. This is the goal of all our Lenten practices.

In the Prayer over the Offerings, we pray for "the right dispositions," the right attitude, as we offer the sacrifice that marks the beginning of the holy season of Lent.

The proper Preface for this First Sunday of Lent reflects on Christ's forty-day fast in the desert. His fast is "the pattern of our Lenten observance." Just as he conquered "the ancient serpent," so we are to "cast out the leaven of malice" from our lives—an allusion to 1 Corinthians 5:6, the same passage we will hear on Easter Sunday. This Preface is found in the Proper of Time.

The lovely Prayer after Communion asks that the "heavenly bread" we have received, which has power to nourish our faith, increase our hope, and strengthen our charity, may also help us to hunger for Christ and live by God's Word.

In the Prayer over the People, we ask God's blessing, that our hope may grow in our trials, and our virtue be strengthened in temptation, and that we come to redemption and eternal life.

Other Ideas

Create a Lenten prayer space in your home, perhaps on a small side table. Use violet cloth and reminders of the liturgical time. A small bowl of sand may remind your family of Jesus's temptations in the desert and his faithfulness to his mission. Add an alms box or basket to hold money saved by simplifying your diet and activities. Read the upcoming Sunday Gospel each week, and decide together on a symbol of its message to add to your prayer space. Gather here mornings and evenings for prayer together.

MON 18 #224 violet
Lenten Weekday

Lectionary for Mass

◆ FIRST READING: Our reading opens with the command to "be holy" (Leviticus 19:2) and continues with the practical spelling out of how to do this as we cooperate with God's grace in heeding his commands. The command is simple: we are to love our neighbor.

◆ RESPONSORIAL PSALM 19: Today's antiphon comes from the Gospel according to John. Jesus's words are indeed Spirit and life! The last stanza of today's Psalm can be seen in connection with the practical commands set forth in today's First Reading regarding our behavior toward others.

◆ GOSPEL: How we treat others in their needs and suffering is the criterion for our judgment at the end of time. Are we among the righteous or the unrighteous, according to Jesus's principles of judgment? His message is simple. What we do—or don't do—for other people in their need is what we do—or don't do—for the Lord. Eternal life or eternal punishment is at stake.

The Roman Missal

Only by conversion and understanding of "heavenly teaching" can we benefit from the good works we offer to God this Lent (Collect).

In the Prayer over the Offerings, we pray that the offering we make to God may change our lives, reconcile us to the Father, and bring us forgiveness.

In the Prayer after Communion, we pray that the power of the sacrament we receive may bring us "help in mind and body" and "the fullness of heavenly healing." The Eucharist is food for body and soul.

The Prayer over the People is a simple prayer that asks that God's people may receive the grace to see what needs to be done—and the strength to do it.

TUE 19 #225 violet
Lenten Weekday

Lectionary for Mass

◆ FIRST READING: The image of rain and snow watering the earth and bringing forth fruit, thus accomplishing the purpose for which they were sent by the Lord, is an apt illustration of the fruitful effect God intends his Word to have in the minds and hearts of those who hear it.

◆ RESPONSORIAL PSALM 34 is a prayer of thanksgiving and praise for God's deliverance. In light of today's First Reading, it is interesting to note the words in the stanzas of the Psalm. There is the Word-in-action of God's deliverance in the first stanza. There are the words of the poor, the just, and the afflicted that are not without fruitful effect when addressed to the Lord.

◆ GOSPEL: One does not need many words for prayer—only confidence and trust. Today Jesus teaches us how to pray. This prayer (Our Father) also requires words-in-action expressed in forgiveness. In fact, our willingness to forgive is the "condition" of God's forgiveness of us—at least in the last line of today's Gospel.

The Roman Missal

We do not undertake "bodily discipline" in Lent for its own sake, like athletes or dieters. Rather, through this observance, we grow in "yearning" for God (Collect).

In the Eucharist, we bring "temporal sustenance," bread and wine, and in his goodness God transforms them into food for eternal life (Prayer over the Offerings).

Controlling our desires can help us to correct our priorities—to "love the things of heaven" (Prayer after Communion).

In the Prayer over the People, we pray that God may be with us in all the trials of life—our consolation in grief, our perseverance in times of trial, our protection in danger.

WED 20 #226 violet
Lenten Weekday

Lectionary for Mass

◆ FIRST READING: The story of Nineveh's immediate faith-filled and penitential response to Jonah's call to conversion is most impressive. And Jonah was only one day into his journey! How quickly Jonah's word had spread. How willingly the Ninevites responded—from the king on down. How quick, how complete is our response to the call of repentance?

◆ RESPONSORIAL PSALM 51 is one of the penitential Psalms, focusing as it does on the humble sinner's plea for God's mercy. Note that the prayer is not only for forgiveness, but also for a renewed and purified heart.

◆ GOSPEL: The people of Jesus's generation could hardly be likened to the Ninevites when it came to responding to God's call. With hearts and minds closed to Jesus's words, they face a judgment of condemnation. The queen of Sheba traveled a great distance to hear the wisdom of Solomon (1 Kings 10). Jesus—greater than Solomon—was in their midst, yet they failed to recognize the wisdom of his teaching.

The Roman Missal

◆ COLLECT: We pray that the Lord may "look kindly" on us, so that our bodily self-restraint may lead to renewal in mind.

◆ PRAYER OVER THE OFFERINGS: For our sake God makes our gifts into the Sacrament of Christ's Body and Blood. We pray that this same sacrament may be for us "an eternal remedy," food for everlasting life.

◆ PRAYER AFTER COMMUNION: We pray that the sacrament we have received may bring us "unending life."

The Prayer over the People is a prayer for forgiveness of sins. This life's trials cannot harm those over whom evil has no dominion.

T H U **21** #227 violet
Lenten Weekday

Optional Memorial of Saint Peter Damian, Bishop and Doctor of the Church / violet

Lectionary for Mass

◆ FIRST READING: Esther was a Jewish woman who became the wife of the Persian king Ahasuerus. As queen, she was in an exceptional position to save her people from the threat of extinction at the hands of Haman, an official in the Persian court. The prayer we hear today was uttered by Esther prior to her audience with the king to intercede on behalf of her people. Note how what Esther learned as a child concerning the saving acts of God in human history gave her strength and courage in her present undertaking.

◆ RESPONSORIAL PSALM 138 is a prayer of thanksgiving for the Lord's favorable answer to a cry for help. The thankful awareness of God's saving deeds in the life of the one who prays is echoed in each stanza. How can we make the awareness, the thanksgiving of this prayer, our own?

◆ GOSPEL: A word of assurance from the Lord: "ask" and you will receive. The heavenly Father wishes only good things for his children. Do we confidently look for the good in whatever the circumstances of our lives?

The Roman Missal

The Collect is a prayer for a new approach to life: we ask for "a spirit of always pondering on what is right / and of hastening to carry it out." In this spirit, recognizing that we cannot live without God, we will live in accordance with God's will.

◆ PRAYER OVER THE OFFERINGS: We implore God's mercy and ask him to convert us: "turn the hearts of us all toward you." In just a moment, in the Preface Dialogue, we will echo the same prayer: "Lift up your hearts." "We lift them up to the Lord."

◆ PRAYER AFTER COMMUNION: God has given us the "sacred mysteries" of the Eucharist as "the safeguard of our salvation," our pledge of future glory. We pray that they may be a "healing remedy" (a phrase that occurs several times in the prayers for Lent), both now and in the future.

The Prayer over the People provides wonderful food for thought about prayer. We ask God to give "mercy" and "the riches of heaven" to those who have prayed to him, that they may know what to pray for as well as how to receive what God gives them.

If the optional Memorial is observed, the Collect is drawn from the Proper of Saints, while the remaining prayers may be taken from the Common of Doctors of the Church or from the Common of Pastors: For a bishop, or from the Lenten weekday. Another option is to use the Collect for Saint Peter Damian as the conclusion of the Prayer of the Faithful.

Today's Saint

Saint Peter Damian (1007–1072), born to a large Italian family, entered a Camaldolese Benedictine monastery of hermit monks who followed an austere life of fasting and prayer. Dedicating himself to the study of Scripture and the fathers of the Church, he gained a reputation among the hermits as a gifted scholar and spiritual guru. Although he lived in a monastery, removed from the world, Saint Peter was a powerful voice of reform in the Church. He spoke out against clerical abuses, challenged bishops to recommit themselves to their vocation, and announced the need for a reformed papacy. Recognized for his ability to lead, he was made abbot of his monastery and later installed as bishop of Ostia. As bishop, he never lost sight of his calling to be a monk. He was so influential in the Church that Pope Leo XII declared him a Doctor of the Church.

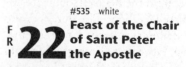

F R I **22** #535 white
Feast of the Chair of Saint Peter the Apostle

Orientation

The chair of a bishop, called the cathedra, is the symbol of his foundational ministry to be a teacher of faith to his church community. What then can we learn from Peter, the rock of our Catholic Church? His extraordinary confession of faith in this passage teaches us courage to confess truth, even if it may sound far-fetched by everyday standards. Peter listened to the Spirit of God in his heart and proclaimed Jesus as Christ, Son of the Living God. When Jesus asks "Who do you say that I am?," each of us is presented with the same question. What is the Spirit of God prompting us to proclaim?

Today's feast, attested to as early as the mid-fourth century, has its roots in the Parentalia, or commemoration of dead relatives and friends celebrated between February 13 and 22. At this commemoration, a chair, or cathedra, was left empty for particular deceased persons. Since the actual date of Peter's death was unknown, it came to be remembered on February 22, eventually becoming a celebration of his taking over the pastoral responsibility of the Church of Rome.

In the Church, "chairs" have great symbolic significance: they represent leadership roles and remind us that the office is greater than the man who fills it. Our cathedrals are reminders of this, named for the cathedra or bishop's chair. This feast, therefore, is not about a piece of furniture—it is about the special role Christ gave to Peter, to be the rock on which the Church is built.

Lectionary

◆ FIRST READING: Peter exhorts his fellow presbyters (those in leadership) to willingly and eagerly shepherd the believers who are entrusted to them. Presbyters are to be examples of service, not domination. Note that although they hold leadership roles, they are nevertheless subordinate to Christ, the "chief Shepherd" (1 Peter 5:4), to whom they are accountable and who will

give them their reward, a share in his glory, when he is revealed at the end of time. Note the twofold mention of this revelation. The early Christians lived in ardent hope and expectation of it.

◆ RESPONSORIAL PSALM 23: Today's Psalm focuses on the Lord as Shepherd, a fitting response to the first reading with its reference to Christ the "chief Shepherd" (see 1 Peter 5:4). Have you ever noticed how much of a servant or minister the shepherd of Psalm 23 is? Everything that he does is for the care and well-being of the sheep. Pray this Psalm, imagining yourself as the sheep who receives such loving care.

◆ GOSPEL: In today's Gospel, Peter confesses Jesus as the Christ or Messiah, the long-awaited son of David—and the Son of the living God. Jesus attributes this profound confession of faith to a gift of grace, a revelation from the Father. Peter was known as Simon when first called by Jesus, and that name occurs in today's text as well. His new name, "Peter," is no doubt derived from the Greek word for "rock"—thus the word play in verses 17–18. Peter is given a foundational role in the establishment of the "church" (and here is the first time the word is used in the Gospel according to Matthew), or the assembly of those who are called, as the Greek word implies. Also implied is a relationship between the Church and the "Kingdom of heaven" (Matthew's phrase for the kingdom of God; see verse 19). The words "bound" and "loose" (verse 19) pertain to the exercise of authority (but see Matthew 18:18 which gives this role to the community). Today, however, Peter's authoritative leadership role is the focus of our feast.

The Roman Missal

The Entrance Antiphon is taken from the words of Christ to Peter: "I have prayed for you that your faith may not fail, / and, once you have turned back, strengthen your brothers" (Luke 22:32). The Antiphon expresses the strength and frailty of Peter, who "turned back" after denying Christ, and became the leader of the early Church.

Even though it is Lent, the Gloria is said or sung today.

In the Collect, we see Peter the rock. His confession of faith that Jesus is the Son of the living God is the rock on which the Church is founded, so firmly that "no tempests" can shake us.

In the Prayer over the Offerings, we see Peter the shepherd. Through the teaching of Peter, the Church "holds the faith in its integrity." His successors, the popes, have continued to safeguard this treasure.

Preface I of the Apostles is used.

The Prayer after Communion on this Feast of the Chair of Saint Peter is a prayer for "unity and peace."

S A T **23** #229 violet
Lenten Weekday

Optional Memorial of Saint Polycarp, Bishop and Martyr / violet

Lectionary for Mass

◆ FIRST READING: The salvation of the present moment, the now, today, is central in our First Reading. We agree to live wholeheartedly as God's people, faithful to the demands of his covenant. God promises us glory and praise if we live as a faithful people, sacred to the Lord.

◆ RESPONSORIAL PSALM: The stipulations of the covenant agreement are spelled out in the law. Psalm 119 acclaims the wisdom of God's law and the blessedness of those who faithfully observe it.

◆ Gospel: The command to hate our enemies is not expressed, at least not in these words, in the Old Testament. Neighbors were members of one's own people. Enemies were those who injured, harmed, or threatened in some way. Certainly we find hatred of the wicked expressed in the Old Testament, but Jesus asks more than did the Law of Moses. One's enemies are to be loved. The heavenly Father loves both the just and the unjust. Jesus's disciples must be as "perfect" (matured) as their heavenly Father.

The Roman Missal

The Collect echoes the Gospel story of Mary and Martha. We pray that we may seek "always the one thing necessary," so that while we undertake works of love, we may worship the Lord.

The Eucharist is the reward of saints, and food for sinners. We pray that these "blessed mysteries" may restore us and make us worthy to receive them (Prayer over the Offerings).

We have been refreshed by a "divine mystery," "imbued with heavenly teaching." We ask that God may accompany us on our way with his consolations (Prayer after Communion).

We long for God's blessing. We ask that his benediction may strengthen us to follow his will, and rejoice in his gifts (Prayer over the People).

If the optional memorial is observed, the Collect is drawn from the Proper of Saints, while the remaining prayers may be taken from the Common of Martyrs: For One Martyr, or from the Common of Pastors: For a Bishop, or from the Lenten weekday. Another option is to use the Collect for Saint Polycarp as the conclusion of the Prayer of the Faithful.

☀ **24** #27 violet
Second Sunday of Lent

Orientation

To fully reveal oneself to one's friends is a risk. In opening up, one hopes to be met with love and trust, but this may not immediately be the case. For this reason, growth in a relationship toward intimacy takes time, until the mutual assurance of love and respect is felt. Jesus may have found such friendship with Peter, James, and John. While they did not fully understand the Transfiguration, Jesus loved and trusted them, and trusted in their faith to handle Calvary. Lent is a time of growth for us in our relationship with Christ as together we approach Calvary, and his love and trust for us strengthens our faith in his powerful presence, even on the cross.

Lectionary for Mass

◆ First Reading: God reiterated his covenant with Abraham several times. Today's reading tells of one such time, emphasizing the numerous descendants that the then childless Abraham would have as the father of the Chosen People. Abraham believed God's promise and thus was deemed "righteous" (Genesis 15:6), that is, in right relationship with God because of his faith and trust in God's Word. The second part of the reading recounts a sacrificial ritual which serves as a sign of the covenant God had made with Abraham. The text speaks of

Abraham's deep religious experience as he waited with his sacrifice.

◆ Responsorial Psalm 27 acclaims the Lord as light—thus evoking the flaming torch in today's first reading. What trust Abraham had in God's Word, what confidence that the promise would be fulfilled, even though he had to "wait" for its fulfilment (note the "wait" in stanza four). Abraham did indeed see the bounty of the Lord (stanza four) in land and descendants.

◆ Second Reading: Both a longer and shorter version of the text is offered. Common to both is Paul's emphasis on the transformation for which we are destined in the age to come—the transformation of our physical bodies into a glorified body such as Jesus manifests in today's account of the Gospel.

◆ Gospel: The Gospel for the Second Sunday of Lent is always the story of Jesus's Transfiguration, when the chosen disciples glimpsed his heavenly glory. Luke emphasizes the fact that Jesus was transfigured during a time of prayer. Note that Moses and Elijah converse with Jesus about his "exodus," that is, his passing over from death to life. There is a deliberate connection with the Old Testament event. Like Abraham before them, the Apostles are overwhelmed by their experience of God's presence. Fear, yes; but joy also: "it is good that we are here" (Luke 9:33). We must hear with them the voice of the Father: "This is my chosen Son; listen to him" (Luke 9:35).

The Roman Missal

◆ "Of you my heart has spoken: Seek his face" (Psalm 27:8/Entrance Antiphon). On this Second Sunday of Lent, we read one of the Gospel accounts of the Transfiguration of the Lord, when Peter, James, and John are privileged to see Christ in his glory—to recognize divinity in the human face of Jesus. Our prayer is that we, too, may seek his face; "hide not your face" (Psalm 27:9).

The second option for the Entrance Antiphon is from Psalm 25 (24).

The Collect shows us the way to see God. God has commanded us to listen to the Word of his Son. We pray that, fed by his divine Word, our sight may be "made pure" so that we too may "behold your glory."

In the Prayer over the Offerings, we ask that our sacrifice may cleanse and sanctify us for the celebration of Easter.

The Preface puts the account of the Transfiguration in context. In all three synoptic Gospels, the Transfiguration follows shortly after the first prediction of the Passion the Lord must undergo. Flanked by Moses and Elijah, "the testimony of the law and the prophets," Christ revealed his glory to his disciples to show them that "the Passion leads to the glory of the Resurrection." The Preface is found in the Proper of Time.

The Prayer after Communion is a simple prayer of thanksgiving for the grace of being "partakers . . . of the things of heaven" while still on earth. The Eucharist is our everyday Transfiguration!

The Prayer over the People also echoes the Gospel account of the Transfiguration, with its prayer that we may be faithful to the Gospel of the Son of God, and one day attain "that glory whose beauty he showed in his own Body."

Other Ideas

Brainstorm ideas for small things that each member of your family can do this week to show love for God and kindness to others, and to help alleviate some of the suffering in the world caused by sin. Make a list with at least one thing for each person each day. Check off your offerings as you complete them. Examples might include offering a

kind word to someone who irritates you, letting someone go ahead of you in line, or praying for someone who cuts you off in traffic.

MON 25 #230 violet
Lenten Weekday

Lectionary for Mass

◆ FIRST READING: Today's First Reading is, in effect, a confession of sin, an acknowledgment that God's people have broken the covenant through their disobedience. They have heeded neither the law nor the prophets. The "scattering" (exile) of God's people (outside the land of Israel) is considered punishment for sin. There is mention of God's mercy, compassion, and forgiveness, but the emphasis in today's text is clearly on the people's guilt.

◆ RESPONSORIAL PSALM 79: Fittingly, our antiphon pleads that the Lord will not deal with his people as they deserve. The context of the Psalm is the aftermath of the destruction of Jerusalem and the Temple which, along with the subsequent exile, are viewed as punishment for sin by biblical authors. The first two stanzas ask for God's forgiveness.

◆ GOSPEL: The Gospel according to Luke stresses the mercy and compassion of God. This is the emphasis in today's text in which Jesus tells his followers to incorporate this same mercy and compassion in their dealings with one another. The last line of the Gospel is a strong call to self-examination.

The Roman Missal

In the Collect, God teaches us to undertake physical penances for the good of our souls. We ask for the strength to "abstain from all sins," and to carry out God's loving commands.

In the Prayer over the Offerings, we pray that all whom God allows to participate in these sacred mysteries may be "set free from worldly attractions."

In the Prayer after Communion, we pray that the Communion we receive may cleanse us of our faults, and "make us heirs to the joy of heaven."

In the Prayer over the People, we pray that with God's grace, we may be faithful in prayer to God, and truly love one another.

TUE 26 #231 violet
Lenten Weekday

Lectionary for Mass

◆ FIRST READING: The cities of Sodom and Gomorrah were notorious for their wickedness, as were the people of Isaiah's day. The first part of today's reading consists of eight commands. In fulfilling these, true righteousness and purity is to be found in God's eyes. In the second part of the reading, God invites us to sit down and talk things over, as it were. God tells us what can "come" to us ("become," mentioned two times) if we listen to him. The possibility is held out to us; the choice is ours.

◆ RESPONSORIAL PSALM 50: Like the First Reading, the Psalm is concerned with true righteousness. The ritual offerings are in place, but the dispositions of heart (the true sacrifice of praise) are not. It is this that God desires. See all of the third part of Psalm 50 for the details of what is required.

◆ GOSPEL: The Pharisees are faulted for their hypocrisy, for calling attention to themselves and expecting preferential treatment. This is not to be the way of Jesus's followers who are called to humble service.

The Roman Missal

Since we will surely fall without God's help, in the Collect, we pray that the Lord may assist us always, protecting us from harm and pointing us toward salvation.

Through this sacred mystery God can work his "sanctification" in us, cleansing us of sin and leading us to heaven (Prayer over the Offerings).

In the Prayer after Communion, we ask that the heavenly "refreshment" we receive at the Lord's table may increase our devotion, and help us with God's reconciling love.

In the Prayer over the People, we ask God to hear the "cries" of our prayer, and lead us from "weariness" to rejoicing.

WED 27 #232 violet
Lenten Weekday

Lectionary for Mass

◆ FIRST READING: Of all the Old Testament prophets, Jeremiah is perhaps the one whose life is most characterized by intense suffering. Today we hear about the incident when the people to whom he was sent to proclaim God's Word openly turn against him and plot to destroy him. We hear also Jeremiah's prayer, beseeching God's intervention and deliverance.

◆ RESPONSORIAL PSALM 31: The antiphon echoes Jeremiah's plea for God's help. The second stanza is a perfect parallel to the first part of the text from Jeremiah. The first and third stanzas speak of the trust the psalmist—and Jeremiah—had in the Lord's deliverance.

◆ GOSPEL: Like Jeremiah, Jesus was a prophet rejected by those to whom he was sent and who plotted to take his life. The chalice spoken of is the cup of suffering which Jesus drinks at his Passion. His disciples, following him, must drink of it as well. Jesus's followers must

be servants who give their life to, and for, others. There is no place for personal aggrandizement in God's kingdom.

The Roman Missal

In the Collect, we ask God to keep his "family," the Church, "schooled always in good works," to surround us with his protection, and to lead us to heaven. Lent is this school for our souls.

The Eucharist is a "holy exchange" (Prayer over the Offerings). We offer to God the sacrifice his Son offered for us, and in return, God gives us forgiveness.

The Communion we have received is our "pledge of immortality." We pray that it may "work for our eternal salvation" (Prayer after Communion).

The Prayer over the People asks God for everything we need to live the Christian life: grace and protection, health, love, and devotion.

THU 28 #233 violet
Lenten Weekday

Lectionary for Mass

◆ FIRST READING: By their fruits you shall know them. Today's First Reading from Jeremiah contrasts the dryness and barrenness of the one rooted in the transitory and mortal with the fruitfulness and stability of the one rooted in the Lord. The word translated as "tortuous" literally means "deceitful" or "fraudulent." The Lord searches out the human mind and heart. In Lent, especially, so must we search our minds and hearts.

◆ RESPONSORIAL PSALM 1: Our antiphon echoes the true blessedness and happiness of the one firmly rooted in the Lord. The stanzas continue this theme and point to God's law as the ground in which we must remain firmly planted.

◆ GOSPEL: In today's parable, the theme we have already heard continues, as Abraham points to the law and prophets as sure guides to everlasting blessedness. The rich man is faulted not because he is rich, but because he looked away from the needy man who was daily at his door. In this, he failed to show the concern for the poor that the law and the prophets command. The poor man, totally ignored in his earthly life, was comforted in the bosom of Abraham.

The Roman Missal

God loves "innocence," and in Jesus Christ, the new Adam, he restores our innocence. We pray that our hearts may be directed to him, and, "caught up in the fire of [his] Spirit," we may be full of faith and good works (Collect).

The Prayer over the Offerings is similar to the Prayer over the People we heard on Friday of the First Week of Lent. We ask God to "sanctify our observance" of Lent, so that our outward disciplines may be accompanied by inward transformation.

In the Prayer after Communion, we ask that the sacrifice we have offered and received may "work ever more strongly within us."

In the Prayer over the People, we ask God's abiding presence with us, so that we may know his "support," "guidance," and "protection."

March
Month of Saint Joseph

FRI 1 #234 violet
Lenten Weekday

Lectionary for Mass

◆ FIRST READING: The jealousy, coldness, and attempt to do away with the one who triggers these emotions is, sadly, perhaps all too common an experience, especially within families. We also hear echoed, or rather, prefigured, what will happen to Jesus, the beloved Son, centuries later, even to being stripped and his garment sold. The reference to Joseph as a dreamer pertains to verses 5–11, which are not included in today's reading.

◆ RESPONSORIAL PSALM 105: Today's Psalm tells a bit more of Joseph's story: how the "evil" inflicted upon him by his brothers worked unto good in the hands of God. It was truly a "marvel done by the Lord," as the antiphon says. Joseph's ability to interpret dreams won his release from his Egyptian prison and led to a position in Pharaoh's royal court.

◆ GOSPEL: Today's text is another example of the destructive power of uncontrolled passions and emotions. By killing the son, the tenants could acquire the vineyard for themselves. Like Joseph's brothers and the chief priests and Pharisees, the tenants plotted the destruction of another for their own gain. Jesus is the Son sent by the Father to obtain the fruit of the work of the tenants. The citation of Psalm 118:22–23 points to Jesus as the rejected stone who became the cornerstone (foundation stone) of God's new people.

The Roman Missal

On this day of fasting, we pray in the Collect that our penance may purify us, and lead us "to attain the holy things to come."

In the Prayer over the Offerings, we ask for God's "merciful grace" to prepare us to celebrate these mysteries, and to lead us to "a devout way of life."

In the Eucharist, we receive a "pledge of eternal salvation" (Prayer after Communion). We pray that we may "set our course" toward the redemption God has promised.

In the Prayer over the People, we ask for "health of mind and body," so that we may use these precious gifts for "good deeds."

S A T **2** #235   violet
Lenten Weekday

Lectionary for Mass

◆ FIRST READING: The reading is a prayer: God is the shepherd, and the people who desire to be led and cared for by him are his flock. What was of old, the marvels of the Exodus, is recalled. The prophet prays to see such wonderful signs again. The prayer arises from a situation of distress and affliction. The second part of the reading/prayer acclaims God as one who forgives and delights in so doing. God will cast the sins of those who repent into the depths of the sea, remembering them no more.

◆ RESPONSORIAL PSALM 103 praises God's benefits: forgiveness, healing, and deliverance from that which threatens to destroy. From the depths of the sea to the heights above the earth, as far as east is from west—it is the image of a cross, his unbounded love, his immeasurable forgiveness.

◆ GOSPEL: The well-known parable of the prodigal son is, perhaps, better named the parable of the lavish and loving father. Once we realize how we have wasted our inheritance, let us make our way to his waiting embrace.

The Roman Missal

Earth and heaven, present and future, meet when we celebrate the Eucharist. We receive "things of heaven," which guide us through this life to the "light" where God lives (Collect).

We ask for the "fruits" of redemption so that we may control "unruly desires" and strive for the "gifts of salvation" (Prayer over the Offerings).

There is no limit to what the Eucharist can do in our lives. In this prayer, we ask that the sacrament "fill the inner depths of our heart"

and work "mightily" within us (Prayer after Communion).

We ask God to open "the ears of [his] mercy" to our prayers, that we may receive what we ask—and ask only what God wants for us (Prayer over the People).

✸**3** #30 or 28   violet
Third Sunday of Lent

Orientation: Year C

In our vocation to live in Christ and to proclaim and work for the kingdom of God, we are led and empowered by the Spirit to bear good fruit. We are not alone in this mission, but neither is God—and we are responsible for cooperating with God's grace offered freely to us. Lent is tilled ground, cultivated by God's nurture through spiritual discipline, inviting us to come to new life at Easter.

Lectionary for Mass: Year C

◆ FIRST READING: Moses, a refugee in the land, has an experience of God that will change his life. One day while shepherding his father-in-law's flock, Moses catches sight of a bush burning but, mysteriously, not being consumed, so he goes over to investigate. Then and there in that holy place, Moses meets God and receives his call to lead God's people out of Egypt. This text tells us two things about God: 1) he is inexpressible mystery, 2) yet known through his actions on behalf of his people.

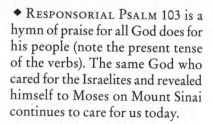

◆ RESPONSORIAL PSALM 103 is a hymn of praise for all God does for his people (note the present tense of the verbs). The same God who cared for the Israelites and revealed himself to Moses on Mount Sinai continues to care for us today.

◆ SECOND READING: Paul invites the Corinthians to learn from the experience of Israel in the desert. These Israelites had passed through the waters of the sea at the time of the Exodus and drank of the water the Lord provided in the desert, yet were punished for their grumbling. We cannot take God's gifts of deliverance and salvation for granted. Paul's reference to the rock following the Israelites is based on rabbinic tradition. "Rock" is an image for God in the Old Testament (see especially Deuteronomy 32:4 and 15; Psalm 18:2–3); Paul transfers this to Christ. At another level, we can see Christ as being the ultimate fulfillment of the story of the water from the rock.

◆ GOSPEL: A tragic incident involving loss of life is reported to Jesus. According to the popular mentality, this was punishment for sin. Jesus warns that a worse fate will come upon those who refuse to take his words to heart and turn from their evil ways (echoes of Paul's similar admonition to the Corinthians in today's Second Reading). Nevertheless, as our Responsorial Psalm points out, God is "slow to anger and abounding in kindness" (verse 8). Like the gardener in the parable, he gives every opportunity, every possibility, for growth and bearing fruit.

Lectionary for Mass: Year A

The commentary for the *Lectionary for Mass*, Year A, was written by Peggy Eckerdt © LTP, 2012. These readings are to be used when the first scrutiny is celebrated.

◆ FIRST READING: We may find it difficult to understand the grum-blings of the people in this passage from Exodus because we live in a country where water and other resources are taken for granted. But if we have ever experienced water rationing or traveled to a country where water resources are in short supply, we might have more sympathy for the nomadic Israelites. Tired and unsure of their future, they demand that Moses fix their intolerable situation. Moses himself is tremendously frustrated and minces no words with God: "What shall I do with this people? A little more and they will stone me." God answers the plea of his messenger with instructions to obtain water from the rock in Horeb. The people demand water, but what they really want is for God to send them a sign of his presence. This is a very human story about how easy it is to trust that God is in our midst when everything is going well in our lives. But when struggle, heartache, and loss occur, we wonder if God is present. In those difficult times, like the Israelites of old, we thirst for reassurance that God is with us.

◆ RESPONSORIAL PSALM: The Psalm builds on the First Reading's theme of trust in God. Considered a song of enthronement, Psalm 95 is sung by a people who have found the one true God. Capturing their sense of wonder and praise, the first verses (1, 2, 6, and 7) jubilantly proclaim loyalty and gratitude. The final verse, however, strikes a different theme as it recounts the desert wanderings of a people who eventually fell apart at Meribah and Massah. There, the Israelites' grumbling and complaining put God to the test. This Psalm's final verse refers to that failure of faithfulness. Even though the Israelites saw God's wonderful works, they openly doubted God's presence and turned away from him with hardened hearts. The Psalm's refrain

calls them (and us) back, encouraging movement from our uncertainties to the freedom of trust. We are called to listen for God's voice in the people and events of each day with open hearts. For God, the rock of salvation, is present in joy and in struggle, and remains the Good Shepherd who will never abandon his flock.

◆ SECOND READING: Paul's writing is complex, but his message is simple: Christ died for all humans and, in doing so, proved God's great and unconditional love for all. That supreme and generous act is the source of our hope and the reason for our trust. While God's love is beyond our imagination, we know his love through human experience. Sometimes, in the best of human circumstances, we can catch a glimpse of what it feels like to be loved by God. Married couples often say that their love for one another makes them better people. This assertion provides an analogy to help grasp divine love: if we truly understood what it meant to be loved by God, we would be nearly perfect people— perfect not for the sake of perfection, but perfect because we want to respond to God's love for us. This selfless love is the true source of our Christian hope.

◆ GOSPEL: Jews were not supposed to speak to Samaritans, much less share drinking vessels with them. Jewish men were never supposed to converse with a woman in public, let alone a Samaritan woman. But cultural division and socially accepted discrimination didn't stop Jesus. He initiates a conversation with a woman of Samaria who is sitting alone at the town well in the noonday heat. She is so dumbfounded by this that she forgets her societal status and blurts, "How can you . . . ask me . . . for a drink?" Thus begins one of the longest and most fascinating conversations in the New Testament. Jesus asks for a drink, but then reveals he is the source of water that will quench thirst for all eternity. The woman then reverses the dialogue and says, "Give me this water." At this point, the conversation shifts and the testimony of faith begins to unfold. Jesus, aware that she has been married five times, tells her to get her husband. In doing so, Jesus recites details of her life that no stranger could know. She asks Jesus if he is the Messiah. And the world is forever changed with these words: "I am he, the one speaking with you." She is the first to hear the news and share it with others. Some say she is the first missionary. What we remember is that this woman stands in a long line of witnesses who have journeyed in faith before us. Buoyed by their faith, we are called to continue that journey today.

The Roman Missal

When the first scrutiny is celebrated today, the prayers for the first scrutiny of the elect, found under Ritual Masses, may be used. The prayers focus on the elect, chosen for the sacraments. There are special insertions for Eucharistic Prayers I, II, and III, which should be used if the Ritual Mass is selected.

There are two options for today's Entrance Antiphon. The second, taken from Ezekiel 36:23–26, is especially appropriate when the scrutiny of the elect is celebrated: "I will pour clean water upon you."

We are burdened by sin, but God has given us a remedy in the Lenten disciplines of prayer, fasting, and almsgiving. We pray in the Collect that we, who are weighed down by a heavy conscience, may be lifted up by God's forgiving mercy.

With the sacrifice we make, we ask God for forgiveness and reconciliation. We who ask these blessings must "take care to forgive our neighbor," as Jesus taught (Prayer over the Offerings).

When the Gospel about the Samaritan woman is read, the proper Preface for the Third Sunday of Lent is used. It is found in the Proper of Time. It reflects beautifully on the encounter at the well. Jesus asks the Samaritan woman for water, and gives living water. Jesus is on fire for her faith, and he gives "the fire of divine love." When this Gospel is not read, Preface I or II of Lent is used.

The Prayer after Communion expresses the mystery of Holy Communion: "we receive the pledge" of what is "hidden in heaven," and are fed on earth with "Bread that comes from on high." We pray that we may come to the "true completion" of this mystery which is already at work in us.

The Prayer over the People echoes the golden rule: we ask this one grace, to abide in love of God and neighbor, and thus to fulfill the whole of God's commandments.

Other Ideas

Jesus broke boundaries when he initiated a conversation with the Samaritan woman. What are the boundaries in your workplace or within your social group? Find a way to break a boundary that will bless another person. Afterward, reflect on how the boundary-breaking blessed you as well.

#237   violet
Lenten Weekday

Optional Memorial of Saint Casimir / violet

Lectionary for Mass

Please note that the optional readings for the Third Week of Lent may be done any day this week (#236).

◆ FIRST READING: The Gentile Namaan is healed of his leprosy by the prophet Elisha. But before he can be healed, he must set aside his own ideas and, listening to the word of the prophet, obey.

◆ RESPONSORIAL PSALM 42: Like the deer that yearns for life-giving streams, the psalmist thirsts for God and prays for enlightenment on the way to God's dwelling place.

◆ GOSPEL: People everywhere have difficulty accepting the word of the prophet, especially when he or she is someone they know. The people of Jesus's hometown are so enraged by his words that they seek to kill him.

The Roman Missal

The Collect is a prayer for the Church, that God may "cleanse and protect" her, and govern her by his grace.

In the Prayer over the Offerings, we ask that what we offer to God may become for us "the sacrament of salvation."

We have shared in the sacrament, and we ask for its fruits: "purification" and "unity," God's gifts (Prayer after Communion).

The Prayer over the People again touches on purification. We pray that God may "purify" and instruct his people, so that they may "reach the good things to come" and find "solace in this life," along the way.

If the optional Memorial is observed, the Collect is drawn from the Proper of Saints, while the remaining prayers may be taken from the Common of Holy Men and Women: For one Saint, or from the Lenten weekday. Another option is to use the Collect for Saint Casimir as the conclusion of the Prayer of the Faithful.

#238   violet
Lenten Weekday

Lectionary for Mass

◆ FIRST READING: The Jewish youth Azariah and his two companions are cast into a fiery furnace as punishment for refusing to worship the idol set up by the king. Acknowledging the infidelities of his people, Azariah begs God to remember his covenant of old and cries out for mercy and deliverance.

◆ RESPONSORIAL PSALM 25: Today's Psalm is yet another plea that God will remember the covenant promises of old and act with mercy. The first and last stanzas reiterate the psalmist's prayer that God will reveal his way.

◆ GOSPEL: The story of the unforgiving servant challenges us to look long and hard at how we treat those who offend us. We have received God's unconditional mercy countless times. We are called to show the same to one another—from our hearts.

The Roman Missal

We pray in the Collect for God's continued grace, that we may dedicate ourselves to his "holy service," and receive his help in our need.

We pray in the Prayer over the Offerings that the sacrifice we offer may cleanse us of sin, and be pleasing to God.

In the Prayer after Communion, we ask for "pardon and protection" through our sharing in the Eucharist.

In the Prayer over the People, we ask God to drive sin away from us, so that we may remain safely under his protection.

WED 6 #239 violet
Lenten Weekday

Lectionary for Mass

◆ FIRST READING: Fidelity to the covenant, expressed in obedience to God's command, is the way to wisdom, to life, and to the realization of all that God has promised. God is especially near to the people he has made his own.

◆ RESPONSORIAL PSALM 147: The heart of the close relationship God has established with Israel is the word, the Law, he has spoken to them.

◆ GOSPEL: Jesus came not to abolish the Law of old, but to fulfill it. In fact, later in this chapter in Matthew's account of the Gospel, he teaches the people that fulfilling the Law means doing more than the letter of the Law requires.

The Roman Missal

Lent is a school in which we learn "holy restraint" (Collect). We pray that we may learn from our Lenten observance, and from God's Word, to be devoted to the Lord and united in prayer.

The Prayer over the Offerings is a prayer for the protection of all those who "celebrate your mysteries."

In the Prayer after Communion, we pray that our sharing in the heavenly banquet may make us holy and cleanse us from "all errors," so that we may see the fulfillment of God's promises in heaven.

Prayer over the People: We ask for "a resolve that is pleasing" to God, for we know that those who are conformed to God's Word will experience his favor.

THU 7 #240 violet
Lenten Weekday

Optional Memorial of Saints Perpetua and Felicity, Martyrs / violet

Lectionary for Mass

◆ FIRST READING: "Listen . . . pay heed . . ." (Jeremiah 7:23–24) so God commanded his people. Yet from the beginning of their existence as a people of God at the time of the Exodus, up to and including Jeremiah's day, they have failed to do so. Can the same be said of us?

◆ RESPONSORIAL PSALM: The theme of listening is echoed in today's Psalm 95, particularly in the antiphon and the last stanza of the Psalm. Only through true obedience to God's Word can we offer a fitting sacrifice of praise; only then, do we truly let ourselves be guided by the Lord our shepherd.

◆ GOSPEL: The controversy surrounding Jesus centers on the source of his power. There are those who would say that he is in league with Satan. But why would Satan weaken his own hold on people? How could others among the Jews have power to cast out demons if it were not for God working through them? The last line of today's text calls us to particular self-examination. Are we with Jesus or against him? How do our everyday lives answer that question?

The Roman Missal

At the midpoint of Lent, we pray that "we may press forward all the more eagerly" to the celebration of the Paschal Mystery at Easter (Collect).

The Prayer over the Offerings is a prayer for cleansing. We must be cleansed "from every taint of wickedness," and freed from "false joys," if we are to bring our gifts to God and receive "the rewards" of his truth.

In the Prayer after Communion, we pray that the sacrament which renews us may bring us salvation. We will know this salvation "in mystery" through the sacraments, but it must also be expressed "in the manner of our life."

God is the source of everything, "all that we are." We ask his grace, that we may "seek what is right" and "do the good we desire" (Prayer over the People)

If the optional Memorial is observed, the prayers are drawn from the Proper of Saints. Another option is to use the prayers of the Lenten weekday, but to pray the Collect for Saints Perpetua and Felicity as the conclusion of the Prayer of the Faithful.

Today's Saints

◆ Saints Perpetua and Felicity: In the year 203, these two women were martyred in the amphitheater at Carthage. Their crime was professing faith in Jesus Christ. Perpetua was a wealthy noblewoman, the mother of a young son; Felicity was a humble slave girl, who gave birth to a daughter just a few days before she died. These women, so different in their circumstances, were united in their death. The names of these heroic women are included in Eucharistic Prayer I, alongside the names of Apostles and martyrs. They lived today's Gospel, praying for their persecutors.

#241   violet
Lenten Weekday

Optional Memorial of Saint John of God, Religious / violet

Lectionary for Mass

◆ First Reading: It is interesting to observe how often the prophet Hosea uses the words heal and return in close proximity. It is only in returning to the Lord that true healing, in every sense of the word, is to be found. The truly wise one knows this and walks in the paths of the Lord.

◆ Responsorial Psalm 81: Returning to the Lord means listening and obeying his Word. We hear the Lord reminding Israel of what he has done for them in the stanzas of today's Psalm and calling them to hear and obey. Then they will find life and blessing. What foreign gods do we worship? What are we called to hear and obey?

◆ Gospel: Omitted from the Lectionary reading is the beginning of verse 28 with its interesting observation: the scribe is drawn to Jesus by the way he so skillfully refuted the Sadducees over the question of resurrection (see Mark 12:18–27). Note also that this same scribe affirms the correctness of Jesus's understanding of the most important commandments of the Law. The scribe, in turn, receives Jesus's affirmation: you are close to the kingdom of God.

The Roman Missal

In the Collect, we ask God to pour his grace into our hearts, for it is only by his grace that we can observe "heavenly teaching," and be "drawn away from unruly desires."

In the Prayer over the Offerings, we ask God to "look with favor" upon the sacrifice we offer, that these gifts may be pleasing to him and bring salvation to us.

We ask for God's strength to "be at work in us," in both mind and body, that we may come to the fullness of redemption (Prayer after Communion).

God has given us gifts, but not for ourselves alone. We need to spread these gifts, "far and wide" (Prayer over the People).

If the optional Memorial is observed, the Collect is drawn from the Proper of Saints, while the remaining prayers may be taken from the Common of Holy Men and Women: For Religious, or For Those Who Practiced Works of Mercy, or from the Lenten weekday. Another option is to use the Collect for Saint John as the conclusion of the Prayer of the Faithful.

Today's Saint

Saint John of God was a Portuguese friar who became a leading religious figure. After a period in the army in Spain, he began to distribute religious books, using the new Gutenberg printing press. At one point, John had an intense religious experience that resulted in temporary insanity. He was thrown into a mental institution, and while there, he realized how badly the sick and the poor were treated. Once he recovered, he spent the rest of his life caring for them. In Granada he gathered a circle of disciples around him who felt the same call and founded what is now known as the Hospitaller Brothers of Saint John of God.

#242   violet
Lenten Weekday

Optional Memorial of Saint Frances of Rome, Religious / violet

Lectionary for Mass

◆ First Reading: The first part of today's reading sounds like true words of repentance, even if the motive does seem a bit self-centered. Perhaps that is why the Lord compares Israel's piety to the morning dew that quickly passes away.

◆ Responsorial Psalm: Our antiphon is the last line of the reading, only here "love" (Hosea 6:6; literally "covenant love") is rendered as "mercy" (antiphon). Psalm 51 is a penitential Psalm. Again, there is the reminder: sacrifice apart from a contrite heart means nothing.

◆ Gospel: Who is righteous (in right relationship) with God? It is God who decides, not us. The Pharisee, even if his assertions were true, looked—and prayed—to himself and not to God. He looked down on the other. The tax collector lowered his eyes before God, acknowledged his sinfulness, and asked mercy. In humbling himself, he was exalted by God.

The Roman Missal

There is joy in Lent! "Rejoicing" in our annual Lenten observance, we pray that we may keep our hearts fixed on Christ's Paschal Mystery, and "be gladdened" by its effect in our lives (Collect).

We pray that we may come to the mysteries of the altar "with minds made pure," and that by reverently celebrating this memorial, we may offer "fitting homage" to God (Prayer over the Offerings).

We pray for the right disposition in receiving Holy Communion: that we may "revere" these gifts and receive them "with abundant faith in our heart" (Prayer after Communion).

We pray that God will reach out to his people with "the right hand of heavenly assistance," so that they may seek what they need, and find it (Prayer over the People).

If the optional Memorial is observed, the Collect is drawn from the Proper of Saints, while the remaining prayers may be taken from the Common of Holy Men and Women: For Holy Women or For Religious, or from the Lenten weekday. Another option is to use the Collect for Saint Frances as the conclusion of the Prayer of the Faithful.

Today's Saint

Saint Frances of Rome (1384–1440) was a wife and mother who dedicated herself to the service of the poor and the sick. She is venerated as the founder of the Congregation of Oblates under the *Rule of Saint Benedict* (also known as the Collatines). She reminds us that no matter what our situation in life is, we can find ways to live the Gospel.

☀ **10** #33 or 31   violet/rose
Fourth Sunday of Lent

Orientation: Year C

Laetare Sunday offers us a moment of joy amidst our somber and introspective Lenten journey, but it is a joyful moment entirely in keeping with Lent. The Gospel reading shows us that the pure joy surrounding the father's welcome of the returning wayward son arises out of reconciliation—out of the acknowledgement of sin, imperfection, and true need, all met by love. Although humbled, the son returns home and is at the mercy of his family. After having spent it all, he expects nothing, yet finds everything in his father's open arms. This is true joy, far surpassing the diversions the son left to seek out.

Lectionary for Mass: Year C

◆ FIRST READING: The Book of Joshua tells of the entrance of God's people into the Promised Land and their observance of the feast of Passover. God's promise of a land, abounding in fruit, had been realized.

◆ RESPONSORIAL PSALM 34: Today's antiphon with its invitation to "taste" (experience) the Lord's goodness is a most appropriate response to Joshua's reference to the produce of the land and Passover, both manifestations of the Lord's goodness to Israel. Note also in the Psalm stanzas the references to

deliverance—Passover is a celebration precisely of that.

◆ SECOND READING: The Death of Christ at the time of Passover was itself a passing over into new life, giving birth to a new creation, a new reality, a new covenant of reconciliation between God and humankind as God no longer holds our transgressions against us. We are to be ambassadors of all that Christ has accomplished on our behalf.

◆ GOSPEL: The parable of the Prodigal Son/Lavishly Forgiving Father should be heard in the context of the introduction given in the first three verses of the text. Tax-collectors, despised both because of their allegiance to the Romans and the use of their position for monetary gain, and sinners, despised by the "self"-righteous Pharisees and religious leaders, come to Jesus who welcomes them and shares table fellowship with them in total acceptance. The Pharisees and scribes mean their complaint to be derogatory, but Jesus uses it as an occasion to teach about God's welcome of sinners—watching, waiting—for them, for us, to return home. In so doing, we are met not with rebuke, not with punishment, but with loving embrace and celebration. At the same time, we have much to learn from the older brother. Are there any traces of his resentment in us? May we always share the Father's joy and delight in our brothers and sisters.

Lectionary for Mass: Year A

The commentary for the *Lectionary for Mass*, Year, A was written by Peggy Eckerdt © LTP, 2012. These readings are to be used when the second scrutiny is celebrated.

◆ FIRST READING: This passage introduces the great King David to posterity. We first find David in the fields tending his sheep, not in royal surroundings. It is a reminder that God's ways often challenge human presumptions. God has sent Samuel to Bethlehem to anoint one of Jesse's sons. Jesse presents seven sons, and Samuel thinks Eliab is the one. But the Lord reminds Samuel that lofty stature is not God's measure of success, for "the LORD looks into the heart," rather than at the exterior appearance. When none of the seven proves to be the chosen one, Samuel asks, "Are these all the sons you have?" Sure enough, there is one more. David, the youngest, is tending the sheep. When David appears, the Lord pronounces, "this is the one!" Samuel anoints David in the presence of his family to establish that David is filled with the Lord. From then on all would know that David's power and authority came from God.

◆ RESPONSORIAL PSALM 23: It is no accident that this Psalm is paired with the Samuel reading, for it continues the shepherd theme, inviting us to reflect on the image of God as our shepherd. Today, shepherds are not a fixture of daily life as they once were. In the time of David, shepherds were guardians and caretakers for sheep, which were dependent on them. The shepherd fed them and protected them. If they were lost, they could not find their way home without the shepherd. The message to us is that the Lord is our shepherd who will walk with us through every dark valley. When we feel lost, he will lead us to safety. When we feel trapped, he will give us courage. When we feel alone, he will lead us to his table of plenty. No wonder this is a beloved Psalm, for indeed, it reminds us that the Lord will always lead us home.

◆ SECOND READING: The letter to the Ephesians is written from a post-Resurrection understanding that Christ Jesus destroyed the power of darkness with his victory over death. The passage for the Fourth Sunday of Lent is part of a section of Ephesians (4:25—6:20) that outlines ethical guidelines for Jesus's followers. Though addressed to the people of Ephesus, this letter has significance for the entire body of Christ, the Church. This particular excerpt advises all to "live as children of light, for light produces every kind of goodness and righteousness and truth" (Ephesians 5:8–9). But what would define a life of light that is "pleasing to the Lord" (Ephesians 5:10)? The beginning of the chapter holds the key: "live in love, as Christ loved us" (Ephesians 5:2). Those who follow Christ the Light will learn that love of each other in the Lord identifies us as Christian.

◆ GOSPEL: For people blessed with eyesight, it can be very difficult to understand what the blind man in this Gospel passage was going through. Think about a man who has been blamed all of his life for his own blindness. Think about his willingness to trust Jesus. Imagine him feeling the mud on his eyes and his walk to Siloam to wash. Consider his feeling of vulnerability as his parents left him on his own to explain this miracle. And think of his courage in response to the Pharisees' questions. He called Jesus a prophet whose power clearly came from God. When asked a second time, his pointed response, "I told you already and you did not listen" (John 9:27), placed him among Jesus's disciples. In his final encounter with Jesus, the former blind man makes a tremendous assent to faith with the words, "I do believe, Lord" (John 9:38). John wanted to address a community dispute between disciples of Moses and Jesus. One group thought Jesus was a sinner; the other, that he was from God. When asked to take a side, the blind man at first ignored the theological dispute: "One thing I do know is that I was blind and now I see" (John 9:25). Pushed further, he said, "we know that God does not listen to sinners" (John 9:31). It's a statement of courage that puts the blind man at odds with the authorities of his faith community. Now he sees. His trust in Jesus filled him with courage to speak the truth. Will we have this same courage?

The Roman Missal

The Entrance Antiphon gives this Sunday its distinctive name, "Laetare," that is, "rejoicing," Sunday: "Rejoice, Jerusalem, and all who love her. / Be joyful, all who were in mourning; / exult and be satisfied at her consoling breast" (from Isaiah 66:10–11). Even in Lent, our time of fasting and penance, we rejoice, because we know that God is love, and our loving God will provide for all our needs.

In the Collect, we ask for "prompt devotion and eager faith" as we hasten toward the "solemn celebrations" to come—the Paschal Triduum of the Lord.

"With joy" on this Laetare Sunday, we bring our offerings to God, and ask that they may be received "for the salvation of all the world" (Prayer over the Offerings).

The proper Preface for the Fourth Sunday of Lent is used when the Gospel of the man born blind is read. If this Gospel is not read, Preface I or II of Lent is used in its place.

The proper Preface does not mention the man born blind, but it speaks of light and darkness. The human race was in darkness, but "by the mystery of the Incarnation" God has led us into the light of faith. We were in slavery, but now have become God's adopted children through the waters of new birth. This Preface is found in the Proper of Time.

The Prayer after Communion resonates with the Gospel of the man born blind: we ask God, "who enlightens everyone who comes into this world," to shine in our hearts, that we may ponder what God loves, and love him in sincerity.

The theme of light continues in the Prayer over the People, as we ask God to "give life by [his] unfailing light" to those who walk in darkness, and bring them to "the highest good."

The prayers for the Second scrutiny of the elect, with the special interpolations for Eucharistic Prayers I–III (found with the ritual Mass for the First scrutiny), may be used in place of the regular prayers at the Mass during which the Second scrutiny is celebrated.

Other Ideas

Write this verse on a small card: "Awake, O sleeper, / and arise from the dead, / and Christ will give you light" (Ephesians 5:14). Put the card next to your alarm and read it when you arise each morning.

M O N 11 #244 violet
Lenten Weekday

Lectionary for Mass

Please note that the optional readings for the Fourth Week of Lent may be done any of the remaining days of this week (#243).

◆ FIRST READING: The prophet's words stem from the period of exile in Babylon and proclaim a message of hope. God is "about" (Isaiah 65:17; an important adverb of time!) to create something new and what joy it brings—both for the people and for God. Note how many times words related to "joy" occur. The past is forgotten as God brings about a new creation.

◆ RESPONSORIAL PSALM 30: Fittingly, today's response is a song of thanksgiving for the experience of deliverance from death (first stanza) and sorrow (second and third stanzas). God has answered the psalmist's prayer.

◆ GOSPEL: Today's text tells of the second sign or miracle Jesus performed in the Gospel according to John (there are a total of seven recorded). Galilee was a region inhabited by many non-Jewish (Gentile) people. The royal official, unlike many of Jesus's own people, believed in his healing power and sought deliverance for his son who was near death (note the link with today's Responsorial Psalm). Unlike many of the Jews we meet in John's Gospel, this official believed in the word which Jesus spoke and his son was healed. What power in Jesus's word! What powerful things can happen as a result of faith in Jesus!

The Roman Missal

Only God can see the big picture. We pray that God will guide the Church according to his "eternal design," and come to our aid in "this present age." God is present, now and for ever (Collect).

By the sacrifice we offer, we pray that we may leave behind "earthly ways" and grow in "heavenly life" (Prayer over the Offerings).

In the Prayer after Communion we ask God to renew us, sanctify us, and lead us to eternal life.

The Prayer over the People continues the theme of renewal present in all today's prayers. We ask God to renew his people "within and without," so that they may not be hindered by the pleasures of the flesh, but persevere in their "spiritual intent"—hope for the life to come.

T U E 12 #245 violet
Lenten Weekday

Lectionary for Mass

◆ FIRST READING: Exiled in Babylon, Ezekiel is led, in a vision, to the Temple in Jerusalem. Accompanied by his heavenly guide, he sees a stream of life-giving water flowing from the Temple where God dwells—a stream so abundant that it becomes a mighty river. On its banks are trees laden with fruit and leaves that bring healing.

◆ RESPONSORIAL PSALM 46 acclaims Jerusalem, the city where God dwells, the city whose strength is the Lord. It is a city watered by life-giving streams. Such was the vision of both Ezekiel in today's First Reading and John in the Book of Revelation (22:1–2).

◆ GOSPEL: What a remarkable thing Jesus has done in today's Gospel. With a word, he healed the man who waited helplessly to be immersed in the healing waters of Bethesda, thus doing the work of the Father. We see in the story the belief that disease was punishment for sin as well as the growing antagonism between the Jews and Jesus because of his healing work on the day of the Lord.

The Roman Missal

We pray that the ancient Lenten practices we observe—"the venerable exercises of holy devotion"—may "shape" our hearts, so that we may come "worthily" to the celebration of the Paschal Mystery (Collect).

We give to God what God has given to us, and we pray for awareness of the Creator's loving care for us, and for the spiritual "healing / that brings us immortality." God cares for us, body and soul (Prayer over the Offerings).

We ask God to purify and renew our minds with the sacrament we share, both now and in the future.

The simple Prayer over the People asks for the grace of perseverance, that God's people may receive the good things God's love and "kindness" wills for them.

WED 13 #246 violet Lenten Weekday

Lectionary for Mass

◆ FIRST READING: The Lord delivers his people from all their afflictions through the life and work of his chosen servant. This is the focus of the first two verses of the reading. Then, we hear what that deliverance and comfort will look like as the people are lovingly shepherded by their God who has not forgotten them, and never will.

◆ RESPONSORIAL PSALM 145: Fittingly, this song of praise highlights the mercy God shows toward his people. The first line of the first stanza, in fact, is the very way God describes himself to Moses on Mount Sinai. The last line of the last stanza, with its theme of calling on the Lord, is a nice connection with the first line of the First Reading.

◆ GOSPEL: Each stanza of today's Responsorial Psalm makes mention of God's work. Today's Gospel, a continuation from yesterday, shares this focus with its emphasis on Jesus doing the work of his Father, in particular, the work of healing and giving life. Do not miss the point: the one who believes in Jesus has eternal life now, the passage from death to life has been accomplished. We wait, of course, for its full realization in the resurrection of life, which is to come after our physical deaths.

The Roman Missal

In the Collect, we call upon God, who rewards the just and forgives the repentant. We pray that we who acknowledge our sinfulness may receive God's pardon.

The Prayer over the Offerings is a prayer for renewal. We ask God to wipe away the old, and increase the "grace of salvation" and new life within us.

The Prayer after Communion echoes Saint Paul: "A person should examine himself, and so eat the bread and drink the cup. For anyone who eats and drinks without discerning the body, eats and drinks judgment on himself" (1 Corinthians 11:28–29). We pray that the sacrament which God gives us as a "heavenly remedy" may not bring us judgment.

We ask God's protection so that we may do "what is good in this world," and so reach God, our "highest good" (Prayer over the People).

THU 14 #247 violet Lenten Weekday

Lectionary for Mass

◆ FIRST READING: The people of Israel forsake God and make an idol in his place with their own hands while Moses is on Mount Sinai. Angered, God is determined to destroy them. Moses pleads on behalf of the people, asking God to remember the covenant he made with their fathers, Abraham, Isaac, and Jacob. God hears and relents.

◆ RESPONSORIAL PSALM 106: This same incident is recounted in today's Responsorial Psalm. Like Israel of old, we have forsaken God and worshipped idols of our own making. We, too, plead for his mercy.

◆ GOSPEL: Still continuing the text of John 5, we hear Jesus confront the Jews on their refusal to believe in him, the one sent by the Father, who comes in the name of the Father and with the voice of the Father, the one who gives life. Jesus is the one to whom the whole Law of Moses points and in whom it is fulfilled. If only they—and we—could hear.

The Roman Missal

In the Collect, we ask God for the grace of perseverance in our "penance" and "good works," that we may come to the celebration of Easter transformed—"corrected" and "schooled" in God's ways.

◆ PRAYER OVER THE OFFERINGS: We pray that the sacrifice of the Mass may cleanse us from evil and bring us God's protection.

◆ PRAYER AFTER COMMUNION: The sacrament we receive has power to purify us, free us, and bring us heavenly help.

The Prayer over the People is a prayer for God's protection: we ask God to "bless," "keep . . . safe," "defend," and "prepare" us so that we may remain in his love.

FRI 15 #248 violet Lenten Weekday

Lectionary for Mass

◆ FIRST READING: The wicked cannot tolerate the just. Their witness condemns them. Accordingly, the wicked seek to destroy the just one to see if God will indeed take care of him.

◆ RESPONSORIAL PSALM 34: The Lord does not abandon the just into the hands of their foes, but delivers them.

◆ GOSPEL: Mistakenly, the Jews think they know Jesus's identity. They fail to realize that he has not come on his own but is sent by the Father.

The Roman Missal

God knows our weakness and prepares "fitting helps" for us in his sacraments. We pray that we may joyfully receive their "healing effects" and reflect them in the way we live our lives (Collect).

We long to be cleansed by the "mighty power" of the sacrifice, so we can come to its source—God—with "greater purity" (Prayer over the Offerings).

The Prayer after Communion reflects the theme of renewal, moving from old to new, which is present in so many of the prayers of Lent. We pray that we may leave behind former ways and "be renewed in holiness of mind."

The Prayer over the People asks God's protection and help for those who trust in his mercy.

S A T 16 #249 violet
Lenten Weekday

Lectionary for Mass

◆ FIRST READING: The prophet is taken by surprise when he realizes the opposition against him. His enemies seek to take his life. Jeremiah can only entrust himself to the Lord.

◆ RESPONSORIAL PSALM 7: The psalmist, too, knows the rage of his foes and cries out for God's help and protection. God is a sure refuge.

◆ GOSPEL: Those who hear Jesus are perplexed. Could Jesus be the long-awaited one, the Messiah? But they didn't expect a prophet, a Messiah, from Galilee. What are they to make of the authority with which he speaks? Who is Jesus for us?

The Roman Missal

We ask God in his mercy to direct our hearts, for without him, we cannot hope to "find favor in his sight" (Collect).

Jesus's prayer in the garden of Gethsemane is one that we have a hard time echoing: "not as I will, but as you will" (Matthew 26:39). The Prayer over the Offerings acknowledges this and asks that "even when our wills are defiant," God may bend them to conversion, to turn toward him.

In the Prayer after Communion, we ask that the sacrament we receive may have an effect in our lives, and make us "fully pleasing" to God.

As Easter approaches, we ask God's grace, so that, knowing his consolations in this life, we may direct our attention to the "higher goods that cannot be seen"—the things of heaven (Prayer over the People).

☀ 17 #36 or 34 violet
Fifth Sunday of Lent

Orienation: Year C

The only one without sin who could have rightfully condemned the woman caught in adultery was Jesus himself. Yet, instead of casting stones and bringing on death, he forgives the woman and renews her in the life of faith. A new chance at life, in which to live justly and to do good is worth more to Jesus than the bloody end of this woman. This reading prepares us to ponder the Paschal Mystery, where death fails to have the last word, and life is given ultimate meaning in the Resurrection. What areas in your life are most in need of such renewal?

Lectionary for Mass: Year C

◆ FIRST READING: Isaiah's words are addressed to an exiled Israel in Babylon. His words are words of hope, for they speak of the Lord's promise of restoration. God is known through his deeds on Israel's

behalf, and the exodus from slavery in Egypt was pre-eminent among them. Once again, God would open a way for his people and do something new—accomplishing their deliverance and salvation.

◆ RESPONSORIAL PSALM 126 celebrates Israel's return to Babylon after the time of the Exile—an event so marvelous that it seemed like a dream. Once again, God has done great things on Israel's behalf. They are filled with joy.

◆ SECOND READING: There is an interesting juxtaposition in today's First and Second Readings. The Israelites lost their land and possessions at the time of the Exile. Paul, in light of his experience of Christ, considers all as loss, mere rubbish in comparison with life in Christ. What Paul wants to gain or possess is Christ and resurrection from the dead. He knows that the way to reach his goal is by being conformed to Christ in his suffering and death. It is a lifelong process, as his words suggest. We must not look at what is behind, but keep our eyes fixed on the goal that is ahead of us: Christ.

◆ GOSPEL: The woman "caught" (John 8:4) in her sin—and where is the man?—seems to be especially singled out for humiliation and shame. At the same time, Jesus is set up for a trap by the self-righteous Pharisees. But Jesus turns the tables and confronts them with the truth of their own sinfulness. They condemned the woman in their self-righteousness. Jesus forgives her—and all sinners—in his love.

Lectionary for Mass: Year A

The commentary for the *Lectionary for Mass*, Year A, was written by Peggy Eckerdt © LTP, 2012. These readings are to be used when the third scrutiny is celebrated.

◆ FIRST READING: Ezekiel served on God's behalf during the time of the Judean exile in Babylon in 593 BC. Like prophets before and since, Ezekiel was both a taskmaster and cheerleader, demanding that the people turn from wayward lives and encouraging them to place their hope in the Lord. This reading conveys a message of hope as it interprets Ezekiel's famous vision of dried bones scattered throughout the plains (37:2–10). The Lord has told Ezekiel to "prophesy over these bones, and say to them: Dry bones, hear the word of the LORD! . . . I will make breath enter you, that you may come to life" (Ezekiel 37:4–5). Even though the people live in exile like dead bones on the plain, God has not forgotten them. He promises that he will raise them from their graves of hopelessness and bring them "back to the land of Israel" (Ezekiel 37:12). He will breathe his spirit into them and give them new life. This story is not intended as a direct commentary on the resurrection from the dead; rather, it is a message of God's faithfulness to the people of Israel. Though bound in exile, they must know and remember that God will set them free.

◆ RESPONSORIAL PSALM: "With the Lord there is mercy, and fullness of redemption" (Psalm 130:7). The Psalm's refrain holds the promise of redemption and new life for the people of Israel. But this Psalm, considered one of seven penitential Psalms, begins with the haunting lament: "Out of the depths I cry to you, O LORD; / LORD, hear my voice!" (Psalm 130:1). In the midst of this plaintive cry, the psalmist expresses a spirit of confidence in the Lord's forgiveness. Vigilant and alert, the psalmist waits on the Lord, trusting that the Lord's generous mercy will bring redemption to his people. It is a statement of faith that we can make our own. No matter what chains restrict us, what illness or worry consumes us,

or what bondage we endure, we can trust in the Lord to walk with us. We can trust the Lord to support and free us.

◆ SECOND READING: In this passage, Paul wants us to know that, through Christ's Death and Resurrection, we now belong to God in a very special way. God has sent his Spirit to remain with us and help us. Paul begins by saying that the goal of human life is to please God. He cautions that self-absorption (living in the flesh) is a big trap that drags us away from God. But Paul also reminds his readers that the Spirit dwelling within all believers is the source of strength for living faithful lives. When distracted by things of the world, God's Spirit will help the faithful focus on what matters most. When tempted to place trust in the things of this world, Christ will help the faithful remain fixed on grace. When selfishness threatens love, the Spirit of God will help the faithful to live for others. Paul promises that, with the Spirit, believers can live righteously and thus participate in divine life.

◆ GOSPEL: Can you imagine receiving a phone call with the news that your best friend, who lives nearby, is dying, and thinking to yourself, "I'll just wait four days and see what happens"? Of course not. That is our clue that John's narrative about Jesus's friend Lazarus speaks not of the bonds of human friendship, but rather of the power of Jesus. It helps to think of this Gospel passage as six acts of a dramatic tableau. The first act establishes the purpose of the drama: "This illness is . . . for the glory of God" (John 11:4). The second recounts Jesus's decision to return to Lazarus's hometown, even though it is dangerous to do so. The third act puts Jesus and the disciples in Bethany, where they learn that Lazarus has been dead for four

days, enough time for the rabbinic scholars to believe Lazarus's soul had left his body. The fourth act introduces Martha, who first chastises Jesus, then professes her belief that his power comes from God. Martha sends for Mary as the scene changes once more, and Mary goes to meet Jesus, with the crowd of mourners accompanying her. These are the people who will return to Jerusalem with news of this miracle, fueling the call to condemn Jesus of Nazareth. The climax of the drama begins with Martha's final assertion of Lazarus's death ("there will be a stench"). Jesus calls on the Father ("that they may believe that you sent me," John 11:42) and then calls for Lazarus. As Lazarus emerges from the tomb, Jesus gives a final instruction: "Untie him and let him go" (John 11:45).

The Roman Missal

Beginning today, we will see a shift in tone in the liturgy of Lent, with an increasing focus on Christ's Passion. In the Entrance Antiphon for today, taken from Psalm 43 (42):1–2, we hear an echo of Jesus's prayer to his Father as the forces of evil begin to close in around him.

In the Collect, we ask God to help us "walk eagerly" in the love of Christ, the same love which prompted him to hand himself over to death.

God has taught us with "the teachings of the Christian faith"; we ask him to purify us by the power of the sacrifice we offer (Prayer over the Offerings).

The proper Preface for the Fifth Sunday of Lent is used when the Gospel of the raising of Lazarus is read. It is found in the Proper of Time. If this Gospel is not read, Preface I or II of Lent is used in its place. The proper Preface speaks of Christ as God and man. As man, he wept for Lazarus; as God, he raised him from the dead. In the same way, Christ takes pity on the human family, and leads us to new life "by sacred mysteries."

Notice that three options are provided for the Communion Antiphon, one for each Gospel that is read on this Sunday. Use the first in Year A or whenever the Gospel of Lazarus is read. The second is proper to Year C, the Gospel of the woman taken in adultery, and the third is for use in Year B.

The prayers for the Third scrutiny of the elect, with the special interpolations for Eucharistic Prayers I–III (found with the ritual Mass for the First scrutiny), may be used in place of the regular prayers at the Mass during which the Third scrutiny is celebrated.

In the Prayer after Communion, we pray that we may always remain in the Body of Christ, for we have communion in him.

In the Prayer over the People, we ask God to grant us what he himself has prompted us to pray for.

Other Ideas

Martha worries that after four days the stench of death will emanate from Lazarus's tomb. Maybe that's what funeral flowers are meant to do—cover up the smell of death. Sweeten the life of someone who has lost a loved one by sending unexpected flowers months after the loss. Sustain the person with prayer throughout the week.

MON 18 #251 violet
Lenten Weekday

Optional Memorial of Saint Cyril of Jerusalem. Bishop and Doctor of the Church / violet

Lectionary for Mass

Please note that the optional readings for the Fifth Week of Lent may be done any of the remaining days of this week (#250).

◆ FIRST READING: Two options are given for today's First Reading about the unjust accusation against the God-fearing (righteous) woman, Susannah, made by two wicked elders of Israel who lusted after her. In the longer form, we hear of their plot to have her as their own and her cry for help. The shorter form begins at this point with her prayer that God will reveal the truth and her life will be spared. The hero of the story is the young Daniel. Endowed by God with wisdom, he objects to the false trial and arranges instead a trial of the two wicked elders, who condemn themselves with their own words. Susannah's life is spared, and the wicked elders receive the punishment they intended to inflict on her.

◆ RESPONSORIAL PSALM 23: How fitting is today's antiphon, for Susannah did indeed walk through a dark valley of unjust accusation which nearly led to her death. Psalm 23 is a song of confidence acclaiming the Lord as Shepherd. He was indeed at her side, hearing her cry for help and rescuing her from death.

◆ GOSPEL: Today's Gospel (John 8:12–20 for Year C) presents Jesus as the Light of the World, the light that overcomes all darkness, the light of life. The mention of testimony and judgment echoes themes in today's First Reading. Jesus, too, knew false accusation. His testimony to the truth was not accepted. In this instance (today's Gospel),

his life is spared for his "hour" had not yet come.

The Roman Missal

The Christian Passover approaches, and our Collect speaks of passing "from former ways to newness of life," so that we may be ready for the kingdom.

Our Lenten observance is not an end in itself, but, as we hear frequently in the Lenten prayers, a school forming and shaping us. We ask that we may bring to God "a joyful purity of heart" as the "fruit" of our penance this Lent (Prayer over the Offerings).

Preface I of the Passion of the Lord is used.

Two options are provided for the Communion Antiphon, depending on which Gospel is proclaimed.

We ask that through "the blessing of [God's] Sacraments," we may be cleansed from sin, and climb toward God in the footsteps of Christ (Prayer after Communion).

We ask God to free us from sin, so that, following a "holy way of life," we may know God's protection "from every trial" (Prayer over the People).

If the optional Memorial is observed, the Collect is drawn from the Proper of Saints, while the remaining prayers may be taken from the Common of Pastors: For a bishop, or from the Common of Doctors of the Church, or from the Lenten weekday. Another option is to use the Collect for Saint Cyril as the conclusion of the Prayer of the Faithful.

Today's Saint

Saint Cyril of Jerusalem (315–386) is well known for his brilliant exposition of the faith to catechumens, which is preserved in 23 homilies. Much of his life was marked by an experience of exile. At three different points during his tenure as bishop of Jerusalem he was exiled by the reigning emperor due to controversy concerning doctrine and authority. Sixteen of his 35 years as rightful bishop of Jerusalem were spent in exile. His life is worthy of emulation, because even though he was continually embroiled in conflict and banished from his home, Saint Cyril remained faithful by never abandoning his convictions and patiently enduring the wrongdoing of others. Stemming from his significant contributions in the area of catechesis, he joined the ranks of many other holy men and women as a Doctor of the Church.

TUE 19 #543 white Solemnity of Saint Joseph, Spouse of the Blessed Virgin Mary

Lectionary for Mass

◆ FIRST READING: David wants to build a "house" or temple for God. Nathan the prophet, instructed by God, tells David that his son will do this. God promises instead to build a house or a dynasty for David. From his line shall come the Messiah, whose kingdom will endure forever.

◆ RESPONSORIAL PSALM 89: The psalmist sings of God's love and fidelity, which is shown in his promise to David of an everlasting covenant and an everlasting kingship.

◆ SECOND READING: Abraham, father of the chosen people, is justified, that is, put in the right relationship with God, not because of his works but because of his faith. Abraham had faith even when—especially when—asked to believe in what seemed impossible.

◆ GOSPEL: Great faith was required of Joseph in the face of the incomprehensible events concerning his espoused wife, and in subsequent years, the actions of her son. Though not understanding, Joseph humbly

and patiently complied with what God asked. In this he is model for us all.

The Roman Missal

The Entrance Antiphon, based on Luke 12:42, speaks of Joseph as the "faithful and prudent steward, / whom the Lord set over his household."

The Gloria is said or sung today.

The Collect presents Joseph as a model for the Church. Just as Joseph watched over Christ in his infancy, so the Church must "watch over / the unfolding of the mysteries of human salvation."

In our ministry at the altar, we pray that we may imitate the "loving care" of Saint Joseph's service of the infant Christ (Prayer over the Offerings).

The Preface is subtitled "The mission of Saint Joseph," and, like the Entrance Antiphon, speaks of Joseph as the steward of God's household, watching "like a father" over the Son of God.

The Prayer after Communion is a prayer for the protection of the Church on this Solemnity of Saint Joseph.

Today's Saint

Joseph was the foster father of Jesus, the man entrusted with his care and upbringing. We know that Joseph was a "righteous man" who protected Mary from disgrace after she was found to be pregnant with Jesus (Matthew 1:19). Like the earlier Joseph in Genesis, he received instruction and reassurance from God through dreams. The Gospel gives little information about him, save that he was an artisan who lived in Nazareth, was a descendant of David, and went to Bethlehem for a census, causing Jesus to be born there in fulfillment of the prophecies. When warned in a dream that Jesus was in danger because of the evil intentions of King Herod, Joseph took Jesus and Mary to live

in exile in Egypt until he learned that Herod had died (see Matthew 2:12–15). As a result, Jesus was spared the fate of the Holy Innocents. After the account of Jesus's being lost and found in the Temple during a pilgrimage, Joseph is not mentioned again. We can infer that he had died before Jesus began his ministry; he was certainly not alive at the time of the Crucifixion, because he would have been the one to claim Jesus's body, not Joseph of Arimathea. Catholic tradition describes him as dying in the arms of Jesus and Mary, and so he is invoked as the patron of a happy death. Because he was a man who worked with his hands, he is the patron of workers and especially carpenters. Devotion to Saint Joseph developed rather late, and was popularized by Saint Bernardine of Siena during the fifteenth century.

WED 20 #253 violet Lenten Weekday

Lectionary for Mass

◆ FIRST READING: Daniel's three companions are condemned to death by being thrown into a fiery furnace for their refusal to worship the idol set up by the Babylonian king, Nebuchadnezzar. They were willing to sacrifice their bodies rather than disobey God's law. God sent his angel to be with them and kept them safe in the midst of the fire. Seeing this, Nebuchadnezzar acknowledged the power of their God.

◆ CANTICLE: Today's text from the book of the prophet Daniel is the hymn sung by the three men in the furnace, when they realized that the flames were not harming them.

◆ GOSPEL: Today's Gospel opens with a beautiful definition of discipleship: remaining in Jesus's word. The rest of today's text focuses on how the Jews misunderstood Jesus's teaching. They still cannot recognize that he is from God, the fulfilment of God's promises all the way back to Abraham.

The Roman Missal

God himself awakens devotion in us. We ask him to enlighten those who have been "sanctified by penance" this Lent, and to hear us when we cry out to him (Collect).

We ask God to "receive back" the sacrifice he has given us, that it may be "for our healing" (Prayer over the Offerings).

The sacrament we receive is "heavenly medicine," purging evil and strengthening us with God's protection (Prayer after Communion).

God has given us our hope in his compassion. In the Prayer over the People, we ask him to let us feel his mercy as well.

THU 21 #254 violet
Lenten Weekday

Lectionary for Mass

◆ FIRST READING: God renews his covenant relationship with Abraham. A covenant is a type of agreement in which two parties pledge themselves to one another and which entails responsibilities on the part of both. God pledges loyalty to Abraham and promises his descendants land. Note the name change, signifying Abraham's special role.

◆ RESPONSORIAL PSALM 105: The psalmist calls the descendants of Abraham to remember their covenant responsibilities and reminds them of all God has done for them.

◆ GOSPEL: The controversy over Jesus's identity continues in today's reading, with the Jews identified as descendants of Abraham. Jesus refers to himself as "I AM," the name by which God revealed himself to Moses. This is who Jesus is, he who is from the beginning.

The Roman Missal

In the Collect, we ask for the grace of perseverance "in holy living," so that we may be "full heirs" of God's promises.

We offer the holy sacrifice not only for our own conversion, but for "the salvation of all the world" (Prayer over the Offerings).

Preface I of the Passion of the Lord is used.

Prayer after Communion: Through the sacrament of which we partake here and now, we pray to be "partakers of life eternal."

In the Prayer over the People, we ask that we may reject those things that displease God, and instead be filled "with delight" in God's commandments.

FRI 22 #255 violet
Lenten Weekday

Lectionary for Mass

◆ FIRST READING: In this text, one of the "confessions" of Jeremiah, the prophet acknowledges the threats of his foes who seek his downfall. He likewise acknowledges his deep trust in the Lord. In the last verse, we hear his acclamation of praise for God's deliverance.

◆ RESPONSORIAL PSALM 18 echoes the prayer of Jeremiah: in the midst of overwhelming distress, trust in God and the experience of God's deliverance.

◆ GOSPEL: In today's Gospel, part of a controversy that actually begins in verse 22, the Jews are in a dilemma over Jesus's identity. They do not understand his claims to be one with the Father, to be the Son of God, to be sent by the Father, even though his works bear witness to this. While some Jews think that he is blaspheming, others believe.

The Roman Missal

There are two options for the Collect today. The first is a prayer for forgiveness and freedom from the bonds of sin. The second invokes the intercession of the Blessed Virgin Mary, whom we "imitate devoutly" in contemplating the Passion of Christ.

In the Prayer over the Offerings, we pray that we may be worthy to serve at God's altar and be saved by our sharing in the sacrifice.

Preface I of the Passion of the Lord is used.

In the Prayer after Communion, we pray that the power of the sacrament we have received may keep us safe from all harm.

The Prayer over the People is a simple prayer for protection from evil, that we may serve God "in peace of mind."

SAT 23 #256 violet
Lenten Weekday

Optional Memorial of Saint Turibius of Mogrovejo, Bishop / violet

Lectionary for Mass

◆ FIRST READING: God's word is addressed to the Jewish nation in exile. The prophets saw the exile as punishment for sin (see verse 23). God promises a return to the land, the unification of all the tribes, the restoration of the Davidic line, and an everlasting covenant.

◆ CANTICLE: Today's response is a canticle taken from the prophet Jeremiah, was spoken during the time of the Babylonain exile, and reiterates the promise of restoration and return.

◆ GOSPEL: Controversy over Jesus heightens after the raising of Lazarus. The Jewish leaders fear the demise of Israel at the hands of the Romans. Ironically, the death of Jesus results not in demise or destruction but in the "gathering" (a motif in each of today's Scriptures) of the scattered people.

The Roman Missal

The Collect echoes 1 Peter 2:9: God has made us "a chosen race and a royal priesthood." We who have been chosen and called ask for the grace to carry out God's commands, so that we may be one in our faith and in our deeds.

We offer the bread and wine "from our fasting" and ask that it may be expiation of our sins and lead us to God's eternal promise (Prayer over the Offerings).

Preface I of the Passion of the Lord is used.

We ask God to "make us sharers of [Christ's] divine nature" through our sharing in his Body and Blood (Prayer after Communion).

We ask God's mercy on the Church, that God not allow those redeemed by the Death of Christ "to be harmed by their sins or weighed down by their trials" (Prayer over the People).

If the optional Memorial is observed, the Collect may be taken from the Proper of Saints, with the remaining prayers drawn from the Common of Pastors or from the Lenten weekday. Another option is to use the Collect for Saint Turibius at the conclusion of the Prayer of the Faithful.

Today's Saint

Saint Turibius de Mogrovejo (1538–1606) was a professor of law at the University of Salamanca, in Spain, until he was called to be bishop of Lima in America. He labored there for nearly thirty years, celebrating the sacraments (he confirmed Saint Rose of Lima), learning the language, and correcting abuses among the clergy.

Gospel with Palms, #37; #38 red

24 Palm Sunday of the Passion of the Lord

Orienation

Branches of palm, olive, or sometimes even budding willow, are ancient symbols of victory and hope, as well as of new life. The procession celebrating Jesus's entry into Jerusalem overflowed with praise and excitement, as onlookers waved these triumphant branches and proclaimed their blessings. Yet, in a few days, they will cry "Crucify him!" The crowd's change of heart illustrates the problem of holding God to our expectations. The crowd expected a liberating leader, the Messiah, to free them from Roman oppression. Jesus instead takes up his cross and invites us to do the same. Through his Death and Resurrection he is indeed a liberator, but from death and sin, not from Rome. But unable to see past their need, the crowd's disappointment turns into anger and a death order. As we enter Holy Week, Palm Sunday teaches us to let God be God, and to trust in God's wisdom not only to meet but shatteringly to exceed our expectations.

Lectionary for Mass

The commentary on the Gospel with Palms was written by Biagio Mazza (© LTP, 2012). The remaining commentaries were written by Anne Elizabeth Sweet, OCSO.

◆ GOSPEL WITH PALMS: As disciples of Jesus, today we imitate his first followers by accompanying him into Jerusalem. Jesus completes his journey to Jerusalem, where he is greeted with great joy as the long-awaited Messiah. A colt never ridden, willing acquiescence to Jesus's directives, cloaks spread out on the road, praise and acclamation boldly proclaimed—all these details affirm his followers' acknowledgement of Jesus as God's Messiah and prophet. How many will be ready to suffer with him as the authorities challenge his person and teachings? This perennial question confronts his followers in every age.

◆ FIRST READING: Today's First Reading is one of the four suffering-servant songs of Isaiah (we will have the others in the course of the week), which depicts a prophet who willingly submits to shame and disgrace in carrying out his ministry, with God's help.

◆ RESPONSORIAL PSALM 22: This is a song of lament uttered in the depths of great distress, which is vividly described and experienced as abandonment by God. Note the confident change of tone in the last stanza.

◆ SECOND READING: Today's Second Reading is an early Christian hymn that concisely summarizes the Christian mystery: though divine, Jesus willingly embraced human likeness and was obedient to God, even unto a shameful death. Exalted by God, all creation reverently acknowledges him as Lord.

◆ GOSPEL: We hear the story of Jesus's Passion according to Luke. In this last day of his life, Jesus's ministry of teaching, healing, and forgiving continues until his Death. On the Cross, he forgives those who crucified him. He trustingly commends his life into the hands of his Father.

The longer version of the Gospel begins with Jesus's Last Supper, a Passover meal, with his disciples before he inaugurated a new covenant, passing over from death to life. Note the teachings Jesus gives to his disciples at this last meal in a sort of farewell discourse: on service rather than domination, on the promise of one day partaking of a meal in his kingdom, on the necessary preparations for their ministry. Note, too, the prayer for Peter's perseverance in faith and Jesus's instruction to him to strengthen his brothers and sisters after his own failure. Other unique touches of Luke's Passion account include the angel ministering to Jesus in the garden and prayer so intense that Jesus's sweat became like drops of blood; Jesus's trial before Herod, who, like Pilate, finds Jesus innocent; the women who followed him on the way to Calvary; the conversation of the two thieves crucified with him, and Jesus's promise of Pariadise to the one thief. Only Luke records that the multitudes who witnessed his death repented after the centurion's proclamation of Jesus's innocence.

The Roman Missal

The liturgy today is divided into three parts: the Commemoration of the Lord's Entrance into Jerusalem, the Liturgy of the Word, and the Liturgy of the Eucharist. As it often does, *The Roman Missal* provides several options for the celebration, to allow for a variety of situations and pastoral needs.

There are three forms for the Commemoration of the Lord's Entrance into Jerusalem: The Procession, The Solemn Entrance, and The Simple Entrance. The Procession, which is strongly encouraged, may take place only once, at the principal Mass. The Solemn Entrance is recommended for the "other Masses that are usually well attended."

◆ THE PROCESSION: The people gather in a place separate from the church—a chapel, a parish hall, perhaps, or (weather permitting) an outdoor gathering place. The people receive branches as they gather (palms are traditional, but the Missal does not specify the type of branches to be carried). The rubrics suggest that the clergy and ministers join them without an elaborate entrance procession—they simply "approach the place where the people are gathered." The celebrant may wear a cope for this first part of the liturgy. After the usual greeting, *The Roman Missal* provides an introduction, which may be freely adapted, about Palm Sunday as both ending and beginning: it is the culmination of five weeks of Lent, and the beginning of Holy Week. The introduction reminds us that what we are about to celebrate is the heart of our faith, the Paschal Mystery of the Passion, Death, and Resurrection of Jesus, and urges us to enter into this holiest of weeks with the right attitude of "faith and devotion." After the introduction the people are invited to hold their palm branches aloft for the Blessing of the Branches. Two options for the Prayer of Blessing are provided. In the first, we pray that we who follow Christ today may one day reach the heavenly Jerusalem. The second urges us to raise up to God the fruit of good works, just as we raise our branches high to honor Christ. Following the blessing the branches are sprinkled with holy water in silence. Then the Gospel of the

Lord's entry into Jerusalem is proclaimed. It is introduced in the usual way, and incense may be used.

Following the Gospel (the Gospel accounts for the blessing of palms are included in the third edition of *The Roman Missal*), a Homily may be given (*The Roman Missal* specifies that it should be "brief"). Then the deacon, priest, or a lay minister invites the people to "go forth in peace" and the procession forms: servers carrying incense, cross (decorated with palm branches), and candles, the deacon carrying the *Book of the Gospels*, the priest and ministers, and finally the whole assembly, carrying branches. The procession moves slowly to the church, accompanied by music (a wide range of antiphons is provided in the Missal, including Psalm 24 (23), Psalm 47 (46), and the text upon which the ancient hymn "All Glory, Laud, and Honor" is based). With careful preparation, you can have groups of singers interspersed through the procession, including at the end, to encourage all to join in song. Keep the music going until everyone has entered the church. The Collect follows, and the Liturgy of the Word proceeds as usual.

The Solemn Entrance may be used when it is not possible to have the procession. The celebrant and ministers gather at a place outside of the sanctuary—for example, at the doors of the church. If possible, the entire congregation, or even a small number, join them. The greeting, introduction, blessing of palms, and Gospel of the Lord's entrance into Jerusalem take place as above. Then all process into the church.

◆ THE SIMPLE ENTRANCE: In the third form of the Commemoration of the Lord's Entrance into Jerusalem, the ministers simply enter the sanctuary as usual. The priest reverences the altar and goes to his place. The Entrance Antiphon about the Lord's entry into Jerusalem is read, then Mass proceeds as usual.

◆ PASSION NARRATIVE: Several options are given for the proclamation of the Passion narrative, which may be read by a deacon or by a priest. If the dramatic form of the Passion is used, lay readers may also share in the Passion, with the part of Christ reserved to the priest, when possible. The Greeting and the Sign of the Cross at the beginning of the account, as well as the incensation, are omitted. When the narrative describes the Death of Jesus, all kneel and pray in silence for a time. At the end of the reading, the deacon or priest says or sings, "The Gospel of the Lord" as usual, but the book is not kissed.

The prayers at the blessing of the palms speak of triumph and exultation; the prayers of the Mass emphasize the Passion of Christ. We contemplate Christ's "example of humility" as he hangs upon the Cross for us, and pray that we may "heed his lesson" and share in his Resurrection (Collect). We do not deserve God's grace, but receive it through his love; in the sacrifice we offer and receive, we already know his mercy (Prayer over the Offerings). The Preface speaks of the saving power of the Passion: by his Death, he "has washed away our sins," and his Resurrection brings "justification"—life with Christ in God. Christ's death has brought us hope for eternal life; we pray that we may have a share in his Resurrection (Prayer after Communion). The Prayer over the People for this solemn feast is simple and beautiful. We ask God simply to "look" upon his "family," the Church, and to remember that Christ suffered the agony of the cross for us. It is the perfect prayer for Holy Week. The Preface is found in the Proper of Time.

Other Ideas

The Suffering Servant of today's First Reading boasts of persevering through persecution and trusting in God's deliverance. Many suffer in the world with little hope of deliverance. Spend time this week reading about an area where people are suffering unjustly and think of how, through prayer or in some other way, you might help them. In the end, Jesus is buried in the tomb under the watchful eyes of two women, Mary Magdalene and Mary, the Mother of Jesus. But many die alone with no watchful, caring eyes upon them. Make a contribution to the bereavement ministry in your parish or pray for those who minister to the dying and the bereaved.

M
O
N **25** #257   violet
Monday of Holy Week

Lectionary for Mass

◆ FIRST READING: We see the gentleness of the servant in dealing with those to whom he is sent. His mission is to bring enlightenment and liberation not only to Israel, but to all the nations. The servant has been chosen by God and endowed with his Spirit.

◆ RESPONSORIAL PSALM 27: With the Lord as light and salvation, the psalmist confidently and courageously faces his adversaries. There is no cause for fear.

◆ GOSPEL: With lavish extravagance, Mary, the sister of Lazarus, washes Jesus's feet and anoints them with costly oil. Jesus interprets her gesture prophetically, associating it with the day of his burial. Judas, Jesus's betrayer, with self-serving concerns, objects to what she has done, but Jesus sets the matter straight.

The Roman Missal

The Solemnity of the Annunciation of the Lord would normally fall on this day. However, because today is Monday of Holy Week, the solemnity is transferred to the first available day on the calendar, which is Monday of the Second Week of Easter.

In the Collect, we pray that we, who fail through our weakness, may be strengthened by Christ's Passion.

We ask God to look upon the "sacred mysteries" we celebrate, and through this holy sacrifice to "cancel the judgment" against us, and bring us to eternal life (Prayer over the Offerings).

Preface II of the Passion of the Lord is used. This preface speaks of the fast-approaching days of the Triduum. We recall the Passion and Resurrection of the Lord, which "vanquished" Satan, "the ancient foe," and we celebrate the redemption Christ has won for us.

◆ PRAYER AFTER COMMUNION: We ask God to "visit" us and protect us, so that we may hold to the pledge of glory we have received in the sacrament.

◆ PRAYER OVER THE PEOPLE: We ask God's protection for those who trust in his mercy, that we may celebrate Easter with "bodily observance" and "purity of mind."

T
U
E **26** #258   violet
Tuesday of Holy Week

Lectionary for Mass

◆ FIRST READING: The Lord's servant addresses both Israel and the nations. Even before he was born he was chosen not only to restore the conquered and exiled Israel, but to enlighten the nations with God's good news of salvation. Though he was disheartened about his ministry, the words of the Lord have given him new courage and vision.

◆ RESPONSORIAL PSALM 71: The Psalmist in distress cries out for God's deliverance. God is—and has been even before the Psalmist's birth—rock, refuge, stronghold, and teacher. The experience of salvation leads to grateful proclamation of the Lord's deliverance.

◆ GOSPEL: Jesus is troubled and distressed, knowing that one of his disciples will betray him and a second will deny him. At the same time, he recognizes that his death will also be his exaltation, his return to the Father, and his glorification. One day, our death will be our return to the Father as well.

The Roman Missal

We pray in the Collect that we may worthily celebrate "the mysteries of the Lord's Passion" and receive forgiveness for our sins.

In the Prayer over the Offerings, we ask for a share in the "fullness" of the "sacred gifts" that we receive in the Sacrament of Christ's Body and Blood.

Preface II of the Passion of the Lord is used.

The Eucharist is the foretaste of the life to come. In the Prayer after Communion, we pray that we who have shared in the "saving gifts" may also have a share in "life eternal."

The Prayer over the People is a prayer for purification in which we ask God to "cleanse" his people of the "seduction of former ways," which still have their hold on us, and to make us "capable of new holiness." Conversion is not a moment in time; conversion is a lifetime.

Lectionary for Mass

◆ FIRST READING: The prophet speaks the word he heard from the Lord, not his own word. The prophet willingly endures the opposition and suffering he experiences in carrying out his mission, knowing that God is his helper.

◆ RESPONSORIAL PSALM 69 is a song of lament, vividly describing the sufferings endured by one of the chosen people—all for the sake of God. The last stanza attests the psalmist's confidence that God will deliver him.

◆ GOSPEL: One of Jesus's own will betray him. Jesus is fully aware of this, yet he does not shun his betrayer, but shares the Passover meal with him.

The Roman Missal

For our sake, God willed that his Son should carry "the yoke of the Cross." We ask for "the grace of the resurrection" (Collect).

In the Prayer over the Offerings, we pray that we who celebrate the Passion of Christ "in mystery" in the sacrifice of the Mass may know its effects in our lives.

Preface II of the Passion of the Lord is used.

The Prayer after Communion is a prayer for faith, that we may have the "firm conviction" that Christ's death brings "perpetual life" to those he redeemed.

The Prayer over the People is a prayer for more faithful and persevering participation in the sacraments, so that "Lenten works" may lead God's people to "newness of life."

Orientation: Chrism Mass

Today no Mass is celebrated before the Mass of the Lord's Supper, except for the diocesan celebration of the Chrism Mass. However, the norms allow for this liturgy to be celebrated earlier in Holy Week (see *Paschale Solemnitatis*, 35). This is because the presence of the diocesan presbyterate and of the faithful, gathered around the bishop, is of key importance to this liturgy. Since the demands of Holy Thursday often make it difficult for priests and the faithful to go to the cathedral, many dioceses celebrate the Chrism Mass earlier in the week. Tuesday is a common day for the celebration.

During this Mass, the holy oils that will be used throughout the coming year are blessed by the bishop:

◆ oil of catechumens, used to anoint those preparing for Baptism (infants, children, and adults);

◆ oil of the sick, used to anoint those who are suffering from serious illnesses;

◆ sacred chrism, used to anoint candidates for Baptism, Confirmation, and Ordination, and to bless and consecrate every new altar.

At the conclusion of the Mass, the oils are distributed to representatives of every parish of the diocese. Since this one Mass touches the sacramental and worship life of all the faithful, they should be informed of the purpose, meaning, time and location of the celebration. Opportunities should be provided to ensure that the faithful can attend this Mass. In most dioceses there is no general invitation, since no cathedral has the physical space accommodate everyone. So, for example, the Archdiocese of Chicago does not issue a general invitation, but gives tickets to each parish instead. You might include a notice in the bulletin throughout Lent, or include short announcements before a Lenten Mass or following the Prayer after Communion. You might even solicit volunteers to organize car pools, especially in areas that are quite far from the cathedral.

Because no morning Mass is celebrated today (save the Chrism Mass at the cathedral), the celebration of Morning Prayer in the place of the usual daily Mass is most appropriate. Many parishes are discovering the role of Morning Prayer during these days of the Triduum. If your parish is not yet accustomed to celebrating the Hours during these days, why not start this year? Introducing an alternative form of offering their thanks and praise to God each day is an excellent way of keeping the faithful connected to the liturgical life of the Church.

If your parish has a school, the students could take part in this celebration of Morning Prayer. All the major Catholic music companies offer a format of sung prayer for the Liturgy of the Hours that is accessible and easy to follow. Familiar settings of the prescribed Psalms (selected from the parish's existing repertoire) can be used. Simple chant tones are available for easy singing of the Psalms and Canticles.

Holy Communion may be given to the sick and homebound.

Both *The Roman Missal* and *Paschale Solemnitatis* note that for pastoral reasons the diocesan bishop may allow another celebration of the Mass of the Lord's Supper earlier in the day: "Where pastoral considerations require it, the local ordinary may permit another Mass to be celebrated in churches and oratories in the evening, and in the case of true necessity, even in the morning, but only for those faithful who cannot otherwise participate in the evening Mass" *(Paschale Solemnitatis,* 47; see also the rubrics

for the Mass of the Lord's Supper under Holy Thursday in *The Roman Missal*).

Lectionary for Mass: Chrism Mass

The commentary below was written by Rev. Thomas P. Looney, CSC (© LTP, 2009).

◆ FIRST READING: As the Church gathers to bless the oil of catechumens, chrism, and the sick for use in its sacramental life, she proclaims in the First Reading Isaiah's prophecy about the Lord's anointed. The fulfillment of Isaiah's prophecy in the life and ministry of Jesus is the foundation of the Church's ministry to the lowly, imprisoned, and sorrowful. Through sacramental signs, the Church celebrates her graced participation in Christ's saving work and the gift of adoption, strengthening, and healing in the life of her own members.

◆ RESPONSORIAL PSALM 89: The Church recalls the anointing of David as King of Israel and God's pledge of fidelity to him. As sharers in God's holy anointing, we recall God's fidelity to us and pray for the grace to remain faithful to God and to one another.

◆ SECOND READING: The book of Revelation announces the glory of the Lord Jesus, who reigns over all the earth and gives us a share in his riches. He has bestowed his royal priesthood upon us so that as the Lord's anointed we may offer fitting praise and worship to the Father. In our service to God and neighbor, we exercise the great privilege of standing in the Lord's presence to offer the praise of the sacrifice of our lives.

◆ GOSPEL: In the Gospel according to Luke, Jesus announces the fulfillment—in his own person—of the ancient prophecy of Isaiah concerning God's anointed. Jesus announces that, in his person and in

relationship to God, divine favor has dawned upon the poor, the imprisoned, and the blind. As sharers in the Lord's anointing through the Sacraments of Baptism and Confirmation, the members of Christ's body are empowered to live and to love as Christ does. May the outpouring of the Holy Spirit enable us to be more effective signs of the abiding presence of the Lord Jesus in the midst of the Church.

The Roman Missal: Chrism Mass

Traditionally, the priests of the diocese and representatives of each parish gather with the bishop in the cathedral church to celebrate the Chrism Mass on the morning of Holy Thursday. During the Mass, the bishop blesses the oil of the catechumens and the oil of the sick, and he consecrates the sacred chrism. In many places, celebrating the Chrism Mass on this day can present undue difficulties, especially in dioceses that are far-flung geographically, so it is sometimes celebrated earlier in Holy Week, or even before Palm Sunday. Even if the Chrism Mass does not take place on Holy Thursday, the Rite of Reception of the Holy Oils at the Evening Mass of the Lord's Supper is encouraged as a way of maintaining the strong link between the Chrism Mass and the Paschal Triduum and of catechizing the faithful about the importance of the holy oils in the sacramental life of the Church.

At the center of the Chrism Mass is the blessing of the oils and the consecration of the sacred chrism. This has a practical purpose, for the oils will be needed all over the diocese for the celebration of the sacraments at the Easter Vigil. The prayers for the blessing of the oils of the catechumens and of the sick are simple. They tell us that the oil of catechumens is to strengthen the catechumens in their resolve, to bring them wisdom, strength, and understanding. The oil of the sick is for healing in body, mind, and soul. The consecration of the sacred chrism is quite different from these simple blessings; it is surrounded by special signs. First a sweet-smelling essence is added to the oil, in a rite not unlike the mingling of the water and the wine during the preparation of the gifts. Then the bishop breathes over the oil, a powerfully symbolic gesture, recalling the Holy Spirit which God breathed over the formless void at the dawn of creation. The solemn prayer of consecration calls down the Holy Spirit upon the oil, which will be used in the Sacraments of Baptism, Confirmation, and Holy Orders, and in the Dedication of a Church and Altar.

In addition to the blessing and consecration of the oils, the Chrism Mass has another purpose. It recalls and celebrates the priesthood: the high priest, Jesus Christ; the royal priesthood of the baptized; the priestly ministry of the ordained. The Entrance Antiphon makes this aspect of the celebration quite clear. There is no mention of oils here; instead, the passage from Revelation 1:6 praises Christ who "has made us into a kingdom, priests for his God and Father." The readings from Isaiah, Revelation, and Luke also recall the royal priesthood of the baptized, received through anointing from on high. In this context, it makes sense that before the blessing and consecration of the oils, there is a "Renewal of Priestly Promises." This is not a renewal of vows, like that made by religious. Instead, the priests express their resolve to unite themselves to Christ, and to sacrifice many of the pleasures of this life to devote themselves to the sanctification of God's people. They resolve to celebrate the Eucharist with devotion and to teach the faith selflessly. The bishop, in turn, expresses his resolve to become more and more a genuine sign of Christ's loving presence in the local Church.

We look to Holy Thursday as the day on which Jesus instituted the Eucharist. But the Church has long seen Holy Thursday as the day on which Christ instituted the priesthood as well. The Preface for the Chrism Mass (found in the Proper of Time) recalls why Jesus chooses "shares in his sacred ministry": to renew "the sacrifice of human redemption" and to "set before [God's] children the paschal banquet." The priesthood is intimately connected to the Eucharist.

When does the blessing of oils take place? *The Roman Missal* provides two different options. The entire rite of blessing may take place following the Liturgy of the Word (which includes the Renewal of Priestly Promises). Or, in keeping with a much more ancient tradition, reaching back to the eighth century, the blessings may take place around the Eucharistic Prayer: "The blessing of the Oil of the Sick takes place before the end of the Eucharistic Prayer, but the blessing of the Oil of Catechumens and the consecration of Chrism take place after Communion."

THE SACRED PASCHAL TRIDUUM

The Meaning / The Lectionary for Mass

THE three days of the Paschal Triduum are one celebration, focusing on three aspects of the same mystery: Christ's passage through death into eternal life. This is the mystery in which we share through our Baptism. This is the mystery into which we are called not only at the moment of our physical death, but throughout our life: allowing ourselves to be handed over by the events and circumstances of life that seem so nonsensical and even unjust; being willing to pass through the darkness of the uncertainties and the unknowns; being raised in the midst of it all into a new life by the power of God at work in us.

The Triduum begins with the Evening Mass of the Lord's Supper on Holy Thursday. The Entrance Antiphon of the Mass calls our attention to what it is all about: the Cross of Christ, our salvation, our freedom, our life (see Galatians 6:14). According to the synoptic accounts of the

Gospel (Matthew, Mark, and Luke), Jesus' Last Supper was a Passover meal commemorating Israel's deliverance from slavery in Egypt (see Exodus 12—15). The Gospel account of John offers a different chronology. The last days of Jesus's life are during Passover time, but the last supper is not a Passover meal. Rather, Jesus dies at the hour the Passover lambs are sacrificed (thus, his title: the Lamb of God).

Accordingly, we hear the account of the first Passover in our First Reading, and our Second Reading is the earliest New Testament account of Jesus's meal with his disciples the night before he died and the institution of our own Eucharistic celebration. Our sharing in this meal is a proclamation of Jesus's Death and points to his coming again in glory.

The Gospel according to John does not contain "an institution account" *per se*, but rather offers an extensive discourse on Jesus as the Bread of Life in chapter 6. At his last meal with his disciples before his death, Jesus washes their feet, the job of a humble servant. His message is loud and clear: this is what they, and we, must do for one another. This service is symbolized in the ritual washing of feet after the homily. In our service to one another, we give our life on behalf of one another, in memory of Jesus. In sharing the bread of his life that is broken for us, in drinking of the cup of his blood that is poured out, we are nourished in eternal life; we are united to him and to one another; we commit ourselves to live in a manner that remembers his presence among us. In so doing, we proclaim his death, and his life of self-giving, until he comes in glory.

After the reception of Holy Communion at Mass, the Blessed Sacrament is removed from the tabernacle and carried in procession to a place readied for its reservation. We gather in this place to watch and pray with Jesus on the eve of his death, recalling that is what he asks of his disciples (see Mark 14:34).

On entering the church on Good Friday, we notice immediately its starkness and emptiness. We can feel the absence of the Blessed Sacrament. The Good Friday celebration is not a Mass, but a three-part ceremony consisting of the Liturgy of the Word, the Adoration of the Cross, and Holy Communion. The readings point to the self-sacrifice of Jesus: as the Suffering Servant described by Isaiah; as the compassionate high priest who himself experienced our weaknesses and struggles and offered his life in obedience to the Father (Hebrews); and in the words of the fourth Evangelist: as the innocent but nonetheless condemned King of the Jews whose Death represents his full accomplishment of the Father's work and the outpouring of the Spirit. From the wound in his side, life-giving water bursts forth.

The Solemn Intercessions on Good Friday are inclusive of the entire human race. We pray for: the Church, the pope, all ministers in the Church, catechumens preparing for Baptism, Christian unity, the Jewish people, all those who do not believe in Christ, atheists, and those in special need.

In the second part of the service, we venerate the cross of Christ, coming forward to kneel before it and kiss it reverently. This part of the service is very old. (See, for example, the account of the fourth-century Spanish nun Egeria who was present in the church of the Holy Sepulchre in Jerusalem for a Good Friday service (*Diary of a Pilgrimage*, chapter 37). Today it is we who proclaim, we who reverence "the wood of the cross on which hung the Savior of the world."

The final part of the service is the Rite of Holy Communion. On this day when Jesus gave his life in death, we share in its mystery, joined to him and to one another.

The Easter Vigil is the high point of the celebration of the Triduum. The service must begin when it is dark. It is the night of the Passover of the Lord, his passage from the darkness of death into the radiant glory of eternal life. The service begins with the blessing of the new fire and the preparation of the paschal candle. Christ is the Alpha and the Omega, the beginning and the end, all time belongs to him, including this year that is our own. As the candle is carried through the darkened church, its light spreads throughout the assembly and we proclaim the Light of Christ. The *Exsultet*, the great Easter hymn of joy, is sung. The light of Christ, the Morning Star, shines brightly in our midst.

In the readings of the Liturgy of the Word, we hear the story of salvation from the beginning of time: creation, the covenant with Abraham, the Exodus, and four prophetic readings set in the time of the Babylonian Exile. God promises to renew and re-create his sinful people in covenant love. All seven readings are integral in the telling of the story and each has its own Responsorial Psalm and prayer. After the seventh, we joyfully sing God's praise in the Gloria. The epistle from the letter to the Romans speaks of our own participation (immersion) in Christ's Death and Resurrection through Baptism. In our Psalm response we hear once again the joyful Alleluia which has been silenced for all of Lent. Finally, we hear the Gospel proclamation of that first Easter morning.

The third part of the Paschal Vigil is the Liturgy of Baptism. How truly blessed are those parishes that will welcome new members into their midst tonight! The water is blessed, becoming the waters of new birth. We call on the intercession of all God's holy ones in the litany of saints. Those to be baptized—and all of us after them—publicly renounce Satan and profess the faith. And then, the moment of new birth: those to be baptized are immersed in the waters of life. There is the anointing, the presentation of the baptismal candle lit from the paschal light, and the clothing with the white garment symbolizing new life. What immense joy is ours as we celebrate these "new births"! Finally, all the assembly is blessed with the new water, the new cleansing prophesied by Ezekiel now come to fulfillment.

The fourth part of the Paschal Vigil is the celebration of the Eucharist. Our new and extended family, our re"new"ed assembly (emphasis added), comes together around the table of the Lord to be nourished with the life that is God's own.

Ideally, all who can should participate in the Paschal Vigil, given its significance in the liturgical year as a whole and its importance for our parish and community life. There is also a Mass for Easter Day with its own readings. The renewal of baptismal promises and the blessing with the new Easter water takes place at this Mass as well.

The Triduum concludes with the celebration of Evening Prayer (Vespers) on Sunday. It was the evening of that first day of the week when Jesus appeared to the disciples (Luke 24:13ff; John 20:19ff). Experiencing him alive, their hearts were filled with joy.

May our participation in this Paschal Triduum strengthen us for all the dyings which will be part of our lives in the coming year. In the face of the darkness, the unknown and the inexplicable, may we know the power of God at work in and through our weakness, bringing us through it to transformed life.

—S. Anne Elizabeth Sweet, OCSO

The Roman Missal

THE Roman Missal is, of course, the place to start in preparing the liturgies of the Sacred Paschal Triduum. In addition to the prayers and texts, *The Roman Missal* includes detailed rubrics for each of the three days. The Missal's brief introduction to the Triduum emphasizes the importance of preparation and understanding for all who participate. "For a fitting celebration of the Sacred Triduum, a sufficient number of lay ministers is required, who must be carefully instructed as to what they are to do . . . . Pastors should . . . not fail to explain to the Christian faithful, as best they can, the meaning and order of the celebrations and to prepare them for active and fruitful participation" (2).

These liturgies are some of the most challenging of the liturgical year. They keep us moving with various processions: processions with the holy oils and the gifts on Holy Thursday, processions with the Holy Eucharist, processions with the cross, processions with the paschal candle. They include elements that happen only once in the course of the liturgical year: the optional washing of the feet, the adoration of the cross, the Baptism of adults. And they demand a careful consideration of the pastoral needs of the community, as the Missal provides a variety of options for the different rites.

Early in Lent, those responsible for preparing the liturgies of the Triduum should begin to meet. If there are to be Baptisms at the Vigil, this meeting should include those who lead the parish's RCIA. A good starting place could be simply reading the rubrics and prayers for each of the three days in *The Roman Missal*, and in the *Rite of Christian Initiation of Adults* (which supplements *The Roman Missal* with detailed rubrics for the celebration of the Baptism of adults). *Paschale Solemnitatis* is also an indispensable resource.

Given the complexities of these liturgies, and the number of possible variations, many parishes prepare a written plan of one kind or another for the liturgies of the Triduum for the use of the priest celebrant and ministers. Sometimes this takes the form of an outline of each liturgy, with notes on where the different liturgical actions will take place. If you use such a "script" or "order of worship," evaluate it carefully each year. Is it clear? Do those who need to use it find it easy to use?

Well-prepared and adequately detailed notes can keep things running smoothly. They can "streamline" the liturgy, saving time by ensuring that the ministers know their cues. But no amount of written instruction can take the place of well-trained masters of ceremonies, who know the liturgies by heart, and can gently and unobtrusively guide the unfolding of these celebrations, which will take us to the very heart of our Christian faith.

Children's Liturgy of the Word

DURING these three days, the Church fasts and prays with anticipation and hope. Although the Easter Vigil with the lighting of the fire, the full initiation of adults and children of catechetical age and the renewal of baptismal promises by the baptized is the center and high point of the Triduum, each day has its own liturgical actions and symbols that draw the assembly more deeply into the mystery of faith. Holy Thursday begins as a rich, colorful feast and ends in somber silence. The Holy Thursday celebration of the washing of the feet and celebration of the Lord's Supper calls us into a deeper commitment to service and doing the things that Jesus did. On Good Friday the church is void of decoration and the prominent symbol is the cross. During the Good Friday liturgy, which is not a Mass but a three-part celebration including proclamation of Scripture and Holy Communion, the assembly processes forward to venerate the cross and to continue to celebrate the salvation won by the sacrifice of Christ.

The joy of the Resurrection is echoed in the songs of Easter Time. The whole of the Triduum celebration invites us to join in praise of the Risen Lord, who died and rose so that we might "live in newness of life" (Romans 6:4.)

Most parishes do not celebrate Liturgy of the Word with children during the Triduum. Families should be encouraged to bring children to the liturgies of the Triduum if the times are appropriate and they are able to attend to what is happening. Ordinarily these celebrations are the most sensate and the music, rituals, and symbols will engage children.

If children are dismissed, think about dismissing them after the Washing of the Feet on Holy Thursday, the Adoration of the Cross on Good Friday, and the lighting of the fire and the procession with the paschal candle at the Easter Vigil. Instead of focusing on the readings, help children break open the rituals and symbols of each day.

The Saints

DURING these three days, we celebrate all saints and no saints. The liturgies of the Triduum take precedence over all saints' days, no matter how significant. And yet, during the Paschal Triduum, we are constantly aware of the great company of witnesses who have gone before us, who have witnessed to the mystery of Christ's Passion, Death, and Resurrection by the holiness of their lives. "May your face thus be our vision, bright in glory, / Christ our God," we sing in the Holy Thursday hymn *Ubi caritas*, "with all the blessed Saints in heaven" (*The Roman Missal*). At the Easter Vigil, we beg the prayers of all the holy men and women throughout the ages in the great Litany of Saints. And the saints are invoked in the Eucharistic Prayer: the "blessed Apostles and Martyrs" (Eucharistic Prayer I), "all the saints who have pleased you throughout the ages" (Eucharistic Prayer II), the saints "on whose constant intercession in your presence / we rely for unfailing help" (Eucharistic Prayer III). Yes, the saints are with us during the Paschal Triduum!

This year, the memorials of Saint Francis of Paola (April 2), Saint Isidore (April 4), Saint Vincent Ferrer (April 5), and Saint John Baptist de la Salle (April 7) are supplanted by the Easter Octave, each day of which ranks as a solemnity. Parishes dedicated in honor of these saints may transfer the celebration of their patronal feast to the nearest available day. This year, that will be Tuesday, April 9, since the Solemnity of the Annunciation of the Lord is transferred to April 8 because March 25 falls during Holy Week.

The Liturgy of the Hours

BECAUSE this three-day liturgy of the Triduum is the pinnacle of the liturgical year, the Liturgy of the Hours provides a way for people to enter into the deep mystery of Christ's Death, Resurrection, and subsequent sending of the Spirit who empowers and invites us to share in Christ's very life. Many parishes will end the Thursday evening celebration of the Mass of the Lord's Supper with Night Prayer. The ritual book for the Liturgy of the Hours states that "Evening Prayer is said only by those who do not participate in the evening Mass of the Lord's Supper" (p. 464), though ending the period of exposition of the Blessed Sacrament with Night Prayer links the official prayer of the Church with the Paschal Triduum.

On Good Friday, the parish could provide Morning Prayer. Note: "Evening Prayer is said only by those who do not participate in the celebration of the Lord's passion" (p. 487). During the Office of Readings, John Chrysostom's mystagogical catechesis links our Baptism to Christ's side, pierced by the Roman centurion, from which blood and water flowed. Water and blood refer to Christ giving to the Church the Sacraments of Baptism (water) and Eucharist (blood) so that we might be united to his very life. We are linked to Christ through communion with him.

On Saturday morning, the parish could gather with the elect who seek to be fully initiated into the Roman Catholic Church to celebrate the Ephphetha Rite from the *Rite of Christian Initiation of Adults* (See RCIA, 185–205). The rite itself is based on a Celebration of the Word, which is basically a Liturgy of the Word with the Ephphetha Rite following. A pastoral adaptation could be to use the Morning Prayer from the Liturgy of the Hours and, after the reading, celebrate the Ephphetha Rite; then after the Ephphetha Rite (but before the Concluding Rite) come the Benedictus, Intercessions, Our Father, Concluding Prayer, and Blessing. Some parishes will then have the rehearsal for the Paschal Vigil following Morning Prayer and the Ephphetha Rite. In other parishes, there is the blessing of the food for Easter that often takes place on Saturday morning. They could be encouraged to come to Morning Prayer and then the blessing of the baskets could take place as part of the concluding rites of Morning Prayer.

Evening Prayer on Easter Sunday evening brings the Paschal Triduum to conclusion. In particular, the newly initiated, their sponsors, family and friends, should be strongly encouraged to be there. In addition, the parish members could gather for the lighting of tapers from the newly blessed paschal candle to renew their baptismal promises along with the newly initiated. Incense, a darkened church, psalmist(s) and accompaniment, all can add solemnity to the importance of the Paschal Triduum. Perhaps a trumpet or brass would add greater solemnity. The end of Evening Prayer includes the Easter dismissal which typically is chanted. The Psalm prayers and concluding prayer could be chanted using the solemn tone from *The Roman Missal* as another way to add solemnity. Especially if a parish regularly celebrates Evening Prayer, adding solemnity will allow this Evening Prayer to really stand out from the other parish celebrations.

The Rite of Christian Initiation of Adults

By this time, the elect are aware of and attentive to the liturgical environment. They will be attentive to the liturgical signs and symbols especially when they are handled and used with reverent, confident gestures. The prayers prayed clearly, the Word proclaimed well and dramatically will hold the attention of adults and children. The elect and catechumens should be dismissed before the Eucharist on Holy Thursday and the Communion service on Good Friday. On Holy Saturday the catechumens should be dismissed at the conclusion of the Liturgy of the Word (if they are not to be initiated that evening). Following the dismissal each day of the Triduum, the catechesis focuses on both the Word and the rituals just experienced.

Holy Saturday is a day of reflection and prayer. Gather the elect, their families, sponsors, godparents, and peer catechetical group on the morning of Holy Saturday for reflection and celebration of the appropriate preparatory rites (RCIA, 185–192). Celebrate the recitation of the Creed only if it has been presented previously. Focus the reflection on the Ephphetha Rite. It's a very simple and effective rite. In the reflection emphasize and discuss the power of words to heal and to motivate others.

Be sure to contact the families, sponsors, and godparents about the Triduum schedule. Include directions for Holy Saturday refection and any other directions. Arrange a time and place for the elect and their families to meet and sit together during the liturgies of Holy Thursday and Good Friday.

Encourage the newly initiated to come to one of the Easter Masses and attend Easter Evening Prayer if your parish celebrates it.

The Sacraments of Initiation

WITHOUT a doubt within these three days one finds a rich liturgical catechesis of the signs and symbols of the Sacraments of Initiation for children and adults.

The liturgies of the Triduum are more solemn and somewhat different from the liturgies of the rest of the year. When the liturgies of the Triduum are well prepared, gracefully celebrated, and musically engaging, they are captivating for children. It might be a good idea if the liturgy and music planners could could find ways to encourage participation by young people preparing for sacraments along with their families. Encourage lavish presentation of symbols and rituals, involvement of some of the candidates and their families as liturgical ministers (lectors and readers, hospitality ministry, choir, art and environment, foot washing).

Encourage children and their families to attend the rituals of the Triduum. Prepare ahead of time for child care during the celebrations. Families with young children will be concerned about that, especially because the celebrations are in the evening and can be longer than other liturgies.

Explain that the celebration of the Easter Triduum, the three days leading up to Easter, is much more than a replay of historical events leading toward Christ's Resurrection. The liturgical celebration of the Triduum makes real God's accomplishments, allowing the assembly to enter into the lived mystery.

Through the symbols of water and the cross, and the liturgical actions of blessing and kissing the foot of the cross, the historical events of Jesus's life, Death, and Resurrection are made real in the here and now. In these liturgical actions the Triduum is more than a reminder of what God did long ago. Instead, it is a continuous celebration of the Church's salvation today.

Although the Easter Vigil is the center and high point of the Triduum, each day has its own liturgical actions and symbols that draw the assembly more deeply into the mystery of faith. Explain what happens each day of the Triduum.

Holy Thursday begins as a rich, colorful feast and ends in somber silence. The Holy Thursday celebration of the washing of the feet and celebration of the Lord's Supper calls us into a deeper commitment to service and to doing the things that Jesus did. Mass may only be celebrated in the evening this day, making it a special memorial of the institution of the Eucharist. Our celebration is wholehearted; we are grateful for the gift of the Blessed Sacrament. But our thanks are tempered as we anticipate the events of the next day with the stripping of the altar and the removal of the consecrated Bread to the altar of repose. We leave without singing a recessional hymn.

On Good Friday the church has no decoration, and the prominent symbol is the cross. During the good Friday liturgy, which is not a Mass but a three-part celebration including the proclamation of Scripture and Holy Communion, the assembly processes forward to adore the cross and to celebrate the salvation won by the sacrifice of Christ on that Cross.

We enter a darkened church on Holy Saturday. With the lighting of the Easter fire, we proclaim our thanks for the Light of Christ. We hear the Scripture stories of creation, the Passover, the wandering in the desert, and redemption through Jesus. We welcome new members, who remind us of the new life Christ received on Easter.

Distribute a simple reflection sheet on the Triduum at the last session before its celebration. Ask young people to note any of their observations about the Triduum and bring their responses back for the next session. Use them for discussion and as conversation starters.

The Rite of Penance

COMMUNAL penitential celebrations "should take place before the Easter Triduum and should not immediately precede the evening Mass of the Lord's Supper" (PS, 37). However, paragraphs 61 and 75 of this document indicate that the Sacrament of Penance may be celebrated on Good Friday and Holy Saturday. This allows pastors to meet a parishioner's pastoral need.

The Pastoral Care of the Sick

ON Holy Thursday "it is more appropriate that the eucharist be borne directly from the altar . . . for the sick and infirm who must communicate at home, so that, in this way they may be more closely united to the celebrating Church" (PS, 53). This will entail some different arrangements for Holy Communion visits with the sick and homebound, but the lovely connection to the community's Eucharist is worth the effort. On Good Friday, Holy Communion "may be brought at any time of the day to the sick" (PS, 59), and on Holy Saturday, Holy Communion "may only be given in the form of Viaticum" (PS, 75). Anointing of the Sick may take place at any time during the Triduum (see PS, 61, and 75).

The Rite of Marriage

THE Triduum is our most solemn time of the liturgical year. These liturgies are meant to yank us out of the usual place and time, unify our hearts and minds, and unite us as one to the joy of the Resurrection. A parish expends a great deal of time and energy to celebrate these liturgies fully. For this reason it is actually forbidden to celebrate Marriages on Good Friday or Holy Saturday (see PS, 61, and 75). While it is possible to imagine a quiet, early marriage in a Liturgy of the Word on Holy Thursday, there would have to be an urgent pastoral need to disturb our focus on that day.

The Order of Christian Funerals

A funeral Mass is not permitted during the Triduum (see OCF, 178). If a funeral service is celebrated on Good Friday, it is "without singing, music or the tolling of bells" (PS, 61). Since the OCF puts great emphasis on the community's role as ministers of consolation (see OCF, 9–11), delaying a funeral until after Triduum will allow more parishioners to be present to the family and to participate in the funeral liturgies.

The Book of Blessings

IF you have invited people to fast on Holy Saturday, they may be going home to a meal after the Vigil. The *Book of Blessings* includes the Order for the Blessing of Food for the First Meal of Easter (ch. 54) and this instruction: "food may be blessed before or after the Easter Vigil on Holy Saturday or on the Easter Morning for consumption at the first meal of Easter, when fasting is ended and the Church is filled with joy" (BB, 1702). Note that this article also cites *Paschale Solemnitatis*, "Festive customs and traditions associated with this day on account of the former practice of anticipating the celebration of Easter on Holy Saturday should be reserved for Easter night and the day that follows" (PS, 76).

The Liturgical Environment

The nature of Holy Week and the Triduum

The singular nature of this week, apart from the fact that it is called "*holy,*" is that it is the only period of time in the liturgical calendar when the whole week is shaped by a series of liturgies that are at the same time distinct but integrated over the course of several days. The liturgies of the Triduum are often referred to as one great liturgy, underscored by the fact that from the opening of the Holy Thursday celebration there is no proper dismissal rite until the conclusion of the Easter Vigil.

As the whole Church enters this week, beginning with the Gospel proclamation of Jesus' entry into Jerusalem until the incredulous announcement that the tomb is empty, the Church is engaged in celebrating the very foundational events of its faith, the Paschal Mystery. The liturgical life of the Church leads to this week, and at the same time flows from its grace and mystery; it is truly a celebration of the source and summit of the Christian tradition.

A Pastoral Insight for Holy Week and the Triduum

The Church traces this week back to the early days of its tradition. Many prayer texts and prescribed Scripture passages in the Lectionary date from the early centuries when the Church's liturgical practice was developing. Selecting Scripture readings, prayers, and hymns deserves careful attention this week. Avoid taking short-cuts in the various celebrations; the richness of the great mysteries of this week deserves full expression and participation.

During the celebrations of this week the full, active, and conscious participation of the liturgical assembly is especially important. The processions, gestures, singing, responses, acclamations, and moments of silence all engage the faithful in the rich and communal worship of this week.

Practical Suggestions

The liturgical environment committee has its work cut out for them during this week. It is important to begin to plan several weeks ahead of time, and to do so with an overall scheme for the whole week. The liturgies of Holy Week involve a number of processions, and liturgical centers in addition to the usual places (e.g., the place for the gathering of those in the Palm Sunday procession; the place for the reservation of the Eucharist on Holy Thursday; the location of the cross for adoration on Good Friday; and the location of the new fire for the Easter Vigil). All these spaces need particular items and liturgical appointments, some need furnishings and vessels (e.g., for the washing of the feet), and each space can have its own liturgical environment. Perhaps a different member of the committee could take responsibility for each liturgy, of course with the assistance of the other members. This may be a good time to enlist a few volunteers with a view toward recruiting new members for the rest of the year!

Holy Thursday

- The Evening Mass of the Lord's Supper on Holy Thursday signals the beginning of the Triduum. The liturgical color is white.

- The liturgical environment for this liturgy moves from the simpler and restrained nature of Lent to a more festive expression. The liturgy will include the ringing of bells and the singing of the Gloria. But this tone will be short-lived—the environment for Good Friday calls for a more somber ambience (see below).

- There is no reason to create an extravagant environment for this liturgy; a few fresh spring flower arrangements can be included, ones than can be incorporated into the Easter setting in a couple of days.

- If the place of reservation is separate from the main body of the church (which it should be), then some decorative items may be placed there. Once again, this space does not need to be busy and cluttered; it is a place for quiet prayer before the Blessed Sacrament (until midnight, or in some parishes until early Friday morning): the focus is on the reserved Eucharist and the place needs to be conducive to prayer.

- The rite for the washing of feet requires a few items: pitchers of water, basins, and towels. The locations for the rite can be marked in some simple fashion; chairs for people to sit, and possibly a lighted candle on a stand nearby. The vessels and towels should be worthy and generous in size. The environment committee will need to work closely with the liturgy coordinator to make sure that all is in place and ready for this rite which takes place after the Homily.

- In some parishes it is the custom to present the blessed oils that have been brought to the church from the Chrism Mass celebrated earlier in the week. The vessels for the holy oils should be worthy containers, and after they are "received" by the parish (see the rite for the presentation of the oils in this section) they are placed in the ambry.

- At the end of the liturgy the altar cloth(s) are removed without any particular ceremony, and when everyone has left the worship space preparations can begin for the Good Friday liturgy.

Good Friday

- The celebration of the Lord's Passion on Good Friday is somber and very moving. The liturgical environment reflects this and, as usual, intends to serve the gestures and mood of the Church's prayer.

- The liturgical color for Good Friday is red; however, the cross is draped in violet.

- When the liturgy begins the altar is bare and the main tabernacle is empty, its door left open. The sanctuary lamp is extinguished and a lighted one is placed in the area where the Eucharist has been reserved since last evening.

- It is appropriate if some of the items from Lent are still in place, and any red accents from Palm Sunday can be included as well.

- A great cross should be carried in procession as it is the primary symbol for this liturgy. It is usual that it is draped with a violet cloth and is unveiled in stages as the acclamation is sung; "Behold the wood of the Cross . . . ." and all respond, "Come, let us adore."

◆ The cross should be placed in such a way as to be accessible for all who come forward to venerate it. Liturgical ministers may stand nearby with lighted candles, an incense brazier may be used, and the cross can be placed upright or held by ministers on a slight angle so that more than one person may touch or kiss the wood of the cross at one time. After the adoration the cross is left in place for the remainder of the day; one or more lighted candles may be placed next to it.

◆ The Communion Rite, which concludes the liturgy today, requires a simple procession with candle bearers, from the place of reservation. A white cloth is placed upon the altar and the Communion vessels and missal are placed there. These are removed at the end of the liturgy.

The Easter Vigil

The celebration of the Easter Vigil is undoubtedly the summit of the Church's liturgical expression. The rich tradition of this liturgy with its processions, Scripture texts, symbols, music, proclamations, and acclamations, comes alive in the full and active participation of the whole assembly. This truly is the night, as the *Exsultet* proclaims, when Christians everywhere are restored to grace and grow together in holiness. No wonder the universal Church and every local Church gives special attention and expends great energy to celebrate this night when heaven is wedded to earth and all human beings are reconciled with God!

All the elements that are needed for the different ritual actions and in the various ritual areas need to be worthy and beautiful.

The blessing of the new fire should be after dusk; the vessel for the fire should be of generous size—a great fire is demanded, and everyone should gather in a place where they can see the opening rites.

◆ It is advisable that a sound system be used so that all can hear the prayers of the blessing over the fire and for the preparation of the paschal candle.

◆ The Easter candle should be a new one and of sufficient scale as to attract attention as it stands in the midst of the people as the Light of Christ. It is placed next to the ambo for the singing of the *Exsultet* and remains there until the feast of the Ascension.

◆ Enough candles should be provided so that everyone can participate in the procession of light; if worship aids are used then there should be enough for everyone as well.

◆ After the singing of the *Exsultet* the candles are put aside for the readings from Scripture. Since these candles are lighted again for the renewal of baptismal promises, they should not be collected at this time.

◆ When the Gloria is intoned, the lights of the church are turned on and the candles in the sanctuary are lighted and bells are rung. Someone needs to be prepared to take care of these actions at the appropriate time.

◆ Since the lectors and readers are proclaiming the Scriptures without the church lights, a small podium light needs to be in place at the ambo.

◆ If the church does not have a permanent immersion font, then a temporary one can be constructed for the Baptisms during the Vigil and left in place throughout Easter Time.

◆ Normally the baptismal font has been emptied and cleaned during Holy Week and is now filled with fresh water.

◆ If adults and/or infants are baptized by the gesture of immersion, then sufficient towels need to be available for use when the newly baptized emerge from the waters of the font.

◆ A suitable pitcher or other vessel is needed for the pouring of the water.

◆ White garments, symbolizing new life, are prepared and given to the newly baptized. These garments are similar to an alb; they should not resemble a stole.

◆ Candles are provided for the newly baptized and are lit from the Easter candle.

◆ The vessels for the holy oils used during the Liturgy of Baptism and the Rite of Confirmation should be readily available; this includes the oil of catechumens and the sacred chrism.

◆ The candles of the assembly are re-lighted for the renewal of baptismal promises. Then they are extinguished and collected. The ushers do this prior to the collection; large baskets work well so that this action doesn't take much time or interrupt the flow of the liturgy.

◆ The priest or the deacon, or both, sprinkles the assembly either while the catechumens are changing from their wet clothing or as the procession returns to the front of the church. Containers for water and sprinklers need to be provided.

◆ The Liturgy of Eucharist proceeds as usual; the altar table could be prepared by several people (placing the altar cloth, the Missal, the Communion vessels) prior to the Preparation of the Gifts.

◆ A special altar cloth may be used at this time, and left on the altar during all of Easter Time.

◆ If the parish can afford a second set of Communion vessels to be used for the more festive liturgies, as at Christmas Time, then they can be used for Easter Time as well.

Pastoral Suggestions

- The liturgical color for the Easter Vigil, Easter Sunday, and all of Easter Time is white or gold or silver.
- Current liturgical documents do not give any principles or restrictions for the environment; however, liturgical environment committees must resist the temptation to overdo the arrangements for Easter. There should be a visual unity between the Masses of the Vigil and Easter Sunday with Easter Time.
- The sanctuary is a ritual area and the principal furnishings are always the center of attention; extravagant displays that turn the sanctuary area into a stage-like setting are never appropriate. Constructing "empty tombs" with fake stones cheapens the Easter mystery and adds unnecessary clutter to the sanctuary. Also, creating "spring gardens" with all manner of objects may be a good idea, but place them in the gathering area or outside in a courtyard, never in the sanctuary.
- It is also helpful to remember that the season lasts for several weeks and that the liturgical environment should remain fresh and in place for that time. Environment committees might want to stretch their resources throughout the season instead of exhausting their budget for the one weekend of Easter.
- It is the custom in some parishes to decorate the main cross/crucifix with swags of white or multi-colored fabric for Easter Time. This is usually not a good idea. The cross is a principal liturgical symbol and almost always a significant work of art. Draping it with white cloths does not make it a symbol of Resurrection; instead it becomes a prop for the environment, turning the profound mystery we associate with the Death and Resurrection of Christ into a literal statement.

The Liturgical Music

ONE of the first things I suggest to anyone preparing the liturgies for Holy Week and the Sacred Paschal Triduum is to read the rubrics, since we are still becoming "at home" with *The Roman Missal*. Of course we know that the typical parts of the Mass changed, but have you considered other changes to the liturgies? Most notably, there are revisions to the Litany of Saints, and to the *Exsultet*. These parts of the liturgy can easily catch us off guard.

These changes force us out of complacency and our comfort zone. In some sense, everyone is a novice again, no matter how many years you've been involved with liturgy or music. We are all scrambling for good resources and can no longer rely on the "we've always done it that way" approach. Now is a good time to look at your liturgies, evaluate what you have been doing, and take the opportunity offered you to grow.

If you have the people and the talent, you may wish to consider keeping the entire Triduum a cappella. In any case ICEL and NPM have prepared samples of many of the official hymns and texts of this time. You can find them at http://www.npm.org/Chants/proper.html.

As a general observation, if your parish holds copyright permissions from more than one publisher, and draws from multiple resources, be sure to communicate clearly where to find music. For example, there are several different hymns called "Servant Song" or "The Servant Song"; GIA has a version of "Tree of Life" by Marty Haugen, and WLP has a totally different piece of the same name by Aaron Thompson. *Ubi Caritas* is the name of an official chant of the Church, a Taizé hymn (GIA), and a composition by Bob Hurd. You would do well to keep your musicians on the same page—literally! Even the same hymn tune may have variations in key, lyrics, or accompaniment depending on which resource is publishing it, so clear communication is a must.

Holy Thursday

Steve Warner's setting, *Mass of Charity and Love*, is based on *Ubi Caritas*. It is very singable and would be a great resource for this evening. Its simplicity and beauty would lend to the entire Triduum. It is based on the common melody, yet also veers away from it enough in the Gloria to keep things interesting.

Remember, that when you bring the Gloria back tonight, the rubrics suggest the use of bells. This may be easier if musicians choose a setting that is "refrain based" rather than through composed. If your pastor does not typically sing the Eucharistic Prayer, work with him and provide him with good recordings so that he can learn the chants of the Missal. A good resource is *Learning the Chants of the Missal, Part I*, by J. Michael Joncas (LTP).

Good Friday

The text for the reproaches and the solemn intercessions has changed with the new Missal. Clear notation is provided if they are to be sung in the solemn tones. If you do not have a deacon capable of singing the opening part, perhaps you could alternate with two cantors (a male and a female voice), with the priest singing the end of each prayer. Chant is also provided for the showing of the cross and the *Crux Fidelis*. The *Stabat Mater* is not an official chant of this day, but works very well for adoration of the cross, as does "Joseph, Take Him Off the Tree," "Tree of Life", and "Behold the Wood." There are significant changes to some texts of *The Roman Missal*, so it might be a good idea not to wander off into musical territory that the congregation will find unfamiliar.

Easter Vigil/Sunday

Randall DeBruyn's setting, *Mass of Resurrection*, is based upon "Duke Street" and would work well for all of Easter Time. Tony Alonso's *Mass of Joy and Peace* (GIA) is available as an SAB arrangement with parts for stringed instruments. It includes a "refrain" Gloria which is easy for the congregation to learn.

J. Michael Joncas has provided a new arrangement of the traditional Roman chant for the *Exsultet* (the official chant is included in *The Roman Missal*). It is an SATB arrangement and can work well with choirs and two cantors (as well as the parts reserved to the deacon or priest).

Every newly published hymnal has revised the Litany of Saints to match the new texts. This included John Becker's popular setting.

Liturgical Ministers

Tʜɪꜱ is the most complex time of the entire liturgical cycle. A few years ago, I counted out all the hours involved in the preparation and execution of the liturgies as well as the total amount of individuals needed to minister and all the individuals necessary to run our parish through the Triduum. Two readers, four greeters, six ushers, ten extraordinary ministers of Holy Communion, musicians and cantor(s), and a sacristan added up to approximately twenty-seven to thirty ministers per liturgy (not to mention the additional readers needed for the Vigil). Multiplying this number by approximately ten hours for each of the Triduum liturgies meant three hundred ministry hours for all ministers combined. To this total may be added thirty choir

members for roughly thirty-two hours of rehearsal time which equalled nine hundred and twenty hours and over twelve hundred hours at the Triduum liturgies. This does not even include those who clean the church, create the liturgical environment, or do so many things behind the scenes, or the contributions of priest and staff. I never stopped to do the math before. Share that with your community so they may appreciate just what goes into making your Triduum happen.

With such a large number of people involved, preparation is a must. Schedule rehearsals and provide outlines, roadmaps, and diagrams. Priest, deacons, liturgical ministers, those involved in the RCIA all need to work closely together. Develop a "cheat sheet" for musicians outlining everything in detail: i.e., cantor (vs. 1), men (vs. 2), all (vs. 3), etc. Prepare cantor books in advance, and clearly mark Lectionary readings and the appropriate texts in other ritual books. Coordinate extra responsibilities with your ushers and greeters.

Take pictures of the liturgical environment, unobtrusively record the liturgy for study later on, and evaluate what needs to be done to facilitate the preparation of next year's celebration. LTP's *The Sacristy Manual* is an invaluable tool for having the right liturgical elements out at each liturgy. It provides clear, succinct lists.

Devotions and Sacramentals

Tʜᴇ liturgies of the great three days are ever powerful, but the Sacred Paschal Triduum is also a time of poignant personal prayer and piety.

Holy Thursday

On Holy Thursday, the liturgy includes the optional washing of feet. We should never try and replicate this gesture with "para-liturgies" or devotions with a watered down "washing of the hands." The foot washing is something that should take place within the liturgy only and not be replicated elsewhere. (Please note: the Spirit of doing likewise, providing charity and love for all, caring for our neighbor, putting others before ourselves should always be our *modus operandi*, not just now at the Sacred Paschal Triduum.)

Agape meal: Celebrate the beginning of Triduum with an agape meal or potluck that commemorates the early Church tradition of gathering for Eucharist. This is much more appropriate to celebrate or commemorate than a seder meal, since we are not Jewish. Some members of the Jewish community may even find our imitation of one of their holiest traditions theologically offensive.

Visiting churches: It has become a custom, especially when churches are in close proximity to each other (in urban areas), to visit seven churches and the altar of repose in each of these churches. Those able to walk from church to church recite prayers, especially the Rosary. Usually the cathedral church (if possible) is included in the walk, being the first or final stop.

Good Friday

There are many devotional elements to this day as one may partake in the *Via Crucis*, that is, the Stations of the Cross, or many other celebrations. In some countries, *Santo Entierro*, or "the procession of the dead Christ," involves carrying a casket with Christ through the streets.

There are several Marian devotions which might be appropriate today. Our Lady of Dolours is often recalled. More information on this devotion is available at www.7dolors.com/seven dolors.htm. Many Catholics know the melody of the traditional *Stabat Mater*, which often accompanies this devotion, and it can be used within the Good Friday liturgy during the Adoration of the Cross. There are beautiful classical arrangements of this hymn. Pergolesi's *Stabat Mater* is an exquisite duet for two female voices, and could be presented along with the seven sorrows either Friday morning or Friday evening. It would be a way to wed popular piety and sacred music.

In many Latino cultures, there is a celebration called *El Pasame*, in which one keeps vigil with the Blessed Mother. *Pasame* means "condolences."

One fun tradition hails from England: "hot cross buns." As children we even sang, "Hot cross buns, hot cross buns, one a penny, two a penny, hot cross buns" These treats are a strange mixture of sweet and spicy, with raisins or currants. They have a cross shape on the top, and are covered with icing.

Easter Vigil

This Saturday is yet one more day where we follow the example of our Mother Mary and simply wait. *Ora Della Madre* teaches us to keep Vigil and stay by the tomb. How are we faithful in our own lives? Every parent who has kept vigil with a colicky baby, or laid awake at night until their teenager returns with the car knows much about keeping vigil.

Truthfully, this author found many references to *Ora Della Madre*, but few examples of how it might be celebrated. Although, here is one idea: observe periods of silence punctuated with brief readings from the Church fathers or other spiritual writers, integrate Pergolesi's *Stabat Mater Dolorosa*, as well as the chanting of Taizé prayers, the Chaplet of Divine Mercy, and the Litany of Our Lady of Sorrows.

While the Church's official liturgy is subject to rubrics and is highly structured, these devotional activities are flexible and allow people a great deal of room for creativity.

Finally, don't forget to invite the faithful to bring home a vial of the newly blessed Easter water.

Easter Sunday

Originating in the Philippines is the custom of processing with an image of the Sorrowful Mother and the Risen Lord. At dawn, two processions form at the church. One procession carries the image of Mary, and the other of our Lord. They go forth in two different directions. Eventually, the two processions meet at the entrance of the church. Flowers are blessed and the *Regina Coeli* is sung. After the procession, Mass at dawn begins. Our sorrow ceases and we now rejoice with the Mother of God!

The Parish and the Home

DURING the final week of Lent, families will want to prepare for the Triduum, sensitizing children to its events, reading the Scriptures in a children's Bible or illustrated version, and arranging the calendar around these high holy days. It begins at sunset on Holy Thursday and concludes with sunset Easter Sunday.

If shared meals were important to Jesus, they should be a high priority for families, no matter how many good excuses get in the way. Children can also learn a great deal from Eucharistic hymns and from observing as the altar cloths are removed after Holy Thursday Mass. This is how the Church expresses its great sadness and emptiness over Jesus' death.

The Good Friday service is stark, beginning in silence. Parents can introduce children to the adoration of the cross by modeling how to touch it or kiss it, and explaining that whatever we suffer takes on meaning in light of Jesus's suffering. Sometimes children's approach to the cross or crucifix is so tender and reverent, it renews the faith of older assembly members. Some parishes also offer the Way of the Cross or a service with other Christian congregations on this day.

For children old enough to attend the Easter Vigil, its symbols will intrigue and communicate without saying a word. The Easter bonfire and lighting of the Easter candle speak of the light dispelling darkness, and Jesus's sacrifice vanquishing death. Spring flowers, the singing of the Gloria and Alleluia for the first time in six weeks, the blessing of the baptismal water, and the exultant Easter hymns: all say more than mere words can about new life. The joy communicated on this night should correct any misperception of Catholicism as being a matter of dour rule-following, or boring drudgery. At this time, we shine: our finest ritual, music and community should draw in families, and encourage their own celebrations to continue at home.

Many parishes celebrate Baptism, Confirmation, and first Holy Communion at the Vigil for people joining the Catholic Christian community, and parishes want to make these sacraments as clear and compelling as possible. Families who know some of the candidates and catechumens who will be fully initiated at the Easter Vigil might want to make "welcome" cards for them. If they haven't yet met, they can congratulate them, or attend a reception for them after the liturgy. If the parish publishes a Holy Week schedule that can be hung on the refrigerator, it's a helpful reminder to keep these days special.

Families may want to build in time at home for children to ask questions or "process" what they have experienced during the Triduum. Children may also wish to display their own illustrations of the events they have witnessed during these three days—both the events of Jesus' life,

and the liturgical celebrations they have participated in.

Mass Texts

◆ SAMPLE PRAYER OF THE FAITHFUL FOR THE EVENING MASS OF THE LORD'S SUPPER

Celebrant:
The love of Christ has gathered us together this night.
With grateful hearts, let us offer our prayers and praise.

Deacon/Lector/Reader:
For the Church, that the Eucharist we celebrate Sunday after Sunday may overflow in generous love for the poor of the world, we pray:

For all who hunger, that through a just and equal sharing of God's gifts, they may be filled with an abundance of good things, we pray:

For the sick, the suffering, and those undergoing spiritual darkness or depression, that they may experience the compassion of Christ and his saving love in body, mind, and soul, we pray:

For Christians, that by our love for one another the world may know Jesus Christ, who on the night before he died prayed that all might be one, we pray:

For all of us, gathered here on this holy night, that there may be an end to bitterness and quarrels among us, and a new beginning of charity and love, we pray:

Celebrant:
God of life and love,
may we who rejoice in the saving love of Christ on this holy night
also serve one another with generous hearts.
We ask this through the One
who gave his life that we might live:
Jesus Christ, our Lord.
Amen.

◆ SAMPLE PRAYER OF THE FAITHFUL FOR THE EASTER VIGIL

Celebrant:
In the fullness of Easter joy, let us bring our needs and hopes to the God of Life.

Our response is

Risen Lord, hear our prayer.

Deacon/Lector/Reader:

For the Church, that we may be renewed in grace on this most blessed of days, we pray:

For the newly baptized, that God will bless them with his own wisdom and peace, on this day and every day of their lives, we pray:

For all who live under the shadow of death and war, that they may experience light, peace, and freedom, we pray:

For the sick, the suffering, the lonely, and the forgotten, that they may feel the joy of this holy night through our prayers and our loving support, we pray:

For all who have died, [especially N. and N.], that they may also share in his Resurrection, we pray:

For all of us, gathered in this holy place, that the surpassing joy of this night may overflow in acts of loving kindness toward all we encounter in our daily lives, we pray:

Celebrant:

Glorious God, your love endures forever.
Raise us in joy with your Son,
so that we may proclaim the Good News of Easter to a waiting world.
We ask this through the One
who is the Resurrection and the life:
Jesus Christ our Lord.
Amen.

◆ **DISMISSAL OF THE CATECHUMENS AND ELECT ON HOLY THURSDAY**

Dear friends, catechumens, and elect,
soon you will join us at our feast of thanks and praise,
where the table is laid with the Bread of Life
and the cup is filled with the Precious Blood of our Lord.
But at this time we send you forth to another place,
once again to ponder and discuss the words you have heard in our midst. Go in the peace of Christ.

◆ **DISMISSAL OF THE CATECHUMENS AND ELECT ON GOOD FRIDAY**

As we send you forth for the last time to consider the readings you have heard,
we pray that you will enter into the deepest of our mysteries:
the mystery of suffering, Death, and Resurrection.
Soon you will be freed from sin and death in the saving waters of Baptism;
until that moment, so near at hand, go in the peace of Christ.

◆ **DISMISSAL OF THE CATECHUMENS FOR THE EASTER VIGIL AND EASTER SUNDAY**

My dear catechumens, it is our deepest longing that you celebrate this Eucharist with us,
that you share in our Easter joy as we give thanks and praise
for the Resurrection of our Lord Jesus Christ.
We send you forth now to another place
so that you may reflect on the great Paschal Mystery,
proclaimed so powerfully in the Scriptures you have heard.
Go now in the peace of the Risen Christ.

March
Month of Saint Joseph

The commentaries pertaining to the Lectionary for Mass for the Evening Mass of the Lord's Supper, Good Friday, and the Easter Vigil were written by Paul Turner © LTP, 2012.

(#39)   white

Thursday of Holy Week (Holy Thursday) / Evening Mass of the Lord's Supper

THU **28**

Orientation

"Do you realize what I have done for you?" This challenging question serves as a most suitable introduction to the Easter Triduum, three continuous days of entering into the mystery of Christ's Passion, Death, and Resurrection in the most profound way. During the elaborate liturgies and varied rituals inviting our participation, Jesus's question remains a constant focal point, reorienting us to the deepest meaning of the celebrations. Making present the culmination of Jesus's life through the liturgies of the Triduum is not an exercise in historical research. The Paschal Mystery touches our lives here and now. Do we realize how Jesus's Passion, Death, and Resurrection involve each of us in a most intimate way?

Lectionary for Mass

◆ FIRST READING: In this reading, God commands Moses and Aaron to institute the feast that would be known as Passover. At the time, the community of Israel was suffering in bondage in Egypt. This passage comes in the midst of the description of the ten plagues which convinced Pharaoh to free the people of Israel from their captivity. Passover came to mean the meal and the date fixed on the Jewish calendar. For the first observance, a family slaughtered a lamb or a goat, eating the meat, but sprinkling the blood on the two doorposts of each home. The blood became a sign for the angel responsible for the tenth plague to "pass over" the homes and spare the life of the firstborn. Ever since this event, the Jewish community has celebrated Passover each year.

◆ RESPONSORIAL PSALM 116: Several verses from a song of thanksgiving form the Responsorial Psalm. The overall purpose of this Psalm is to give thanks to God, but the Lectionary designates these verses because they especially fit the themes of Holy Thursday. The psalmist gives thanks by taking up "the cup of salvation" (116:13). The Psalm proclaims, "Precious in the eyes of the LORD / is the death of his faithful ones" (116:15). These verses foreshadow the Eucharistic cup that Jesus shared at the Last Supper, as well as his own Death looming on Good Friday. The refrain is lifted from the same epistle that gives us the Second Reading; it is not a verse from the Psalm. As Christians experiencing anew the last days of Jesus, rooted in the meal traditions of our ancestors, we sing, "Our blessing-cup is a communion with the Blood of Christ." Normally, the Responsorial Psalm echoes a theme from the First Reading or the Gospel. This is a rare instance when it pertains to the Second Reading, which is yet to be proclaimed.

◆ SECOND READING: Saint Paul tells how Jesus instituted the Eucharist. With minor variations, this account also appears in Gospel accounts by Matthew, Mark, and Luke. Scholars tell us, however, that Paul wrote these epistles before the evangelists wrote their Gospel narratives. Therefore, this is the oldest account of what happened at the Last Supper, the version that lies closest to the years of Jesus's life. At this point in his letter, Paul is probably responding to some specific questions from the Corinthians. Apparently, they had asked about the proper way to celebrate the Eucharist. Paul hands on to them what others had told him. Paul says that the supper took place on the night before Jesus was betrayed, that Jesus took bread, gave thanks, said, "This is my body that is for you," and commanded his followers to "do this in remembrance of me" (11:24). Jesus repeated this command upon taking up the cup, which he called "the new covenant in my blood" (11:25). Paul says we proclaim the death of the Lord until he comes whenever we "eat this bread and drink the cup" (11:26). These words address the heart of Catholic faith. We believe that our Eucharist is the Body and Blood of Christ, that Jesus told us this, and that he commanded us to eat and drink in remembrance of him. This passage is the key that unlocks the meaning of Holy Thursday.

◆ GOSPEL: Jesus gives his followers a model of discipleship when he washes their feet. In John's account of the Gospel, at the Last Supper, when the reader expects to find the institution of the Eucharist that appears in Matthew, Mark, and Luke (the synoptic accounts of the Gospel), and even in Paul's First Letter to the Corinthians, it is not there. Instead, John gives a mystical interpretation of the Eucharist in the washing of the feet. Just as Paul's letter unlocks the meaning of Holy Thursday, John's narrative unlocks its implications. As Jesus stoops to wash feet, Simon Peter resists until Jesus warns him, "Unless I wash you, you will have no inheritance with me" (13:8). His statement probably alludes to Baptism, which became an initiation rite for all the followers of Jesus. Importantly, Jesus advises the disciples, "If I, therefore, the master and teacher, have washed your feet, you ought to wash one another's feet" (13:14). Whenever we engage in selfless, humble service to our neighbor, we follow the model that Jesus gave.

The Roman Missal

The Entrance Antiphon for Holy Thursday from Saint Paul's Letter to the Galatians perfectly express-es the paradox of our faith, which is also the paradox of the Sacred Paschal Triduum: "We should glory in the Cross of our Lord Jesus Christ, / in whom is our salvation, life and resurrection, / through whom we are saved and delivered." We are not ashamed of the Cross; rather, we glory in it, because through the Paschal Mystery, the instrument of death has become the sign of Resurrection, life, and grace. What Pius Parsch called "the double strain" of this liturgy is clear from the first moments: joy and sorrow, love and suffering (Vol. II, p. 326).

This Mass marks the beginning of a new liturgical time. Gone are the violet vestments of Lent, and in their place are vestments of white and gold (white is proper; gold and silver are allowed for solemn feasts). The procession should feel different also—it should be both solemn and grand, befitting the occasion. The Gloria returns; sing it with joy and with the ringing of bells. If you have a set of bells outside the church, let them ring immediately following the absolution of the Penitential Act, so that the people inside can hear

them. Then ring all the bells inside: the choir might ring handbells, and the servers could ring the sanctus bells. At the end of the Gloria, all the bells fall silent until the Easter Vigil. Then the Mass continues much as usual, with the Liturgy of the Word and the Homily.

The rubrics of *The Roman Missal* seldom comment on the Homily, but tonight the Missal indicates that the Homily should shed light on "the principal mysteries that are com-memorated in this Mass, namely, the institution of the Holy Eucharist and of the priestly Order, and the commandment of the Lord con-cerning fraternal charity" (9). In a sense, the Homily should do what Jesus did for his disciples in to-night's Gospel: it should answer the question, "Do you realize what I have done for you?"

The optional washing of the feet may follow the Homily. After the reading of the Gospel account of Christ washing the feet of his dis-ciples, this rite will require no in-troduction or explanation—it will speak for itself. After a period of silence following the Homily, the priest simply stands, removes his chasuble, and, accompanied by the servers, begins the ritual action of the Washing of the Feet. The Gos-pel does not tell us how many of his disciples' feet Jesus washed, nor does *The Roman Missal* specify how many the priest will wash. In keep-ing with an ancient custom, many parishes choose 12 people to have their feet washed. Those chosen should reflect the diversity of the parish community: young and old, different races and nationalities. Choose different people each year. You might ask the coordinators of the various ministries in the par-ish to suggest names. Perhaps include one of the elect or one of those recently received into Full Communion.

Give those who are to have their feet washed some simple instructions before Mass begins: when to move to the place for the foot-washing, when to remove their shoes and socks, when to put them back on, and when to return to their seats.

In preparing for this rite, con-sider visibility. Will it work best to have all those whose feet are to be washed near the sanctuary? Or, can stations be set up throughout the church, with the priest and minis-ters processing to different places, so that everyone in the assembly has a clear view of the ritual?

Think through the logistics of the rite as well. Who places the chairs or stools for those to have their feet washed? Will these chairs need to be removed afterward? Is there enough room for the priest to kneel in front of the people comfortably? How many servers will be needed to carry the pitcher of water, the basin, the towel? Will the water need to be replenished along the way? Will the basin need to be emptied? Who will see that this happens?

The important thing is that the meaning of the washing of the feet shines through clearly in the ritual action: it "represents the service and charity of Christ, who came 'not to be served, but to serve'" (*Paschale Solemnitatis*, 51).

The Roman Missal provides seven different antiphons to be sung dur-ing the Washing of the Feet, an indication that there is no need to hurry through the rite. These texts, drawn from the Gospel according to John and from 1 Corinthians, emphasize again and again the meaning of this rite: Christ's love for us; the love we must have for one another.

At the conclusion of the washing of the feet, *The Roman Missal* spec-ifies that the priest washes and dries his hands, then puts the chasuble back on before returning to his chair for the Prayer of the Faithful.

The Creed is not said tonight, and the Prayer of the Faithful follows the washing of the feet. If there are elect, dismiss them just before the Prayer of the Faithful.

Following the Prayer of the Faithful, the altar is prepared and there may be a procession of the faithful with gifts for the poor, "presented with the bread and wine" (RM, 14). These gifts are different from those we offer every Sunday; they are "those collected during Lent as the fruit of penance" (PS, 52). If the parish participates in Operation Rice Bowl for Catholic Relief Services or a similar program, encourage the people to bring their Rice Bowl with them tonight, and carry it forward in procession. Please note that extra help will be needed to receive the gifts. Since the baskets are not passed through the pews, the ushers may be free to assist.

The Roman Missal suggests the singing of the great hymn *Ubi Caritas* during this part of the liturgy. The refrain "Where true charity is dwelling, God is present there" forms a powerful accompaniment to the procession of gifts and the preparation of the altar for the celebration of the Eucharist.

There is an optional Rite for the Reception of the Blessed Oils and the Sacred Chrism (it can be found at page 161 of this *Sourcebook*). If this rite takes place during the Evening Mass of the Lord's Supper, it should happen just before the gifts procession.

On Holy Thursday, as at every Mass, the Lord's Supper is not past, but present. The celebrant's prayers for this holy day emphasize this. In the Collect, we recall this "sacrifice new for all eternity, / the banquet of his love," which Christ gave to the Church when he was about to die. This ever-new mystery is the source of "the fullness of charity and of life" for us. The Prayer over

the Offerings is a prayer for awareness: we ask that we may "participate worthily" in this mystery, for here, "the work of Our redemption is accomplished"—not *will* be, but *is*. And the Prayer after Communion asks that we who celebrate the Lord's Supper here and now may "enjoy his banquet for all eternity." What we do now, in this liturgy, is a glimpse and a foretaste of what we hope to share forever in heaven.

On Holy Thursday, the Preface of the Holy Eucharist is used. This Preface (found in the Proper of Time) draws together in a powerful way the primary threads of this liturgy: sacrifice and memory, love and service. The Proper of Time for Holy Thursday includes the entire text of the Roman Canon, including the special forms of the *Communicantes* or "In communion with those whose memory we venerate" and of the *Hanc igitur* or "Therefore, Lord, we pray" for Holy Thursday. The Celebrant is free to choose another Eucharistic Prayer as well.

Notice that the *Sanctus* bells are not rung at the elevations tonight, although incense may be used.

After Holy Communion, the ciborium containing the hosts for Good Friday is left on the altar. "At an appropriate moment during Communion," the priest may give the Eucharist to ministers to the homebound, who will immediately go forth to carry Communion to them (RM, 33).

Following the Prayer after Communion, which is said at the chair as usual, the priest goes to the altar and, kneeling, incenses the Blessed Sacrament. Then he receives the humeral veil, takes the ciborium, and the procession to the altar of repose begins. *The Roman Missal* provides a number of details about the order of procession. After the cross-bearer, who is accompanied by two candle-bearers, come "others carrying lighted candles" (38), including any concelebrants or

deacons. Then comes an altar server, carrying "a smoking thurible," immediately in front of the priest carrying the Blessed Sacrament. "All in the procession carry lighted candles, and around the blessed sacrament torches are carried" (*Ceremonial of Bishops*, 307).

All sing during the procession. Any Eucharistic hymn may be chosen. The chant suggested in *The Roman Missal* is *Pange lingua*, all except the last two verses (those beginning "Tantum ergo" and "Genitori, genitoque," which are saved for later). At the altar of repose, as the ciborium is placed in the tabernacle, these final two verses of the hymn are sung. The priest celebrant incenses the Blessed Sacrament again, then he or an assisting deacon closes and locks the tabernacle. The priest celebrant and ministers may remain in silent adoration as long as they see fit. Then they simply genuflect and return to the sacristy, without procession. Adoration continues into the evening, but not after midnight: for at midnight the day of the Lord's Passion has begun.

Notice that there is no formal dismissal at the end of tonight's liturgy; indeed, we will not be formally dismissed until the end of the Easter Vigil. In essence, the Paschal Triduum is one great liturgy.

At an appropriate time following the Mass, hence during the period of adoration, the altar is stripped, the crosses are veiled, and candles are extinguished before the shrines of saints. In ancient times, Psalm 22 was recited as the altar was stripped: "They divide my garments among them" (Psalm 22:19)

The period of adoration may take place in silence. However, you might consider offering the Office of Night Prayer at some point during the period of adoration, perhaps just before its conclusion at midnight. Another possibility is to mark the beginning of each hour by reading some part of the Gospel according to John, chapters 13–17, the Book of Glory. These readings take us from the Gospel we heard at Mass tonight, through Judas's betrayal, the prediction of Peter's denial, the Last Supper discourses, and the great high priestly prayer of Jesus in John 17 (see PS, 56).

Other Ideas

Over the next three days when watching the news, listen for stories that manifest the presence of evil in the world. Discuss in a small group how those events challenge your Christian faith and your belief in the Resurrection.

#40   red

F
R   **29** Friday of the Passion
I   of the Lord/
            Good Friday

Orientation

Behold Jesus, our crucified king! Even at his execution, the people surrounding Jesus struggle with the truth of his identity. The title of king, used to mock and reject Jesus by the crowd, suddenly becomes a transcendent symbol of truth when Pilate orders it affixed on Jesus's Cross. "Jesus of Nazareth King of the Jews," often abbreviated as INRI in Christian art, unexpectedly reveals the horrific truth of the Crucifixion to Jesus's adversaries,

as they promptly demand the sign's removal. Pilate, in pursuit of truth at the trial of Jesus, now gains a sense of it as he persists in keeping the sign. The truth stated on the simple sign holds the power to stir the heart and conscience of all who behold it. In coming before the cross today, what sense of truth are you gaining?

Lectionary for Mass

◆ FIRST READING: The Lectionary subtitles this passage the fourth oracle of the Servant of the Lord, but it is often called the fourth song of the Suffering Servant. Near the end of the book of the prophet Isaiah, we meet a figure called God's servant, who represents God but suffers greatly for the sins of others. The figure may have been a historical person at the time of Isaiah or a representation of the people of Israel. Christians read these four passages with a very specific insight: they prophesy Jesus, the servant of the Father, who suffered for our salvation. The passage opens with a startling description of this servant. He was "spurned and avoided by people, / a man of suffering, accustomed to infirmity" (Isaiah 53:3). In the most moving verses, read with a lump in our throats, we realize that the servant's suffering should have been ours: "Yet it was our infirmities that he bore, / our sufferings that he endured . . . / We had all gone astray like sheep . . . / but the LORD laid upon him / the guilt of us all" (Isaiah 53:4, 6). On Good Friday, these verses come to fulfillment in the crucified Jesus.

◆ RESPONSORIAL PSALM 31 appeals to God for rescue. The psalmist is desperate, "an object of reproach, / a laughingstock to my neighbors, and a dread to my friends" (Psalm 31:6). But the Psalm does not dwell in despair. It trusts that God will redeem the one in distress. This singer is so convinced of salvation

that the Psalm concludes with an exhortation to the hearer: "Take courage and be stouthearted, / all you who hope in the LORD" (Psalm 31:25). The refrain for the Psalm comes from the Gospel according to Luke. It was spoken by Jesus on the cross. Jesus, who must have known its words by heart, quotes Psalm 31 when he makes his appeal for rescue: "Father, into your hands I commend my spirit" (Luke 23:46).

◆ SECOND READING: The sufferings of Jesus enabled him to empathize with our weakness, making him a powerful mediator of mercy and grace. The Letter to the Hebrews explains the role of Jesus as the greatest of all high priests. This passage describes the events of Jesus's Passion: "In the days when Christ was in the flesh, he offered prayers and supplications with loud cries and tears to the one who was able to save him from death" (Hebrews 5:7). These words resemble the Gospel accounts of Jesus suffering his agony in the garden of Gethsemane. But the passage does not linger on Jesus's suffering. "[H]e was heard" (Hebrews 5:7). The Father, who could save Jesus from death, did, through his Death and Resurrection.

◆ GOSPEL: This passage in the Gospel according to John is one of the most sublime testimonies to the glory of God. The narrative moves through several scenes, but it constantly teaches the meaning of Jesus's life, death, and Resurrection. We hear it each year on Good Friday.

Early on, John presents "Jesus, knowing everything that was going to happen to him" (John 18:4). Jesus is no innocent bystander. He is the omniscient God in control of the events that follow. Three times in the opening confrontation he says, "I AM," boldly claiming the name that God revealed to Moses in the burning bush. His enemies end up proclaiming the truth about Jesus in spite of themselves. Caiaphas had told the Jews that, "it was better that one man should die rather than the people" (John 18:14), fulfilling Isaiah's fourth oracle. Pilate, unable to get a straight answer from Jesus about his identity, asks, "What is truth?" (John 18:38). But it is Pilate who has an inscription made for the cross that calls Jesus, in three languages, the King of the Jews. The soldiers plait a crown from thorns and wrap Jesus's aching body in purple cloth, intending to mock, but instead acknowledging his kingship.

While the enemies of Jesus unintentionally speak the truth, his friend Peter intentionally denies Jesus three times. From the cross, Jesus takes matters into his own hands, entrusting his mother and the disciple whom he loved to each other. From these faithful disciples the Church will be born. Before he dies, Jesus says, "It is finished" (John 19:30). That doesn't mean, "It's over." It means, "It is accomplished," or "It is perfected." He has completed the task he was given. He hands himself over to God. John has Jesus dying on the cross on preparation day, the day before Passover, so that we will see in the slaughtering of the Passover lambs a contemporaneous symbol of the One who gave his life that others might live.

The Roman Missal

Today's celebration of the Lord's Passion has no Entrance Procession, no cross and no candles. Instead, "The Priest and the Deacon . . . wearing red vestments as for Mass, go to the altar in silence and, after making a reverence to the altar, prostrate themselves" while the people kneel. The prostration should last long enough so that the echoes of banging kneelers and rustling programs have died out of our ears, and so we have time to pray. According

to *Paschale Solemnitatis*, the prostration, which "should be strictly observed" (PS, 65), has a dual meaning. "It signifies both the abasement of 'earthly man,' and also the grief and sorrow of the Church" (PS, 65). It is a sign of humility, a posture of prayer, a gesture of grief. (*The Roman Missal* provides priests and deacons with the possibility of kneeling before the altar when prostration is not possible.)

The prayer is said when the priest returns to his chair. It is not called the "Collect," nor is "Let us pray" said at the beginning. There is no Sign of the Cross, no Penitential Act. The beginning of this liturgy—different from any other day in the entire year—reminds us that the Church is already at prayer. Two options are given for the prayer. The first prayer is simpler, and asks God to "sanctify" his servants, for whom Christ shed his blood and "established the Paschal Mystery." The second option speaks of how Christ "abolished the death inherited from ancient sin." We pray that we who "have borne . . . the image of the man of earth," Adam, may now "bear the image of the Man of heaven," Christ.

The Liturgy of the Word proceeds as usual, with the Passion according to Saint John. The same options are provided as for the proclamation of the Passion on Palm Sunday. Following the reading of the Passion, there is a "brief homily" and a time for silent prayer.

The Solemn Intercessions follow. There are three parts to each of these intercessions: an introduction, which may be sung or spoken by a deacon or by a lay minister, if no deacon is present; a prayer, sung or spoken by the priest; and the people's response, "Amen." In addition, following each of the introductions, the people may be asked to kneel for a few moments of silent prayer.

There are ten prayers in the Solemn Intercessions, and the local bishop has the option of adding another if there is a special need. We pray for the Church; for the pope; "for all orders and degrees of the faithful": bishops, priests, deacons, and laity; for catechumens; for the unity of Christians; for the Jewish people; for those who do not believe in Christ; for those who do not believe in God; for those in public office; and finally "for those in tribulation": the imprisoned, the hungry, travelers and pilgrims, and the sick and dying

Following the intercessions, all are seated. Then the Adoration of the Holy Cross begins. The rite is divided into two parts: the showing of the holy cross, and the adoration of the cross. The Missal provides two options for the showing of the holy cross. In the first form, the cross, "covered with a violet veil," is carried before the altar, accompanied by servers with lit candles (note the change from red to violet). The priest or deacon uncovers the upper part of the cross, raises it high, and sings, "Behold the wood of the cross, on which hung the salvation of the world." All respond, "Come, let us adore," and kneel in prayer. *The Roman Missal* specifies that a deacon or even the choir may assist with the singing of the invitation, if necessary. Then the priest uncovers the right arm of the cross, lifts it up, and repeats the invitation to prayer. Finally, he uncovers the entire cross. Following the third acclamation, the cross is set in place for individual veneration.

In the second form of showing the cross, the cross is not veiled. Instead, three stops are made, beginning at the doors, then in the middle of the church, and finally at the entrance to the sanctuary. The same invitation and response are sung at each stop.

Immediately following the showing of the cross, individual adoration begins. There are no rules for individual veneration, but a simple genuflection, and touching or kissing the cross, would be appropriate.

The rubrics very clearly state that only one cross should be used for the adoration, and *Paschale Solemnitatis* states unequivocally that "personal adoration of the cross is the most important feature in this celebration" (PS, 69). *The Roman Missal* provides a good deal of music to be sung during the veneration: the antiphon *Crucem tuam adoramus*, "We adore your Cross, O Lord"; the "Reproaches," with the ancient acclamation "Holy is God," called the Trisagion; and the hymn *Crux fidelis*, "Faithful Cross." The abundance of musical options suggests that it is reasonable to allow a fair amount of time for individual adoration.

There is no Mass on Good Friday! The way we pray the Communion Rite can help the assembly understand the difference between Mass and this Communion service. *The Roman Missal* certainly urges us to see the difference. Following the period of adoration, the altar is prepared with the utmost simplicity. The altar cloth, corporal, and Missal are placed. The deacon or priest, accompanied by two ministers with lit candles, brings the ciborium to the altar in a simple procession, "by a shorter route" than was taken last night in the Eucharistic procession. The candles are placed on or around the altar, and the ministers retire. The ciborium is uncovered, the priest comes to the altar, genuflects, and without any preamble invites the people to pray the Lord's Prayer. Following the doxology, the Sign of Peace, and Lamb of God are omitted. The priest simply takes a host from the ciborium, raises it slightly, and says, "Behold the Lamb of God," to which the people give the usual

response. He receives Holy Communion, and Holy Communion is then given to the people.

The Good Friday liturgy begins unlike any other liturgy of the year; it ends differently, too. Following Holy Communion, the priest returns to his place and the usual period of silence is observed. The Prayer after Communion is said, and even as we recall the Lord's Passion we are never unaware that the Risen Lord is with us: God has "restored us to life / by the blessed Death and Resurrection of . . . Christ." There is no dismissal; its place is taken by a Prayer over the People, prayed with hands extended over the congregation. We ask God for "pardon," "comfort," and "holy faith" for all who have "honored the Death" of Christ, "in hope of their resurrection." There is no concluding procession and no music at the end of the liturgy; the ministers simply genuflect before the Cross and "depart in silence." We will not be dismissed until tomorrow night, at the conclusion of the great Easter Vigil.

When is the collection? Because there is no procession with the gifts on Good Friday, there is no obvious place for the collection. It might be taken up as people leave the church following the liturgy. Alternately, it might be taken up during a hymn or choral motet sung following the Homily, the intercessions, or the period of veneration.

Other Ideas

On this day when we participate in Christ's great sacrifice and remember all he gave and suffered for our sakes, the author of Hebrews tells us to approach confidently the throne of grace. We're not told to languish in remorse nor to dwell on guilt. Instead, we are invited to contemplate God's gracious mercy. What better day than this, then, to

extend to others the mercy so generously shared with us. Think of someone with whom you need reconciliation, and no matter who hurt whom, write that person a brief note of apology or forgiveness.

S A T **30** #41 violet/white
Holy Saturday/ Easter Vigil

Orientation

"Why do you seek the living one among the dead?" This pointed question of the two in dazzling garments challenges faith calcified in routine and empty ritual. The Easter Vigil retells the story of God and God's people, culminating in the Paschal Mystery. For many of us, these are stories and rituals we have seen and heard many times before, and they can even become objectified as "things that the Church does at Easter," losing their powerful impact on our present context. To participate in the Easter Vigil, to hear again the many readings recounting God's continued relationship with humankind, to witness sacraments of new life in Christ: these hold the power to rouse us all to new life in robust faith. The rituals of the Church are not about looking back, but rather about making the past powerfully present in our here and now. The Risen One is not an artifact of the past, but here among us today. Alleluia!

Lectionary for Mass

◆ FIRST READING: The entire Bible opens with an account of how and why all things came to be. The heavens and the earth exist by the will of God. At the time these verses were written, science had not advanced beyond a rudimentary understanding of biology and zoology. The Catholic Church does not expect members to believe literally in the words of this story. Genesis, however, defends a vital belief that we recite at the beginning of our weekly Profession of Faith: God is the Creator of heaven and earth. The Easter Vigil is the pivotal night of the entire liturgical year. Lent has led up to this night; even Advent and Christmas Time have been preparing for this night. Everything we celebrate for the next 50 days results from our belief that Jesus is risen from the dead. Christ's Resurrection from the dead makes our own resurrection possible. As faithful followers, we believe that God created us, and that God will re-create us at the end of time. Our destiny is prefigured in the Baptisms we celebrate in Catholic churches throughout the world on this night. To reaffirm the foundation of our belief in a new creation, the Easter Vigil offers us the story of the first creation. Since God created everything out of nothing, it is not so hard to believe that God can re-create everything out of something.

◆ RESPONSORIAL PSALM, OPTION 1: Psalm 104 is a song of praise to God for the wonders of creation. It imagines the earth fixed upon a foundation, covered with the waters of the oceans, surmounted by waters enclosed in the sky, high above the tops of the mountains. Water, birds, cattle, and grain all supply the needs of humanity, the crown of God's creation. It would be enough if this Psalm praised God for the wonders of nature, but it does something more. It praises God for the way nature is renewed each year and from one generation to the next. The verse we use for the refrain calls upon God to send the Spirit to renew the face of the earth. This quality of creation, its inherent ability to renew, makes this Psalm a perfect choice for the Easter Vigil. On this night, we praise God for the Resurrection of Christ, for the new life bestowed upon the newly baptized, and for the promise of eternal life revealed throughout God's Word.

◆ RESPONSORIAL PSALM, OPTION 2: As an alternative to Psalm 104, a different song of creation may follow the First Reading: Psalm 33. It, too, praises God for the wonders of nature. This Psalm envisions that the waters of the ocean are contained as in a flask, confined as though in cellars in the deep. Notably, Psalm 33 includes morality among God's creations. God's word is "upright," all God's works are "trustworthy," God loves "justice and right," and the earth is full of God's "kindness." Here is echoed the belief from the First Reading that what God made is "good." We praise God not just for the things that are, but for the goodness of things that are. Christians interpret one of the verses of this Psalm as a prophecy for our belief in the Holy Trinity: "By the word of the LORD the heavens were made; / by the breath of his mouth all their host." In one verse we find references to the Lord, the Word, and the breath, images of the Triune God, preexisting all that is.

◆ SECOND READING: This is one of the most difficult passages in the entire Bible, and it is hard to hear it without feeling squeamish about the God who would make this request, Abraham who would fulfill it, and Isaac who would be the innocent victim. There is a happy ending, but not before the story turns our stomachs. Adding to the grim nature of God's request is that Abraham had no son until he was over one hundred years old. God had promised that Abraham's progeny would be as numberless as the sands on the shore of the sea, but the patriarch was not yet a father of one. Now, at incredibly advanced ages, Abraham and Sarah had become first-time parents, and this was the son God wanted him to sacrifice. The story is retold at the Easter Vigil because it foreshadows the life of Jesus. He was an only child, as was Isaac. He was innocent, yet walked up a hill carrying on his shoulders the wood of his sacrifice. But there, the similarities end. Isaac was saved from death; Jesus was saved through death.

◆ RESPONSORIAL PSALM: Those in the most difficult circumstances yearn for the confident trust of Psalm 16. When things go wrong, we turn to God for assistance. Sometimes we demand help; often we hope against hope for it. But Psalm 16 exudes confidence: "with [the Lord] at my right hand I shall not be disturbed." This Psalm flows naturally from the story of Abraham and Isaac. Abraham, too, possessed the charism of confidence. He believed that, even in the most difficult circumstances, God would be faithful to the covenant. Psalm 16 fits the Easter Vigil because of its references to death and life. This Psalm appears each week in Thursday's night prayer from the Liturgy of the Hours. Before going to bed, Christians pray these words, confident that wakefulness will follow sleep, and life will follow death.

◆ THIRD READING: This paradigmatic reading from the Old Testament must be proclaimed in every celebration of the Easter Vigil. The liturgy encourages the use of all the Old Testament readings at the Vigil, but permits a smaller number for exceptional circumstances. This reading is never omitted because it roots our understanding of Baptism and resurrection. In the story, Egypt has enslaved the Israelites, and God has appointed Moses to lead them from the clutches of Pharaoh into freedom. Their only route traverses the Red Sea, which parts for their passage, but returns to swallow up the pursuing forces of Pharaoh, his chariots, and his charioteers. On the other side of the waters, Israel is poised to enter the Promised Land. The *Exsultet* and the blessing of baptismal water, which are both heard in the Vigil, point out the significance of this passage, and hence of this night. God freed Israel from its foes through water, and God will free the catechumens from the clutches of Satan and sin through the waters of Baptism. Set free from Pharaoh, Israel entered the Promised Land. Set free from sin, the neophytes enter the life of grace as members of the Body of Christ. At the center of all this imagery is Jesus Christ, who was set free from death to life through the mercy of the Father.

◆ CANTICLE: The Responsory that follows this reading from Exodus also comes from Exodus. It is the very song that Israel sings upon reaching the dry shores on the other side of the Red Sea. It retells the events of this Passover night: the loss of Pharaoh's chariots in the Red Sea and the redemption of God's Chosen People when God "planted them on the mountain" (Exodus 15:17). Throughout the song, the people give praise to God. It is the Lord who has covered himself in glory. Yes, they have experienced freedom from slavery, but they do not rejoice in their own accomplishment. They praise God.

◆ FOURTH READING: This passage from the prophecy of Isaiah meets Israel at a very different moment in history. Many years have passed since the dramatic rescue of the Chosen People from the hand of

Pharaoh. The people have dwelled in the Promised Land and have enjoyed too much prosperity. They have been lured away by other beliefs. But God did not relinquish the covenant. Isaiah uses a startling image: "The Lord calls you back, / like a wife forsaken and grieved in spirit" (Isaiah 54:6). God says through Isaiah, "For a brief moment I abandoned you, / but with great tenderness I will take you back" (Isaiah 54:7). God compares this event to the days of Noah, when God swore never again to cover the earth with the waters of wrath. God is not angry with the Chosen People. God takes them home. God still takes pity on us in our sin. Even those who have not yet been baptized are God's children. God is yearning to receive them with great tenderness as they enter the waters of Baptism. Catholics who have spent this Lenten season in repentance can hear these consoling words and take heart that God has noticed their penance, heard their prayers, and is anxious to renew with them the everlasting covenant of mercy.

◆ RESPONSORIAL PSALM: We thank God for release from a serious threat, not for just any unexpected gift. The writer of Psalm 30 experienced death threats from enemies. Death seemed near, but somehow God rescued the singer "from among those going down into the pit" (Psalm 30:4). At the time, it seemed as though there was no way out, but in retrospect, it seems as though God's anger lasted "but a moment" and his good will lasts "a lifetime" (Psalm 30:6). This Psalm takes up the main theme of the Easter Vigil: the triumphant Passion of our Lord Jesus Christ. He could have sung this Psalm himself: "O LORD, you brought me up from the netherworld. . . . / At nightfall, weeping enters in, / but with the dawn, rejoicing" (Psalm 30:4, 6). All the participants in the Easter Vigil can sing this along with Christ.

Those to be baptized are to be lifted from their former way of life to membership in the body of Christ. Those who have already been baptized have expressed sorrow for their sins and experienced the joy of God's mercy. With Christ, we are all brought up from the netherworld on this night that shines more brightly than the dawn.

◆ FIFTH READING: Isaiah offers a second prophecy for our reflection. It extends again to a people who had drifted from the covenant, but who discover that God's mercies are without end. The prophecy opens with an invitation to drink water, a symbol that will occupy center stage at the Easter Vigil in the next part of the ceremony. We cannot live without water, and our relationship with God slakes our spiritual thirst. The Lord is near, and Isaiah urges us to call upon him, forsaking the ways of sin. The Risen Christ is very near to all who seek him. Catechumens have left the desert of life-without-Christ, and the faithful have abandoned their sins through the penance of Lent. The waters of the covenant will renew us. Strengthening the image of water, God speaks through Isaiah about the effectiveness of rain and snow. They come down from the heavens and do not return there "till they have watered the earth, / making it fertile and fruitful." God's word does that in our lives. It comes to us like living water, and it produces the effect for which it was sent.

◆ CANTICLE: Isaiah supplies not just the two previous readings, but also the Responsory for the second one. Like the passage from Exodus that follows the Third Reading, this canticle resembles the structure and content of a Psalm, but it exists in another book of the Bible. The Lectionary offers us this passage to follow the previous reading because of the similarity in the way it applies the image of water, and because it comes from the same biblical book. The Canticle rings forth with praise of God. The singer proclaims, "I am confident and unafraid" (Isaiah 12:2). God is the source of salvation, just as a fountain is the source of life-giving water. On this Easter night, preparing for the celebration of Baptism, we are reminded of all that God promises, and how confidently we stand in faith.

◆ SIXTH READING: Changing the tone of the evening, the prophet Baruch chides Israel for forsaking the fountain of wisdom. He ascribes the troubles of Israel to the people's infidelity to the covenant. The solution? "Learn where prudence is, / where strength, where understanding" (Baruch 3:14). To know wisdom is to know God. Just as creation unveils the wisdom of God, so to know the wisdom of God is to draw near to our Maker. On this wondrous night, we grasp the wisdom of God's plan. The plan existed from the beginning of creation, but it was revealed to human beings slowly, through history. At the time of Baruch's prophecy, people still did not fully comprehend that Jesus would reveal the resurrection. Yet even without complete knowledge, people were able to perceive the wisdom of God in imperfect ways. Hearing this reading, and standing on the other historical shore from the Passion of Christ, we praise God for the gift of revelation made plain to us. Those who are approaching the waters of Baptism have come to the same insight. They put their faith in the Resurrection of Christ, and they participate in his life because of the interior wisdom they have received.

◆ RESPONSORIAL PSALM: Psalm 19 has two parts, and these verses come from the section that revels in the beauty of God's word. It resembles

Psalm 119, the longest in the Bible, which meditates line by line on the word of God through a variety of synonyms and attributes. These verses of Psalm 19 praise the "law," "decree," "precepts," "command," and "ordinances" of the Lord; they gladden the heart and enlighten the eye. This Psalm builds upon the theme of wisdom from the previous reading. We come to know God through meditation on his decrees. God revealed these to us in the covenant, so they detail the wisdom that exudes from the very being of God. For Christians, Jesus Christ is the perfect expression of God's wisdom. He is God's wisdom. He is the Word made flesh. For this reason, the Lectionary gives us a refrain taken from the Gospel according to John, not from the Psalm itself. The verse is spoken by Peter after Jesus has given the discourse on the Bread of Life. The teaching revealed the very reason Jesus came: to offer us eternal life through the eating of his body and drinking of his Blood. Many of those who heard him speak these words, however, turned away. Jesus looked fearfully at his closest followers and asked if they, too, were going to leave him now. Peter said no: "You have the words of everlasting life" (John 6:68c). That statement of faith becomes the refrain we sing to a Psalm that praises the wisdom of God. It also foreshadows the initiation of those who will share Holy Communion for the first time at this Mass.

◆ SEVENTH READING: The prophet Ezekiel addresses a people who had experienced exile from their homeland because of their infidelity, but learned now that God had not abandoned them. As a sign of renewing the eternal covenant, God offered the people cleansing and renewal through the gift of a new spirit. Israel's sin was not covered up, but it was forgiven, and the people grew stronger in faith. On a night when the waters of Baptism

contain the symbolism of new life, this passage prophesies all that Christianity has to offer. Those who have failed to love God as they should are cleansed from all sin. Some are baptized and others will renew their baptismal covenant through promises and holy water. All will experience the gift of the new spirit that God places in the heart of believers. God never goes back on the covenant; it is eternal. Even though we sometimes fail to keep the covenant, God always gives us the opportunity to renew it.

◆ RESPONSORIAL PSALM, OPTION 1: The Lectionary offers three possible Responsories to the Seventh Reading. The first, from Psalm 42, is sung whenever Baptism will be celebrated at the Vigil. The Psalm asks God for the gift of God's light and fidelity, so that those who receive it may approach the dwelling place of God, and specifically the altar of God. These verses eloquently prophesy the journey of the catechumens, who thirst for the waters of Baptism, and attain it through the light and fidelity that God extends to new believers through the covenant. Having been refreshed by the waters of Baptism, the neophytes come to the altar of God, where they participate in Holy Communion, the intimate union that makes them fully the body of Christ, a dwelling place for God most high.

◆ CANTICLE, OPTION 2: In this song of praise, we thank God for all that he has accomplished. This is exactly the Responsory that follows the Fifth Reading of the Easter Vigil. It is offered again as one of the alternatives following the Seventh Reading. In practice, it could logically be sung here whenever the seven readings are abbreviated and the Fifth Reading has been eliminated. But the Responsory may be used twice on the same night. Here, the English Lectionary recommends it as one of the options if Baptism is not celebrated during the Vigil. This may seem puzzling because the image of water is so strong at the beginning of these verses. In fact, the liturgical books are not consistent on this point. The *Ordo Lectionum Missae* actually recommends this Psalm, not the previous one, when Baptism is to be celebrated.

◆ RESPONSORIAL PSALM, OPTION 3: Tradition calls seven of the 150 Psalms penitential. This one is perhaps the greatest of them. It expresses the remorse we feel after sinning and our cries for forgiveness. These particular verses, coming at the end of the Psalm, focus on renewal. Although we have sung this text often during Lent, we may complete its sentiments at the Vigil, when we put our sinful ways behind us and seek a clean heart. These verses work well after the passage from Ezekiel, which employs a similar image—a new heart. In reestablishing the covenant with us, God remakes us. We reenter the covenant not as the same people, but as those who have known sin, repented of it, received forgiveness, and resolved not to sin again. This Psalm is recommended for an Easter Vigil that does not include Baptism. It more nearly suits the faithful Christians coming for renewal after observing a rigorous Lent.

◆ EPISTLE: Through Baptism, we enter the mystery of his Death and Resurrection. After hearing and singing up to fourteen passages from the Old Testament (seven readings and seven responsories), the New Testament makes its bright appearance. We hear Paul say, "We know that Christ, raised from the dead, dies no more; death no longer has power over him" (Romans 6:9). This is the first scriptural proclamation from tonight that Jesus is risen. Paul compares the Resurrection of

Christ and Baptism. This passage underscores our liturgical practice of celebrating Baptism at the Easter Vigil. It also affirms our preference for baptizing infants on any Sunday, our weekly observance of the Resurrection.

◆ RESPONSORIAL PSALM/GOSPEL ACCLAMATION: This Psalm gives many reasons for thanksgiving. It opens with the simple assertion that the Lord is good, and that "his mercy endures forever" (Psalm 118:1). It then announces the power and deeds of God's right hand. Two of the verses prophesy the meaning of this Easter night. You can imagine Jesus singing this Psalm: "I shall not die, but live, / and declare the works of the LORD" (Psalm 118:17). Christians can affirm, "The stone which the builders rejected / has become the cornerstone" (Psalm 118:22). His enemies thought they had put Jesus to death, but he has become the cornerstone of life. The refrain for this Psalm is a triple Alleluia. It doubles as the Gospel Acclamation. No words can fully express the joy of this night, so we resort to a Hebrew acclamation that needs no translation: Alleluia! Throughout Lent, we have abstained from singing that word. We have introduced the Gospel with a different acclamation of praise. But now, the word returns. Our "fasting" from the Alleluia is over. We rejoice that Christ is risen.

◆ GOSPEL: Jesus is risen from the dead. Jesus's Resurrection was so unexpected that Luke used stereotypes of women to explain it. He presumes that women are mourners; have limited powers of deduction; are terrified, not emboldened, by danger; are forgetful; and should not tell men the news. Luke accepts some stereotypes and rejects others. The women do not roll away the stone, but they do roll away unbelief. At first the two men in dazzling garments chide them: "Why do you

seek the living one among the dead?" The question contrasts unbelievers who never seek with believers who seek in the wrong place. The women inhabit a middle territory, believers not yet enlightened by Resurrection. They become Apostles to the Apostles. At this pivotal moment, Luke reveals three of their names: Mary Magdalene, Joanna, and Mary the mother of James. The Apostles thought their story was nonsense. Peter, the flawed leader, fearful he has missed out, runs to the tomb and beholds the scene. Without the testimony of women, the man called the first pope would not have heard of the Resurrection or investigated its report. Easter celebrates new life for all who feel underappreciated, terrified, inadequate, or just plain forgetful.

The Roman Missal

Tonight's liturgy is divided into four principal parts: the first and shortest of these is the Lucernarium; the second, and longest, is the Liturgy of the Word. Next comes the Baptismal Liturgy followed, finally, by the Liturgy of the Eucharist.

This liturgy is long—there is no way around this. But careful pacing of the various elements can ensure that people will come away feeling that it wasn't a moment too long. Pay special attention to the transition moments. Prepare in advance so that ministers know exactly when the next element in the liturgy begins. Some questions to consider:

How does the light get spread to the people following the second "Light of Christ"? The priest should begin this action. The deacon, priest, or cantor who is chanting "Light of Christ," should carry a candle (if he is not carrying the paschal candle), but probably should not help spread the light lest the procession get unduly slowed down.

When does the deacon approach the priest for a blessing before the

Exsultet? Immediately after placing the candle in the stand? Or after all the people have their candles lit? It makes sense to do this immediately following the placing of the candle. The light can continue to spread quietly during the incensation of the paschal candle and the beginning of the *Exsultet*.

During the sequence of readings, Psalms, and prayers, keep things moving. The First Reading can begin as soon as all are seated with their candles extinguished. The Psalm can follow after a short pause. "Let us pray" can come shortly following the Psalm. As the Collect begins, the next reader should be ready to move into place and begin the reading after a suitable pause for silence. You can also keep things lively by having eight different readers do the readings. It would be tedious to hear even the most gifted reader do all or most of the readings alone.

During the Baptismal Liturgy, streamline the action by making sure all is carefully arranged in the rooms where the neophytes will change into their white robes. Is there someone there to help them, hand them towels, collect wet towels, and the like? What is the assembly doing while it waits for them to enter? What is the cue for the entrance of the newly baptized? Will music accompany their entrance? How do the musicians know when this music begins? After the Confirmations, where do the neophytes go during the intercessions? Where do they go to present the gifts? Careful preparation really does make a difference. Let the moments of silence be intentional times of prayer—not the confusion of wondering what is coming next!

◆ The Solemn Beginning of the Vigil, or Lucernarium: The Easter Vigil begins in darkness. In that darkness, a fire is kindled, and is used to light the Easter candle, from which, in turn, light is spread to the entire assembly. Fire becomes

the symbol of the Resurrection of Jesus Christ from the dead; and as the Prayer of Blessing suggests, fire also reminds us to rekindle our desire and to purify our minds as we celebrate the Lord's Resurrection.

For the symbols of light and darkness to speak, they need to be real. The fire should be a real fire (*The Roman Missal* says a "blazing fire"); it should "be such that they [the flames] genuinely dispel the darkness and light up the night" (PS, 82). And that means that the Vigil should begin not in the glow of a lovely spring evening, but at night. The candle which will represent the Risen Christ must be a genuine sign that "Christ is the light of the world" (PS, 82): made of wax, new each year, large in size, and worthy in its design (see PS, 82).

There is no formal procession to the fire—no cross or candles are carried; but the priest, deacon, and the minister carrying the candle could be led to the fire by a server carrying the thurible. The clergy are already wearing their white Mass vestments. At the fire, the priest greets the congregation in the usual way with the Sign of the Cross and "The Lord be with you." An instruction follows. (The celebrant may use the words provided, or compose his own introduction.) It reminds us of why we gather "on this most sacred night": "to watch and pray" in memory of Christ's passover "from death to life." We believe that if we remember his Death and Resurrection, as he commanded, "then we shall have the sure hope / of sharing his triumph over death / and living with him in God."

Next comes the blessing of the fire. Then follow the beautiful rites for the preparation of the candle (with *The Roman Missal*, these rites are no longer optional). The candle is inscribed with a cross, the numbers of the current year, and the Greek letters alpha and omega. The

priest may inscribe the design in the candle with a stylus, or, if the candle has been prepared ahead of time, he may simply trace the letters and numbers with his finger. The prayer that accompanies this rite tells us that time itself belongs to the Risen Lord. It is a reminder of what we hear throughout this evening's liturgy: that "this is the night," that Christ's passover, his Passion, Death, and Resurrection, are not things of yesterday but of today.

After inscribing the candle, the priest inserts five grains of incense into the candle, representing the five wounds of Christ. The candle is then lit from the new fire, and the procession into the church begins. The priest takes burning coals from the fire and places them in the thurible, then adds incense. In this way, all the flames in the church—even the coals in the thurible—are lit from the newly blessed fire. This server leads the way into the church, followed by the minister carrying the paschal candle, and then by all the faithful.

On Good Friday, there are three showings of the cross; on Holy Saturday, there are three showings of the candle. The first stop is at the door of the church. The candle is raised high, and the deacon or priest sings, "The Light of Christ," to which all respond, "Thanks be to God." Then the priest lights his taper from the paschal candle. The procession continues, and in the middle of the church the candle is raised high once again, with the same acclamation. At this point (not before), all the faithful light their candles. At the altar, the candle is raised for the third and last time, and then placed in the stand, which may be placed either near the ambo, or in the middle of the sanctuary.

When should the lights be turned on? The rubrics tell us that the lights in the church may be turned on as the candle is placed in its stand, with the exception of the candles around the altar, which are lit during the Gloria. But since all are holding lighted candles (they will not be extinguished till after the *Exsultet*) it makes sense to wait to turn on the electric lights until the Liturgy of the Word begins. But still another possibility is implied by the rubrics. The paschal candle is traditionally placed near the ambo, clearly to give light to the readers and cantors, and the altar candles are not lit until the Gloria. Some parishes therefore celebrate the first part of the Liturgy of the Word by the light of the paschal candle alone, not bringing up the electric lights until the Gloria. If you use a single, simple refrain for the psalmody, the people will not need light to follow along in missals or programs.

The Easter Proclamation (*Exsultet*) is the splendid song of praise which the Church offers to Christ on the night of his rising. This great poem, a rhapsody in the best sense of the word, urges us to rejoice with all of creation in the Resurrection of Jesus Christ from the dead. It begins with a series of exuberant exclamations, calling on "the hosts of heaven," "Angel ministers," "all corners of the earth" and "Mother Church" to rejoice in the glory of Christ's light. The song then takes us through the long journey of humanity, from God's favor to the Chosen People of old, to the Passion of Christ, who now rises triumphant from the grave. Out of suffering, God has brought forth goodness in overwhelming measure: "O happy fault," the minister sings, for it was that "truly necessary sin of Adam" that gained for us our glorious Redeemer. The *Exsultet* ends with a cosmic look into the future, to the second coming of Christ.

The *Exsultet* is a song, and it should be sung. This is clear from the rubrics, which indicate that the deacon should sing it, and if no deacon is available, then a priest, and if no priest, then a cantor. If it is impossible to have the proclamation sung, it may be read. But that should only be a last resort!

With the singing of the *Exsultet*, the Lucernarium comes to an end; the people extinguish their candles, and the Liturgy of the Word begins. The priest invites the people to the celebration of the Word with a short introduction. As Saint Augustine urged his congregation many centuries ago: "Watch, I tell you, and pray. Let us celebrate this vigil internally and externally. Let God speak to us in these readings. Let us speak to him in our prayers. If we hear his words obediently, he to whom we pray will dwell in us" (Sermon 219; quoted in Johnson, p. 94).

◆ LITURGY OF THE WORD: All are seated, and the Liturgy of the Word begins, with a reading, a Responsorial Psalm, and a prayer, for which all stand. This pattern is repeated for all seven of the Old Testament readings. Following the last of these prayers, the Gloria is sung, then comes the Collect, the epistle, the Alleluia (Psalm 118), and finally the Gospel. If need be, the seven Responsorial Psalms may be omitted, and a period of silence observed instead. However, the Psalms offer such a rich counterpoint to the readings that they should only be omitted for serious pastoral reasons.

The rubrics around the Liturgy of the Word offer a rather bewildering range of options. All seven Old Testament readings should be read, but for pastoral reasons, the number may be reduced. We should hear at least three of the readings, but the reading of Exodus 14 should "never" be omitted (RM, 21). If your parish has typically not used all the readings, find out why. If these readings are indeed the fundamental element of the Easter Vigil, as *The Roman Missal* tells us, then the reasons for omitting any of them should be pretty good ones—and not just that

the first Mass the next day begins at 8:00 AM, or that young children are being baptized at the Vigil, or that the pews are uncomfortable, or that people simply don't want to stay up late.

The Gloria follows the Collect to the Seventh Reading. The bells ring out again (if you have sanctus bells, ring them; if you have outdoor bells, ring them, too. Depending when the Vigil begins, you may need to arrange for a sound variance with the local authorities). Servers take the light from the paschal candle, and light the altar candles. At the Easter Vigil, the Gloria should truly be glorious, proclaiming to all that Christ is risen—the waiting is over; now the outpouring of grace begins!

Following the Gloria, the priest celebrant prays the Collect, and all are seated. The epistle follows, then the Easter Alleluia (Psalm 118). *The Roman Missal* is very clear that the priest intones the Alleluia three times, singing it a step higher each time. If necessary, it may be intoned by the cantor, who also sings the verses of Psalm 118. The Gregorian Alleluia included in *The Roman Missal* is used only at the Easter Vigil. Savor every syllable and make the return of the Alleluia a moment of true joy!

The Gospel procession takes place during the Alleluia Psalm (notice that the *Book of the Gospels* will have been placed on the altar before the liturgy begins, since it does not figure in the procession with the paschal candle). This procession is quite different from the usual. No candles are carried, because the paschal candle, which is placed near the ambo, is the central symbol of tonight's liturgy. But the thurifer can lead the priest or deacon to the ambo, and the procession could be accompanied by servers without candles. Some parishes extend this procession and carry the *Book of the Gospels* through the congregation. If you do this, you might pause at the same places in the church where you paused with the cross on Good Friday, and the candle at the beginning of tonight's liturgy.

The Gospel is proclaimed in the usual way, and the Homily follows.

◆ Baptismal Liturgy: Following the Homily, we move into the third part of the Vigil, the Baptismal Liturgy. If you do not have elect to be baptized or candidates to be received, the Litany of Saints "is omitted, and the Blessing of Water takes place at once" (RM, 42).

If you do have elect to be baptized, please note that you will want to be guided by the *Rite of Christian Initiation of Adults* (RCIA), 206–243, for this part of the celebration. It provides significantly more detail than *The Roman Missal*. However, in cases where a text is in both the RCIA and *The Roman Missal*, you must use the texts from *The Roman Missal*.

◆ Calling of the Candidates and Litany of Saints: Several options are given for how the rite begins. The priest and ministers may simply go to the baptismal font after the Homily, and call the candidates for Baptism from there. The elect then come forward and take their places near the font with their godparents. After all have been called, the Litany of Saints begins. If the Baptisms take place in the sanctuary (which is recommended if the font of the church is not "in view of the faithful" [RCIA, 218]), the calling of the candidates happens immediately following the Homily; the candidates come forward and take their places, not blocking the view of the assembly, and the Litany of Saints follows. A third option is a procession to the baptismal font. After the calling of the candidates, a minister carrying the paschal candle leads the candidates with their godparents to the font, with the priest bringing up the rear of this procession. The Litany of Saints is

prayed with the entire group gathered around the baptismal font.

The Litany of Saints is prayed at many of the key moments of the liturgical year. It is prayed at every celebration of the Sacrament of Baptism; it is prayed at the Ordination of priests, at the consecration of men and women in the religious life, and at the Dedication of Church buildings. Tonight, the litany invokes the intercession of all the saints for those to be baptized and for the community. The litany concludes with a series of petitions that beg the Lord to "bring these chosen ones to new birth through the grace of Baptism."

The blessing of water follows. Use the new translation from *The Roman Missal*, not the RCIA. The Missal includes a chant setting of the prayer. The text of the blessing reminds us where we have been during the Easter Vigil, taking us from the very beginning of creation, through the waters of the Red Sea, to the Resurrection of the Lord. All three options for the Prayer of Blessing invite the participation of the people, not only with their "Amen" but with sung acclamations.

After the blessing of the water, the celebrant turns to the elect, and invites them to make their Profession of Faith. The introduction to the rite emphasizes the importance of this moment. "Adults are not saved unless they come forward of their own accord and with the will to accept God's gift through their own belief. The faith of those to be baptized is not simply the faith of the Church, but the personal faith of each one of them and each one of them is expected to keep it a living faith" (RCIA, 211). The Renunciation of Sin and Profession of Faith at this point are for the elect alone—the rest of the congregation will make a profession later in the liturgy. By this point in their preparation, their response "I do!"

should ring through the church, loud and clear.

Baptism follows without further ado. If candidates are baptized by full immersion, be sure to have a place designated for them to change after their Baptism. If they are baptized by pouring, have a minister ready to hand them a towel, and to lead them to where they need to be for the Explanatory Rites.

The term "Explanatory Rites" covers several post-baptismal rites. If the candidates are to be confirmed immediately (this is the norm for adults baptized at the Easter Vigil), the usual anointing with sacred chrism following Baptism is omitted. The clothing with a white garment is optional. If the newly baptized receive their white garment in the changing rooms rather than in the midst of the assembly, you might encourage the godparents to use the simple prayer provided in the rite as they help the newly baptized to dress. The third of the explanatory rites is the presentation of a lighted candle. The godparents come forward, and the candles are lit from the paschal candle. The godparents then present the candle to the newly baptized.

Confirmation comes immediately following the presentation of the lighted candle. There is a brief instruction, addressed to the newly baptized; and then the entire assembly is invited to join in prayer for those to be confirmed. The Prayer of Confirmation follows (notice that the laying on of hands is corporate, not individual), and then the anointing with chrism. Following their Confirmation, the neophytes could help spread the light to the entire assembly.

After the Rites of Baptism and Confirmation are complete, all present, holding lighted candles, renew their baptismal promises. Then the assembly is sprinkled with baptismal water, and the Prayer of the Faithful follows.

◆ COMBINED RITES: If the Rite of Reception into the Full Communion of the Catholic Church is celebrated at the Vigil as well, the sequence of events is somewhat different. The rites proceed as noted above through the Explanatory Rites. Then, following the presentation of the lighted candle, the candidates for full communion are called forward. The entire congregation, including the candidates, holds lighted candles. The candidates join in the renunciation of sin and the profession of faith with the entire community. All are sprinkled with baptismal water. Following the sprinkling comes the act of reception for the candidates. Then neophytes and candidates, accompanied by their sponsors, approach the celebrant for the Sacrament of Confirmation. Following Confirmation, all take their places in the assembly, and the Prayer of the Faithful follows.

◆ LITURGY OF THE EUCHARIST: Following the intercessions, the altar is prepared for the celebration of the Eucharist. It is suggested that the neophytes (and newly received) present the gifts of bread and wine; it is also recommended that the community receive Communion under both kinds at this celebration (RCIA, 594).

Preface of Easter I is used, with the words "on this night above all." Eucharistic Prayers I, II, and III all have special interpolations for the newly baptized which can be used tonight. The text can be found in *The Roman Missal* under "Ritual Masses: Baptism." Note that Eucharistic Prayer I also has a special form of the *Communicantes*. *The Roman Missal* suggests that just before the Agnus Dei, "the Priest may briefly address the newly baptized about receiving their first Communion and about the excellence of this great mystery, which is the climax of Initiation and the center of the whole Christian life" (RM, 64).

◆ CONCLUDING RITES: The Solemn Blessing of Easter (you'll find it in the Proper of Time, among the prayers for the Easter Vigil) provides a fitting conclusion to this most solemn liturgy of the year. The Easter form of the dismissal, with its double Alleluia, is used beginning tonight and at each Mass until next Sunday, the conclusion of the Easter Octave.

Other Ideas

Invite your child to point out to you any changes he or she notices in the decor of your parish church. The new liturgical color, white, signifies joy! Tell your child to listen for the singing of the Gloria after the Lenten abstinence and to note how many times the Church sings "Alleluia," a word we neither spoke nor sang during Lent. Encourage your child to watch for other signs that indicate the celebration of a great Church feast, like the Rite of Blessing and Sprinkling of Water, the Baptism of adults, incense, and so on.

#42, Gospel #41 or 46   white
☀31 Easter Sunday of the Resurrection of the Lord

Orientation

This Gospel passage names three people discovering the empty tomb of Jesus: Mary of Magdala, Simon Peter, and the Beloved Disciple. They are first to see evidence of the Resurrection, the greatest miracle of salvation history, yet they hesitate and defer entry into the tomb to one another. Were they each wrestling with fear and hope, fearing to see a desecrated tomb, and yet hoping that somehow Jesus is alive after all? In an internal battle between faith and reason, none of the three yet knew how to make sense of it all, as they deferred to each other not just for entry, but for leadership in this perplexing situation. Like all of us, these first Christians only came to an understanding of the depths of the Paschal Mystery gradually, with each Easter as another chance to enter more fully into this culminating moment of salvation.

Lectionary for Mass

The commentaries for the First Reading, Responsorial Psalm, and Second Reading were written by S. Anne Elizabeth Sweet, ocso © LTP, 2012. The commentaries for the Sequence and the Gospel were written by Paul Turner © LTP, 2012.

◆ FIRST READING: On this Easter morning, we are invited to place ourselves among the people of the household of Cornelius as they gathered to hear Simon Peter talk about the ministry of Jesus. Both of these men—Peter and Cornelius—received a divinely inspired vision that led them to one another. They must have recognized the gift of that grace because it was extremely unlikely that a Jew (Peter) would be a guest in a Gentile home. What they heard remains ours today as we hear the First Reading: Jesus of Nazareth, anointed by God with the Holy Spirit, healed many people. He was put to death but was raised by God. We have seen him and have eaten with him. He has sent us to preach this Good News. And this is the truth we speak to you today: "Everyone who believes in him will receive forgiveness of sins through his name." Peter took a very bold step that day to broaden the mission of the followers of

Jesus. Because of the vision he received, Peter had come to believe that all people were to be included in the great work of preaching the story of Jesus Christ. The Good News could not and should not be contained, for it is meant for all people for all time.

◆ RESPONSORIAL PSALM: This song of thanksgiving was the accompaniment for a procession to the Temple to celebrate a victory. The psalmist gives voice to the great joy of the people, expressing their overwhelming gratitude for the faithfulness of the Lord. That joy spills out in their song. The psalmist might well have been rejoicing because a once-defeated king later rose to power. But the early Christian community heard in these words vindication that relieved the sting of Jesus's rejection and execution. For those who have been rejected for living as Jesus did—for feeding the hungry, living simply, championing the marginalized, loving unconditionally, and pursuing the cause of peace—the words help stay the course. For one day all will come to know that those rejected in God's name are the cornerstones of faith. On that day, all people will sing with the psalmist: "This is the day the Lord has made; / let us rejoice and be glad."

◆ SECOND READING. OPTION 1: The Colossians reading urges us to die to self in order to focus on the Lord, for having been baptized in Christ, the concerns of the world should diminish in meaning. For those who are caught up in the things of this world, however, this reading is an invitation to reorder our lives. On the day of glory, the worldly things that can consume human hearts will have no significance.

◆ SECOND READING, OPTION 2: Some have called this Corinthians reading the first Easter sermon. Leading up to this passage, Paul has

chastised the people for their wicked behavior. Now he makes it clear that to honor the paschal sacrifice and live as the new life demands, Christians have a responsibility to one another to live with sincerity and truth.

◆ SEQUENCE: This Sunday, the Church sings a sequence—an ancient, poetic song that precedes the singing of the Gospel acclamation. The Easter Sequence, *Victimae paschali laudes*, is a song of praise to the Paschal Victim that also reflects the Gospel account of Mary's encounter with the Risen Lord. It may be sung throughout the Octave of Easter.

◆ GOSPEL: Mary Magdalene is the first person at the tomb in all four Gospel accounts. In the synoptic accounts, she brings oil to anoint the body of the Lord. In John's account, the anointing has already taken place, but Mary is still the first person on record to go to the tomb. She is the messenger who then brings Peter and the Beloved Disciple to see that the stone has been moved. There are no angels in this story to suggest that a body has inexplicably been raised. There are only cloths that lay on the ground, the head cloth arranged in a separate place, all to indicate that this is not the scene of a robbery. In those first moments, what it all means is unclear, and only the Beloved Disciple "saw and believed." Time and future appearances of the Lord will add believers to the community. As we gather on this Easter day, we remember and celebrate that Jesus is indeed risen and walks among us still. Yet, it is only with eyes of faith that we recognize him—in the breaking of bread, in the preaching of his Word, and in the presence of his people gathered in his name.

The Roman Missal

The texts for this liturgy are found following those for the Easter Vigil. Both the Easter Vigil and Easter

Sunday are found in "Easter Sunday of the Resurrection of the Lord." Easter Sunday is "At the Mass during the Day."

On Easter Sunday, the liturgy is quite simple, and with the exception of the Rite of the Renewal of Baptismal Promises (which takes place after the Homily), it is "Mass as usual." Yet it is not as usual, of course! This is a day for incense and the grandest of processions. It is a day for pulling out all the stops, not only on the organ but in every other way!

The Entrance Antiphon forms a dramatic beginning to the liturgy—in it we hear the voice of Christ: "I have risen, and I am with you still, Alleluia . . . ." The Rite of Blessing and Sprinkling of Water may be substituted for the Penitential Act, but *The Roman Missal* suggests that in the United States, where the Renewal of Baptismal Promises takes the place of the Creed, the sprinkling with baptismal water follow that renewal instead. In that case, the Penitential Act is prayed at the beginning of Mass as usual. The Gloria should be sung with gusto, as it was last night at the Vigil.

The Collect for Easter Day praises Christ, who "conquered death / and unlocked for us the path to eternity." We pray for a share in Christ's Resurrection, that we may be renewed by the Holy Spirit, and, like Christ, "rise up in the light of life." The Collect, like many of Vigil texts, emphasizes that Easter is now: it is "on this day" that Christ conquers death for us.

Following the Homily, the Creed is not said. Instead, the priest celebrant invites all present to renew the promises of their Baptism. The texts for the renewal are found in *The Roman Missal* among the prayers for the Easter Vigil. Following this renewal, the people are sprinkled with baptismal water from the font. Let the people see that the water comes from the font by having servers process to the font, perhaps during the renewal of promises or immediately following the Homily, and bring the filled vessels back to the priest celebrant's chair. Use a fresh branch for the sprinkling, perhaps interwoven with flowers and tied with ribbon.

After the sprinkling, the Prayer of the Faithful is recited or sung. Our prayer should always embrace the whole world; on Easter, when we celebrate the saving sacrifice of Christ, that is especially important. Some models for this prayer are found in Appendix V to *The Roman Missal* which may be used as they are or adapted.

Preface I of Easter is used throughout the Easter octave. If the Roman Canon is used, the special insertions should be included today and throughout the coming week.

The Solemn Blessing of Easter (again, turn back to the prayers of the Easter Vigil to find it) forms a fitting end to the Mass. It reminds us of where we have been—"the days of the Lord's Passion"—where we are—"the gladness of the Paschal Feast"—and where we are going— "to those feasts that are celebrated in eternal joy"! The Easter form of the dismissal, with its double Alleluia, is used again today and throughout the octave of Easter.

Other Ideas

Help your child understand the connection between the Good News of Easter and natural symbols of new life such as spring flowers, eggs, baby animals, and so on. Even the natural world reminds us of God's gift of new life that springs from the barren landscapes of winter. Prominently display a cross in your home, surrounded by these reminders of God's goodness and the sacredness of life. Make an Easter centerpiece using dyed eggs (either boiled or hollowed). Write words on them that you have heard during Lent about God, perhaps an image or description, such as *Good Shepherd, forgiving,* or *source of life.* Display it at the family meal table and use it as a basis for your mealtime prayer.

Proclaim the Good News. For your front door, cut a long banner from white or golden-yellow felt. Cut or purchase letters to spell "Alleluia!" and affix these down the center of the banner. Provide glue and felt shapes, stick-on "jewels," and other decorations.

Write a card to someone who might need to hear joyful words. It might be a homebound person from your parish, a neighbor, or a family member. Make the words your own, but convey the Easter message of Good News that Jesus entrusted to his disciples.

The Reception of the Holy Oils
Blessed at the Chrism Mass

Introduction

1. It is appropriate that the oil of the sick, the oil of catechumens, and the holy chrism, which are blessed by the bishop during the Chrism Mass, be presented to and received by the local parish community.

2. The reception of the holy oils may take place at the Mass of the Lord's Supper on Holy Thursday or on another suitable day after the celebration of the Chrism Mass.

3. The oils should be reserved in a suitable repository in the sanctuary or near the baptismal font.

4. The oils, in suitable vessels, are carried in the procession of the gifts, before the bread and wine, by members of the assembly.

5. The oils are received by the priest and are then placed on a suitably prepared table in the sanctuary or in the repository where they will be reserved.

6. As each of the oils is presented, the following or other words may be used to explain the significance of the particular oil.

7. The people's response may be sung.

Presenter of the Oil of the Sick:

The oil of the sick.

Priest:

May the sick who are anointed with this oil experience the compassion of Christ and his saving love, in body, mind, and soul.

The people may respond:

Blessed be God for ever.

Presenter of the Oil of Catechumens:

The oil of catechumens.

Priest:

Through anointing with this oil may our catechumens who are preparing to receive the saving waters of baptism be strengthened by Christ to resist the power of Satan and reject evil in all its forms.

The people may respond:

Blessed be God for ever.

Presenter of the Holy Chrism:

The holy Chrism.

Priest:

Through anointing with this perfumed Chrism may children and adults, who are baptized and confirmed, and presbyters, who are ordained, experience the gracious gift of the Holy Spirit.

The people may respond:

Blessed be God for ever.

The bread and wine for the eucharist are then received and the Mass continues in the usual way.

EASTER TIME

The Meaning

To his disciples, Christ's suffering, Crucifixion, and Death seemed to be the end of the world. The Messiah had been ridiculed, tormented, tortured, and put to death. To them, this must have been a shocking ending to the actions of teaching, healing, and forgiveness Jesus had accomplished during his life. They cannot envision what is next. Then the unimaginable happened: life from death, light from darkness, and hope from despair. The women, the first visitors to the tomb, hear the astounding announcement that he has risen, and when they actually meet Jesus on the way, he sends them to announce the Good News of his Resurrection.

The Easter story is beyond our comprehension. We, too, are told not to be afraid and are invited to hear with new ears that Jesus Christ is risen! Then we also are sent to announce the Good News of Christ's Resurrection to the world. God's triumphant action in the world must be announced and Good News must be proclaimed. Like the disciples, we are promised the presence of the Holy Spirit as we witness and work to continue Christ's mission to all the ends of the earth.

Easter Time is a powerful time for us disciples in the twenty-first century. We will hear countless Scripture readings about the Apostles and early disciples of Jesus attempting to understand his words and follow him as well as minister to the very first Christian communities. Unlike Peter and Mary Magdala, early followers of the Risen Christ who knew him directly, we do not. But it is because of their faith that we are here as believers. The accounts of the post-Resurrection appearances of Jesus inspire us so that, like the early witnesses of the Risen Lord, we can carry the message of God's justice and mercy to those we meet. The Scriptures we will hear during Easter Time repeatedly reflect Jesus's words of instruction or prayer for the ones who will carry on his mission after his Ascension. But the power of Easter is realized fully only when we take the message of Jesus's Death and Resurrection out into the world as Paul did to the early communities. Paul, earlier known as Saul, was at first a persecutor of Christians. He did not know Jesus personally, but rather saw the testimony of Jesus's followers. Yet after his conversion, Paul was relentless in carrying Christ's message to the known world at the time. Now it is our turn to go and do the same!

The Roman Missal

Easter Time brings with it some changes in the liturgy. The paschal candle is lit "at least in all the more solemn liturgical celebrations of the season until Pentecost Sunday, whether at Mass or at Morning and Evening Prayer" (PS, 99). After Pentecost, the candle is moved to a place of honor near the baptismal font. It will still be lit at the "little Easters" of the parish—Baptisms and funerals.

The solemn dismissal, with its double Alleluia, is used at all the Masses of the Easter Octave, the Second Sunday of Easter, and the solemnity of Pentecost.

The Rite of Blessing and Sprinkling Holy Water may be used in place of the Penitential Act. This is especially fitting in Easter, which begins with the renewal of baptismal promises. On Easter Sunday, all needed prayers are found in the Proper of Time. During the rest of the season, you'll find the prayers for the Rite for the Blessing and Sprinkling of Water in Appendix II, including a special Easter form of the Blessing of Water.

The Mass prayers for Easter Time are quite varied. Each day has its own unique Collect, with the Prayer over the Offerings, and the Prayer after Communion repeated in a regular rotation, as in Advent and Christmas Time. The prayers emphasize the grace of Baptism with many references to the newly baptized (see, for example, the Collects for Monday, Thursday, and Saturday of the Easter Octave; and the Second, Third, and Fifth Sundays of Easter—just a few examples of this predominant theme). The Prefaces of Easter (there are five to choose from) emphasize the saving sacrifice of Christ. Just as the disciples recognize the Risen Lord when he shows them his wounds, so the Prefaces view the Resurrection of the Lord through the lens of his Passion: "By dying he has destroyed our death" (Preface I of Easter); "His Death is our ransom from death, / and in his rising the life of all has risen" (Preface II of Easter); "he is the sacrificial Victim who dies no more, the Lamb, once slain, who lives for ever" (Preface III of Easter); he is "the Priest, the Altar, and the Lamb of sacrifice" (Preface V of Easter). To celebrate the Resurrection of the Lord means to remember the entirety of Christ's Paschal sacrifice, his Passion, Death, and glorious rising from the dead.

A seasonal solemn blessing is provided for Easter Time (#6). It echoes all the major themes of this joyful season: "redemption," "adoption," "freedom," "Baptism," and rising with Christ. There are also blessings for the Ascension of the Lord (#7) and for Pentecost ("The Holy Spirit," #8).

The Lectionary for Mass

The celebration of Easter always has a note of glory and splendor about it, and well it should. The Risen Christ has broken the bonds of sin, passing through the darkness of death into the brilliant light of eternal life. Flowers and banners adorn our churches. Triumphant and joyful hymns acclaim the Risen Lord! Nevertheless, we must not lose sight that his new life is accomplished by God's power at work in the very wounds of sin and death. Look again at the Easter candle signed with the cross and grains of incense marking the wounds. Transformed life comes only through the pain of suffering, through the experience of dying, in the ultimate surrender of all of our efforts and plans to the wisdom and mystery of God.

Although we are an Easter people, we are at the same time a sinful people, still in the process of conversion. If Lent bids us focus more on repentance and conversion, Easter would have us keep our goal in mind: transformation with and in Christ, accomplished by the power of his Spirit at work within us—and what tremendous openness and readiness to use the gifts of God's Spirit we must have. We sing *Alleluia* not only because of what Christ has done, but because of the hope that is held out to us that we, too, can become like Christ. When tragedy strikes, whether it be the result of sin, accident, sudden and unexpected illness or death, we are stretched to go more deeply into the hope and assurance that is Easter's gift to us.

A careful reading of the Gospel texts reveals that the evangelists see Jesus's Death, Resurrection, Ascension, and glorification, and the pouring out of the Holy Spirit, all as integrally related, even in some cases simultaneous, if we can use that word as we pass over into the realm of the eternal! The evangelists search for the words to convey what they have experienced and know to be true, and it is not an easy job! At times, the details are inconsistent; for example, Luke's situating the Ascension on Easter night in his Gospel account (24:50–51; so also John 20:19–23) but having it 40 days later in his second volume, the Acts of the Apostles (1:1–10). It is not so much chronology that is important—40 days is a symbolic number—as is the meaning of the message and the experience that underlies it.

During the Octave, the eight days after Easter, our Gospel readings tell of the appearances of the Risen Lord. Repeatedly, we hear of the simultaneous fear, struggle to believe, and overwhelming joy the Apostles and disciples experienced. The Gloria is sung at every Mass. *Victimae paschali laudes,* or the Easter sequence, may also be sung or recited on each day of the Octave. This centuries-old hymn is a song of praise to the victorious Lamb of God, the Risen Christ. The Alleluia verse before the Gospel is the same as for Easter Day: *This* is the day the Lord has made! The solemn Easter Alleluias are joined to the closing verses of the liturgy. How can we not put our all into the celebration of Christ's victory over death, a victory in which we have already begun to share?

The First Readings during the Octave are from the Acts of the Apostles as they are throughout Easter Time. We begin with the Apostles preaching on the day of Pentecost after they have received the Holy Spirit. The Church, the community of those who believed that the Risen Christ was Lord and Messiah, had its beginning at this time. Throughout Easter Time, our readings from Acts of the Apostles tell of the Church's expanded growth and those individuals who were instrumental in the spreading of the faith: Peter, James, John, Philip, Paul, Barnabas, Prisca and Aquila, to name but a few. The Responsorial Psalms are all Psalms of victory and deliverance.

Beginning in the second week of Easter, our Gospel readings are all from John. It is interesting to hear them in light of the Resurrection. From John 3: God so loved the world that he sent Jesus—not to condemn, but to give life to all who would receive it. Christ is the Bread of Life, heavenly food for our earthly journey, the food of eternal life, so proclaims John 6 in the third week of Easter. In the fourth week, we see him as our Risen Shepherd who goes before us, offering us life in all its fullness (John 10), as the paschal Light of the World who overcame the darkness (John 12), as the one who prepares a heavenly place for us and will come back to take us with him (John 14), as the one who instructs his followers to continue his work, empowered by his presence and his Spirit (John 14). In the fifth, sixth, and seventh weeks we hear from Jesus's last discourse in John's account of the Gospel (chapters 15–17). Note the references to the presence and work of the Holy Spirit as we draw closer to Pentecost.

On the Sundays of Easter we hear John's account of Jesus's Easter evening appearance to the fearful disciples gathered in the locked room. He wishes them his peace and bestows his Spirit on them. Thomas was absent, so the Gospel for the Second Sunday continues with another appearance a week later. On the Third Sunday, we hear again from John's Gospel account, the story of the Risen Christ's appearance to the disciples as they came in from a night's work fishing, having caught nothing. At Jesus's word they throw in their nets and haul in a miraculous catch of fish. Jesus invites them to share a meal of bread and fish with him on the shore. The longer form of this reading includes Jesus's three-fold commission to Peter to feed his sheep and the prediction of Peter's death. The theme of sheep is also prominent on the Fourth Sunday of Easter (John 10). Jesus is the Good Shepherd who lovingly tends the flock given to him by the Father. His sheep listen to his voice and follow him . . . into eternal life. We listen again to words from Jesus's last discourse to his disciples (John 13–17) on the Fifth, Sixth, and Seventh Sundays of Easter, hearing them now as spoken and realized by the Risen Lord: his glorification (through the cross) and his new commandment of love (Fifth Sunday); Jesus's indwelling with the Father in the heart of the believer, his promise of the Holy Spirit, and his gift of peace (Sixth Sunday); and his prayer that his disciples be united as one on the Seventh Sunday (John 17).

The Ascension of the Lord, marking the end of the "40" period of appearances of the Risen Christ as Luke recounts it in Acts of the Apostles, is celebrated either on the Sixth Sunday of Easter or on Thursday, depending on the diocese. As we would expect, the First Reading is Acts' account of the Ascension and the Gospel excerpt is about the Risen Christ's commissioning of his disciples before being taken up to heaven on Easter evening, as recounted at the end of the Gospel according to Luke. Note that this Gospel ends on a note of joy and praise.

Easter Time closes with the Solemnity of Pentecost. The First Reading, of course, is Acts' account of Pentecost after Jesus's death when the promised Holy Spirit was poured out on the Apostles, Mary the Mother of Jesus, the women who had journeyed with Jesus to Jerusalem (Luke 8:1–3; 23:49), and members of his family (see Acts of the Apostles 1:11–14). The Gospel reading is again from Jesus's last discourse in John and his promise that the Father will send another Advocate to be with them, the Holy Spirit. In the Second Reading, Paul tells the Romans that this Spirit is the same Spirit who raised Christ from the dead and who will give life to our mortal bodies as well. It is likewise the Spirit through whom we intimately call out to our God as *Abba*, which is best translated as "daddy." There is also a sequence for this day, the ancient hymn which prays for the coming of the Holy Spirit who enlightens, comforts, heals, and transforms.

As noted above, Mary the Mother of Jesus was among those gathered to receive the promised Spirit. This same Spirit overshadowed her at the time of the Annunciation, when Jesus was conceived in her womb. The Solemnity of the Annunciation is transferred this year to Monday of the second week of Easter.

The three feasts of the season, Saint Mark (April 25), Saints Philip and James (May 3), and Saint Matthias (May 14) point to the continuation of Jesus's ministry and the proclamation of the Gospel after his return to the Father through the work of the evangelist and these Apostles. That task is ours as well in our own day, in whatever circumstances of life we find ourselves. We, too, have received the empowering gift of the Spirit. We, too, have been sent in Jesus's name. Let us not neglect the mission that is ours; let us not treat lightly the tremendous gift we have been given. The gift we have received is a gift to be shared.

Children's Liturgy of the Word

EASTER is the most joyful time of the liturgical year. The signs and symbols of Easter all contribute to the atmosphere of joyful celebration. Easter Time lasts for the 50 days following the Triduum and concludes with Pentecost. The joy of Easter is reflected in decoration, song, and action. Churches are adorned with lilies and other spring flowers; Alleluias are sung; the Gloria returns to the liturgy. All express the joy of the Body of Christ in the Resurrection of Jesus.

One of the central motifs of Easter Time is the new life of Baptism. Through Baptism, we come to share in the life of the Risen Christ. Baptisms often take place during Easter Time, and the Rite of Blessing and Sprinkling of Water is frequently used at the beginning of Mass in place of the Penitential Act. In the *Rite of Christian Initiation of Adults* the term *mystagogia* is used as a name for Easter Time. *Mystagogia* means to "uncover the mysteries." It is a time for the newly baptized and the assembly to share the Eucharist, reflect on the Sunday readings, and do acts of service as a means to more fully uncover the mystery and meaning of their Baptism. The Solemnity of Pentecost concludes Easter Time and celebrates the descent of the Holy Spirit, the birth of the Church, and the gifts for mission and ministry given to the Church as a whole and to baptized individuals.

Readings

You will notice that the First Readings of Easter Time are taken from the Acts of the Apostles. They present the story of the growth, triumphs, and struggles of the early Church after the Resurrection. One of the major themes is how the early Church formed community and brought the Good News to others in spite of persecution and martyrdom. There are lessons here for children. They like to know how things begin, they are fascinated by stories of people of long ago, and they need to be reminded that they, too, have a mission to spread the Good News.

The Gospel accounts of Luke and John unpack the meaning of the Resurrection and emphasize both the presence of the Risen Christ and his promise to remain with his disciples. Children benefit from being reminded that the Risen Christ is still present in the Church and, for them, as a Good Shepherd. They are also helped to see that actions of loving are ways to bring the Good News to others, which is the mission of the baptized in this period of mystagogy.

Environment

One of the theological themes of Easter is movement from death to new life. The season of spring echoes this theme of new life. As winter gives way to spring the earth comes to life again. Fresh green grass, budding trees, and flowers are signs of new life. The earth joins in celebrating the Resurrection. The liturgy uses elements from the created world to praise God for his saving actions in history. Water, light, candles, flowers, song, and silence are all part of the environment for worship at this time.

During Easter Time, focus on bringing these elements into the worship environment. The liturgical color for this season is white (gold and silver may also be used). The banners and cloths on the lectern and prayer table should be white, except on Pentecost when the liturgical color is red. You may wish to highlight the white with gold and silver cloths, and with red on Pentecost. Place a clear glass bowl of holy water and a large white candle in a visible space in the worship area. Explain that the Easter candle in church is always lit at Baptisms and funerals and that the newly baptized receive baptismal candles that are lit from the paschal candle, and become children of the light in Christ.

Music

Easter Time and Pentecost lend well to additional musicians and voices. Ask your parish liturgy or music director if there is someone who can accompany children or be a cantor. Also check with the parish youth director. There may be teens who have music ability or band experience who could share their talents with the children on these days. Sung Alleluias are good way to help children be aware of the joy and importance of Easter Time. Use suggestions given in *Children's Liturgy of the Word: A Weekly Resource* from LTP or make music selections from your parish repertoire.

The Saints

WE celebrate the saints not on the day of their birth, but on the day of their death, that is, the day of their entry into heaven. To celebrate the saints is not only to honor the holy men and women who have gone before us and who teach us how to live, how to pray, how to believe: it is to profess our faith in the Resurrection of Christ.

Easter Time gives us many opportunities to celebrate the saints. There are three feasts—Saint Mark, Evangelist on April 25, Saints Philip and James on May 3, and Saint Matthias on May 14—and three obligatory memorials: Saint Stanislaus on April 11, Saint Catherine of Siena on April 29, and Saint Athanasius on May 2. And there are many optional memorials during Easter Time as well.

In addition to the celebrations of the saints during this time, there are two other special observances to be noted. The Second Sunday of Easter is called the Sunday of Divine Mercy. (Read more about the Divine Mercy and the associated devotions in the calendar for April 7). And the month of May, like the month of October, is a time specially dedicated to the Blessed Virgin Mary. For ideas about honoring Mary during Easter Time, see below under Devotions and Sacramentals.

The Liturgy of the Hours

EASTER is the continuation of 50 days of praise and thanksgiving for Christ who broke the chains of sin so that we might enter into greater communion with God the Father through the power of the Spirit. If at all possible, the parish should strive to celebrate Evening Prayer on the Sundays of Easter Time, not only in Advent or Lent, to mark the liturgical time. In addition, the parish worship commission might think about ways the domestic church—the household—might observe Morning Prayer and Evening Prayer within the homes; thus, Sunday would be the parish celebration.

The Liturgy of the Hours provides Easter hymns that are rich in what Easter means. Of course, other Easter hymns could be used rather than the suggested evening hymn. Particularly in the Octave of Easter, "Jesus Christ Is Risen Today" would fit perfectly.

The antiphon for all of the Psalms for Easter Time is the triple Alleluia.

The Office of Readings provides rich fare on the tradition of the Church. Anastasius of Antioch links Christ's Incarnation to his Death and Resurrection. The readings from the *Jerusalem Catechesis* break open the meaning of Baptism and Eucharist and would be great catechesis not only for the neophytes but for the entire parish as well. A parish could offer adult formation, linked to the Office of Readings, that would allow participants to reflect from experience on the various rich texts from the early Church.

The Sunday of the Octave of Easter (Second Sunday of Easter) has a quite appropriate reading from Saint Augustine on the meaning of the Octave as an eighth day on the first of the week. Those baptized, he notes, are new in the life of Christ; they are "a new colony of bees, the very flower of our ministry and fruit of our toil, my joy and my crown" (p. 635–636). Like Easter Sunday, the canticle of the Magnificat can be substituted with a *Te Deum*. In addition to the chanted version, a slight adaptation would be to use "Holy God, We Praise Thy Name" as the *Te Deum*. There are other arrangements of the *Te Deum* on the market as well. The Octave is still part of Easter Sunday, so adding incense, psalmists, a trumpeter (brass), and so forth would heighten its solemnity.

While the Liturgy of the Hours encourages the use of the Easter dismissal rite during the Easter Octave, this Easter dismissal could be used throughout all of Easter Time as the dismissal for the Hours.

The neophytes are delving into mystagogical or post-baptismal catechesis. Mystagogy could easily fit into the context of Evening Prayer, unless a great many people would be there.

The various and many texts from the early Church connect the mystery of Christ's death and Resurrection to a deepening of our communion with God. The cross bears fruit in our lives, says Theodore the Studite, and "opens the way for our return" to paradise (p. 677). Gregory of Nyssa, in the Seventh Week of Easter, connects the mystery of Christ to the God of Love: "When love has entirely cast out fear, and fear has been transformed into love, then the unity brought us by our Savior will be fully realized, for all men will be united with one another through their union with one supreme Good" (p. 957–958).

Easter Time concludes with Evening Prayer on the Solemnity of Pentecost. The *Rite of Christian Initiation of Adults* notes that "to close the period of postbaptismal catechesis, some sort of celebration should be held at the end of the Easter season near Pentecost Sunday" (249). Some dioceses offer such a service at the cathedral church. However, if not, then the parish could easily prepare Evening Prayer with perhaps a closing blessing for the neophytes that marks their transition from intense mystagogy to less formal mystagogy.

The Rite of Christian Initiation of Adults

YEARS ago when the RCIA was just beginning to be implemented and people were having difficulty with new terms like "catechumen" and "mystagogia," I was at a restaurant involved in a conversation defending the keeping of what in those days were really foreign-sounding terms. When the server approached our table I asked her, "Have you ever had a mystagogia?" She paused and then said, "No, but it sure sounds like fun!" In a way it should be fun. It is a time for the community and neophytes (adults and children) to deepen their understanding of the Paschal Mystery and make it a part of their lives through meditating on the Gospel, sharing in the Eucharist, and doing works of charity (see RCIA, 244).

The "success" of this period for the neophyte is very dependent on what has occurred during the initiation process. Have the children developed skills in reflecting on the Sunday readings and are they able to relate them to their own lives? Have they developed an appreciation and motivation to be a part of the Sunday assembly? Do they have some beginnings of a relationship with the wider parish community and their Catholic peers? Have they been introduced to doing works of charity? Ideally you would answer "yes" to all those questions. By its very nature, and especially because children and families are involved, the initiation process is usually not "ideal." In planning mystagogical or post-baptismal catechesis, start where they are and with what you see as their needs. The rite provides some practical guidelines.

Liturgical Catechesis

Gather the neophytes and those involved in the Easter Vigil, including members of the assembly, to reflect on their experience of the celebration. Ask questions such as: What was the best thing about the celebration for you? How did you feel? What did you see, hear, and smell that was different? Did anything surprise you? What did the celebration tell you about God? About Jesus? About the Church? About your faith? Using their responses, instruct participants on the meaning of the Vigil and the Paschal Mystery for the Church today.

The main setting for catechesis is the Sunday assembly. Meet long before Easter with the liturgy director, music director, homilist, and director of the adult group to help facilitate the inclusion of child neophytes in the Easter Time Masses.

Together with the liturgy director and music director plan a celebration for the end of Easter Time to send the neophytes to preach the Good News (see RCIA, 249).

Invite the neophytes, their family members, and members of the assembly to a short reflection and social time after a Sunday Mass. Have them gather in small groups over coffee and juice to talk about the readings and/or some liturgical element of the Sunday liturgy.

If you feel there is a need for more instructional catechesis, plan sessions over the summer.

Include family members and peers from the religious education program and/or Catholic school.

Invite members of the parish social action committees and charitable organizations to a gathering with neophytes and their families to explain their goals and invite them to join in some practical projects.

Plan several reflective and social gatherings during the year following initiation.

The Sacraments of Initiation

ONE of the central motifs of Easter Time is the new life of Baptism. Through Baptism, we come to share in the life of the Risen Christ. Baptisms often take place during Easter Time, and the Rite of Blessing and Sprinkling Water frequently replaces the Penitential Act at the beginning of Mass.

Parishioners renew their baptismal commitments in the Rite of Sprinkling. The Gospel readings unpack the meaning of the Easter event and help the assembly to celebrate and remember that what God the Father did in his Son Jesus is being done in our lives today. The period from Easter Sunday to Pentecost is the ideal time to celebrate the Sacraments of Initiation in the midst of the assembly.

Work with the liturgy and music directors to emphasize the Rite of Sprinkling and the renewal of baptismal promises at the Masses where Baptism, first Eucharist, and Confirmation are celebrated.

Parishes have varied practices for the celebration of first Holy Communion. Some celebrate in a large group and others celebrate individually with families or throughout Easter Time with smaller family groups. If at all possible do not celebrate first Holy Communion at a Mass separate from the Sunday assembly. A "first" Eucharist is the first time a person shares fully at the table, and this should happen on Sunday, the Day of the Lord, when the community gathers for the central act of worship. To separate them from the assembly does not make good liturgical sense.

Plan the celebration(s) with the liturgy and music directors. If you have a large number of children celebrating, you may want to look at the relevant directives in the *Directory for Masses with Children*. This directory is available in the first volume of *The Liturgy Documents* from Liturgy Training Publications. Since initiation is a call to mission, develop a specific final blessing and dismissal that explicitly includes the first communicants.

Since most Confirmations are presided over by the bishop, it is not always possible to celebrate during Easter Time, but it is appropriate if possible to arrange it.

During the week before Pentecost or the week before Confirmation, plan an afternoon or evening of reflection with the Confirmation candidates and their sponsors on the theme of being anointed for service as an element of initiation into the Christian community.

member to trace the Sign of the Cross on their forehead. The parish might send some flowers to individuals who receive regular visits from the ministers of care. It would be lovely if the choir recorded a song or two from the Easter repertoire on a CD for these persons.

Invite the sick and homebound to participate in the Church's prayers for the neophytes, first communicants, and candidates for Confirmation. Perhaps they could be given a list of names to remember in their prayers.

If the Sacrament of Anointing of the Sick is celebrated, mention that the oil (oil of the sick) was blessed at the cathedral in the Chrism Mass during Holy Week and received by the parish on Holy Thursday.

The Rite of Penance

A joyful grace for Catholics is the knowledge that when we come to Holy Communion with a properly disposed heart, we become so close to Christ that our venial sins are wiped away (See CCC, 1391 and 1394). These are two of the fruits of Holy Communion and a teaching the faithful should be celebrating. However, this does not abrogate our responsibility to constantly examine our lives for the places that still need conversion.

Invite the neophytes to prepare for the Sacrament of Reconciliation. All sacraments express what we believe about God, and catechesis should emphasize this sacrament as the sign of our belief in God's unlimited mercy. The catechumenate period and the scrutinies will have helped the neophytes understand Christ's call to conversion.

Certainly, young people preparing for Confirmation and their sponsors and families would benefit from an invitation to gather for the Sacrament of Reconcilaition.

The Pastoral Care of the Sick

T AKE some Easter holy water to the sick and homebound in this liturgical time. They can use it to bless themselves, or they can ask a family

The Rite of Marriage

A s with our other times of the year, if a couple is married at a Mass celebrated on Saturday evening, Sunday, or on a solemnity, the readings and prayers of the day must be used. This is also true of the weekdays in the Octave of Easter from April 9 to 14 (see GIRM, 372). However, it is permitted to substitute one reading from the *Rite of Marriage*. This restriction does not apply if the wedding is celebrated outside of Mass.

Some parishes gather couples at various times of the year to talk about how the parish does weddings. Consider beginning with the *Book of Blessing*'s Order for the Blessing of an Engaged Couple (ch. 1, VI).

The Order of Christian Funerals

C ATHOLICS never get stuck at the foot of the cross. This is beautifully expressed in OCF, 1: "In the face of death, the Church confidently proclaims that God has created each person for eternal life and that Jesus, the Son of God, by his death and resurrection, has broken the chains of sin and death that bound humanity." We proclaim this at every funeral throughout the year with the white pall, holy water, and paschal candle, but it is particularly clear in Easter. In the Northern hemisphere even the earth proclaims our theology of new life.

The participation of the assembly is essential at all times (see *Sing to the Lord: Music in Divine Worship*, 11) but especially at funerals. We encourage participation in the sung parts of the liturgy by having a good cantor at every Mass. However good the musician is as a singer, the musician is not the best choice to lead an assembly, especially a grieving one. The cantor needs to be clearly seen by the people, and be clear about where the music may be found. (A separate worship aid in which the music is printed is the best option. It can be a simple, folded piece of paper.) The cantor makes it clear the assembly is invited to sing, with strong gestures and clear instructions, if needed. The comment "they never sing at weddings and funerals" will remain true as long as we handicap the assembly by depriving them of the words and proper leadership.

The Book of Blessings

THE *Book of Blessings* is bursting with ideas for gathering and blessing people around the themes of spring and newness! The Order for the Blessing for Fields and Flocks (chapter 26) and the Order for the Blessing of Seeds at Planting Time (chapter 27) are perfect at this time of year, even if farmers and those with gardens have already begun planting. Invite people to bring seeds and seedlings to Mass one day or give each parishioner a seedling or packet of seeds to take home. Bless them before the final blessing of Mass.

Many new babies are expected in spring and summer. Consider gathering new mothers together with experienced ones and doing some theological reflection on the experience of birth and motherhood. Use the Order of Blessing of a Mother Before Childbirth (chapter 1, VIII, A.) to begin.

Many people move into new homes at this time of year. It would be wonderful to offer the Order of Blessing of a New Home (chapter 11) when new people come to register with the parish. This is a good way for a priest, deacon, or lay minister to make a personal connection with the family.

The Liturgical Environment

The Nature of the Liturgical Time

In Easter Time, we continue to rejoice in the glory of new life. The liturgy through its prayers, hymns, Scripture texts, and preaching unfolds the meaning of the wonders that God has bestowed on humanity through the Death and Resurrection of Jesus Christ.

The Church continues to journey with the newly baptized, the neophytes, as they reflect on their new life in Christ. Indeed, all the baptized continue to renew their promises of Baptism throughout Easter Time and enter deeper into the work of shaping the kingdom of God in the world. The Gospel passages recount several of the post-Resurrection encounters with the Risen Lord, and the readings from the Acts of the Apostles recall for us the life of the early Church and its coming together in the name of the Risen Lord.

A Pastoral Thought

The 50 days of Easter Time are always a busy period in the life of the parish. It is a time for many joyful celebrations: first Holy Communion and Confirmation liturgies; Baptism celebrations that have been awaited since the beginning of Lent; graduations and weddings—all continue the joyous nature of Easter Time.

The baptismal font figures prominently in the Sunday liturgy as the Rite of Sprinkling may be done as part of the Entrance Procession. Even in the celebration of funerals during this time, people are made more aware of the promise and gift of new life through Christ. The greeting of the funeral liturgy should take place at the font (especially if the font is located near the entry to the church) and the placing of the pall takes on an added connection to the baptismal garments that were given to the newly baptized at the Easter Vigil. These connections can be noted in the Homily as part of the mystagogy that is developed during the Easter season.

Practical Suggestions

◆ The main task of the liturgical environment committee during Easter Time is maintaining the elements of the environment for several weeks.

- During this time the wisdom of budgeting with the liturgical environment in mind becomes evident. New arrangements will be needed; adding new spring plants, and making sure that other decorative items are fresh looking and still attractive is important.

- This is a time when donations of spring potting plants can be solicited from parishioners; these can be arranged in groupings inside and then planted outside to beautify the grounds throughout the summer and into the early fall.

- Some additional items may be added for special liturgies during Easter Time, but these need to be carefully monitored so that the liturgical space is always suitable for the liturgy and never converted into an exhibition space.

- The Solemnity of Pentecost marks the end of Easter Time; the liturgical color is red. The addition of red accents such as flowers and fabric pieces can give a new face to the liturgical environment at this time.

- The more specific elements of the Easter Time environment could be removed from the liturgical space and plans made for the transition to the summer segment of Ordinary Time.

The Liturgical Music

EASTER Time seems like it should be so straightforward liturgically: just sing Alleluia and Psalm 118. But it never is that easy. The Sunday of the Divine Mercy falls on the Octave of Easter. Then there is a backlog of Baptisms from babies born during Lent, first Holy Communions, May crownings, and Confirmations. To this is added those non-liturgical elements of spring that creep into the liturgy, such as Mother's Day, which falls on Ascension Sunday. Easter is early this year, so those elements may seem even more complex than usual. Pentecost is May 19th. Much will be crammed into these great 50 days!

Since Vatican II, every document referring to the liturgy and liturgical music has encouraged the use of the vernacular, while still recognizing the importance and beauty of Gregorian chant (STL 72–80). STL even went so far as to suggest a basic chant repertoire for school children. This highlights the official Church's stress that we maintain ties with our musical and liturgical roots.

Through the years, the Easter sequence has been set to a number of hymn tunes but the richness of the chant prevails. Whether it be in English or Latin, learn the melody for *Victimae paschali laudes.* If your congregation is not ready for it, then engage your choir or small scholas. Even children can master it. If you look at the text carefully, the Easter sequence can easily be divided into parts; for example, a narrator on verse one, choir on verses two and three, male voice on verse four and six, female voice on verses five and seven, and the choir on verse eight. It also works well to sing the "Amen, Alleluia," and then go directly into the "Easter Alleluia" without a pause.

Similarly, your congregation could easily learn (or relearn) *Regina Caeli* or *Salve Regina* to use at the May crowning. There is something so pure and sweet about hearing children's voices singing these hymns. If they learn them now, they will also stay with the child as a prayer, a hymn, a memory for a lifetime.

Use traditional hymns, but don't forget those wonderful new compositions. If you are able to work in a bilingual arrangement of some of them, even better! OCP's *Resucitó* or *Alabaré* is always a lot of fun and can be sung with just a Spanish refrain, or a mixture of English and Spanish verses. In their brand new *Gather* and *Worship* hymnals, GIA has even made "Sing With All the Saints in Glory" bilingual. When you add language to a hymn the congregation already knows, you are taking away half of the battle of learning a new text and will meet with less resistance.

"We Walk By Faith" is always good as is "O Sons and Daughters" with Marty Haugen's driving setting to the same tune as "Easter Alleluia." Pull both hymns together and you will have fifteen verses to use for a great Communion procession!

In most cases, congregations appreciate familiarity in the liturgy. It is the musicians who are often looking for something new and exciting, especially if you play for multiple services on weekends, or have been working with the same hymnal resource for many years. Be kind to your choral budget: go back and dust off some oldies. Your choir will appreciate it, and it will save you time and energy.

Similarly, look for musical selections which may have more than one use. For example, WLP publishes a version of "Hail Thee, Festival Day" which has refrains and verses for Easter, Ascension, and Pentecost. What a great way to save practice time and energy, and create a semblance of seasonal familiarity in the liturgy. Another example would be a fine piece by Kevin Keil (OCP) which

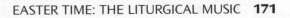

uses "Llanfair" and "Christ the Lord is Risen Today" and "Hail the Day That Sees Him Rise" with a great little choral introduction of "Cantate Domino" that sounds incredibly festive and triumphal.

Liturgical Ministers

DURING this Easter Time, the Sunday liturgies may include first Holy Communions, May crownings, Confirmations, many Baptisms, and anniversary blessings. Often, these liturgies can become more like an "event." There are many guests, and people are excited. Encourage hospitality ministers to help people find their way around the parish. Have musicians provide an extended prelude to "tame the crowd."

Are there special needs for audiovisual ministers on these days? Provide a "script" for those who may be involved, and help them know where the liturgical action will be taking place. Communication is so critical in liturgy.

As the weather becomes more pleasant, families get "spring fever" and take off for the weekend. Remind ministers to find substitutes, or for other parishioners to check in as they attend church to make sure all ministerial roles have been accounted for. Moving to a ministry scheduling program or an e-mail listserv will allow people to find substitutes quickly and effortlessly. This might also be a good time to schedule a training period so that you have enough ministers to carry you through the summer. It is important to remember though, that any time you change procedures there will be a period of growing pains and adjustment. Be patient, laugh a lot, listen to suggestions, and learn much. Trial and error will get you a long way!

Devotions and Sacramentals

THE Sunday of Divine Mercy was established by Pope John Paul II as "a perennial invitation to the Christian world, to face with confidence in divine benevolence, the difficulties and trials that humankind will experience in the years to come" (23 May 2000, the Congregation for Divine Worship and the Discipline of the Sacraments). In a way similar to Palm Sunday (Passion Sunday) or the Fourth Sunday of Easter (Good Shepherd Sunday), the Second Sunday of Easter bears the additional title of Divine Mercy Sunday. This is not a new solemnity or feast, nor does it celebrate a new or separate mystery of redemption, but rather, it leads into the continuing celebration of God's mercy during Easter Time. As the Octave day of Easter, the Lectionary readings and prayer texts highlight the mystery of divine compassion that underlies the Church's Easter faith.

The month of May has been devoted to the Blessed Virgin Mary for centuries, as has been the month of October, the month of the holy rosary. The *Directory on Popular Piety and the Liturgy* invites us to focus on "Our Lady's participation in the Paschal mystery . . . and the Pentecost event" (191). Possible devotions include praying the Rosary and litanies of the Blessed Virgin Mary; recitation of the *Regina Caeli*, Queen of Heaven; and crowning an image of the Blessed Virgin Mary. For more on May crowning, see Celebrating the Marian Year (USCCB, 1987). Your parish should have a devotional area devoted to Mary, where an artistic icon, image, or statue may be placed and honored with candles and flowers. Let it be a place where people can easily stop and pray.

As one prepares for Pentecost, consider making a Novena to the Holy Spirit. It is built upon the pillars of the seven fruits of the Holy Spirit and is a wonderful opportunity to reflect on each of them. It is also a great example of how our prayer flows to and from the liturgy as it prepares us for Pentecost.

If your church does not celebrate an extended Pentecost liturgy for the Vigil, then consider having some other form of communal prayer in preparation for the coming of the Holy Spirit. You could print holy cards with devotions to the Holy Spirit. This could include Saint Alphonsus Liguori's famous prayer or a prayer of consecration to the Holy Spirit. Traditional prayers can also be wedded with communal elements such as Taizé prayer.

The Parish and the Home

EASTER abounds with so many wonderful symbols, it's perfect for family celebrations. Simply going for a walk is a way to rejoice in new life. Children will be especially eager to identify new buds, shoots, bird songs, grasses, and flowers, all signs of hope after the dreary landscapes of winter. The images speak more clearly than words can say: forsythia, crocuses, jonquils, and tulips emerge in a blaze of color from what appears lifeless. In the same way, those who seemed to be dead rise into a glorious dawn and the final goal of humanity: union with God our Creator. Just as we cherish the Christmas crèche, so an abundance of images, stories, and music can decorate the home and fill the family discussion for Easter.

Even young children can learn the traditional Easter greeting, passed down for centuries: "The Lord is risen. Alleluia!" "He is truly risen. Alleluia!" All can learn to sing the refrains of Easter hymns too, so that songs sung at the parish can carry over into the home. To help children visualize the scene where the disciples discovered an empty tomb, have them create an Easter garden, perhaps on a cookie sheet or box lid covered with sand or green material. With pipe cleaners and fabric scraps, they can create the angels and humans. Use rocks to represent the tomb, a few small pieces of cloth for the linen wrappings, and lots of twigs, greenery, and flowers for the surrounding garden. Gardens have a long history in Hebrew-Christian symbolism. After Adam and Eve lost Eden, Jesus regained it. The Cross on which he died became a tree of life. This is a wonderful time to plant gardens, depending on the climate. Later in the summer, when the family eats homegrown tomatoes or green beans, or brings in bouquets of flowers, they can remember how the seeds were sown during Easter Time.

Just as families may have decorated a bare branch with symbols from the Lenten Scriptures, so they may want to create an Easter tree. "Planting" a branch in a large coffee can filled with pebbles or sand can help prevent its toppling over when lots of decorations are hung there. Then decorate it with eggs, butterflies, flowers, birds— all crafted from paper, felt, or foam board.

Within the home, reverently place a bowl of water, candle, crucifix, perhaps arranged in the prayer corner on white or gold cloth, the liturgical colors of the season. Read from the Acts of the Apostles, if possible an illustrated children's version. Or invite the children to tell or act out the Easter story from the point of view of Mary Magdalene (John 20:11–18), Mary the Mother of Jesus, the beloved disciple, Peter, or the disciples who walked to Emmaus with a "stranger" whom they recognized in the breaking of the bread (Luke 24:13–35). They might especially like to dramatize the disciples, at Jesus's directive, catching more fish than they could haul in, Peter putting on clothes and jumping into the lake, then Jesus barbecuing breakfast on the shore (John 21:1–19).

Throughout Easter Time, concrete Scriptures such as the Good Shepherd, and the vine and branches lend themselves to decoration and illustration. LTP publishes *The Garden of the Good Shepherd* by Tomie de Paola, a sticker calendar to mark Easter's 50 days. Pentecost coincides with the Jewish feast Shavuot which celebrates the grain harvest. It is the time to appreciate seasonal treats: strawberries, asparagus, lettuce, rhubarb, cheesecake or ice cream from "the land flowing with milk and honey." Fly kites, sing "Come, Holy Spirit" or other hymns to the Spirit, wear red, and talk about the gifts of the Spirit.

In medieval times Easter was the time for telling jokes—because the ultimate joke is on death. Christians delighted in poking fun at the devil defeated by Christ. Now's the time for the corny humor and outrageous puns kids love— there are 50 days for rejoicing!

Mass Texts

◆ SAMPLE PRAYER OF THE FAITHFUL FOR EASTER TIME

Celebrant:

To the Lord who comes to us and makes his dwelling with us, let us pray.

Deacon/Lector/Reader:

For the Church, that in the midst of doubts and difficulties, we may be open to the workings of the Holy Spirit, Risen Lord:

For all the afflicted of our world; for those who live in conditions of violence, oppression, famine, or disease; that God will use us to reach out to them in their need, Risen Lord:

For mothers who have lost a child; that Mary, who stood by the cross of her Son, may be their consolation, Risen Lord:

For the continued protection of God's creation, Risen Lord:

For those affected by the recent flooding; for all who are suffering; for rescue workers, health care providers, and those who provide comfort; and for those who have died, Risen Lord:

For all our beloved dead, [for N._____ and N._____], and for all our mothers who have died, that God may gather them into the embrace of his love, Risen Lord:

For all of us, gathered in this holy place, that we may be instruments of Christ's peace in our families, our communities, and our world, Risen Lord:

Celebrant:

Good and gracious God,
your love has gathered us together today.
May the joy and hope you have given us in Christ
shine forth in our lives for all the world to see.
We ask this through the same Christ our Lord.
Amen.

◆ DISMISSAL TEXT FOR CATECHUMENS

The Church knows no greater rejoicing than
the Easter feast:
nothing stirs us like the victory song of
the Lamb, slain but now risen in glory.

Yet your desire to bond yourself to Christ and
to join the ranks of his saints
fills heaven with splendid joy and swells
the sound of the angelic chorus.
Let God's Word be your nourishment and
our fellowship be your bond
that a special place has been prepared for you
in the kingdom in which we all hope to rejoice
with the One who conquered death and called
us to himself.

◆ DISMISSAL TEXT FOR CHILDREN'S LITURGY OF THE WORD

The Church chants Alleluia during this very
happy time
because the joy of Resurrection fills our hearts,
and God loves us more than we can imagine.
Go listen to God's Word and hear him speak
to you.
He wants to tell you of his love for you
and teach you how to be like Jesus,
the Son who did everything his Father asked
of him
and made us all children of the Resurrection.

◆ DISMISSAL TEXT FOR EXTRAORDINARY MINISTERS OF HOLY COMMUNION

The human heart knows endless hunger
that only heaven's Bread can gratify.
In Christ's name and ours,
go to those who could not worship here today.
Share the Word of life with them,
and nourish them with the Bread of ages.
May your presence be as Christ to them,
reassuring them of their oneness with us
in spirit and in hope.

April
Month of the Holy Eucharist

MON 1 #261 white

Solemnity of Monday within the Octave of Easter

Lectionary for Mass

◆ FIRST READING: A great crowd of Jews gather in Jerusalem for the feast of Pentecost (a day commemorating the giving of the law on Mount Sinai). Sounds of a strong wind and the different languages spoken by the Apostles draw them to where the Apostles are staying (see Acts of the Apostles 2:1–11). Filled with the Holy Spirit, Peter proclaims the Gospel to the crowds: the Jesus whom they crucified has been raised up and exalted. He is the fulfillment of all that was promised under the old covenant.

◆ RESPONSORIAL PSALM 16: Today's response, a song of confidence prayed in a time when sickness and death were life threatening, is actually cited in the First Reading. It is fulfilled par excellence in Jesus.

◆ GOSPEL: A wide range of emotions and responses to the news of Christ's Resurrection are evident: the simultaneous fear and joy of the women, the panic of the chief priests and elders, their frantic attempt to cover up and explain the empty tomb. What incredible joy the women must have experienced when they saw the Risen Christ and touched him. What they must have felt as they fulfilled the mission: "Go tell my brothers"!

The Roman Missal

Our long journey through the desert has brought us "into a land flowing with milk and honey"—Easter (Entrance Antiphon)!

At every Mass this week, the Gloria is said or sung, but the Creed is not said. Preface I of Easter is used. If the Roman Canon is used, the Easter forms of the *Communicantes* and *Hanc igitur* are said. The Easter form of the dismissal with double Alleluia is used throughout the Octave.

We praise God who adds "new offspring" to the Church through Baptism, and we pray that all remain faithful to their Baptism throughout their lives (Collect) and "attain unending happiness" (Prayer over the Offerings). We pray for the abounding grace of the "paschal Sacrament" (Prayer after Communion) we receive on this Easter day.

TUE 2 #262 white

Solemnity of Tuesday within the Octave of Easter

Lectionary for Mass

◆ FIRST READING: Today's First Reading is a continuation of Peter's Pentecost speech. The hearts of many of those who heard Peter's proclamation of Jesus as Lord and Messiah were opened to repentance and the gift of faith. Some three thousand people were baptized.

◆ RESPONSORIAL PSALM 33 is a song of confidence. In his love, the Lord desires that all turn to him in trust. Only in the Lord is their salvation. His goodness fills the earth.

◆ GOSPEL: At the tomb, Mary Magdalene is greeted by the Risen Christ, though she does not recognize him until he calls her by name. She is sent to announce Christ's return to the Father. She becomes the "apostle to the Apostles," the first to announce the Good News of Christ's Resurrection and exaltation.

The Roman Missal

God gives us "paschal remedies" that we may have "perfect freedom" and rejoice both on earth and in heaven in Christ's Resurrection (Collect). We pray that God may protect us (Prayer over the Offerings) and prepare us for eternal life (Prayer after Communion).

WED 3 #263 white

Solemnity of Wednesday within the Octave of Easter

Lectionary for Mass

◆ FIRST READING: Peter and John give a gift far greater than alms to the crippled man at the gate of the Temple. Raised up by the hand of Peter in the name of Jesus, he is completely healed.

◆ RESPONSORIAL PSALM 105: This song of thanksgiving is a most appropriate response. For truly, the formerly lame man, now walking and praising God with joy, announces his deeds among the peoples.

◆ GOSPEL: Two of Jesus's disciples, discouraged by the happenings of the previous few days, are desolately leaving Jerusalem. Meeting them along the way and speaking with them about Scripture, Jesus enlivens their hearts. They recognize him in the breaking of the bread.

The Roman Missal

Each year the Church is gladdened by the celebration of Christ's Resurrection; we pray that we may experience the joys that Easter promises (Collect). We ask for "salvation of mind and body" (Prayer over the Offerings), that we may be cleansed of our former way of life and transformed into "a new creation" (Prayer after Communion).

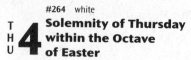

T H U 4 #264 white Solemnity of Thursday within the Octave of Easter

Lectionary for Mass

◆ FIRST READING: Having drawn a crowd by the miraculous cure of the lame man, Peter addresses them in the Temple. Though Jesus was the servant of the God of Abraham, Isaac, and Jacob, and the "Author of Life," the leaders of his people rejected him, handing him over to death. God raised him from the dead and offers forgiveness and life to all who repent and believe in his name.

◆ RESPONSORIAL PSALM 8 praises and acclaims the name of God and God's goodness to the human creature, whom he crowns with glory and honor. This Psalm is eminently fulfilled in Jesus. His is our destiny as well.

◆ GOSPEL: The two disciples who met Jesus on the road to Emmaus return to Jerusalem and announce the Good News of Christ's Resurrection to the other disciples. As they are speaking, Jesus suddenly stands in their midst. He assures the disciples that he is really alive and speaks to them of the fulfillment of Scripture.

The Roman Missal

We continue to pray for the neophytes and for all the baptized, that we may be one in faith and in "the homage of their deeds," the praise they offer to God by the good work they do (Collect). We offer the sacrifice of the Mass for the newly baptized and for ourselves (Prayer over the Offerings). We pray that the "holy exchange" of the Eucharist may bring us present help and "eternal gladness" (Prayer after Communion).

F R I 5 #265 white Solemnity of Friday within the Octave of Easter

Lectionary for Mass

◆ FIRST READING: Despite their arrest, Peter and John proclaim the Gospel, which draws more believers. Note the emphasis given to the name of Jesus in their witness before their accusers.

◆ RESPONSORIAL PSALM 118: Our response is from the same Psalm cited by Peter in the First Reading. We give thanks to the Lord for his goodness, for his wonderful work in establishing the rejected stone (Jesus) as the cornerstone (Lord and Savior).

◆ GOSPEL: The Apostles have returned to their former occupation as fishermen—in this instance, with little success. Jesus gifts them with a miraculous catch of fish, then nourishes them with food for body and spirit. The disciples know, without a doubt, that it is the Lord.

The Roman Missal

The Paschal Mystery is God's covenant with us, to reconcile us to himself. We pray that we may profess our faith in this great mystery, and express our faith in the way we live our lives (Collect). We pray that our offering may draw our minds from earth to heaven (Prayer over the Offerings). We ask God to redeem all he has saved through Christ's Passion, that they may rejoice in his Resurrection (Prayer after Communion).

S A T 6 #266 white Solemnity of Saturday within the Octave of Easter

Lectionary for Mass

◆ FIRST READING: The consternation of the Jewish leaders focuses on the proclamation of the name of Jesus. The disciples are warned to speak it no more, but they only respond that they must—in obedience to God.

◆ RESPONSORIAL PSALM 118: The disciples experience the truth of the psalmist's prayer: their strength is the Lord, who has rescued them from death. They acclaim the work of the Lord.

◆ GOSPEL: This portion of the longer (and probably later) ending of Mark's account of the Gospel summarizes stories which the other accounts tell in more detail: the Lord's appearance to and commission of Mary Magdalene, his appearance to the disciples on the road to Emmaus, and his appearance to the disciples at table. Jesus takes them to task for their stubbornness and lack of faith in refusing to believe the news of his Resurrection. Having seen and believed, they are sent to proclaim the Gospel to the world.

The Roman Missal

In many of our parishes, we saw the newly baptized in white garments as they emerged from the waters of new life. In the Collect, we pray that those who have been reborn in Baptism may be clothed "with blessed immortality." The prayers echo the "delight" and "joy" of Easter Time (Prayer over the Offerings), as we pray that all who are renewed by the sacraments may share in the resurrection of the body (Prayer after Communion).

#45   white

7 Solemnity of the Second Sunday of Easter / Sunday of Divine Mercy

Orientation

Through Christian art and cinema, we have come to imagine the Risen Christ as whole, glowing, transcendent and powerful, the opposite of the Man of Sorrows suffering through the Passion. Yet the wounds on Jesus's hands, feet, and side remained on his risen body as signs of the suffering he endured and the death he conquered. The Apostles are encouraged by seeing his wounds, though they are also confronted with the mystery of the bodily Resurrection. Jesus is not a disembodied spirit, a ghost walking around. He is entirely risen and embodying a whole new reality. When Thomas exclaims, "My Lord and My God!" (John 20:28), he is sensing something greater than he had ever experienced before, something heralding a new creation. During Easter Time, we also sense this new realty, finding glimpses of the reign of God in the new life around us.

Lectionary for Mass

◆ First Reading: Today's reading begins and ends with the signs and wonders worked by Peter and the other Apostles, especially healing and exorcisms. In between, there are the somewhat contradictory verses concerning the fear that many

people had of joining them and the fact that many did! We find all kinds of emotions, all kinds of signs and wonders in the nascent church and in our own lives as well.

◆ Responsorial Psalm 118: The psalmist acclaims God's everlasting love and invites his hearers to give thanks. The rejected stone is now the cornerstone, and the psalmist experiences life, not death, on this day of salvation. Truly this was the experience of those who heard the Apostles' words and witnessed their marvelous works.

◆ Second Reading: Easter's victory comes only after the Cross. So it was for Jesus, so it will be for John, who is imprisoned on the island of Patmos because of his witness to Jesus. His vision of the victorious Lord sustains and encourages him. His vision is likewise a call to make known what he sees and hears.

◆ Gospel: The Risen Christ comes into the midst of his fearful disciples, bringing them peace, gifting them with his Spirit, and sending them to bring forgiveness. Thomas, who was absent, does not believe the witness of the others. A week later, he is with the disciples gathered again behind locked doors. Jesus invites Thomas to see, to touch, and to believe; Jesus pronounces a blessing on all who will believe without seeing. We are among them.

The Roman Missal

The splendid Collect is a prayer for the grace to recognize the Christ in whom we have been baptized, whose Spirit gives new life, and whose blood redeems us.

The Prayer over the Offerings includes a special optional insert for the newly baptized.

Preface I of Easter, with the words "on this day above all," is used, as on Easter Sunday. If the Roman Canon is used, the Easter form of

the *Communicantes* and *Hanc igitur* are said.

The simple Prayer after Communion asks that the "paschal Sacrament" may have an ongoing effect on our hearts and minds.

The Easter form of the dismissal, with double Alleluia, is used at Masses today.

Other Ideas

Identify something you believe in without ever having seen it, like ghosts, atoms, bacteria, planets, aliens, and so on. Discuss with someone why you don't need physical evidence to persist in your belief.

Celebrate this Sunday of Divine Mercy by inviting each family member to perform a secret kindness for someone who has hurt or aggravated him or her. Discuss ideas and share suggestions, but don't tell the names of the recipients of your gestures, and make sure these recipients don't know who performed the secret kindnesses. Consider saying special prayers for someone, tucking a small gift in a coworker's mail slot, picking up trash in a neighbor's yard when no one is home, or performing some other small act of generosity.

#545   white

MON 8 Solemnity of the Annunciation of the Lord

Orientation

Through the angel Gabriel, the Spirit of God comes to Mary in the most unfeasible way, asking the impossible. As a young woman engaged to be married, being found pregnant would have meant her death in the culture of the time. She risks hurting Joseph, bringing shame on their families, and setting herself up for execution, because she is sure of one thing: God calls her to be Mother to the Son of God. Mary is special because her faith is stronger than her fear. She does not see the road ahead but knows that God wills for her to journey it nonetheless. Trusting in God above all, she consents her will, becoming the first and most important vessel of bringing Christ's presence into the world.

Lectionary for Mass

◆ FIRST READING: Christian tradition has long seen this text of the prophet Isaiah fulfilled in Mary of Nazareth. In his account of the Gospel, Matthew says so explicitly (1:22–23). In its original context, the child to be born was the son of Ahaz the king and would be heir to the Davidic throne at a time when the kingdom of Judah feared total annihilation. It was a sign of assurance that God's promises would be fulfilled. God was indeed still with his people and acting on their behalf.

◆ RESPONSORIAL PSALM 40: Today's antiphon is particularly appropriate given Mary's acceptance of the angel's word. God desires a listening heart, an obedient heart above all.

◆ SECOND READING: Our responsorial Psalm 40 is cited in today's Second Reading from Hebrews. Jesus's obedient response, "Behold, I come to do your will," echoes that of his mother. How much her faith and devotion to God must have been a living example for her son as she taught him by word and deed from the earliest days of his life to be an obedient servant of the Lord. His obedience to his heavenly Father, even to the point of giving his own life as a sacrifice, inaugurated a new covenant with our God.

◆ GOSPEL: The word of the Lord is sent to yet another woman betrothed to one of David's descendants. God has not forgotten his promise of an everlasting throne of David. The humble virgin of Nazareth has found favor with God. She shall conceive by the power of the Holy Spirit and bear a son. He will

rule over God's people. His kingdom shall be everlasting. Truly, as no other Davidic king before him, he is indeed the Son of God in a most unique way.

The Roman Missal

Because March 25 fell on the Monday of Holy Week, the Solemnity of the Annunciation of the Lord is transferred to today. The Preface and other prayers are found in the Proper of Saints.

The Annunciation is a feast of the Word made flesh, and the prayers are rich in allusions to the Incarnation. God willed that his divine Word "should take on the reality of human flesh" in Mary's womb; just as he shared our human nature, we pray that we may share in his divine nature (Collect). The Church rejoices in this solemnity because she recognizes that the Incarnation of Christ is where "her beginnings / lie" (Prayer over the Offerings). Mary heard and believed the word of the Angel that the Christ was to be born among us and for us, and she carried him in her womb so that the promises of God and the "hope of nations" might be fulfilled (Preface). We pray that we who acknowledge our faith in the Incarnation may experience the "saving power of his Resurrection" (Prayer after Communion).

T U E **9** #268 white
Easter Weekday

Lectionary for Mass

◆ FIRST READING: The community of believers was completely united in mind and heart, and held all possessions in common. We are introduced to Barnabas, future companion of Paul, who gave the proceeds from the sale of his field to the community. He exemplifies what it means to hold all things in common. The Apostles continued their witness to the Risen Christ.

◆ RESPONSORIAL PSALM 93 extols the glorious majesty of God the King. This is also an appropriate response to the proclamation of the Risen Christ: he who was crucified as the King of the Jews is now exalted at the right hand of the Father.

◆ GOSPEL: Jesus teaches Nicodemus about the necessity of being born again, born of the Spirit, born from above. Jesus speaks of himself as the one who has descended from heaven, the Son of Man whose lifting up on the cross will also be his lifting up in glory.

The Roman Missal

On the weekdays of Easter Time, the Prayer over the Gifts and the Prayer after Communion are repeated week by week. Commentaries are included for these prayers on the Easter Sundays when they occur. Each day has its own unique Collect, however, which is briefly commented on below.

"With great power the Apostles bore witness to the resurrection of the Lord Jesus," we hear in today's First Reading (Acts of the Apostles 4:33). The Collect for today reminds us that we, too, are called to that apostolic task, "to proclaim the power of the risen Lord."

W E D **10** #269 white
Easter Weekday

Lectionary for Mass

◆ FIRST READING: The signs and wonders worked by the Apostles in the name of Jesus draw great crowds. Filled with jealousy, the high priests and the Sadducees (who deny the Resurrection) arrest the Apostles. They are delivered from prison by an angel of the Lord and are sent to continue their proclamation of the Gospel.

◆ RESPONSORIAL PSALM 34: The Lord did indeed hear the cry of his poor Apostles and sent his angel to deliver them. The Apostles themselves have experienced (have "tasted") and "seen" the goodness of the Lord.

◆ GOSPEL: God's love for the world was so great that he sent his only beloved Son, not to condemn the world, but to give light and life to all who believe.

The Roman Missal

Easter is the new creation, as the dignity of human nature is restored by "the hope of rising again" (Collect)

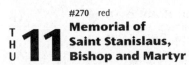

#270   red

T H U 11 Memorial of Saint Stanislaus, Bishop and Martyr

Lectionary for Mass

◆ FIRST READING: The high priests and council interrogate the Apostles, who can only respond that it is God whom they must obey. Enraged, the Jewish leaders want to destroy them.

◆ RESPONSORIAL PSALM 34: As yesterday, we have Psalm 34 again with its strong confidence in the Lord and his deliverance of the just.

◆ GOSPEL: The Son is from above, sent by God, to give eternal life to all who believe. Do we "accept his testimony" (John 3:33)?

The Roman Missal

The Collect for the memorial is taken from the Proper of Saints, with the remaining prayers taken from the Common of Martyrs: For One Martyr or the Common of Pastors: For a Bishop.

Today's Saint

Noted for his compassionate concern for the poor and for his wise counsel, Saint Stanislaus (1030–1079) was appointed bishop of Krakow. The people were overjoyed by his consecration as bishop. While serving as bishop he spoke out against King Boleslaus, an unjust and cruel man who terrified the people of Poland with his oppressive behavior. Saint Stanislaus declared that an unjust king had no place in the Church. In response, the king defamed his reputation, eventually ordering guards to kill him, but they refused. The king took matters into his own hands by stabbing him with a sword. Saint Stanislaus, the martyr, is the patron saint of Poland and the city of Krakow.

#271   white

F R I 12 Easter Weekday

Lectionary for Mass

◆ FIRST READING: Gamaliel, a revered teacher of the law, wisely addresses the Sanhedrin: if the witness of the Apostles is of divine origin, then the Sanhedrin will have no power over it. In fact, they may even be fighting God. If it is of human origin, in time it will destroy itself. Though persuaded, the Sanhedrin have the Apostles flogged (as was Jesus). What do we make of their joy that they are found worthy to suffer for the name of Jesus? Would that same joy be ours?

◆ RESPONSORIAL PSALM 27: Our First Reading ends with the Apostles continuing their proclamation of the Gospel in the Temple (the house of God) as well as in their own homes. Thus, today's Responsorial Antiphon: "One thing I seek: to dwell in the house of the Lord." The verses speak confidently of the Lord as one's refuge and salvation.

◆ GOSPEL: The feeding of the multitude is a story that beautifully illustrates that, in Jesus, whatever one has is enough to satisfy any need. Who of us cannot identify with Philip and Andrew? How are we going to do this? If this is all we have, what good is it when so much more is needed? If only we could have the mind of Jesus, take what is at hand, and give thanks. Would we, too, find that it is more than enough?

The Roman Missal

In the Collect, we ask God for hearts disposed to prayer and praise.

#272   white

S A T 13 Easter Weekday

Optional Memorial of Saint Martin I, Pope and Martyr / red

Lectionary for Mass

◆ FIRST READING: We hear of complaints among the early Christians, a bit of tension between those of different nationalities. If the basic needs of all are to be met, the Apostles need assistants. Stephen, who figures prominently in this and the next chapter of Acts of the Apostles, is chosen, along with other men who are reputable, wise, and filled with God's Spirit.

◆ RESPONSORIAL PSALM 33 picks up on the need for food, a concern expressed in today's First Reading. The concern for "justice and right" (second stanza) is likewise addressed by the Apostles in today's First Reading. Those who place their trust in the Lord will not be confounded.

◆ GOSPEL: Today's Gospel is the sequel to yesterday's Gospel, where the disciples see and experience Jesus's signs and wonders. Jesus's power over the sea (raging powers of destruction) is like that of God the Creator (see Job 9:8). Seeing and experiencing this, the disciples are fearful. "It is I," says Jesus (John 6:20). The words in the Greek text are the ones used of God's name in Exodus 3:14 (Moses and the burning bush). May we see and hear the powerful presence of Jesus in all the turbulent situations in our lives.

The Roman Missal

There are two options for today's Collect. In the first, we beg God to "set aside . . . / the bond of sentence" written by our sins and cancel it through the Resurrection of Christ. In the second, we see "the gates of mercy" flung wide through the Paschal Mystery, and we pray that we may "never stray from the paths of life."

Today's Saint

As pope, Saint Martin I (+655) found himself at great odds with the reigning emperor, Constans II, who was a proponent of monothelitism, which articulated that Jesus did not have a human nature (only a divine nature). The Church, represented by Saint Martin I and a synod of bishops, affirmed the two natures of Jesus, ultimately denouncing the belief in only one nature as heresy. The emperor did everything he could to undermine the power of the pope, which included rallying the bishops to revolt against him, but his attempts proved unsuccessful. Saint Martin I was placed in solitary confinement, starved, and publicly stripped of his episcopal garments. He was put on trial and sentenced to death, but after a plea on behalf of the pope by the patriarch of Constantinople, the sentence was changed to exile. Saint Martin died from harsh treatment while in exile. He is venerated as the last martyred pope.

☀ 14 #48 white Third Sunday of Easter

Orientation

Peter had been with Jesus from the beginning. He long ago heard the call to follow him, and based on their close relationship, he had assumed Jesus sensed his love and devotion. In this scene, however, Peter is called to express three times his sincere love for the Lord and the willingness to serve and follow him. Peter is hurt, and wonders: Doesn't he know? Indeed, the Risen Lord knows Peter's heart. He knows that in our life of faith, we face highs and lows, and for a constant relationship with God, it does us well to recall our vows of faith. During Easter Time, we recall our baptismal vows and get sprinkled with holy water to remind us of the day we became God's in the font of Baptism. God already knows we belong to him. But it does our faith well, as it did for Peter, to recall who we are in Christ, and what we are called to do.

Lectionary for Mass

◆ FIRST READING: In between the event described in last Sunday's reading and today's text, the Apostles have been arrested, imprisoned, and miraculously released to resume their proclamation of the Gospel. As today's reading begins, they are apprehended again. Always, there is the shadow of the Cross—Jesus's, the disciples', and our own. Would that we, too, could rejoice in our sufferings for the sake of Jesus.

◆ RESPONSORIAL PSALM 40 is a song of praise celebrating God's deliverance of his people and, particularly in today's liturgy, of the Apostles. Surely the words of the psalmist sustained them, giving them courage and hope in all they would endure.

◆ SECOND READING: In a vision, John, the Christian prophet, sees God's heavenly throne surrounded by the elders, the living creatures, and countless angels. They sing praise to the victorious Lamb of God. All creatures in heaven and on earth join in the triumphal hymn.

◆ GOSPEL: The Apostles have returned to their former occupation as fishermen—in this instance, with little success. Jesus gifts them with a miraculous catch of fish, then nourishes them with food for body and spirit. The disciples know, without a doubt, that it is the Lord. The longer option includes Jesus's triple questioning of Peter's love for him (paralleling his earlier threefold denial). Peter likewise receives a threefold commission to shepherd Jesus's flock. Peter's destiny is the focus of the final verses. His martyrdom, like Jesus's own Death, would glorify God. Today's Gospel ends with the command and invitation to "Follow me" (John 21:19). The way of the disciple can be none other than the way of Jesus.

The Roman Missal

The Collect is full of joy—the joy of "the restored glory of our adoption" in Christ, the joy of "the day of resurrection," the joy of a new "youthfulness of spirit."

Joy is the keynote of the Prayer over the Offerings as well: the Church exults in great gladness, and we pray that the gifts we bring will "bear fruit in perpetual happiness" for us.

In the Prayer after Communion, we ask that all who share in the "eternal mysteries" may one day know the resurrection of the body.

Other Ideas

In point form, jot down things that strengthen your faith that Jesus Christ is the Son of God and Savior of the World. If you can't come up with more than three reasons, ask others for their thoughts and add them to your list until it grows to six or more items. This is an excellent group activity. Share your reflections with each other.

M O N 15 #273 white
Easter Weekday

Lectionary for Mass

◆ FIRST READING: Stephen continues the Spirit-filled ministry of Jesus and, like Jesus, encounters opposition and false accusation. Through it all, his countenance was "like the face of an angel" (Acts of the Apostles 6:15), centered in the deep peace that is the gift of the Spirit within.

◆ RESPONSORIAL PSALM 119: Virtually every verse focuses on some aspect of the Law and the psalmist's relationship to it. The Law, for Israel, was a guide on the way through life, a priceless treasure. In today's verses, the psalmist also prays for deliverance from false accusers, treasuring God's truth above all.

◆ GOSPEL: The crowds pursue Jesus after he so miraculously fed them. Jesus questions them on their motives for seeking him. And what about us: why and what do we seek? Let us hear Jesus's words and seek what endures forever—eternal life.

The Roman Missal

We must leave behind the "old self with all its ways" and "live as Christ did." Our sharing in "the healing paschal remedies" is transformative, making us more like Christ (Collect).

T U E 16 #274 white
Easter Weekday

Lectionary for Mass

◆ FIRST READING: Today's First Reading is the conclusion of Stephen's address to the Sanhedrin, or Jewish council, before whom he is tried. He, however, becomes *their* accuser. His words challenge us as well. Are we among those who "always oppose the Holy Spirit" (Acts of the Apostles 7:51)? Note his prayer as he dies. Note also the introduction of Saul (Paul) at the end of the reading.

◆ RESPONSORIAL PSALM 31: The response is the words of both Jesus and Stephen as they die, taken from Psalm 31, a song of trust in God's deliverance.

◆ GOSPEL: The Jews seek signs (miracles) that they might "see and believe" (John 6:30). Jesus invites them to "see" with their minds and leads them to a deeper faith. The true Bread from heaven is not the manna God provided for the Israelites in the desert, or even the bread with which Jesus fed the multitudes, but Jesus himself, sent to give life to the world. May we too say, "Sir, give us this bread always" (John 6:34). May we know that it is offered to us each day.

The Roman Missal

God opens "wide the gates of the heavenly Kingdom / to those reborn of water and the Holy Spirit" (Collect). We ask for an increase of grace so that, purged of all sin, we may attain to the promises of God.

W E D 17 #275 white
Easter Weekday

Optional Memorial of Blessed Kateri Tekakwitha, Virgin / white (Canada)

Lectionary for Mass

◆ FIRST READING: Stephen's death marks the beginning of a severe persecution of the Jewish Christians spearheaded by Saul. Acting out of his zeal for Judaism and convinced that those who believed Jesus was the Messiah were in error, Saul sets out to destroy this perceived heresy and threat to Judaism. This time of great suffering and dispersion of the disciples nevertheless gives rise to new life and wholeness as the Gospel is proclaimed in new places.

◆ RESPONSORIAL PSALM 66: Today's Psalm echoes the joy in the last line of the First Reading. Notice the emphasis on the deeds and works of the Lord, given new meaning in the healings accomplished in the name of Jesus. The God who miraculously led Israel out of Egypt continues to work marvels in their midst.

◆ GOSPEL: "Comings" abound in today's Gospel: that of Jesus into the world, that of the believer to Jesus, and that of the believer to the Father and to eternal life. How strong, how real is our belief in Jesus? Jesus was solely about the will of his Father when he came to earth. Are we?

The Roman Missal

We have received the gift of faith; we ask for what our faith promises— "an eternal share in the Resurrection" (Collect).

Today's Saint

Kateri Tekakwitha (1656–1680), called the "Lily of the Mohawks," is the first Native American to have been beatified, and is on the road to possible canonization as a saint.

The daughter of a Mohawk chief and Christian Algonquin, she vowed to live as a virgin, and eventually decided to convert to Christianity after a few encounters with Jesuit missionaries. Her decision to convert was not received well within her community because Christianity was seen as the religion of the oppressors. Blessed Kateri was a pious woman who attended daily Mass, fasted twice a week, taught children, and cared for the sick. After she died, a number of miracles and visions were attributed to her intercession.

THU 18 #276 white
Easter Weekday

Optional Memorial of Blessed Marie-Anne Blondin, Virgin / white (Canada)

Lectionary for Mass

◆ FIRST READING: Today's account of Philip and the Ethiopian eunuch is a beautiful account of the impact God's word can have on us if only we are open to it and eager to understand. On hearing Philip's proclamation about Jesus, the eunuch immediately believes, requests, and receives Baptism. The reference to Philip being snatched up evokes other accounts of heavenly translation in Scripture (such as Elijah's; see 2 Kings 2:11). This happening is a witness to the tremendous power of God's Spirit at work in the life of Philip.

◆ RESPONSORIAL PSALM 66: Today's Responsorial Psalm, a call to all the earth to cry out with joy to the Lord, is aptly chosen as a response to a reading about the conversion of the Ethiopian eunuch. As a result of his conversion, the man receives new life (first stanza) and continues on his way rejoicing.

◆ GOSPEL: Faith in Jesus is first of all the result of the Father's initiative in drawing people to his Son, a point beautifully illustrated in today's First Reading. Faith in Jesus leads to eternal life. Within the context of chapter 6 of John's Gospel, having faith in Jesus means recognizing and receiving him as the Bread of eternal life, the Bread that is his very own life given for us.

The Roman Missal

Easter is the season of God's great compassion. We pray that all whom God has "freed from the darkness of error" may cling to his truth (Collect).

Today's Saint

Born in 1809, Esther Blondin was a French Canadian who learned from the Sisters of Notre Dame to read and write—at age 22. Although she wanted to join this community, her health prohibited it. As a teacher in the parochial school, she realized that high rates of illiteracy were due to Church policy that girls be taught only by women and boys only by men. She founded an order of religious sisters to offset illiteracy and instruct boys and girls together, a new idea for the time.

Her order was called the Congregation of the Sisters of St. Anne, and she took the name Marie-Anne. However, she faced stiff opposition from their chaplain, who prevented her from taking any administrative position. She spent 32 years doing the laundry, convinced that "there is more happiness in forgiving than in revenge."

FRI 19 #277 white
Easter Weekday

Lectionary for Mass

◆ FIRST READING: In this rather long reading, we hear the first of three accounts in Acts of the Apostles regarding Saul's conversion to Jesus. It is important to note that Saul was a deeply religious man prior to this experience on the road to Damascus, zealous for the traditions of his ancestors, and convinced that those who followed the way of Jesus were in error. Notice the interplay of the themes of light and darkness, of blindness and sight, of ignorance and understanding. Notice also the role of hearing, of being led by the hand, and of being healed through the laying on of hands. What openness to God's at times perplexing ways was demanded of both Saul and Ananias!

◆ RESPONSORIAL PSALM 117: Today's Responsorial Psalm is a fitting response to the account of Saul's conversion, for it is exactly what he did for the rest of his life: he went out and proclaimed the Gospel of Jesus to all the world.

◆ GOSPEL: The controversy between Jesus and the Jews continues. How can Jesus give them his flesh to eat and his blood to drink? How can the food he gives be better than the manna God gave to Israel in the desert? Jesus is true bread from heaven. Jesus's very life is nourishment for the world. Jesus's body, given in his sacrificial death, passed over into glorious new life. Partaking of his body and blood, given for believers in every age, is assurance that we share in this glorious new life now and forever.

The Roman Missal

The grace of Easter is not a moment in time, but a lifetime! We have already come to know "the grace of the Lord's Resurrection," yet we continue to pray that "through the love of the Spirit" we may "rise to newness of life" (Collect).

S A T **20** #278 white
Easter Weekday

Lectionary for Mass

◆ FIRST READING: After Saul's conversion, the Church experiences a time of peace. The Church was "built up" (Acts of the Apostles 9:31) not only in number, but in conviction and virtue. The Apostles continued to work signs and wonders in the name of Jesus. Today we hear of two such incidents: the paralyzed man Aeneas and the woman disciple, Tabitha, who had fallen sick and died.

◆ RESPONSORIAL PSALM 116: Today's Responsorial Psalm is one of thanksgiving, fittingly prayed by Aeneas, Tabitha, Peter, and all believers, with gratitude for all the good the Lord has done for us.

◆ GOSPEL: Today's Gospel is the conclusion of the sixth chapter of John's account of the Gospel, and we hear verses that might appropriately be entitled "the struggle to believe." Those who hear Jesus's words are faced with a decision: Shall we stay with him? Or, do we return to our former way of life? What is our response?

The Roman Missal

The Collect is a prayer for the protection of those "reborn in Christ," that they may be victorious in combating error and "preserve the grace" God has given them.

☀ **21** #51 white
Fourth Sunday of Easter

Orientation

The Fourth Sunday of Easter generally focuses on the image of Christ as the Good Shepherd. Even though in our modern world we would rarely, if ever, encounter a shepherd, the image of the Good Shepherd still evokes comfort, protection, guidance, and divine care. Sheep wander the pasture all day and rely on the voice of the shepherd to guide them back to safety for the night. Similarly, God lets us exercise our freedom and meander through life, but if we go astray, we can always rely on the Word of God to guide us back to the Way in Jesus Christ.

Lectionary for Mass

◆ FIRST READING: We witness the popularity of Paul and Barnabas, chosen by the Holy Spirit as missionaries of the Gospel (see Acts of the Apostles 13:2). After an introductory verse (14), the reading skips over Paul's speech in the synagogue on their first Sabbath in Antioch and resumes with a description of its effect on many who heard them (verse 43, the second line of today's reading). Their popularity soon led to opposition from the Jews, and even persecution. Paul and Barnabas read this as a sign that they should go to the Gentiles.

◆ RESPONSORIAL PSALM 100: The first antiphon option is particularly apropos in light of both today's Second Reading (last line) and Gospel. Note also the reference to "flock" in the second stanza of this joyful hymn of praise.

◆ SECOND READING: Our reading from Revelation echoes the theme of persecution heard in today's text from Acts of the Apostles. Only here, the focus is the eternal reward enjoyed by those who are victorious. The Lamb who was sacrificed is at the same time the Shepherd of his people.

◆ GOSPEL: The reference to "follow" in today's Gospel harks back to today's First Reading (those who "followed" Paul and Barnabas). Those who heard these missionaries, in effect, heard the word of God which they spoke. In the Word of God proclaimed in the Liturgy, we likewise hear the voice of the Lord our Shepherd.

The Roman Missal

On this "Good Shepherd Sunday," the texts are full of images of shepherds. In the Collect, we pray that "the humble flock" may follow "the brave Shepherd" (Christ) to where he has gone—to the very "joys of heaven." The Prayer over the Offerings is one of "delight," "renewal," and "joy." The Prayer after Communion, addressed to God, the "kind Shepherd," asks that the whole flock redeemed by Christ's Blood may come to "eternal pastures."

Other Ideas

Tomorrow is Earth Day. Look for other ways to treat fellow human beings, the earth, and all its creatures with justice. Discuss recycling, reusing, and repairing for the good of the earth. Commit yourself to purchasing fair trade products that help eliminate unjust labor conditions and ensure fair wages for workers. Learn about factory farming and how your purchasing power can make a difference in the treatment of animals, while increasing for yourself the health benefits of eating foods that contain fewer chemicals.

MON 22 #279 white
Easter Weekday

Lectionary for Mass

◆ FIRST READING: The Gentiles' (non-Jews') acceptance of the Gospel was something the first Christians had not expected. This becomes, in fact, a struggle for them. For example, Gentiles did not observe the Mosaic laws (in this instance, dietary laws are of particular concern). Peter himself did not observe them when he ate with the Gentiles. When confronted by the others, Peter can only respond that he had done as he was instructed in prayer. The subsequent pouring out of God's Spirit was confirmation of his mission's divine origin. Who was he to hinder God!

◆ RESPONSORIAL PSALM 42: All people have an innate thirst or desire for God. Through the words and deeds of Peter in today's First Reading, God's light and fidelity led Cornelius's household to faith (see chapter 10 of Acts of the Apostles). This is true cause for thanksgiving.

◆ GOSPEL: Several words and images occur repeatedly in today's Gospel, thus emphasizing their importance: "listen," "voice," and "gate." Imagine an enclosed area, providing security and protection for a flock. Jesus is presented both as the "gate"—the way in and out—and the shepherd, the one who knows his sheep by name and cares deeply for them, even to the point of laying down his life. He came that we might have life abundantly.

The Roman Missal

◆ COLLECT: It is by God's gift that we celebrate the Paschal Mystery here on earth; we pray that we may "rejoice in the full measure of . . . grace / for ages unending." Time intersects with eternity.

TUE 23 #280 white
Easter Weekday

Optional Memorials of Saint George, Martyr / red; Saint Adalbert, Bishop and Martyr / red

Lectionary for Mass

◆ FIRST READING: The number of believers continues to grow not only among the Jews, but among the Gentiles. The disciples recognize this growth as indeed the Lord's work. Barnabas and Saul spend a year in Antioch teaching the first "Christians" as they came to be known, those first followers or disciples of Christ.

◆ RESPONSORIAL PSALM: The verses of today's response are from Psalm 87, a Psalm acclaiming Jerusalem (Zion) as the "mother" of those who know the Lord. How fitting, given that Jesus's Death, Resurrection, Ascension, and the pouring out of his Spirit took place there. The antiphon is from Psalm 117, a song of praise, very appropriate as today's First Reading invites all nations (Gentiles) to praise the Lord.

◆ GOSPEL: The feast of the Dedication (Hanukkah) celebrated the purification of the Temple after its desecration by Gentiles (see 1 Maccabees 4:36–59). The Temple was that sacred place where God dwelt with his people. In today's Gospel, the Jews fail to recognize that Jesus is the very embodiment of God's presence with his people, God's Word in their midst.

The Roman Missal

If one of the optional memorials is observed, the Collect is found in the Proper of Saints, with the remaining prayers drawn from the appropriate Common.

Today's Saints

Saint George was a soldier in the Guard of Emperor Diocletian. When ordered to persecute the Church, he refused and admitted that he was also a Christian. An enraged Diocletian ordered his execution.

Saint Adalbert came from a wealthy Czech family. He became bishop of Prague but resigned because paganism persisted among the Christians there. Adalbert went to Rome and became a Benedictine monk, but the pope sent him back to Prague to resume his role as bishop. He founded the first monastery in the Czech region but was martyred when he tried to bring the Gospel to Prussia.

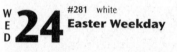

WED 24 #281 white
Easter Weekday

Optional Memorial of Saint Fidelis of Sigmaringen, Priest and Martyr / red

Lectionary for Mass

◆ FIRST READING: The Lectionary omits the prophetic prediction of a famine in the land, and the disciples' decision to send aid to those affected (Acts of the Apostles 11:27–30). This is the "relief mission" referred to in today's reading (Acts of the Apostles 12:25). Emphasis, however, is given to the continued fruit of their mission of proclaiming the Gospel. We get a glimpse of the importance of prayer and fasting for ministers in the early Church. This disposes them to receptivity to the Holy Spirit. Note also the sacramental gesture of the laying on of hands as a way of designating persons chosen by God.

◆ RESPONSORIAL PSALM 67 calls all nations to praise the Lord. The Psalm prays that God's ways be known upon the earth. This wish is fulfilled through the proclamation of the Gospel.

◆ GOSPEL: Today's Gospel speaks of the intimate union and solidarity of the Father and the Son. To believe in Jesus is to believe in God. To see Jesus is to see God. To hear Jesus is to hear the Word of God. Jesus, sent by the God of life and light, comes to bring life and light to all.

The Roman Missal

If the optional memorial is observed, the Collect is found in the Proper of Saints, with the remaining prayers drawn from the Common of Martyrs: For One Martyr During Easter Time or of Pastors: For One Pastor.

Today's Saint

Saint Fidelis was a German Capuchin. His baptismal name was Mark, but when he joined the order, he took the name Fidelis, which means "faithful." Fidelis was known for his charity and prayer, and when he became superior of a Capuchin friary, many in the local area returned to Catholicism as a result of his influence. At the behest of the Habsburgs, who ruled parts of Europe at the time, Fidelis went to the north of France to reconvert the people there. Although he was protected by Austrian soldiers, he was captured by Calvinists, who murdered him when he refused to renounce his faith.

THU 25 #555 red
Feast of Saint Mark, Evangelist

Lectionary for Mass

◆ FIRST READING: We hear of Mark in the closing greeting of Peter's letter. In the preceding verses, Peter exhorts believers to humility, to trust in the Lord, to discipline and vigilance, and to being on guard against the devil. Heavenly glory awaits us after our suffering.

◆ RESPONSORIAL PSALM 89: Through their written accounts of the Gospel of the Lord, the evangelists did indeed sing the goodness of the Lord. Their words are light through which we may walk in the light of the Lord's countenance, rejoicing in his name all the day.

◆ GOSPEL: The Risen Christ commissions his Apostles to proclaim the Gospel to the whole world, promising them the assurance of signs and wonders as confirmation of their message. Having sent the Apostles as his messengers, the Risen Christ ascends to heavenly glory.

The Roman Missal

The prayers for the feast are found in the Proper of Saints. The Gloria is said or sung today. Preface II of Apostles is used.

In the Collect we pray that we may learn from the Gospel according to Mark to "follow faithfully in the footsteps of Christ." The Prayer over the Offerings is a prayer for the Church, that she may "always persevere / in the preaching of the Gospel." We pray that the Communion we have received may make us strong in the faith which Saint Mark proclaimed (Prayer after Communion).

Today's Saint

According to tradition, Matthew and John were Apostles. Mark was not, although he could have been an eyewitness to the events he describes in his Gospel. He is thought to have been a friend and disciple of Peter, and we know from New Testament references that he ran into some difficulties with Paul. We know that his account of the Gospel of Jesus Christ was written in Rome between 60 and 70 AD, following the martyrdom of Peter and Paul. Mark's symbol is a winged lion, an allusion to the desert wilderness with which his Gospel begins. Mark is the patron saint of Venice, and his relics are venerated in the great cathedral of San Marco.

FRI 26 #283 white
Easter Weekday

Optional Memorial of Our Lady of Good Counsel / white (Canada)

Lectionary for Mass

◆ FIRST READING: Today's First Reading is a continuation of Paul's address to the Jews and Gentile "God-fearing" in the synagogue at Antioch. Drawing upon the history and Scriptures of Israel of old, Paul demonstrated that Jesus is the fulfillment of God's promises. Psalm 2, cited at the end of today's text, is a royal Psalm extolling the special relationship God established with the anointed Davidic king, now his son, a text eminently fulfilled in Jesus.

◆ RESPONSORIAL PSALM 2: God has established his Anointed One and made firm his rule. All kings and rulers of the earth must hear, understand, and respond accordingly.

◆ GOSPEL: This text, which is part of the Last Supper discourse, points to Jesus's death. In it, Jesus speaks of his return to the Father. This was Jesus's way, and it is ours as well. How comforting it is to know that he will journey with us, taking us to himself.

The Roman Missal

◆ COLLECT: We pray that all who have been redeemed by the blood of Christ may have life and protection from God, "author of our freedom and of our salvation."

Today's Optional Memorial

Today in Canada the Blessed Virgin Mary is honored under the title Our Lady of Good Counsel. In this well-loved image, Mary embraces the child Jesus, who has his arm around her neck. She seems to be leaning down to hear what the Child Jesus has to say—to listen to his words of "good counsel." The original image is found in Genazzano, near Rome, but the devotion has spread all over the world. Many schools, colleges, and parishes are dedicated to Our Lady under this title, and Pope Pius XII was devoted to Our Lady of Good Counsel. Our Lady of Good Counsel, pray for us, and for the people of Canada.

S A T 27 #284   white
Easter Weekday

Lectionary for Mass

◆ FIRST READING: What conflicting emotions pervade today's reading: the jealousy and vengeance of some of the Jews toward the Apostles in their proclamation of the Gospel, the joyful acceptance of those who believe, and the disciples' joy in the face of persecution. At the heart of it all is the conviction that the call, the command, to proclaim the Gospel comes from the Lord, whose salvation extends to Gentiles as well as Jews, offering eternal life to any who believe.

◆ RESPONSORIAL PSALM 98: This universal offer of salvation is proclaimed in today's Psalm. God is king of all nations: God has fulfilled his promises to the Jews and stretched out his loving embrace to people of *all* nations.

◆ GOSPEL: Today's Gospel focuses on the Father, and more specifically, Jesus's relationship with the Father—a unity so complete, that to see Jesus is to see the Father; to hear Jesus is to hear the Father. The Father works in and through Jesus. Jesus invites his disciples to allow

his work to continue in them, through their union with him, and through prayer in his name.

The Roman Missal

◆ COLLECT: We pray that what we do today—"our present observance" of the Paschal Mystery of Christ—may benefit us for eternity.

☀ 28 #54   white
Fifth Sunday of Easter

Orientation

"As I have loved you, so you also should love one another" (John 13:34). The love we have known through Jesus Christ is the most profound and unconditional divine gesture. This love accepts us in our iniquity and offers the first step toward reconciliation; it is a hopeful love that sees not what we have done but the best we are capable of. It sees in us our God-given beauty and dignity, even if we are unaware of this ourselves; thus, it is a joyful love that celebrates the life and spirit of each of us. Above all, it is an enduring love, a love that never fails and remains with us through thick and thin as a lifeline of grace. The love of God in Jesus Christ, the cause and culmination of his self-gift, continues to surround us in the genuine relationships we share with others. To love as Jesus did not only binds us to one another, but also evokes the Holy Spirit in our midst.

Lectionary for Mass

◆ FIRST READING: Again and again in the stories of Acts of the Apostles we hear of the trials and sufferings endured by the first Christian missionaries because of their proclamation of Jesus. A perusal of chapters 13 and 14 of Acts of the Apostles reveals that such was the case in each of the cities named in today's reading. These first missionaries realized that hardship was an inevitable, indeed necessary, part of Christian discipleship. Such had been, after all, the way of their Lord and master. The Gentiles' faith in Jesus seems to have been one of the most unexpected happenings in these early days, despite numerous Old Testament texts which point to it. This, too, became cause for rejoicing and praising the Lord.

◆ RESPONSORIAL PSALM 145: This hymn of praise celebrates the goodness of the Lord to all. We hear this today with reference to the first Jewish Christian missionaries, who spoke of the glories of God's kingdom not only to the Jews, but also to the Gentile "children of Adam."

◆ SECOND READING: Throughout Easter Time, we celebrate the passing away of the reign of death and the new creation of life eternal with God. The vision of John we hear today looks to fulfillment in the full realization of the new creation at the end of time when all is transformed and made new.

◆ GOSPEL: The first part of today's Gospel, spoken by Jesus to the disciples at table with him the night before he died, takes us back to the painful moment of Judas's betrayal and Jesus's imminent death on the cross. In John, this is the moment of Jesus's glorification. This same reality must be lived out by his missioned disciples, as we heard in today's First Reading. It is interesting to hear the "love commandment," the second focus in today's Gospel, in these last days of Easter Time ("the little while") prior to Jesus's Ascension. To love one another as Jesus loved them is the parting command that the Risen Christ gives us today.

The Roman Missal

We ask God to "constantly accomplish the Paschal Mystery within us," so that all the baptized may bear fruit and come to eternal life (Collect). The Paschal Mystery of Christ's life, Death, and Resurrection is not something that happened: it is something that is happening.

.It is a "wonderful exchange" indeed that has made us "partakers of the one supreme Godhead"! And yet, that is what we are through our sharing in the Eucharist (Prayer over the Offerings).

Every day is Passover, in the sense that every day we are called "to pass from former ways to newness of life" (Prayer after Communion).

Other Ideas

At home and at work, look for situations in which you fall short of living out your convictions, or situations in which you live the Gospel in words, but not in deeds. Don't let the list get too long. Pick one item from the list that you want to work on so that what you say and what you do correspond.

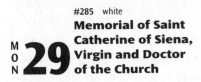

#285   white

Memorial of Saint Catherine of Siena, Virgin and Doctor of the Church

MON 29

Lectionary for Mass

◆ First Reading: Paul and Barnabas have two disparate experiences. On the one hand, the perceived threat to their lives in Iconium causes them to flee from the city. On the other hand, as a result of the miracle performed on the lame man at Lystra, they are hailed as the incarnation of Greek gods. Though mistaken in their conclusion, the people at Lystra were on to something. God *had* come in human form, but in Jesus of Nazareth. It is his Good News that is proclaimed by the disciples; it is the power of his name that brings healing.

◆ Responsorial Psalm 115: The words of today's text could well be the response of Paul and Barnabas to their experience in Lystra: Not to us, but to God give glory! In worshipping Zeus, the people bowed down to an idol. All people are called to acknowledge the true God, the creator of heaven and earth.

◆ Gospel: The Gospel today stresses the strong connection, almost identification, between loving Jesus and keeping his word or commandment, especially his commandment to love others. Jesus and his Father come to us in and through this love with a power and a presence that is gift and lasting presence.

The Roman Missal

The prayers for the memorial are found in the Proper of Saints. They speak of Catherine's "contemplation of the Lord's Passion" and her love for and service of the Church (Collect), and her extraordinary wisdom which continues to teach us (Prayer over the Offerings). The sacrament from which Saint Catherine drew life is the same "heavenly table / at which we have been fed" (Prayer after Communion).

Today's Saint

Catherine of Siena (1347–1380) was a Dominican tertiary and mystic, the twenty-fourth of 25 children. Against family opposition, she dedicated herself to Christ at a very young age. At 16 she withdrew from her family to lead a life of intense prayer. When she emerged, she began to dedicate herself to care of the sick and poor. Her joyful spirit attracted a number of followers.

After a series of mystical experiences, Catherine felt compelled to write letters to those in secular and Church authority, which she dictated to her friend, the Dominican Raymond of Capua. Her influence became so great that papal legates consulted her. At this time, the papal residence had moved from Rome to Avignon, France. Catherine begged Gregory XI to return to Rome, which he did in 1377. Saint Catherine died in 1380 at the age of 33, leaving behind her writings, *The Dialogue: A Treatise on Divine Providence*, letters, and prayers. She is represented in art holding a lily and wearing the habit of a Dominican tertiary, and is the patron of Europe and Italy. In 1970, Pope Paul VI made her a Doctor of the Church, one of the first women, along with Teresa of Avila, to be so honored.

#286   white

TUE 30

Easter Weekday

Optional Memorial of Saint Pius V, Pope / white ◆ *Optional Memorial of Blessed Marie of the Incarnation, Religious / white (Canada)*

Lectionary for Mass

◆ First Reading: Today's First Reading is a continuation of yesterday's reading. The arrival of some Jews who opposed Paul quickly puts an end to the worship he and Barnabas had almost received from the people at Lystra. In fact, Paul is stoned and left for dead. With the support of the disciples, he recovers, and he and Barnabas continue their journey proclaiming the Gospel. Note how they perceive all that happens as part of their following of Jesus. Note, too, their concern that each local community have leaders (presbyters) and that prayer and fasting are important in choosing and installing them.

◆ RESPONSORIAL PSALM 145: The antiphon "Your friends make known, O Lord, the glorious splendor of your kingdom" evokes Jesus's reference to his Apostles as "friends" (John 15:15). And certainly, Paul's and Barnabas's proclamation of the Gospel is a proclamation of God's kingship and kingdom.

◆ GOSPEL: Today's reading is a continuation of Jesus's "farewell discourse" at the Last Supper (see John 13–17). Peace is his farewell gift to his friends. Peace is their lasting inheritance from him. They must stay centered in this peace, not letting troubles or fears disturb it. He is returning to the Father, but he will come back to them and take them to himself (see John 14:3).

The Roman Missal

We ask for "constancy in faith and hope," so that we may never doubt the promises of our faith (Collect).

◆ U.S.A.: If the optional memorial is observed, the Collect is found in the Proper of Saints, with the remaining prayers drawn from the Common of Pastors: For a Pope.

Today's Saints

Saint Pius V (1504–1572) was a Dominican theologian, elected pope in 1566. His primary task as pope was to implement the reforms of the Council of Trent, which had concluded three years before. During his pontificate, seminaries were reformed, a new Missal was published, and the Catechism and Breviary were also revised. Pius retained his white Dominican habit when he became pope; since that time all the popes have worn white.

Marie of the Incarnation (1599–1672), was born in Tours, France. She married and bore a son. After her husband died, she devoted herself to religion and entered the Ursulines in 1620, first arranging for the care of her son. Around 1638, Marie experienced visions in which she was instructed to go to Canada and found a convent. In 1639, she set off with two other nuns, landing at Quebec in August and settling in the section of the city that is today called Lower Town. She studied with the Jesuits to learn the indigenous languages, becoming so proficient that she wrote dictionaries in Algonquin and Iroquois, as well as a catechism in Iroquois. She spent the last 33 years of her life teaching and catechizing. Marie of the Incarnation died in Quebec in 1672 and was beatified by Pope John Paul II in 1980. Her numerous letters are an indispensable resource for Canadian colonial history.

May
Month of Our Lady

W E D 1 #287 white
Easter Weekday

Optional Memorial of Saint Joseph the Worker (#559) white

Lectionary for Mass

◆ FIRST READING: The early chapters of Acts of the Apostles paint such idyllic pictures of the first Christian community, that we tend to forget that internal conflict was a part of their lives as well. Since Jesus and his first followers were Jewish, and Jesus as Messiah was the fulfillment of the promises of old, Gentile believers came as somewhat of a surprise. The question arose: must they become Jews (i.e., be circumcised) to be followers of Jesus? Consultation with the leaders of the community was needed.

◆ RESPONSORIAL PSALM: The house of the Lord, or Temple, is in Jerusalem. Psalm 122 is a pilgrimage Psalm, sung by pilgrims as they made their way to the city of Jerusalem where the Temple was located. The first Christians continued their observance of Jewish rituals and went daily to the Temple (see Acts of the Apostles 2:46).

◆ GOSPEL: This is the same Gospel as we heard on Sunday. In addition to the thoughts given in Sunday's reflection, we might also ponder the question: What does it mean for us to glorify the Father? What kind of fruit glorifies God? Notice that Jesus makes a connection between bearing fruit and *becoming* disciples in the last line of the Gospel. They had been with him for several years and were still becoming disciples. Why does Jesus speak of discipleship as something they, and we, become?

The Roman Missal

God has set us free "from the darkness of unbelief." We pray that he may guide us to him by the light of truth (Collect).

If the optional memorial is observed, the Preface and other prayers are found in the Proper of Saints. This Mass (in contrast to the Solemnity of Joseph, Spouse of the Blessed Virgin Mary, celebrated on March 19) points to Joseph as a model for all workers. Work is God's law, and we pray that with Joseph as our model and patron, "we may complete the works you set us to do" (Collect from the Proper of Saints).

Today's Saint/ Optional Memorial

Today you may celebrate the optional Memorial of Saint Joseph the Worker, a relatively new addition to the calendar. It was introduced by Pope Pius XII in 1955, as an alternative to secular May Day celebrations of the worker, which originated in Communist countries and which did more to promote Communist propaganda than to promote the worker. Pope Pius XII urged workers to look to Saint Joseph, the carpenter, and to see the dignity inherent in human labor, which could become a source of holiness.

THU 2 #288 white
Memorial of Saint Athanasius, Bishop and Doctor of the Church

Lectionary for Mass

◆ FIRST READING: Yesterday's reading continues. The solution to the dilemma caused by the Gentiles' reception of the faith and the question of circumcision does not come easy to the Jewish Christian leaders. "Much debate" (Acts of the Apostles 15:7) takes place. We hear the words of Peter and James, who insist that the Gentiles' faith is from God. Salvation comes through grace for all. According to this text from Acts of the Apostles, Gentile believers are asked to observe Jewish dietary laws, avoid idolatry, and refrain from marriage within the prohibited degrees of circumcision, but were not required to be circumcised.

◆ RESPONSORIAL PSALM 96, with its exhortation to proclaim God's salvation to all the nations (i.e., Gentiles), is a fitting response to today's First Reading.

◆ GOSPEL: Reflect on how deep is the love that the Father has for Jesus, how intimate the union between them. That, says Jesus, is the love that he has for each and every one of his disciples, regardless of nationality or ethnic origin. Disciples are to remain (to "live" or "abide," as the Greek verb is sometimes translated) in this love. Jesus also tells us the way to do it: keep his commandments.

The Roman Missal

The prayers for the memorial are drawn from the Proper of Saints. They recall that Athanasius championed Christ's divinity in a time when the Church was divided by heresies. We "profess, as he did, an unblemished faith" (Prayer over the Offerings) in "the true divinity of" Christ (Prayer after Communion).

Today's Saint

Saint Athanasius (293/6–373), bishop of Alexandria and Doctor of the Church, contributed immensely in the areas of doctrine and spirituality. In terms of doctrine, he defended the teaching of the First Council of Nicaea (325 AD) that Jesus was both fully human and fully divine. The Arians, who advocated that Jesus was not divine, unleashed a series of attacks on Athanasius, resulting in his exile not just once, but five times in his life. During one period of exile, he wrote a biography of the renowned hermit and monk, Saint Anthony of Egypt. This spiritual classic, entitled *Life of Antony*, continues to be a source of inspiration for people longing to remove worldly distractions that prevent them from mystical union with God. He is also noted for two other writings: *On the Incarnation and Discourses Against the Arians*. Many titles have been bestowed upon him, including defender of faith, champion of orthodoxy, mystical theologian, and spiritual master.

FRI 3 #561 red
Feast of Saints Philip and James, Apostles

Lectionary for Mass

◆ FIRST READING: Note that in this our earliest scriptural account of the Resurrection of Christ, a man named James is identified as someone to whom the Risen Lord appeared. We can easily become confused in trying to sort out "who's who" in the various appearances named, most of which we find recounted only by Paul. Are the James and the Apostles of verse 7 to be understood more broadly than the Twelve of verse 5? Paul used the term "apostle" with reference to himself and others who had not known Jesus before his Resurrection (see 1 Corinthians 15:9). The answer doesn't really matter. What is important is the experience of the Risen

Christ that gives rise to deep personal faith and becomes the impetus for the proclamation of the Gospel.

◆ RESPONSORIAL PSALM 19: Today's acclamation is an apt summary of the whole apostolic missionary endeavor, even though the verse itself comes from an Old Testament Psalm originally referring to creation as bearing witness to God's glory! The Apostles speak in this same tradition and to the ends of the earth, our own land included, and their voice resounds through the ages.

◆ GOSPEL: Today's reading singles out Philip, the one whose question at the Last Supper not only reveals his own lack of comprehension of Jesus's message, but also leads to further explanation and teaching from Jesus. May we, like Philip, ponder the words of Jesus our Master and take his words to heart.

The Roman Missal

The prayers for the feast are found in the Proper of Saints. One of the Prefaces of the Apostles is used. The Gloria is said or sung, and the Solemn Blessing of the Apostles may be used at the end of Mass.

The Collect asks for "a share in the Passion and Resurrection" of Christ through the prayers of Philip and James. The Communion Antiphon is taken from Philip's words to Jesus, and the Lord's reply: "Lord, show us the Father, and that will be enough for us. / Whoever has seen me, Philip, has seen the Father also, alleluia."

Today's Saints

Two of the chosen Twelve, Saints Philip and James (first century), grace the liturgical calendar today. Although few details are known about Saint Philip, Scripture portrays him as one who leads others to Christ. Saint Philip introduces his friend Nathaniel to Jesus, and points to Jesus as the source of nourishment in the feeding of the five thousand. He also highlights Jesus as the path to the Father in the Last Supper account. Saint James "the Lesser"—not to be confused with Saint James "the Greater" (he is honored on July 25)—was gifted with a special appearance of the Risen Christ (see 1 Corinthians 15:7). Throughout history it was believed that he authored the letter of James, but recent biblical scholarship considers this to be unlikely. Both Saints Philip and James died as martyrs, shedding their blood for the sake of the Gospel. They are most likely celebrated together because the Basilica of the Twelve Apostles in Rome is dedicated to them.

**S
A 4** #290   white
T Easter Weekday

Optional Memorial of Blessed Marie-Léonie Paradis, Virgin / white (Canada)

Lectionary for Mass

◆ First Reading: Perhaps the most striking point in today's reading is Paul's total openness to the direction of the Spirit of God in his ministry of preaching the Gospel (i.e., what to do, where to go). We witness his pastoral concern that there should be no stumbling block for believers. Today we meet Timothy, Paul's soon-to-be traveling companion and assistant.

◆ Responsorial Psalm 100: Our Psalm response once again reaches out to all lands and nations, calling all to know whose we are and to acclaim and serve him joyfully.

◆ Gospel: Today's Gospel is a grim message, in the midst of the many upbeat assurances we've heard in recent days: expect persecution and rejection. As Jesus was received, as he was treated, so will his disciples be. As the Father sent Jesus, so Jesus sends the disciples to continue his ministry.

The Roman Missal

Through Baptism, God gives us "heavenly life" and makes us "capable of immortality." We pray that we may "attain the fullness of glory" (Collect).

Today's Saint

Elodie (Marie-Léonie) Paradis was born in 1840 in the village of L'Acadie in the province of Quebec, Canada. Her parents were poor, but they wanted their daughter of have a good education, so they sent her to a boarding school run by the Sisters of Notre Dame. Elodie was so inspired by religious life that she asked to join the Sisters of the Holy Cross in 1854 and took the name Marie-Léonie. In spite of her youth and poor health, she was accepted by the founder, Basile Moreau, at the age of fourteen. At first her parents were against it, but they later accepted it, and she made her vows in 1857. After working in Canada as a teacher, she was sent to New York and later transferred to the Province of Notre Dame, Indiana. When the Holy Cross sisters dropped their ministry of serving priests by managing their households, Sister Leonie felt that the work to which she was called was no longer possible there. In 1880, under the direction of Father Camille Lefebvre, Blessed Marie-Léonie founded a new religious order, the Institute of the Little Sisters of the Holy Family, dedicated to assisting priests and seminarians by serving as housekeepers, and in 1896, the new order gained official recognition. In spite of poor health, which she suffered throughout her life, Blessed Marie-Léonie spent her life in service to her sisters and the people of God, finishing the Rule for her order just a few hours before she passed away on May 3, 1912 at the age of 71 in Nebraska. Since her death, her order has spread throughout Canada, the

United States, Rome, Honduras, and Guatemala. She was beatified by Blessed Pope John Paul II on September 11, 1984.

5 #57   white
**Sixth Sunday
of Easter**

Orientation

The Holy Spirit, the third person of the Trinity, is the life-force of the early Christian community, encouraging and empowering these disciples to solidify as a Church and to carry out their mission of proclaiming the Gospel. Today's Gospel passage refers to the Spirit specifically as Advocate, as Christ assures the disciples of the enduring presence of this Spirit, who will guide them in understanding and exploring the mysteries of the faith. The Spirit as Advocate evokes the image of a supportive voice, one seeking to protect and promote the rights and interests of another. It is a great comfort to us, as individuals and as a community of faith, to think of God's Spirit in this way.

Lectionary for Mass

◆ First Reading: One of the most pressing issues for the earliest Christian community, and indeed, the subject of the first church "council" as Acts of the Apostles tells the story, pertained to Gentile Christians. Jesus, his disciples and Apostles, and the first members of the Christian community were all

Jewish. Now the new community has to decide: Must Gentiles who come to have faith in Jesus also become Jews (i.e., be circumcised according to the law of Moses)? We hear today the decision of the Apostles and elders of the community: what is asked of Gentile believers is observance of dietary laws, avoidance of idolatry, and prohibition of Marriage within certain degrees of kinship, but not circumcision.

◆ RESPONSORIAL PSALM 67: This joyful hymn of praise acclaims God's salvation for all the nations (Gentiles) in each stanza and, indeed, in almost every line.

◆ SECOND READING: The universal theme is likewise found in the description of the glorious, heavenly Jerusalem, whose gates, marked with the names of the ancestors of Israel, open in every direction, toward all peoples. The walls of the city are inscribed with the names of the Apostles. Jesus, who brought salvation to all, is the fulfillment of the promises first made to Israel. The city gleamed with the glory of God who was its light, and the Lamb, who was its lamp.

◆ GOSPEL: The strong connection, almost identification, between loving Jesus and keeping his word is stressed. Jesus and his Father come to us in and through this loving obedience and dwell within us. Jesus tells his disciples here, the night before he dies, that the Father will send the Holy Spirit, an Advocate on their behalf, just as he had sent Jesus. The Holy Spirit will teach them and help them to remember all that Jesus told them. Jesus's farewell gift to them is a deep and abiding peace. His return to the Father should be a source of great joy. He has accomplished the mission for which he was sent. They will not be left alone.

The Roman Missal

◆ COLLECT: We pray that we may not only celebrate Easter, but live it, so that "what we relive in remembrance / we may always hold to in what we do."

◆ PRAYER OVER THE OFFERINGS: We pray that our prayers may rise up with our offerings, so that we may be transformed as they are, "conformed to the mysteries of your mighty love."

◆ PRAYER AFTER COMMUNION: We ask for an increase in the fruits of the Eucharist, which is the "paschal Sacrament."

Other Ideas

We see signs of new life all around us during this liturgical time. Pope Benedict has called us as Catholics to become more aware in our care and stewardship for the environment. How does your family or church act as a good steward for the environment? Do you recycle and reuse? Do you pass along things you no longer need? How else can you take the responsibility to heart?

As we prepare to celebrate the coming of the Holy Spirit at Pentecost, we celebrate the diversity of the many members of the one body of Christ. Visit a church other than your own. Participate in their celebration of the liturgy or evening prayer. Discuss with a group or reflect individually on how this parish is similar to your own and how it is different.

Individually or as group, decide on an issue of justice that needs attention. The Campaign for Human Development (sponsored by the United States Conference of Catholic Bishops), your parish bulletin, or diocesan newspaper or website will have some ideas. Decide how you can make a difference by doing such things as writing to your congressional representative, volunteering, or collecting goods. Be an advocate for something.

Find someone who is alone (for example, someone who is ill or in assisted living). Make a card or visit them. Let them know someone cares.

MON 6 #291 white
Easter Weekday

Optional Memorial of Blessed François de Laval, Bishop / white (Canada)

Lectionary for Mass

◆ FIRST READING: Continuing from Saturday's reading, we see Paul and his companions embarking for Macedonia (present-day Greece) and arriving at Philippi. Paul seeks out a Jewish community for prayer and encounters Lydia, the "worshiper of God" (which means God-fearing Gentile), the business woman and dealer in textiles. She obviously was a woman of prominence. She and her household, whose hearts were opened to receive the Word, came to faith through the proclamation of Paul.

◆ RESPONSORIAL PSALM 149: Though the word "delight" is not mentioned in today's First Reading, we can imagine the joy that filled Lydia's house, perhaps even with singing and dancing, as they celebrated a festive meal. Even so, how much greater is God's delight in his people.

◆ GOSPEL: In contrast to today's First Reading which speaks of people coming to the Word, today's Gospel warns against the dangers of falling away in the face of persecution. The Jewish-Christian/Jewish rift was so strong that in time, Jewish Christians were expelled from their synagogues by Jews of good faith and zeal for their ancestral traditions. Be prepared, says Jesus, and stay rooted in the spirit of truth.

The Roman Missal

We ask for "the fruit produced by the paschal observances," that Easter may have an effect in our lives (Collect).

Today's Saint

Blessed François de Laval (1623–1708), was the first Roman Catholic bishop of Canada. He was born in France, a member of the noble Montmorency family, who are believed to go back to pagan Gaul. In spite of its rank, the family was not wealthy, and when his older brothers were killed in battle, François inherited the responsibility for his family and interrupted his studies for the priesthood in order to arrange for their financial security. In 1658, he was appointed vicar apostolic for New France, as French Canada was then known. In spite of difficulties caused by politics, both ecclesiastical and secular, Bishop Laval traveled extensively, confirming hundreds, founding parishes, and instituting a seminary. Seeing the damage caused to indigenous peoples by alcohol, he worked to stop traders from paying them with liquor for their furs. As a result of his work, at the time of his retirement the number of parishes had increased from five to 35, the number of priests from 24 to 102, and the number of religious women from 32 to 97. He was known for his holiness, his spirit of poverty, and his generosity to the poor. Exhausted from his work, Bishop Laval died in 1708. The people immediately acclaimed him a saint. He was beatified by Blessed Pope John Paul II in 1980.

T U E 7 #292 white
Easter Weekday

Lectionary for Mass

◆ FIRST READING: Acts of the Apostles 16:16–21 is omitted by the Lectionary. These verses explain the reason for the imprisonment of Paul and Silas mentioned in today's reading. Paul had healed a demon-possessed slave girl who brought great profit to her owners. Enraged, they had them arrested for creating a disturbance. The high point of the story is not so much the miraculous opening of the prison, as the prisoners remaining in their cell and using the occasion to proclaim the Gospel to the jailer, who on hearing the word of the Lord, was baptized with all his household. Note the jailer's care of Paul and Silas and his household's rejoicing and celebration at having come to faith.

◆ RESPONSORIAL PSALM 138: Paul and Silas surely witnessed the saving power of the Lord in their experience of imprisonment and their jailer's conversion. It was indeed true cause for rejoicing and gladness.

◆ GOSPEL: Sadness fills the hearts of the Lord's disciples at the thought of his departure, yet he must return to the Father so the Spirit may be sent in his place.

The Roman Missal

The Collect is a simple prayer for a share in the Resurrection of Christ.

W E D 8 #293 white
Easter Weekday

Optional Memorial of Blessed Catherine of Saint Augustine, Virgin / white (Canada)

Lectionary for Mass

◆ FIRST READING: We hear of Paul's arrival in Athens (verse 15). The Lectionary omits verses 16 to 21 describing his distress at the sight of so many idols in the city and his debating with the local people. Yet Paul's approach is to meet them where they are, so to speak, using their cult of an unknown God as a springboard to proclaim the Good News of Jesus of Nazareth, thus making known the true God whom they had previously not known. He is the one in whom "we live and move and have our being" (Acts 17:28).

◆ RESPONSORIAL PSALM 148 is a song of praise. The heavens and the earth and all who dwell therein are called to praise the Lord. Note how Paul's speech to the Athenians echoes the themes of today's Psalm.

◆ GOSPEL: What is the truth that Jesus speaks of today? Why is it too heavy for the disciples to bear without the Holy Spirit? Today's Gospel leaves us pondering. How can we grasp the reality of the intimate communion of life and knowledge between the Father and the Son, and between the Son and the believer, in and through the Holy Spirit?

The Roman Missal

◆ COLLECT: Through the liturgy, we "celebrate in mystery" the Resurrection of Christ. We pray that when Christ comes "with all the Saints," "we may be worthy / to rejoice."

Today's Saint

Catherine (1632–1668) was born near Cherbourg, France. Her family was very devout, and she learned to care for the sick from her grandmother, who used to take invalids into her home. In 1644, Catherine entered the Augustinian Hospitaller Sisters, an order dedicated to caring for the sick. In spite of her family's opposition—her father even went to court to stop her—she volunteered for the mission in Quebec, and arrived there in 1648. Upon her arrival, she dedicated herself to working in the newly founded hospital, the Hôtel-Dieu de Québec. Throughout her life, Catherine suffered from physical illness and spiritual trials, which she offered for the new colony until her death in 1668 at the age of 36. She was beatified by Blessed Pope John Paul II in 1989.

THU 9 #58 white
Solemnity of the Ascension of the Lord
HOLYDAY OF OBLIGATION

In some dioceses, today is celebrated as an Easter Weekday (#294) white

Orientation: Ascension

Being clothed with power from on high foretells the coming of the Holy Spirit to fill the disciples with power to proclaim the Gospel at Pentecost. The image of being clothed also evokes a new start and a new look, a new way of being perceived. As the Holy Spirit filled the disciples, they seemed remarkably different to the people around them. Their divine mission shone through them, and they matured in their identity as Christians to take charge of their evangelizing mission. As Jesus ascends to heaven, the disciples are filled with joy in anticipation of this heavenly gift.

Lectionary for Mass: Ascension

◆ FIRST READING: In his introduction to the second volume of his work, Luke again begins by addressing the man who sponsored his work. He then picks up where his Gospel account left off, only with a slightly different chronology concerning Jesus's return to the heavenly realm. In Acts of the Apostles, this takes place after "forty days," that Biblically significant number. His point: the Apostles experienced the presence of the Risen Christ with them over an extended period of time. His parting words to them: "wait" for the promised Holy Spirit, later described as "power" (the Greek word is *dynamis*). The Holy Spirit is the "power" they will need to be his witnesses, not only to the Jews, but to the Gentiles as well.

◆ RESPONSORIAL PSALM 47: Returning to heaven, Jesus is enthroned at the right hand of his heavenly Father. Today's Psalm breaks forth in a joyful hymn of praise.

◆ SECOND READING: The Letter to the Hebrews speaks of Jesus's passage through death into life and his return to the heavenly realm as his entrance, as supreme high priest, into the heavenly tabernacle. Throughout the letter, Hebrews develops the theme of Jesus's sacrificial offering of himself and of his priesthood, as fulfilling and, indeed far surpassing, the priesthood and sacrificial rites of the Law of Moses. Jesus's self-sacrifice is a once-and-for-all sacrifice. What this means for us is confidence and hope, a point especially emphasized in the second part of the reading. We can and should be confident: Christ has opened the way for us.

Note that the Second Reading from Year A may also be used today. Saint Paul prays that the Christian community at Ephesus may receive "a Spirit of wisdom and revelation resulting in knowledge" (Ephesians 1:17). Knowledge and understanding will lead to hope in Christ, who has been raised and now sits at the Father's right hand. Christ has ascended but is still very present to them. As Saint Paul emphasizes, the Church herself is "the fullness of the one who fills all things" (Ephesians 1:23)

◆ GOSPEL: In his Gospel, Luke situates the Ascension on Easter evening, shortly after he appeared to the disciples and shared a meal with them (24:36–45). He interprets the Scriptures for them, showing that his Death and Resurrection have fulfilled them. He commissions them, but instructs them to wait until they receive the "power from high," that is his Holy Spirit. His final act toward them is blessing; theirs to him, adoration.

The Roman Missal: Ascension

There are two complete sets of prayers for the Ascension. Those for the Vigil Mass can be used on the afternoon or evening before the Solemnity, including at an anticipated Mass on a Saturday evening.

Vigil Mass

The lovely Collect asks that we may be worthy for Christ to live with us on earth, and for us to live with him in heaven, in keeping with his promise to be with us always.

The Prayer over the Offerings echoes Hebrews 4:16: since Christ, "our High Priest," is seated at God's right hand, we can "approach with confidence the throne of grace" and ask God's mercy.

Preface I or II of the Ascension is used. If you choose the Roman Canon, be sure to use the proper form of the *Communicantes*.

In the Pryaer after Communion, we pray that the sacrament we have received will "kindle in our hearts a longing for the heavenly homeland," so that we may follow where Christ has gone.

The Solemn Blessing of the Ascension of the Lord may be used.

Mass during the Day

The Collect is full of gladness, "holy joys," and "devout thanksgiving," because where Christ, "the Head," has gone, the Church, his Body, will follow. The alternate Collect is a prayer that our hearts and minds may ascend with Christ, who is "already in heavenly realms" and dwell with him there in spirit.

Through the "holy exchange" of the Eucharist, we pray that "we, too, may rise up to the heavenly realms" where the ascended Christ has gone (Prayer over the Offerings).

Preface I or II of the Ascension is used. If you choose the Roman Canon, be sure to use the proper form of the *Communicantes*.

Even on earth, God gives us the "divine mysteries" to celebrate. We pray that hope may lead us to heaven, where our humanity is one with God's divinity in our risen and ascended Lord (Prayer after Communion).

The Solemn Blessing of the Ascension of the Lord may be used.

Other Ideas: Ascension

Every Mass ends with our being sent forth on a mission. Help your child listen for this sending forth. What words are used? How can we live out this mission? Discuss how the liturgy prepares us for this important undertaking. Talk about how we're fed, body and soul, on the Word, and how the Eucharist strengthens us for this task. Do we burst forth from our spiritual revival at Mass, on fire with desire to spread the Good News and prepare for Christ's return? Can everyone see that we're on a mission?

Lectionary for Mass: Easter Weekday

◆ FIRST READING: Paul is depicted as an ordinary working man, practicing his trade to make a living. Like the other early Jewish Christians, he continues to attend services in the synagogue and uses this as an occasion to testify to the fact that Jesus is the Christ (Messiah). Meeting with opposition, Paul decides to devote himself totally to the Gentile mission. Note the introduction of Aquila and Priscilla, Jewish Christians who shared Paul's trade. They will come to figure prominently in the ministry of evangelization.

◆ RESPONSORIAL PSALM 98: The Lord's faithfulness to Israel is manifest in the arrival of the promised Messiah, Jesus Christ. His salvation is now made known to all nations (Gentiles) through the missionary activity of the first Jewish Christians.

◆ GOSPEL: We should find comfort in knowing that even Jesus's first disciples had trouble understanding his words! Perhaps part of discipleship is precisely that: to be willing to stand in the mystery, pondering it in our hearts. Absence, sorrow, and grief are givens. But Jesus promises that the "grief will become joy" in the mystery, in the manner that is his.

The Roman Missal: Easter Weekday

God has made us "partakers in . . . redemption." For so great a gift, we should "perpetually render thanks" (Collect).

Optional Memorial of Saint Damien de Veuster, Priest / white

Lectionary for Mass

◆ FIRST READING: Today's reading, a continuation of yesterday's, contains important information which may be missed if the Ascension was celebrated yesterday. First is the introduction of Aquila and Priscilla, the husband and wife who shared Paul's tent-making trade. Paul stayed and worked with them for a year and a half in Corinth. He continued his ministry of proclaiming the Gospel in the synagogues. Eventually—and here is where today's reading begins—opposition to Paul arises. As was the case with Jesus, the civil authority found nothing with which to charge Paul. Are we surprised that the civil authorities did nothing when the innocent Sosthenes, the synagogue official, is beaten by the Jews, presumably for allowing Paul to teach the Gospel among them? How many, in our own day, are charged unjustly and suffer undeservedly on behalf of the Gospel?

◆ RESPONSORIAL PSALM 47: Our Psalm is the same as we had on the Ascension. We are reminded that God is king, more powerful than any ruler on earth. All will one day be subjected to him.

◆ GOSPEL: In his last discourse to his disciples in John's account of the Gospel, Jesus speaks of the pain and anguish they will experience at his Passion and perhaps at their own as well. It is a life-giving pain, however; that is the nature of the Paschal Mystery.

The Roman Missal

Notice that there are two options for the Collect today, to be used depending on when the Solemnity of the Ascension of the Lord is observed.

If the optional memorial is observed, the Collect is found in the Proper of Saints, with the remaining prayers drawn from the Common of Pastors: For Missionaries.

Today's Saint

Saint Damien Joseph de Veuster of Moloka'i: After years of missionary work in the Hawaiian Islands, Damien (1840–1889), a young priest from Belgium, sought to align himself even more with the "crucified" in society. He requested to be stationed on the island of Moloka'i where the lepers and diseased were sent to die. Outraged by the deplorable conditions of the island, he sought to restore a sense of dignity. Within a short period of time, the sick were living in clean houses instead of caves, and upon death they were given a proper burial rather than being dumped into mass graves. Even though leprosy was highly contagious, he chose to remain in close contact with the people. Damien eventually contracted the disease and died from it. He was recently canonized by Pope Benedict XVI on October 11, 2009.

SAT **11** #296 white
Easter Weekday

Lectionary for Mass

◆ FIRST READING: After briefly mentioning Paul's missionary travels proclaiming the Gospel and strengthening the disciples (for the sufferings they would endure), today's reading focuses on Apollos. This eloquent speaker was well-versed in the Scriptures and knew about Jesus and was zealous in his teaching. Recognizing his giftedness, and his ignorance about certain aspects of the Gospel message, Priscilla and Aquila took him aside and taught him. He received full support from the community to continue his apostolic activity on behalf of the Gospel.

◆ RESPONSORIAL PSALM 47: Again, we have the Ascension Psalm which celebrates God's kingship, and in the context of our liturgical cycle, the enthronement of Jesus in the heavenly realm.

◆ GOSPEL: We hear the promise of Jesus, the reminder in this post-Resurrection time: ask and we will receive. In his last words to his disciples before his Death, Jesus speaks of his return to the Father. Ask and we will receive. He desires that our joy be complete.

The Roman Missal

Notice that there are two options for the Collect today, to be used depending on when the Solemnity of the Ascension of the Lord is observed.

When he ascended into heaven, Christ promised his Holy Spirit to the Apostles. We ask for a share in those same "spiritual gifts" (Collect).

12 #61 white
Seventh Sunday of Easter

In some dioceses, today is celebrated as the Solemnity of the Ascension of the Lord. Please see above on May 9 for commentary. What follows pertains to the Seventh Sunday of Easter.

Orientation

Jesus's prayer to the Father in this passage transcends the Gospel narrative and touches our lives directly. After reading it one cannot help but feel the stirring of the Holy Spirit, pointing to one truth: Jesus prayed to his heavenly Father with all his future followers in mind, including you and me. Millennia before our present day, Jesus Christ already held us in his heart and offered us in prayer to God—this is a truly mysterious and amazing thing to ponder. To be a Christian is to enter into this living mystery, which reaches out to embrace us from Christ's earthly time in our midst. Before we begin to imagine ourselves in the presence of Jesus Christ, we are already held by his love.

Lectionary for Mass

◆ FIRST READING: Today's first reading from Acts of the Apostles recounts the death of Stephen, the first martyr in the church. It is an interesting choice for this second to last Sunday of Easter Time. Perhaps Stephen's vision of God's glory prompted its choice since Jesus prays in today's Gospel that his followers will see the glory which the Father has given him. This is precisely what Stephen sees in his vision. Stephen's death and Jesus's reception of his spirit, marks the completion of his journey to his heavenly home. So it will be for us.

◆ RESPONSORIAL PSALM 97: Today's Psalm celebrates God's kingship. Although kingship is not specifically mentioned in today's first reading, it is implied: e.g., Jesus, standing at the right hand of God. The language evokes the prophet Daniel's vision of the exaltation of the Son of Man.

◆ SECOND READING: The verses chosen for today's reading come from the end of Revelation, a book filled with descriptions of heaven and of the rewards given to those who are judged righteous after their death. Note the names given to Jesus, especially Alpha and Omega: these very words are used in the preparation of the paschal candle at the Easter Vigil. Note also the prominence of the word "come." Jesus promises to come soon. The Church prays, "come, Lord Jesus." How deep is our longing, our prayer, for his coming?

◆ GOSPEL: Today's Gospel is set in the context of Jesus's last words to his disciples the night before he died. Here Jesus is speaking not only to the disciples, but to the heavenly Father. In his prayer, Jesus asks that his followers will be united as one, more specifically, as he and the Father are one. The unity of his followers will give witness to the world that the Jesus in whom they believe, and whose teachings they follow, was indeed sent by the Father. The unity of the Father and the Son, the love between the Father and the Son—this is the same unity and love that Jesus prays will be the experience and the witness of all who believe in him.

The Roman Missal

We believe that Christ has risen and ascended to his Father; in the Collect, we pray that we may experience his abiding presence in our midst.

We pray that the "acts of devotedness" we bring to God in the celebration of the Eucharist may help us to "pass over to the glory of heaven" (Prayer over the Offerings).

Use the Prefaces of Easter or of the Ascension.

The Ascension is a fact, and a promise of future glory, because we believe that "what has already come to pass in Christ," the Head of the Church, "will be accomplished in the body of the whole Church" (Prayer after Communion).

Other Ideas

Include in your family prayers intercessions for the Church, the nations of the world, your local community, and the poor, sick, and lonely. Include individuals you personally know who are in special need at this time, and all those whose needs are known to God alone. Use the same pattern of response that's used in your parish.

MON 13 #297 white
Easter Weekday

Optional Memorial of Our Lady of Fatima / white

Lectionary for Mass

◆ FIRST READING: Faith is a process of growth, as today's account of the Ephesian disciples makes clear. Coming to faith needs the assistance of others who will proclaim a word and minister a moment of sacred encounter with the Lord.

◆ RESPONSORIAL PSALM 68: Sing to God all nations—God gives a home to the forsaken, a home through faith and the indwelling presence of God in our life.

◆ GOSPEL: That you might have peace in me, despite the troubles, despite the sense of abandonment and confusion. Peace is the gift the Risen Christ desires for all. He was not alone in the time of his anguish and suffering, for the Father was with him. Neither are we alone.

The Roman Missal

If the optional memorial is observed, the Collect is found in the Proper of Saints, with the remaining prayers drawn from the Common of the Blessed Virgin Mary.

Today's Optional Memorial

The Blessed Virgin Mary appeared to three shepherd children (Lucía dos Santos and her cousins, Francisco and Jacinta Marto) at Fatima, Portugal, starting on May 13, 1917.

World War I was raging at the time, and Our Lady asked the children to say the Rosary every day for world peace. Devotion to the Blessed Virgin Mary under this title (Our Lady of Fatima) became important after World War II at the onset of the Cold War. One of Our Lady's requests was the consecration of Russia to her Immaculate Heart. Francisco and Jacinta (beatified in 2000 by Pope John Paul II) died during the influenza epidemic of 1919, but Lucía became a Carmelite nun and died in 2005 at the age of 91.

TUE 14 #564 red
Feast of Saint Matthias, Apostle

Lectionary for Mass

◆ FIRST READING: After Jesus's Ascension, the men and women who followed him gathered together in prayer. Peter recognized the need to find a replacement for Judas among the Apostles and cited scriptural evidence in support. The qualifications: the person should have accompanied Jesus during his time on earth, from his baptism until his Ascension. Notice the petition of their prayer: "You, Lord . . . show which one . . . you have chosen." It is the Lord who chooses; the praying assembly must be open and receptive.

◆ RESPONSORIAL PSALM 113: Matthias, counted among the twelve leaders of God's people, gives new meaning to the words of this song of praise. Notice the reference to the enthroned Lord in the third stanza, now understood with reference to Jesus.

◆ GOSPEL: The one sent in Jesus's name must be centered (remain, dwell) in Jesus's love. Here is the source of joy, the sustenance needed for bearing fruit. It is Jesus who has chosen that person to be friend, to be messenger, to love as he or she is loved by Jesus.

The Roman Missal

The prayers for the feast are found in the Proper of Saints. The Gloria is said or sung today. One of the Prefaces of the Apostles is used.

The Collect alludes to the fact that Saint Matthias was chosen by lot to take the place of Judas among the Twelve. We pray that, through his intercession, we may "be numbered among the elect."

Today's Saint

According to the Acts of the Apostles (1:15–26) Saint Matthias (first century) was chosen as the successor to Judas. The Apostles selected him because he met the following two qualifications: he had been (1) a disciple from the time of Jesus's baptism to his Ascension and (2) a witness to Jesus's Resurrection. Historical details around his apostolic activity are vague, but there is some evidence that he may have preached in Judea and later in Cappadocia near the Caspian Sea. The apocryphal Acts of Andrew and Matthias speak of a mission to evangelize cannibals. Regarding his death, tradition has it that he was martyred at Colchis or Jerusalem by crucifixion, while artistic representations point to a death by axe or halberd.

WED 15 #299 white
Easter Weekday

Optional Memorial of Saint Isidore / white

Lectionary for Mass

◆ FIRST READING: Today's First Reading is Paul's final commission to the leaders of the Church of Ephesus. Note the imagery used: the presbyters, or overseers, are to be vigilant shepherds who protect their flock. They are to help the weak and the poor. Significantly, they are to be built up by the word of God for the carrying out of their mission. Their deep love for Paul, their teacher and leader, is obvious.

◆ RESPONSORIAL PSALM 68: Today's Psalm invites all kingdoms of the earth, all peoples, to praise the Lord. God's power, mentioned in each stanza, is a particular reason for praise. Juxtaposed with today's First Reading, we are reminded of the power of the Holy Spirit operative in the Church's leaders (Paul included!) as well as the power of God's word in building them up.

◆ GOSPEL: Just as we are, Father, so may they be. Such is Jesus's prayer for his disciples. May they be united as one, filled with joy, consecrated in truth, and made holy.

The Roman Missal

If the optional memorial is observed, the Collect is found in the Proper of Saints, with the remaining prayers drawn from the Common of Holy Men and Women: For One Saint.

Today's Saint

Today we honor Isidore the Farmer, rather than the Doctor of the Church, Isidore of Seville, whose April 4 memorial falls on a Sunday this year. Isidore the Farmer was born in Madrid to poor parents who sent him to work for a landowner. He was very devout and married a like-minded woman, Maria, who also became a saint. Isidore attended daily Mass and was often late arriving at the fields, but he managed to get his work done nonetheless. He shared the little he had with the poor. He is the patron of farmers; it is fitting to remember him in the northern hemisphere's agricultural season.

THU 16 #300 white
Easter Weekday

Lectionary for Mass

◆ FIRST READING: The Lectionary skips over chapter 21 and much of chapter 22 of Acts of the Apostles. It picks up with Paul in the hands of the Roman cohort in Jerusalem, after having nearly caused a riot when he went into the Temple area. Though perplexed as to what Paul had done, the cohort commander convenes the Jewish leaders trying to get to the truth. Quite cleverly, Paul manages to set the Pharisees and the Sadducees, two sects within Judaism with opposing views on the Resurrection, against one another. Such an argument ensues that the Roman becomes Paul's rescuer. In the midst of it all is the Lord's word to Paul: "Take courage. For just as you have borne witness to my cause in Jerusalem, so you must also bear witness in Rome" (Acts of the Apostles 23:11).

◆ RESPONSORIAL PSALM 16: This prayer of confidence is most fitting. The word Paul received from the Lord during the night is nothing less than the counsel of the Lord spoken of in the second stanza. Acts of the Apostles presents Paul as having a clear picture of the suffering and death which awaits him in Rome. In light of Christ's Resurrection, he knows that he will enjoy life and joy in God's presence forever.

◆ GOSPEL: Jesus's prayer embraces disciples in every age, including us! Do we grasp the significance of what he says? Of who we are? Note how many times the word "one" occurs. Jesus prays first and foremost for the unity of his followers. How is that unity realized among us today?

The Roman Missal

◆ COLLECT: As we draw nearer to Pentecost, our prayers are full of the Spirit. We pray that we may be powerfully imbued "with spiritual gifts," that our minds may be pleasing to God and our lives conformed to his will.

F
R 17 #301 white
I **Easter Weekday**

Lectionary for Mass

◆ FIRST READING: Paul is in Caesarea, having been secretly transported there by the Romans for his protection. They continue to be baffled by the Jews' accusations against him (see Acts of the Apostles 23:12–35). Paul is led before one ruler after another. The heart of the controversy is Paul's proclamation of the Resurrection. Today's reading simply advances both the story and the journey to Rome.

◆ RESPONSORIAL PSALM 103: This song of praise with its mention of the Lord's enthronement fittingly follows today's First Reading; first, because of Acts of the Apostles' implicit reference to the Resurrection and Ascension of Christ and, second, because of the contrast between the thrones of earthly rulers before whom Paul stands now, and the throne of God, before which Paul one day, at the conclusion of his earthly journey, shall stand.

◆ GOSPEL: Today's Gospel focuses on Peter's destiny, one which is similar to Paul's in that both will be martyred because of their witness to Jesus. Peter's death, like that of Jesus, would glorify God. Peter receives a triple commission to shepherd Jesus's flock (paralleling his earlier threefold denial?). Today's Gospel ends with the command and invitation to "Follow me" (John 21:19). The way of the disciple can be none other than the way of Jesus.

The Roman Missal

Through Christ's Resurrection and the Spirit's light, "the gates of eternity" stand open before us. We pray that our sharing in God's great gifts may deepen our devotion and strengthen our faith.

S
A 18 #302 white
T **Easter Weekday**

Optional Memorial of Saint John I, Pope and Martyr / red

Lectionary for Mass

◆ FIRST READING: Today's reading, the conclusion of the Acts of the Apostles, ends on a rather open-ended note. Paul is under house arrest in Rome, awaiting his trial before the emperor. His ministry of proclaiming the Gospel continues unimpeded, his very imprisonment perhaps being at its service. Can we, like Paul, see the potential for all things in our lives to work for good, to be an occasion for speaking and living the Gospel message?

◆ RESPONSORIAL PSALM 11: Today's responsorial antiphon echoes the theme of Paul's righteousness and of his innocence of the charges against him. Although Paul is in the hands of human courts, the judgment of the Most High is what ultimately matters. Those who are just and upright will see the face of God.

◆ GOSPEL: We might also think of today's Gospel as having an open ending. It begins with a typical Petrine comment. When seeing the beloved disciple following them, Peter, having just heard about the nature of his own death, asks Jesus what will happen to the beloved disciple. What good advice Jesus's comment is for us all. He basically says to Peter, "Never mind! Just follow me—that's more than enough for you to do!" A second main concern of these closing verses of John's Gospel account is to verify the authenticity of the witness, the author of the Gospel.

The Roman Missal

If the optional memorial is observed, the Collect is found in the Proper of Saints, with the remaining prayers drawn from the Common of Martyrs: For One Martyr or of Pastors: For a Pope.

Today's Saint

The papacy of Saint John I (+526) took place amid the Arian controversy. King Theodoric the Goth, an Arian ruler tolerant of Catholics, employed the help of John in trying to negotiate an end to the persecution of Arians in the Eastern part of the empire. John went to Constantinople to present the demands of Theodoric to Emperor Justin I, the initiator of the persecutions. Justin agreed to all of the demands except allowing Arians who had converted under pressure to return to their heretical ways. The king was infuriated that John failed in his attempt to bring about resolution; therefore, he sentenced him to prison where he eventually died. Saint John is not only revered as "a victim for Christ," but also remembered for introducing the Alexandrian system of calculating the date of Easter.

☀ **19** #62 or 63   red
Solemnity of Pentecost

Orientation

As the 50 days of celebrating Christ's Resurrection comes to a close today, another new beginning bursts forth powerfully into our lives: the coming of the Holy Spirit. Pentecost recalls and makes present in our lives the advent of the Spirit, which empowered the followers of Christ to proclaim the Gospel message and carry it throughout the world. Reminiscent of the confusion of tongues at the tower of Babel, the Spirit restores God's order at Pentecost by empowering the Apostles to communicate the Good News of God's salvation to all without the hindrance of language barriers. Truly, the Spirit demonstrates God's power to teach and communicate to all. Pentecost invites us to consider the movement of the Spirit in our own lives as well: in Baptism and Confirmation we have welcomed the Spirit, who continues to vivify the Christian life, thus enabling us to proclaim the Good News today.

Lectionary for Mass: Vigil

The commentary below was written by Paul Turner © 2012, LTP.

◆ FIRST READING OPTIONS: The Lectionary provides four optional First Readings for the Vigil Mass of Pentecost. These comments will focus on the reading from the Book of Genesis. This is the first time since the Easter Vigil that we hear a text from the Old Testament. The Church's liturgy during Easter focuses our attention on the unfolding story of the power of Christ's Resurrection. As we come to the end of Easter Time, the readings take us back to primeval salvation history. In Hebrew rhetoric, an author repeats a word or phrase for the sake of emphasis. Though slightly unclear in the English translation of this passage from Genesis, the Hebrew word for "language" or "speech" recurs five times, and of those, the phrase "the same language" appears twice (11:1, 6). Language, which had been the fundamental means of communication and communion, has become a source of confusion and disunity.

◆ RESPONSORIAL Psalm 104 is a hymn recounting the wondrous works of God and the wisdom with which God has ordered creation in harmony and goodness. The opening phrase, "Bless the Lord, O my soul!" (104:1), is a powerful expression of praise. The Hebrew word for soul, nefesh, refers to that part of the human person which sustains life and vitality, the life force within an individual. Here the psalmist is calling to his own inner being, that which gives and sustains his life, to lift up praise to God. The first three stanzas of the Responsorial Psalm give the psalmist's reasons for giving voice to this praise. The last stanza twice employs the word "spirit," in Hebrew, ruach. This word can variously refer to one's breath, the wind, or the spirit. In the Hebrew imagination, both human breath and the wind were

mysterious things. In Genesis 1:2, a mighty "wind" swept over the chaotic waters. In Genesis 2:7, the Lord God blew "breath" into a mass of earth and it became a living being, Adam. Likewise in this verse, when God sends forth "spirit," things are created and the face of the earth is renewed. Such images from the Old Testament serve as a prelude to the act of new creation by which Jesus sends his Spirit upon Mary and the Twelve, and the people in Jerusalem to celebrate Pentecost.

◆ EPISTLE: Saint Paul writes about the human condition, specifically, our fragility and weakness in the lifelong process of growth into Christ. Yet as Jesus promised, he has not left us orphans (John 14:18–26). He has given us the Holy Spirit as the pledge of his presence, as a helper in time of distress, and as a guide to live faithfully as his disciples. This same Holy Spirit teaches us to pray, even when we feel our prayer to be inadequate. Saint Paul speaks of the Spirit who "intercedes with inexpressible groanings" within us (8:26). Paul is here referring to that ache we experience in prayer when we cannot even find words to wrap around what we know we should pray for, yet the feeling stays within us, almost haunting us. That is the Spirit praying in us, leading us to intercession, to praise, to gratitude, and to whatever might draw us into that intimate communion with God that is true prayer. Such a gift is reason for great hope and comfort.

This very short Gospel is packed with meaning appropriate to our celebration of Pentecost. "The last and greatest day of the feast" refers to the last day of the festival of Tabernacles, or Sukkoth in Hebrew. This feast commemorated the wandering of the Hebrew people in the desert on the way to the Promised

Land. It also eventually came to be associated with the end-of-the-year gathering in of the harvest. It was marked by seven days of grateful rejoicing for God's abundant goodness to them. So when Jesus exclaims, "Let anyone who thirsts come to me and drink," he is asserting that he has something far greater than what is being celebrated during these festive days. A new harvest of grace is to be received by those who believe. Jesus's words about "rivers of living water" (7:38) can be understood as a reference to Baptism, that initial sacrament which imparts the gift of the Holy Spirit. It is worthwhile to meditate on how the evangelist John has placed the Bread of Life discourse (John 6) immediately adjacent to this chapter on Baptism and the Holy Spirit.

Lectionary for Mass: Mass During the Day

The commentary below was written by S. Anne Elizabeth Sweet, osco © 2012, LTP.

◆ FIRST READING: Pentecost was one of the three pilgrimage feasts of the Jews, when all who were able came to the Temple in Jerusalem; thus, the presence of so many foreigners in Jerusalem that day. "All" the disciples were gathered in one place. Acts of the Apostles 1:13–14 identifies these disciples as the Eleven, Mary the Mother of Jesus, the women who journeyed with Jesus from Galilee to Jerusalem (Luke 8:1–3; 23:49), and his relatives. The cosmic sign of the strong driving wind attracted the crowd. (In Greek, the language in which Acts of the Apostles was originally written, the same word is used for both "wind" and "spirit.") Note also the sign of "fire." The fruit of the Spirit's presence and work is the disciples' ability to proclaim the Gospel in various tongues and be understood by those who heard them.

◆ RESPONSORIAL PSALM: As at the Vigil Mass, Psalm 104 is used, along with the same antiphon. There is some variation in the stanzas. Today's addition in the last stanza voices the desire that both God's glory and God's joy in his creation endure. The psalmist is intent on being "pleasing" to the Lord and finding joy in him. A beautiful theme for each of our lives!

◆ SECOND READING: Paul makes a sharp contrast between living according to the flesh (by worldly standards) and living according to the Spirit, the gift of God's presence, life, and power within us, received at Baptism. Note that this is the same Spirit, the same Power, that raised Jesus from the dead. That's powerful power! The Spirit within us also prays within us, as it gently leads us back to our God. The Aramaic word Abba is best rendered as "Daddy." How intimately God has united us to himself.

◆ GOSPEL: Twice in today's Gospel, the Holy Spirit is referred to as an "Advocate." The Greek word *paraklētos* means "one who intercedes or acts for the good of another." In other words, God's Holy Spirit continues Jesus's work on our behalf, the work of bringing us the fullness of life. Our job is to listen to the words spoken by God and obey them.

The Roman Missal

This great solemnity marks the conclusion of Easter Time. *The Roman Missal* includes prayers and rubrics for a solemn Vigil Mass, paralleling the Easter Vigil. This Vigil is optional, and a simpler Vigil, with the usual number of readings, may be celebrated instead.

Extended Vigil

The circular letter *Paschale Solemnitatis* says: "Encouragement should be given to the prolonged celebration of Mass in the form of a Vigil, whose character is not baptismal as in the Easter Vigil, but is one of urgent prayer, after the example of the Apostles and disciples, who persevered together in prayer with Mary, as they awaited the Holy Spirit" (PS, 107). The procession, Greeting, and Penitential Act or Sprinkling Rite take place as usual. Following the Penitential Act, the second Collect for the Vigil of Pentecost is said. Then the priest celebrant invites the people to "listen with quiet hearts" to God's words, pondering what God did for his people in times past, and praying for the gifts of the Spirit as Mary and the disciples did. (*The Roman Missal* also includes instructions for beginning the Vigil with First Vespers of Pentecost.) The Liturgy of the Word follows. It parallels the Easter Vigil, with the four readings alternating with Psalms and collects. Following the last Collect, the Gloria is sung. Then the Collect for the Vigil (first option) is prayed. The reading from Romans follows, and Mass proceeds as usual.

Vigil (Simple Form)

There are two options for the Collect of the Mass. The first echoes the Old Testament account of the confusion of tongues at Babel. We pray that from "the confusion of many tongues" may arise "one great confession" of God's name. The second is a prayer that, by the power of the Holy Spirit, the light of Christ may shine in the hearts of all reborn by the grace of Baptism (a nice echo of where this Easter Time began, with the solemn procession of the Paschal candle—Christ the light—in the darkness). In the Prayer over the Offerings, we ask God to send the Spirit upon the gifts we offer, and to fill the Church "with such love" that God's truth may "shine forth for the whole world." In the Prayer after Communion we pray that the same fire which burned in the disciples at Pentecost may burn in us as well.

Mass During the Day

The prayers for Pentecost Sunday have a different emphasis. The Collect asks for the Holy Spirit's gifts on the Church throughout the world, so that the hearts of believers may be touched, even as they were "when the Gospel was first proclaimed."

The Prayer over the Offerings echoes John 16:13: "But when he comes, the Spirit of truth, he will guide you to all truth." We ask the Spirit to "reveal to us more abundantly / the hidden mystery" of the sacrifice we offer, and "lead us to all truth."

The Preface, found with the other prayers in the Proper of Time, speaks of Pentecost as the "completion" of the Paschal Mystery. Through the Spirit, we are united with Christ and with each other.

In the Prayer after Communion, we ask God to "safeguard" the gifts he has given to the Church, so that "the gift of the Holy Spirit . . . may retain all its force," and the heavenly food by which the Church is fed "may gain her abundance of eternal redemption."

A splendid Solemn Blessing, invoking the enlightenment of the Holy Spirit on the assembly, is provided for this Pentecost Sunday.

The Easter Dismissal with its double Alleluia is used at the conclusion of all Masses of Pentecost.

The Roman Missal notes that in places where it is customary to attend Mass on the Monday or Tuesday after Pentecost (the so-called "Pentecost Monday" and "Pentecost Tuesday"), the Pentecost Mass may be repeated.

Other Ideas

Celebrate the Holy Spirit by wearing red to church today. Have a picnic, serving red foods on a red tablecloth, and light a red candle. Blow bubbles, fly a kite, make a windsock, or find other ways to enjoy playfulness in the wind and air. Breathe in deeply, and feel the air fill your lungs. The Spirit of God is closer to you than the air. Breathe in the love of God and breathe out anything that threatens to come between you and that love.

ORDINARY TIME DURING SUMMER AND FALL

The Meaning

Our journey of faith through the liturgical year returns to Ordinary Time. The Lectionary resumes with the continuous reading of the Gospel according to Luke. In many places, the return to Ordinary Time this year also coincides with the end of the school year and the beginning of summer break. The rhythms of life change for the summer and we find ourselves moving into a more relaxed mode. This can also be true in our celebration of the liturgical year, but it is also an opportunity to reflect more consciously on the meaning of Sunday as the Lord's Day.

The Sundays of Ordinary Time present us with the opportunity to let each Sunday nourish our faith life. This is a noble idea to ponder during the summer's Ordinary Sundays because for the Christian no time is "ordinary." Every day is "extraordinary" because every day God is acting in our lives. God is sustaining us. God is re-creating us.

Nothing is ordinary about people of faith who gather each Sunday to become who we are destined to be by virtue of our Baptism—the Body of Christ. Sunday is the original feast day, the only feast day for the Church in its first several hundred years following the death and Resurrection of the Lord. From the time of the New Testament, we have known it as the Lord's Day.

"On the first day of each week, which is known as the Day of the Lord or the Lord's Day, the Church, by an apostolic tradition that draws its origin from the very day of the Resurrection of Christ, celebrates the Paschal Mystery. Hence, Sunday must be considered the primordial feast day" (UNLYC, 4). In the slower and more relaxed pace of our summer days, our Sunday gathering for worship is a perfect opportunity to keep our focus on the Paschal Mystery of Jesus and living out that mystery in our everyday lives. In turn, we go forth into our world proclaiming the kingdom of God. This is not ordinary! We have the opportunity to do extraordinary things. The love and forgiveness of God celebrated in Christ every Sunday will help us to proclaim God's love and forgiveness in word and deed, to carry on what Jesus began. This is our extraordinary vocation. This is the power of Ordinary Time!

In the busyness that autumn can bring, our Sunday gathering for liturgy is a perfect opportunity to keep our eyes fixed on the presence of God and our ears attuned to his life-giving Word so that we are able to go forth into our world proclaiming and witnessing to his kingdom. This is not ordinary. We have the opportunity to do extraordinary things. The love and forgiveness of God celebrated in Christ every Sunday will help us to proclaim his love and forgiveness in word and deed until Christ comes again in glory. When we do this, we carry on what Jesus began. This is our extraordinary vocation. This is the power of Ordinary Time.

Fall can seem like a contradiction. We harvest the land, trees lose their leaves, and we prepare for winter. But at the same time, many individuals and families prepare for beginnings as a new school year or semester starts. As a Church, we continue Ordinary Time that we celebrate throughout the liturgical year, culminating with the final feast of the year, the Solemnity of Our Lord Jesus Christ, King of the Universe.

Over these weeks of Ordinary Time we will hear Jesus instruct his disciples about how they must act. Jesus often surprises religious authorities and disciples as he preaches, tells parables, heals those who are in need, and eats with sinners. He will speak of God's justice, having faith, and forgiveness. We will see where following Jesus leads when we celebrate Christ the King and hear Luke's account of the Gospel about Jesus's final act of forgiveness as he is dying on the Cross. Along with the disciples, there will be many times this season that we will hear Jesus's invitation to come after him. May we open our eyes and ears and listen carefully so that we may find our own way to follow him into the light.

The Roman Missal

ORDINARY Time offers many opportunities to explore the riches of *The Roman Missal*. On weekdays, the options for presidential prayers are almost endless. You can use the prayers for the current week, or for any of the Ordinary Sundays; you can also choose from a huge variety of Masses for Various Needs and Occasions and Votive Masses.

In the history of the liturgy, weekdays, especially the weekdays of Ordinary Time, were slow to develop a "liturgical character" of their own (Adolf Adam, *The Liturgical Year*, p. 52). When they did, they looked like a "faint copy of Holy Week" (Jungmann, quoted in Adam, p. 52). Just as every Sunday is a celebration of the Resurrection—in a sense, every Sunday is Easter—the other days of the week also came to reflect aspects of the Paschal Mystery. Wednesday and Friday, the days of Christ's betrayal and his Passion, acquired a penitential character. Thursday, the day of the Last Supper, became associated with the Eucharist and Christ's priesthood. Saturday was Mary's day. The 1570 Missal even assigned special devotions to Mondays (the Blessed Trinity) and Tuesdays (the Angels), thus giving a unique character to every day of the week.

In the current Missal, the Votive Masses are not limited to specific days of the week, as before, but can be celebrated on any weekday which is not an obligatory memorial, feast, or solemnity. Friday and Saturday, however, retain a certain special character. The Votive Mass of the Holy Cross, the Precious Blood, and the Sacred Heart are all especially appropriate for Fridays, and the Memorial of the Blessed Virgin Mary on Saturdays is still a well-loved aspect of the Church's prayer. *The Roman Missal* significantly expands the variety of Marian prayers. Eleven Masses are found in the Common of the Blessed Virgin Mary: eight for use during Ordinary Time and one for Advent, Christmas Time, and Easter Time. Three more are found among the Votive Masses: Our Lady, Mother of the Church, The Most Holy Name of Mary, and Our Lady, Queen of Apostles.

Please note that Votive Masses call for a change in liturgical color, and most have their own Preface. Just before the Votive Masses begin, *The Roman Missal* provides some details about when Votive Masses are, and are not, permitted.

The Masses for Various Needs and Occasions do not require a change in liturgical color (though you can heighten any celebration by using more festive vestments). During election season, you might choose #21, For the Nation or State, or #22, For Those in Public Office. After the election, or at a time of crisis, #24, For the Head of State or Ruler, may be used. The prayers for the Preservation of Peace and Justice (#30), especially in conjunction with one of the Eucharistic Prayers for Reconciliation, are powerful in times of conflict and division, whether on the local or the national scale. The prayers for Giving Thanks to God for the Gift of Human Life (#48/1), for Persecuted Christians (#19), for Those in Prison (#44), for Refugees and Exiles (#32), and for Those Suffering Hunger (#33), make us more aware of global concerns. There are prayers for more homey occasions, too: for anniversaries of Ordination (#7C) or Marriage (#11), for a Spiritual or Pastoral Gathering (#20), for Fine Weather (#36), at Seedtime (#27), and at Harvest (#28). Judicious use of these prayers during the long weeks of Ordinary Time can help us to widen our awareness and to embrace the whole world with our prayer.

The Lectionary for Mass

WE enter once again into Ordinary Time, on the heels of Easter Time, gifted with the Spirit's Pentecost gifts. Catholic tradition has long spoken of the gifts (see Isaiah 11:1–3a) and fruits of the Holy Spirit (see Galatians 5:22–23). If we are attentive, we find wonderful illustrations of these very gifts in the stories that the Lectionary sets before us in the weeks and months ahead.

The giftedness of our life in Christ is also highlighted by the solemnities and feasts we celebrate in this Ordinary Time's first few weeks. This year the readings for the Solemnity of the Most Holy Trinity focus on the Wisdom of God and the power of God's Spirit at work in our lives. We give thanks for the nourishment of God's life received in the Eucharist at every Mass, but in a special way on the Solemnity of the Most Holy Body and Blood of Christ the following Sunday. We commemorate as well the Body of Christ which we are called to become by virtue of his life within us and the working of the Holy Spirit. All is the gift of God's love, manifested in the Incarnation of Jesus, who was and is for us the Good Shepherd leading us to everlasting life, as we hear on the Solemnity of the Most Sacred Heart of Jesus on the Friday after the Solemnity of the Most Holy Body and Blood of Christ.

Each month we celebrate the feast of an apostle or evangelist who worked to spread the Good News of Jesus Christ and build up the Body of Christ, the Church: Saints Peter and Paul (June 29), Saint Thomas (July 3), Saint Bartholomew (August 24), Saint Matthew (September 21), Saint Luke (October 18), Saints Simon and Jude (October 28), and Saint Andrew (November 30). The Memorial of Saint Mary Magdalene, the Apostle to the Apostles with her announcement of the Resurrection of Christ, is celebrated on July 22. The seeds of their words and deeds have flourished, enabling us to receive the gifts God so desires to give us.

Our Gospel accounts throughout Ordinary Time, this year from the Gospel according to Luke on Sundays, set before us the ministry of Jesus and his teachings on discipleship. Do we see ourselves among those whom he desires to teach and to heal? Do we reckon ourselves among the "rich" who are called to share with those less fortunate? Are we aware of our own call to continue the spread of the Gospel by our words and deeds? Do we think of our own life as a journey with Jesus to Jerusalem, with many passovers through death into life with Christ, before that final passage into the glory of his heavenly kingdom?

Several of Ordinary Time's feasts focus our attention on those who have accomplished the passage from death to the fullness of life. We glimpse the glory that Jesus entered into on the

Feast of the Transfiguration (August 6). Preeminent among those who followed after him is, of course, his Mother Mary, whose Assumption we celebrate on August 15 (a solemnity). She enjoys already the fullness of resurrected life.

So many faith-filled witnesses have gone before us—a multitude from every age and every nation throughout the ages (All Saints, November 1). And then there are the saints we have known personally, and though not "officially" canonized, their witness of fidelity strengthens our own faith. We need these models of people ever open to the call of the Lord, whatever may be asked of them in "ordinary" life, thus making it an "extraordinary" time of grace for them. And so we turn to the Scriptures, particularly as found in the Lectionary, offering us both models and "mirrors" for our own life of faith and discipleship, and inviting us to be receptive to the power of God's Spirit at work in our lives. God's Pentecost gift is meant for each one of us!

In the seventh and eighth weeks, we hear Sirach's praise of Wisdom and his discussion of her role in the life of God's people. (The word for Wisdom is feminine in gender in both Hebrew and Greek.) We hear also Sirach's exhortation on how to live a life of service to the Lord in our daily lives.

In the ninth week we hear the story of Tobit, acclaimed for his piety and acts of mercy, particularly what we have traditionally called the corporal works of mercy. We hear both of his sufferings and the healing God rendered to him through Raphael, the angel who journeyed with his son Tobiah. (Archangels: Raphael, Michael, and Gabriel have a feast of their own on September 29.)

Paul's Second Letter to the Corinthians is read in the tenth and eleventh weeks, a letter which exhorts the gifted and prosperous to generous concern on behalf of others. Are we, too, not gifted and prosperous, especially in comparison with the many, many people throughout the world, and indeed in our own cities, with such great needs? We hear also in this letter Paul's testimony of the afflictions and endurance, the joys and personal transformation that have been part of his own ministry on behalf of the Gospel.

In the twelfth week, we return to the Old Testament, and to the story of God's people beginning with Abraham and Sarah in Genesis 12. Does not their openness to God's call as it manifests itself in daily life, and their willingness to respond, challenge us all? The Genesis accounts of the patriarchs and their families continue through the fourteenth week.

We are with Israel in Egypt in the fifteenth week and then on through the exodus, the Sinai experience, and the settlement in the land through the twentieth week. Can we see Israel's story as our own? Can we see our own life's journey reflected in their story? Our fidelity and infidelities in theirs?

At the end of the twentieth week, we read from the book of Ruth. It is a very short book, only four chapters. Ruth's story is marked by grief and poverty, and at the same time, by deep faith and loyalty. Widowed and having suffered the loss of her two sons, Naomi returned to Bethlehem with her Moabite daughter-in-law Ruth, who later married one of Naomi's kinsmen. They had a child, Obed, who was the father of Jesse who was the father of King David. Note that Ruth is one of the four women named in Matthew's genealogy of Jesus (1:5).

In the twenty-first week, we return to Paul's writings, beginning with 1 Thessalonians, his earliest writing with its concerns about those who have died and his expectations of an imminent return of the Lord. Then on to Colossians, a later letter, with its beautiful Christological hymn in the first chapter and its practical instructions on daily life throughout the letter.

An even later period of the early Church is the subject of the First Letter to Timothy, read in the twenty-third and twenty-fourth weeks. We hear of the concern for well-qualified ministers in the Church and of the threat posed by false teachers. All believers are exhorted to strive to lead "quiet and tranquil" lives "in all devotion and dignity" (Monday, twenty-fourth week).

It is back to the Old Testament in the twenty-fifth and twenty-sixth weeks, and jumping far ahead of where we left off (with the birth of King David's grandfather). The books of Ezra and Nehemiah deal with the Israelites' return to their own land around 539 after their time of Babylonian exile (Jerusalem was conquered in 586). One of the first tasks they undertook, as we hear from the books of Ezra, Nehemiah, and the prophet Haggai, was to rebuild the Temple in Jerusalem. It would be a place of prayer not only for Jews, but a place where the Gentiles would seek the Lord as well (so the prophet Zechariah).

In the twenty-seventh week we hear from several of the "minor" prophets, so-called because their works are much shorter than the "major" prophets (Isaiah, Jeremiah, Ezekiel, and Daniel). Jonah is a delightful tale about a prophet who tried to escape from his prophetic call by boarding a ship headed in the opposite direction from that to which he was called! He was not at all ready to see the Ninevites, the enemies of Israel, repent and be saved! The story challenges us to examine our own attitudes toward those who do wrong as well as to doing the difficult things the Lord asks. The prophets Joel and Malachi direct our thoughts to the coming Day of the Lord, a prominent theme in these last weeks of the liturgical year.

Returning to the New Testament in the twenty-eighth week, we read from the Letter to the Romans, Paul's longest, and for some, the most theologically developed letter. In many ways, it is a summation of many of the major teachings in his other letters: salvation by faith for both Jews and Gentiles, the presence and power of the Spirit in the life of a Christian, the gifts of the Spirit in the life of the community, and the behavior appropriate for Christians. In the concluding chapter of Romans—read on Saturday of the thirty-first week, Paul greets any number of people active in the church at Rome by name. Note well their names and roles: we may be surprised at the number of women who are named, including one who is called an apostle! Yes, the faith is spread, the church grows in numbers, and its members in holiness through fidelity in the ordinary activities of everyday life—an important message for us since most of the liturgical year, and most of our own lives, is "ordinary."

We return to the Old Testament and the Wisdom literature in particular, in the thirty-second week when we hear from the Book of Wisdom, dating from the second century before Christ and perhaps written in Alexandria (Egypt). We might think of it as a theological reflection on the nature of human life and destiny in relationship with God. The role of God's wisdom, at times personified, in human life and history is given special focus.

In the second century before Christ, the Jews in Palestine were enduring great suffering and distress under Greek rulers. In the thirty-third week, we hear the stories of those who lost their lives rather than disobey the law of God and of their attempts to resist and overthrow the Gentile and foreign rulers. Some of our readings from the Book of Daniel (the thirty-fourth week) stem from this same period. The second part of the Book of Daniel is apocalyptic in style and tone, giving us a "vision" of the events of the end time (see the readings for Friday and Saturday) and setting the stage for us to have this same focus as we begin the season of Advent once again.

The readings we hear throughout these weeks of Ordinary Time speak to us of both the linear and cyclical dimensions of human life and history, particularly salvation history. Yes, there is a chronological history and we are moving forward in time, awaiting the coming of the Lord in glory. At the same time, as the saying goes, history repeats itself—in recurring cycles. We hope there is a spiraling dimension as well to our "histories" both as individuals and as Church, that as we continue to hear the stories read we may hear them more deeply in our hearts and be continually transformed into the people God so desires that we become. May Ordinary Time be a time of "extraordinary" grace and growth for us all, through the power of God's Spirit, our wonderful Pentecost gift.

Children's Liturgy of the Word

Summer

It is important to remember that Sunday was always the Church's day of celebration even before the Church celebrated Easter or Christmas. Ordinary Time is the "season of Sundays," days which celebrate the Risen Christ among us. The *Constitution on the Sacred Liturgy* (106) states:

> By a tradition handed down from the Apostles and having its origin from the very day of Christ's resurrection, the Church celebrates the paschal mystery every eighth day, which, with good reason, bears the name of the Lord's Day or Sunday. For on this day Christ's faithful must gather together so that, by hearing the word of God and taking part in the eucharist, they may call to mind the passion, the resurrection, and the glorification of the Lord Jesus and may thank God . . . . Hence the Lord's Day is the first holy day of all and should be proposed to the devotion of the faithful and taught to them in such a way that it may become a day of joy and freedom from work.

Readings

The Tenth Sunday of Ordinary Time begins this segment of Ordinary Time. During the summer the Gospel stories of Luke unfold the public ministry of Jesus through his miracles and parables. Luke's emphasis on the people who were ordinarily excluded from Jewish society, such as Gentiles, widows, and sinners is very obvious as is his focus on the call and cost of discipleship. Both of these themes are relevant and interesting to young children. They want to be included and they know what it feels like to exclude or be excluded. They also need to be aware that following Jesus is not always easy. We go back to the Old Testament for the First Readings and their themes integrate with the Gospel readings.

Environment

The liturgical color is green. The banners and cloths on the lectern and prayer table should be green. Enthrone the Lectionary or *Book of the Gospels* along with a candle and clear glass bowl of holy water. Use fresh garden flowers for decoration. Create an environment of welcome for children who are vacationing or visiting relatives. Encourage children to bring their friends to join them at the Liturgy of the Word. Summer and the Liturgy of the Word with children are good opportunities for evangelization.

Music

For music selections use suggestions given in *Children's Liturgy of the Word: A Weekly Resource* from LTP or make music choices from your parish repertoire. If children are not familiar with the music, take a few minutes to go over the songs with them. When appropriate, use gestures with the songs or responses and have children follow with you.

Fall

The liturgical year follows the natural rhythms of life—periods of intense concentration and celebration followed by times of quiet reflection and maturation. Ordinary Time expresses the Church's faith outside the "high seasons" of Advent, Christmas Time, Lent, Sacred Paschal Triduum, and Easter Time.

The Sundays of Ordinary Time are numbered consecutively. Unlike the other liturgical times Ordinary Time does not always have the same number of weeks. It can be 33 or 34 weeks long depending on when Easter is celebrated.

The fall weeks of Ordinary Time coincide with the beginning of the school year. In many parishes Liturgy of the Word with Children is not celebrated in the summer months. While the Church is coming to the end of the liturgical year, many children and leaders of the celebrations are just beginning.

Preparation

◆ If this is the case, new leaders need some preparation and training about the celebrations. Important points to stress are:

◆ This is a catechetical liturgical experience, not a religious education setting. Stress the importance of creating an environment of prayer and reverence for the Word through processions to and from the assembly, enthronement of the Lectionary or *Book of the Gospels*, and times of quiet.

◆ Stress the importance of music in the celebrations. Music should be liturgically appropriate. Music serves the liturgy, and is not an addition. The music selection for children should follow the liturgy's various genres: acclamations, Responsorial Psalms, and hymns. Encourage leaders to use suggestions given in *Children's Liturgy of the Word: A Weekly Resource* from LTP or make music choices from the parish repertoire and explain what the different options are for live music during the celebrations and for support for those who are not musically inclined.

◆ Encourage leaders to help children break open the Word through dialogue and reflection on experience during the reflection/Homily as well as guided meditation. Use suggestions given in *Children's Liturgy of the Word: A Weekly Resource*.

◆ Show priest celebrants how to set up a worship space with a prayer table and/or lectern. Explain the use of different color cloths and banners for each liturgical time. If a classroom is being used give options for rearranging chairs and making the space appropriate for worship.

The Saints

IN Advent, Christmas Time, Lent, and Easter Time, the ferial prayers and readings most often take precedence over the saints' days, and rightly so. But in Ordinary Time, we are free to celebrate the saints. The saints of summer and fall come from every corner of the globe and from every era in history. They were missionaries, mystics, bishops, religious, and laypeople. Some were brilliant scholars, others humble laborers. But all these saints have one thing in common: each of them lived the Christian life remarkably well.

Celebrating them, we not only ask their intercession, but look to their example for help in living our faith more and more deeply.

◆ THERE ARE TWO HOLYDAYS OF OBLIGATION: The Solemnity of the Assumption of the Blessed Virgin Mary on August 15 and the Solemnity of All Saints on Friday, November 1. All Souls Day is technically a "commemoration," and while the Church doesn't call it a Holyday of Obligation, the faithful have made it one by popular acclaim. It falls on a Saturday this year, which means that an evening Mass should be that of All Souls, not an anticipated Mass of the Thirty-First Sunday in Ordinary Time. Check your local *Ordo* for additional details.

◆ WEEKDAY SOLEMNITIES AND FEASTS: In addition to the Holydays of Obligation, the Visitation of the Blessed Virgin Mary (May 31), the Most Sacred Heart of Jesus (June 7), the Nativity of John the Baptist (June 24) and his Passion (August 29), Saints Peter and Paul, Apostles (June 29), the Transfiguration of the Lord (August 6), the Exaltation of the Holy Cross (September 14), and the Dedication of St. John Lateran (November 9) are significant observances that occur during Ordinary Time. Each calls for special attention in preparing the liturgy (see the notes in the Introduction, above, on the concept of "progressive solemnity"). Do something, however small, to set these days apart from the regular weekdays. Encourage the faithful to attend. If you don't have regular daily Mass, see if you can schedule one. If you don't normally have servers and musicians at your weekday Masses, arrange for them to come. Sing the Gloria. In the absence of a priest, invite the faithful to pray the Liturgy of the Hours together—the antiphons and readings will take you straight to the heart of the feast. Add a bit of solemnity to these solemnities and feasts!

◆ HONORING THE BLESSED VIRGIN MARY: There are many feasts and memorials of the Blessed Mother during the coming months. We will recall Mary's Presentation in the Temple (November 21), her Assumption (August 15), and her Queenship (August 22); we will give honor to her Holy Name (September 12) and her Immaculate Heart (June 8). We will honor her under the title of Our Lady of the Rosary (October 7), and we will recall the dedication of a great basilica in her honor, St. Mary Major in Rome (August 5).

In addition to these special observances, Mary also has a month and a day in her honor during Ordinary Time. The month of October, like the month of May, is traditionally associated with Mary. It's an ideal time for Marian devotions; for example, singing an antiphon to Mary following the dismissal at Mass, praying the Angelus or the Litany of Loreto, or having a rosary procession. And every Saturday is traditionally a day to honor Mary. Except when an obligatory memorial falls on a Saturday, the optional Memorial of the Blessed Virgin Mary can be observed each Saturday during Ordinary Time. The Collection of Masses of the Blessed Virgin Mary has a wonderful variety of prayers, offering a many-faceted view of Christ's Mother and ours.

◆ WEEKDAY MEMORIALS: The weeks of summer and fall are full of memorials of the saints, too many to list here. The saints' days add color to the weekdays of Ordinary Time. If you have images of the saints in your church, call special attention to them on the day of the memorial. Place flowers, candles, or prayer cards near the image. The ministers might pause at the image for a moment of prayer in the concluding procession.

◆ PATRONAL SOLEMNITY: The abundance of saints' days means that many parishes celebrate their patronal solemnity over the summer as well. If you don't usually make much of your patronal solemnity, consider doing so this year. It's an opportunity for the community to feel their special connection with the saint or mystery the parish is named for. And in becoming aware of the special charism of the saint, you have an opportunity to reflect on how that charism is lived out in the parish. Note that your patronal solemnity takes precedence, in your parish, over any of the Sundays of Ordinary Time. If your patronal feast falls on a weekday this year, it can still be observed on the nearest Sunday, and the prayers and readings of the day may be replaced with those of the feast.

The patronal feast is an ideal time to take stock of the parish community. Weather permitting, schedule your parish picnic or ministries fair to coincide with the celebration. Small communities could arrange a group picture on this day, and add it to the parish archives. Parishes small and large can take the opportunity to collect stories and photos. The patronal feast is also a good time to install new members of the parish council. The *Book of Blessings* includes a simple blessing for this purpose (chapter 64).

◆ CIVIC MOMENTS: We will encounter a number of civic holidays during the months of summer and fall. The Fourth of July falls on a Thursday this year. It's a great day for hot dogs and fireworks, and for prayer. Labor Day, on September 2, is ideal for the blessing of workers. September 11 marks the twelfth anniversary of the terrorist attacks, and, with Veterans' Day (November 11), has become a national day of remembrance. Thanksgiving Day comes at the very end of this liturgical time on November 28. It's a time for feasting, but also a time to give thanks for all God has done for us in the past year, and to be challenged to do as much as we can for others.

The Liturgy of the Hours

THE summer time in many parishes is "down time." In the United States, often times our parish calendars are set to the school year rather than to the liturgical year. Thus, summer and/or fall Ordinary Time can be a challenge in preparing the Liturgy of the Hours. The Hours are the official prayer of the Church and mold us, form us or "school" us in the ways we not only praise and thank the Triune God but also in living our faith in all we do. Our spiritual lives are strengthened because the Hours are deeply scriptural: the Psalms, the canticles, the readings, the prayers themselves that cite or allude to passages of Scripture. Moreover, the great sermons by those of the Church's early tradition provide rich sources for living our faith. Thus, the Liturgy of the Hours is something that can also be prayed in the homes as well as at the parish. Encouraging people to pray at set times with the official prayer of the Church integrates the baptized into the life deepened by the Scriptures and the Church's tradition. This is why Robert Taft, sj, could write these words: "In every time, in every land and from every race: in the privacy of the home, in desert or cave, in peasant hut and hermit cell, in Gothic choir or country chapel, in concentration camp or jungle mission-station; at every hour around the clock someone raises his or her voice in the prayer of the Church, to join with the heavenly and earthly choirs down through the ages in the glorification of almighty God" (*The Liturgy*

of the Hours in East and West: The Origins of the Divine Office and Its Meaning for Today, Second Edition. [Collegeville, MN: Liturgical Press, 1986/1993], pp. 370–371).

For the Eighteenth Sunday of Ordinary Time we move from volume three to volume four. During Ordinary Time perhaps the music for the evening hymn, Psalms, canticles, and intercessions could be easily sung a cappella if there is no accompaniment available or with simpler settings in order to convey progressive solemnity. Moreover, changing those musical settings during the autumn of Ordinary Time would provide a connection to the changes in the season.

The Hours can school us in praising and glorifying the God who has liberated us from death; they can also lead us to grow in communion with the Triune God. During the summer and autumn, the worship commission should perhaps think about the place of the Hours in the parish and how they can strengthen the relationship of the faithful with God and the Church.

The Rite of Christian Initiation of Adults

Summer

When Easter Time concludes, the RCIA and the Sunday celebration of the Eucharist do not. If you are one of the lucky parishes with an ongoing RCIA, you will have children catechumens at Mass every Sunday who experience dismissal catechesis. During the summer the Gospel stories of Luke unfold the public ministry of Jesus through his miracles and parables. Catechumens will be introduced to Luke's emphasis on Jesus's outreach to those who were ordinarily excluded from Jewish society, such as Gentiles, widows, and sinners as well as his focus on the call and cost of discipleship. Combined with these readings you may wish to invite children and their families to become involved in an outreach project. Consult with the liturgy and music directors to plan a celebration of commissioning: anoint the group when the project begins, and bless its members when the project concludes.

Often these are the months when parents begin to ask about the Christian initiation of their children. Set aside time to visit and invite them into the process. If the parish already has a pre-catechumenate structure in place, invite them to a session and introduce them to the team and to other inquirers. If not, plan some times when those inquiring can meet and greet children and family members who have already been through the process to share their story.

Plan a picnic or pot luck for families of neophytes, catechumens, inquirers, and others who have recently been through the process.

Remember, baptized children are candidates—not catechumens. Their initiation may or may not be part of the process. It is important to meet with the family to discern the best way to prepare them for reception into full communion.

If you have not yet included peer companions in the initiation process, think about some ways to do that (RCIA, 252, 254). You will find them a valuable part of the process. There are different ways of involving young people. The parish director of religious education or the principal of the Catholic school may have some ideas about involving child catechumens in upcoming prayer activities, outreach projects, or social gatherings. They may also know individual young people who could be a more consistent presence in inquiry and catechumenal sessions. Are there ways to include catechumens in first Holy Communion or Confirmation preparation sessions? Your goal is to help inquirers, catechumens, and family members develop a relationship with other children and families in the parish.

Liturgical catechesis is the heart of RCIA formation. Summertime is a good planning time. Meet together with the parish liturgy director, music director, and director of the adult catechumenate. Discuss the calendar. If you have a year-round catechumenate, choose times during the year to celebrate the Rite of Acceptance. Talk about how to celebrate the minor rites well. Plan for the training of catechists who will preside at dismissal and some of the minor rites. Are there ways to involve music more during the catechetical sessions? Discuss the best ways to celebrate the rites with children, and think about times when adults and children catechumens can celebrate. The more that those involved in formation all work together, the better the process will be.

Fall

While fall is the period when the liturgical year is nearing its end, the parish is coming alive after the summer. The pre-catechumenate and catechumenate will become more formalized at this point. This is a good time to touch base with those who were initiated during the Easter Vigil to see if they are comfortable in the parish and actively part of the Sunday assembly.

Liturgical Catechesis

At some time before the First Sunday of Advent there should be an opportunity for those who are ready to celebrate the Rite of Acceptance. Although the Rite of Christian Initiation of Adults (see 257, 260) recommends that the rites for children not be celebrated with the whole parish community since it might make the children "uncomfortable." However, the general practice in the United States is to celebrate the rites in the midst of the community. There is a great value to this practice for both the children and the community. Children are formed by full ritual experience and they learn from it. I remember a specific instance in a parish when after the celebration of the Rite of Acceptance at a Sunday assembly, the children were asked, "What did you learn about the Church?" A seven–year–old girl responded: "They are all my family and they want me here." What better catechesis!

When a congregation is present and involved, children "catch it." The assembly benefits and is catechized too. There is something very formative about hearing children respond to the questions "What do you want to become?" and "Why?" There is something salvific about watching a parent or sponsor sign a child's senses, then responding in song. No amount of reading or teaching can match that experience. Children in RCIA are being initiated into the Body of Christ and the Sunday assembly. It does not make sense to separate them as part of the process.

If your process has a group of peer companions, talk with the liturgy director about finding a way to involve them in the celebration of the rite. Companions are mentioned in the Rite of Acceptance (see 269), but it doesn't say how. One possible adaptation is to have the companions sign the senses after parents, sponsors, or catechists have signed them.

A major part of liturgical formation for the catechumenate period is the celebration of the minor rites. If done well they are very beneficial to the faith development of children. Good celebration adds to the sense of prayer and reverence.

Work with the liturgy director to suggest appropriate times and circumstances to celebrate the minor rites and to train catechists to be confident and competent in planning and leading the rites.

The Sacraments of Initiation

Summer

The summer and fall months of Ordinary Time are also times when Confirmation is celebrated. Acquaint yourself with the rite. You will want to confer with the directors of liturgy and music to prepare the celebration. The Rite of Confirmation is very clear, but depending on the size of the group you still need to look at options for calling the candidates forward.

You will also need to look at space in the Church. Where will the candidates and their sponsors be seated? Appropriate space for the bishop, and the priests and deacons participating in the liturgy, is required. Sacramental symbols should be lavish and visible. Prepare candidates ahead of time so they are familiar with the flow of the ritual and their responses.

Involve candidates as liturgical ministers in this Eucharist as readers, music ministers, and gift bearers.

Summer is a good time for gathering people for picnics or ice cream socials. Invite parents of infants who have been baptized in the last year to a social gathering. Include a clothes and toy swap. At some point during the social, plan a blessing for families. Confer with the liturgy and music directors to design a short but reverent and prayerful blessing. Consult the *Book of Blessings*.

Planning is also a summer task. Take time this summer to review your Baptism preparation program. Survey parents who have been through it. Ask what they liked, what was helpful, and what was not. See if there are ways to introduce more rituals into the preparation process to help young parents better understand the meaning of the Rite of Baptism. Evaluate ways you have been able to keep in contact with families and involve them in parish life.

This is also a time to recruit catechists and group leaders for sacramental preparation. Look at the parents, sponsors and older teens who have

been actively involved in parish life. Would any of them be enthusiastic about taking on a different role?

Fall

While this may be the beginning of the end of the liturgical year it is also the time when parish life comes alive after the summer. Most of the sacramental preparation programs will become more formalized at this point.

At some point during this time it is good to touch base with those who celebrated first Holy Communion and Confirmation last year to see if they are participating in the Sunday assembly and other areas of parish life. If not, reach out to them.

Most preparation programs have rituals of enrollment. Talk with the liturgy director to see if some of these can be celebrated at a Sunday liturgy. Remember: there are usually ways making adaptations that will allow everyone preparing for sacraments of initiation to be enrolled at the same liturgy.

If you are using a liturgical catechetical model for sacramental preparation, set up a workshop for catechists who will lead the session celebrations. Show them how to set up a worship space with a prayer table and /or lectern. Explain the use of different color cloths and banners. If a classroom is being used, give options for rearranging chairs and space so it is appropriate for worship. Invite the liturgy director to give them tips on presiding, proclaiming the Word, and doing liturgical gesture. Have the music director talk about using music from the parish repertoire and suggest ways to lead singing during the sessions.

Plan a meeting for parents of children in the preparation programs. Use the first session to explain the program and process, give them a schedule, and be upfront about expectations. Go through the child's book and show them the family sections. Conclude the session with a prayer of blessing.

The Rite of Penance

CONTINUE to offer regularly the first form of the Rite of Penance: private confession and absolution. Most parishes make the sacrament available on Saturdays, but any day is suitable.

Also, post the times when the rite is offered in neighboring parishes in the bulletin and on the door of the church.

The Pastoral Care of the Sick

VIATICUM, Holy Communion for the dying, may be offered by a priest, deacon, or lay minister at any time. Take the time to explain to the parish why the term "Last Rites" is no longer used and what pastoral care is all about. The prayers for the sick and dying in the rite can richly contribute to the ministry of those who visit and care for the sick.

Note, however, only the priest can administer the Sacrament of the Anointing of the Sick. This may take place any time of the year for the good of those who are ill or dying. The summer season, when there are fewer solemnities or big liturgical events, may be the perfect time for the communal celebration of this sacrament. This could be done at daily Mass.

The Rite of Marriage

THIS is the season when Saturday weddings fill up many parish calendars. While we are still awaiting the official English translation of the revised *Rite of Marriage*, catechesis can begin now on the rite's greater emphasis on the role of bride and groom as primary ministers of this sacrament, and their liturgical procession together into the church. What a powerful (and startling) statement of welcome is made by the bride and groom when they greet their wedding guests at the door before they enter!

For couples with differing religious backgrounds, I strongly recommend (as does the rite itself) the use of Form II, the Celebration of Marriage outside of Mass. When a large majority of guests and family members are not Catholic, a Liturgy of the Word puts everyone on an equal footing and no one feels excluded. It is also hospitable since many people will not be able to go to Communion. Perhaps the assembly can have a

more specific role in the liturgy by lighting and holding congregational candles during the Rite of Marriage.

At a Saturday evening celebration of Marriage, the wedding Mass readings and prayers may replace those of an Ordinary Time Sunday without a solemnity.

The Order of Christian Funerals

DURING the summer months, consider developing various funeral ministries such as a funeral choir, ministers of hospitality who greet and seat, and teams who prepare a meal or reception after the funeral. A cantor is invaluable in making a grieving and disparate group feel comfortable by letting them know when to sing, sit, or stand. You might also consider urging retired parishioners to represent the greater parish community and simply attend funerals. Their role is to sit near the front of the church and model singing and participation. There is nothing sadder than a parish funeral liturgy with several family members, many of whom may not be Catholic, seated alone in the front row, and separated by an ocean of pews from the few Catholics sitting at the back.

Be sure that the terminology in the obituary section of the newspaper is correct. Remember that a Mass of Resurrection is what we celebrate every Sunday, whereas a Mass of Christian Burial is the liturgy for the deceased. Take the summer months to catechize about the first of the three funeral liturgies, the Vigil (*Order of Christian Funerals*, 54–97). This "wake" service is a Liturgy of the Word that does not include the recitation of the Rosary, although this practice is still quite commonplace. It may, however, include a eulogy, which is more appropriate here rather than at the conclusion of the funeral Mass. A deacon or a lay leader of prayer may lead the Vigil in the absence of a priest. The service can be greatly enhanced by the ministry of a good cantor who can lead a cappella singing. Some parishes now celebrate the Vigil in the church. Consider this with your pastor and liturgy committee. With its liturgical furnishings and symbols, a church is more conducive to prayer. Prepare to celebrate the vigil first, then follow it with visitation. The Rosary, if requested, is perhaps best prayed by the family and a few parishioners beforehand.

The Book of Blessings

DURING this season there are several occasions for blessing groups. Engaged couples could be blessed (BB, 195–214) and wedding anniversaries celebrated (chapter 1). During the months of summer and autumn, the *Book of Blessings* can be an invaluable resource for the worship life of the parish. As you prepare for the season, be sure to include these occasional rites, either during Mass or at parish gatherings, scheduled prayer services, catechetical meetings with catechumens or adults, and the like.

As the summer begins to wind down and the parish readies for school to begin, a blessing of students and teachers may be used on the Sunday preceding the first day of school (chapter 5). During the final week of Ordinary Time, a blessing of food for Thanksgiving Day helps the parish to observe this important civic holiday (chapter 58).

Remember that the various cycles of family and parish life can be sanctified through celebrations marked by special blessings. For blessings of people during times of sickness, pregnancy and birth, birthdays, and anniversaries, consult the *Book of Blessings*.

Blessings provide an opportunity to see God's extraordinary presence and action in the ordinary experiences of life. They are times to gather, share fellowship, and give God thanks and praise.

The Liturgical Environment

THE summer weeks of Ordinary Time are somewhat less hectic in the life of most parishes. Nonetheless, there is any number of celebrations to deal with: school graduations, weddings, parish social events, the end of the school year and its beginning a few weeks later, and of course, the normal life of the parish that never really takes a break!

There are a number of significant feasts during these weeks (see section on "The Saints" on page XX above) and these can be opportunities for special liturgical celebrations that can be festive occasions in the midst of Ordinary Time. In addition, if the solemnity of the patron of the parish falls during these weeks, or the anniversary of the dedication of the church, or any other important event in the history of the parish, then these would be good opportunities to make Ordinary Time a little more extraordinary for the whole parish community.

Practical Suggestions (Summer)

◆ The liturgical color remains green, but the palette of tones and hues is extensive, drawn from the colors and elements of nature which afford a wonderful variety of choices for the components of the liturgical environment.

◆ Fresh–cut flower arrangements can be expensive if they are used on a regular basis; look for more economical sources like neighborhood markets, or invite parishioners to donate a bundle from time to time. Another source is the leftover arrangements from summer weddings. But someone needs to rearrange these so that they have a fresh appearance and appear as though they were done with the liturgical space in mind. The same is true of floral displays left behind after funerals. Again, lavish displays are not necessary and grouping green plants and fresh flowers can be as attractive as setting individual containers off by themselves, especially in a larger space.

◆ The colors of nature, in both the summer months and the weeks of autumn, can be a good clue for the coordinating colors that work well in the environment, especially in the choice of fabric accents.

◆ At the beginning of the summer invite parishioners to donate one or two potted plants to the liturgical environment committee who will in turn fashion colorful planters that can be placed both outside and inside, even changing them around from time to time.

◆ This is a good time to pay extra attention to the outdoor environment. Keeping the church grounds clear of litter, marking the pathways with colorful planters, using colorful outdoor banners on light standards, making sure that access ramps are free of obstacles, adding extra foliage to any outdoor shrines or sitting areas—all help to extend hospitality to members and visitors alike.

◆ These weeks could be a time for the liturgical environment committee to do a slightly delayed "spring-cleaning" of its resources and storage rooms. Are some items no longer needed? Are there unused items that are no longer appropriate for the liturgical space? Do some things need to be repaired or cleaned? Is it time to invest in any new items, like altar linens, vestments, items for later in the year, and so forth? What about Advent candles? And don't forget to do a complete inspection of the vestment closets and cupboards in the sacristy for items that need repair, cleaning, or discarding.

Practical Suggestions (Fall)

◆ As the autumn weeks unfold the colors and textures of nature change and they can be a source of inspiration for the liturgical environment.

◆ The liturgical color is still green, but a more subdued tone could be used after the brighter green that may have been dominant during the summer. Fabric swags and hangings offer ample varieties of green tones that would work well with this time of year and also complement the vesture in the space. When shopping for fabric, it's a good idea to take a color sample along to make sure that the new textiles work with the existing ones.

◆ This is a good time to decorate some of those forgotten places in the building—back corners, hallways (being attentive to safety requirements), doorways, alcoves (that sometimes attract clutter), chapels, and gathering areas. Large urns with fall grasses and fall branches can make these spaces attractive and add a point of interest as people walk through the space.

◆ There are a number of feast days during these weeks that can be highlighted by a little extra attention to the environment. On feast days in honor of the Blessed Mother, extra decorations could be added to the Marian shrine. On the Feast of the Exaltation of the Holy Cross (September 14) perhaps a large cross could be placed in the gathering area (if the parish uses one for Lent) and attention drawn to it in some appropriate way on this day.

◆ During the month of November many parishes place a *Book of the Names of the Dead* in a prominent location. It should be arranged so people can add names of loved ones who have died; a large candle can be placed near the book stand, or the stand can be placed next to the font where the Easter candle is already located.

◆ Another custom at this time is the arranging of a shrine-like setting that follows the Mexican tradition of the *Día de los Muertos* (the Day of the Dead). Those familiar with this custom can help with the appropriate arrangements.

◆ Every parish celebrates Thanksgiving near the end of November. This is often a time to collect food items for local food pantries. Perhaps the liturgical environment committee can help arrange the donations into containers suitable for incorporation into the liturgical environment. Note that not all the donations need to overtake the sanctuary—only enough to symbolize the connection between the celebra-tion of Eucharist (as thanksgiving) and the obligation we have to give thanks for the bounty of God's blessings by sharing with our brothers and sisters.

◆ The last Sunday of the liturgical year, and Last Sunday of Ordinary Time, is the Solemnity of Our Lord Jesus Christ, King of the Universe; the liturgical color is white.

◆ It's now time for a significant "make-over" of the liturgical environment as a new liturgical year has arrived and the ministry of the liturgical environment committee once again addresses how the place where the Church gathers serves well its worship and praise of God.

The Liturgical Music

Now almost two years since the implementation of *The Roman Missal*, it might be helpful to revisit the idea of chant. *The Roman Missal* suggests that the congregation should be able to chant some parts of the Mass. This brings unity to the sung prayer of the universal Church. The new chants have been revised into English from some of the Gregorian chants. Many of the melodies will sound familiar to parishes that are already familiar with singing the Gregorian chants in Latin.

Chants are natural melodies, most having only four or five musical notes. The chants are sung in unison and are usually done without accompaniment. The distance between the notes, small steps of a second, third, or fifth, makes it easy to sing and to learn.

What are some ways to teach the chants to our assemblies? Here are a few ideas:

◆ The organist could start using the chant melodies as prelude and meditation music during the Mass. Doing this will make the melodies more familiar to the assembly.

◆ The choir could use the chant tones as vocal warm-up exercises, familiarizing themselves with the tones and melodies so they can confidently, without hesitation, support the congregation in the new chants until they learn them.

◆ The cantors could teach the assembly the chant parts of the Mass from the Missal (Responses; Holy, Holy, Holy; Memorial Acclamations; and Gloria) in October and November.

Of course, other musical settings besides the chanted Mass parts are also available. Nonetheless, every parish should learn the chant settings for use at Sunday liturgies and at diocesan celebrations where familiar music is important for active participation.

The priest, in particular, should learn to use the chants in *The Roman Missal*. Because chanting is done slowly and reverently, it can be easier than saying the text. The priest should practice the chants so that he is able to sing his parts confidently and without hesitation. This will help the assembly in singing their parts well.

Chants have been a part of our Catholic tradition for centuries. We now have another opportunity to grow deeper in our faith and knowledge of our Catholic heritage. Using *The Roman Missal* in this way helps us to particpate in the Mass more fully, actively, and consciously by chanting the praises of God together in song.

—John Mark Klaus, TOR

Liturgical Ministers

Summer

Do current ministers sign in? If not, try this for a while. You may find that the same people are consistently absent or don't find a substitute. Perhaps it is time to call them and find out if they want to be involved in the ministry and remove inactive minsters from your list. Summer is typically the time of year that many kids go off on vacation, so you may need to train altar servers. And if you do, be sure to schedule a new server with a more experienceed one. Perhaps you could schedule a summer ministry picnic as a way for people involved in ministry to get to know each other. Or, you might consider putting out a summer newsletter to remind people of any changes in procedure, to encourage and thank them, or to note any areas that need to be tightened up a bit. Provide a list of helpful web links to their areas of ministry, or testimonials from those who have been involved in the ministry for a long time. Let people share what it means to them!

Summer adds the additional weight of multiple weddings and many funerals. Compile a "call list" of servers and readers for these services. Does your parish have volunteer sacristans? Have multiple people available to assist so no one person is overwhelmed. As a liturgist or scheduling minister, do not be afraid to ask for help. Too many

martyrs have canonized themselves! People are more than willing to help. What may seem like one more mammoth task to you as liturgist might end up being a simple 15-minute session of phone calls to members of your choir. Be grateful for those involved in ministry, and tell them so—repeatedly.

Fall

As surely as the leaves change in autumn, there are changes in our lives. Kids grow up and move on, jobs change, people are married or widowed, and interests shift. When we think of liturgical ministries, it is not a one-size-fits-all proposition.

Saint Paul reminded his people, "There are different kinds of spiritual gifts but the same Spirit; there are different forms of service but the same Lord" (1 Corinthians 12:4–5). For Saint Paul, ministry is not about holding an office or being in a position of honor; it is about action, about doing, about serving God in both a universal and diverse fashion.

In Paul Bernier's powerful text, *Ministry in the Church*, (p. 24, Twenty-Third Publications), he points out five things to remember from Saint Paul's theology of "one body":

1. Paul is speaking of organic unity. In a body all of us parts are interconnected, and when one is sick we are all sick.

2. Each part is necessary. There are no higher and lower functions, and the diversity of gifts is necessary to keep the whole body functioning smoothly.

3. The different gifts that each possesses are not for one's own use but for the good of the whole.

4. Human beings are never defined autonomously. We are relational. It is in being brother and sister and how we actively look out for one another that matters.

5. What enables the body to function is mutual love and concern.

Sometimes love may involve painful honesty in helping someone to grow beyond an identity in a ministry which God may no longer be calling them to. Since we are working with the sensitivies of volunteers, "performance" issues must be handled carefully. One way to proceed is to ask the person to consider where God may be calling him or her to serve now, and then tactfully to help the person move in that direction.

For example, maybe someone no longer has the voice to be a solo cantor. Could they be a reader, or an extraordinary minister of Holy

Communion? Or perhaps after connecting with the larger congregation for so many years, they could engage in some one-on-one ministry as a greeter.

Devotions and Sacramentals

◆ MEMORIAL DAY: In many parts of the world, there is a custom in which people visit the cemetery and honor their dead. Church tradition reserves November 2 for this opportunity. However, in the United States, we remember those who died in the service of our country on this day, so it would be appropriate to use the Blessing of a Cemetery from chapter 43 of the *Book of Blessings*.

◆ MOST HOLY TRINITY: In the Eastern rites of the Catholic Church, there is much reflection on the Trinitarian aspect of married life and how couples are a reflection of the Trinity. Blessing of Married Couples, *Book of Blessings*, chapter 1, reiterates this Trinitarian view of couples in their growth in Christian love.

◆ MOST HOLY BODY AND BLOOD OF CHRIST: See the order in *Holy Communion and Worship of the Eucharist Outside Mass* (101–108) as well as the *Ceremonial of Bishops* (387–394). It may be helpful to have various parish groups at stations along the route of the procession with the Blessed Sacrament (in a monstrance) ready for a priest or deacon to bless the people. Ask a neighboring parish to join in the celebration by processing from one church to the other, having one church celebrate the Order for Solemn Exposition of the Holy Eucharist to end the prayer time and devotion together. Conclude with a light reception to celebrate your unity as the Body of Christ.

◆ MOST SACRED HEART OF JESUS: This devotion became popular in the seventeenth century through Saint Mary Margaret Alacoque (memorial is October 16) who said that in one of her visions Christ told her "Behold the heart that has loved people so, yet is loved so little in return." In *Catholic Household Blessings & Prayers*, there is a Litany of the Sacred Heart. It may also be helpful to have an extended period of prayer in the presence of the Blessed Sacrament or with the parish's image of the Sacred Heart. Remind parish-

ioners of the importance of the practice of first Fridays (see DPPL, 171) and first Saturdays (see DPPL, 174).

◆ NATIVITY OF SAINT JOHN THE BAPTIST: Many communities celebrate infant Baptism this day. Families who have celebrated a Baptism within the year still require support in their lives as Christian parents. To mark this solemnity, invite them to a continuing education or formation session followed by a potluck. It may be an opportunity for an evening bonfire, as has been a custom, since John's mission was to witness to the light. During these bonfires, the Church prays that we "may overcome the darkness of the world and reach the 'indefectible light' of God" (see DPPL, 225).

There are summer blessings for fun, teens, cars, and more. See the *Book of Blessings*, chapter 21, for the Blessing of the Various Means of Transportation (bikes, cars, skateboards, etc.), chapter 22 for the Blessing of Boats and Fishing Gear, chapter 23 for the Blessing of Technical Installations or Equipment (iPod™, stereo equipment, etc.), chapter 24 for the Blessing of Tools or Other Equipment for Work, chapter 29 for the Blessing of an Athletic Event (or Field at chapter 20), chapter 44 for the Blessing of Religious Articles, or chapter 46 for the Blessing and Conferral of a Scapular.

◆ INDEPENDENCE DAY: See the *Book of Blessings*, 1965, A or E, for a special blessing that could be used as part of a prayer service for home on this special day in American history.

◆ TRANSFIGURATION OF THE LORD: There is a tradition of having a vigil service on the eve of the Transfiguration with candlelight, Scripture readings, and intercessions for peace. It is especially poignant considering the tragic anniversaries on this date (first use of the electric chair in 1890 and the drop of the atomic bomb on Hiroshima in 1945).

◆ ASSUMPTION OF THE BLESSED VIRGIN MARY: Because Our Lady is the "highest fruit of the redemption" (see DPPL, 180), a custom for Blessing of Produce (or herbs) has been remembered each year in many countries. See the *Book of Blessings*, chapter 26 or 28. A Litany of Mary is also found in *Catholic Household Blessings & Prayers*.

◆ LABOR DAY: The Book of Blessings, chapter 24, includes a helpful prayer and note about the importance of the dignity of work. Use these intercessions to support a prayer service reminding us of how we are partners with God in serving the earth with our labors. Encourage praying (exposition or some other time in church) in the presence of the Blessed Sacrament to support those looking for meaningful employment.

◆ EXALTATION OF THE HOLY CROSS: Most of the year we take for granted the Sign of the Cross or in Lent the Stations of the Cross. Here is an opportunity to help the community focus on the significance of the cross in their lives, perhaps through another celebration of the Way of the Cross.

◆ MONTH OF THE HOLY ROSARY: Throughout the month of October say the Rosary as a prayer for peace.

◆ MISSION SUNDAY is celebrated on the Third Sunday of October. See the websites at www.usccb.org or vatican.va for more information on this annual reminder that we are one, universal Church, supporting each other in the mission to evangelize.

◆ PRAYER FOR THE DEAD: The colorful customs surrounding the Mexican *Día de los Muertos*, the Day of the Dead, celebrated on November 2, are growing more familiar and more popular. Keep in mind that this is primarily a family and community celebration, not a liturgical one: the liturgical celebration of those who have gone before us takes place on November 1, All Saints, and November 2, All Souls' Day. Careful catechesis can help families understand how the remembrance of deceased relatives fits into the Catholic tradition. The pious practice of offering Masses for the deceased is another beloved tradition.

—John Thomas Lane, sss

The Parish and the Home

DURING the summer, families will naturally celebrate time outdoors—with picnics, barbecues, travel, boating, hiking, camping. It's the perfect chance to enjoy the beauty of God's creation: meadows, orchards, beaches, forests, rivers, mountains, lakes, farms, and oceans. With less pressure from school schedules and homework, people can relax and rejoice in each other. They can also eat healthy, fresh foods from home gardens or farmers' markets.

During summer, in a prayer corner draped in green one could place shells (symbol for John the Baptist, who baptized Jesus, and James; also a symbol for pilgrims) and fishing nets or small boats to honor Peter, the fisherman, and Paul who traveled many miles around the Mediterranean to spread the Gospel. Later, since Kateri Tekakwitha combined Native American and Christian spirituality, display Native American art, pottery, or designs. Because Martha is patron saint of cooks, arrange a display of kitchen tools in her honor: spatula, plate, measuring cup—or have a lovely meal. Jesuit parishes, schools, or retreat centers in the area may have celebrations for Ignatius, their founder.

For Italians, the optional Memorial of Our Lady of Mount Carmel (July 16) occasions carnivals or fairs where the food is excellent and the music is lively. August 6, the Feast of the Transfiguration, recalls Jesus's radiance and the voice of God calling him "Beloved." Peter wanted to set up booths on the mountain top where this occurred, because he was remembering the Jewish festival of Sukkot when tents are constructed and people live outdoors as a reminder of the Israelites' exile in the desert. The Solemnity of the Assumption of the Blessed Virign Mary expresses the Church's belief that when Mary died, God raised her into heaven. Because of the time it occurs, it's a harvest feast, when people often place flowers, herbs, and vegetables around a statue of Mary.

In fall, when school starts, ritualize the event. Rather than grumbling that summer is over, celebrate the new learning and growth that will occur during the academic year, blessing the children as they leave for their first day back.

Some important feasts during September are the Nativity of Mary, the Exaltation of the Holy Cross, and the Archangels Michael, Gabriel and Raphael. The prayer corner at home can be decorated with a statue or picture of Mary, then a crucifix and finally, figures or pictures of angels.

Many of autumn's saints had a particular concern for the poor: Saint Vincent de Paul, Saint Francis of Assisi, Saint Frances Cabrini, Saint Margaret of Scotland, Saint Elizabeth of Hungary, and Saint Rose Philippine Duchesne. Families can decide what cause to support and what activity to do: could a local soup kitchen use help? What about visiting a retirement home, or working at a parish soup supper, potluck, or pancake

breakfast? Could the family start a collection of used clothing or canned goods for a homeless shelter? Then use the feasts as checkpoints or stepping stones to renew a commitment and praise the progress.

Saint Thérèse of Lisieux and St. Teresa of Avila are such outstanding women saints. Find a children's biography of each at the library, or read a brief summary of their lives at www.americancatholic.org/Features/Saints.

We not only celebrate the harvest, we also prepare for next year. Children who plant bulbs in autumn, then see them blossom in spring, have a direct and wordless demonstration of resurrection. From a brown and seemingly lifeless bulb springs the colorful flower. LTP's *Blessings and Prayers through the Year* has a blessing for flower bulbs (page 12) and one for pets on the memorial of Saint Francis of Assisi (page 14).

On the Solemnity of All Saints, November 1, we celebrate even those whose names may not be remembered, but who are always remembered by God. It's a good reminder to the family that we are all called to share in God's holiness and become saints. For All Souls' Day families might want to set up shrines for the dead, with mementos, photos, or a blank journal in which the names of the beloved dead are recorded.

Mass Texts

◆ SAMPLE PRAYER OF THE FAITHFUL

Celebrant:

Let us open our hearts in prayer to the needs of the Church, the world, and all gathered here.

Our response is:

Hear our prayer.

Deacon/Lector/Reader:

For the Church, the body of Christ,
that we may live each day in God's presence,
trusting in the Lord's power to guide us,
generous God:

For the world,
that there may be peace in every land
and every human heart,
generous God:

For the poor, blessed by God,
that we may find ways to share our abundance
with them,
generous God:

For our beloved dead, [especially
N._____],
that they who have died with Christ in Baptism
may rise with him to new and everlasting life,
generous God:

For all of us, gathered in this holy place,
that we may seek the things that are above,
generous God:

Celebrant:

Generous God,
gifts without measure flow from your goodness.
Guide our life's journey,
and teach us to share the good things you have
given us
with a generosity like your own.
We ask this through Christ our Lord.
Amen.

◆ DISMISSAL TEXT FOR THE CATECHUMENS (SUMMER)

The longer days and warmth of summer
free us to explore the beauty of God's creation.
Now, you go forth to explore the beauty of
God's Word
that you might be freed to become the beautiful
creation God calls you to be.
Supported by our prayer and encouraged by
our fellowship,
go seek together the meaning of God's saving
Word.
May it sustain you until the day when you can
feast with us
at the table of his Body and his Blood.

◆ DISMISSAL TEXT FOR CHILDREN'S LITURGY OF THE WORD (SUMMER)

The summer months bring children rest from
school and lessons,
but we never rest from learning of God's
goodness and of his love for us.
Because we long for you to know Jesus as your
brother and your friend
we send you now to hear his Word.
Listen well, for he will come to you through
those words
and he will teach you how to find him in your
family and your friends,
in our community, and in our world.

◆ DISMISSAL TEXT FOR EXTRAORDINARY MINISTERS OF HOLY COMMUNION (SUMMER)

Our homebound neighbors and those of our
    community who are ill
are deprived of some of summer's rich delights,
but not of the rich fare which we are privileged
    to receive
at the altar of sacrifice and love.
As the first disciples went from home to home
    to bring the Good News of the Gospel,
go to our absent members with word and
    sacrament
that they, too, may feast on the Bread that comes
    from heaven.

◆ DISMISSAL TEXT FOR THE CATECHUMENS (FALL)

Autumn's winds and the trees' willingness to lose
    their leaves
    remind us that we, too, must be shaken
and we, too, must shed those things that don't
    reflect God's love.
As you go forth to delve more deeply into
    God's Word,
let him delve deeply into your hearts
so you may joyously proceed toward the pool
    of Baptism
and humbly wear the garment of salvation.

◆ DISMISSAL TEXT FOR CHILDREN'S LITURGY OF THE WORD (FALL)

Animals prepare for winter by growing thicker
    coats and setting food aside,
and teach us that no one is free from work and
    constant preparation.
Your minds and hearts are young,
but not too young to hear God's Word,
to learn God's ways, and follow his commands.
Your special time now is very holy,
for you go to hear God speak to you and to call
    you to his heart.

◆ DISMISSAL TEXT FOR EXTRAORDINARY MINISTERS OF HOLY COMMUNION (FALL)

The table has been set and we've been nourished
by the Lord who gave his life for us.
But not all who would have dined were with
    us here,
so now you venture forth to share with them
what God has shared with us.
Bring them the fire of God's Word
and the Bread that is Christ's very flesh.
Bring them our prayers as well, and the assurance
    of our mindful love.

May
Month of Our Lady

Except for the days of the First and Thirty-fourth Weeks in Ordinary Time, The Roman Missal does not provide prayer texts for the weekdays in Ordinary Time. Instead, priest celebrants and those who prepare the liturgy may select from among the prayers provided for the Sundays in Ordinary Time. Your diocesan Ordo will provide suggestions for which prayers to use. On days celebrated as optional memorials, prayers may be from the Sundays of Ordinary Time, the Proper of Saints, or the Commons. On all Saturdays during Ordinary Time that do not have an obligatory memorial, a memorial to the Blessed Virgin Mary may be celebrated. The prayers may be selected from the Common of the Blessed Virgin Mary.

M O N 20
#341 green
Weekday / Seventh Week in Ordinary Time

Optional Memorial of Saint Bernardine of Siena, Priest / white

Lectionary for Mass

◆ FIRST READING: Today's reading is the beginning of the book of Sirach (Ecclesiasticus), one of the Wisdom writings of the Old Testament. Wisdom is an attribute of God. At times, the biblical authors personify her (the Hebrew word for wisdom is feminine in gender), that is, depict her as a person. Today's text speaks of her as created by God and created by God through the Holy Spirit. She existed "before all time." God has poured wisdom out on all his creation and "lavished her upon his friends." Truly she is gift.

◆ RESPONSORIAL PSALM 93: This Psalm acclaiming God's kingship is a fitting response to our reading, which speaks of God as "all-powerful creator-king." Note also the reference to God as creator in the second stanza.

◆ GOSPEL: Today's Gospel follows immediately upon Mark's account of the Transfiguration. Peter, James, and John were with him, and there on the mountain they saw his transformed glory. Perhaps it was a bit of this radiance still on Jesus's face that amazed the crowds in the beginning of today's text. The issue of concern is the disciples' inability to expel an unclean spirit which had taken possession of a boy.

Who is the "faithless generation?" Was it the disciples? (They are characterized this way elsewhere in the Gospel.) Was it the crowd? No matter, the point is clear: faith is needed to receive the power of God. One must pray and rely on God's power, not one's own, if healing is to be accomplished.

Today's Saint

Saint Bernardine was an Italian Franciscan, a priest, and preacher. Orphaned at a young age, he was raised by a pious aunt. While still a student, he helped care for the sick during an outbreak of bubonic plague, caught it, and almost died. Bernardine joined a strict branch of the Franciscans, called the Observants, around 1402. Known as the "apostle of Italy," he preached devotion to the Holy Name of Jesus, popularizing the use of the monogram, I.H.S. (*Iesus Hominum Salvator*).

T U E 21
#342 green
Weekday

Optional Memorial of Saint Christopher Magallanes, Priest, and Companions, Martyrs / red

Lectionary for Mass

◆ FIRST READING: The teacher of wisdom tells a young disciple that when one aspires to serve the Lord and live an upright life, he can expect that it is going to be difficult. Not an inviting message, perhaps, but it is certainly reassuring when trials do come. They serve to prove the quality of one's commitment and integrity.

For Sirach and the other wisdom authors, "fear of the Lord" is perhaps best understood in the sense of reverence for God. Several motifs occur repeatedly in today's reading: fear, trust, waiting for the Lord, and hope. The bottom line: God will not let you down. No one who hopes in the Lord has ever been disappointed.

◆ RESPONSORIAL PSALM 37: This same sense of God's total trustworthiness is voiced in today's Responsorial Psalm. This song of instruction on the wisdom of God's ways assures faithful disciples that they will receive the blessings of salvation and deliverance.

◆ GOSPEL: Today's Gospel consists of two separate incidents: the first, as Jesus and his disciples are traveling through Galilee on a journey which will eventually end in Jerusalem, in the southern part of the country; the second, in Capernaum, the seaside city where Jesus makes his home. In the first incident, Jesus tells his discples about his upcoming Passion and Resurrection, a teaching they fail to understand. The second incident gives much insight into the character of Jesus's disciples: they seek greatness. They have yet to grasp the way of their master, a way of service and self-giving.

Today's Saint

Saint Christopher Magallanes (1869–1927), a priest, and 24 other companions were martyred for standing up to the anti-Catholic Mexican government of the time. Outraged by attempts on the part of the government to eliminate the Catholic faith (i.e., bans against Baptism and the celebration of Mass), he joined the Cristero movement which pledged an allegiance to Christ and the Church to spread the Good News. The slogan of the Cristero uprising was "Long live Christ the King and the Virgin of Guadalupe!" After years of secretly ministering to Catholics, he was imprisoned and executed without a trial. Prior to his death he said, "I am innocent and I die innocent. . . . I ask God that the shedding of my blood serve the peace of our divided Mexico" (quoted in the BCL Newsletter, August 2002: www. usccb.org/ liturgy/ innews/ 082002. shtml).

W E D 22 #343 green
Weekday

Optional Memorial of Saint Rita of Cascia, Religious / white

Lectionary for Mass

◆ First Reading: Once again we meet a personified Wisdom, here depicted as a mother giving life. Notice the close relationship between Wisdom and the Lord: to love and serve one is to love and serve the other. Note the verbs which indicate how the would-be wise disciple is to act: seek, hold fast, serve, love, obey, hearken (listen), trust. As on Monday, we are warned of the trials that one who seeks wisdom must undergo. These only serve to test the integrity and trustworthiness of the disciple, who will be rewarded or punished accordingly.

◆ Responsorial Psalm: In the Old Testament, God's wisdom is revealed preeminently in the Law. Psalm 119 acclaims the wisdom of the Law and uses a variety of synonyms to speak of it. Note the ones used today. What rewards are promised to the one who is faithful in keeping the Law?

◆ Gospel: Today's text offers us another insight into the very human character of the disciples (remember how Jesus called them faithless in Monday's text?). Today, they see themselves as a rather elitist group. No, Jesus tells them. If someone has performed an act of power in Jesus's name, that person is one with and for Jesus.

Today's Saint

Saint Rita of Cascia (1381–1447) was born to a peasant family in the region of Umbria, Italy. From an early age, she longed to consecrate her life to Christ as a religious, but in obedience to her parents she married instead. Her husband was harsh and sometimes violent, but over the years Rita's unfailing faith and gentleness began to have its effect, and her husband slowly changed. He was stabbed to death in a dispute, and shortly thereafter both Rita's sons died as well. She entered an Augustinian convent, where she remained for 40 years. She was especially devoted to the Passion of Christ. It is said that while praying, she received the stigmata of Christ's wounds. The stigmata remained for 15 years, until her death. Given her life story, it is little wonder that Saint Rita is the patron saint of difficult marriages, abuse victims, and lost causes.

T H U 23 #344 green
Weekday

Lectionary for Mass

◆ First Reading: The first three admonitions in today's reading are exhortations against relying on one's self rather than on the Lord. The remaining verses deal with the subjects of sin, forgiveness, and conversion, and they warn against overconfidence in God's mercy without sincerity and commitment to conversion.

◆ Responsorial Psalm 1 acclaims the blessedness of the person who delights in and lives by the Law of the Lord. He or she is like a verdant, fruit-bearing tree; not so the wicked, those who refuse to obey the Law of the Lord.

◆ Gospel: Commitment to conversion and integrity is likewise the subject of today's Gospel. Nothing at all is worth the cost of losing everlasting life! (Gehenna, or hell, is its opposite.) Jesus is not suggesting self-mutilation, but he is clearly putting things in vivid perspective! The final line of today's Gospel is likewise a vivid image: live so as to be a "good" seasoning, a "good" preservative for peace in your dealings with one another.

F R I 24 #345 green
Weekday

Optional Memorial of Blessed Louis-Zéphirin Moreau, Bishop / white (Canada)

Lectionary for Mass

◆ First Reading: Friendship, its blessings, its pitfalls, and dangers, is the topic of the wisdom teacher's discourse in today's First Reading. Does the teaching resonate with your own experience? Whom do you consider your faithful friends? Take a moment to tell them how much they mean to you!

◆ RESPONSORIAL PSALM 119: Today's First Reading ends with a two-fold mention of fear of the Lord. The fear spoken of is really a sense of reverence for God and the recognition that one must be obedient to him. Today's antiphon picks up on this motif with a prayer for guidance in God's ways. Psalm 119 acclaims the wisdom of God's law and voices the desire to know it and live by it.

◆ GOSPEL: Jesus asks more of his disciples than did the Law of Moses. The case in point in today's Gospel is divorce. According to the Law of Moses, this is permissible on certain grounds. According to Jesus, who came to fulfill the law, it is not.

Today's Saint

Louis (1824–1901) was from a large Canadian farming family. A delicate child too frail for farm work, he was fortunately intelligent enough to be sent to be educated. He was ordained to the priesthood in 1846; unfortunately, his theological training was shortened by his ill health. In 1852, he became advisor to the bishops of Saint-Hyacinthe and administered the diocese when the bishops' were absent. He earned a reputation for hard work and administrative efficiency and skill. When serving as parish priest, he became concerned about the financial condition of workers, and he established the Union Saint-Joseph, a society that provided protection from unexpected events such as unemployment, accidents, and premature death. In 1876, Louis was consecrated fourth bishop of Saint-Hyacinthe and administered the diocese for 25 years. During this time, he built a cathedral, founded two orders of sisters, and worked to support the priests of the dioceses spiritually and intellectually by instituting conferences and retreats for them. Bishop Moreau's health began to fail around 1896,

and he died in 1901. He was beatified by Blessed Pope John Paul II in 1987.

S A T

25

#346   green

Weekday

Optional Memorials of Saint Bede the Venerable, Priest and Doctor of the Church / white; Saint Gregory VII, Pope / white; Saint Mary Magdalene de'Pazzi, Virgin / white; Blessed Virgin Mary / white

Lectionary for Mass

◆ FIRST READING: Sirach reflects on the human person as a creature of God, made in God's image and gifted in many ways. His reflection is obviously rooted in the narratives of Genesis 1 and 2. Midway through the text, Sirach turns his thoughts to the covenant God made with Israel on Mount Sinai, and the inherent judgment on Israel's fidelity or infidelity.

◆ RESPONSORIAL PSALM 103: Several themes from the First Reading are echoed in today's Responsorial Psalm: the human creature as dust, the covenant, and fear of the Lord. Those who fear the Lord are obedient and the Lord's everlasting kindness rests upon them.

◆ GOSPEL: If only we knew the reasons why the disciples objected to people bringing children to Jesus! Whatever the reason, Jesus did not approve of their so doing. Jesus wanted people to bring children to him. More important than knowing why the disciples objected is knowing why a child is the model of acceptance of the kingdom for disciples of all ages. What do you think?

Today's Saints

The life of the Venerable Bede (672/73–735), a Doctor of the Church, demonstrates that one really can transform the Church from the quiet of a monastery. As a Benedictine monk at the Abbey of Jarrow in England, he devoted his life to scholarly pursuits, including the study of Scripture, the composition of commentaries based on the ideas of Church fathers, and extensive research and writing about the history of the Church in England. He is credited with educating over six hundred monks and popularizing the use of AD (*Anno Domini*—in the year of our Lord) to refer to the Christian era. Although known as "Venerable," this title is not in reference to the ranking of canonization. Saint Bede was canonized in 1935.

Saint Gregory VII (540–604) joined the Benedictine monks, but was eventually called beyond the cloister to serve the larger Church as pope. Recognized as one of the greatest reformer popes, Saint Gregory instituted what is known as the Gregorian reform. Through this reform he wanted to end rampant and widespread abuses in the Church; in particular, nepotism, clerical marriage, and lay interference in the appointment of bishops and abbots. He was removed from the papal office twice by bishops under the control of Emperor Henry IV due to his arduous efforts to eliminate the power of temporal rulers in Church matters.

Mary Magdalene de'Pazzi (1566–1607), daughter of a noble Florentine family, was a Carmelite mystic who prayed tirelessly for the Church.

☼ **26** #166 white
Solemnity of the Most Holy Trinity

Orientation

Today's solemnity commemorates the central dogma of Christianity: the Trinity. This dogma says that there is one God in three divine persons, the Father, the Son, and the Holy Spirit. "The faith of all Christians rests on the Trinity" (*Catechism of the Catholic Church*, 232, quoting Saint Caesarius of Arles, Sermon 9, Exp. symb.: CCL 103, 47).

One of the greatest gifts of the Christian faith is the dogma of the triune God: God is three (tri) in one (une). The Christian God—Father, Son, and Holy Spirit—is relational. How amazing and wonderfully mysterious at the same time!

The readings for this solemnity speak of all aspects of the Holy Trinity. In the First Reading, we hear of the work of the Creator God, the Lord who established the heavens and the earth. We hear of the wisdom of God, an expression of God's Holy Spirit, at work even before the creation of the world. In the Second Reading, we hear of Jesus Christ through whom we have been justified and been offered peace with God. Paul also tells us of the Holy Spirit through whom the love of God has been poured into our hearts. In the Gospel reading, we hear of the Spirit of truth who will come to teach us even more about

God, leading us into a deeper relationship with the Father through Jesus.

Human beings were created to be in relationship with God from the beginning. May our relationships with each other reflect the relationships of the divine persons of the Trinity.

Lectionary for Mass

◆ FIRST READING: In today's reading, the personified wisdom of God speaks. She—both the Hebrew and Greek words for wisdom are feminine—is begotten by God in the very beginning of time, even before the creation of the earth. What is more, Wisdom is present at creation, serving as God's craftsman. Our reading concludes on a note of joy: God's delight in Wisdom and Wisdom's delight in human creatures. God delights in us. We can take these words to heart.

◆ RESPONSORIAL PSALM 8: All creation is crafted by the hand of God. Its beauty and magnificence move us to awe. Who are we in the face of all of this? God has made humankind the high point of creation, making the human creature in God's own image and giving this human creature authority and responsibility for all other creatures.

◆ SECOND READING: Paul's words delve deeply into the mystery of the Trinity at work in our lives. We are set in the right relationship with God through faith in the Lord Jesus Christ and the reconciliation he accomplished through his Death and Resurrection, our hope of glory. God has poured the gift of his Holy Spirit into our hearts. Suffering afflictions serves only to prove the genuineness of our faith and make us ever more ready to be transformed in the glory of God.

◆ GOSPEL: The words of today's Gospel are from Jesus's last discourse to his disciples the night before he died. Today's verses focus on the Holy Spirit, who will be sent by the Father and given by Jesus to those who are his own. The work of the Spirit is to guide us to the truth, speaking in the name of Jesus. In the truth that is revealed, we are set free. In this truth, Jesus is glorified.

The Roman Missal

By sending his divine Word and sanctifying Spirit into the world, God has given us a glimpse of the "wondrous mystery" we honor today: the three Persons of the Holy Trinity (Collect). We pray that we may hold to our profession of faith in the Trinity and adore the one God.

In the Prayer over the Offerings, we ask God to sanctify the gifts we offer "by the invocation of your name." The name of God is blessing and power.

The proper Preface, subtitled "The Mystery of the Most Holy Trinity," expresses what we believe about the Trinity: God is "one substance," but not "a single person." Rather, God has revealed that he is three divine Persons, Father, Son, and Holy Spirit, and what he has "revealed to us" of his glory, "we believe equally of your Son / and of the Holy Spirit."

We ask for the fruits of the Eucharist: "health of body and soul" (Prayer after Communion).

M **27** #347 green
O **Weekday /**
N **Eighth Week in Ordinary Time**

Optional Memorial of Saint Augustine of Canterbury, Bishop / white

Lectionary for Mass

◆ FIRST READING: God provides a way back to those who sin: namely, that the sinner turn *from* sin and turn *to* God. This is the meaning of conversion. Having turned to

God, one must stand firm, facing the direction God has revealed. In the second part of the reading, we hear the Old Testament understanding of Sheol, the netherworld, the realm of the dead. Here there is neither life nor praise of God. Conversion and praise are ours to do while we live on the earth.

◆ RESPONSORIAL PSALM 32: This penitential Psalm celebrates God's forgiveness and is a fitting response to today's First Reading. Confession and acknowledgement of sin are an important first step. We are open to receive God's forgiveness. We grow in self-knowledge and are readied for conversion, knowing that we need God's help.

◆ GOSPEL: Eternal life is the desire of this would-be disciple of Jesus, a man faithful to the Law and commandments, but whose heart is deeply attached to all that he owns, so much so that he is unable to follow Jesus. It is indeed hard to enter the kingdom of God, to let go of everything that God might be all in all for us.

Today's Saint

Saint Augustine, born in the first third of the sixth-century, was a Benedictine monk who became the first archbishop of Canterbury in 598. He was prior of a monastery in Rome when Saint Gregory the Great, after seeing blonde Saxon slaves in the market, chose him to lead a mission to England. Augustine worked in Kent in the south of England. When he converted King Aethelberht, the rest of Kent followed. He died in 605 and was buried in the abbey church at Canterbury, which became a place of pilgrimage. The shrine was destroyed during the English Reformation.

TUE 28 #348 green
Weekday

Lectionary for Mass

◆ FIRST READING: Sacrifice was an important part of Israel's worship. Sirach's words broaden the scope of what constitutes sacrifice. Obedience to the Law, works of charity, almsgiving, refraining from evil, and avoiding injustice—all can be "offerings to the Lord." At the same time, the ritual sacrifices prescribed according to the Law are to be rendered joyfully. Regardless of how much or how little we have or bring to the Lord, we will be repaid abundantly.

◆ RESPONSORIAL PSALM 50: In our Responsorial Psalm, God takes his people to task for offering their sacrifices without having their hearts turned toward God in praise.

◆ GOSPEL: There is something so human and real about Peter. He tells Jesus that "we have given up everything and followed you"—unlike that man who couldn't part from his possessions. He asks him, "What are we going to get in return?" And the Lord says, "All that you have given up will return to you in abundance and you will have eternal life. There is also something else: Persecutions. You will suffer because you follow me" (author's paraphrasing). The members of Mark's community know the reality of persecution because of their faith in Jesus. In the early Church, this faith can cost you your life. But the return will be abundant: eternal life.

WED 29 #349 green
Weekday

Lectionary for Mass

◆ FIRST READING: Today's reading is a prayer for God's help, for deliverance in a time of affliction, for an act of power that will give witness to all the nations that the Almighty God is indeed the God of Israel. The mention of signs and wonders evokes the time when Israel was enslaved in Egypt and God delivered them in the marvels of the Exodus. What Israel needs now—possibly at the time of the Greek domination of the land of Israel and oppression of her people in the second century before Christ—are new signs and wonders. The people express their trust in God's abiding graciousness toward them and their hope for deliverance from their enemies.

◆ RESPONSORIAL PSALM: Our antiphon is the first line of the First Reading from Sirach. The verses are from Psalm 79, an oppressed (first stanza) people's prayer for deliverance. In return for God's deliverance through an act demonstrating his power, the people promise perpetual praise.

◆ GOSPEL: Today's text follows immediately upon yesterday's Gospel. By his mention of persecution, Jesus has engendered fear in the disciples. Today he teaches them that this is the lot he will suffer, and all who follow him must share in it. Jesus came precisely that he might give his life to redeem others.

THU 30 #350 green
Weekday

Lectionary for Mass

◆ FIRST READING: Today's text is actually part of a discourse on the glory of God as revealed in all of creation, a discourse which includes all of chapter 43 of Sirach as well. God's omnipotence, his knowledge of all creatures and all time, his wisdom and understanding are also treated in this discourse.

◆ RESPONSORIAL PSALM 33: Echoing a verse from today's First Reading, our responsorial antiphon acclaims the creative word of the Lord. The Psalm is one of praise and thanksgiving for all the works of creation.

◆ GOSPEL: In restoring the sight of the blind Bartimaeus, Jesus continues the creative work of God. Bartimaeus "sees" with insight, not only physically. He became a disciple, one who follows Jesus on his way.

FRI 31 #572 white
Feast of the Visitation of the Blessed Virgin Mary

Orientation

What a gift it must have been for these two women to spend time together. Given their miraculous pregnancies and unique experiences of God, they could only turn to each other to ponder and process what was happening. As God brought them together, their companionship during this time must have been a source of mutual comfort, encouragement, and joyful anticipation. Praise be to God for knowing our needs even before we are aware of them, and caring for us through the love and friendship of those around us.

Lectionary for Mass

◆ FIRST OPTION FOR FIRST READING: A spirit of joy pervades this reading from the prophet Zephaniah—both God's joy in Zion (Jerusalem) and Zion's joy in God. Jerusalem's salvation is at hand; the Lord is in her midst. We find these same themes in the feast we celebrate today: the joy of the two women miraculously with child, the joy of the Baptist in the womb of Elizabeth when he hears Mary's greeting. The Lord is in their midst, the Lord is within Mary.

◆ SECOND OPTION FOR FIRST READING: The behaviors prescribed in Paul's words to the Romans are demonstrably manifest in today's Gospel. What sincere love and mutual affection existed between Mary and Elizabeth, these two humble servants of the Lord. In coming to assist her elderly and pregnant cousin, Mary contributed to the needs of the holy ones and Elizabeth received her in gracious hospitality. Fervent in spirit, they served the Lord and one another.

◆ CANTICLE: Today's Canticle is from a hymn from the prophet Isaiah. Mary and Elizabeth could fittingly make this prayer their own. How truly God is among them in Mary's unborn child. Both women break forth in praise.

◆ GOSPEL: As we would expect for today, we hear of the meeting between the pregnant Mary and the pregnant Elizabeth. Each has conceived through the marvelous working of God in her life. Each knows that she is indeed blessed by the Lord and sings God's praise.

The Roman Missal

The Entrance Antiphon from Psalm 66 perfectly captures the joy of Mary and Elizabeth, who both speak words of faith at their holy meeting: "Come and hear . . . I will tell what the Lord did for my soul."

The Gloria is said or sung on this feast.

The Collect is full of echoes of the Gospel account of the Visitation. Just as Mary visited her cousin in response to the Spirit's urging, we pray that we may be "faithful to the promptings of the Spirit." Just as Mary praised God in her Magnificat, we pray that we may "magnify [God's] greatness / with the Virgin Mary."

We ask God to receive what we offer, just as he received "the charity" of Mary (Prayer over the Offerings).

Preface II of the Blessed Virgin Mary is used.

The Prayer after Communion echoes the language of Mary's Magnificat: "May your Church proclaim your greatness, O God, / for you have done great things for your faithful." We pray that we may be like John the Baptist in his mother's womb, aware of "the hidden presence of Christ," and rejoice to receive him in the Sacrament of his Body and Blood.

June
Month of the Sacred Heart

SAT 1 #352 red
Memorial of Saint Justin, Martyr

Lectionary for Mass

◆ FIRST READING: This reading from the concluding chapter of the Book of Sirach is actually a prayer of thanksgiving for the much sought-after gift of wisdom. Note the diligence and hard work required for the pursuit of wisdom! What qualities are important if one is to attain wisdom?

◆ RESPONSORIAL PSALM: These verses from the second half of Psalm 19 acclaim the wisdom of the Law of the Lord. God's Law is a source of joy for the psalmist. It is more precious than gold; it is more pleasing to the taste than even the sweetest honey.

◆ GOSPEL: The Jewish authorities try to trick Jesus, and he in turn catches them in their own ruse.

The Roman Missal

The prayers, which emphasize the wise teaching and doctrine of Saint Justin, are found in the Proper of Saints. The Preface of Holy Martyrs is used.

Today's Saint

Saint Justin (103–165) was a philosopher who became one of the Church's first apologists, exploring the rational basis of faith and arguing that true philosophy would lead to Christ. We are also indebted to Justin for one of the earliest descriptions of the Mass (it can be found in the Office of Readings for the Third Sunday of Easter). His memorial is a good day to pray for theologians, philosophers, and for ourselves—that we will seek God not only with our hearts, but also with our minds.

#169   white

Solemnity of the Most Holy Body and Blood of Christ / Corpus Christi

Orientation

In the reading from the Gospel according to Luke, the Twelve have five loaves and two fish and so they tell Jesus to send the crowds away to find their own lodging and food. Jesus, however, wishes to do otherwise. Earlier, Jesus had instructed the Twelve for their mission saying, "Take nothing for the journey, neither walking stick, nor sack, nor food, nor money, and let no one take a second tunic" (Luke 9:3). It seems they have quickly forgotten they need not worry about having enough to eat.

With the small amount of food, Jesus feeds all five thousand. An impossible task becomes possible through Christ! On the Solemnity of the Most Holy Body and Blood of Christ, we celebrate with great joy the gift of the Eucharist. Jesus, by giving us his Body and Blood, gave us the possibility of new life. Go forth from the Eucharist following Jesus's command to his disciples to share what we have received. Trust God and there will even be leftovers!

Lectionary for Mass

◆ FIRST READING: We meet the mysterious figure of Melchizedek who appears rather suddenly with no introduction other than that he is king of Salem (Jerusalem) and a priest of God the Most High. He blesses Abraham and brings gifts of bread and wine. The sparse detail about Melchizedek (no information on birth, death, family, etc.) was interpreted in Jewish tradition as signifying that his was an eternal priesthood, as is said in Hebrews 7 where he is presented as a figure of Christ. This, plus the mention of bread and wine, is no doubt the basis for the choice of this reading for today's feast.

◆ RESPONSORIAL PSALM 110: This royal Psalm acclaims the priestly role of the Davidic kings, in line with Melchizedek's royal priestly service. The Psalm was perhaps used on the day of the king's coronation. In Hebrews 7, the words of this Psalm are applied to Christ.

◆ SECOND READING: This text is the earliest account of the institution of the Eucharist. Paul "hands on" the tradition which he has first received from the Church, the body of Christ, concerning the meal Jesus shared with his disciples the night he was "handed over." The bread that he gives is his very own Body. The cup of wine is the cup of his Blood, the blood of the new covenant. Whenever we eat of this bread and drink of this cup, we proclaim the Lord's death, his total gift of self to us and for us, until he comes again.

◆ GOSPEL: The early Christians saw each of the Gospel scenes where Jesus fed the crowds with bread and fish as prefiguring the Eucharist. Note the details of the miracle: "looking up to heaven" and saying a blessing. Note, too, the context of the story: Jesus is teaching about the kingdom of God and curing those in need of healing. Is this not also what our own celebration of the Eucharist is about? ("but only say the word and I shall be healed . . .")

The Roman Missal

The prayers for this solemnity are thought to have been composed by Saint Thomas Aquinas, and they are rich in Eucharistic theology.

The "wonderful Sacrament" which we celebrate on this day, and at every Mass, is "a memorial," a living remembrance, of the Passion. We pray that we may "revere the sacred mysteries" and "experience in ourselves" the promised redemption (Collect).

The sacrament of Christ's Body and Blood is a sign "in mystery" of the "unity and peace" for which the Church longs (Prayer over the Offerings).

Preface I or II of the Holy Eucharist is used.

In our sharing in the Body and Blood of Christ, we receive a pledge of future glory. The "divine life" is "foreshadowed in this present age" in the Eucharist we receive. We pray that we may "delight" in its fulfillment "for all eternity" (Prayer after Communion).

The Roman Missal states, "It is desirable that a procession take place after the Mass in which the Host to be carried in the procession is consecrated." The procession may begin immediately, or after an extended period of adoration. In either circumstance, the Concluding Rites of the Mass are omitted. As soon as Communion is over, the deacon or priest exposes the host in the monstrance, which is placed on the altar. Then the Prayer after Communion is said, and the procession begins. The *Ceremonial of Bishops* includes much more detail about the order of the procession, which concludes with Benediction, either in another church, outside, or even back in the church where the procession began (see Chapter 15, paragraphs 385–394).

Other Ideas

Does your parish do a procession for the Most Holy Body and Blood of Christ? If so, attend it this week. If not, talk with friends about their experiences of the procession and ask if it might be possible to revive this tradition in your parish.

This week spend some time before the Blessed Sacrament, perhaps taking with you today's Scriptures for meditation. Then write in your journal or talk to a friend about your experience.

Receiving the Eucharist each week is the most essential and intimate part of our faith. Our experience and understanding of the sacrament will grow over time. Write in your journal or talk with a trusted friend about what it is for you at this moment, and then repeat this exercise six months from now.

The disciples wanted to dismiss the crowds to take care of themselves. Jesus wanted to do otherwise. Who gets dismissed by our society or even by us? Who does Jesus invite us to consider feeding (literally or figuratively)?

Abram gave a tenth of everything in gratitude for Melchizedek's priestly service. Abram acted in a spirit of stewardship by doing this, giving something from his own sustenance. You might also read the story of the widow's offering in Luke 21:1–4 for another example of stewardship. What do you believe about stewardship? What effort do you make to tithe your time, talent, and treasure? Examine your own or your family's effort to give in these three ways to your parish and other charities.

Bring food or a meal to a sick neighbor, soup kitchen, local pantry, or a family with a new baby.

#353   red
Memorial of Saint Charles Lwanga and Companions, Martyrs / Ninth Week in Ordinary Time

M O N 3

Lectionary for Mass

◆ FIRST READING: In today's reading, we are introduced to the acts of piety and good deeds performed by Tobit, a deportee from Israel living in the land of Assyria. He is faithful to the celebration of Jewish festivals and shares what he has with the poor. Another of Tobit's good deeds was to bury the dead, but this got him into trouble with the Assyrian authorities prior to the celebration of Pentecost spoken of in today's text. When the king had members of his people executed, Tobit would take the bodies and bury them as soon as possible. If he had not, the Assyrians might have treated the bodies with disrespect or at best, not properly cared for them. Tobit was not to be put off by fear of the consequences, to his neighbors' great amazement.

◆ RESPONSORIAL PSALM 112 is an apt description of Tobit! As the story unfolds throughout the week, we shall see how much he is blessed

for faithfulness to God. For centuries, this just person has been remembered for his fear and reverence of the Lord—in both Jewish and Christian tradition.

◆ GOSPEL: We hear the parable of the vineyard (a symbol for Israel in Isaiah 5:1–7) told to Israel's religious leaders. The tenants' rejection of the numerous servants evokes Israel's rejection of the prophets sent by God. Perhaps the one beaten over the head is John the Baptist (see Mark 6:17–29). In the Gospel accounts, Jesus is the Beloved Son (see Mark 9:7). The verse from Psalm 118 cited in today's Gospel was much used by the early Church with reference to Jesus. Finally, we have a view of the outreach of the Gospel to the nations with the reference to the vineyard being given to others.

The Roman Missal

The prayers are found in the Proper of Saints. The Preface of Holy Martyrs is used.

Today's Saints

Along with his 22 companions, Saint Charles Lwanga (1860/1865–1886) is considered a proto-martyr and is one of the first African martyrs. Saint Charles, a native of Uganda, served the kabaka, or king, as a master of pages whose primary task was to train young people in royal service. Unfortunately, he was thrust into this position during the reign of the anti-Christian king, Mwanga. As a recent convert, he felt impelled to catechize the young pages in the ways of Christianity, which led to several Baptisms. When the king found out about his actions, he demanded that Saint Charles and the newly baptized renounce their faith, but they remained steadfast in their beliefs, resulting in their arrest and sentence to death. Saint Charles and six others were wrapped in a reed mat and burned to death. His final words were *Kotonda wange*, "My God."

T U E **4** #354 green
Weekday

Lectionary for Mass

◆ First Reading: Tobit hardly seems blessed for his good deeds in today's First Reading, and one can even wonder about his "true character" because of the way he treats his wife and his inability to believe her word. Though we may perform many good deeds, there is always room for conversion!

◆ Responsorial Psalm 112: Today's Psalm is the same as yesterday's. We can think of Tobit as one whose trust in the Lord is firm.

◆ Gospel: In this controversy with the hypocritical Pharisees and Herodians, Jesus is clearly set up: "You don't care what people think. . . . Status means nothing to you. . . . So, tell us, should we pay taxes to the Emperor?" (author's paraphrasing). Jesus's clever reply acknowledges the legitimate authority of society and takes the discussion a step further. Where do we find the image of God? In the human person!

W E D **5** #355 red
Memorial of Saint Boniface, Bishop and Martyr

Lectionary for Mass

◆ First Reading: Today's reading follows upon yesterday's text and is, in fact, a prayer of lamentation. Tobit acknowledges the sins of his people as well as his own. He prays for death, a much better option than his blindness. Perhaps the "insults" he refers to are those spoken by his wife in yesterday's text. The second episode in today's reading focuses on the lament of another person

who has had to endure insult because of her fate. Sarah, too, prays for death. God heard the prayer of both Tobit and Sarah and sends his angel to heal them both. What is more, Sarah will become the wife of Tobit's son.

◆ Responsorial Psalm 25: This song of confidence is somewhat of a contrast with Tobit's and Sarah's prayers for death. Nevertheless, they both entrusted their lot to the Lord, rather than take their own lives. Both waited for the Lord, who answered their prayers in ways they could never have expected.

◆ Gospel: Today's Gospel reading is yet another controversy story, another set-up. The Sadducees were a group within Judaism who adhered only to the teachings of the Torah as found in the first five books of the Bible. They did not embrace later developments in religious thought as did the Pharisees. The Sadducees, who reject the idea of resurrection, pose what seems like an insurmountable problem. But they do so because they think of life only as we know it. Jesus makes it quite clear: in the age to come, we will be transformed spiritual creatures.

The Roman Missal

The Collect is drawn from the Proper of Saints, with the remaining prayers taken from the Common of Martyrs or of Pastors. The Preface of Holy Martyrs or of Holy Pastors may be used.

Today's Saint

Saint Boniface started life as Winfrid, a member of a Benedictine monastery in England. He was elected abbot, but resigned in order to become a missionary. The pope gave him the name Boniface and sent him to Germany, where he served as bishop for 30 years. It is said that he won the confidence of the people when he took an ax to

the sacred oak of Thor, and it immediately crashed to the ground. He was martyred on June 5, 754, as he was preparing to administer the Sacrament of Confirmation.

T H U **6** #356 green
Weekday

Optional Memorial of Saint Norbert, Bishop / white

Lectionary for Mass

◆ First Reading: The Lectionary, going from chapter 3 to chapter 6 of Tobit, omits details of the story that provide the setting for today's reading. In chapter 4, Tobit recalls that he had left a large sum of money in Media and decided to send his son in search of it. When Tobiah went in search of a travelling companion, he met Raphael, the angel of God in disguise. Raphael then led him to the house of Raguel where he met Sarah his future wife. Their prayer together on their wedding night delivered them from the demon who had stricken Sarah's previous husbands.

◆ Responsorial Psalm 128: Indeed Sarah and Tobiah deeply reverenced the Lord and lived according to God's Law. Those who do so will receive blessings from the Lord in descendants and prosperity.

◆ Gospel: Note the interesting dynamic between the scribe (scholar of the Law) and Jesus. It is the scribe who affirms Jesus's wisdom and teaching. Jesus returns the compliment, if you will, when he sees that the scribe has moved beyond the mere letter of the Law with his additional comment that the law of love is worth more in the eyes of God than ritual sacrifices.

Today's Saint

Saint Norbert (1080–1134), a subdeacon and canon in the Rhineland, had a conversion experience similar to Saint Paul, in which he was thrown from a horse during a violent thunderstorm. Following this event he had a change of heart. He became increasingly aware of the need to renounce the trappings of the world and to preach reform to the canons. His preaching led him to the valley of Premontre where he laid the framework, along with 13 disciples, for a reform movement that became known as the Canons Regular of Premontre, the Premonstratensians, or Norbertines. These Norbertines lived together according to the *Rule of Saint Augustine*, wore a simple white habit, and challenged the clergy through preaching and example to recommit themselves to celibacy and simplicity. Although their message was not always well received by the clergy, more and more young men felt called to join the Norbertines. Because of his extraordinary leadership and reforming spirit, Saint Norbert was appointed archbishop of Magdeburg, Germany.

FRI 7 #172 white
Solemnity of the Most Sacred Heart of Jesus

Orientatation

Saint Margaret Mary Alacoque, in late seventeenth-century France, had a vision of the Sacred Heart of Jesus. She felt compelled to spread the word about Jesus's mercy and love for all humanity. The devotion was officially recognized in 1765. In the early twentieth century, with the approval of Pope Pius X, Father Mateo Crawley-Boevey in South America proposed that all Christian families formally acknowledge the sovereignty of the Heart of Jesus over their homes with enthronement ceremonies.

Lectionary for Mass

◆ FIRST READING: What consoling words we hear: God will be the shepherd of his flock. We are comforted by the images of the tender care this good shepherd gives his

flock: rescuing, leading, gathering together, pasturing them on good grazing ground, seeking the lost, healing the injured. Which of these images have you experienced in God's care for you?

◆ RESPONSORIAL PSALM 23 likewise acclaims God as the good shepherd. It is a beautiful prayer of confidence prayed by one who has personally experienced God's tender care for his flock.

◆ SECOND READING: Paul reflects on the tremendous love of God in sending us his Son who died that we might be reconciled to him and who has also poured out the gift of his Holy Spirit, his love, into our hearts.

◆ GOSPEL: The lost sheep is the subject of today's Gospel. No shepherd would nonchalantly write off the loss of a sheep. Neither would God. Jesus's parable focuses on the joy of finding what is lost, especially the joy in heaven over the repentance of one sinner who had strayed away.

The Roman Missal

The Solemnity of the Sacred Heart of Jesus is all about the incredible love of Christ for humanity. The Entrance Antiphon speaks of this love in the words of Psalm 33: "The designs of his Heart are from age to age, / to rescue their souls from death, / and to keep them alive in famine."

There are two options for the Collect. The first speaks of the Heart of Jesus as a fount of grace. We pray that we who "glory" in the Sacred Heart of Jesus may remember his goodness, and be worthy to receive "an overflowing measure of grace / from that fount of heavenly gifts." The second emphasizes the suffering of Christ, whose heart is "wounded by our sins" and yet who gives us "the boundless treasures of . . . love." We pray that we may

make reparation to him as we offer our devotion.

In the Prayer over the Offerings, we ask God to look at his Son's love for us in his Heart—and to let our offering be "an expiation of our offenses."

The proper Preface is subtitled "The Boundless Charity of Christ." In Christ, raised high on the cross, pierced by the soldier's lance, we behold "the wellspring of the Church's Sacraments," a fountain of salvation open to all. Christ's Sacred Heart is an "open heart," offering love and life to every person.

The familiar image shows the Sacred Heart of Jesus on fire, a sign of his suffering and his love. In the Prayer after Communion, we pray that we may also be "fervent with the fire of holy love," and be so drawn to Christ that "we may learn to see him in our neighbor" (Prayer after Communion).

Other Ideas

To celebrate the Sacred Heart of Jesus, the Lectionary offers us readings that focus on Christ as the Good Shepherd. Ezekiel and Luke both describe the shepherd as fully committed to his sheep, concretely demonstrating care and compassion through unmistakable acts of love. Cut out a large paper heart and invite family members throughout the week to jot down the specific acts of love—corporal or spiritual works of mercy—they have done in imitation of the Good Shepherd who has opened his Sacred Heart to all of us.

SAT 8 #358, Gospel #573 white
Memorial of the Immaculate Heart of the Blessed Virgin Mary

Lectionary for Mass

◆ FIRST READING: Because of yesterday's solemnity, we missed the reading about Tobiah's homecoming. Tobiah's attempt to pay Raphael for his services becomes the occasion for instruction on the praise and thanksgiving that are God's due as well as on the acts of piety that those who fear God are to perform. Raphael also reveals to Tobit and Tobiah that he is one of the seven angels who serve the Lord.

◆ CANTICLE: Our response is from Tobit's hymn of praise after Raphael's ascent to heaven. Notice how Tobit's hymn reflects his own life experience and how he invites others to join in his hymn of praise and thanksgiving.

◆ GOSPEL: Jesus warns his listeners against taking on the hypocrisy of the scribes who grasp at honor and notoriety for themselves in the name of religion. The second part of the Gospel is particularly interesting. What did Mark mean by saying that Jesus observed how financial offerings were made in the Temple? Were the rich likewise trying to get honor and acclaim by their large donations? Jesus did not praise the rich with their sizeable offerings but the poor widow and her meager offering. Her gift, insignificant as it was, was indeed a true gift, for it came from her very livelihood.

The Roman Missal

The prayers for this memorial are found in the Proper of Saints, immediately following the prayers for the Visitation of the Blessed Virgin Mary on May 31.

God made Mary's Immaculate Heart "a fit dwelling place for the Holy Spirit." We, too, are formed to be a "temple of [God's] glory" (Collect).

In the Prayer over the Offerings, we pray that the prayers and offerings we make on this memorial may be pleasing to God, and bring us "help and forgiveness."

Through the sacrament we share, we are "partakers of eternal redemption" (Prayer after Communion.) We pray that God's grace may increase in us.

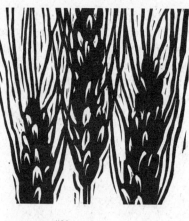

9 #90   green
Tenth Sunday in Ordinary Time

Orientation

As Jesus raises the dead son of the widow of Naim, he reveals God's power over life and death. This passage, however, also teaches something about God's loving disposition toward humankind. Even though filled with the authority of divine power, Jesus was moved with pity toward the mourning widow and offered her kind words of comfort. He knew he had the power to help her, but compassion still filled his heart as he did so. In this, Jesus reveals to us a God who is not only all-powerful, but who is also deeply concerned for us as his beloved sons and daughters.

Lectionary for Mass

◆ FIRST READING: The marvelous signs worked by the prophets bear witness that the power of God is active in their ministry. The plight of the woman in today's story is particularly poignant since she is a widow, helpless and powerless, having no husband to provide for her and her son. God shows a special concern for the helpless and powerless (widows, orphans, and the poor). Elijah's prayer is heard and the child revives.

◆ RESPONSORIAL PSALM 30: This song of thanksgiving for deliverance in a time of sickness and death is most fitting given the miracle accounts in both the First Reading and the Gospel. The sons in both stories are raised from the netherworld of death and their mothers' mourning changes to joy.

◆ SECOND READING: For the next five Sundays, we hear from Paul's Letter to the Galatians. (We missed the beginning last week, because of the solemnity.) In the section for today, we hear Paul's own account of his apostolic call to ministry to the Gentiles. He contrasts his former way of life as a zealous persecutor on behalf of Judaism, with his new way after his experience of a revelation of Jesus. What is striking in Paul's account is the fact that he needed time, some three years in fact, just to "be" with the revelation before acting on it. What a powerful, overwhelming experience it must have been!

◆ GOSPEL: Luke's account of Jesus raising the widow's son from the dead has many parallels with today's First Reading, including the attribution of the title "prophet" to Jesus. Note also the acclamation of God's presence in their midst in the person of Jesus.

The Roman Missal

The Collect praises God, the source of "all good things," and asks that with God's help we may "discern what is right," and, with God's guidance, do it.

Prayer over the Offerings: We pray that we may grow in charity through the sacrifice we offer.

The short and simple Prayer after Communion asks God to free us from evil, and "lead us to what is right."

Other Ideas

Schedule a retreat day for yourself to get away and rest with the Lord. Even if it's in your own home or apartment, give yourself the time and space just to be for a whole day.

MON 10 #359 green
Weekday

Lectionary for Mass

◆ FIRST READING: Encouragement is without doubt the predominant motif in this reading from the second letter of Paul to the Corinthians. The word (in some form) occurs at least ten times. Paul has received comfort and encouragement from God so that he in turn might encourage others who are suffering. Suffering is part and parcel of Christian life, and of the Paschal Mystery. But suffering is not the end; suffering can open up to encouragement and to life.

◆ RESPONSORIAL PSALM: The experience of encouragement is certainly a pleasant one, so today's responsorial antiphon invites us to "taste and see." Psalm 34 is a prayer of confident praise from one who has experienced deliverance by the Lord.

◆ GOSPEL: "Blessed are . . ." To be blessed in the Beatitude sense is to experience the deep happiness that comes from God alone. The categories singled out as blessed call us to examine our own manner of life. Note that seven of the Beatitudes speak of future reward; two, of present reward. Nine Beatitudes? Yes, our Gospel includes a ninth.

TUE 11 #580, Gospel #360 red
Memorial of Saint
Barnabas, Apostle

Lectionary for Mass

◆ FIRST READING: Barnabas was a Levite from Cyprus who in the very first days of the Church sold his farm and gave the money to the

Apostles. He was involved in the early Christian community from then on, and it is he who first introduces the newly converted Saul to the other Apostles. The context of today's reading is the dispersion of some members of the Jerusalem community after the death of Stephen, the first martyr. Some went to Antioch, where a great number of people received the Good News of the Gospel and believed. As a result, Barnabas is sent there to teach. Barnabas enlists Saul's help and they remain in Antioch for a year. There, the Christain community heard the voice of the Spirit commissioning Barnabas and Saul for further missionary journeys. With prayer, fasting, and the laying on of hands, the community sends them on their way.

◆ RESPONSORIAL PSALM 98: Already in the Old Testament, there is testimony that all nations—and not just the Jewish people—will receive the revelation of the Lord's saving power. Today's Psalm is a case in point. And certainly, the missionary journeys of Barnabas, Saul and their companions are further realization of this promise. The Apostles did indeed journey to the ends of the earth—at least as it was known in their day—to proclaim the salvation accomplished by Jesus of Nazareth. For those who received their message, praise and thanksgiving are the only fitting response.

◆ GOSPEL: Jesus compares the presence and ministry of his disciples to salt (which enhances the taste of food) and to light (which allows us to see in the dark). If salt or light lose their effectiveness, they are worthless. So, too, with the disciples—and we are among them.

The Roman Missal

The prayers are found in the Proper of Saints. The Collect is a prayer for the continued spread of the Gospel, both "by word and by deed." We

ask that our offering may "set us on fire / with the flame of your love," the same fire which burned in Saint Barnabas (Prayer over the Offerings). The Preface of the Apostles is used.

Today's Saint

Even though Saint Barnabas (first century) was not one of the original Twelve Apostles, he was given the title of "Apostle" by Saint Luke and the early Church Fathers, due to his apostolic endeavors on behalf of Christianity. His original name was Joseph, but the Apostles gave him the surname Barnabas, meaning "son of encouragement," probably due to his friendly disposition. Together with Saint Paul, he extended the missionary efforts of the Church beyond Jerusalem to Antioch, and after much success moved onto other places throughout Asia Minor. After parting ways with Saint Paul over issues regarding circumcision and the Mosaic Law, Saint Barnabas embarked on missionary journeys with John and Mark (see Acts of the Apostles 15:36–40). Tradition indicates that Saint Barnabas was stoned to death, and his remains were taken to Constantinople where a church stands in his honor.

WED 12 #361 green
Weekday

Lectionary for Mass

◆ FIRST READING: It is God who has called Paul and his travelling companions to their ministry on behalf of the Gospel, and it is God working through them who accomplishes anything they do. Having made that point, Paul goes on to compare the new covenant which they proclaim with the old covenant of Mt. Sinai, focusing on the glory of the two covenants. Note that "glory" occurs some nine times in the second part of the reading. The

glory of the new covenant far surpasses that of the old.

◆ RESPONSORIAL PSALM 99: Having heard of the glory of God's covenant in the First Reading, we acclaim now the holiness of God. The Psalm tells of God's giving the covenant to Moses on Mt. Sinai and God's forgiveness of the people's infidelities.

◆ GOSPEL: A key issue in Matthew's account of the Gospel is Jesus's attitude to the law. Does he ignore it or abolish it? Subsequent verses in chapter 5 of the Gospel make it perfectly clear: far from abolishing the law, Jesus demands even more than the letter of the law. It is the observance of this "more" that makes one truly a disciple, and great in the kingdom of heaven.

THU 13 #362 white
Memorial of Saint Anthony of Padua, Priest and Doctor of the Church

Lectionary for Mass

◆ FIRST READING: The contrasting of the old covenant (Sinai) with the new covenant inaugurated by Jesus continues in this reading. All of us, and not just a chosen few, can gaze on the glory of God and be transformed in radiance. (Remember the glory on Moses's face when he spoke with God on the mountain? See Exodus 34:29). To see God's glory is to be transformed, through the power of God's Spirit at work in our hearts.

◆ RESPONSORIAL PSALM 89: Our antiphon acclaims the glory of God dwelling among us. The stanzas of the Psalm describe the characteristics of the full realization of this glory in our midst.

◆ GOSPEL: We hear the first examples of Jesus's teaching on the Law, where he asks for something more than the letter of the Law. Today's Gospel focuses on anger toward

another, on speaking offensively to another, on holding grudges. Jesus prohibits them all and calls for rather strong evidence of amendment: "[L]eave your gift . . . at the altar . . . go first and be reconciled . . . then come and offer your gift" (Matthew 5:24).

The Roman Missal

The Collect, which emphasizes Saint Anthony's powerful preaching and intercession, is found in the Proper of Saints, with the remaining prayers drawn from the Common of Pastors, of Doctors of the Church, or of Holy Men and Women.

Today's Saint

Saint Anthony of Padua (1195–1231), a member of a noble Portuguese family, joined the Canons Regular of Saint Augustine at a young age, but later joined the Franciscans to engage in missionary work. Although his missionary dreams were halted due to illness, he received public acclaim for his preaching style, which led to the conversion of many and the end of heresy, earning him the title "the Hammer of the Heretics." He had the privilege of meeting Saint Francis of Assisi in person and was later elected provincial of Northern Italy. His writing is extensive, especially in the area of sermons; therefore, he was named a Doctor of the Church. People invoke his name when trying to find lost items. This is due to an event when a novice took Anthony's Psalter, eventually returning it because of a distressing apparition.

FRI 14 #363 green
Weekday

Lectionary for Mass

◆ FIRST READING: Today's First Reading plants us firmly on the earth, not on the mountain of glory! Yes, we see the glory of God, we hold that treasure in our hearts, but

our hearts are contained in fragile, and sometimes cracked, earthen vessels. Our fragility is tested by the trials we experience, but it is through these trials that we are transformed in Jesus's very own life. Let us give thanks to God for these challenging realities!

◆ RESPONSORIAL PSALM: We offer thanks to God in a sacrifice of praise in the words of Psalm 116. The psalmist kept faith even in a time of affliction and experienced the Lord's deliverance.

◆ GOSPEL: Jesus asks more of his disciples than the mere letter of the Law. Today's Gospel is concerned with the laws pertaining to adultery and divorce. Jesus prohibits adultery in one's heart. Divorce is prohibited except when the marriage violated the kinship prohibitions in Jewish law.

SAT 15 #364 green
Weekday

Optional Memorial of the Blessed Virgin Mary / white

Lectionary for Mass

◆ FIRST READING: The death of Christ has given birth to a new creation, a new reality, a new covenant of reconciliation between God and humankind. The love of Christ drives Paul—both Christ's love for Paul and Paul's love for Christ—to be an ambassador for God in his apostolic ministry. What love God has shown us in the Incarnation, Death, and Resurrection of Christ!

◆ RESPONSORIAL PSALM 103: The Lord is indeed kind and merciful in all he has done for us. Let us never forget his forgiveness of our transgressions.

◆ GOSPEL: Jesus speaks against false oaths, exhorting his disciples to speak in truth and integrity.

16 #93 green
Eleventh Sunday in Ordinary Time

Orientation

A penitent woman is washing Jesus's feet at the house of the Pharisee. People are judging her and showing disdain, so Jesus relates a parable to explain that she is showing and experiencing deep gratitude for her reconciliation with the Lord. Those who have been lost in the depths of shame and despair surely rejoice more for rediscovering the path toward right relationship with God; therefore, instead of judgment and disdain, they deserve our attention and imitation. All of us are alike in the need for forgiveness. Those who have been forgiven for more are role models for the rest of us, not because they have sinned more, but because of the profound sense of joy they have come to know in light of God's forgiveness.

Lectionary for Mass

◆ FIRST READING: Today's First Reading and Gospel place two sinners in bold contrast: the one, the famous King David, greatest of Israel's kings, and the other, an unnamed woman who anoints Jesus's feet when he is at table in the home of a Pharisee (perhaps the third sinner in today's reading, guilty of self-righteousness if nothing else). The First Reading begins with a recital of all God has done for the seemingly thankless David. Nevertheless, when he acknowledged his sin, David was forgiven.

◆ RESPONSORIAL PSALM 32: Our antiphon is a confession of sin, as is the second stanza chosen from this penitential Psalm. The first, third, and last stanzas focus on the joy and gladness—indeed, blessedness—of the one who acknowledges sin and is forgiven.

◆ SECOND READING: One of the major issues in the Letter to the Galatians is that of justification, being in the right relationship with God. Is it by observance of the Law (according to the Jews) or by faith in Jesus? A problem had arisen in the Galatian community because of the presence of Judaizing missionaries who say that to be Christian, Gentiles must first convert to Judaism. Paul's emphasis is strong: we are put in the right relationship with God through faith in Jesus, not circumcision.

◆ GOSPEL: The story of the encounter between Jesus and the sinful woman highlights not only Jesus's compassion and his authority to forgive sins, but also the woman's great love which is much more significant to Jesus than her sins. (It is not so from the perspective of Simon. As a Pharisee, he would pride himself on his separation from sinners.) The longer form of today's Gospel includes an important text regarding the women disciples who journeyed with Jesus and the other disciples from Galilee to Jerusalem. They are there at the Crucifixion and burial of Jesus. They come to the tomb on the morning of the first day of the week. They are with the others, awaiting the promised Holy Spirit on Pentecost.

The Roman Missal

Without God, we "can do nothing." We ask for God's grace, that we may follow God's commands and be pleasing to him "by our resolve and our deeds" (Collect).

The Eucharist is food for body and soul. We pray that this "sustenance . . . may not fail us in body or in spirit" (Prayer over the Offerings).

Holy Communion is a foretaste of the promise of our union with God. We pray that this sacrament may "bring about unity in your Church" (Prayer after Communion).

Other Ideas

During this week, make time for quiet prayer before the Blessed Sacrament. Use the time to thank God for the gift of the Eucharist and ask God to deepen your faith.

Simon invited Jesus to teach him (Luke 7:40). Learning from the forgiveness Jesus taught, think about a person to whom you need to offer forgiveness and decide on a way to do so.

Several women's names are listed at the end of the Gospel passage. Among the names is Mary Magdalene. Mary of Magdala is often confused with other Marys in the Gospel accounts. Sometimes, she is incorrectly thought to have been a prostitute. She is often referred to as a disciple and has a significant role in the Gospel according to John as a witness to the Risen Christ. Read the references to Mary Magdalene in the Scriptures (Matthew 27:56–61; 28:1; Mark 15:40–47; 16:1–9; Luke 8:2; 24:10; John 19:25; 20:1–18). What do you learn about discipleship from her actions? Journal or discuss the meaning of discipleship with a small group or a friend.

M O N 17 #365 green
Weekday

Lectionary for Mass

◆ First Reading: Today's reading follows upon the text we heard on Saturday. Having spoken about the new creation that is in Christ and the call to reconciliation, Paul urges the Corinthians not to receive God's grace in vain. In other words, recognize the power of God that could be operative within us, if only we are open to it and willing to cooperate with it. Paul then lists all that he and his companions have endured for the sake of spreading the Gospel. Theirs is a sharing in the paradox of the Gospel: it is in dying that we live; it is in losing all that we gain everything.

◆ Responsorial Psalm: Today's responsorial antiphon echoes the theme of salvation heard in the First Reading. Psalm 98 is a hymn of praise to God for his fidelity to Israel and for the salvation offered to all nations.

◆ Gospel: Like deserves like, deemed the Law in terms of retaliation for evil, but Jesus radically overturns this: Do not give like for like; rather, absorb the evil and respond in love. Give more than what is asked of you. This is the radical nature of the law of love in the kingdom of God.

T U E 18 #366 green
Weekday

Lectionary for Mass

◆ First Reading: Chapters 8 and 9 of 2 Corinthians are concerned with a collection for the church in Jerusalem. In today's reading, Paul holds up the generosity of the Macedonian churches for the community in Jerusalem—despite their own poverty—as an inspiration and encouragement to the Corinthians. Even more should Jesus be their model in giving graciously on behalf of others.

◆ Responsorial Psalm 146: The stanzas of this song of praise speak of God's gracious concern for those who are in any need. Throughout the Scriptures, God calls on his people to demonstrate this same concern.

◆ Gospel: How easy it is to love those who love us, to show kindness to those who are kind to us. How hard it is to love those who act otherwise. But only in loving and showing kindness to those who are mean or unkind to us are we like our heavenly Father who acts in just this manner. The Greek word for perfection, in the last line of today's text, means not so much flawlessness as maturity and wholeness.

W E D 19 #367 green
Weekday

Optional Memorial of Saint Romuald, Abbot / white

Lectionary for Mass

◆ First Reading: Paul encourages the Corinthians to be generous in their contributions for the Church in Jerusalem, and to do so with joy and gladness. They can be assured that God will provide for their needs and, even more, reward them abundantly.

◆ Responsorial Psalm 112 acclaims the blessedness of the one who fears the Lord and who finds joy in the commandments of the Lord, particularly regarding generosity toward the poor. God will give so much more to the one who gives to others.

◆ Gospel: This proclamation is also heard on Ash Wednesday. While we may associate fasting, almsgiving, and prayer with Lent, they are works that should characterize Christian life at all times. The importance of our not making a public display of these actions is stressed repeatedly. We should seek reward from the heavenly Father, not from others.

Today's Saint

Aristocratic-born Romuald led a wild life as a young person in tenth-century Italy. This changed at age 20 when he saw his father murder another man. Filled with horror, Romuald fled to a Benedictine monastery to do penance for his father's actions. Even monks found him uncomfortably holy, so he left and wandered throughout Italy, establishing his own monasteries and hermitages along the way. He eventually formed the Order of Camaldoli, a religious group of men who combined the cenobitic tradition of communal living with the eremitical (hermit) life of the Eastern monks. He lived a long life, dying of natural causes in 1027.

T H U 20 #368 green
Weekday

Lectionary for Mass

◆ First Reading: Paul must contend with the accusations of other evangelists and missionaries who consider him inferior in some way, perhaps in terms of rhetorical eloquence (see verse 6). These people have apparently come into Corinth, attracting members of the local church. What is worse, some were preaching falsehoods (see verse 13, not included in today's Lectionary). In today's reading, Paul defends the credibility of his knowledge and his message. His concern stems from his love for the community, which he has brought into faith and intimate union with Christ the Lord (see verse 2),

◆ Responsorial Psalm 111: Truth and justice, both issues in today's First Reading, are found in the responsorial antiphon. This hymn of thanksgiving acclaims the reliability of God's words and works.

◆ GOSPEL: In teaching his disciples about prayer, Jesus tells them that their heavenly Father so cares for them, that he knows their needs even before they ask. If we look closely at the Lord's Prayer, we see not only the words with which to pray, but also the spirit in which we are to approach God: as a trusting child, mindful of God's holiness and reverent before him, aware of our failures and seeking his forgiveness and protection. Especially emphasized is the forgiveness we are to show to others, for in our prayer we ask God to forgive us just as we forgive others. Today's Gospel calls us to examine how we are doing at forgiving others.

#369   white
FRI 21   Memorial of Saint Aloysius Gonzaga, Religious

Lectionary for Mass

◆ FIRST READING: Paul's self-defense continues from yesterday's reading. First, he asserts his Jewish background; then, all that he has endured in his ministry of proclaiming the Gospel. Can any of his opponents make these same claims? It is in and through the experience of his weakness and all that he has endured that the power of God worked within and strengthened him.

◆ RESPONSORIAL PSALM 34: Paul experienced the deliverance of the Lord on more than one occasion! Thus, today's responsorial verse is most apropos. Notice how the theme of deliverance and rescue is heard in both the second and third stanzas of this song of praise and thanksgiving.

◆ GOSPEL: "Where is your treasure?" asks Jesus in today's Gospel. "On what is your heart set?" (author's paraphrase). By answering honestly, we will discover what we value the most. Does our honest reflection call for any changes?

The Roman Missal

The prayers are found in the Proper of Saints. The Collect speaks of the "wonderful innocence of life" of Saint Aloysius Gonzaga, and asks that we "may imitate him in penitence," who have not imitated his innocence. The Prayer over the Offerings asks that we may come to this banquet "clothed always in our wedding garment," free from sin.

The Preface of Virgins or of Holy Men and Women is used.

Today's Saint

Raised in a wealthy aristocratic family in Italy, Saint Aloysius Gonzaga (1568–1591) became aware at age seven that treasures in this lifetime cannot satisfy the longings of the heart. Much to the disappointment of his father, Aloysius renounced his inheritance to join the Society of Jesus. His short life as a Jesuit was marked by austere piety, theological study, and service to the sick. Sometimes his piety was a bit severe, so his spiritual director, Saint Robert Bellarmine, mentored him in the way of moderation. Saint Aloysius's love of study, especially the *Summa Theologiae* and the Bible, led to him being declared patron of college students. While ministering to the sick in a Jesuit hospital, he contracted a plague, which led to his death. Because his death is attributed to a plague, he, along with Saint Camillus de Lellis, is considered the patron of AIDS patients. He is also considered patron of the young, due to his youthful zeal.

#370   green
SAT 22   Weekday

Optional Memorial Saint Paulinus of Nola, Bishop / white; Saints John Fisher, Bishop, and Thomas More, Martyrs / red; Blessed Virgin Mary / white

Lectionary for Mass

◆ FIRST READING: In today's reading, Paul speaks of the mystical experience of being "caught up to the third heaven," though "whether in the body or out of the body, I do not know . . . ." However, this is not the subject of Paul's boast to the Corinthians and to his opponents; rather, he boasts of his weakness. As blessed as he was by these marvelous ecstatic experiences, Paul was tormented by an irritation that the Lord would not remove, "a thorn in the flesh," most likely a person who created problems for him. But this struggle, this "weakness," was precisely the place where Paul would know the power of God. Of himself, Paul could not deal with the problem/person alone, but only with the help and grace of God.

◆ RESPONSORIAL PSALM 34: The words "taste and see" point to Paul's experience of the Lord's presence and power, here with particular reference to a time of need. The second stanza attests that God will supply the needs of those who fear (reverence) him. In God, with God, there is life and prosperity.

◆ GOSPEL: Serving mammon leads to great anxiety and worry; serving God implies deep trust. The heavenly Father who so lovingly provides for the seemingly insignificant sparrow will do that and more for his children

Today's Saints

Saint Paulinus (354–431) was raised in a family of wealthy politicians in Bordeaux. His interests were varied; everything from practicing law to writing poetry, from traveling to governing. After the death of a newly born son, he and his wife, Therasia, gave away the family fortune to the poor and to the Church. Saint Paulinus and Therasia moved to Italy where they began to live, along with some other friends, a life of prayer and service. They lived in a two-story building in which the first floor provided a place of rest for the wayward and the lost, and the second floor was their place of residence based on the rhythms of monasticism. Gaining a reputation for holiness, Saint Paulinus was ordained a priest and was eventually made bishop of Nola.

Saint John Fisher (1469–1535) and Saint Thomas More (1478–1535) lived during a time of great upheaval and reformation. Both were friends and consultants to King Henry VIII, and both were executed because they would not declare the king's supremacy over the Church. Saint John Fisher, born in Yorkshire, was an astute scholar recognized for his profound insight into the complex questions of life. He held many positions of esteem, including tutor to the young Henry VIII, Chancellor of Cambridge University, and bishop of Rochester.

Saint Thomas More, born in London, was a family man characterized by a deep affection for his wife and three daughters. He, too, held many powerful positions in the Church and in society, in particular, a Parliament lawyer, Speaker of the House of Commons, and Chancellor of England.

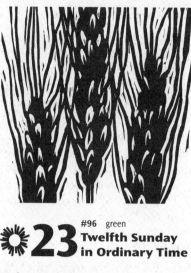

☀ 23 #96 green Twelfth Sunday in Ordinary Time

Orientation

Why does Jesus rebuke the disciples for proclaiming he is the Christ of God? In his wisdom, Jesus must have had a sense of optimal timing for God's revelation to be communicated most fruitfully; the hearers of the Word had to be ready to receive it. This is an important lesson for all of us who by virtue of our Christian identity are called to proclaim the Gospel. Evangelization is a true communication of the Gospel, in that it presumes the openness of its audience. Before the disciples were ready to proclaim Jesus as the Christ, true and trusting relationships needed to be established with others, so that the message could really be heard. The same holds for our own mission to evangelize: in sharing the Good News, the relationships we establish with those around us pave the way for the authentic communication of God's Word.

Lectionary for Mass

◆ FIRST READING: Despite its somber tone, today's First Reading is filled with hope. God will pour out a spirit of grace and petition on the people of Jerusalem through the death of one who was "pierced." A fountain of purification from sin shall be opened to them. The identity of the person of whom Zechariah speaks is unknown. In the context of today's liturgy, however, the juxtaposition of this reading with today's Gospel points to Jesus, who is the fulfillment of all of the prophetic texts of old.

◆ RESPONSORIAL PSALM 63: The imagery of deep longing for the Lord in this Psalm has connections with all of today's readings: thirst, water, gaze, and clinging. For the psalmist, the Lord is a greater good than life itself.

◆ SECOND READING: Baptism annuls all distinctions among us based on ethnic origins, social status, and gender. This was an important point that the Galatians, both Jewish and Gentile Christian, had to learn. In Christ, we are all equal; we are all children of God; we are all one in him.

◆ GOSPEL: Often in the Gospel according to Luke, we see Jesus going off by himself to pray. This time with his heavenly Father enabled him to know himself and his Father's will for him; it also gave him the strength to undertake his ministry. In today's text, Peter has come to know Jesus's identity as the Christ or Messiah, the one long awaited by Israel. But Jesus has to teach his disciples what his messiahship means: taking up the cross and losing one's life, in order to save it.

The Roman Missal

We pray that we may honor God's name and, "set firm on the foundation of [God's] love," know his guidance (Collect).

We offer "the sacrifice of conciliation and praise," and pray that it may so work in our lives that we may offer to God "a heart pleasing" to him (Prayer over the Offerings).

The Eucharist renews and nourishes us. We pray that this sacrifice "may be our sure pledge of redemption," the promise of eternal life (Prayer after Communion).

Other Ideas

Most parishes have outreach programs that collaborate with local Catholic organizations working for justice in the community. Find out how you can become involved. Even young children can help organize and shelve donations at food pantries. If you have a branch of the Interfaith Hospitality Network in your community, hosting churches often appreciate having older children come in to play games for an hour with the children of hosted families.

Make an image of the cross by using pictures of people's faces cut from magazines or the newspaper. Try to find images from different parts of the world, including your own. Hang your cross on a wall where you can prayerfully reflect on it this week. Think about the diversity of people that God loves and has come to save. Pray for the people of the world.

#586, #587 white

24 Solemnity of the Nativity of Saint John the Baptist

MON

Orientation

Zechariah had questioned the message of the angel, expressing doubt and asking for more proof that he would indeed father a child. When the boy is born, Zechariah finally confirms all that Gabriel has predicted. He names his son John and his voice returns. Zechariah is a leader in the community and a priest in the sanctuary of the Lord. His muteness is less a punishment than an appropriate time-out during which his faith and trust in God matures and deepens.

Lectionary for Mass

Vigil

◆ FIRST READING: The prophet Jeremiah was quite young when he received his prophetic call. In fact, as he himself saw it, he was too young to do what the Lord asked. Nevertheless, the Lord reassures him that it will be the Lord's word he speaks, not his own. What is more, he will not be alone; the Lord is with him.

◆ RESPONSORIAL PSALM 71: The reference to the mother's womb in the antiphon and in the third stanza is fitting for this solemnity that celebrates the birth of John the Baptist, who, as Luke attests, even in his mother's womb bore witness to his Lord. The pleas for deliverance are likewise applicable to John the Baptist, who was put to death because of the word he spoke.

◆ SECOND READING: The themes of joy and the working of the Spirit in God's prophets link today's Second Reading with the Gospel announcement of the birth of John the Baptist. Believers in every generation are among those who rejoice because of the salvation that is theirs in Christ.

◆ GOSPEL: The birth of John the Baptist was announced to his elderly father, Zechariah, in a vision as he offered incense in the temple. As it was the case with other visionaries before him, the experience evokes fear, but God's messenger immediately reassures him and speaks of the joy that he and so many others will have because of his son. The messenger speaks of the child's future role: he will be dedicated to God as the Nazirites of old (no wine, strong drink; see Numbers 6) and will be instrumental in the conversion of many in Israel. The Spirit of the Lord will be upon him, even in his mother's womb.

Mass During the Day

◆ FIRST READING: Three motifs from this "servant song" of the prophet Isaiah are particularly apropos for today's feast: being called from birth, being "named" by God (see Luke 1:13 and today's Gospel), and the mission to Israel (see Luke 1:17, 68–79; 3:3, 7–12). The text from Isaiah also mentions a mission to Gentiles, and Luke has John preaching even to the soldiers (see Luke 3:14).

◆ RESPONSORIAL PSALM 139: The psalmist acclaims God's knowledge of and plan for him, even from birth. How true this is for he who was the forerunner of Jesus!

◆ SECOND READING: Today's Second Reading is a brief summary of the Gospel proclamation of Jesus as the promised Davidic Messiah, whose coming was heralded by John the Baptist. Note that John's proclamation (see Acts of the Apostels 13:26) is both to the children "of the family of Abraham" (the Jews), and to the "God-fearing" (Gentiles who were associated with the synagogue).

◆ GOSPEL: Fittingly, we hear of the birth of John the Baptist. Note the emotions the event generates among Elizabeth and Zechariah's family and friends: joy, amazement, and even fear and uncertainty as to what it all means. Perhaps we have reacted in the same way to God's marvelous deeds in our own lives. Like John the Baptist, we too must grow and become strong in spirit if we are to accomplish the work God has entrusted to us

The Roman Missal

The prayers are found in the Proper of Saints. There are two complete sets of prayers. The prayers for the Vigil are to be used on the afternoon or evening of June 23; the prayers for the Mass During the Day on June 24. The same proper Preface is used with both Masses.

In the prayers for this Solemnity, we see John the Baptist not as a figure from the past, but as a saint who continues to teach the Church today. In the Collect at the Vigil we pray that we may be "attentive to what Saint John the Precursor urged," and so "come safely to the One he foretold." In the Prayer after Communion for the Vigil, we ask that his "marvelous prayer" may "accompany us," and that he who recognized Jesus as the Lamb of God may pray for us to God.

The Preface of John the Baptist traces the "singular honor" God gave John "among those born of women." While still in his mother's womb, he recognized Christ's presence and leapt for joy; he pointed to Christ as "the Lamb of redemption"; he "baptized the author of Baptism"; and he shed his blood for him.

T U E 25 #372 green Weekday

Lectionary for Mass

◆ FIRST READING: Because of yesterday's solemnity, we missed the beginning of the Abraham narratives in Genesis 12. When the Lord called Abraham to leave his homeland for a new land, his nephew Lot went with him. Both had livestock and many possessions; so many, in fact, that the land could not sustain them both. For the sake of peace, they parted and dwelt in separate parts of the land. At the end of today's reading, God renews his covenant with Abraham.

◆ RESPONSORIAL PSALM 15: Today's reading portrays Abraham as a man who promotes peace within the family by his willingness to yield freely to the wishes of another. Is this not a man of justice as today's antiphon proclaims? Abraham personifies the qualities of justice set forth in Psalm 15.

◆ GOSPEL: Today's Gospel consists of three sayings from the Sermon on the Mount. The first evokes a parable found later in the Gospel, in which the kingdom of heaven is likened to a pearl of great price. The second commands that the same love and respect that we desire for ourselves be given to others. The third warns that passing through the gate to enter into the kingdom can be demanding.

W E D 26 #373 green Weekday

Lectionary for Mass

◆ FIRST READING: Abraham is a most realistic man, whom the biblical author portrays as speaking in a very direct manner to God! The chances of having an heir seemed rather slim to Abraham, since he and his wife Sarai were both elderly and childless. Perhaps what is most beautiful and moving in today's reading is that Abraham was able to trust God's promise, despite the seeming impossibility of its fulfillment. In fact, God promises Abraham not just one child but countless descendants. The perhaps strange to us sacrificial ritual (cutting up the animals) described in the second part of the reading was common at the time. The fire, of course, was a sign of God's presence and ratification of the covenant.

◆ RESPONSORIAL PSALM 105: Our responsorial acclamation is a fitting proclamation of the faith and trust that Abraham showed: "The Lord remembers his covenant forever!" God's covenant with Abraham is at the same time a covenant with all his descendants. This response in faith and trust that Abraham showed should be ours as well.

◆ GOSPEL: By their fruits, the goodness or wickedness, the fidelity or infidelity of a person shall be known. What are our fruits?

T H U 27 #374 green Weekday

Optional Memorial of Saint Cyril of Alexandria, Bishop and Doctor of the Church / white (U.S.A.) ◆ Optional Memorial of Blessed Nykyta Budka and Vasyl Velychkovsky, Bishops and Martyrs / red (Canada)

Lectionary for Mass

◆ FIRST READING: Sarah's action in giving Hagar to Abraham was an acceptable practice at the time. Nevertheless, problems arose when Hagar began to disdain Sarah, and Sarah became abusive toward Hagar—all too human, perhaps too common, emotional responses. Note that Hagar has a vision of a messenger of the Lord. The messenger assures Hagar that the Lord has heard her prayer and he gives her the name for her son. From this son numerous descendants would come.

◆ RESPONSORIAL PSALM 106: The thanksgiving voiced in today's antiphon is a most fitting response to the promises of God's covenant. Note also the references to "people" and "inheritance" in the last line of the Psalm.

◆ GOSPEL: The saying of Jesus in the first part of today's Gospel reading and the parable in the second part both stress the importance of doing the will of the Father as opposed to only hearing it. Are we hearers or doers? Is our foundation sand or the rock that is Christ?

Today's Saints

Saint Cyril (378–444), the patriarch of Alexandria, was an avid defender of the faith; therefore, he was no stranger to conflict. He found himself at odds with Nestorius, the archbishop of Constantinople, who advocated that the Blessed Virgin is the mother of Christ (Christokos) not the Mother of God (Theotokos). Saint Cyril presided over the First Council of Ephesus (431), which condemned this particular belief, known as Nestorianism, as heresy and proclaimed Mary as the Mother of God. The Council of Chalcedon (451) based its teachings regarding the two natures of Christ on the thought of Saint Cyril. Due to the breadth of his writing on the Incarnation and the dignity of the human person, he was declared a Doctor of the Church.

After studies in Vienna and Innsbruck, Nykyta Budka received his doctorate in Theology and was ordained a priest in 1905. After his consecration as bishop, he became the first leader of the Ukrainian Catholic Church in Canada. But he lacked organizational skills. A trip to Rome to report on conflicts in the Canadian Church led to his resignation and reassignment. He was arrested by the Soviets in 1945, and sentenced to eight years in a concentration camp where he died a martyr four years later. Vasyl Velychkovsky, CSsR, a Ukrainian priest of the Byzantine Rite, was arrested by Communist secret police and served ten years at hard labor before his sentence was commuted. In 1963, he was secretly consecrated the archbishop of Moscow. Suffering from heart disease, Velychkovsky was deported to Winnipeg, Canada, where he died in 1973. Both priests were beatified in 2001 by Pope John Paul II.

#375   red

28 Memorial of Saint Irenaeus, Bishop and Martyr

F R I

Lectionary for Mass

◆ First Reading: God renews the covenant he made with Abraham and prescribes circumcision as the sign of the covenant. Abraham is promised a son, born of his wife Sarah. (Note the name change as she assumes a new role in God's plan of salvation.) Through their son, God will fulfill his covenant promises. Abraham is dubious and even laughs. How can this be? Both he and Sarah are old. Nevertheless, nothing is impossible with God. Ishmael, too, will be blessed; but the covenant promises are fulfilled through Isaac.

◆ Responsorial Psalm 128: In today's First Reading, God commands Abraham to be blameless. This is one aspect of "fear of the Lord." Today's Psalm reiterates how such people are blessed. Note in particular the reference to children in the second stanza.

◆ Gospel: The leper is likewise one who "fears" (reverences) the Lord—he did him homage. The blessing he receives is healing, cleansing from his leprosy. When he is declared "clean" by the priest (see Leviticus 14) he will be restored to the community, no longer isolated because of his leprosy.

The Roman Missal

The prayers are found in the Proper of Saints. The Preface of Holy Pastors or of Holy Martyrs is used.

Today's Saint

Saint Irenaeus was the bishop of Lyons, France, a disciple of Saint Polycarp of Smyrna, and one of the first Christian theologians. His best known work, *Against Heresies*, is an attack on the gnostics, who claimed to have a secret oral tradition from Jesus. Irenaeus refutes them by pointing out that we know who the bishops are back to the Apostles, and that none was gnostic. He is an early witness to the recognition of the four accounts of the Gospel, to the unique importance of the Bishop of Rome, and to the apostolic succession—the uninterrupted transmission of authority from the Apostles themselves to present-day bishops.

#590, #591   red

29 Solemnity of Saints Peter and Paul, Apostles

S A T

Orientation / Today's Saints

Today we commemorate Peter and Paul, martyred around the year 64 AD during Nero's persecution following the Great Fire of Rome. Tradition says that Peter fled Rome to avoid arrest and saw Jesus on the road. "Where are you going, Lord," Peter asked. Jesus replied, "I am going to Rome to be crucified again." Peter turned back and was crucified upside down because he felt unworthy to meet his death the same way as Christ. Paul was arrested in Jerusalem and was sent to Rome, where he was placed under house arrest. He was slain by beheading, because as a Roman citizen he could not be subjected to the indignity of crucifixion.

Lectionary for Mass

Vigil

◆ First Reading: Today's First Reading is the story of the crippled beggar who lies at the gate of the Temple. Instead of receiving alms, as expected, he receives the gift of healing in the name of the Lord Jesus from the hands of Peter. What better way to give God praise than by fully using what is restored to full health! The man walks and jumps with joy, giving God praise.

◆ Responsorial Psalm 19: All creation declares the glory of God. In the light of today's First Reading, "their" (antiphon) refers not to creation, but to the voice of the Apostles.

◆ Second Reading: Paul speaks to the Galatians of his encounter with the Risen Christ, a revelation that changed his life. Paul turned from persecutor to missionary of the Gospel, sent by the 13 to the Gentiles.

◆ GOSPEL: This is John's account of the Risen Christ's commissioning of Peter, entrusting to him care for the sheep of his flock. Jesus also speaks of how Peter will one day follow him, led by another to death, and ultimately to glory.

Mass During the Day

◆ FIRST READING: Even in these early days, the persecution of Christians was at times for political reasons. Was it not that way with Jesus as well? As with Jesus, the persecution of the Apostles takes place at the time of the Passover, the feast of Unleavened Bread. As God delivered Israel of old from slavery in Egypt, so God delivered Peter from the hands of Herod. Peter's following of the angel is but one incident in his following of the Lord Jesus in the ultimate passage from death to life.

◆ RESPONSORIAL PSALM 34: A song of praise celebrating God's deliverance of his chosen through the intervention of a heavenly messenger—a most appropriate response for today's First Reading.

◆ SECOND READING: Paul's words reflect his awareness of his imminent death, his "departure" for the heavenly kingdom. In language echoing the ritual sacrifice in the Temple, he speaks of his life's ministry as a sacrificial offering "poured out," given to God. He also uses the athletic imagery found elsewhere in his writing: the competition, the race, the winner's crown.

◆ GOSPEL: "Who do you say that I am?" asks Jesus of his disciples. In today's Gospel we hear Peter's profound confession: "You are the Christ (Messiah) . . . the Son of the Living God." As Peter confesses Jesus, Jesus commissions Peter: "[Y]ou are Peter and upon this rock I will build my Church" (Matthew 7:24). The powers of evil shall not prevail against it.

The Roman Missal

Two complete sets of prayers are provided for this great solemnity. The Vigil Mass may be offered on the afternoon or evening of June 28; the prayers for the Mass during the Day are used on June 29.

The Gloria and the Creed are said or sung today.

Vigil

We pray that we may be "sustained / by the intercession" of the great Apostles, through whom the Church received "the foundations of her heavenly office" (Collect).

In the Prayer over the Offerings, we pray that we may not be weighed down by "doubt of our own merits," but rather "rejoice" in the saving kindness of God.

We have been "enlightened with the teaching of the Apostles," we pray that we may be strengthened by the sacrament we receive (Prayer after Communion).

Mass During the Day

In the Collect, we pray that the Church may remain faithful to the teaching of these Apostles, through whom the Church first received the faith.

In the Prayer over the Offerings, we ask the intercession of the Apostles, that we may offer the sacrifice with devotion.

Peter and Paul are like two halves of one whole: together they helped establish the infant Church. Peter was the first to confess the faith; Paul was that faith's "outstanding preacher." Peter drew into the Church "the remnant of Israel"; Paul preached to the Gentiles. Each in his way "gathered together the one family of Christ" (Preface).

The Prayer after Communion echoes Acts of the Apostles 2:42: we pray that we may be faithful in breaking the bread, and listening to the teaching of the Apostles, and so grow in unity and love.

A Solemn Blessing for this solemnity can be found following the Order of Mass (#16).

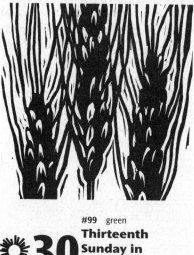

#99   green

☀ 30 Thirteenth Sunday in Ordinary Time

Orienation

In this passage, Jesus demonstrates his firm resolution to carry out his salvific mission. As he heads to Jerusalem, he carries a clear sense of purpose, which influences all his interactions and activities. He has come to submit to the cross in order to rise again and invite us into eternity with him. His acute focus invites us to consider what the overall goal and purpose of our life is in him, while prompting us to imitate his commitment and resolution to see it through.

Lectionary for Mass

◆ FIRST READING: With symbolic gestures, Elijah designates Elisha as his prophetic successor. In response, Elisha totally renounces his former way of life. Making a sacrificial offering of his oxen and tools, he leaves his family to follow Elijah as his servant and attendant.

◆ RESPONSORIAL PSALM 16: How fittingly this song of confidence can be a response to our reading about Elisha, whose portion is no longer among his own people or his own possessions, but with the Lord.

◆ SECOND READING: Paul warns the Galatians against the very real danger of allowing themselves to be bound—enslaved—by a sinful way of life, losing sight of the real meaning of their freedom in Christ. This is manifest in their "biting and devouring" one another, an image of slander and gossip. Such behavior hardly accords with life in the Spirit. Paul's words call us all to self-examination.

◆ GOSPEL: Jesus's journey to Jerusalem—and his Passion and Death—would take firm and resolute determination. There was some danger in traveling through Samaria due to antagonism between the Samaritans and the Jews going back to the time of the Babylonian Exile. This, however, is not the issue in today's Gospel, but rather the disciples' desire to seek revenge. The second half of this Gospel account is more related to today's First Reading. As Jesus continues his journey to Jerusalem, someone comes up and announces his intended discipleship. But Jesus wants to know if he is willing to be homeless. Another would-be disciple has a stipulation: "I will follow you, Lord, but first let me . . . ." The answer is no. Jesus asks more of his followers than did Elijah. The response must be immediate and total, with no stipulations. The kingdom of God has priority over all.

The Roman Missal

The Collect contrasts light and darkness. God has chosen us as "children of light." We pray that we may not be "wrapped in the darkness of error," but remain in the "bright light of truth."

We pray that our "deeds" may be worthy of the "sacred gifts" we receive in this sacrifice (Prayer ove the Offerings).

We pray that the "divine sacrifice" we have received may so "fill us with life" that we may "bear fruit

that lasts forever" (Prayer after Communion)

Other Ideas

Create a drawing or a mind map that outlines your life as a path to God. Draw images or use words or events to show your life experiences. Mark the places where you have sought insight or understanding. List the times or places in which, to your surprise, you found God. Talk about your journey with your family, a friend, or a small faith community.

Learn about the life of the prophet Elijah. You can read about him in the first and second books of Kings. What was his life as a prophet like? What do you think he wrestled with in order to follow God? What advice might he offer to his successor and us?

Psalm 16 says that God is our inheritance. An inheritance can mean a birthright, legacy, or heritage. What do you think the psalmist means? How is God your inheritance?

July
Month of the Most Precious Blood

M O N 1   #377   green
Weekday

Optional Memorial of Blessed Junípero Serra, Priest / white

Lectionary for Mass

◆ FIRST READING: Because of Saturday's feast, we missed the first part of today's reading (Genesis 18:1–15) which tells of Abraham and Sarah's three visitors. They are, in fact, messengers of the Lord. Note the reference to Abraham's role in the history of salvation: "I have singled him out . . . ." Nevertheless, it is not Abraham's role as the father of many nations that is singled out today, but his intercessory role as

he somewhat boldly pleads for the sake of the just, however few they may be. The Lord grants his request.

◆ RESPONSORIAL PSALM 103: The Lord's kindness and mercy abound in his willingness to spare Sodom and Gomorrah. Today's Psalm calls us never to forget these qualities of our God, particularly as they are manifest in his forgiveness of sin. He does not deal with us as we deserve.

◆ GOSPEL: "Follow" is a key word for discipleship. Today's Gospel touches upon what it means in terms of its practical implications: a certain "homelessness" when following Jesus the itinerant preacher, a new relationship with Jesus which takes precedence over all others.

Today's Saint

Blessed Junípero Serra (1713–1784) was a Spanish Franciscan friar, best known for founding the string of 21 missions that stretch from San Diego to Sonoma, California. Junípero was born in Majorca. At age 16 he entered the Franciscans. After completing his theological studies, he served as professor of philosophy at Majorca before volunteering for the missions in the "New World." Upon arrival, he went to Mexico City to dedicate his mission at the shrine of Our Lady of Guadalupe. Serra founded his first mission at San Diego in 1769, and worked his way up the coast along El Camino Real, making converts as he went. In spite of a leg injury he suffered at the beginning of his ministry, he traveled on foot whenever possible, eventually covering 24,000 miles. The chapel at Mission San Juan Capistrano is believed to be oldest standing building in California, and the only one left where Serra is known to have celebrated the liturgy. He was beatified by Pope John Paul II in 1988.

T U E 2 #378 green
Weekday

Lectionary for Mass

◆ FIRST READING: The wickedness of Sodom is evident in the attempt made to abuse Lot's visitors This incident is described in the verses that precede today's Lectionary text. So great was its wickedness, that God determined to destroy the city. However, God spared Lot and his family because they were just. This was in keeping with God's promise to Abraham as we heard in yesterday's reading.

◆ RESPONSORIAL PSALM 26: God's mercy is evident in sparing Lot and his family. Today's Psalm calls us to continued fidelity and uprightness, to walk according to God's truth and not in the way of wickedness. We need God's mercy and help as we make our way to him.

◆ GOSPEL: The mercy of God is likewise manifest in today's Gospel reading as Jesus calms the storm at sea, delivering his terrified disciples from their fear of perishing. Note that Jesus calls the disciples people of "little faith." This story has much to teach us about of the presence of Jesus in the storms that come up in our lives. May we always remember that he has power over these storms.

W E D 3 #593 red
Feast of Saint Thomas, Apostle

Lectionary for Mass

◆ FIRST READING: Our unity in Christ abolishes all former distinctions. We are now one with all who believe. Through our common faith, we are united to Christ and to one another: as brothers and sisters in the family of God, fellow citizens of God's holy city, the household of God, a temple or dwelling place of God. On this feast of Saint Thomas, are we aware of how our faith today has been built on the foundation of the Apostles' witness centuries ago?

◆ RESPONSORIAL PSALM 117: Our antiphon, drawn from Mark's account of Jesus's commission of the Apostles, is precisely what Thomas and the other Apostles did for the rest of their lives. As a result, all nations know the Lord's fidelity and loving kindness, which are true cause for praise.

◆ GOSPEL: Something absolutely unheard of . . . a resurrection from the dead! Who of us cannot identify with Thomas's doubt? Yet this is the reality that gives our life meaning and our faith hope. Blessed are we who believe without seeing, for one day we shall see him who is our Lord and our God.

The Roman Missal

Entrance Antiphon: The words of Psalm 118 recall "doubting Thomas's" profession of faith—"My Lord and my God!"

The Gloria is said or sung today.

The Collect echoes John 20:31, which follows immediately upon Thomas's profession of faith in Christ. We ask that, with the prayers of Saint Thomas to help us, we too may believe and "have life / in the name of Jesus Christ."

In the Prayer over the Offerings, we ask God to "keep safe" the gifts he has given us, so that we may offer to him "a sacrifice of praise."

In the sacrament, we receive the very Body and Blood of the one whom Thomas called Lord and God. We pray that we may recognize his presence "and proclaim him by our deeds and by our life" (Prayer after Communion).

Today's Saint

Thomas, also called "Didymus" or "the Twin" (John 11:16) was one of the Twelve Apostles. He is remembered for doubting the Resurrection of Christ: "Unless I see the mark of the nails in his hands and put my finger into the nail marks and put my hand into his side, I will not believe." The following week, Thomas was with the Twelve, when Jesus appeared and chided him for his lack of faith: "Have you come to believe because you have seen me? Blessed are those who have not seen and have believed" (John 20:25–29). After seeing the Risen Christ alive, Thomas exclaims "My Lord and my God!" According to tradition, Thomas is the only apostle who went outside the borders of the Roman Empire to evangelize.

Although there is a Gospel account attributed to him, it is not accepted in the canon of Scripture, and is, in fact of gnostic origin. The people of Kerala in South India fervently believe that it was Thomas who evangelized them. He is represented in art with a spear, the instrument of his martyrdom. He is the patron of architects and builders, and of India, where today is a solemnity.

T H U 4 #380 green
Weekday

Optional Proper Mass for Independence Day #882–886 or #887–891 / white

Lectionary for Mass

◆ FIRST READING: Abraham's obedience to what God asked and his total trust in God's fidelity are powerfully evident in today's text. Abraham was called by God to be the father of his chosen people. The fulfillment of God's promises rested on Abraham's son Isaac. God's request in today's reading is unexpected and makes no sense: he asks Abraham to sacrifice his beloved and only son. Who cannot but be astounded by Abraham's obedience and total trust in the Lord? He was rewarded not only by the preservation of Isaac's life but also by the promised blessing of countless descendants.

◆ RESPONSORIAL PSALM 115: Today's antiphon can easily be applied to both Abraham and Isaac: Abraham for his total obedience; Isaac, in his deliverance from death. The stanzas of today's Psalm contrast the powerlessness of idols with the glory of the God of Israel.

◆ GOSPEL: In the Gospel readings over the past few days, we have seen Jesus exercise power over nature and over demons. Today, his power over sin, his power to forgive sin, is demonstrated. In Jesus's day, people considered illness to be a punishment for sin. Thus, forgiveness and healing go hand in hand.

The Roman Missal

For the optional Mass for Independence Day, the Gloria is said or sung.

Two complete sets of prayers are provided in the Proper of Saints.

The first option for the Collect is a prayer that God's "peace may rule in our hearts" and God's "justice guide our lives." The second option gives thanks for all that has been accomplished, and calls on us to share the blessings we have received "with all the peoples of the earth."

The first option for the Prayer over the Offerings asks God to lead us to "true justice and lasting peace" through the Gospel. The second echoes the familiar motto, *E pluribus unum* (from many, one): God has "molded into one our nation, drawn from the people of many lands." Just as the "grains of wheat become one bread," and "the many grapes one cup," we pray that we may, as one, be "instruments of . . . peace."

The first option for the Preface speaks of Christ's message of peace as the beginning of "the vision of our founding fathers," a message that "lives on in our midst," both today and tomorrow. The second focuses on Christ's love for all peoples, "his witness of justice and truth." We are "reborn in the Spirit," and like the Spirit we are to be "filled with love for all people."

The first option for the Prayer after Communion is a prayer for unity, that together we may "build the city of lasting peace." The second is a prayer that as a nation we may trust in God, and do God's will.

A proper Solemn Blessing is provided, which focuses on harmony, wisdom, love, and unity.

Other Ideas

What were the initial values of the American founders? How do we practice those values today? Explore how other countries may celebrate their independence. What did those countries' founders want to accomplish in their own history? How do the values the Christian faith relate to the values of the United States? Talk over what you have found with a friend or small group.

F R I 5 #381 green Weekday

Optional Memorials of Saint Anthony Zaccaria, Priest / white; Saint Elizabeth of Portugal / white

Lectionary for Mass

◆ FIRST READING: We hear of the death of Sarah and of Abraham's instructions to his servant regarding a wife for Isaac. Note Abraham's insistence that his son stay in the land which God promised them, and that his wife be from his own people, not the Canaanites. Note also his trust that God will provide a wife for Isaac. This did indeed happen, but is recounted in verses not included in today's reading (see Genesis 24:10–61).

◆ RESPONSORIAL PSALM 106: Thanksgiving is indeed an apt response for all that God did for Abraham, Sarah, and their son Isaac. They knew firsthand of the mighty deeds of the Lord; they experienced his blessings and grace.

They strove to observe what was right in all their doings.

◆ GOSPEL: It was so very hard for the Jewish officials to be reconciled with Jesus's welcoming and acceptance of everyone, including sinners and even the despicable tax collectors (who worked for the Roman government and supplemented their own income as well). In fact, Jesus not only accepted Matthew the tax collector, he called him to be his disciple.

Today's Saints

Anthony Mary Zaccaria (1502–1539) was from Cremona, Italy. He was born into a noble family, and dedicated himself to the Lord from a young age. He studied philosophy, went to study medicine at the University of Padua, and practiced for three years before deciding to become a priest. Anthony had already done so much study that he was ordained quickly, in 1528. He founded three religious orders: the Barnabites or Clerics Regular of Saint Paul—the first order named for Saint Paul—the Angelic Sisters of Saint Paul for nuns, and a lay community. The three groups worked together to reform society.

Because of the implied criticism of abuses in the Church, Anthony was investigated for heresy twice, but was acquitted both times. In addition to founding the Barnabites, he popularized the forty-hour devotion of exposition of the Eucharist. In 1539, he became ill with a fever, and because his health had been undermined by his penitential practices, he died at the age of thirty-seven. Anthony is the patron of his order, the Barnabites, and is represented in art wearing a cassock and with a lily, a cross, or a symbol of the Eucharist. Today the Barnabites can be found in sixteen countries, including Italy, the United States, Brazil, and Afghanistan.

Saint Elizabeth of Portugal (1271–1336) was the grandniece of Elizabeth of Hungary and is known by the Spanish version of her name, Isabel. When very young, she was married to the King of Portugal.

Elizabeth had been raised to be devout, but at her husband's court, she found much corruption and immorality. In spite of this, she managed to continue her life of prayer, penance, and devotion to the care of the sick. This caused resentment in the court, which Elizabeth bore quietly. After her husband, the king, died, she went to live in a convent of Poor Clares that she had founded, and she took the habit of a Third Order Franciscan. Throughout her life she was well known for her peacemaking skills, most importantly when she prevented a war between Portugal and Castile in 1336. The exertion weakened her health, and she died soon after and is buried at Coimbra. Elizabeth of Portugal is a patron of Franciscan Tertiaries.

 #382 green
6 Weekday

Optional Memorials of Saint Maria Goretti, Virgin and Martyr / red; Blessed Virgin Mary / white

Lectionary for Mass

◆ First Reading: At times, the words and actions of the biblical characters can be most enigmatic, and today is a case in point. What are we to make of the deceit in today's text? The scheming and dishonesty cannot be denied yet God's plan and purposes are furthered despite the weakness and sinfulness of his chosen ones. The blessing, whose words are inherently powerful, signified the passing on of a spirit of life from one generation to the next, and it cannot be revoked. God's covenant promises will be fulfilled through the line of Jacob.

◆ Responsorial Psalm 135: This hymn of praise celebrates Jacob's role in God's plan of salvation. He is God's chosen one through whom God's covenant promises will be realized.

◆ Gospel: The image of Jesus as Bridegroom echoes an Old Testament image for God (see Isaiah 54:6). Similarly, the glory of the end time is depicted as a wedding feast (see Revelation 21). When Jesus lived on earth, the divine Bridegroom was one of us and dwelt among us. It was indeed the beginning of a new creation.

Today's Saint

Maria Goretti (1890–1902) is one of the youngest saints to be canonized. She died of stab wounds after she resisted a rapist. Maria came from a poor Italian family. They lost their farm and a few years later, her father died of malaria. In spite of their hard existence as farm laborers, the family was close-knit and devout. By 1902, the family was sharing a building with another family of farm workers, one of whom was Alessandro Serenelli, who made it a habit to sexually harass Maria. One day, finding her alone, he threatened to kill her if she did not submit to him. Maria protested that what he asked was a mortal sin. Alessandro choked, and then stabbed her, leaving her bleeding to death. She was taken to the hospital, but she could not be saved and died forgiving her murderer. Shortly after Maria died, Alessandro was arrested, charged with her murder, and sentenced to twenty years in prison. He remained unrepentant until Maria appeared to him in a dream. Upon his release, he went to Maria's mother and asked for forgiveness. Eventually he became a Capuchin lay brother and was present at Maria's canonization in 1950, as was her mother. Maria Goretti is the patron of rape victims

and teenage girls and is shown in art dressed as a peasant farmer, holding lilies. Her story has prompted thought on the broader meaning of chastity, integrating sexual purity with personal integrity, and self-determination.

#102 green
7 Fourteenth Sunday in Ordinary Time

Orientation

In commissioning the 72 to go and proclaim the kingdom of God, Jesus instructs them to focus on the mission at hand. Forget about carrying money and other belongings, greeting passers-by on the way, or worrying about food and lodging—all of this could easily take up their mental and physical energy, as it does for most of us every day. For us as well, it is all too easy to go about our lives pursuing our essential comforts, letting our chores and quotidian tasks take over our lives. Jesus assures the 72 that these essentials will be provided for, freeing these Apostles up to focus on proclaiming the kingdom. In the same way, this passage reminds us in the midst of our busyness to open ourselves up to the greater eternal reality of which we are a part.

Lectionary for Mass

◆ First Reading: Today's reading opens on a note of overwhelming joy, a joy even more poignant since it is proclaimed some forty years after the destruction of Jerusalem and the holy temple by the Babylonians. Once again, Jerusalem shall become a life-giving mother. Once again, her inhabitants, returned from the exile, shall know comfort. Their hearts shall rejoice, their strength be renewed.

◆ RESPONSORIAL PSALM 66: Today's antiphon echoes the theme of joy. Not only Jerusalem, but all the earth is called to rejoice in the marvelous works of the Lord. For the Jews, the return from Babylon was like a second Exodus (note the reference to the Exodus in the third stanza). In the experience of God's wonderful deeds on their behalf, Israel can only break forth in praise.

◆ SECOND READING: In his concluding words to the Galatians, Paul reiterates that salvation is not a question of circumcision or uncircumcision, but of faith in Jesus Christ. Paul focuses in particular on the cross of our salvation. In Baptism, we are crucified with Christ. We are marked with his wounds, which are for us the source of true and everlasting life.

◆ GOSPEL: Jesus sends some of his followers out to proclaim the Good News of the kingdom of God which is at hand, to bring peace, and to heal. In fulfilling their ministry, they must be totally dependent on the Lord, and on the hospitality they receive from others. They must trust that the Lord will provide for them. The theme of joy heard in the longer form of the Gospel is a link with today's First Reading. The source of their joy must be rooted in the Lord—it is his power at work in them, not their own. It is not success in their mission that is of utmost importance, but rather, their own faith and commitment to the Lord.

The Roman Missal

The Collect uses imagery of high and low: Christ became low in "abasement" that "a fallen world" might be "raised up." We who have been rescued from "slavery to sin" ask for the "holy joy" of the redeemed.

◆ PRAYER OVER THE OFFERINGS: We pray that by the power of this sacrifice, our daily lives may reflect the "life of heaven."

◆ PRAYER AFTER COMMUNION: "Replenished" by the Eucharist, we pray that we may attain to salvation, and praise God without ceasing.

Other Ideas

Gardeners know they must plant now to prepare for a harvest in late summer and fall. In the same way, Jesus knows that to have an abundant harvest disciples must plant now. We are called to plant the word of God deep in the ground of our hearts in order to bear fruit. How are you planting God's word in your life?

M
O
N **8** #383 green
Weekday

Lectionary for Mass

◆ FIRST READING: A reading of Genesis 27:41—28:5 gives helpful background to today's text. We hear of Esau's grudge toward Jacob and witness Rebekah's ongoing role in determining the events. Jacob is sent to Abraham's homeland to procure a wife; his absence also serves to protect him from his brother's wrath. Jacob is God's chosen one, and in today's text, he has an experience of God in a dream. God renews the covenant made with Abraham and Isaac with him. Setting up a memorial stone as a sign of the sacredness of the place, Jacob promises fidelity to God if God is with him on his journey.

◆ RESPONSORIAL PSALM 91: Our Psalm response echoes the trust that Jacob has voiced. The stanzas stress the theme of God's protection of the one who dwells with him and is faithful to him.

◆ GOSPEL: Touching Jesus and being touched by Jesus brings healing and life—to the woman with the hemorrhage and to the official's daughter who had died. What in us is in need of Jesus's healing, life-giving touch? We need only seek it in faith!

T
U
E **9** #384 green
Weekday

Optional Memorial of Saint Augustine Zhao Rong, Priest, and Companions, Martyrs / red

Lectionary for Mass

◆ FIRST READING: The Lectionary omits most of the five chapters of the Jacob story which tell of his arrival in his ancestral homeland, his marriages to Leah and Rachel, and the prosperity he achieved. In today's text, after a lapse of some fourteen years, Jacob is en route back to Canaan and has already sent gifts ahead to Esau, hoping to be well received. Alone in his camp, he has another experience of God and is portrayed as wrestling with God's messenger. Jacob asks and receives a blessing, and his name is changed to Israel, a name coming from the Hebrew words for "contend" and "God."

◆ RESPONSORIAL PSALM 17: Our antiphon echoes Jacob's words that he has seen God. Notice the implicit reference to struggle (testing) in the first stanza and the theme of calling on the Lord and being heard. Similarly, Jacob had to flee from his foe (Esau).

◆ GOSPEL: We see Jesus's power over the realm of Satan and the demons in his cure of the man who was mute. We also hear the opposition of the Pharisees. Perhaps the most touching line in today's Gospel is the depiction of Jesus as one whose heart was moved with compassion for the many people who came to him to hear his word and to be healed. Are we among them? And what is in our heart toward the people we meet every day?

Today's Saints

Between 1648 and 1930, 87 Chinese Catholics and 33 Western missionaries, some of whom were Dominicans, Franciscans, Salesians, Jesuits, or Vincentians, were martyred for their ministry or for refusing to renounce their Christian faith. Many of the Chinese converts were killed during the Boxer Rebellion, a xenophobic uprising during which many foreigners were slaughtered by angry peasants. Augustine Zhao Rong was a Chinese diocesan priest who was tortured and killed in 1815, after the Emperor Kia-Kin issued decrees banning Catholicism. Augustine Zhao Rong and the other Chinese martyrs were canonized in 2000 by Pope John Paul II.

W E D 10 #385 green Weekday

Lectionary for Mass

◆ FIRST READING: We really jump ahead in the Genesis narrative today—over the details of how Joseph, the son of Jacob, came to be in the land of Egypt (sold into slavery by his jealous brothers) and how he came to prominence there (his ability to interpret dreams). Once again we see how God uses all the circumstances of life, even those resulting from the envy of siblings or others, to bring about good. We also witness the deep goodness of Joseph and his willingness to forgive. Indeed, he loved his brothers regardless of what they had done to him.

◆ RESPONSORIAL PSALM 33: The Israelites in Canaan, suffering from famine, had need of grain for food. They needed God's mercy and the mercy of the one who had provisions. The thanksgiving of today's Psalm can be understood in light of the ways God's plan for his people unfolded in the life of Joseph. The evil plans of his jealous brothers were thwarted as God brought about the accomplishment of his own plan of salvation. Israel, through Joseph, would be saved from famine.

◆ GOSPEL: Jesus commissions his Twelve Apostles (called disciples here) but insists that they continue to learn from him. After giving them authority over evil spirits and the power to heal, Jesus sends them to the house of Israel, to those to whom God's promises were first made. (Antagonism toward Samaria, seen here and elsewhere in the Gospel, dates back to the time of the Babylonian Exile, when the inhabitants of this central part of Israel remained in their homeland and intermarried with foreigners who subsequently settled there.)

T H U 11 #386 white Memorial of Saint Benedict, Abbot

Lectionary for Mass

◆ FIRST READING: Today we witness the depth of Joseph's love for his father and his forgiveness of his brothers. "I am your brother Joseph whom you once sold into Egypt." He is not dead, contrary to what Judah had explained! Joseph's conviction that God's providence is at work, no matter the magnitude of the wrongdoing, is a call to us all to have this same trust.

◆ RESPONSORIAL PSALM 105: It is indeed a marvel of the Lord that Joseph had such an important position in Egypt, and was able to provide for the welfare of his family. Today's Psalm recounts how this came about.

◆ GOSPEL: Today's text is a continuation of what we heard yesterday about Jesus's instruction to his newly commissioned Apostles (who are also called laborers here). Jesus warns that not everyone will receive them. Particularly poignant are Jesus's words: "Without cost you have received; without cost you are to give" (Matthew 10:8). Do we see the relevance of that statement for our own lives?

The Roman Missal

The prayers are found in the Proper of Saints. The prayers for today are full of references to the teachings of Saint Benedict. He was "an outstanding master in the school of divine service" (Collect), and we pray that we may be "attentive" to his teaching (Prayer after Communion) and, following his example, seek the Lord (Prayer over the Offerings).

Today's Saint

Saddened by the immoral state of society, Saint Benedict of Nursia (480–553/7) left the city to live as a hermit at Subiaco. In time, more and more men were attracted to his charismatic personality as well as to his way of life. He eventually moved a group of monks to Monte Cassino, near Naples, where he completed the final version of his rule, now known as *The Rule of Saint Benedict*, on the fundamentals of monastic life, including the day-to-day operation of a monastery. The rule asserts that the primary occupation of the monk is to pray the Divine Office in tandem with a vowed life of stability, obedience, and conversion of life. The whole of the monastic vocation can be summarized in the opening line of his rule, "Listen carefully." Saint Benedict is considered the father of Western monasticism.

F R I **12** #387 green
Weekday

Lectionary for Mass

◆ FIRST READING: In verses not included in the Lectionary (see Genesis 45:9–20), Joseph sends for his father and family. Pharaoh gave them the best land in Egypt for their home. Today's reading tells of their migration to Egypt and the moving encounter of Jacob and Joseph.

◆ RESPONSORIAL PSALM 37: God's providence was at work in the lives of Joseph and all his family, as it is in our own. We need only to trust. Notice the references to "famine" and "be[ing] fed" which evoke the plight of Joseph's family as well as the motifs of land, refuge, salvation.

◆ GOSPEL: Today's text continues from the previous two days' texts. It focuses on the persecution and suffering Jesus's Apostles must endure. In the midst of it all, there is the powerful promise: "it will not be you who speak but the Spirit of your Father speaking through you" (Matthew 10:20). Jesus asks his disciples not to worry, but to trust in the providential care of their heavenly Father.

S A T **13** #388 green
Weekday

Optional Memorials of Saint Henry / white; Blessed Virgin Mary / white

Lectionary for Mass

◆ FIRST READING: Jacob instructs his sons to bury him in Canaan, the land promised to Abraham and Isaac, and indeed in the same grave. The second part of the reading treats of the understandable guilt and fear of Joseph's brothers after the death of their father. Again we see the depths of Joseph's forgiveness and his trust in divine providence. After a passage of several

generations, the time for Joseph's death is drawing near. He instructs his brothers to bury him in Canaan, with Abraham, Isaac, and Jacob and tells them that God, in his providence, will lead them back to the land of their ancestors.

◆ RESPONSORIAL PSALM: There is much cause for joy in today's First Reading! The stanzas of today's response are the beginning of Psalm 105, a hymn recounting God's marvels in Israel's history from the time of Abraham to the Exodus and reentry into the Promised Land.

◆ GOSPEL: Once again we hear an installment from Matthew's account of Jesus's commissioning of his Apostles. Yesterday we heard of the opposition and persecution that the disciples can expect. Today's reading opens with an explanation why: as it was for the teacher, so it will be for the disciple. Our way must be that of Jesus—there is no other way. The disciple is not to fear (an injunction occurring three times) the opposition, but rather, to fear the loss of life and soul in Gehenna as a result of infidelity.

Today's Saint

Henry II (972–1024) was a German king and Holy Roman Emperor, the only German king to be canonized.

Henry had considered becoming a priest, but when his father died, he inherited his father's title of Duke of Bavaria. He became king of Germany in 1002 and married Cunegunda, who is also a saint. He had a reputation for being learned and pious, and was a positive influence in Church–state relations.

At that time, secular authorities appointed bishops and often selected their political allies. Henry appointed bishops who would be good pastors, and supported them in their work. Although he waged

many wars, he was not the aggressor but fought only to protect his borders and preserve peace. Henry is a patron of Benedictine oblates and is invoked against infertility, for he and his wife were childless.

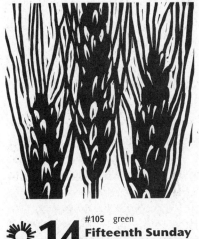

 **14** #105 green
Fifteenth Sunday in Ordinary Time

Orientation

Jesus presents the story of the Good Samaritan in response to a scholar's question about whom we should consider to be our neighbor. The story of the Good Samaritan is a challenging response to this, as it demands from all of us an honest look at our boundaries of care and compassion. We are happy and relieved to read that the Samaritan traveler helped the poor robbery victim, but as the story draws us in, it addresses us, and leaves us wondering: would I have stopped to help? The fact that help arrives from the unlikeliest of sources also asks us to humble ourselves before the grace and goodness of God working through others, especially those whom we judge as inferior and easily dismiss.

Lectionary for Mass

◆ FIRST READING: There is a simple and profound beauty in these words which Moses speaks to the people: the word of God is very near to us; in fact, it is within us, in our minds and hearts. If only we would listen to his voice with the ear of our hearts and do whatever he asks, we will find life and blessings in abundance.

◆ RESPONSORIAL PSALM 69: Today's responsorial antiphon (from the Gospel according to John) highlights the life-giving power (Spirit) of God's Word. The first three stanzas of the Psalm focus on the Word of the Lord as expressed in the Law; the last, on the value and delight that is to be found in it.

◆ SECOND READING: This hymn found at the beginning of the Letter to the Colossians acclaims Christ as the image of God and the fullness of God, the one in whom and through whom all things were created and who sustains them in existence. Through him, our reconciliation to God was accomplished. Christ is the first fruit of the new creation, the firstborn from the dead. He has revealed and made possible the destiny that is ours.

◆ GOSPEL: Today's Gospel presents us with a man who has listened to the Word of God and knows it well. All that remains is for him to do it (note the threefold reference to "do" in today's Gospel). The scholar of the Law wants to be precise in his keeping of the Law: who is my neighbor? There are several surprising elements in the parable Jesus tells. The official religious personnel pass by the man in need; contact with a corpse would have rendered them defiled and therefore unfit for Temple worship. Samaritans were looked down upon by the Jews for both historical and religious reasons, yet the Samaritan traveler is the one who does what the Law requires! What must I do? Show mercy.

The Roman Missal

Because of our faith, we are called "Christian." We pray that all who bear this holy name may reject what is contrary to Christ's name and seek whatever honors it (Collect).

We pray that the "offerings of the Church . . . / may bring ever greater holiness" to all who receive them (Prayer over the Offerings)

We pray for an increase in the "saving effects" of the Eucharist we share (Prayer after Communion).

Other Ideas

Read the farewell speech Moses gave to the Israelites before they entered the Promised Land (Deuteronomy 29:1–30:20). Talk with others about Moses and the guidance he gives in the speech. What does he hope they will remember after he is gone? What do you imagine it meant for him to lead them here but not enter the Promised Land himself? What does it say of Moses's faith in God?

Find examples in history or the news where people who were enemies treated one another as loving children of the same God. What do you think it cost them? Who do you think their example touched?

Find a place in your community where suffering persons are treated with compassion and love. Your parish or Catholic Charities would have a list of places. Talk about the reasons for their suffering. Who are the people trying to make a difference in their lives? Can you make a difference?

#389   white
Memorial of Saint Bonaventure, Bishop and Doctor of the Church

MON **15**

Lectionary for Mass

◆ FIRST READING: The story of Israel in Egypt continues, several generations after Joseph. God's promise of numerous descendants for Abraham is being realized, and this is a threat to the Egyptians.

Pharaoh takes steps to keep Israel "oppressed" by enslaving them. The order to kill the firstborn males is likewise an attempt to thwart Israel's increase in number.

◆ RESPONSORIAL PSALM 64: Today's Psalm is an apt description of what must have been Israel's prayer and experience during their enslavement in Egypt and their exodus through the waters into the freedom of new life in the Promised Land. Had the Lord not been with them—and rescued them—they would indeed have perished.

◆ GOSPEL: We are still hearing from Matthew 10, Jesus's commission of the Apostles. Today the emphasis is first of all on the opposition his disciples will encounter, even from their own family members. Yet no relationship can have priority over one's relationship with Jesus. The second part of the text focuses on the blessings that the people to whom the Apostles are sent will receive—if they are receptive to their words.

The Roman Missal

The Collect is found in the Proper of Saints, with the remaining prayers taken from the Common of Pastors: For a Bishop or the Common of Doctors of the Church.

Today's Saint

Saint Bonaventure (1221–1274), scholastic theologian and philosopher, was born in Italy and joined the Franciscans in 1243. He studied theology at Paris with his great contemporary, Thomas Aquinas. After teaching for a time, he was chosen Minister General of the Franciscans in 1257, at a time when the order suffered from divisions, which he was able to do much to heal. Later, he was named cardinal bishop of Albano. Bonaventure was declared a Doctor of the Church in 1588 by Pope Sixtus V, and is called the "Seraphic Doctor" because his love of God is so evident, even in his philosophical writings. When the Council of Lyons was called to bring the Greek and Latin churches back together, Bonaventure went at the request of Pope Gregory X, but he died before the Council's work was finished, receiving the Sacrament of the Sick from the pope himself. Saint Bonaventure is shown in art dressed in a Franciscan habit and wearing a cardinal's hat.

T U E 16 #390 green **Weekday**

Optional Memorial of Our Lady of Mount Carmel / white

Lectionary for Mass

◆ FIRST READING: The infant Moses is miraculously saved from Pharaoh's command to kill male babies by the ingenuity of his mother and sister, and the compassion of Pharaoh's daughter. In today's reading we also meet the adult Moses, passionate over the well-being of his people and fearful that his revenge against the Egyptians would lead to trouble. He was right. Moses fled for his life into the land of Midian.

◆ RESPONSORIAL PSALM 69 is a song of lament by one who is in the depths of despair and oppressed by others. God is the only one who can help. Notice the change of tone in the middle of the third stanza, when suddenly the psalmist senses that God will indeed hear the prayer of his poor one. Praise is the only fitting response.

◆ GOSPEL: The signs and wonders performed by the Lord call those who receive and benefit from them to faith and conversion. Today, Jesus takes to task those cities noteworthy for their lack of faith.

Today's Optional Memorial

Mount Carmel is part of a mountain range in northern Israel, significant to Christians for its biblical association with the prophet Elijah (see 1 Kings 18). In the twelfth century, the Carmelites were founded at a site reputed to have been Elijah's cave. They soon built a monastery here. The Carmelites honor the Blessed Virgin Mary under the title Our Lady of Mount Carmel. The English Carmelite, Saint Simon Stock, is believed to have been given the brown scapular by Our Lady, and those who wear it believe they can be sure of her help at the hour of their death.

W E D 17 #391 green **Weekday**

Lectionary for Mass

◆ FIRST READING: Moses, a refugee in the land, has an experience of God that will change his life. One day while shepherding his father-in-law's flock, Moses catches sight of a bush burning though mysteriously not being consumed, so he goes over to investigate. Then and there Moses meets God and receives his call to be the one who will lead God's people out of Egypt.

◆ RESPONSORIAL PSALM 103 is a hymn of praise for all that God has done for Israel. The verses chosen for today's response focus on God's deliverance of his people through Moses his servant.

◆ GOSPEL: The wisdom of Jesus's teaching is quite different from what the world esteems as wise. Jesus calls his disciples to a simplicity that renders them receptive to what God will reveal.

T H U 18 #392 green **Weekday**

Optional Memorial of Saint Camillus de Lellis, Priest / white

Lectionary for Mass

◆ FIRST READING: The story of Moses and the burning bush continues. Today, God reveals his name to Moses: "I am who I am." The name is a mystery; God is so much more than anything or anyone we can imagine. At the same time, he is God-in-relationship: to Abraham, to Isaac, to Jacob, to Moses, and to Israel as a people. He is a God of action, a God who will deliver his people from oppression, no matter the obstacles, and lead them into a glorious new land.

◆ RESPONSORIAL PSALM 105: This song of thanksgiving and praise celebrates the fidelity of God who remembers his covenant to Abraham and Isaac. The second stanza focuses on the realization of the promise of many descendants; the third, on his choice of Moses and Aaron as his instruments in the land of Ham (Egypt).

◆ GOSPEL: The words of today's Gospel are tremendous comfort for anyone feeling burdened by his or her life situation. Who does not long for the rest (Matthew 11:28)—the restoration and peace that God alone can give!

Today's Saint

Laying aside a life of violence and gambling, Saint Camillus de Lellis (1550–1614) was ordained a priest and later founded the Order of Clerks Regular Ministers to the Sick (the Camillians), a religious order dedicated to the sick, especially those afflicted with the plague. Whether they were ministering in a hospital or tending to the wounded on the battlefield, the Camillians were easily identified by their black habit with a large red cross on the breast. Saint Camillus implemented many innovative approaches to hospital care, including proper ventilation, suitable diets, and isolation of people with infectious diseases. He is also credited with inventing field ambulances and military hospitals. Along with Saint John of God, he is patron of hospitals, nurses, and the sick.

F R I 19 #393 green Weekday

Lectionary for Mass

◆ FIRST READING: The Lectionary omits the accounts of the first nine plagues that God wrought against the land of Egypt. The story resumes with the account of Moses receiving instructions from God for the Passover just prior to the last plague, when God's angel "passed over" the dwellings of the Israelites that were marked with the blood of the sacrificial lamb and brought death to the Egyptian households. In the wake of this, the Egyptians would allow the Israelites to leave their land. The celebration of Passover was to be an annual celebration in memory of what God did for Israel in Egypt. And so it is today.

◆ RESPONSORIAL PSALM 116: The "cup" in today's antiphon refers to a cup that was shared as part of a sacrificial meal. This particular thanksgiving sacrifice celebrated the Lord's deliverance from death.

◆ GOSPEL: Throughout the Gospel according to Matthew, the Pharisees fault Jesus for his apparent failure to observe the Law. Today is one such incident. In response, Jesus chides them on their failure to recognize the deeper spirit of the Law. Jesus makes the weight of his authority clear: the Son of Man is Lord of the Sabbath.

S A T 20 #394 green Weekday

Optional Memorials of Saint Apollinaris, Bishop and Martyr / red; Blessed Virgin Mary / white

Lectionary for Mass

◆ FIRST READING: After the death of the first-born among the Egyptians, the Israelites were not only allowed to leave Israel, but actually sent on their way during the night. It was a night of vigil for the Lord as he kept watch over the Israelites. It was to be a night of vigil for the Israelites for coming generations, as they remember and celebrate what God had done for them.

◆ RESPONSORIAL PSALM 136: This joyful hymn of thanksgiving celebrates God's remembrance of his covenant promises, showing mercy to Israel and delivering them from oppression in the land of Egypt. The second stanza speaks of the tenth plague—the death of the Egyptian first-born. The third stanza speaks of Israel's safe crossing of the Red (literally "reed" in the Hebrew text) Sea and of the Egyptians' subsequent destruction in its waters.

◆ GOSPEL: The opposition between Jesus and the Pharisees increases to the point where they plot his death. Jesus knows it and quietly withdraws, while still continuing his healing mission to those who would receive him. The text from Isaiah cited by Matthew focuses on the mission of the Servant chosen by God; endowed with his Spirit he promotes justice and proclaims God's good news of salvation even to the Gentiles. Jesus is this servant par excellence.

Today's Saint

Not much is known about Saint Apollinaris except that he was from Antioch, a Syrian, and the first bishop of Ravenna. Tradition says he was appointed bishop by Saint Peter himself. Apollinaris was exiled with his people during the persecution of Emperor Vespasian. As he left the city, he was identified as the leader of the Christians. He was tortured and executed with a sword. Saint Apollinaris is a patron of those suffering from epilepsy or gout, and is shown in art with a sword, the instrument of his martyrdom.

21 #108 green Sixteenth Sunday in Ordinary Time

Orientation

Martha and Mary are often put forth as symbols of the active and the contemplative life in faith. Yet, this dichotomy would ring truer if both Martha and Mary found joy and true encounter with the Lord through their particular ministries. It seems that only Mary does, while stressed and anxious Martha complains by giving her sister a hard time, while her duties as a hostess call her away. Would Martha truly wish to hinder her sister's encounter with the Lord? Not at all! Her complaint is rather about herself, as in the midst of her duties, worries, and anxieties, she has lost focus and is missing out on a similarly profound encounter. Jesus sees the worries and restlessness surrounding Martha and he refocuses her heart by pointing out that there is need of only one thing. This one thing, the source and center of our lives, installs peace and joy into our hearts no matter what our duties and challenges are at hand. Mary has found it at the feet of her Lord, and invites Martha to the same stillness in the presence of God, whether in the kitchen, or in Jesus's direct company.

Lectionary for Mass

◆ FIRST READING: Today's reading offers us a beautiful example of hospitality, or more precisely, of welcoming strangers, which is the literal meaning of the Greek word for hospitality. The Letter to the Hebrews (13:2), in encouraging the practice of this virtue, alludes to this incident from Genesis, pointing out that some have entertained angels without realizing it. Abraham's generosity is rewarded. He and Sarah are promised a son.

◆ RESPONSORIAL PSALM 15: Hospitality to the stranger was commanded in the law of old. Abraham exemplifies righteousness in this regard. The stanzas of today's Psalm list other characteristics of the righteousness which must be observed if one is to live in the presence of the Lord.

◆ SECOND READING: Paul's enigmatic words about suffering serve as an invitation for us to see whatever suffering is ours as a share in the sufferings of Christ, a suffering with him, a suffering for his Body, the Church. It is mystery, this movement through death to life. The "perfect" of the last line does not mean "flawless" but "fully mature."

◆ GOSPEL: The beginning of today's Gospel raises the question: is this the first time Jesus met Martha and Mary? This story is another example of hospitality—and the stranger or traveler they welcomed was the Lord! (Something similar happens in the Emmaus story in Luke 24.) Hospitality requires effort and attention to the guest, and

it is easy to get caught up in the practicalities of the meal. Jesus's words teach us that presence and listening to the other are what is most important.

The Roman Missal

We ask to be "made fervent" in the theological virtues of faith, hope, and charity, so that we may keep God's commands (Collect).

In the sacrifice of the Mass, God "brought to completion" all the "offerings of the law." We pray that God may receive the sacrifice we offer as he received "the gifts of Abel," so that what each of us brings may "benefit the salvation of all" (Prayer over the Offerings)

We pray that all who are "imbued with heavenly mysteries" by sharing in the Eucharist may leave behind "former ways" and walk in "newness of life" (Prayer after Communion).

Other Ideas

The Gospel reading for this Sunday is unique to Luke. Read some of the passages which are only found in Luke's account of the Gospel: Luke 1:26–56; 2:8–52; 7:36—8:3; 12:16–21; 13:6–17; 15:1–32; 16:19–31; 18:1–14; 24:13–35. What is Luke saying to his audience with these stories? What image of discipleship does he convey?

The custom of using luminarias (lanterns) is a practice among Hispanics at Christmas Time. Luminarias are a sign of hope that the love of the Christ child will find its way into the homes and places outside of which the luminarias are present. Luminarias can be made by weighting brown paper bags down with sand and placing a small candle or other light inside of them. During the summer, make luminarias for a gathering of friends. When your guests arrive, have a discussion about how we light the way for one another as a sign of hospitality. Give them each a luminaria to take home.

Spend five or ten minutes silently listening to God's voice. If you are distracted, try to let go of the distraction and then continue in silence. What did you hear?

MON 22 #395, Gospel #603 white
Memorial of Saint Mary Magdalene

Lectionary for Mass

◆ FIRST READING: After the Israelites departed from Egypt, Pharaoh realized that he had just lost his work force. He and his army set out in pursuit. The Israelites cried out in fear but Moses reassured them. The Lord would win victory for Israel. When, at the word of the Lord, Moses lifted up his staff and stretched out his hand over the sea, the waters parted and a path was opened for the Israelites right through the sea.

◆ CANTICLE: Today's canticle from the book of Exodus is the hymn sung by Moses and the Israelites in praise of what the Lord had accomplished on their behalf at the parting of the sea. When the Egyptians tried to pass through, the waters enveloped them.

◆ GOSPEL: We hear of the appearance of the Risen Christ to Mary Magdalene. She recognizes him only when he calls her by name. The Risen Christ commissions her to be the "apostle to the Apostles."

The Roman Missal

The prayers are found in the Proper of Saints.

Mary Magdalene is often called "the apostle to the Apostles." The Collect speaks of Mary as the one "entrusted . . . before all others" with the Good News of the Resurrection. We are to follow her example and "proclaim the living Christ" (Collect)

We ask God to receive our offerings, as Christ received the "homage of charity" of Saint Mary Magdalene, an allusion to Luke

7:36–38, when a penitent woman, traditionally associated with Mary Magdalene, anoints Jesus's feet with her tears, and dries them with her hair (Prayer over the Offerings).

The Preface of Holy Men and Women is used.

After his Resurrection, Mary clung to Jesus, her Master. We pray that we may be filled with that same "persevering love" (Prayer after Communion).

Today's Saint

Mary Magdalene was one of the followers of Jesus and one of the few witnesses of his Crucifixion and burial. At dawn on the third day, she went to anoint the body and was the first to see the empty tomb. She immediately ran to tell Peter and John (John 20:1–2)—for this reason, she has been called the "apostle to the Apostles" by Saint Bernard of Clairvaux, among others. One tradition puts her in Ephesus after the Ascension, but the French believe she sailed to Marseille in a small boat, accompanied by her brother Lazarus, and lived in a cave doing penance for the rest of her life.

TUE 23 #396 green Weekday

Optional Memorial of Saint Bridget, Religious / white

Lectionary for Mass

◆ FIRST READING: The reading is a more detailed account of the event celebrated in yesterday's Responsorial Psalm. All that happens—the Israelites' deliverance, the Egyptians' destruction—is the work of the Lord, the Savior of Israel. Notice that the reading ends with the beginning of the hymn of praise which was yesterday's response and is today's as well.

◆ CANTICLE: Today's verses are a continuation from yesterday's text. Note the vivid imagery used in the hymn. The last stanza looks ahead to the settlement of Israel in the Promised Land.

◆ GOSPEL: At first glance, the words of today's Gospel can seem heartless. Is Jesus really ignoring his own family? The evangelist stresses an important point: fidelity and obedience to God's word establishes a closer relationship with Jesus than the ties of blood within one's biological family.

Today's Saint

Saint Bridget of Sweden (1303–1373), a wife and mother of eight children, joined a Cistercian monastery after the death of her husband. After a series of visions, she founded the Bridgettine Order, a double monastery for men and women, living in separate enclosures, dedicated to learning. In another vision, she was instructed to heal the schism of the Avignon papacy by warning Pope Clement VI to return to Rome from Avignon. She was not canonized for her many and varied visions and revelations she believed herself to have had, but for her heroic virtue.

WED 24 #397 green Weekday

Optional Memorial of Saint Sharbel Makhlūf, Priest / white

Lectionary for Mass

◆ FIRST READING: What a radical change in tone between the readings of yesterday and today! Yesterday we had songs of praise. Today we hear complaints from the discontented children of Israel, overwhelmed by famine. Still, God was faithful to them and provided food, at the same time testing their fidelity and obedience. Even as they grumbled, God let them see his glory. What an amazing, merciful, and loving God!

◆ RESPONSORIAL Psalm 78 recounts the history of Israel from the Exodus to the settlement of the land. Today's verses focus on the story we heard in the First Reading. Despite Israel's rebellion and murmuring, God provided food from heaven in abundance.

◆ GOSPEL: We hear the first part of the parable of the sower and the seed. The crowds who listened to Jesus on the shore of the Sea of Galilee had only to turn around and see the fields on the hillside for a living illustration of the parable he told. Perhaps the sight of this prompted the imagery he used! What kind of soil is our heart for the seed of God's Word?

Today's Saint

Saint Sharbel Makhlūf Joseph Zaroun was a Maronite Catholic, born and raised in a small Lebanese mountain village. As a child he led a pious life of prayer and solitude. His favorite book was *The Imitation of Christ* by Thomas à Kempis. When he entered the Monastery of Saint Maron at 23, he took the name Sharbel after the second-century martyr of the Antioch Church. He lived an austere life as a hermit, eating only one meal of vegetables each day, sleeping on a pillow of wood and a duvet filled with dead leaves. His time was devoted to prayer, contemplation, and manual labor. Many came to him for counsel and blessing. He died in 1898 on Christmas Eve.

25 THU #605 red
Feast of Saint James, Apostle

Lectionary for Mass

◆ FIRST READING: Paul's words are aptly chosen for this Apostle, who was martyred because of his faith in the Lord Jesus and his proclamation of the Gospel (Acts of the Apostles 12:2). James, like the other Apostles and each of us, was a fragile earthen vessel. Yet, he was sustained by his conviction that he, too, would be raised with Jesus.

◆ RESPONSORIAL PSALM 126 celebrates the deliverance of the Israelites from their exile in Babylon. Note the marked contrast between the weeping of their exile and the rejoicing of their return to their homeland.

◆ GOSPEL: What mother cannot identify with the mother of James and John, wanting the ultimate best for her son! Jesus's response to her leaves no doubt: glory comes only after drinking the cup of suffering and after self-emptying service.

The Roman Missal

The prayers are found in the Proper of Saints. The Gloria is said or sung on this feast.

Saint James was the first of the Apostles to give his life for Christ. We pray that the Church may be strengthened by his faith, and protected by his intercession (Collect).

James announced himself capable of drinking the cup of the Lord, and he did "drink of Christ's chalice of suffering." We pray that we may be cleansed "by the saving baptism" of Christ's Passion, as James was (Prayer over the Offerings).

The Prayer after Communion is a simple prayer for God's help through the intercession of the Apostle James.

Today's Saint

The Saint James we honor today is the brother of the Apostle John, one of the "sons of thunder" (Mark 3:17) who were privileged witnesses of some of Jesus's greatest signs: the raising of the daughter of Jairus from the dead, the Transfiguration, and the agony in the garden. James was the first apostle to suffer martyrdom, slain by Herod's orders as described in Acts of the Apostles. According to legend, his remains were carried away by his friends in a rudderless boat, which drifted all the way to Spain. Many centuries later his remains were discovered, and a great cathedral was built over the spot where they were found (Santiago de Compostela, which became one of the most popular pilgrimage destinations of the Middle Ages). To this day, hundreds of thousands of pilgrims make their way to that remote corner of Spain to venerate the relics of Saint James.

26 FRI #399 white
Memorial of Saints Joachim and Anne, Parents of the Blessed Virgin Mary

Lectionary for Mass

◆ FIRST READING: God gives the Ten Commandments to Moses on Mount Sinai. Note God's self-identification: "I, the LORD, am your God, who brought you out of the land of Egypt . . . ." Note that the text is longer than the simple list we learned as children. The expansions help us to understand the reasons underlying the various commandments.

◆ RESPONSORIAL PSALM: The words of God's covenant are words that lead to life. Today's response is from the Gospel according to John. The stanzas from the latter part of Psalm 19 acclaim the wisdom of the law of God. Note the adjectives used to describe God's Law.

◆ GOSPEL: We hear Jesus's explanation of the parable of the sower and the seed. What type of soil has our heart for receiving the seed of God's Word?

The Roman Missal

The prayers, found in the Proper of Saints, place Joachim and Anne in the long line of ancestors who faithfully awaited the coming of the Messiah. We pray that we may attain the promised salvation (Collect) and share the blessing promised "to Abraham and his descendants" (Prayer over the Offerings). The Prayer after Communion expresses the wonderful paradox of the Incarnation: God wills that Christ be "born from among humanity" so that "humanity might be born again from you."

Today is a feast in Canada.

Today's Saints

The information we have regarding Saints Joachim and Anne, the parents of the Blessed Virgin Mary, comes from an unreliable source known as the Gospel of James. They are portrayed as an old and barren couple who long to bring life into the world. Through an angelic messenger they are told they will bear a child—not just any child, but one who will be revered for all time. A following developed around both of them, but it seems that Saint Anne had a stronger following, which continues to flourish, especially in Canada. She is the patron of childless women, expectant mothers, and women in labor.

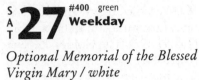

S A T #400 green
27 Weekday

Optional Memorial of the Blessed Virgin Mary / white

Lectionary for Mass

◆ FIRST READING: The "words and ordinances" Moses recounts to the people of Israel are those he received from the Lord on Mount Sinai. Today he has come down to the foot of the mountain and related these words to the people, who affirmed their acceptance of them and promised their obedience. The covenant agreement between God and Israel was then sealed by the blood of the sacrificial offering.

◆ RESPONSORIAL PSALM 50: Today's Psalm opens with a word of summons for judgment. If we read the Psalm in its entirety, we see that while Israel was faithful in offering sacrifices, the people's way of life did not reflect a fidelity to the spirit and intention of the covenant laws. The third stanza of today's response reiterates the importance of obedience to God's law. Then call on the Lord for help in times of distress.

◆ GOSPEL: Today's parable bids us to take a good look at the field of our lives. Do we know what has been sown there and by whom? Are there good seeds bringing forth grain that nourishes, or are there weeds in our hearts?

#111 green

☀ 28 Seventeenth Sunday in Ordinary Time

Orientation

Jesus Christ witnessed for us the importance of prayer, and he taught us explicitly to pray in the Lord's Prayer. Prayer is like an encounter with a beloved friend. Even though there is a friendship between us, we still need to make time to meet and to enjoy one another's company. These meetings help us to grow deeper in the relationship we enjoy. In prayer, meeting with God is like meeting with a beloved friend. Like a meeting, prayer can take many forms, as long as it contributes to the relationship of love that exists between God and us. Like seeing a beloved friend, time spent with God in prayer is essential for our relationship to grow, mature and continue to support us throughout our lifetimes.

Lectionary for Mass

◆ FIRST READING: Hearing of the sinfulness of the cities of Sodom and Gomorrah, the Lord sets out to determine if the accusations are indeed true. If so, the citizens of those cities deserve to be punished. Abraham enters into dialogue with God, a bit boldly perhaps, but nonetheless with moving concern for the innocent ones who dwell among the wicked. God accedes to his request . . . even for the sake of only ten innocent people.

◆ RESPONSORIAL PSALM 138: This song of thanksgiving is fitting response to the account of the Lord's merciful response to Abraham's plea. The Hebrew word translated as "kindness" in the second and last stanzas of today's Psalm is *hesed,* or covenant love. Mercy has its source in love. Confident in God, the psalmist is assured of God's protection. The one who prays knows that he or she is the work of God's hands.

◆ SECOND READING: In Baptism, we die and rise with Christ into a newness of life. Even before we were baptized, by his Death on the Cross, Christ inaugurated a new experience of life, a life reconciled to God, a sharing in the life that is God's own.

◆ GOSPEL: There is a beautiful simplicity in the disciples' request as they watched Jesus pray: "Lord, teach us to pray." He gives them not only words for prayer, but a relationship to God: he is Father, they are his sons and daughters. The subsequent parable and teachings illustrate the confidence disciples should have when they pray. Our Father desires to give us his Holy Spirit if only we ask.

The Roman Missal

Without God, nothing is firm, nothing is holy. We pray that we may use the things of this world in such a way that we grasp, even now, the things of heaven—the things "that ever endure" (Collect)

From among God's many gifts to us, we bring our offerings. We pray that through his grace, these offerings may make us holy, and lead us home to him (Prayer over the Offerings).

The Eucharist is the "perpetual memorial of the Passion," and the everlasting sign of Christ's "love beyond all telling." We pray that this unsurpassed gift may lead us to salvation (Prayer after Communion).

Other Ideas

Paragraph 2635 of the *Catechism of the Catholic Church* talks about intercession, or asking God for something on behalf of someone else. Read this paragraph, either in print or online, and discuss with a friend or a group how this might direct who we remember in our prayer.

Take the phrases of the Lord's Prayer from the Gospel reading for this Sunday. Reflect on each individual phrase. What does it mean to you? Discuss your different ideas with a group.

Create a time to pray daily. Ask for what you need to continue to serve as Jesus's disciple. Reflect on how God responds to your prayers.

M O N 29 #401 or Gospel #607 white Memorial of Saint Martha

Lectionary for Mass

◆ First Reading: Though not a part of the Lectionary text, after the sacrificial ratification of the covenant which we heard about in Saturday's reading, Moses went back up the mountain. Today's reading begins as he comes back down—and hears the sounds of revelry in the camp. Already, Israel had turned to idolatry, worshiping a calf of molten gold. Today's reading omits the account of Moses separating the people into those who were "for" the Lord and those who were not. The latter were killed. Moses intercedes for the people with God, seeking to make atonement for them. Notice the intensity of his plea! If God will not forgive, then Moses asks to be written off as well.

◆ Responsorial Psalm 106 is another historical Psalm. Today's verses recount the incident of the golden calf and Moses' intercession. The first stanza speaks of their exchanging their glory—the glory of God—for the image of a bull. Are

we ever tempted to exchange our glory? For what?

◆ Gospel: Today's Gospel relates two parables, both focusing on very tiny things that have tremendous power for life-giving growth in the right environment (good soil, warm water). So it is with the kingdom of heaven (God) in the lives of those who hear and receive God's Word.

The Roman Missal

The prayers, found in the Proper of Saints, are full of allusions to the Gospel accounts of Martha, who welcomed Christ to her home, and who believed in him as the Son of God.

Martha welcomed Christ as a guest. We pray that we may so serve Christ in our brothers and sisters, that God may welcome us to "the halls of heaven" (Collect)

Martha's "homage of love" was pleasing to the Lord. We pray that "our dutiful service" may likewise "find favor" in God's sight (Prayer over the Offerings).

Earth and heaven are contrasted. We pray that we may turn away from the things of earth to the things of heaven. At the same time, we must follow the example of Saint Martha, growing in sincere love for Christ on earth so that we may behold him in heaven (Prayer after Communion).

Today's Saint

Martha was the sister of Lazarus and Mary, friends of Jesus. She appears to have been a practical-minded woman, for she seems to have organized the dinner in Luke 10:38–42, and she protests when Jesus commands that the stone be rolled from the entrance to her brother's tomb after he'd been dead for three days. At the same time, however, she is one of the few in the Gospel to profess her faith in Jesus as the Messiah: "Yes, Lord. I have come to believe that you are the

Messiah, the Son of God, the one who is coming into the world" (John 11:27). The Golden Legend records the tradition that Martha, with her sister, Mary, and brother, Lazarus, fled Judea after the death of Jesus and landed at Marseilles. Martha is supposed to have traveled to Avignon, where she converted many to Christianity. Saint Martha is shown in art bearing the tools of a housekeeper—keys or a broom—and is a patron saint of domestic servants, homemakers, cooks, and single laywomen.

T U E 30 #402 green Weekday

Optional Memorial of Saint Peter Chrysologus, Bishop and Doctor of the Church / white

Lectionary for Mass

◆ First Reading: Today's reading is excerpted from two chapters in the book of Exodus. The first, from chapter 33, speaks of the cloud as a symbol of God's presence at the Tent of Meeting, where God would speak with Moses. Take note of the reverential awe of the people when they witnessed the cloud, and also of the familiarity between God and Moses. The second part, from chapter 34, takes us to the top of Mount Sinai. Though not evident in the Lectionary, there is a cloud on Mount Sinai when God speaks to Moses. What a beautiful definition, or rather, self-identification of who God is: merciful, gracious, patient, kind, faithful, forgiving. At the same time, he is a just God, who will punish the unrepentant guilty.

◆ Responsorial Psalm 103: Today's Psalm response is almost a recapitulation of the First Reading: the revelation to Moses, the description of God as merciful, gracious, patient, forgiving, kind, and compassionate.

◆ GOSPEL: Last Saturday, we heard the parable that is interpreted in today's Gospel. The harvest is the end time judgment, with its subsequent punishment of consuming fire or its heavenly reward of the shining fire of transformation and glorification—as bright as the sun.

Today's Saint

Saint Peter Chrysologus (380–450), born in Imola in northeastern Italy, was appointed Archbishop of Ravenna by Emperor Valentinian III. His orthodox approach to the Incarnation and other Church doctrines earned him the support of Pope Saint Leo the Great. He was given the title "Chrysologus," meaning "Golden-worded," due to his flair for preaching. This title may have been given to him so that the Western Church would have a preacher equal to Saint John "Chrysostom" ("Golden-tongued") of the East. Most of his writings did not survive, but the Church is graced with a number of his sermons. The remaining sermons are written with pastoral sensitivity and optimism, while challenging people to conversion and repentance.

#403   white

WED 31

Memorial of Saint Ignatius of Loyola, Priest

Lectionary for Mass

◆ FIRST READING: This is the second time Moses has come down the mountain with tablets of the commandments! The emphasis in today's texts is not so much on the tablets which Moses carried—though the text does mention his relating to the people the words of the Lord, but on the radiance of his face after being in the presence of God.

◆ RESPONSORIAL PSALM 99: Upon seeing the holiness of God on the mountain, Moses was radiantly transformed. We are all called, like Moses, Aaron, and Samuel, to come into the presence of God and worship him.

◆ GOSPEL: Two images convey the sense of the immense value of the kingdom of heaven (God). Having "discovered it," the seeker is willing to relinquish all other possessions in order to obtain it.

The Roman Missal

The prayers for the memorial are found in the Proper of Saints. The Collect is rich in allusions to the mission of the great saint. He worked "to further the greater glory of [God's] name." We pray that we, like him, may fight "the good fight."

Today's Saint

Women, gambling, and sword fights filled the early life of Saint Ignatius of Loyola in the Spanish court. This changed while he was recuperating from a leg injury. With nothing else to do, he hesitantly began reading a book about Christ. This changed him. He retreated into a cave and contemplated how to live an exemplary Christian life while developing his renowned *Spiritual Exercises*. After inspiring a pilgrimage to Rome, he studied for the priesthood and started the Society of Jesus (the Jesuits) to assist the pope in missionary work and other projects. It has become the largest Catholic order with 18,139 priests, brothers, and men in training. They serve in more than 112 nations.

August
Month of the Immaculate Heart of Mary

#404   white

THU 1

Memorial of Saint Alphonsus Liguori, Bishop and Doctor of the Church

Lectionary for Mass

◆ FIRST READING: Moses is obedient to God's command regarding the erection of the Tent of Meeting. In addition to being the place where God and Moses met, the Tent also housed the Ark of the Covenant (commandments). The cloud which descended upon the tent symbolized the presence of God. Note God's fidelity to his people, guiding them along their journey in a cloud by day and pillar of fire at night.

◆ RESPONSORIAL PSALM: The beauty of God's temple, God's dwelling place—of which the Tent of Meeting was a forerunner—is the focus of Psalm 84. If we read the text of Exodus 40 in its entirety, we note that there was an altar there as well. The last line of the third stanza evokes the sense of progression, moving forward, like Israel on their journey.

◆ GOSPEL: Jesus uses the things of everyday life to teach about the kingdom of God. Today, it is the fisherman's net, something used every day by many of Jesus's listeners. Many would have sat on the shore separating their fish—and herein lies the Gospel's important point: the good and the bad will be separated and justly rewarded or punished at the end of time.

The Roman Missal

The prayers for the memorial are found in the Proper of Saints. They echo some of the principal themes of the saint's life: zeal for souls (Collect), self-offering (Prayer over the Offerings), and frequent reception of Holy Communion (Prayer after Communion).

Today's Saint

Following a successful career as a lawyer, Saint Alphonsus Ligouri (1696–1787) lost a legal case which he believed to be a sign from God that he should change his ways and study for the priesthood. At the suggestion of a bishop friend, he founded the Congregation of the Most Holy Redeemer, also known as the Redemptorists, a community of priests dedicated to preaching, hearing confessions, and administering the sacraments. One of his most important contributions to the Church is his prolific writing in the area of moral theology. Also included among his writings are many devotional works on Mary and the saints. He influenced the Church not only through his writings, but also through his leadership as a bishop. Due to his many accomplishments, he was declared a Doctor of the Church and is recognized as one of the greatest moral theologians in Church history.

F R I 2 #405 green
Weekday

Optional Memorials of Saint Eusebius of Vercelli, Bishop / white; Saint Peter Julian Eymard, Priest / white

Lectionary for Mass

◆ FIRST READING: Israel is commanded by the Lord to observe four major holy days: Passover, commemorating the exodus from Egypt; Pentecost, the fiftieth day harvest feast; the Day of Atonement, a day of fasting and penance; and the Feast of Booths, a fall harvest festival which also commemorated Israel's wanderings in the desert. Note that three of these were to be observed for seven days!

◆ RESPONSORIAL PSALM 81: Today's Psalm is an invitation to praise the Lord. Note the mention of musical instruments! The third stanza reminds Israel that such celebrations are commanded by the Lord their God, who led them out of Egypt and who is the true God (fourth stanza).

◆ GOSPEL: In today's Gospel, Jesus, the prophet, is rejected by his own people in his hometown. In effect, they say: "Who does he think he is!" (author's paraphrase). Not only do Jesus's people reject him, they are offended by him. Did his words touch too close to home? How hard it is to recognize and to receive what those closest to us may have to give us.

Today's Saints

Saint Eusebius (283–371), the first bishop of Vercelli, spent much of his life trying to settle conflicts between Catholics and Arians. (Arians denied the divinity of Christ.) Because Saint Eusebius actively supported the views of the Catholic Church, as expressed in the Nicene Creed, he was severely persecuted by Arian proponents, by means of starvation and exile. It is believed that he contributed to the composition of the Athanasian Creed.

Saint Peter Julian Eymard (1811–1868) changed immensely after he had an overwhelming experience of God's love while carrying the Blessed Sacrament during the Corpus Christi procession. He decided to leave the Marist order to found the Blessed Sacrament Fathers, a community dedicated to perpetual adoration of the Eucharist. Later, he established a foundation of sisters, known as the Sisters of the Blessed Sacrament, and a confraternity of laypeople. He believed adoration of the Eucharist was not an end in itself, but a means to evangelization and service.

S A T 3 #406 green
Weekday

Optional Memorial of the Blessed Virgin Mary / white

Lectionary for Mass

◆ FIRST READING: The fiftieth year, the jubilee year, is sacred to the Lord. Note its purpose: liberty, return to one's family estate, rest, fairness in buying and selling—all in a spirit of reverence before the Lord.

◆ RESPONSORIAL PSALM 67: This hymn of praise, although not specifically about the jubilee year, points to it as cause for joy and blessings for all people—not only Israel, but all nations as well. Note the references to abundant crops and awareness of blessings. As God deals with equity, so must Israel.

◆ GOSPEL: The question of Jesus's identity leads to the telling of the story about John the Baptist's death. Today's Gospel presents a challenge to us: Are we ever like Herod, compromising what we know to be the truth for the sake of our own reputation and esteem?

4 #114 green
Eighteenth Sunday in Ordinary Time

Orientation

The rich man of this parable has more than enough: his storehouses cannot hold all of the bountiful harvest his lands have produced. He has many blessings, but in deciding to build larger storehouses to hold his surplus, he does not recognize these blessings as gifts to be shared. Jesus teaches us that the surplus the rich man piles up in his new storehouses is not what true wealth is all about. Had the rich man shared his surplus with those in need around him, he would have gained much more—he would have experienced the reign of God through sharing in love with his neighbors. Wealth is fleeting, but love carries us into eternal life.

Lectionary for Mass

◆ FIRST READING: The book of Ecclesiastes (Qoheleth) opens with a reflection on the recognizable patterns and transitory nature of human life. Vanity can also be translated as vapor or breath. In other words, all is a mere bit of moisture that can evaporate or a puff of air. Today's text focuses in particular on the pains and difficulties of human labor. When all is said and done, what is there to show for it? The words can sound depressing, but they wisely call us to focus on the ultimate and most important (eternal) realities in life.

◆ RESPONSORIAL PSALM 90: The theme of the transitoriness of human life is clearly echoed in the first two stanzas of Psalm 90. A prayer for wisdom about the true meaning of life is voiced in the third stanza, and for prosperity in the fourth. The antiphon, from Psalm 94, calls us to hear the wisdom of God. This call is particularly stark in light of the First Reading. In contrast to the dismal tone of Ecclesiastes, Psalm 90 is permeated with joy. God our Creator is our Savior and Shepherd. He will lead us into his presence if we respond to his call and live by his wisdom.

◆ SECOND READING: Our Baptism meant dying with Christ and being raised with him in newness of life. Ours, too, is the hope of glory. We must now live accordingly. Today's reading offers some very specific instructions on how we are to live and become the new self that we have received in Baptism, one in the image of our creator.

◆ GOSPEL: The situation at the beginning of today's Gospel is sadly an all too familiar one. Jesus's parable touches deeply into the truth regarding riches. Ultimately earthly wealth does not matter—we cannot take it with us into the next life. Let us labor, instead, for riches in what matters to God.

The Roman Missal

God is our "Creator and guide." We ask him to "restore" us, his creation, and to keep us safe (Collect)

We ask God to accept our "spiritual sacrifice," and to make us an "eternal offering" to himself (Prayer over the Offerings).

We ask God to be with us with his protection, and to make us worthy of "eternal redemption" (Prayer after Communion).

Other Ideas

Listen to a song about being open to God's call to live in right relationship or to walk in God's ways of justice and healing; for example, "Open My Eyes" (Manibusan), "The Harvest of Justice" (Haas), "All That We Have" (Ault), or "If Today You Hear God's Voice" (Farrell). What is God telling you through the music or the lyrics?

Journal for yourself and then discuss with a group how pressure from peers, family members, or our culture or society in general makes us want more. Where does this desire come from? What is the Gospel response to this desire?

Make a list of your possessions in one dresser, one closet, a backpack, or in the basement or garage. Look over your list and reflect on which of these is essential for your life in God.

MON 5 #407 green Weekday

Optional Memorial of the Dedication of the Basilica of Saint Mary Major / white (U.S.A.) ◆ *Optional Memorial of Blessed Frédéric Janssoone, Priest / white (Canada)*

Lectionary for Mass

◆ FIRST READING: Buried in the midst of all the complaining in today's reading, we find a beautiful image used with reference to God's people. Don't miss it! Israel is the child conceived by the God who gave them birth. Moses is subsequently cast in the role of foster father and charged with carrying them close to his heart until they reach the Promised Land. The children, however, have become ungrateful and rebellious. And Moses tells God, he has had enough of this responsibility and would just as soon die.

◆ RESPONSORIAL PSALM 81: Juxtaposed with the reading above, today's antiphon is jarring! Yet perhaps therein is a message for us. In difficult times we must believe that God is our help and sing for joy. If only we will listen to him and not harden our hearts, we will experience his providential care in all of our needs.

◆ GOSPEL: We hear Matthew's account of the feeding of the five thousand. The beginning of the story is telling. Jesus has just heard of the death of his friend and cousin, John the Baptist. He goes off by himself—but a vast crowd gets there before him, and the compassionate heart of Jesus is touched. He heals them and then feeds them.

Today's Optional Memorial

Today we celebrate one of Rome's most prestigious churches, the Basilica of Saint Mary Major, formerly called Our Lady of the Snows. Among its most prized possessions are relics of the manger in Bethlehem. Saint Mary Major sits on the horizon of the seven hills that form Rome, along with three other papal basilicas: Saint John Lateran, Saint Peter, and Saint Paul Outside the Walls.

Today's Saint

Blessed Frédéric Janssoone (1838–1916) was born in Flanders to a family of wealthy farmers, the youngest of 13 children. When his father died, he left school to help support his family, even though he was only nine years old. When his mother died in 1861, he realized that he was called to be a religious and, after considering the Trappists, joined the Franciscans. After ordination, he was sent to the Holy Land where he ministered to pilgrims and revived the custom of making the Stations of the Cross in the streets of Jerusalem. In 1881, Frédéric was sent to Canada to raise funds for the Holy Land mission, and in 1888, he returned to minister there for the rest of his life. He was instrumental in strengthening the Franciscan presence in Canada, especially by encouraging the growth of the Third Order and writing and distributing Catholic literature. He built the shrine to Our Lady at Cap-de-la-Madeleine in the diocese of Trois-Rivières. Blessed Frédéric was a friend of Saint André Bessette who testified to his holiness. He was beatified by Pope John Paul II in 1988.

#614   white

T U E **6**
Feast of the Transfiguration of the Lord

Orientation

On the mountaintop, Peter, James, and John see Jesus Christ in a new way. Christ, their friend and teacher, visits with the greatest prophets of old and shines in heavenly glory as the voice of God proclaims: "This is my chosen Son; listen to him." The Feast of the Transfiguration of the Lord reminds us about the depth of mystery that surrounded Jesus Christ—mystery in the sense that we can never exhaust who he really is or categorize him in any way. Fully human, he may indeed have needed a tent or a place to camp on the mountain, like Peter asked. But just when the Apostles may have been getting really comfortable with their understanding of Jesus as friend and teacher, they catch a glimpse of his heavenly glory, challenging them to remain open to Christ communicating to them who he is as Son of God. We have moments like the Apostles each time we encounter and grapple with a new and challenging image of God in the Scriptures. Remaining humble and open to the revelatory action of God's Word and Spirit is a way to enter ever more deeply into the mystery of who God is for us in Jesus Christ.

Lectionary for Mass

◆ FIRST READING: In his night vision, Daniel sees God, the Ancient of Days, enthroned in the heavens. A second person is introduced, "[o]ne like a son of man" (Daniel 7:13)—like a human being—who is presented before God, honored, glorified, and established as king of all nations. In the Gospel accounts, "son of man" (Daniel 7:13) is a title used in reference to Jesus.

◆ RESPONSORIAL PSALM 97: This Psalm celebrating God's kingship is well chosen in light of Daniel's reference to the "one like a Son of man" receiving heavenly kingship.

◆ SECOND READING: Peter attests to his mountaintop experience when he glimpsed the glory of the transfigured Jesus and heard the Father's voice affirming him. This experience became a guiding light for Peter's discipleship, as he hoped it would be for the community to whom he writes.

◆ GOSPEL: As Jesus prayed, his face became radiant in the experience of love and communion with his heavenly Father. Even his clothing became dazzling white, as is often described of heavenly beings. With Peter, James, and John we get a glimpse of Jesus's heavenly glory! Note that Moses and Elijah, who are also gloriously transformed, converse with Jesus about his "exodus," Luke's word for Jesus's passage through death into life. The word, of course, evokes the exodus of Israel centuries earlier. As was the case then, the cloud which enfolded them was a sign of the presence of God. And from the cloud, the disciples heard the voice of the heavenly Father. Jesus is his chosen Son.

The Roman Missal

The prayers and Preface are found in the Proper of Saints. The Gloria is said or sung today.

The Collect speaks of the mystery of the Transfiguration as prophecy and fulfillment. The "witness of the Fathers," Moses and Elijah, points to Jesus as the fulfillment of all that was promised. At the same time, the Transfiguration "wonderfully prefigured our full adoption to sonship"—our bodies are destined for glory, to shine like the human body of Jesus in glory. We pray that we may listen to him, as God commanded from the cloud, and "become co-heirs."

The Prayer over the Offerings asks that the cleansing light of Christ's "radiant splendor" purify us from "the stains of sin."

Jesus revealed his glory to "chosen witnesses," Peter, James, and John, so that "the scandal of the Cross" would not prevent them from recognizing him. One day his Mystical Body, the Church, will fulfill "what so wonderfully shone forth first in its Head" (Preface).

The Prayer after Communion is a prayer that we, too, may be transfigured: the Eucharist we have shared has the power to transform us "into the likeness" of Christ.

WED 7 #409 green
Weekday

Optional Memorials of Saint Sixtus II, Pope, and Companions, Martyrs / red; Saint Cajetan, Priest / white

Lectionary for Mass

◆ FIRST READING: The scouts who reconnoitered God's promised land returned with word of abundant fruit and flowing streams and of its powerful inhabitants. Israel was unable to see beyond their own seemingly insufficient power. How easily Israel doubted God's word. How readily they grumbled against him. Their sin would not go unpunished.

◆ RESPONSORIAL PSALM 106: Again, our Psalm stands in stark contrast with the First Reading, even though the stanzas talk about the sin of Israel described in the First Reading. Notice that the First Reading from Numbers is excerpted. The reference to Moses's intercession, in the last stanza of the Psalm, is recounted in verses excluded from today's reading.

◆ GOSPEL: Jesus is imaged as shepherd. The woman in today's Gospel actually serves to broaden our understanding of his mission. She is not of Israel, but she has faith and is persistent in her request.

Today's Saints

◆ SAINT SIXTUS II: This third-century pope was best known for solving the controversy surrounding Baptism performed by heretics. He stated that the validity of Baptism should be based on the recipient's desire to be Christian and not on the errors of the baptizer. This decision restored relations with the African and Eastern Churches. Sixtus was pope for only a year before he and six of his deacons were beheaded by Emperor Valerian.

Today's other saint, Cajetan, is known for establishing the Theatines, a pioneer religious order of the Counter-Reformation, whose mission was to bring clergy back to a life of prayer, Scripture study, preaching, and pastoral care.

THU 8 #410 white
Memorial of
Saint Dominic, Priest

Lectionary for Mass

◆ FIRST READING: The journey to the Promised Land was characterized by continual grumbling against the reality of their desert environment and a longing for the life they left behind—even though it was one of slavery. Again, Moses and Aaron intercede for the people before the Lord. And again, God provides. Whether Moses's act of striking the rock twice was at odds with God's command is unclear. What is evident, however, is that Moses and Aaron are judged to be unfaithful. As punishment, they will not be allowed to enter the Promised Land.

◆ RESPONSORIAL PSALM 95: A hardened heart is not an obedient heart. The incident named in the First Reading is the subject of the last stanza of today's Responsorial Psalm. The first two stanzas describe the thoughts and actions of an obedient heart.

◆ GOSPEL: The Gospel question concerning Jesus' identity continues. John the Baptist had been beheaded; Elijah had been mysteriously taken up to heaven, thus giving rise to the tradition that he would likewise return before the coming of the Messiah (2 Kings 2:11, Malachi 3:23); Jeremiah was the suffering prophet par excellence. Peter, however, has been gifted with the Father's revelation of Jesus' identity.

The Roman Missal

The prayers for the memorial are found in the Proper of Saints. The Entrance Antiphon, based on Sirach 15:5, is the perfect beginning to this Mass in honor of the founder of the Order of Preachers: "In the midst of the Church he opened his mouth, / and the Lord filled him with the spirit of wisdom . . . ."

Today's Saint

Saint Dominic (1170–1221), a contemporary of Saint Francis of Assisi, founded a mendicant order (those who rely on the charity of others) of men, called the Order of Preachers, or Dominicans, to preach against theological error. One of the pressing issues facing the newly established order was the Albigensian heresy, claiming that matter, specifically the body, is evil. Contrary to this heretical thinking, the Black Friars, as they were commonly known, went from town to town preaching the goodness of the body. In order to preach sound doctrine with clarity, Saint Dominic exhorted his sons to engage in rigorous academic study. He eventually started a contemplative female branch of the Dominicans to support the apostolate of the men through prayer.

F R I **9** #411   green
Weekday

Optional Memorial of Saint Teresa Benedicta of the Cross, Virgin and Martyr / red

Lectionary for Mass

◆ FIRST READING: We begin a series of readings from Deuteronomy, a book cast as Moses's farewell address to the Israelites before his death and their entrance into the Promised Land. As we might expect, Moses exhorts the people to be faithful and obedient to the Lord their God. In so doing, they will be blessed. In today's text, we hear of the "privileged" status of the Israelites as the chosen people. They must never forget how awesome God is and all of the things that he has done for them.

◆ RESPONSORIAL PSALM 77: Today's antiphon and the first stanza of the Psalm pick up on the theme of remembering. The second stanza stresses the awesome power of God, and the third focuses on his deeds for the chosen people.

◆ GOSPEL: Discipleship demands self-denial and a willingness to take up our cross—whatever it may be—if we are to follow Jesus. Only by losing our life will we receive our promised reward when the Son of Man comes in glory.

Today's Saint

Saint Teresa Benedicta of the Cross was born Edith Stein at Breslau in 1891 into an observant Jewish family, but by the time she reached her teens, she had become an atheist. She went on to study philosophy and received her doctorate at Freiburg under the philosopher Edmund Husserl but left her university career to teach at a girls' school when Husserl did not support her further studies. Influenced by her study of Thomism and spirituality, she became a Catholic in 1922. In 1932, she became a lecturer at Munster, but anti-Semitic laws passed by the Nazis forced her to resign, and she entered the Carmel at Cologne in 1933. In an attempt to protect her from the Nazis, she was transferred to a Carmel in the Netherlands, but when the Dutch bishops condemned Nazi racism, the Nazis retaliated by arresting Jewish converts. Edith, along with her sister Rosa, who had also become a Catholic, was deported to Auschwitz and died in the gas chamber on August 9, 1942. She was canonized by Pope John Paul II in 1998.

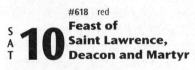

S A T **10** #618   red
Feast of Saint Lawrence, Deacon and Martyr

Lectionary for Mass

◆ FIRST READING: The context of today's reading is Paul's plea for the Corinthians' generosity in contributing to the needs of the Church in Jerusalem. This focus on those in need is particularly appropriate since Saint Lawrence the deacon was known for his great concern for the poor. Paul's words challenge us about both almsgiving and serving others. We are never diminished by our self-giving, but rather enriched by God because of it.

◆ RESPONSORIAL PSALM: The theme of concern for the poor continues. Psalm 112 acclaims the "wisdom" and happiness of one who heeds God's command to help those in need.

◆ GOSPEL: "The blood of the martyrs is the seed of the Church," wrote an early Church father. Lawrence was put to death because he was a Christian. His life was the grain of wheat that bore witness and gave life—new life to the Church, and eternal life to himself.

The Roman Missal

The prayers for the feast are found in the Proper of Saints. The Gloria is said or sung. The Entrance Antiphon alludes to "the treasure of the Church," recalling one of the favorite stories told of this beloved saint. The simple petition in the Collect might be spoken of any saint: "grant that we may love what he loved / and put into practice what he taught."

Today's Saint

Saint Lawrence (+ 258), one of the seven deacons of the Roman Church, fell victim to the anti-Christian persecutions launched by the emperor Valerian. Although little is known about the events leading up to his death, legend claims that he was martyred by being roasted on a gridiron. However, most historians believe he was beheaded several days after Pope Sixtus II was. According to tradition, his death brought an end to idolatry and led to the conversion of Rome. His life has been the subject of many artistic masterpieces, including the paintings of Fra Angelico.

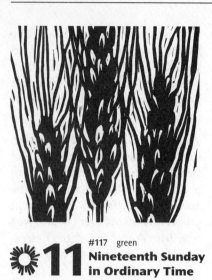

11 Nineteenth Sunday in Ordinary Time
#117   green

Orientation

This passage reminds us to continue to await, in faith and in hope, the return of the Risen Christ at the end of the age. Living in the hope of Christ's return means that we become increasingly conscious of Christ's presence in our midst. Christ is present in countless ways around us, and knocks at the door of our hearts day after day. Where can we encounter Christ? In the faces of joy and love, Christ is there. In the faces of suffering and sadness, Christ is there also. In word and in sacrament, Christ is always there. If we become aware of Christ already here, no longer will we be surprised by the arrival of the Son of Man. Awareness of his presence in our midst is our preparation.

Lectionary for Mass

◆ FIRST READING: The celebration of the first Passover is the subject of today's First Reading, but faith is the focus here and in the Second Reading as well. The faith of the Israelites in God's word spoken through Moses gave them the courage to move forward in obedience to what God had commanded. Their faith was not disappointed. They experienced the salvation hoped for as they passed over into freedom while their Egyptian enemies were destroyed.

◆ RESPONSORIAL PSALM 33: The people of Israel were the people God has chosen. This motif recurs again and again; it is, in fact, the story of the Old Testament. Throughout their history, the Israelites experienced his blessings and salvation. In return, they were called to be an obedient people of praise who fear and reverence the Lord.

◆ SECOND READING: We hear of the faith of Israel's patriarchs and matriarchs, Abraham and Sarah in particular. Today's reading tells of their call and migration to the promised land, the birth of their son, Isaac, their obedience to whatever God asked. They lived and died in faith, looking to the fulfillment of God's promises in a land yet to be entered, the heavenly city of God.

◆ GOSPEL: Yet another journey of faith is highlighted at the beginning of today's Gospel—our journey as we respond to the call of discipleship and move on to our heavenly home. The words "gird your loins" evoke the instructions of that first Passover. Jesus's instructions focus on the importance of being ready to receive him at his coming, however unexpected it may be. We must be faithful and prudent servants, good stewards of the tremendous riches of God with which we have been entrusted.

The Roman Missal

The Collect echoes Saint Paul's words in Galatians 4:6: "As proof that you are children, God sent the spirit of his Son into our hearts, crying out, 'Abba, Father!'" We are "taught by the Holy Spirit" and "dare to call [God] our Father." We ask God to bring to perfection within us this "spirit of adoption," that we may come to our promised inheritance.

◆ PRAYER OVER THE OFFERINGS: We ask God to receive the offerings of his Church, the gifts he himself has given and will transform for us, for our salvation (Prayer over the Offerings).

We ask God to save us and teach us through the sacrament we have received (Prayer after Communion).

Other Ideas

Do some research on an immigrant or group of immigrants who have settled in a new country. The library or Internet can help you find some. See what you can find out about their faith or faith traditions. How did they believe or trust in God?

Make a list of the things that God trusts us to do in the world. List the messages about God's kingdom that we are called to proclaim. List the virtues we are called to practice. Share your list with a friend or group.

12 Weekday
MON   #413   green

Optional Memorial of Saint Jane Frances de Chantal, Religious / white

Lectionary for Mass

◆ FIRST READING: What does God ask of his chosen people? Fidelity, obedience, and reverence. Note that Jesus quotes from today's text when teaching about the most important commandments in the law. Note also the mention of God's special concern for foreigners (the alien), orphans, and widows—those with particular needs for whom Israel must also show the same concern that God has for them. In remembering all that God has done for them, let them not forget that they, too, were once aliens, helpless and powerless.

◆ RESPONSORIAL PSALM 147: The only response Israel can give in light of all that God has done for them is praise. Note how the Psalm lists specific reasons for praise. Note also the allusion to Israel's privileged chosen status in the last stanza.

◆ Gospel: Today's Gospel consists of two separate scenes. The first is Jesus's prediction of his Passion and Death, which overwhelms the disciples with grief. Note also the reference to the Resurrection. Do they hear this? The second concerns the temple tax, which all Jewish men were required to pay (see Exodus 30:11–16). Jesus's response can seem enigmatic, yet it demonstrates both his obedience to the law and his concern not to give offense.

Today's Saint

Under the influence of her spiritual director Saint Francis de Sales, Saint Jane (1572–1641), a wealthy widow and mother from France, founded the Congregation of the Visitation of the Virgin Mary. Unusual in its time, this new community of cloistered nuns welcomed individuals with frailties due to health and age, and who were often refused admittance by other cloistered orders. She was no stranger to pain, from the death of her husband and some of her children, to the death of her dear friend Saint Francis, but she transformed her experiences of sorrow into moments of transformation and service to the sick.

T U E **13** #414 green
Weekday

Optional Memorial of Saints Pontian, Pope, and Hippolytus, Priest, Martyrs / red

Lectionary for Mass

◆ First Reading: Moses exhorts both the Israelite people and Joshua, his successor, who will lead the people into the Promised Land, to have courage. They have nothing to fear. God himself goes before them.

◆ Canticle: Today's response is from a hymn in the book of Deuteronomy, purported to be sung by Moses. The hymn emphasizes God's choice of Israel as his people among all the peoples of the earth.

◆ Gospel: Today's Gospel consists of several separate sayings. The first addresses the perhaps somewhat lost—and certainly difficult—practice of mutual correction. It can only be done in humility and love. The power and authority given to the Church in terms of binding and loosening as community is significant.

Today's Saints

Saints Pontian and Hippolytus (+ 235) became the target of Emperor Maximinus Thrax who despised Christians, especially their leaders. Pope Pontian and the priest Hippolytus differed in terms of orthodoxy, so much so that they rivaled each other as leaders. Hippolytus did not acknowledge Pontian as the true pope, resulting in a schism in the Roman Church and leading to Hippolytus's reign as the antipope. They eventually reconciled during their exile to Sardinia, known as the island of death, where they were harshly treated and died as martyrs.

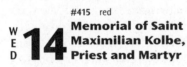

W E D **14** #415 red
Memorial of Saint Maximilian Kolbe, Priest and Martyr

Lectionary for Mass

◆ First Reading: After seeing the Promised Land from afar, Moses died. The people obediently follow the lead of Joshua, Moses's designated successor. Deuteronomy attests to Moses's unique and powerful role in Israel's history. He has no equal.

◆ Responsorial Psalm: Today's Responsorial Psalm, a combination of two verses from Psalm 66, alludes to Moses as one who was aflame

with the love and power of God. The Psalm is one of praise to God for his marvelous deeds on Israel's behalf. Moses was truly an instrument God used to accomplish his work.

◆ Gospel: Jesus wants the Church, the community of his disciples, to be characterized by forgiveness and reconciliation. Today, he sets forth practices by which this might be accomplished. The first is to speak privately to a brother who has given offense to you. If that doesn't work, enlist the help of one or two others, more if needed. Forgiveness and reconciliation must be sought no matter what. If a brother or sister obstinately refuses to hear, he or she should be expelled from the community lest the whole community be harmed.

The Roman Missal

The prayers for the memorial are found in the Proper of Saints. They speak of the saint's "burning love for the Immaculate Virgin Mary" (Collect), his example of self-offering (Prayer over the Offerings), and the "fire of charity" that consumed him (Prayer after Communion).

Today's Saint

Polish-born Maximilian was a Conventual Franciscan friar whose devotion to Mary continues to affect the Church today. He established the Militia of the Immaculata, a Marian apostolate that uses prayer as its main weapon in spiritual battles. His extensive writing on Mary's role as mediatrix and advocate later influenced the Second Vatican Council. He was eventually arrested and sent to Auschwitz. He volunteered to die in place of another prisoner and was put in the starvation bunker. Still alive two weeks later, Maximilian was injected with a lethal dose of carbolic acid, dying with a radiant, calm look upon his face.

Vigil, #621; Day, #622 white
THU 15 Solemnity of the Assumption of the Blessed Virgin Mary
HOLYDAY OF OBLIGATION

Orientation

This day we celebrate the promise of God expressed fully in the life of Mary, the Holy Mother of God. God invites us to eternal life, to enjoy the glorious new creation of his Son in body, soul, and spirit. Our final hope is the resurrection of our own bodies at the end of time to exist forever in this new order of creation. The Solemnity of the Assumption is our great celebration of this final hope. Mary is a pioneer for us in faith. She was the first among us to accept Jesus Christ into her life. In her bodily assumption, she is also the first fully to enjoy eternal life at the side of her Risen Son in the glory of heaven. Where she has gone, we hope to follow. We rejoice in the fulfillment of God's promise in her, as we turn to her to guide us to the side of her Risen Son who reigns in heaven.

Lectionary for Mass

Vigil

◆ FIRST READING: Today's First Reading recounts David's enthronement of the Ark of the Covenant (the chest containing the tablets of the law) in the tent he had prepared for it. Mary, the Mother of Jesus, has traditionally been invoked as the Ark of the New Covenant; thus, the reading from 1 Chronicles is particularly appropriate as we celebrate the heavenly enthronement of the Blessed Virgin Mary who was the Ark of the Living Lord.

◆ RESPONSORIAL PSALM 132 was sung by Jewish pilgrims as they made their way to the temple. It recounts David's concern to establish a home for the Ark of the Covenant. Today we celebrate Mary being taken up into the heavenly temple, enjoying her heavenly rest there with her risen and glorified Son.

◆ SECOND READING: All of 1 Corinthians 15 deals with the subject of the resurrection of the body. These concluding verses celebrate the victory Jesus has won over death. Assumed into heaven, Mary is clothed with immortality.

◆ GOSPEL: Today's Gospel seems to put Mary in the background. The opposite is true, though. It brings all believers into the foreground with her. The heavenly glory she enjoys will likewise be ours if we hear God's Word and keep it.

Mass During the Day

◆ FIRST READING: In approaching today's text from Revelation, one must remember that it is part of a vision the author had; thus its highly symbolic language. The description in Revelation 12:1 has given rise to countless artistic representations of Mary, the Mother of Jesus. The chapter recounts both the divine deliverance of the woman and her child, as well as the cosmic battle between good and evil, in which God triumphs over Satan and the powers of evil, thus inaugurating the kingdom of God.

◆ RESPONSORIAL PSALM 45 is a royal wedding song, and Mary, the Mother of Jesus, is traditionally spoken of as Queen of heaven and earth. Assumed into heaven, Mary has entered into the Father's house, into the palace of the King.

◆ SECOND READING: Paul speaks here of the order or sequence in which the resurrection of the dead will occur. Christ is first. Today we celebrate the teaching of our Catholic tradition that Mary enjoys the fullness of resurrected life.

◆ GOSPEL: Today's solemnity celebrates Mary's glorification at the end of her life. The Gospel reading takes us back to that moment in her life when she responded to God's special call to be the mother of the Lord. We hear her hymn of praise, now fulfilled in a way we cannot even begin to comprehend.

The Roman Missal

The Prayers and Preface for the solemnity are found in the Proper of Saints. The Gloria and the Creed are said or sung today. Please note that there are two full sets of prayers. Those of the Vigil can be used on the afternoon or evening of August 14, with those of the Day reserved for August 15.

Vigil

The Collect echoes Mary's Magnificat. God looked "on the lowliness of the Blessed Virgin Mary, / [and] raised her to this grace." We pray that, with the help of her prayers, we, too, may be saved and "exalted . . . on high."

The sacrifice we offer today is "the sacrifice of conciliation and praise." We pray that we may both know God's "pardon" and rejoice "in perpetual thanksgiving" (Prayer over the Offerings).

The Communion Antiphon echoes the Gospel for the Vigil Mass of the Assumption: "Blessed is the womb of the Virgin Mary."

The Prayer after Communion is a simple prayer for protection as we honor Mary's Assumption into heaven.

The Solemn Blessing of the Blessed Virgin Mary may be used.

Mass During the Day

There are two options for the Entrance Antiphon. The first is taken from Revelation 12:1, the First Reading at the Mass. The second calls on the Church to rejoice with the angels in Mary's Assumption into heaven.

◆ COLLECT: Mary has gone "body and soul into heavenly glory." We pray that we may keep our eyes fixed where she has gone, "attentive to the things that are above," and come one day to share her glory.

◆ PRAYER OVER THE OFFERINGS: Through Mary's intercession, we pray that our hearts may be "aflame with the fire of love" and longing for God.

◆ PREFACE: God would not allow decay to touch Mary's body, because from her body Christ, "the Author of all life," was born. In Mary's Assumption, we glimpse our own destiny—"the beginning and image / of your Church's coming to perfection / and a sign of sure hope and comfort to your pilgrim people."

◆ PRAYER AFTER COMMUNION: We ask Mary's intercession, that "we may be brought to the glory of the resurrection." The Solemnity of the Assumption flows from the Resurrection of Christ, in which Mary already shares, body and soul.

Other Ideas

Tally up the number of "reversals" promised in Mary's Magnificat. Memorize the one that you find most meaningful or poignant.

FRI 16 #417   green
Weekday

Optional Memorial of Saint Stephen of Hungary / white

Lectionary for Mass

◆ FIRST READING: Because of yesterday's feast, we missed the Lectionary's introduction to Joshua and his role in leading the people across the Jordan and into the Promised Land. It is well worth a perusal. Today's text comes from the last chapter of the book of Joshua, which describes an assembly of all the Israelites (all ages) for a ceremony of covenant renewal. The verses chosen as today's reading recount all that God had done for his people beginning with the call of Abraham.

◆ RESPONSORIAL PSALM 136: Today's Psalm is one of thanksgiving for what God has done for his people, focusing in particular on his fidelity to them in their desert journeys to the Promised Land. The word translated as "mercy" is *hesed* in the Hebrew text, literally, loving kindness in covenant fidelity.

◆ GOSPEL: The question of divorce is an issue in today's Gospel. Moses and the law allowed it. What is Jesus's position? Jesus demands more than what the law required and reminds his hearers of the Creator's original intent: "what God has joined together, man must not separate." The one exception allowed by Matthew is "unlawful" marriage (Matthew 19:9), that is, marriage between those with close kinship ties (see Leviticus 18:6–18).

Today's Saint

Saint Stephen (975–1038) Christianized the people of Hungary, specifically a pagan group from Asia known as the Magyars. By the time of his coronation as king of Hungary, he had already, as a duke, established numerous dioceses and monasteries. With the goal of unifying the people, he ended tribal divisions, limited the power of the nobility, and suppressed pagan practices. He had a special love for the needy, and, often in disguise so people would not recognize him, he gave them money. Saint Stephen is also recognized as a saint of the Orthodox Church.

SAT 17 #418   green
Weekday

Optional Memorial of the Blessed Virgin Mary / white

Lectionary for Mass

◆ FIRST READING: The reading is the conclusion of yesterday's account about the ceremony of covenant renewal. Today's verses focus on what is being asked of the people if they wish to renew their covenant relationship with God, namely, to put away their idols or foreign gods. They can have no other God than the God who has done such marvelous deeds for them. The renewal ceremony concludes with the erection of a large stone in the sanctuary of the Lord as a reminder to the people of their covenant with the Lord.

◆ RESPONSORIAL PSALM 16 is a song of confidence in the Lord who leads and guides us. In the covenant relationship, God is our inheritance. Perhaps possession is too strong a word, but indeed there is the sense of God and the Israelites belonging to one another.

◆ GOSPEL: We see the gentleness of Jesus, his delight in the simplicity of the children, his eagerness to have them come to him for his blessing. Today's Gospel makes children a model for all who would enter the kingdom of heaven.

☀ 18 #120 green
Twentieth Sunday in Ordinary Time

Orientation

This tough reading is a reality check for us about the life of faith. Coupled with the promise of God's eternal love in heaven is the vision of the rift between those who accept God's invitation and those who do not. Salvation in Jesus Christ invites our consent and our participation, and some people freely chose not to accept it. In proclaiming this message, Jesus speaks to us from the long tradition of prophets who courageously spoke the truth, even when they knew it would be difficult for their listeners to accept. Instead of sowing discouragement, this message calls each of us with urgency to continue to share Christ's loving invitation through our words and deeds. People respond to God freely in faith. Yet, our hospitality as the People of God may encourage those around us to accept the invitation to eternal love more readily.

Lectionary for Mass

◆ FIRST READING: Jeremiah, more so than any other prophet, met with opposition and rejection from his own people. Today we hear of a plot to put him to death, despite his intention of warning the people to flee for their lives. In a move orchestrated by individuals not pleased with his prophecy about the siege and capture of Jerusalem, Jeremiah was seized and thrown into a cistern. He was rescued through the intervention of a member of the court who realized the wrong that had been done.

◆ RESPONSORIAL PSALM 40: Today's Psalm is a prayer of gratitude for God's deliverance. The images of "pit" and "mud" in the first stanza echo Jeremiah's plight in today's First Reading. The rescue leads to praise and thanksgiving (stanza 2) and the psalmist prays for God's continued help (stanza 3).

◆ SECOND READING: Today's reading looks back to the persons named in the previous chapter of the Letter to the Hebrews as models of a life of faith and it looks ahead to Jesus, the one who leads us in faith and brings it to maturity and full realization (i.e., perfection). Looking at Jesus, we see the cross, and beyond it, glory at the right hand of the Father. That destiny of suffering and glory is ours as well.

◆ GOSPEL: Today's Gospel is somewhat unsettling with its presentation of opposition and division, a theme found in the other two readings as well. As Simeon prophesized, Jesus would be a sign of contradiction (Luke 2:34); his presence would lead to opposition from those who would not, could not, accept him or those who believed in him. Sadly, such was the reality some of the early disciples of Jesus experienced within their families.

The Roman Missal

The Collect is a prayer of praise and yearning for God. "No eye can see" what God has prepared for those who love him (see 1 Corinthians 2:9). We pray that we may love God "in all things and above all things," and come to the promises of God, which surpass all our human desires.

The Prayer over the Offerings speaks of the "glorious exchange" of divine and human in the Eucharistic sacrifice. This prayer occurs frequently in Christmas Time.

We pray that we may be "conformed" to the image of the Christ we receive in the sacrament and that we merit to be his "coheirs" in heaven (Prayer after Communion).

Other Ideas

We are reminded today that truth divides and alienates. Speaking the truth is no protection for a prophet, not even from harsh judgment or reprisal from other family members. Speaking the truth can involve great risk. Make a list of people you truly admire who had the courage to speak the truth and suffered for it. Post the list where you can see it every day this week and pray for the courage they demonstrated to speak the truth despite the cost.

M O N 19 #419 green
Weekday

Optional Memorial of Saint John Eudes, Priest / white

Lectionary for Mass

◆ FIRST READING: The Israelites had not been long in the Promised Land before they turned to the worship of the god Baal and the goddess Ashtaroth. As punishment God let them fall into the hands of their enemies. Yet, God did not abandon them. Time and again he raised up judges, Spirit-filled military leaders who would call them to fidelity to the God of the covenant. Time and again, the people listened for awhile, but soon fell back into their evil ways.

◆ RESPONSORIAL PSALM 106 recounts the history of Israel, in particular, the history of their infidelities from their time in Egypt through their settlement in the Promised Land. This latter is the focus of the verses chosen for today.

One can almost wonder how Israel could dare to ask God to remember them (our antiphon) given their repeated infidelities. The answer is in the last stanza. As often as they turn to him, God will turn to them and deliver them.

◆ GOSPEL: What must I do? Like the young man in today's Gospel, we want certainty and assurance; we want to be able to measure ourselves against a norm. And measure himself he could, but Jesus asks for more. Jesus asks for all. The young man's possessions got in the way of his relationship with Jesus and the kingdom of heaven. May it never be so for us.

Today's Saint

Saint John Eudes (1601–1680), a successful preacher in France, cared for plague victims physically and spiritually. The Protestant Reformation convinced him that the academic and spiritual training of priests needed to be strengthened, so he established a society of diocesan priests, the Congregation of Jesus and Mary, commonly called the Eudists. Their sole purpose was directed toward the foundation of new seminaries where future priests would be equipped with the necessary tools to respond pastorally to the turbulent times. He eventually established a religious community of women, the Congregation of Our Lady of Charity of the Refuge, dedicated to the rehabilitation of prostitutes.

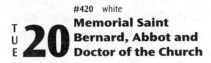

#420 white

20 Memorial Saint Bernard, Abbot and Doctor of the Church

TUE

Lectionary for Mass

◆ FIRST READING: Gideon was one of the Judges God raised up to deliver Israel. Today's reading recounts his call and the miraculous sign God gave to confirm it.

◆ RESPONSORIAL PSALM 85: What words of hope in today's antiphon, juxtaposed with the oppressed status of Israel in today's First Reading. God does desire peace for his people. The Hebrew word for peace is *shalom*, connoting not only the absence of war and conflict, but total and complete well-being. The second and third stanzas name some of the characteristics of a time of peace.

◆ GOSPEL: Today's text follows up on yesterday's Gospel. Jesus makes it quite clear that riches are a major obstacle to discipleship, a point evident from the young man's response. The saying elicits Peter's boast of having given up all to follow Jesus (unlike the young man), as well as Peter's concern for reward. Jesus promises that the reward for such renunciation will indeed be great.

The Roman Missal

The prayers for the memorial are found in the Proper of Saints. They speak of Saint Bernard as "a light shining and burning" (Collect), a tireless advocate for "order and concord" in the Church (Prayer over the Offerings), and a man "caught up in love of your incarnate Word" (Prayer after Communion).

Today's Saint

Saint Bernard (1090–1153) joined the Cistercian abbey at Citeaux, known for its strict and austere way of life. Within a short time he was noticed for his leadership abilities; hence, he was appointed abbot of a new monastery at Clairvaux. His monastic vision at Clairvaux led to the foundation of several monasteries throughout France, Britain, and Ireland. In the solitude he wrote numerous theological and spiritual classics, including his treatise *On Loving God*, 86 sermons on the Song of Songs, and a major work

entitled *On Consideration*, a reflection on papal spirituality. Saint Bernard had a special devotion to Mary, earning him the titles "Our Lady's faithful chaplain" and "Mary's harper." Due to his abundant writing and influence upon the Church, he was declared a Doctor of the Church.

#421 white

21 Memorial of Saint Pius X, Pope

WED

Lectionary for Mass

◆ FIRST READING: A bit of introduction is needed to today's reading. Abimelech was one of Gideon's sons. The incident recounted today took place after Gideon's death. While he lived, Gideon refused to be king over the Israelites or allow any of his sons to be king because he believed that the Lord alone was king of Israel. In today's text, however, one of his sons successfully sought this position for himself. Not mentioned in today's text is the fact that all of his brothers, with the exception of Jotham, were killed as a result. There is a bit of sarcasm in the parable. Good faith was not evident in all that had happened.

◆ RESPONSORIAL PSALM 21 acclaims God's blessing and protection of Israel's king when he trusts in the Lord and worships him alone.

◆ GOSPEL: Yet another image for God is found in today's Gospel: that of a landowner. As parables are wont to do, this one completely overturns what we, like the workers, would reckon to be just and fair. The landowner is fair as he himself points out. God is extraordinarily generous. What is our response when we see such generosity extended to others?

The Roman Missal

The prayers for the memorial are found in the Proper of Saints. The Collect alludes to the pope's motto—"to restore all things in Christ." We pray for reverence in approaching the Eucharist (Prayer over the Offerings) and for constancy in faith and the unity of the Church (Prayer after Communion).

Today's Saint

Known as the pope of the Eucharist, Pius X is remembered for promoting frequent reception of the Eucharist. He did this when Jansenism, a heresy that believed Holy Communion should be reserved for only a select few, was prevalent. Stating that "Holy Communion is the shortest and safest way to heaven," Pius X issued a decree to combat Jansenism, allowing children to receive Holy Communion when they reached the age of reason (age seven), rather than waiting until they were older. Pius X's other accomplishments include reforming the liturgy, encouraging priests to give simple homilies, reintroducing Gregorian chant into services, revising the Roman Breviary, and developing a new catechism.

#422   white
T H U 22 Memorial of the Queenship of the Blessed Virgin Mary

Orientation

Mary is truly the "Favored One of God." Her relationship with Jesus Christ was like no other, and God filled her life with grace from beginning to end because of her Son. Today we celebrate her at her Son's side in heaven. As Christ reigns in heaven, tradition teaches that God continues to favor the Mother of God, crowning her queen alongside her Son. Even in heaven, her relationship with Jesus Christ fills Mary's life with grace. On this memorial we rejoice in the fullness of hope and promise God shows us in Mary's life. She is Queen of Heaven, as God holds nothing back

from her in the glory of heaven. Mary's joy is our hope as she lovingly guides us to join her at the side of her Son in eternity.

Lectionary for Mass

◆ FIRST READING: Today's reading is perhaps one of the most enigmatic texts in the Bible. Its cultural context and the rite of human sacrifice are totally alien to our own religious practice. Do not let this obscure the text's underlying message: Jephthah was a man faithful to the promise he made to his God, no matter what the cost. His daughter was of the same mind, even if the cost was her life.

◆ RESPONSORIAL PSALM 40: These words can readily be placed on the lips of both Jephthah and his daughter, particularly if doing God's will meant fidelity to one's vow to him. What the Lord desires is not ritual sacrifices devoid of personal meaning, but rather, obedient hearts.

◆ GOSPEL: Throughout the Scriptures, God's covenant with Israel is likened to a marriage bond. Today's parable appropriates this imagery and speaks of future reward as a wedding banquet. The main focus of the parable is on the manner of response to the invitation. It calls us to serious self-examination.

The Roman Missal

The prayers are found in the Proper of Saints. Mary is both "our Mother and our Queen," and she prays that we may come to the heavenly kingdom (Collect). In the Prayer over the Offerings, we ask to "be given strength by the humanity of Christ" as we offer the unending sacrifice which is Christ's sacrifice on the cross. Appropriately, we are reminded of Christ's humanity on this memorial honoring Mary, in whom the Word became flesh.

F R I 23 #423   green
Weekday

Optional Memorial of Saint Rose of Lima, Virgin / white

Lectionary for Mass

◆ FIRST READING: Leaving the Book of Judges, we move into the Book of Ruth. Notice that the story is situated in this same time period. The book tells the story of Naomi, a Jewish woman from Bethlehem who moved to Moab with her husband and two sons in search of food during a time of famine. In the course of their years there, both her husband and her sons died. As a childless widow, she made preparations to return to her homeland. Her daughters-in-law wished to accompany her. As the story goes, only one actually did, and her name is Ruth. In the course of time, Ruth married one of Naomi's kinsmen and became the mother of the father of Jesse, the father of David. Ruth is named in Matthew's account of Jesus's ancestors.

◆ RESPONSORIAL PSALM 146: This Psalm is a hymn of praise extolling God's care for the poor and oppressed who place their trust in him. The mention of strangers (3rd stanza) and widows (last stanza) are particularly relevant in light of our reading from Ruth.

◆ GOSPEL: The Pharisees, those strict adherents of the Law, set out to test Jesus. The Lectionary omits the incident immediately preceding today's Gospel, in which the Sadducees put Jesus to the test on the question of resurrection. Today's question concerns what is most important in the Law. Jesus responds not only in terms of the greatest commandment, but adds another that is just like it.

Today's Saint

During Saint Rose of Lima's (1586–1617) brief life, people noticed her physical beauty, declaring her *coma una rosa* ("like a rose"), but the beauty of her soul far surpassed her physical appearance. Saint Rose longed to live solely for God, so she renounced the institution of marriage by claiming Christ as her spouse. Basing her life upon Saint Catherine of Siena, she lived a penitential life, setting up an infirmary in the family home to care for impoverished children and the sick. She gained popularity due to her selfless service to the needy. As the first canonized saint of the Americas, she is the patron of South and Central America, the Philippines, and the West Indies.

#629   red

S A T 24 Feast of Saint Bartholomew, Apostle

Lectionary for Mass

◆ FIRST READING: In today's First Reading, John, the Christian prophet, is shown a vision of the heavenly Jerusalem. He describes the walls of this heavenly city in great detail. Fittingly, the names of the Twelve Apostles are inscribed on the foundation stones of the wall. How true it is that the Church is founded upon the witness of these Apostles, sent out by the Risen Christ to all the nations.

◆ RESPONSORIAL PSALM 145: The responsorial antiphon evokes a text from John's account of the Gospel where Jesus tells the Apostles they are his "friends" (John 15:15). In the context of the Psalm, God's friends are his faithful ones who praise God and speak of his name and kingdom. A fitting description of Jesus's Apostles!

◆ GOSPEL: Tradition associates Bartholomew with Nathanael, thus the choice of this text for today's Gospel. Can you imagine Philip's excitement when he went to Nathanael? The latter is a man of caution, and a messiah from Nazareth is not his understanding of what the Scriptures prophesy. It is in the moment of personal encounter with Jesus that Nathanael comes to believe. Our faith will grow and deepen in precisely the same way.

The Roman Missal

The Prayers for the feast are found in the Proper of Saints. The Gloria is said or sung today. The Preface of the Apostles is used. We pray that God may strengthen us in the faith to which the Apostle Bartholomew "clung wholeheartedly" (Collect) and that through his prayers we may know God's help (Prayer over the Offerings).

Today's Saint

There is little reference in the Gospel to Saint Bartholomew (first century), other than the fact that he was one of the original Twelve Apostles. He is also mentioned in the Acts of the Apostles as one of the disciples waiting for the descent of the Holy Spirit. According to the second-century Alexandrian teacher Pantaenus, an early Christian community in India claims Saint Bartholomew as its founder. Tradition states that he preached throughout Persia, Mesopotamia, Lycaonia, and Phrygia. It is believed that he was skinned alive and beheaded at Albanopolis, on the west coast of the Caspian Sea.

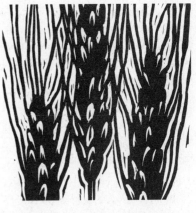

#123   green

☀ 25 Twenty-first Sunday in Ordinary Time

Orientation

Today's Gospel reminds us that we live the life of faith by participation. God has abundant graces for our lives, countless gifts every day that enable us to live life to the fullest. But we have to accept these gifts to live the life of faith; our free choice and willing consent is a crucial step in conversion to Jesus Christ. Those who ate and drank with Jesus and overheard his teachings in passing are not the same as those believers who recognized, accepted, and followed him as the Son of God. Jesus Christ calls us to enter into a loving relationship with God, not just to be aware of God's existence in a way that may or may not have true impact on our lives. Jesus invites us to participate in the life of faith, by saying yes to this relationship every day through our words and deeds.

Lectionary for Mass

◆ FIRST READING: The Jews were God's chosen people to whom he revealed himself and made known his plan of salvation. Nonetheless, starting with the call of Abraham it is clear that God's plan of salvation embraces people of all nations. This same word is heard in the text from the prophet Isaiah today. All nations shall worship the Lord in Jerusalem, just as Israel does.

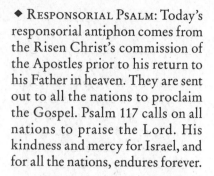

◆ RESPONSORIAL PSALM: Today's responsorial antiphon comes from the Risen Christ's commission of the Apostles prior to his return to his Father in heaven. They are sent out to all the nations to proclaim the Gospel. Psalm 117 calls on all nations to praise the Lord. His kindness and mercy for Israel, and for all the nations, endures forever.

◆ SECOND READING: Today's text from Hebrews exhorts us not to weaken in the face of trials as we go forward on our Christian journey. Our trials, in fact, are meant to discipline us, that is, to teach us. They will help us grow in righteousness, that is, in a "right" relationship with God marked by fidelity to his teaching, and bring us healing and wholeness.

◆ GOSPEL: Jesus's words speak not only of the presence of people from all nations at the banquet of the kingdom, but perhaps surprisingly, of the exclusion of some who thought they should have been there. The entrance into the kingdom is narrow. To pass through requires that we listen to Jesus's words and put them into practice.

The Roman Missal

God is the giver of unity. Gathered together in his name, we pray that "amid the uncertainties of this world," we may desire only what God wills, "our hearts . . . fixed on that place / where true gladness is found" (Collect).

The Prayer over the Offerings is a prayer for the "unity and peace" of the Church.

We ask God to "perfect and sustain us" through the "healing work" of his mercy (Prayer after Communion).

Other Ideas

God's message of love is universal. He shows a preferential love to the poor, lost, broken-hearted, and oppressed. As we approach the season of autumn, find a place you can go with a group to offer God's love in a concrete way. You might volunteer monthly at an area pantry or soup kitchen. You might visit a nursing home or collect school supplies for children. The list of places where God's love needs to be carried is endless. Ask your parish or local Catholic Charities for suggestions.

Search newspapers or magazines for a week. What places in the world are in need of urgent care or attention due to war, poverty famine, or disease? Discuss with your family or small faith group what God wants us as Catholics to do in these places that may be very far from our home.

MON 26 #425 green Weekday

Lectionary for Mass

◆ FIRST READING: We begin reading from Paul's first Letter to the Thessalonians. As is typical of the structure of a letter in his day we have first, the identification of the sender and, second, the name of the addressee. Paul begins every letter but one with a prayer of thanksgiving for the community to whom he is writing. The Thessalonians are commended for their faith in action and endurance.

◆ RESPONSORIAL PSALM 149: As Paul takes delight in the Thessalonians, so too does the Lord in his people. Psalm 149 is a hymn of praise calling all Israel to take delight in the Lord. Notice how the theme of joy permeates the verses of today's response.

◆ GOSPEL: All of chapter 23 of Matthew's account of the Gospel is a condemnation of the hypocrisy of the Scribes and Pharisees. What

a stark contrast between the life-giving silent witness of the Thessalonians in today's First Reading and the death-dealing, at times not so silent, behaviors of the scribes and Pharisees. We glimpse their myopic vision which has lost sight of the breadth, mercy, and integrity of the kingdom of heaven.

TUE 27 #426 white Memorial of Saint Monica

Lectionary for Mass

◆ FIRST READING: What deep love Paul and his companions have for the Thessalonians. How tender the image used for their ministry: gentle nursing mothers nourishing their children's new life of faith. Paul's ministry was one of service not of domination.

◆ RESPONSORIAL PSALM 139: Today's Psalm is a beautiful and deeply personal prayer to the God who knows his creatures intimately.

◆ GOSPEL: In their hypocrisy, the scribes and Pharisees are caught up in externals, thinking that literal observance of the letter of the Law renders them righteous. On the contrary, they have observed the letter but not the heartfelt integrity manifest in mercy, fidelity, and right judgment. These are the weightier matters of the Law. External observances without these mean nothing.

The Roman Missal

The Collect for the memorial is found in the Proper of Saints, with the remaining prayers from the Common of Holy Men and Women. The proper Collect speaks beautifully of Monica's "motherly tears . . . / for the conversion of her son Augustine." We ask the intercession of both mother and son that we, too, may repent of our sins, and "find the grace of . . . pardon."

Today's Saint

Much of what we know about the fourth-century Saint Monica comes from the writings of her son, Saint Augustine of Hippo (see biography on August 28). An Algerian-born Christian, she married a pagan named Patricius and they had three children: Perpetua, Navigius, and Augustine. Perpetua and Navigius entered the monastic life. Monica spent hours in prayer asking for the conversion of her husband and her son. Patricius converted on his death bed, but Augustine continued living an immoral lifestyle and following the gnostic beliefs of the Manicheans. Monica prayed, fasted, and begged priests and bishops to pray for Augustine. Eventually he met Milanese Bishop Ambrose (see biography on December 7) and decided to change his life. Monica died shortly after his conversion.

#427 white

W E D 28 Memorial of Saint Augustine, Bishop and Doctor of the Church

Lectionary for Mass

◆ FIRST READING: In today's text, Paul and his companions use the image of father with reference to their ministry among the Thessalonians. Note how they repeatedly speak of the toil and hardship they endured in their work of proclaiming the Gospel. Nonetheless, they are filled with thanksgiving at the Thessalonians' reception of it.

◆ RESPONSORIAL PSALM 139: Today's Psalm is a continuation of yesterday's. The responsorial antiphon is the same.

◆ GOSPEL: We hear Jesus's accusations against the hypocrisy of the Scribes and the Pharisees. In their rejection of Jesus, they are as guilty as their ancestors who murdered the prophets.

The Roman Missal

The prayers for the memorial are found in the Proper of Saints. The Collect echoes a passage from the saint's Confessions: we pray that "we may thirst" for God, and "seek . . . the author of heavenly love." The Prayer after Communion also alludes to the saint's words about Holy Communion: ". . . being made members of his Body," we pray that "we may become what we have received."

Today's Saint

Saint Augustine was born to a pagan father and a devout Christian mother. This wild, unruly young man later became one of Western Christianity's most influential figures. He tried it all—living with a woman, fathering a child out of wedlock, and dabbling in Manichaeism, a heretical belief similar to gnosticism. Through his mother's prayers and a friendship with Ambrose, he eventually converted to Christianity, was ordained a priest, and then became bishop of Hippo in 396. His prolific writing formulated theories and doctrines on original sin, just war, human will, divine predestination, the Trinity, and Christology.

#428, Gospel #634 red

T H U 29 Memorial of the Passion of Saint John the Baptist

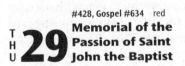

Orientation

For speaking the truth, John the Baptist is imprisoned, and eventually beheaded. The story of his death cries injustice to this day. Yet the courage of John the Baptist to speak the truth to Herod is also inspiring and awesome. How did he find the courage? Did he have a sense of what would be at risk? What might have sustained his spirit in prison? To answer these questions, we could look to the many people,

such as political prisoners or victims of religious intolerance or ethnic persecution, who are imprisoned unjustly today for daring to speak the truth. People like Oscar Romero, Edith Stein, and Dietrich Bonhoeffer are modern-day John the Baptists who continue to remind us of the power of the Holy Spirit that accompanies us even in the most difficult circumstances. Trusting in God's Spirit, we, too, may find the courage to speak and act for God's goodness and truth.

Lectionary for Mass

◆ FIRST READING: The news Paul and his companions hear about the fidelity of the Thessalonians is comfort to them in their present trials and they give thanks to God. They long to visit the community again and pray that God will help make their way clear.

◆ RESPONSORIAL PSALM 90: Today's antiphon acclaims God's love as the source of all joy. The first stanza of today's Psalm reflects on the transitoriness of human life; the second prays for true wisdom in the face of this reality; and the last asks for God's blessing on all human endeavors.

◆ GOSPEL: As we celebrate the memorial of the Passion of John the Baptist, it is only fitting that we read Mark's account of his death. What a juxtaposition of reactions to his preaching and proclamation of the truth! Herod feared John, knowing him to be a just and holy man. Herodias had a grudge against him because he had pronounced her marriage to Herod unlawful. In the end, Herod set aside both truth and John's life for the sake of saving face. For his disciples, John was a revered teacher. They dared to come forward and ask for his body to bury it.

The Roman Missal

The prayers and Preface for the Memorial are found in the Proper of Saints. The Collect speaks of John as the forerunner, whom God sent to "go ahead" of Christ "both in his birth and in his death." We pray that, like him, we may "fight hard" for what we believe. The Prayer over the Offerings asks that we may be taught by John, "that voice crying in the desert," to "make straight" the path of the Lord.

Today's Saint

"I tell you, among those born of women, no one is greater than John," Jesus told the crowds (Luke 7:28). John the Baptist, the forerunner, came to prepare the way of the Lord, and he did that from the first moments of his life. In his mother's womb, he leapt for joy at the nearness of the Lord. He preached repentance to the people, preparing them for the coming of the kingdom, and baptizing them with water so that they might be prepared to receive baptism "with the Holy Spirit and with fire." Even in his death, John prepared the way for the Lord. He boldly told Herod that he was violating the Law in taking his brother's widow as his wife, and Herod had him arrested and imprisoned and then executed. Even in his martyrdom, he prepared the way of the Lord, pointing to the way of the Cross.

F R I **30** #429 green Weekday

Lectionary for Mass

◆ FIRST READING: Paul and his companions affirm the Thessalonians for the way they are following their instructions on living as Christians and encourage them to make even more progress. The second part of the reading focuses on specific behaviors, particularly with regard to marriage. Finally, the

Thessalonians are reminded that the instructions they have received from Paul and his companions are not just from them, but from God.

◆ RESPONSORIAL PSALM: All who live justly are called to rejoice in the Lord! The stanzas of Psalm 97 acclaiming God's kingship focus on his just judgments and his protection of those who are faithful.

◆ GOSPEL: The parables of Matthew 25 look to the Parousia, or Second Coming, of the Lord at the end of time. Today, his coming is likened to that of a bridegroom who comes to meet his bride. Preparation for his coming and vigilance is of utmost importance if we are to enter into the wedding feast in the age to come.

S A T **31** #430 green Weekday

Optional Memorial of the Blessed Virgin Mary / white

Lectionary for Mass

◆ FIRST READING: Paul and his companions are well aware of the Thessalonians' mutual love for one another and encourage them to make even more progress in so doing. They are also exhorted to live peaceful lives and not to become involved in things that do not concern them. In addition, they are to support themselves through their own labor.

◆ RESPONSORIAL PSALM 98: Once again today's Psalm emphasizes the theme of God's just judgments and the joy of the righteous as a result. It is not only the just who rejoice in the presence of the Lord, but all creation.

◆ GOSPEL: This second parable from Matthew 25 deals with the servants' stewardship of what their master has entrusted to them. Clearly, the master expects good stewardship manifest in productivity and profit. Those who prove faithful are rewarded; the "useless"

(no productivity, no profit) are punished. Darkness, wailing, and grinding of teeth are all images associated with the punishment of the end time. With what are we entrusted? How will the Lord judge our stewardship?

September
Month of Our Lady of Sorrows

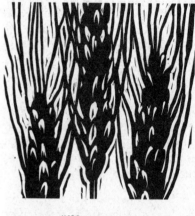

☼ **1** #126 green Twenty-second Sunday in Ordinary Time

Orientation

Anyone who has ever planned a wedding or another big celebration knows the important role seating arrangements can take on. The head-table and other seats of honor indicate who the most distinguished people are at the banquet. Playing with this metaphor, Jesus teaches us a great lesson: in the kingdom of God, the humble, the poor, and the needy are the ones who hold these honored places. Through his life, Death, and Resurrection, Christ invites us to the great heavenly banquet table, and in doing so, calls each of us to humility. A humble person recognizes his or her limitations, weakness, and poverty before God. Humility, though, is far from despair: along with a sense of finitude comes the recognition of God's grace in our lives abundantly meeting our needs. To assume the place of honor is to miss the opportunity of letting God's Spirit animate our lives and lead us well beyond our selfish ambitions.

Lectionary for Mass

◆ FIRST READING: We might think of today's readings as consisting of several independent sayings. The first is concerned with humility (verses 17–18). Sirach's wisdom is rooted in life experience: no one likes to be around an arrogant person who is into self-exaltation. Verse 20 has to do with knowing one's place in the larger scheme of things and coming to a sense of awe, mystery, and humble reverence. Verse 27 encourages an active search for wisdom with the help of sages and proverbs. Verse 29 makes an interesting parallel between water putting out a fire and almsgiving atoning for sin.

◆ RESPONSORIAL PSALM 68: Today's antiphon with its focus on the poor picks up on the last line of the First Reading (alms). Psalm 68 is a hymn of praise (see the first stanza of today's response). The second stanza focuses on God's providential care for the poor. The "needy" of the last stanza refers to all God's people ("your flock").

◆ SECOND READING: Today's text from Hebrews contrasts Israel's experience of God on Mount Sinai with our experience of God on Mount Zion in the heavenly Jerusalem (now). The reading invites us to think about when and how we approach the heavenly Mount Zion. Take note of all those gathered there with God and Jesus.

◆ GOSPEL: Today's First Reading and Gospel are nice complements to one another: the warning against self-exaltation, the exhortation to concern for the poor, and the mention of seeking wisdom through the advice of the Wise Person (Jesus). The reference to the resurrection

of the righteous provides a nice link to the Second Reading, specifically, to God the judge and the spirits of the just (righteous). Jesus is very clear on what is expected of those who want to enter into the new covenant and be counted among the righteous.

The Roman Missal

We pray for a love of God's holy name and a deeper reverence, so that God may "nurture" what is good in us, and keep us safe (Collect).

We ask for "salvation" through the "sacred offering," that we may experience the power of what we celebrate "in mystery" (Prayer over the Offerings).

The Eucharist is "the food of charity." We pray that it may inspire us to greater service of God "in our neighbor" (Prayer after Communion).

Other Ideas

Create a list of people God might want you to invite to the table. This list can be a literal or symbolic list. Share your list with your family or a small group, inviting others to talk about who is on their list.

As Catholics we believe in the God-given dignity of every human person. The Catholic Worker Movement puts this belief into practice. Research the movement on the internet and volunteer at a Catholic Worker house. If you don't have one locally, try a local soup kitchen. Reflect on your experience of the guests.

The Responsorial Psalm speaks of orphans, widows, prisoners, the forsaken, and the needy. Find out what your community or parish is doing for one or all of these groups. How do they need our special care? What can you do to practice humility as you care for them?

2 MON #431 green
Weekday

Optional proper Mass for Labor Day #907–911 / white (U.S.A. and Canada)

Optional Memorial of Blessed André Grasset, Priest and Martyr / red (Canada)

Lectionary for Mass

◆ FIRST READING: Today's text addresses the sorrow and grief the Thessalonians experience at the death of their loved ones. They are assured that they and their loved ones will be together again with the Lord when he comes in glory.

◆ RESPONSORIAL PSALM 96: Once again, the theme of the Lord's judgment is heard in the Responsorial Psalm. The Lord will come as judge. All creation rejoices in his presence.

◆ GOSPEL: This text from Luke's account of the Gospel is a sort of programmatic statement for the whole of Jesus's ministry and teaching. Empowered by God's spirit, he is sent in particular to those who are poor or imprisoned, physically disabled, or in need of consolation from the Lord. Note that Jesus is in the synagogue in his hometown of Nazareth, and he gets mixed reviews. Jesus, well-versed in the Scriptures, knows that it is often the lot of prophets to be rejected by their own. On this day, those who could not receive his word were so enraged that they tried to kill him. This is a hint of what will happen later in the Gospel.

Labor Day/The Roman Missal

The Mass "For the Sanctification of Human Labor" (Masses for Various Needs and Occasions, #26) may be used on this Labor Day, with the Preface for Independence Day and Other Civic Observances, I or II.

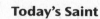

Today's Saint

Brother André served in the archdiocese of Sens, France. He was one of 191 Martyrs of September who were imprisoned by the Legislative Assembly because they refused to take an oath which supported the civil constitution of the clergy. This act, condemned by the Vatican, would give the state control over priests. Scholars are still debating whether they died for political reasons or for their refusal to submit to the civil authorities because it meant surrendering their religious independence. Grasset was killed on this date in 1792, (during the French Revolution) in Paris. He and his companions were canonized by Pope Pius XI on October 17, 1926. Though he died in France, Grasset was the first Canadian-born saint. A college in Montreal is named for him.

#432   white

TUE 3   Memorial of Saint Gregory the Great, Pope and Doctor of the Church

Lectionary for Mass

◆ First Reading: The Thessalonians are exhorted to be watchful for the coming of the Lord, for he will come when least expected. They must continue to live as children of light and support and encourage one another.

◆ Responsorial Psalm 27: Today's Responsorial song of confidence can easily be understood in terms of the age to come, although in its original context, its reference was this life. We long to dwell in the heavenly house of the Lord forever.

◆ Gospel: Today's Gospel is an account of Jesus's healing of the man with an unclean spirit. Jesus's word has power over the evil spirits and is capable of restoring the man to health.

The Roman Missal

The prayers for the Memorial are found in the Proper of Saints. The Entrance Antiphon speaks of Saint Gregory as one who "sought always the beauty of the Lord" and "lived in celebration of that love." The Collect asks Gregory's intercession for all who govern the Church.

Today's Saint

Saint Gregory the Great (540–604) was a mayor, a monk, a pope, and a writer. Unhappy with his life as mayor of Rome, Saint Gregory allocated half of his fortune to the poor and the other half to the foundation of seven monasteries. After joining a monastery in pursuit of a simple life, he was elected to the papacy. As pope, he cared for the poor, implemented the Gregorian reforms to improve Church governance and clerical behavior, promoted the monastic vocation, and renewed the liturgy. His name is associated with Gregorian chant (plainsong) and Eucharistic Prayer II (along with Saint Hippolytus). A prolific writer and Doctor of the Church, Saint Gregory composed numerous theological texts and is cited 374 times in Saint Thomas Aquinas's *Summa Theologiae*.

#433   green

WED 4   Weekday

Optional Memorial of Blessed Dina Bélanger, Virgin / white (Canada)

Lectionary for Mass

◆ First Reading: We begin the Letter to the Colossians. Paul is filled with thanksgiving for this community that has faithfully received the word of the Gospel from Epaphras. His testimony about the community's Christian life is encouragement and consolation to Paul and Timothy, his travelling companion.

◆ Responsorial Psalm 52: The image of the green olive tree suggests life, growth, and fruit—which is what the First Reading says about the Gospel. Our faith in the Lord is first and foremost his gift, received through the ministry of others. May we always be thankful for what God has done and proclaim his goodness to others.

◆ Gospel: Jesus heals the mother of Peter's wife. Word of his healing activity spreads quickly, and many bring their loved ones to him. Jesus must have continued his healing work throughout the night, for at daybreak we see him seeking solitude. In what little time he has to commune alone with God, he comes more and more in touch with his mission to proclaim the kingdom of God.

Today's Saint

A contemporary of Saint Thérèse of Lisieux (she's known as the "Little Flower of Canada"), Blessed Dina Bélanger was born in Quebec City, Canada in 1897. When Bélanger's brother died at three months old, her grieving mother starting visiting the poor and ill, bringing nourishment and compassion. Dina often went with her, which must have had a profound impact on the young girl. Discovering she didn't have a patron saint, she resolved to be the first Saint Dina.

Gifted in music, Dina studied piano at the Conservatory of Music in New York from 1916 to 1918. But instead of becoming a concert pianist, she entered the convent of Jesus and Mary in 1921 and taught music there. A great mystic, she revealed her intimacy with God in her diaries and autobiography. In prayer, she heard Jesus say, "You will do good by your writings." She died at age 32.

THU 5 #434 green
Weekday

Lectionary for Mass

◆ FIRST READING: What a beautiful and consoling message it is to hear that someone is praying for us, and that is exactly what Paul tells the Colossians. The words of his prayers are ones we can easily pray; they ask for the wisdom and knowledge to live in a manner worthy of the Lord, bearing the fruit of good works, and growing in the knowledge of God. Those who belong to Christ belong to the kingdom of light.

◆ RESPONSORIAL PSALM 98: The Lord has made known his salvation through the word of the Gospel which the Colossians have believed. Today's song of praise, prayed by Israel centuries ago, anticipated the inclusion of the Gentiles in God's plan of salvation.

◆ GOSPEL: Jesus is a man who speaks the word of God. His message and his authority attract people. Simon must have likewise been attracted by Jesus's word: he willingly offers his boat to facilitate Jesus's teaching of the crowd, and he obeys Jesus's command even though it is at odds with his own experience (they have caught nothing all night). Seeing what Jesus's word can accomplish, Peter and his companions leave all to follow him and work on his behalf.

FRI 6 #435 green
Weekday

Lectionary for Mass

◆ FIRST READING: Today's text highlights Jesus's pre-existence as God, his role in creation, and his work of sustaining it and holding it together. He who is the image of God became visible to us when he became flesh and reconciled all things to God.

◆ RESPONSORIAL PSALM 100: Once again we hear the call to all the nations to join in the joyful praise of God, our Creator, Shepherd, and Savior.

◆ GOSPEL: It must have been difficult for the people to understand why Jesus's disciples seemingly acted so differently from both the followers of John the Baptist and the Pharisees. On one occasion when he was questioned about this, Jesus answers by comparing himself to a Bridegroom, thus drawing on an image of God in the biblical tradition (see Isaiah 54:6).

SAT 7 #436 green
Weekday

Optional Memorial of the Blessed Virgin Mary / white

Lectionary for Mass

◆ FIRST READING: Today's reading focuses on God's reconciling work accomplished in Christ. It is hard to comprehend the tremendous change in our very being that happens in Baptism when God shares his very life with us. Yes, something of the divine is within us. May we always live faithfully, mindful of the gift we have received.

◆ RESPONSORIAL PSALM: God himself is our helper in every aspect of our lives. Without him, we are and can do nothing. How can we not offer a sacrifice of praise in thanksgiving?

◆ GOSPEL: Too literal, too legal a mindset can block the recognition of the ultimate meaning and significance of the Law, and even more, the underlying mercy of God for all his creatures. The person and authority of Jesus has priority over the letter of the Law. If exceptions are allowed even in the Old Testament for the man who was king (David), how much more so for the one who is the Son of Man and Lord?

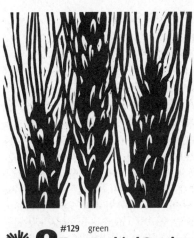

8 #129 green
Twenty-third Sunday in Ordinary Time

Orientation

Jesus reminds us about the Cross today, an image central to his life, and the life of those who follow in his name. In this world we will have trouble: suffering, loss, and finitude are part and parcel of the human experience. While most of our worldly efforts center on avoiding or escaping this harsh reality, Christianity has a radical challenge for us: embrace it, and trust in God to get you through. Only by taking up the Cross, that symbol of the frailty of the human condition, can we look with hope beyond it. Christ took up the Cross and rose to glory, shattering the bonds of death over all of creation. His victory gives us hope, because we now know that the troubles of this world no longer have the final say over our lives.

Lectionary for Mass

◆ FIRST READING: Wisdom's author is in touch with the uncertainties and anxieties of human existence. If we are unable to understand the ways of life on earth, how can we begin to fathom heavenly things? Only through God's gift of wisdom and his divine Spirit is this possible.

◆ RESPONSORIAL PSALM 90: The transitoriness and fragility of the human creature are the focus of the first two stanzas of this Psalm's realistic appraisal of human life. The psalmist is indeed a wise man, recognizing his dependence on God and his need for God's guidance, teaching, and mercy. We pray for God's blessing on all the days of our lives and on the work of our hands.

◆ SECOND READING: Paul writes these words from prison, where he was on more than one occasion because of his proclamation of the Gospel, or more precisely, because of the turmoil and unrest it created. Paul was no stranger to the difficulties of being faithful to the Lord's call. Even prison, however, could not impede his proclamation of the Word. Onesimus, a runaway slave, hears and believes. Paul beseeches Philemon, Onesimus's master, to receive him as Paul's child of faith and as a brother in Christ.

◆ GOSPEL: The First Reading puts into perspective Jesus's hard sayings in today's Gospel. Only in the wisdom of God and through the power of God's spirit can we hear, not to mention do, what Jesus asks. To become his disciple, one must first accede to Jesus's demand to renounce all possessions, and indeed one's very self. Only then can we be as available and open as God requires.

The Roman Missal

Through adoption, we have become God's "beloved sons and daughters." We pray that we may come into the "freedom" and "inheritance" God has promised (Collect).

We pray that through our offering, we may "do fitting homage" to God and be "faithfully united in mind and heart" (Prayer over the Offerings)

In the liturgy God nourishes us with "the food of the Word and heavenly Sacrament." We pray that we may benefit from these "great gifts" and come to "an eternal share in his life" (Prayer after Communion).

Other Ideas

Read Paul's Letter to Philemon, the shortest book in the Bible. In it, he writes about Onesimus, a former slave now converted to Christianity. Paul asks Philemon to treat him as a brother. Discuss the situation Paul speaks about. What do you think happened when Onesimus met Philemon? How does becoming a Christian and following Christ transform human relationships?

Make a cross (you might use construction paper, clay, or wood). Place it somewhere you can see it during the week or fall season. Let it remind you of the cross of discipleship Jesus invites us to carry. Pray especially for those who are ridiculed for following Christ.

Take time to go through some of your possessions. Donate your things to a place that could benefit from them. What is the mission of the place? Who does it serve? Is your help needed?

MON 9 #437 white
Memorial of Saint Peter Claver, Priest

Lectionary for Mass

◆ FIRST READING: Paul's words today encourage us to see our own suffering, offered for the sake of the Church. It is not that Christ did not do enough—but rather, that the Church is still in the process of becoming. Sufferings offered as a prayer or sacrifice for another can give pain meaning and purpose. Such is the example of Christ. Note that the word "mystery" occurs three times in today's reading. God and his plan of salvation for us, the subject of his Word to us in the Scriptures, is so much more than anything we can ask or imagine.

◆ RESPONSORIAL PSALM 62: So much in life is mystery, especially the ultimate things. Only in God will we find the answers, the way, and peace. Psalm 62 is a song of confidence in God alone.

◆ GOSPEL: The details in today's Gospel are interesting. Was the man right-handed? If so, that would be a serious impairment. The Pharisees and the scribes are watching closely to see what Jesus would do. Jesus questions them on their interpretation of Sabbath observance and acts in accord with the mercy and loving kindness of the Lord.

The Roman Missal

Saint Peter Claver called himself "the slave of the slaves for ever." The Collect echoes his words, speaking of Peter as the "slave of slaves," a man of "wonderful charity and patience." We pray that we may imitate him in "seeking the things of Jesus Christ" and loving "our neighbor in deeds and in truth." The remaining prayers are drawn from the Common of Pastors or the Common of Holy Men and Women.

Today's Saint

Saint Peter Claver (1581–1654), a Spanish Jesuit priest, spent his life tending to the needs of African slaves in Colombia. While serving as a missionary, he ministered to the slaves by providing them with food and medicine, washing their wounds, preparing them for Baptism, and witnessing their marriages. He actively pursued lawyers to plead the cases of imprisoned slaves and prepared criminals for death. He also preached missions to plantation owners and sailors. The "saint of the slaves," as Saint Peter is often called, died after contracting a plague.

TUE 10 #438 green
Weekday

Lectionary for Mass

◆ FIRST READING: The first part of today's reading refers to a Christian's manner of life, as the words "walk" and "philosophy" indicate. Pay particular attention to the verbs in the second part of the reading, which stress what has happened to us as a result of Christ's saving Death and Resurrection in which we share in Baptism.

◆ RESPONSORIAL PSALM 145: Today's Psalm is fittingly one of praise. Surely it was the Lord's compassion for all that he made that led to such marvelous gifts as described in the First Reading. We, like the Colossians Paul addresses, are to be people of thanksgiving.

◆ GOSPEL: It is interesting to note how many times in the Gospel Jesus goes off by himself to spend time with his heavenly Father in prayer, particularly before important decisions or moments in his life. As a result of prayer, he named his disciples. Through prayer, he knew of his mission to heal and he experienced God's power working through him.

W E D **11** #439 green
Weekday

Lectionary for Mass

◆ FIRST READING: Today's text is one of the options for the Second Reading on Easter Sunday. Yes, through Baptism, the reality of our life has been changed because of what Christ has done for us. We must live accordingly. The second part of the reading details what our manner of life should be like.

◆ RESPONSORIAL PSALM 145: Today's response is the same as yesterday, only the last stanzas are different. Our lives should be such that we make known God's kingdom in word and deed.

◆ GOSPEL: Luke's version of the Beatitudes differs slightly from Matthew's. We see here, for example, his concern for the poor and

those who are in need of any kind. These are the ones who are acclaimed blessed and promised that their needs will one day be met. Correspondingly, those who have great possessions now risk woe and doom if they neglect the needs of others.

T H U **12** #440 green
Weekday

Optional Memorial of the Most Holy Name of Mary / white

Lectionary for Mass

◆ FIRST READING: The instructions on a Christian manner of life continue. This chapter from Colossians makes an excellent examination of conscience. How do we measure up in fulfilling what Paul prescribes?

◆ RESPONSORIAL PSALM 150: Today's response is from the great hymn of praise which closes the entire Psalter and which flows naturally from the last line of today's reading. May all that we do and say praise the Lord.

◆ GOSPEL: Today's Gospel is a series of sayings that stress loving those who mistreat us and giving selflessly regardless of cost. Above all, believers must be merciful, for this is one of God's main attributes. What we do to others will be done to us.

Today's Optional Memorial

The Most Holy Name of Mary is the counterpart to the optional Memorial of the Most Holy Name of Jesus celebrated on January 3. Both of these optional memorials had been removed from the general calendar after the reform of the liturgical calendar in 1969. The memorials were restored with the promulgation of the third edition of *The Roman Missal.*

#441 white
F R I **13** Memorial of Saint John Chrysostom, Bishop and Doctor of the Church

Lectionary for Mass

◆ FIRST READING: In the greeting at the beginning of his first Letter to Timothy, Paul emphasizes that his ministry on behalf of the Gospel results from God's command, God's mercy, and God's grace. Paul's experience of the 13 totally changed the direction of his life.

◆ RESPONSORIAL PSALM 16: Indeed, the Lord was Paul's inheritance and all that mattered to him in life. Today's Psalm expresses confidence in God. Within the context of today's liturgy, we can easily understand this as a reference to Jesus. See how the words of the stanzas are borne out in Paul's life.

◆ GOSPEL: Jesus's words call for clear-sighted vision of one's self, particularly of weaknesses and sinfulness. How easy it is to focus myopically on the speck in the other's eye and miss the beam in our own!

The Roman Missal

The prayers for the memorial are found in the Proper of Saints. The name Chrysostom means "Golden-tongued." It was given to John to honor his great eloquence in preaching the Gospel. The Collect speaks not only of his "wonderful eloquence" but of "his experience of suffering" and "invincible patience" (Collect). Taught by him, we pray that we may also dedicate ourselves to praise of God (Prayer over the Offerings).

Today's Saint

After a short stint as a monk, Saint John Chrysostom (347–407), whose surname means "golden mouth," returned to Antioch where he was ordained a priest and became a noted preacher. During his free time, he wrote commentaries on the Pauline letters as well as the Gospel accounts of Matthew and John. Due to his reputation for preaching and writing, he was appointed bishop of Constantinople. As bishop, he initiated a program of reform that challenged clerical abuses and the extravagant lifestyle of the upper class. His reforms were not always received well, especially on the part of Empress Eudoxia; therefore, he was exiled from the city for a period of time. Saint John Chrysostom bears two distinctive titles in the Church: father of the Church and Doctor of the Church.

SAT 14 — #638   red
Feast of the Exaltation of the Holy Cross

Orientation

The cross is one of the most complex symbols we have as Christians. Literally, it is an instrument of torture. Symbolically, it is a sign of our salvation. Culturally, it is a mark of Christian identity. The cross depicts horrid suffering at the same time as immense love. It is a sign of utter humility and powerful victory. It holds together death and eternal life all in one. Today's feast day invites us to ponder this complex symbol, which we exult as a sign of Christ's victory. The symbol of the Cross is a source of enormous hope for our lives, that whatever burdens and sufferings we endure, whatever crosses we bear, can be transformed through God's grace into glorious relics of victory.

Lectionary for Mass

◆ FIRST READING: A tired and discouraged Israel let itself slip into a rebellious attitude toward God and his servant Moses. God punished the Israelites through the bites of poisonous serpents. Only then did they acknowledge their sin. God, in his mercy, allowed those bitten by the snake to be healed simply by looking at a bronze replica of the serpent, raised up on a pole at his command.

◆ RESPONSORIAL PSALM 78: The source of difficulties described in the First Reading was precisely that Israel *forgot* the works of the Lord. The psalmist has learned from Israel's experience and calls on all who hear him to do likewise.

◆ SECOND READING: This early Christian hymn acclaims the self-emptying of Christ, who relinquishing his heavenly glory, became one of us that he might show us the way to God through his obedience, Passion, and Resurrection.

◆ GOSPEL: Jesus's words to Nicodemus recall the incident in today's First Reading. The Greek verb translated as "lifted up" means both to raise up as on a staff or a cross and to exalt. The "lifted up" Son of Man is now the source of salvation and life for all the world.

The Roman Missal

The prayers and Preface are found in the Proper of Saints. The Gloria is said or sung today.

Only through the Cross did Christ "save the human race," and we, too, must pass through the cross, "his mystery on earth," if we hope to "merit the grace of his redemption in heaven" (Collect).

Christ's self-offering "on the altar of the Cross / canceled the offense of the whole world." This sacrifice, renewed on our altar today, has power to "cleanse us . . . of all our sins" (Prayer over the Offerings).

The Preface speaks of the Cross as a tree of glory. In Eden, "the evil one . . . conquered on a tree"; on the tree of the Cross, evil is defeated. The Cross is not dead wood, but a living tree and a source of life

We pray that all whom Christ has redeemed "by the wood of [his] life-giving Cross" may also follow him "to the glory of the resurrection" (Prayer after Communion).

Other Ideas

Sometimes people talk about taking up the cross as a burden to be borne or endured. Jesus referred to it as a kind of self-sacrifice. What does it mean to deny oneself and take up the cross daily to follow Christ? Journal about this or discuss it with a small group.

☀ 15 — #132   green
Twenty-fourth Sunday in Ordinary Time

Orientation

In today's busy world, we spend much of our time rushing, multitasking, and making do, so that things get done. With such a mindset, 99 out of a hundred is pretty good; few of us would be driven enough to aim for the perfect number. Yet in today's parable Jesus supposes just that. What would make a shepherd go after the one sheep with a flock of 99 safely in the corral? One missing sheep may not seem so serious to the shepherd or the rest of the sheep, but being the one missing number from the flock certainly matters to the lost sheep. This compassionate shepherd recognizes that the lost sheep may be hurt, terrified, and in danger somewhere, so rather than count it as an unfortunate loss, he sets out to help. This parable reveals something to us about our compassionately loving God. Each of us matters to God, especially when we are lost, and God rejoices when we find our way back.

Lectionary for Mass

◆ FIRST READING: How quickly the Israelites turned away from the God who had revealed himself to them and created their own god! How quickly they forsook the covenant so recently made. They are, as the Lord described them, a "stiff-necked" people. God's anger is understandable, his threatened punishment, justifiable. Today we witness both the power of Moses's intercession and God's merciful fidelity to the covenant.

◆ RESPONSORIAL PSALM: Although today's antiphon is taken from the Gospel, it is nonetheless a fitting response from a stiff-necked people. The verses are from Psalm 51, a prayer of repentance.

◆ SECOND READING: Paul's words acknowledge his previous ignorance regarding his treatment of Christians before his own personal experience of the 13. The saying he quotes about Jesus coming into the world to save sinners is amply illustrated by today's Gospel.

◆ GOSPEL: The parables in chapter 15 are unique to Luke's account of the Gospel. Note, first, the setting: the tax collectors and sinners, people considered as outcasts by the official religious establishment, are receptive to Jesus's word. He, in turn, is receptive to them, even sharing meals—a sign of acceptance and

fellowship—with them. Two options are given. The longer includes the parable of the prodigal son (the merciful father? the stiff-necked and unforgiving elder brother?). All three focus on the joy in heaven over the repentance of sinners.

The Roman Missal

We pray that we may "serve [God] with all our heart" and so "feel the working" of his mercy in our lives (Collect).

We pray that the offering of each of us "may serve the salvation of all." We are one body in Christ: the love and faith, the needs and hopes we each bring to our prayer touches others in ways we cannot imagine (Prayer over the Offerings).

We pray that the "heavenly gift" we have received may so work in us that God's will may prevail over our own desires (Prayer after Communion).

Other Ideas

Listen to a hymn about God as a shepherd, such as "Like a Shepherd" (Dufford). What images do you hear in the words and music?

Find a story about someone who either changed his or her life because of an experience of God or who went beyond the normal expectations of society to help someone else. There are stories of individuals who saved people dying of starvation or poverty, or who helped rescue Jews during the Holocaust. You may know a story of a local person. Your local librarian can help you find some books or movies.

Write another chapter to the story of the father with two sons. What does the elder son say to his brother? What does the younger son say to his older brother? What does the father say during conversation between his sons? What do you think they are each feeling? Discuss your ideas with a group or your family.

#443   red

Memorial of Saints Cornelius, Pope, and Cyprian, Bishop, Martyrs

MON **16**

Lectionary for Mass

◆ FIRST READING: In the early days of the Church—as in some countries in our world today—Christians were not always and everywhere accepted or welcomed; thus, the importance of intercessory prayer, especially for rulers and civil officials. The intent is that Christians might be able to practice their faith and live in peace. Their example is likewise to speak of the goodness and truth of their way of life and bear testimony to Jesus.

◆ RESPONSORIAL PSALM 28: Today's Psalm echoes the gesture of prayer mentioned in today's First Reading: the lifting up of hands. The antiphon is a prayer of thanksgiving (a theme likewise found in the First Reading). The stanzas speak of confident trust in God's care for his people.

◆ GOSPEL: A Roman centurion, a Gentile, believing in what he had heard about Jesus as a healer, asks some of the Jewish elders to ask Jesus to come and heal his dying slave. (Note the good word the elders put in for the centurion, obviously a benefactor of the local synagogue and perhaps himself a God-fearer.) Jesus sets out to do so, only to be met by friends of the centurion who had been sent to tell Jesus not to inconvenience himself by coming to the house, but only to say a word of healing. The centurion believes in the power of Jesus's word. Jesus not only heals the slave, he pronounces the Gentile centurion a model of faith to his Jewish contemporaries.

The Roman Missal

The prayers for the memorial are found in the Proper of Saints. The Collect speaks of these saints as "diligent shepherds and valiant Martyrs." We pray that we may "spend ourselves without reserve / for the unity of the Church" (Collect), be "steadfast in all trials" as they were (Prayer over the Offerings), and be strengthened by the Spirit so that we may "witness to the truth of the Gospel" (Prayer after Communion).

Today's Saints

Saint Cornelius (+ 253) and Saint Cyprian (+ 258) lived during the persecution by the Emperor Decius. Saint Cornelius, the pope, faced the issue of whether or not Christians who renounced their faith during the persecutions should be welcomed back into the Church. With great compassion he publicly declared that these individuals may return to the Church after a period of penance. Saint Cyprian, bishop of Carthage, spent much of his life in hiding due to the persecutions, but this did not stop him from offering pastoral guidance and dispensing wisdom to the people of his diocese. Through letters he urged the people to remain faithful to their Christian call. Both Saints Cornelius and Cyprian shared the same fate—a martyr's death.

T U E 17 #444 green **Weekday**

Optional Memorial of Saint Robert Bellarmine, Bishop and Doctor of the Church / white

Lectionary for Mass

◆ FIRST READING: Paul sets forth the criteria for those chosen as bishops and deacons. The qualifications reveal a life-situation in the early Church different from our own.

◆ RESPONSORIAL PSALM 101: Today's Psalm echoes the qualities set forth in today's First Reading. How important that those who minister and serve in the Church be people of blamelessness and integrity of heart.

◆ GOSPEL: Perhaps it is the mother who is the focus in today's Gospel, rather than the son. She is a widow and now has lost her only son. In the society of her time she would be totally helpless, with no means of financial support. When Jesus saw her, he was moved with pity for her. Raising her dead son to life, he gives him to her. What needs do we have that the Lord looks on in his mercy? What gifts does the Lord give us to meet these needs?

Today's Saint

Saint Robert Bellarmine (1542–1621), bishop and Doctor of the Church, was an astute scholar with a knack for diplomatically responding to the controversies of his day. As a Jesuit priest embroiled in the Protestant Reformation, he sensitively communicated through word and writing the Catholic perspective, especially regarding the relationship between Church and state. One of his most important contributions to the Church is a three-volume work, *Disputations on the Controversies of the Christian Faith*, which explained Catholic fundamentals in a non-defensive, systematic way. Saint Robert, a devotee of Saint Francis of Assisi, demonstrated heroic virtue by praying for his opponents, living simply, and embracing spiritual discipline.

W E D 18 #445 green **Weekday**

Lectionary for Mass

◆ FIRST READING: Throughout this letter, Paul is concerned with the behavior of Christians, members of the household of God. He likewise continually reiterates the centrality of Jesus, who dwelt among us and now reigns in heavenly glory.

◆ RESPONSORIAL PSALM: The antiphon is an acclamation of praise for the great works of God. Juxtaposed with the First Reading, it points to Jesus and his saving Gospel. The Psalm, appropriately, is one of thanksgiving for all that God has done for his people. Pray it bearing in mind what God has done for us in Christ.

◆ GOSPEL: The Lectionary omits Luke 7:18-30 which recounts Jesus's response to the questions of John the Baptist as well as his commentary on John's mission. Jesus speaks of his contemporaries (those who hear his preaching and those who heard John the Baptist) as children, in this instance, as children dissatisfied with what is offered them. Jesus calls this generation to be children of wisdom instead, open to his teaching and to his work.

T H U 19 #446 green **Weekday**

Optional Memorial of Saint Januarius, Bishop and Martyr / red

Lectionary for Mass

◆ FIRST READING: Given his young age, Timothy must have been an exceptionally gifted individual to hold the position and ministry he did in the Church. His youth, says Paul, should not be an obstacle for himself or for others. He was to persevere diligently in the task with which he was charged; his was the ministry of salvation.

◆ RESPONSORIAL PSALM: What Timothy received, like all that had been given to God's people throughout the ages, was the gift and work of the Lord. Preeminent among these is the gift of salvation. Praise and thanksgiving are fitting response. Gospel: Jesus paints quite a contrast between Simon the righteous Pharisee and the unnamed sinner who washes the feet of his guest with her tears and anoints them with oil. Though Simon invited Jesus to his home for dinner, it is the woman who welcomed and received him into her heart. She was the one who received salvation and forgiveness because of her great love.

Today's Saint

Saint Januarius (+ 305) was bishop of Benevento in Italy during the Diocletian persecutions. After suffering the fate of a martyr, being thrown to wild beasts and then beheaded, his relics were transported to Naples, where it is said that a vial of his blood liquefies on three feast days related to his life: today, the day he supposedly prevented an eruption of Mount Vesuvius in 1631 (December 16), and the Saturday before the first Sunday in May, commemorating the transfer of his relics. He is the patron saint of blood banks and Naples, where he is referred to as San Gennaro.

#447   red

Memorial of Saints Andrew Kim Tae-gŏn, Priest, and Paul Chŏng Ha-sang, and Companions, Martyrs

F R I 20

Lectionary for Mass

◆ FIRST READING: Sound teaching is a prominent concern in the pastoral epistles (1 and 2 Timothy, and Titus), as the Church at the time

was particularly threatened by heresies. False teachings only lead to corruption and division in the Church. So, too, do discontent and the love of money. Paul's words call us to examine the desires and motivations of our hearts.

◆ RESPONSORIAL PSALM: Today's Psalm comes from the Gospel according to Matthew, addressing the poverty of spirit as described in today's First Reading (contentment with having what is needed; disinterest in amassing wealth). The verses of today's Psalm associate fleeting wealth and riches with those who are at enmity with God. True riches are found in the salvation God gives.

◆ GOSPEL: Today's Gospel focuses on the many women among Jesus's disciples who journey with him from Galilee to Jerusalem, and are present—albeit from a distance—at the Cross. Note that the only thing said about Mary Magdalene is that she had been healed of evil spirits and infirmities. She is not to be confused with the sinful woman in yesterday's Gospel.

The Roman Missal

The prayers for this memorial are found in the Proper of Saints. "The blood of the Martyrs" is "a most fruitful seed of Christians" (Collect). The faith for which they died has come to flourish through their witness.

Today's Saints

During the eighteenth and nineteenth centuries, approximately eight thousand adherents to the Catholic faith in Korea were martyred, 103 of whom were canonized by Pope John Paul II in 1988. The canonized martyrs were victims of a particularly heinous series of persecutions happening between 1839 and 1867. During this time period, Korea was ruled by an anti-Christian

dynasty that did everything possible to eliminate Catholic ideology and influence, including the malicious mass murder of Christian missionaries and their followers. Two of the more notable martyrs are Saint Andrew Kim Tae-gŏn (1821–1846), a priest, and Saint Paul Chŏng Ha-sang (1794/5–1839), a layman, both of whom were dedicated to the revitalization of the Church in Korea.

#643   red

Feast of Saint Matthew, Apostle and Evangelist

S A T 21

Lectionary for Mass

◆ FIRST READING: Everyone in the community is gifted by God's grace. Everyone! This is God's Word to us. Each *has* received and *continually receives* God's grace—the *gift* of God's grace. There are various gifts in the community, but all are necessary. Everyone has a responsibility to "build up" the community which long ago was built on the foundational work of the Apostles.

◆ RESPONSORIAL PSALM 19: How far away our land is from that where Jesus and his Apostles lived. We give thanks that the Apostles proclaimed his message "through all the earth" and that it has reached us.

◆ GOSPEL: Tax collectors were looked down upon in Jesus's day. They were agents of a foreign (Gentile) government and they supplemented their income with what they superimposed on the taxes of others. Through table fellowship with tax collectors, Jesus showed his acceptance of them. This was not to approve of their wrongdoing but to offer them the opportunity to convert and be healed. This can happen only in the face of love and acceptance.

The Roman Missal

The prayers are found in the Proper of Saints. The Gloria is said or sung today.

The Collect emphasizes the "untold mercy" of God, who chose Matthew "the tax collector" to be both Apostle and Evangelist. We pray that we may imitate him, and "hold firm in following" the Lord.

The Prayer after Communion echoes the Gospel account of the call of Saint Matthew: Jesus is glad to dine with this tax collector, because he "did not come to call the righteous but sinners" (Matthew 9:13). Just as Matthew rejoiced to welcome "the Savior as a guest in his home," so we rejoice to welcome Christ who has come to dwell with us through the sacrament we share.

The Solemn Blessing of the Apostles may be used.

Today's Saint

Matthew (first century), referred to as the tax collector, is one of the twelve Apostles and and traditionally honored as the author of the first of the four accounts of the Gospel. His Gospel has a twofold purpose: one, to announce that Jesus is the eternal king of all creation; and two, to encourage faith in the face of doubt, especially regarding persecution. We have very little information about him, other than he invited Jesus to his home to dine with societal outcasts (see Matthew 9:9–13), and that he preached the Good News after the Resurrection. Tradition says he began preaching in Judea, then moved on to Ethiopia, Persia, Syria, Macedonia, and possibly Ireland. He is venerated as a martyr, even though there is no historical evidence to validate this claim.

#135   green

✳22 Twenty-fifth Sunday in Ordinary Time

Orientation

At the heart of today's Gospel is the importance of integrity. Integrity is the courage to be who we are, and it honors God, our neighbors, and ourselves. A person of integrity honors God by trusting in God's unique gifts that characterize who he or she is. In the same way, the person of integrity honors self by accepting these gifts and using them for the life of the world. Finally, the person of integrity honors others, who do not have to fear duplicity or deception when interacting together. Integrity makes one trustworthy and true, and in this, the person imitates God.

Lectionary for Mass

◆ FIRST READING: God's words are justly severe to those who with full forethought defraud the poor, all the while observing, at least outwardly, the ritual celebrations as prescribed in the law. God's word is strong: he will never forget this injustice. One day, God's people will pay for their sins of iniquity.

◆ RESPONSORIAL PSALM 113: It is the poor, taken advantage of by the wicked depicted in the words of Amos, who are the recipients of God's blessing and deliverance. Today's song of praise can seem jarring when it is juxtaposed with Amos's words; indeed, it would be for the wicked. For the oppressed poor, the Psalm's message is a word of Good News: God will raise them up.

◆ SECOND READING: Paul stresses the importance of prayer for all civil leaders that through their government, religious tolerance and peace will abound for all people. Such is the will of Christ Jesus who wants all people to be saved and to know the truth revealed in the Gospel.

◆ GOSPEL: There is a certain irony in today's Gospel depiction of the steward who loses his position because of his wasteful management of the master's property and who, prior to leaving his job, insures his own well-being by drastically writing off the debts owed to his master, thus incurring additional losses for his master. When the master became aware of his actions, he praised him for his astuteness. (We aren't told whether or not he received his job back!) Described in the parable as a "child of the world," he stands in contrast to "the children of light" and of God. Several sayings attributed to Jesus, all concerning wealth, follow the parable. All call us to examine our attitude toward, and use of, money.

The Roman Missal

In the Collect we pray that, keeping this great commandment, "we may merit to attain eternal life."

We pray in the Prayer over the Offerings that what we believe in may be ours through our sharing in the Eucharist.

In the Prayer after Communion, we pray that we may truly live the mystery we celebrate and receive in the Eucharist.

Other Ideas

Watch a movie about the poor, such as *Romero*, *Gandhi*, or *Slumdog Millionaire*. What is the daily life of a poor person like? What do the poor have to do to survive? How do you think God acts in their lives?

Paul urges prayers for rulers and those in authority. As you read the newspaper or listen to the news this week, make a list of people in positions of authority. The list might include judges, mayors, police officers, Church leaders, or teachers. You can name groups or individuals. It does not matter if you agree with their politics or religion, just ask God to be with them in their decisions.

Where do you invest your money? Does your bank or retirement fund invest in companies with fair and just practices? You may wish to research your own investments.

M O N 23 #449   white
Memorial of Saint Pius of Pietrelcina, Priest

Lectionary for Mass

◆ FIRST READING: Due to the victory of Cyrus of Persia over the Babylonians, the Jews in exile in Babylon were allowed to return to Jerusalem. Among their first tasks was to rebuild God's temple that had been destroyed by the Babylonians. Note that the biblical author interprets this as the charge God gave (inspired) Cyrus. The Jews receive gifts from their Babylonian neighbors to help rebuild the temple.

◆ RESPONSORIAL PSALM 136 celebrates the end of the Babylonian exile, a dream come true for Israel. What marvels the Lord had done for them; what joy marked their return to their homeland.

◆ GOSPEL: "Take care . . . how you hear" (Luke 8:18, emphasis added). In one ear and out the other? Or, do we listen with the ear of the heart and shine forth with the light of love for God and others?

The Roman Missal

The Collect for the memorial is found in the Proper of Saints. The Collect speaks of the "singular grace" by which the saint was given "a share in the Cross." We pray that we, too, in our own way, may be "united constantly to the sufferings of Christ." The remaining prayers are drawn from the Common of Pastors: For One Pastor or of Holy Men and Women: For Religious.

Today's Saint

Early in life Saint "Padre" Pio of Pietrelcina (1887–1968), a Capuchin priest from Italy, demonstrated an unquenchable thirst for God. While praying one day before a crucifix, he received the visible wounds of crucifixion that Christ bore in his Passion and death, known as the stigmata. After an examination by a doctor, it was determined that there was no natural explanation for the wounds. Along with the stigmata, he experienced other mystical phenomena, including bilocation, the ability to be in two places at the same time, and "reading the hearts" of those who sought counsel and forgiveness in the Sacrament of Reconciliation. These two miraculous gifts enabled him to lead both the sinner and devout closer to God. Upon his death the stigmata were no longer visible.

T U E 24 #450   green
Weekday

Optional Memorial of Blessed Émilie Tavernier-Gamelin, Religious / white(Canada)

Lectionary for Mass

◆ FIRST READING: Ezra's account of the rebuilding of the temple and the support of the Persian kings continues. The dedication of the temple was celebrated with great joy. How special that first celebration of Passover back in their homeland and in their temple must have

been, as they continued to witness God's marvelous deeds for them.

◆ RESPONSORIAL PSALM 122 is a hymn that pilgrims sang as they joyfully made their way to the temple in Jerusalem. It is a fitting response to the account of the temple's rebuilding and dedication.

◆ GOSPEL: Hearing and doing the word of God puts one in a relationship with Jesus that is tighter than the bonds of natural family ties.

Today's Saint

At the age of 18, Émilie Tavernier moved in to help her widowed brother on one condition: they must set a table for the hungry, called "The Table of the King." In 1823, Émilie married Jean-Baptiste Gamelin, an apple grower, and they had three children. But her husband and children all died at about the same time. Instead of being consumed by grief, she came to see the poor as, in a sense, her husband and children. They filled her home: the unemployed, indigent, elderly, orphans, people with handicaps, prisoners, immigrants. They came to call it the House of Providence and for 15 years, she opened more and more homes. Eventually, those who helped her formed a religious community, the Sisters of Providence, who now work internationally. She died in the cholera epidemic of 1851.

W E D 25 #451   green
Weekday

Optional Memorial of Saints Cosmas and Damian, Martyrs (Canada)

Lectionary for Mass

◆ FIRST READING: In the midst of the joy and the hope of a new beginning for Israel, we find Ezra's honest acknowledgement of the guilt of his people and the deserved punishment of their servitude in Babylon. Confession of our sinfulness makes us even more aware of the gifts and graces God gives us.

◆ CANTICLE: Today's prayer is a hymn found not in the Psalter but in the Book of Tobit. It acclaims God's deliverance of his people among the Gentiles (non-Jews), an example of which is described in the First Reading.

◆ GOSPEL: The Apostles sent in Jesus's name are empowered by him in their mission of healing and proclamation of the Gospel. He asks for radical trust and contentment with what is offered them by those who receive them. If rejected, they must testify against those who would not receive them.

Today's Saints

Saints Cosmas and Damian (+ 287) were brothers, possibly twins, who practiced medicine without accepting money for their services, which is why they are known in the East as the anargyroi, meaning "moneyless ones" or "moneyless healers." As vibrant witnesses to the Christian faith, they were arrested during the Diocletian persecutions. When they refused to renounce their faith and engage in idolatrous worship, they were beheaded and cast into the sea. They are patron saints of twins, confectioners, the sightless, and many medical professions (e.g., physicians, nurses, and dentists). Their names are included in Eucharistic Prayer 1.

T
H **26** #452 green
U **Weekday**

Optional Memorial of Saints Cosmas and Damian, Martyrs / red (U.S.A.) ◆ Feast of Saints John de Brébeuf, Isaac Jogues, Priests, and Companions, Martyrs, Secondary Patrons of Canada / red

U.S.A.: Lectionary for Mass

◆ FIRST READING: Today, we backtrack a bit in history with the prophet Haggai to the time before the temple was rebuilt. Here it seems that the people did not first set about rebuilding the temple upon their return; rather, they started constructing houses for themselves. They are called to repentance and to begin building a house for the Lord.

◆ RESPONSORIAL PSALM 149: The Lord takes pleasure in his people, a sentiment echoed at the end of the First Reading and in today's antiphon. The verses speak of joyful praise of God in a liturgical assembly with song and dance.

◆ GOSPEL: The question of Jesus's identity pervades the Gospels. In today's text, it is Herod the tetrarch, who is perplexed about him.

Today's Saints

See biographies above.

F
R **27** #453 white
I **Memorial of Saint Vincent de Paul, Priest**

Lectionary for Mass

◆ FIRST READING: For those who remembered the splendor of Solomon's Temple, the sight of the post-Exilic Temple paled in comparison. The prophet speaks a word of hope and encouragement with the promise that in days to come, the glory of the Temple would exceed even that of Solomon's time.

◆ RESPONSORIAL PSALM 43: The Psalm encourages hope in the Lord's promise, for he is our Savior. The stanzas progress from the experience of being threatened by the deceitful and impious to the confident hope of one day offering a joyful sacrifice of thanksgiving for God's deliverance.

◆ GOSPEL: No doubt the people of Jesus's day had never met anyone quite like him. Who is this? they asked. In today's Gospel—and note the context, prayer—Jesus asks his disciples what people were saying about him. He asks them as well:

What do you say? Peter confesses that Jesus is the Christ, the messiah. Lest his disciples misunderstood the nature of his messiahship, Jesus is quick to tell them that he will suffer and be killed, but also that he will be raised on the third day.

The Roman Missal

The prayers for the memorial are found in the Proper of Saints. The texts for today speak of Saint Vincent's wonderful love for the poor. "Let them thank the Lord for his mercy, / his wonders for the children of men, / for he satisfies the thirsty soul, / and the hungry he fills with good things" (Communion Antiphon).

Today's Saint

Saint Vincent de Paul (1580–1660), a French priest, gradually became aware of the growing disparity between the rich and poor; therefore, he laid the framework for a confraternity of caring, called the Servants of the Poor, which provided for the physical needs of the poor. Recognizing the call to care for not only their physical needs, but also their spiritual needs, he established a society of priests, the Congregation of the Mission (Vincentians), dedicated to preaching to peasants, catechesis of the marginalized, and other charitable works. In collaboration with Saint Louise Montfort de Marillac, he founded the Daughters of Charity, a community of sisters not bound by traditional vows or enclosure, and devoted to the sick, orphaned, and imprisoned. Saint Vincent is the patron of charitable societies. Many day cares, hospitals, thrift stores, and soup kitchens are named in his honor.

SAT 28 #454 green
Weekday

Optional Memorial of Saint Wenceslaus, Martyr / red; Saint Lawrence Ruiz and Companions, Martyrs / red; Blessed Virgin Mary / white

Lectionary for Mass

◆ FIRST READING: The word of the prophet assures God's people of a future day of glory for Jerusalem, God dwelling in her midst. What is more, the Gentile nations will join themselves to Israel and together they will praise the Lord.

◆ CANTICLE: Today's canticle, from the Book of Jeremiah, speaks of the return of God's people to Jerusalem. God is imaged as the shepherd who gathers his flock and redeems them from the hand of the conqueror. Zion is another name for Jerusalem.

◆ GOSPEL: Jesus keeps telling his disciples what kind of messiah he will be. Right now they are full of amazement at his mighty deeds; but Jesus says, "Pay attention to what I am telling you" (Luke 9:44): the Passion is coming. But the disciples do not understand; in fact, they are afraid to understand.

Today's Saints

◆ SAINT WENCELSAUS: Most people are familiar with Wenceslaus (903–935), due to the popular Christmas carol "Good King Wenceslaus." Although this ancient carol is not based on historical events, it illustrates the fame King Wenceslaus received because of his heroic life. As a Christian king in Bohemia, a primarily pagan country, he worked fervently to Christianize his people. His attempt to evangelize the Bohemians was not received well by some, including his brother who eventually murdered him. As he was dying, he prayed that God would forgive his brother. Shortly

following his death, people proclaimed him a martyr.

Saint Lawrence Ruiz (1600–1637), a married man with three children, fled to Japan from Manila to escape an unjust charge. Upon arrival he was greeted with hostility, due to a recent edict that banned Christianity. When he and 15 other companions would not adhere to the state religion and trample on religious images associated with the Catholic faith, they were executed. Saint Lawrence and his companions join 231 other Catholics martyred in Japan between the sixteenth and seventeenth centuries.

☀ 29 #138 green
Twenty-sixth Sunday in Ordinary Time

Orientation

How could the rich man possibly have missed the sick, suffering and hungry beggar right at his door? From the afterlife, the rich man begs Abraham to send Lazarus to warn his brothers. His request tells us that he simply did not notice or did not take seriously this opportunity for compassion and service during his life. The warning may not have reached the rich man's brothers, but it does reach us. His unawareness challenges us to open our eyes to the Lazarus at our door. The rich man had more than enough food to share with Lazarus—what surpluses do we have in life? Who might be grateful even for a scrap of these?

Lectionary for Mass

◆ FIRST READING: God's special concern for the poor and helpless is evident throughout the Scriptures. God's law ordains that those who have earthly goods should be mindful of those who do not. But Israel did not always heed God's word. In today's text from the prophet Amos, God's word of judgment is spoken against those who ignore the poor.

◆ RESPONSORIAL PSALM 146 is a song of praise to God who shows tremendous care and concern for the poor, the oppressed, the powerless, and those in any need.

◆ SECOND READING: Paul's exhortation to Timothy is applicable to us all. We are all men and women of God. Let us live now, striving to love and serve God and others, as we await the coming of our Lord.

◆ GOSPEL: Jesus's parable points to God's loving concern for those who are in need now and to the abundance and consolation they will receive in the age to come. Similarly, those who refuse to show mercy to those in need will be punished forever.

The Roman Missal

God shows his power "by pardoning and showing mercy." We ask God to pour out his grace upon us so that we may be "heirs to the treasures of heaven" (Collect).

The sacrifice we offer is Christ, "the wellspring of all blessing." We ask God to open this source of blessing for us (Prayer over the Offerings).

We pray that we may be "coheirs in glory with Christ," whose death we have proclaimed in our celebration of the Eucharistic mystery (Prayer after Communion).

Other Ideas

Take a walk or drive around your neighborhood. What do you notice that you never saw before? Where do people gather? Where are they being helped or served? What places are offering support? What do we often overlook?

Discuss in a group how people react when they see a beggar. What emotions do people feel when they see a person in this kind of need? What judgments do they make? What creative ways have they offered to help?

MON 30   #455   white   Memorial of Saint Jerome, Priest and Doctor of the Church

Lectionary for Mass

◆ FIRST READING: We hear words of promise for Jerusalem about the return of her citizens after their exile in Babylon. The Lord will again dwell within the temple in Jerusalem. Even if this seems impossible to the people, nothing is impossible for God.

◆ RESPONSORIAL PSALM: The antiphon reiterates the Lord's promise of the restoration of Jerusalem. The verses come from the end of this song of lament, perhaps from the time of the exile, and state confidently that the Lord will answer the people's cry for deliverance and restore Jerusalem. All nations (Gentiles) will come to know the Lord and revere him.

◆ GOSPEL: Perhaps it may seem strange to think of Jesus's disciples arguing among themselves, but that is exactly what is happening in today's Gospel reading. To make matters worse, they are arguing about who is the greatest in the presence of he who came to serve. They have really missed the point of Jesus's teaching. The disciples should not be concerned with greatness, but

rather, with lowliness. Jesus is dead set against any kind of elitism.

The Roman Missal

The prayers for the memorial are found in the Proper of Saints. They speak of Saint Jerome's great love for the Word of God, his "living and tender love for Sacred Scripture" (Collect). We pray that we may find in God's word "the fount of life" (Collect), and that our meditation on the Scriptures may fill us with eagerness to offer "the sacrifice of salvation" (Prayer over the Offerings).

Today's Saint

Saint Jerome (345–420) is the patron saint of scholars and librarians. With a great love of learning and books, as a monk and priest he developed a passion for the interpretation of Sacred Scripture. With a comprehensive knowledge of classical languages, Saint Jerome produced a Latin text of the entire Bible eventually known as the Vulgate. He wrote numerous commentaries on several books of the Bible, including a highly reputable work on the Gospel according to Matthew. Along with writing, he provided spiritual guidance to wealthy widows and mentored young monks in monastic discipline. Saint Jerome joins three other saints (Ambrose, Augustine, and Gregory the Great) as the first Doctors of the Church.

October
Month of the Most Holy Rosary

TUE 1   #456   white   Memorial of Saint Thérèse of the Child Jesus, Virgin and Doctor of the Church

Lectionary for Mass

◆ FIRST READING: What a vivid picture is presented in these words from Zechariah. Gentile peoples have become missionaries to one another, announcing that God is with his people and leading one another to Jerusalem.

◆ RESPONSORIAL PSALM: Today's antiphon, adapted from the First Reading, echoes the announcement of God's salvific presence with his people. Psalm 87 celebrates the glory of Jerusalem, particularly her motherhood. She has become home to people from countless nations.

◆ GOSPEL: Jesus's journey to Jerusalem—and his Passion and Death—would take firm and resolute determination. There was antagonism between the Samaritans and the Jews stemming from the time of the Babylonian Exile. The issue here, however, is not so much this antagonism but the disciples' desire to seek revenge for the Samaritans' lack of hospitality. Jesus rebukes his disciples for their violent thoughts.

The Roman Missal

The prayers for the memorial are found in the Proper of Saints. They are rich in allusions to the writings of this great saint of modern times. The Entrance Antiphon, speaks of God as "an eagle spreading its wings," a favorite image of the saint. We pray that we may "follow trustingly in the little way of Saint Thérèse" (Collect), and burn, as she did, for the salvation of all (Prayer after Communion).

Today's Saint

Saint Thérèse of Lisieux of the Child Jesus (1873–1897), known as the "Little Flower," was a spiritual athlete, but not in the same way as her contemporaries. Contrary to the spirituality of her time, which favored self-mortification and miraculous phenomena, she approached God through the ordinary experiences of everyday life. As a Carmelite nun, she coined the phrase the "Little Way," referring to her belief that every act, no matter how small, is an opportunity to meet and praise God. While struggling with the debilitating disease of tuberculosis, she wrote her spiritual autobiography, *The Story of a Soul.* Her autobiography, translated into over fifty languages, has inspired faith in the skeptic and strengthened the soul of the believer. She is patron saint of the missions and a Doctor of the Church.

W E D 2 #457, Gospel #650   white
Memorial of the Holy Guardian Angels

Lectionary for Mass

◆ FIRST READING: The book of Nehemiah offers yet another perspective on the rebuilding of the city of Jerusalem after the Babylonian Exile. Nehemiah was a servant in the court of the Persian king. He received official approbation and support to go and help rebuild the walls of the city of Jerusalem. Nehemiah interpreted the king's favor toward him as an indication of the favor of God upon him.

◆ RESPONSORIAL PSALM 137, prayed by the Jews exiled in Babylon, laments their misery in not being at home in Jerusalem, as well as the destruction of the city and its Temple. Nehemiah, in today's First Reading, exemplifies one who has not forgotten the city and seeks to restore it as soon as possible.

◆ GOSPEL: The Gospel text draws upon the Jewish tradition that every nation has an angel in heaven. Here, each person has a guardian angel. Most of the text focuses on the child and the necessity of becoming like a child—simple, open, and trusting.

The Roman Missal

The prayers and Preface for the memorial are found in the Proper of Saints. We pray that we may know the protection of the angels now, and enjoy their company in eternity (Collect). In the "dignity and splendor" of angels, we see "how infinitely great" is God (Preface).

Today's Memorial

Today we honor the countless unnamed angels assigned to guide, guard, and protect us throughout our lives. The belief in angels is supported by their mention in the Psalms and other books of the Old Testament, as well as the Gospel, as in today's passage from Matthew 18:10.

T H U 3 #458   green
Weekday

Lectionary for Mass

◆ FIRST READING: When the walls of the city of Jerusalem had been rebuilt, Ezra the priest gathered all the people for a public reading of the Law of God. In fact, the description of the event suggests a liturgical assembly. We might think of it as comparable to our own Liturgy of the Word. Note, too, that there is instruction based on the Law (perhaps like our Homily?). People of all ages, even children, were part of the assembly. Did the weeping reflect the people's sadness in realizing how far they were from being faithful to the Lord? Even this realization can lead the people to joyful thanksgiving for all that God has done for them—and for us, despite our infidelities.

◆ RESPONSORIAL PSALM 18 acclaims God's Law as a source of joy, as indeed it was in today's First Reading. The stanzas highlight all that the Lord can do for us and all that he should mean to us.

◆ GOSPEL: Jesus sends some of his followers out to proclaim the Good News of the kingdom, to bring peace and to heal. The harvest is great.

F R I 4 #459   white
Memorial of Saint Francis of Assisi

Lectionary for Mass

◆ FIRST READING: We return to the Babylonian captivity. The prophets, and in today's First Reading, the people as well, clearly perceived it as a time of punishment for Israel's infidelities.

◆ RESPONSORIAL PSALM 79: The people pray for the deliverance that they know they do not deserve. They appeal to God's glory, that it might be manifest among them, and among the nations too.

◆ GOSPEL: In this chapter on the mission of the disciples, Jesus speaks of both the reception and the rejection of their message. Acts of power and healing should lead to repentance. The rejection of the Gospel by the contemporaries of Jesus is far worse than the sins of Tyre and Sidon.

The Roman Missal

The prayers for the memorial are found in the Proper of Saints. They speak of Francis's love of poverty (Collect), his charity (Prayer after Communion), and his love for the cross (Prayer over the Offerings). The Entrance Antiphon offers a brief biography, of sorts: "Francis, the man of God, left his home behind, / abandoned his inheritance and became poor and penniless, / but the Lord raised him up."

Today's Saint

As the son of a wealthy Assisi merchant, Saint Francis (1182–1226) was destined for grand homes, exquisite clothing, and fine food. After a conversion experience he relinquished the trappings of this world to minister to lepers and preach to the spiritually hungry. His home was the earth; his clothing, humility; and his identity, that of an impoverished beggar seeking God. Many young men joined Saint Francis in this new way of life, leading to the foundation of the *frati minori* ("lesser brothers"), which eventually became known as the Friars Minor. He is perhaps one of the most popular saints in Church history, due to his love of creation as exemplified in his famous "Canticle of the Sun." Pope Pius XI described Saint Francis as *alter Christus*, meaning "another Christ."

SAT 5 #460 green
Weekday

Optional Memorial of the Blessed Virgin Mary / white

Lectionary for Mass

◆ FIRST READING: Comforting words of hope and promise addressed to the Israelites in captivity in Babylon are heard in today's First Reading. Israel's sins are acknowledged and she is encouraged to repent and return to God. As Israel's Savior, God will bring the Israelites back to their homeland.

◆ RESPONSORIAL PSALM: The theme of returning to the Lord (i.e., seeking the Lord) recurs in the first stanza of today's Psalm, with the promise that the Lord hears the prayer of those who are in need. We hear again God's promise to rebuild Jerusalem and the cities that were destroyed. The exiled people will be restored to their homeland.

◆ GOSPEL: Jesus instructs his disciples to rejoice, not so much in the acts of power they perform but, rather, in the fact that their names are written in heaven. Jesus's prayer in the second part of the Gospel stresses that the revelation the disciples have received is a gift from the Lord and a source of blessing for them.

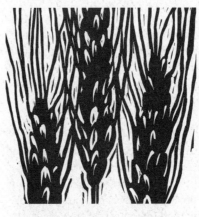

#141   green

6 Twenty-seventh Sunday in Ordinary Time

Orientation

Jesus Christ was a great teacher, and the metaphor of the mustard seed is another example of his wise approach to teaching the faith. Mustard seeds are tiny, making it an encouraging and accessible image for those who hear it. Even a tiny bit of faith is enough for the radical transformation to begin in us toward the fullness of life promised by God. Faith is our response to God's invitation to eternal life, an invitation that is continual and comes in so many ways. Like a mustard seed, the seed of faith will mature and flourish as we grow in our relationship with God through Jesus Christ.

Lectionary for Mass

◆ FIRST READING: It takes great faith not to lose hope in God in times of deep suffering and affliction. Habakkuk, in today's First Reading, exhorts his hearers to faith and hope. We may think of the word

"vision" (which occurs twice) as all God has promised, all, that hope encompasses. This hope has its time—it *will* come to fruition. The promises will be fulfilled. We must only have faith.

◆ RESPONSORIAL PSALM: Hear the word of the Lord and receive it—in your heart. Psalm 95 calls us to humble obedience to the God in whom we find strength.

◆ SECOND READING: Bear your hardships, encourages Paul, fan into even stronger flames the fervor of your zeal for the Gospel. Embrace in your heart the rich deposit of faith the Church teaches.

◆ GOSPEL: Today's Gospel consists of two rather independent sayings or teachings. The first begins with a request or prayer: "Increase our faith." Jesus's response points out the strength and power of even a little faith. The second part of the Gospel is the parable of a servant. How easy it is to think only of what we shall receive in return for whatever we do. Before the Lord, however, we are servants and whatever we do is only what we have been commanded.

The Roman Missal

We are burdened with guilt and fear, and, in the words of Saint Paul, "we do not know how to pray as we ought" (Romans 8:26). We ask God's mercy, to forgive "what conscience dreads," and to grant what we dare not ask (Collect).

Obedient to God's command, we celebrate the sacred mysteries. We ask God to "complete the sanctifying work" of redemption in us (Prayer over the Offerings).

The Prayer after Communion asks simply that we may become what we receive in the Eucharist.

Other Ideas

What stories do you know about people who, after suffering from pain or violence, have not fallen into despair but rather have renewed their faith in God? Some examples might be young people growing up in dangerous neighborhoods or soldiers at war. Can you find such a story and share it with a group or your family?

In Paul's opening lines to Timothy, he remembers Timothy's "sincere faith that first lived in your grandmother Lois and in your mother Eunice" (2 Timothy 1:5). Who has taught you faith like Timothy's grandmother and mother did? Make an effort to thank or commemorate that person this week.

Do one thing this week that demonstrates what you believe about your life as a disciple.

M O N 7 #461 white Memorial of Our Lady of the Rosary

Orientation

Pope John Paul II called the Rosary "the school of Mary," a special devotion that teaches us about the profoundly close relationship Mary shared with her Son, Jesus Christ. More than this, praying the Rosary invites us into this relationship, nurturing our faith and deepening our understanding of who Jesus Christ was for the world. The Church celebrates Our Lady of the Rosary in order to honor Mary's example and guidance to her Son. May we learn in her school how to open our lives to her Son Jesus, and how to imitate his example of sharing God's love with the world.

Lectionary for Mass

◆ FIRST READING: Today we begin the story of the prophet Jonah, a delightful and somewhat humorous story with a very strong message! Perhaps we can identify with Jonah's desire to flee from what the Lord was asking of him—at least at one time or another in our lives! As

Jonah soon discovered, there is no running away from the Lord. In today's reading, we hear of the Lord's care for this rebellious prophet who resisted his call.

◆ CANTICLE: Today's canticle is Jonah's prayer from the belly of a fish. Remember that the sea is a symbol of chaos and destruction. We know from the last line of the First Reading that the Lord heard Jonah's prayer.

◆ GOSPEL: What must I do? Tell me exactly. We all want certitude regarding what we have been asked to do, especially when it is a matter of eternal life. There are several surprising elements in the parable in today's Gospel. Why did the official religious personnel pass by the man in need? If he were dead, contact with a corpse would have rendered them defiled and therefore unfit for temple worship. But even more surprising is the way in which the question changes from "Who *is* my neighbor?" to "Which of these . . . *was* neighbor" (author's emphasis)? Jesus couches the command in a new way: *Be* neighbor by showing mercy.

The Roman Missal

The prayers for the memorial are found in the Proper of Saints. We have heard the Good News of the Incarnation of Christ; we pray that we may follow him in his Passion and Cross, and so come to "the glory of his Resurrection." It is an appropriate prayer as we honor Mary as Our Lady of the Rosary, for in the Rosary, through the Joyful, Luminous, Sorrowful, and Glorious Mysteries, we follow Christ from the Incarnation to the glory of heaven.

T U E 8 #462 green Weekday

Lectionary for Mass

◆ FIRST READING: The Lord tries again with Jonah, commissioning him to preach repentance to the Ninevites in the country of Assyria. In contrast to Jonah, the Ninevites are immediately obedient to the Lord's command. Both humans and animals underwent a period of fasting and repentance. Seeing this, the Lord relents—has a change of heart—and does not inflict the punishment that was threatened.

◆ RESPONSORIAL PSALM 130: This song of repentance is most apropos given the reading's account of the repentance of the Ninevites. Acknowledging their sins, repenting in sack cloth and ashes, fasting from food and drink, the Ninevites waited for—and received—merciful deliverance from the Lord.

◆ GOSPEL: What an interesting study in personalities is set before us today. Both Martha and Mary have great love for Jesus. Martha seems to be the manager of the home; Mary is the more quiet one. Martha's perhaps understandable reaction is: "Tell her to help me" (Luke 10:40). Her reaction reminds us how easy it is to get caught up in anxieties. In listening to Jesus, Mary has chosen the better part.

W E D 9 #463 green Weekday

Optional Memorials of Saints Denis, Bishop, and Companions, Martyrs / red; Saint John Leonardi, Priest / white

Lectionary for Mass

◆ FIRST READING: Perhaps we are surprised at Jonah's reaction when he witnesses God's merciful response to the Ninevites. Does Jonah's anger and resentment come from a bit of self-righteousness?

Jonah is more concerned with himself than with the people to whom he was sent. But God is concerned with the Ninevites and looks on them with mercy.

◆ RESPONSORIAL PSALM: The Lord is indeed merciful and gracious as the First Reading proclaims, echoing words that God himself spoke to Moses at Mount Sinai. Today's Psalm is a prayer of confident trust in the mercy of the God.

◆ GOSPEL: What a beautiful image! The disciples want to pray in the same manner that they see Jesus praying. The prayer that Jesus teaches them is what we know as the Our Father. God is Father, source of life and provider of our needs. He loves us so much! To the Father we are more important than the wrong we do, but we must turn to him for forgiveness.

Today's Saints

◆ SAINT DENIS: In Paris there still stands one of the world's oldest churches still in continuous use, the Royal Abbey of Saint Denis. Its first stones were laid in the third century. Renowned as the major burial place of the French monarchy, it owes its establishment and subsequent prestige to the presence of the relics of Saint Denis, first bishop of Paris, martyred during the third century. The legend surrounding the saint's life is complex, as three historical figures appear to have been conflated into one legendary figure. He is portrayed as Dionysius, the evangelizer of Gaul; Dionysius the Areopagite, a disciple of Paul; and later as Pseudo-Dionysius the Areopagite, the author of mystical works. Who was the real Saint Denis? Historians have not reached a consensus, partly because the stories are too good not to be told. The favorite of the French is about the beheading of Bishop Denis on the hill of Montmartre; he did not lose his head, however, for he picked it

up and walked two miles, his lips chanting the Psalms, until he reached his chosen burial spot. There his relics have remained ever since. This miracle of *céphalophorie* (picking up your head after being decapitated and walking away) is well attested to in hagiographical accounts and in medieval iconography. Besides being the patron saint of those with headaches, he is the patron of France and of the city of Paris.

Saint John Leonardi, founder of Clerks Regular of the Mother of God of Lucca, was born in Tuscany and ordained in 1572. He founded the Confraternity of Christian Doctrine and the College for the Propagation of the Faith, an important part of the Counter-Reformation.

THU 10 #464 green Weekday

Lectionary for Mass

◆ FIRST READING: "What's the use?" Haven't we all felt that way at one time or another? In today's reading, the Israelites, who have been engaged in penitential practices that are seemingly to no avail, ask this same question. The Lord did not seem to respond. To the contrary, though, the Lord did see and hear—and noted those who reverenced him and trusted in him. Their prayers would be heard, and they would be spared on the day of judgment.

◆ RESPONSORIAL PSALM 1: Today's Psalm proclaims the blessedness of all who trust in the Lord. They are like a fruitful tree planted near running waters.

◆ GOSPEL: Jesus encourages his disciples to be persistent in prayer through the parable of the persistent friend. If human parents demonstrate such watchful care for their children, how much more attentive will the heavenly Fahter be, who

gifts all who believe in Jesus with his Holy Spirit.

FRI 11 #465 green Weekday

Lectionary for Mass

◆ FIRST READING: The prophet Joel warns of an imminent day of the Lord—a day of judgment and destruction. All are to prepare for it through repentance and prayer.

◆ RESPONSORIAL PSALM: The theme of the Lord's judgment is echoed in today's antiphon. Surprisingly, perhaps, the first stanza speaks of thanksgiving, but so it should. Those who trust in the Lord have no reason to fear. They will witness God's judgment against the wicked.

◆ GOSPEL: What is the source of Jesus's power over evil? It can only be from God. The two parables at the end of the Gospel remind us that we must be ever watchful of the strength of the evil one who strives to separate us from God.

SAT 12 #466 green Weekday

Optional Memorial of the Blessed Virgin Mary / white

Lectionary for Mass

◆ FIRST READING: Joel's words announce the imminence of the day of the Lord, a time marked by signs in the heavens and on the earth, when all the nations who have done violence against God's chosen people in Judah will be judged. On that day, God, who dwells in Zion, will be a refuge for his people and they will be vindicated.

◆ RESPONSORIAL PSALM 97: Today's Psalm celebrates God's kingship and just judgments. Note the repetition of the cosmic elements mentioned in today's First Reading. On the day of judgment, God's people have every reason to rejoice.

For them, it is a day of deliverance and reward, a day of thanksgiving.

◆ GOSPEL: Faith in Jesus establishes new relationships, transcending even natural family ties. Note the emphasis on hearing the Word, and even more importantly, on doing it.

#144   green

☀13 Twenty-eighth Sunday in Ordinary Time

Orientation

Jesus heals ten lepers, restoring their health but also re-establishing them in their community, from which they had been marginalized because of their disease. The story is about healing but also about inclusion. When the one grateful leper returns to thank Jesus, we learn that he is a Samaritan, making him a double outcast as both an unpopular foreigner and a leper. Jesus shows us that through sharing in the goodness and love of God, we will learn to recognize the "other" as a cherished brother or sister made in the image and likeness of God. God's love transforms alienation and separation into community and fellowship.

Lectionary for Mass

◆ FIRST READING: Today's reading begins midway through the story of Naaman, whose skepticism in the face of the prophet's command, among other details of the story, is omitted. The focus is rather on the moment of healing. Elisha's selflessness in the face of Naaman's gratitude reminds us of the servant's response in last Sunday's Gospel reading. He was only doing what was required. Overwhelmed by the power of God at work in his life, Naaman, the Gentile, promises to worship him alone.

◆ RESPONSORIAL PSALM 98: Both the First Reading and the Gospel show God's power at work in the lives of Gentiles through the hands of Israelite intermediaries. As a result, people from all the nations sing the praises of God.

◆ SECOND READING: Never forget, writes Paul to Timothy, that Jesus Christ rose from the dead. One wonders, how could we? This belief is the cornerstone of his Christian faith. It spurs Paul on in his ministry even though it meant imprisonment; it is the source of his endurance. Paul knows that we can depend on the promises of Christ.

◆ GOSPEL: What faith these lepers had—first in approaching Jesus, believing he could cure them, and then obediently doing what he told them. A priest would have to declare them clean before they could re-enter the Israelite community. Realizing that he had been healed, one returned to thank Jesus before going to the priest.

The Roman Missal

We ask that God's grace may be with us always, going before and following after us, and that we may be "determined / to carry out good works" (Collect). It is the perfect formula for a holy life!

We ask God to accept our prayers together with the "sacrificial offerings" we present, that we may "pass over to the glory of heaven" (Prayer over the Offerings).

We pray that we who receive the Body and Blood of Christ in the Eucharist may also be "sharers of his divine nature" (Prayer after Communion).

Other Ideas

Leprosy, also known as Hansen's Disease, does not affect many people today. But Saint Damien of Moloka'i, who lived from 1840 to 1889, was a Belgian missionary priest who ministered on the Hawaiian Island of Moloka'i to inhabitants quarantined because of this disease. In 1889, he contracted leprosy and died. He was canonized on October 11, 2009. You may wish to read more about him.

Dr. Albert Schweitzer won the 1952 Nobel Peace Prize for humanitarian medical missionary work in Africa from 1933 to 1965, helping those in need. In 2004, Wangari Maathai became the first African woman and environmentalist to win. Research other Nobel Peace Prize winners. How have some been role models of caring for the poor or the earth?

#467   green

M O N 14 Weekday

Optional Memorial of Saint Callistus I, Pope and Martyr / red

Lectionary for Mass

◆ FIRST READING: Today we begin Paul's letter to the Romans. Paul begins his letters with a salutation which often names his co-workers and stresses some aspect of his ministry. In the Letter to the Romans, Paul stresses his call to be an apostle of Jesus, who is the fulfillment of all that was prophesied in the Scriptures. In particular, Paul is an apostle to the Gentiles (non-Jews). Paul also speaks of the Romans' vocation to belong to Jesus and to be holy.

◆ RESPONSORIAL PSALM 98: How fitting is today's responsorial antiphon! The Lord has indeed made known his salvation to both the Gentiles (the "nations" in the second stanza, the "ends of the earth" and the "lands" in the third) and the Jews (Israel, second stanza). We sing God's praise for all his marvelous deeds.

◆ GOSPEL: Jesus speaks to the crowd, drawing upon the heritage of the Old Testament to demonstrate that he is greater than Jonah, who preached repentance to Nineveh, and greater than Solomon, whose reputation for wisdom drew people from distant lands.

Today's Saint

Following a life of slavery and hard labor, Saint Callistus I (+ 222) was appointed deacon in charge of the Christian cemetery on the Appian Way, now called the catacomb of San Callisto. Recognized for his abounding wisdom and natural bent for leadership, he was eventually elected pope. He had many critics, due to his liberal stance regarding the forgiveness of those who had apostatized during times of persecution. Saint Callistus, heeding the commands of Christ, believed the repentant should be forgiven and welcomed back into the Church. Tradition maintains that he began the Ember Days, periods of fasting and abstinence, which are no longer observed among Catholics. He is commemorated as a martyr; he was probably killed during a public disturbance.

#468 white

TUE 15 Memorial of Saint Teresa of Jesus, Virgin and Doctor of the Church

Lectionary for Mass

◆ FIRST READING: The Jews believed that they were righteous, that is, in the right relationship with God through observance of the Law. Paul, drawing on the words of the prophet Habakkuk asserts that righteousness comes through faith (2:4). In subsequent verses, Paul attests to the revelation of God manifest in creation. As a result, those (Gentiles) who worshipped idols rather than God are not to be excused. They received the punishment they deserved. We may fittingly ask ourselves what idols we worship.

◆ RESPONSORIAL PSALM: Today's Psalm 18, a song of praise, reiterates the theme of today's First Reading: all of creation bears witness to the glory of the Creator God.

◆ GOSPEL: Jesus is once again at a meal, sharing table fellowship with his Pharisee host, a strict adherent to the law. Though welcoming his guest, the Pharisee at the same time judges him. Jesus confronts him for his hypocrisy. What matters is not what is on the outside, but what is within, particularly as expressed in loving concern for the poor through almsgiving.

The Roman Missal

The prayers for the memorial are found in the Proper of Saints. They are rich in allusions to the writings of the foundress of the Discalced Carmelites. Teresa shows the Church "the way to seek perfection" (Collect), and we hope together with her to "sing of your mercies for all eternity" (Prayer after Communion).

Today's Saint

Saint Teresa of Jesus (1515–1582), more commonly known as Saint Teresa of Avila, joined the Carmelite Convent of the Incarnation at the age of 21. Disheartened by convent life, in particular, its spiritual laxity, opulent nature, and overly social atmosphere, she began a reform movement that provided the framework for the Discalced Carmelites. Members of this new branch of Carmelites modeled themselves on the poor and crucified Christ, adopting a life of poverty and abstinence. In collaboration with Saint John of the Cross, Teresa helped bring this new way of life to the male Carmelite communities. Their reforms met with great resistance, but they moved forward with faith and persistence. Among her many writings, she is well known for two classics: *The Way of Perfection* and *The Interior Castle*.

#469 green

WED 16 Weekday

Optional Memorial of Saint Hedwig, Religious / white; Saint Margaret Mary Alacoque, Virgin / white (U.S.A.) ◆ *Memorial of Saint Marguerite d'Youville, Religious / white (Canada)*

Lectionary for Mass

◆ FIRST READING: Paul's words express an uncomfortable and disturbing message to all who pass judgment on other people without recognizing their own sin and hypocrisy. Paul voices an urgent call to repentance. We must not presume on the mercy of our impartial God at the time of judgment. All will be repaid accoring to their works.

◆ RESPONSORIAL PSALM 62: The Psalm is one of confidence and trust in God. Only one who is truly just can face God's judgment with confidence and peace.

◆ GOSPEL: Controversy between Jesus and the scribes and Pharisees pervades the Gospels. While observing the letter of the law, they miss the deeper call to love, to be righteous, and to be open to God's love and mercy. Self-justification is always dangerous.

Today's Saints

Saint Hedwig married the Duke of greater Poland, with whom she lived a pious life. Together they founded a Cistercian convent, which Hedwig entered when she was widowed.

Saint Margaret Mary Alacoque was a French Visitation nun and mystic who promoted devotion to the Sacred Heart of Jesus. In a series of visions, the form of this devotion was revealed: Holy Communion on the first Friday of each month, and the institution of the Solemnity of the Sacred Heart. Margaret Mary was criticized by the other nuns but had the support of the community's confessor, Blessed Claude de la Colombière.

Saint Marguerite d'Youville (1701–1771) is the Canadian founder of the Grey Nuns of Montreal. She was born in the Montreal suburb of Varennes and received two years of schooling at the Ursuline convent in Quebec City. At the age of 21, she married François d'Youville, a bootlegger and fur trader, with whom she had six children before his death in 1730. Before she was 30, Marguerite had experienced the loss of her father, husband, and four of her children, but her sufferings brought about a religious conversion. In 1737, her two surviving sons having entered the priesthood, Marguerite co-founded a group dedicated to helping the poor, which developed into the order known as the Grey Nuns. Saint Marguerite d'Youville died in 1771 in Montreal and was canonized by Pope John Paul II, the first Canadian to be so honored. She is a patron of widows and of those in difficult marriages.

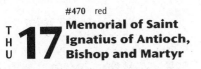

#470   red

17 THU Memorial of Saint Ignatius of Antioch, Bishop and Martyr

Lectionary for Mass

◆ FIRST READING: Our reading picks up on a theme from the beginning of Paul's letter (see Tuesday's reading): we are made righteous through faith in Jesus. There is no longer any distinction between Jews and Gentiles; all are sinners, all can be justified through faith in Jesus.

◆ RESPONSORIAL PSALM: Our antiphon acclaims God as the source of mercy and redemption. Psalm 130 is a prayer of lament, voiced by one who is conscious of sin and confidently prays for forgiveness.

◆ GOSPEL: Jesus continues his harsh condemnation of the scribes and Pharisees. They give honor to the prophets of the past, but fail to recognize the prophet who is in their midst. They seek to control access to knowledge: without striving after wisdom themselves, they try to prevent others from learning the ways of God.

The Roman Missal

The prayers for the memorial are found in the Proper of Saints. The Communion Antiphon is drawn not from Scripture, but from the words of the saint: "I am the wheat of Christ to be ground by the teeth of beasts, / that I may be found to be pure bread." This same image is repeated in the Prayer over the Offerings, which refers to Ignatius as "the wheat of Christ." We pray that the "heavenly Bread" we receive may "make us Christians in name and in deed" (Prayer after Communion).

Today's Saint

Saint Ignatius was born in the year 50 and died somewhere between 98 and 117 in Rome. An Apostolic Father and possible disciple of John the Evangelist, he served the community of Antioch as bishop. Living during the anti-Christian reign of the Roman emperor Trajan, he was sentenced to be fed to animals in the Roman Colosseum because he refused to engage in idol worship. His journey to Rome was marked by extensive writing in which he composed seven letters. These letters, directed to various churches, emphasized the humanity and divinity of Christ, the centrality of Eucharist, and the importance of Church unity.

#661   red

18 FRI Feast of Saint Luke, Evangelist

Lectionary for Mass

◆ FIRST READING: Paul always ends his letters with very personal notes, and today we hear of Luke's loyalty and fidelity in remaining with Paul even though others have deserted him. It is this mention of Luke that results in today's text as the first reading. We can surmise that it is through the presence of Luke that Paul experienced the strength of the Lord, enabling him to continue his proclamation of the Gospel to the Gentiles.

◆ RESPONSORIAL PSALM 145: Today's responsorial verse calls to mind Jesus' reference to the disciples in John's account of the Gospel as his "friends." Certainly, in writing the Gospel accounts and Acts of the Apostles, Luke makes known the glorious splendor of God's kingdom. The first two stanzas of today's Psalm could well be a description of what a Gospel "does."

◆ GOSPEL: We hear of Jesus' sending out seventy two disciples ahead of his own intended visit to various towns and places. Clearly they are to prepare his way. They are to be unencumbered by possessions, realistic about meeting opposition, people of peace, healers of the sick and proclaimers of God's kingdom.

The Roman Missal

The prayers for the feast are found in the Proper of Saints. The Gloria is said or sung today. Preface II of the Apostles is used.

One of the distinctive characteristics of the Gospel according to Luke is its portrayal of Christ as the healer who reaches out to the poor and the afflicted. The Collect speaks of Luke as the one chosen to reveal "the mystery of [God's] love for the poor." We pray that we may be true to the faith he proclaimed (Prayer after Communion).

Today's Saint

Where would we be without Saint Luke? Think how the Church's prayer would be impoverished without Mary's Magnificat, Simeon's canticle of praise on holding Jesus in his arms, and Zechariah's thanksgiving for the birth of John the Baptist. Think how our knowledge and love of the Mother of God would be diminished without Luke's accounts of the infancy of Christ, the Annunciation, the Visitation, the shepherds in the fields at the birth of the Lord, the Presentation and the finding in the Temple. Tradition tells us that Luke was a physician and artist who lived in Syria and who wrote at the end of the first century, completing Luke and Acts of the Apostles, a two-volume work, about 80 or 90 AD. He was highly educated, a gifted writer, and a knowledgeable historian as well. He probably knew, and perhaps worked with, Saint Paul.

#472   red
SAT 19 Memorial of Saints John de Brébeuf and Isaac Jogues, Priests, and Companions, Martyrs

Lectionary for Mass

◆ FIRST READING: Paul holds up Abraham as an example of one who was in right relationship with God because of his faith.

◆ RESPONSORIAL PSALM: The history of Israel is recounted in Psalm 105 and today's verses focus in particular on God's covenant with Abraham and Isaac his son. The last stanza actually refers to the exodus event, but we can hear it in today's liturgy as God leading forth his people throughout history in the joy of salvation.

◆ GOSPEL: Jesus promises a heavenly reward to those who acknowledge him before others. This is the witness to which we are called. But woe to those who are closed to the workings and movements of God's Holy Spirit.

The Roman Missal

The Collect for the memorial is found in the Proper of Saints, with the remaining prayers drawn from the Common of Martyrs: For Missionary Martyrs.

Today's Saints

We celebrate the Martyrs of North America (1642–1649), six Jesuit priests and two lay missionaries, who were killed for evangelizing New France, known today as Canada. Their missionary endeavors were successful on many levels, especially with the Huron tribe, but they were despised by the Iroquois and Mohawks, the enemies of the Hurons. The anti-Christian sentiment of the Iroquois and Mohawks led to the killing of seven priests and laypeople over an eight-year period of time. Two of the more notable figures, Saint John de Brébeuf (1593–1649) and Saint Isaac Jogues (1607–1646), both priests, formed the backbone of the mission. Three of these martyrs were killed in what is now New York state.

#147   green
☼ 20 Twenty-ninth Sunday in Ordinary Time

Orientation

In today's parable, the dishonest judge finally helps the widow because of her persistence. Jesus teaches us an important lesson: if a fallible and dishonest judge can be persuaded to do the right thing because of persistence, just think of how much more we can expect from our heavenly Father. God in heaven is the perfect judge, merciful and just, who surrounds us with his abundant grace. Jesus assures us that God hears our prayer and reaches out to us swiftly and lovingly. The story of the widow and the dishonest judge encourages us to dare to expect more when it comes to God's love for us.

Lectionary for Mass

◆ FIRST READING: The lifting up of arms and hands in the air is an ancient gesture of prayer, one that the priest still uses today at Mass. In our First Reading, Moses raises his hands in prayer, interceding with God for Israel's success in battle. Today's text teaches us to persevere and to support one another in prayer.

◆ RESPONSORIAL PSALM: The Israelites prayed today's Psalm as they journeyed on pilgrimage to the temple in Jerusalem. Note that the Psalm speaks of lifting up the eyes in prayer. We should pray this song often as we make our way through life, since it both asks for and assures God's protection on the journey.

◆ SECOND READING: Earlier in this letter, Paul specifically names Timothy's mother Eunice and grandmother Lois as his teachers (see 2 Timothy 1:5). Paul encourages Timothy to be faithful to the Scriptures that he learned in his youth and to persevere in proclaiming and teaching the Word at all costs.

◆ GOSPEL: What a comparison Jesus makes between the dishonest judge and God! We all know the feeling of being ready to do almost anything if it will mean someone will stop bothering us! How much more will God, who loves us, hear our prayers. The point of the parable is given at the outset: persevere in prayer.

The Roman Missal

We pray that our will may be what God wills, and that we may serve God "in sincerity of heart" (Collect).

The second part of the Prayer over the Offerings is a formula that occurs frequently in *The Roman Missal*. We pray that "we may be cleansed by the very mysteries we serve": the power of Christ's sacrifice on the cross, renewed at the altar, can heal, cleanse, and renew.

By the "heavenly things" in which we share, we receive present help and are prepared for eternity (Prayer after Communion).

Other Ideas

Create an outline of the story of your life using images or words. Have there ever been times when you worried that God would not be with you? In your story or on your picture, mark the times that you were uncertain, anxious, or afraid.

Widows in Jesus's time were defenseless and often unable to care for themselves. Since they usually had neither property nor the guaranteed support of family ties, they were forced to beg or become destitute. The judge was supposed to offer care and compassion to one in such need. Who in our society is in such desperate need? What does God ask us to do?

Parables such as this one were meant to move people to act. What other parables did Jesus tell that invited his disciples to reflect and respond?

#473 green
21 MON Weekday

Lectionary for Mass

◆ FIRST READING: Once again, Abraham is held up as a model of faith. Despite the fact his barren wife Sarah was well beyond childbearing age, Abraham believed against all odds that God's promise of an heir would be realized (see Genesis 15:3–6). It was truly an act of faith—Abraham was "empowered" by it. Because of this faith, he was deemed righteous. Believers of every race and time are also deemed righteous because of their faith in Jesus Christ, risen from the dead.

◆ CANTICLE: Today's response is from a canticle in the New Testament, Zechariah's hymn of praise when his son, John (the Baptist), was born. The child's birth was the fulfillment of a promise God made to Zechariah that he and his wife Elizabeth would have a child despite their old age (see Luke 1:5–25). We can also hear the words of today's canticle as ultimately fulfilled in Jesus.

◆ GOSPEL: Sadly, the situation at the beginning of today's Gospel is all too familiar. Jesus's parable touches deeply into the truth regarding riches. Ultimately earthly wealth doesn't matter, since we can't take it with us into the next life. Let us labor, instead, for riches in what matters to God.

#474 green
22 TUE Weekday

Solemnity of the Dedication of Consecrated Churches whose Date of Consecrations Is Unknown / white (Canada)

Lectionary for Mass

◆ FIRST READING: Beginning in Romans 5:12, Paul contrasts Christ with Adam, the first human creature. Through Adam, sin came into the world, through Christ, justification and life; through Adam, death; through Christ, everlasting life. How very much more has Christ done for us! His grace overflows into the lives of all who believe.

◆ RESPONSORIAL PSALM 40: Today's responsorial verse is a concise summary of the life and death of Christ: Here am I, Father, I came to earth to do your will. Christ's obedience was the perfect sacrifice, acceptable to God and accomplishing salvation.

◆ GOSPEL: We are called to be vigilant no matter how long into the night we must wait for the Master, for the coming of the Lord. The heavenly reward envisaged in this parable is a banquet served by the Master become servant himself.

Today's Solemnity

Every parish, large and small, has a solemnity on its calendar, which is its very own: its anniversary of dedication. In the *Rite of Dedication of a Church*, a church building is consecrated to divine worship, its walls are anointed with sacred Chrism, and Mass is offered on its altar for the first time. A church's dedication day is something like a birthday. It is a time to reflect on the history of the parish community and to give thanks for the great "cloud of witnesses" who have worshipped there over the years and to pray that the Gospel may continue to be preached there for generations yet to come. When the date of dedication of the church is known, this solemnity is usually celebrated on the anniversary. But for parishes whose date of dedication is not known, it is customary to celebrate the solemnity sometime in October. In Canada, that day is today!

W E D 23 #475 green Weekday

Optional Memorial of Saint John of Capistrano, Priest / white

Lectionary for Mass

◆ FIRST READING: In the verses immediately preceding today's reading, Paul speaks of our death to sin and new life in Christ as a result of our Baptism. Thus, as he says today, "we have been raised from the dead to life." Now we must live accordingly, obedient to the teachings of the Christ in whom we are baptized.

◆ RESPONSORIAL PSALM: Psalm 124 celebrates the Lord's deliverance of Israel out of Egypt. Christ's Paschal Death and Resurrection have made our passage from death to life possible. We share in this new life this through the saving waters of Baptism. Our help, our salvation, is in the name of the Lord Jesus, risen from the dead.

◆ GOSPEL: Chapter 12 of Luke contains several parables of vigilance. We hear another one today. Does our Master's (Lord's) delay in returning (to the earth at the end of time) result in our being careless? Perhaps even abusing people and things? We must be prepared to render an account. We know not the time of our Master's coming.

Today's Saint

Saint John of Capistrano was born in Italy and entered the Franciscans in 1416. He was drawn to the ascetic life and became a follower of Saint Bernardine of Siena. After his ordination, John traveled throughout Italy, Germany, Bohemia, Austria, Hungary, Poland, and Russia, preaching penance and establishing numerous communities of Franciscan renewal. When Mohammed II threatened Vienna and Rome, John, then 70, was commissioned by Pope Callistus III to lead a crusade against the invading Turks. Marching at the head of an army of 70,000 Christians, he was victorious in the battle of Belgrade in 1456.

Roman Missal Update: Possible Inclusion of an Optional Memorial for Blessed Pope John Paul II (U.S.A.)

At the time of this printing, the United States Bishops have approved the insertion of an optional Memorial for Blessed Pope John Paul II. It is awaiting approval from the Vatican. Please check www.RevisedRomanMissal.org for updates concerning the proper texts to use for his memorial from *The Roman Missal* and the Lectionary for Mass.

To tell of John Paul II's 26 years of Petrine ministry is to provide a litany of encyclicals, travels, and historic events. Not only was John Paul II the first pope to enter a synagogue since Saint Peter, but he appealed to both Jews and Christians to be "a blessing to one another," and offered repentance in the name of the Church for the Shoah. From the moment Karol Wojtyla was elected pope in October 1978, the man who had entered a clandestine seminary while living under Nazi occupation mesmerized the world. In the early years, Catholics and non-Catholics alike were attracted to the athletic man who sneaked out of his villa to ski and reached out to the young at World Youth Days.

People of many faiths prayed for him when he was shot in St. Peter's Square and were awed with the mercy he granted his assailant. And none escaped the poignancy of a feeble John Paul II praying at the Western Wall in Israel, leaving a prayer inside the wall. Even a scant follower of the pope knew that the man who forgave his assailant, traveled the world to evangelize, and sought healing in relations with the Jewish people looked to the Blessed Virgin as a model of faith. A week after taking on the Chair of Saint Peter, he brought reporters to the Marian Shrine of Mentorella outside of Rome. "I wanted to come here, among these mountains," he told them "to sing the Magnificat in Mary's footsteps." On that date, too, he told of his love for the Rosary, a remark that he recalled 24 years later in his apostolic letter *Rosarium Virginis Mariae* (RVM): "The Rosary is my favorite prayer. A marvelous prayer! Marvelous in its simplicity and depth." In that letter, he explained the Christocentric nature of the prayer. "With the Rosary, the Christian people sit at the school of Mary and are led to contemplate the beauty on the face of Christ and to experience the depths of his love." In RVM, he notes Mary's conformity to Christ: "Mary lives only in Christ and for Christ!" It is such conformity that John Paul II sought. His motto was *Totus Tuus* ("all thine"). To John Paul II, the woman who carried the Savior in her womb, who first gazed on him at birth, and stayed with him by the cross, is the person who can bring followers closest to Christ. In the apostolic exhortation *Ecclesia in America*, he called Mary "the sure path to our meeting with Christ." In *Ecclesia in America*, the pope noted that Our Lady of Guadalupe's meeting with Juan Diego evangelized beyond Mexico and voiced hope that the Mother and Evangelizer of America would guide the Church in America, "so that the new evangelization may yield a splendid flowering of Christian life."

The pope credited Our Lady of Fatima with saving his life when he was shot on May 13, 1981, the anniversary of the first apparition at Fatima. He believed that Mary guided the bullet away from his vital organs. A year after the shooting, he placed the bullet that was taken from him among the diamonds in the crown of the statue of Our Lady of Fatima (see page XX). "I wish once more to thank Our Lady of Fatima for the gift of my life being spared," he said. With the Church, many surely are thanking the man who espoused the Rosary for modeling a life of faith.

THU 24 #476 green
Weekday

Optional Memorial of Saint Anthony Mary Claret, Bishop / white

◆ LECTIONARY FOR MASS FIRST READING: It seems that the Romans were struggling to break with their pre-baptismal patterns of life. Paul encourages them to live their life for God in Christ, no longer as slaves to sin. Sin leads to death; God's gift, to eternal life.

◆ RESPONSORIAL PSALM I: Today's antiphon is Psalm 40:5, from the same Psalm that we had on Tuesday. If we look at the verse in its entirety, we see that the Psalmist contrasts the blessed one who hopes in the Lord with the person who is idolatrous or strays after falsehood, which is exactly what Paul says to the Romans. The stanzas of today's response are from Psalm 1, which likewise contrasts the just person who delights in the law of the Lord with the wicked.

◆ GOSPEL: Sadly, commitment to the Lord can sometimes result in family divisions. This was a reality in Luke's community and is still the case today. Let us pray for our families and for perseverance for those who face opposition in their commitment to the Lord.

Today's Saint

Saint Anthony Mary Claret, the son of a Spanish weaver, wanted to be a Jesuit, but ill health prevented him from entering that religious order. Instead, he became a secular priest, overseeing a parish in Spain before heading to Catalonia and the Canary Islands as a missionary. He established the Congregation of the Immaculate Heart of Mary (the Claretians), a group of priests and brothers dedicated to seeing the world through the eyes of the poor. They operate a diverse number of ministries throughout the world. Saint Anthony was instrumental in spreading the devotion to the Immaculate Heart of Mary and the Rosary.

FRI 25 #477 green
Weekday

Lectionary for Mass

◆ FIRST READING: Paul acknowledges that all people, himself included, struggle against sin. It takes real effort to live a Christian life and to avoid evil. Good intentions are not enough. Christ has already accomplished the victory and he is ready to help us. As long as we are in this mortal body, we must fight against sin and seek the help of God's grace and life within us.

◆ RESPONSORIAL PSALM 119, like Psalm 1, acclaims the Law of the Lord as the source of life. In the light of the Christ event, we can pray this Psalm to the Lord Jesus, the teacher of the new Law. In our struggle against sin, we need his compassion, his kindness, his saving help.

◆ GOSPEL: Jesus chides the crowds; they are capable of interpreting the signs of nature, but can't discern the sign of the present moment marked by his presence among them. The saying at the end of the Gospel encourages Jesus's listeners to work out their differences and to seek reconciliation among themselves rather than resort to law courts, which will only result in punishment.

SAT 26 #478 green
Weekday

Optional Memorial of the Blessed Virgin Mary / white

Lectionary for Mass

◆ FIRST READING: "If the Spirit of the one who raised Jesus from the dead dwells in you"—what powerful words at the conclusion of today's reading! And let there be no doubt—the Spirit of the One who raised Jesus from the dead does indeed dwell in us through Baptism. Yes, we live in mortal bodies, we struggle against the flesh (Paul's word for anything which stands in opposition to the Spirit of God), but we are victorious in the spirit of Christ. He is our life now and will raise us to eternal life in the age to come.

◆ RESPONSORIAL PSALM: Today's Psalm speaks of the deep human longing to see the face of God. Psalm 24 is a processional Psalm used in the Temple liturgy. The second stanza calls our attention to what is required of the one who would be in the presence of the Lord. Is not our life a "procession" to the heavenly Temple where we will be in the presence and see the face of the living God?

◆ GOSPEL: A tragic incident involving loss of life is reported to Jesus. According to the popular mentality, this was punishment for sin. Jesus warns that a worse fate awaits those who refuse to take his words to heart and turn from evil.

Perhaps Jesus and our heavenly Father are a bit like the gardener in the parable in the second half of the Gospel: ever patient, always providing opportunities for growth and repentance.

☀ 27 #150 green
Thirtieth Sunday in Ordinary Time

Orientation

In a culture that values independence and self-sufficiency, it can be hard to keep in mind our utter dependence on God's grace in our lives. God gives us life, and invites us to live it to the fullest by loving and serving those around us. All life is a response to God's grace, a humble acceptance of the greater reality that God has revealed to us through Jesus Christ. When we brag like the Pharisee does in today's parable, we fool ourselves about the nature of our relationship with God. The tax collector, more conscious of his shortcomings and limitations than the Pharisee, also has a better sense of the truth: that we are utterly reliant on God's help to get us through, because we are too limited to do it on our own.

Lectionary for Mass

◆ FIRST READING: Though not "unduly partial," God does show special care for the poor, the oppressed, and the helpless—those with no one to provide for their needs. This is clear not only from God's actions in the history of Israel, but also in the commands of his law (see, for example, Exodus 22:21). The Lord hears and answers their cries for help.

◆ RESPONSORIAL PSALM: What we might call God's preferential option for the poor and helpless is evident in today's Responsorial Psalm as well, a hymn of praise confessing God's justice and deliverance of those who are oppressed. The psalmist's confession of what God has done is meant as a witness and incentive to hope for others (end of first stanza).

◆ SECOND READING: What Paul says about himself to Timothy conveys the image of one who serves God willingly. Paul uses both the cultic language of sacrifice and images from athletic competition (the race, the crown) in speaking of his own discipleship. As in both the First Reading and the Responsorial Psalm, Paul likewise attests to his experience of the Lord's deliverance from all that threatened him.

◆ GOSPEL: The introduction to today's parable warns about being overly convinced of our own righteousness. The Pharisees took great pride in their observance of the Law and so considered themselves to be in right relationship with God because of it. Note, however, that the Pharisee prayed not to God, but to himself (Luke 18:11). The tax collector is the one who prayed to God willingly in humility and repentance. By doing so, this outcast and reputed sinner is the one who receives mercy and justification from God.

The Roman Missal

We pray for an increase in the theological virtues of faith, hope, and charity. Loving what God commands, we hope to inherit what God promises (Collect).

We pray that everything we do in God's service may be done for God's glory (Prayer over the Offerings).

The sacraments bring us the real but veiled presence of Christ. We ask God to bring his sacraments to perfection in us, so that we may one day "possess in truth" what we now "celebrate in signs" (Prayer after Communion).

Other Ideas

Read the four brief chapters of Paul's second Letter to Timothy. In a group, discuss the images Paul uses, such as the image of running a race. How do his words give hope and resolve to disciples who are trying to live as witnesses to Christ?

Make a list of things that you profess to believe about your faith. Make a second list of the actions that you must take to live out your beliefs. Discuss your lists with a friend. How does the faith you profess match the actions you take?

On a page of drawing paper or newsprint, jot down some ways of offering praise and thanksgiving to God. Post the paper in your home and add to it during the week. Ask your family or household members to add to it as well.

M O N 28 #666 red
Feast of Saints Simon and Jude, Apostles

Lectionary for Mass

◆ FIRST READING: Our unity in Christ abolishes all distinctions between us. Through our common faith, we are united to Christ and to one another: as brothers and sisters in the family of God, fellow citizens of God's holy city, the household of God, a temple or dwelling place of God. On this feast of Saints Simon and Jude, are we aware of how our faith today has been built on the foundation of the Apostles' witness centuries ago?

◆ RESPONSORIAL PSALM 19: In its original context, today's Psalm spoke of the witness of the heavens to the glory of the Creator God. On this feast of Saints Simon and Jude, we celebrate the witness of the Apostles who brought the Gospel message throughout all the earth.

◆ GOSPEL: Little is known about the Apostles whose feast we celebrate today. Simon is identified as a zealot, someone zealous to re-establish the nation of Israel and be rid of Roman domination. We might even go so far as to think of him as somewhat of a revolutionary. Of Jude, we know only that he is the son of James. Jesus chose these and the other Apostles after spending a night in prayer.

The Roman Missal

The prayers on this feast of the two Apostles are found in the Proper of Saints. The Gloria is said or sung, and one of the Prefaces of the Apostles is used. Simon and Jude are mentioned in Eucharistic Prayer 1.

Today's Saints

Today we honor two Apostles about whom we know very little. Tradition maintains that Saint Simon the Zealot preached missions throughout Persia and Egypt. Saint Jude, not to be confused with Judas Iscariot, is the patron of hopeless causes and is called Thaddeus in the Gospel according to Matthew and the Gospel according to Mark. It is believed that he engaged in missionary work in Mesopotamia and Persia. Both Apostles are thought to have been martyred in Persia, and their relics were transferred to Saint Peter's Basilica in Rome sometime during the seventh or eighth century.

TUE 29 #480 green
Weekday

Lectionary for Mass

◆ FIRST READING: All creation—nature and humankind—is being transformed. Creation is in labor like a mother giving birth, as we come to be in the new life God has ordained for us. The Spirit is within us, pushing us on to this new life. All that we must suffer now pales in comparison with the life that is coming to be.

◆ RESPONSORIAL PSALM: In its original context, Psalm 126 celebrated Israel's deliverance from exile in Babylonia. Christian tradition has long viewed our life on earth as a sort of exile from our heavenly homeland. The Psalm speaks of joy in light of what the Lord has done and prays for full restoration. The juxtaposition of weeping and sadness with joy is yet another link with the First Reading.

◆ GOSPEL: There are two images for the kingdom of God in today's Gospel, and Jesus's Palestinian listeners would be familiar with both from everyday life: a mustard seed and grains of yeast. Though small at first, they eventually have tremendous effects. The tiny mustard seed grows into a large bush, which provides shelter and a home for the birds of the air. The small grains of yeast cause flour to expand and become bread for human nourishment. And so it is with the kingdom of God.

WED 30 #481 green
Weekday

Lectionary for Mass

◆ FIRST READING: Much of Romans 8 has to do with the powerful presence of God's Spirit in our lives. Today's text focuses on the help that the Spirit gives us in our weakness and in our prayer. Do we recognize what is available to us? Do we draw on it? Do we truly believe that with the Spirit's help and power, all things in our life can work together for good?

◆ RESPONSORIAL PSALM 131: Today's Psalm is a cry for help against the threat of enemies. The psalmist is confident in God's mercy and help. When it is received and the enemy is overcome, the psalmist will sing God's praise with thanksgiving.

◆ GOSPEL: Entering the kingdom of God demands the spiritual strength that comes from faithful adherence to the words and commands of the Lord. Many who are self-assured by virtue of their religious practices may not be as secure in the eyes of the Lord as they are in their own. Similarly, some of those deemed unfit for the kingdom by self-appointed judges may, in fact, be worthy of a higher place.

THU 31 #482 green
Weekday

Lectionary for Mass

◆ FIRST READING: Paul is all too familiar with opposition and suffering in his life, especially from those who did not receive his message about Jesus Christ. No matter how great the difficulties experienced, no matter how overwhelming the suffering, Paul is convinced that the love of Christ Jesus the Lord remains with us. Nothing, absolutely nothing, can separate us from that love.

◆ RESPONSORIAL PSALM 109: Today's Psalm is a prayer that cries out for God's mercy and deliverance in times of distress. If we look at the Psalm in its entirety, we discover that the psalmist identifies the suffering as a result of false accusation. The psalmist has fasted in prayer for God's deliverance and promises to thank God publicly for his help.

◆ Gospel: Like today's psalmist and like other prophets before him, Jesus knew false accusation and opposition. Herod, in particular, is mentioned in today's text. Jesus senses the imminence and inevitability of his death. Yet, in fidelity to the call he has received he must continue on his journey to Jerusalem. In today's text, Jesus employs the image of a mother hen carefully gathering and protecting her chicks under her wing to speak of his longing to gather Jerusalem's children into the fullness of life and salvation. Though acclaimed the messenger of salvation as he enters Jerusalem, he is ultimately rejected and put to death.

November
Month of the Holy Souls

FRI 1 #667 white
Solemnity of All Saints
HOLYDAY OF OBLIGATION

Orientation

Christian iconography has long solidified for us what a saint is through specific imagery: halos, expressions of ecstatic joy or stark, pious serenity, and a general otherworldly appearance. Saints are people who seem to have transcended our world, even in their lifetimes. Stories of their miracles, ascetic practices, and martyrdoms abound. Because of these extraordinary details, it is easy to put our saints in heaven in some category other than our day-to-day experience. But it would be a mistake to do so. In today's Gospel passage, we hear the Beatitudes: Jesus's descriptions about a holy, saintly life. Meekness, faithfulness, righteousness, peacefulness, and cleanliness of heart are virtues we can all strive for in our lives, and we honor our saints for having done so in theirs. Each honored saint in heaven lived a life like you and I, but through God's grace lived it to the fullest.

May they show us the way to the everyday holiness that will lead us into their company in heaven.

Lectionary for Mass

◆ First Reading: John recounts his visions of two groups of people who are gathered in heaven in the presence of the victorious Lamb of God and the enthroned God. The 144,000 evokes the fullness of the 12 tribes of Israel whose faithfulness is rewarded. The universal scope of salvation includes every nation, race, and people. All have been faithful. All have been victorious, having endured a time of great distress.

◆ Responsorial Psalm 24: Today's antiphon perhaps best describes us as we wait to enter our heavenly home and be counted among those in the presence of God. The second stanza directs our thoughts to what is required of those who would dwell in the Lord's presence.

◆ Second Reading: We are already children of God in the here and now, says John. But his words also touch on the unfathomable mystery of what we have yet to become: we shall be like God and we shall see God as he is.

◆ Gospel: In today's Gospel reading we hear the Beatitudes from Matthew's account of the Gospel. Notice that there are nine in today's text, the last one being a reference to those who are persecuted—also a link with today's First Reading. The first and eighth Beatitudes speak of the blessedness, or happiness, of those who are poor in spirit (who know their need for and dependence upon God) or who suffer because of their righteous conduct. It is an inner happiness that God alone can give, and it is the realization of life in God's kingdom. The other Beatitudes speak of the heavenly reward that is yet

to be realized. Suffering and sorrow are inevitable on the way to the kingdom. Meekness, mercy, integrity, and "making peace" must all be manifest in the one who would dwell on God's mountain.

The Roman Missal

The prayers and Preface are found in the Proper of Saints. The Gloria and the Creed are said or sung today.

This great solemnity of all the saints is a gift to us from God. In the Collect, we ask God to grant us reconciliation with him through their prayers.

We believe that the saints are already with God in heaven, "assured of immortality." In the Prayer over the Offerings, we pray that we may "experience their concern for our salvation" through their powerful intercession.

The Preface offers a beautiful vision of heaven, not as a far-off destination, but as home. The city of God is "our mother," filled with a great array of the saints, "our brothers and sisters." We are on a homeward journey, "pilgrims advancing by faith," with all the saints to give us the example of holy lives and the help of their prayers.

The Prayer after Communion echoes the language of pilgrimage in the Preface: We pray that "we may pass from this pilgrim table / to the banquet of our heavenly homeland." In honoring the saints, we adore God, who is "wonderful" in his saints.

Other Ideas

This is a good opportunity to learn more about the saints. Find books at your parish or public library, or use your favorite search engine to find brief biographies of saints that interest you. Particularly striking artistic depictions of the saints can be found on the tapestries decorating the nave of Our Lady of the Angels Cathedral in Los Angeles.

From the main page of the website (http://www.olacatheddral.org/), click on "art," then "tapestries," and then choose "view north tapestries gallery" and "view south tapestries gallery." These are people you want to befriend!

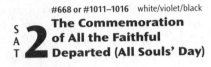

#668 or #1011–1016   white/violet/black

2 SAT
The Commemoration of All the Faithful Departed (All Souls' Day)

Orientation

The Commemoration of All the Faithful Departed, or All Souls' Day, is a moment in the Church's calendar to recognize God's enduring love that binds us all together. As we learn from Saint Paul in the First Letter to the Corinthians, love is eternal: it endures when all else passes away. This eternal love compels us to keep our beloved dead in mind on this day. Out of love, we recall and pray for our beloved dead, hoping and trusting in God's mercy to welcome them into the glory of heaven. May all of God's people, past and present, continue to share in God's love now and forever.

Lectionary for Mass

Please note that a wide selection of readings is offered in Lectionary #668. What follows are the author's suggestions.

◆ FIRST READING (WISDOM 3:1–9): In appearance, death can seem to be the absolute end of life, beyond which there is nothing more, as the first lines of this reading suggest. This is far from the truth, as the first-century author of the Book of Wisdom realized. There is hope of immortality and everlasting blessing. What beautiful images for death: God "took one" to himself (Wisdom 3:6); God's faithful people "abide with him in love" (Wisdom 3:9). Note also the references to shining and darting about like sparks (Wisdom 3:7). This is an image of the transformation that the just will undergo in the age to come; they will be like the angels who are described with similar imagery in the Scriptures.

◆ RESPONSORIAL PSALM 23 is a much loved prayer of confidence, whose image of the dark valley represents all our fears and unknowns regarding death. But there is no need to fear; we are led by the Lord to a place of rest and joyful fullness of life in the house of the Lord.

◆ SECOND READING (PHILIPPIANS 3:20–21): God's word assures us that our weak and lowly bodies will be transformed to conform to the image of the glorious Risen Christ. Our eyes have yet to see what is in store for us in the age to come.

◆ GOSPEL (JOHN 14:1–6): What Jesus has to say to the disciples at the Last Supper reflects his awareness of the imminence of his own death. Perhaps what can speak to us the most on All Souls' Day is the image, repeated here yet again, of Jesus coming to take us to himself at the time of death (see John 14:3). He is the way to the Father, the way to our heavenly home.

The Roman Missal

Three complete sets of prayers are provided in the Proper of Saints, and any of the Prefaces for Masses for the Dead may be used. On this commemoration, we pray that we may have new faith in Christ, risen from the dead, and new hope for our departed brothers and sisters (Collect I). We offer the sacrifice of the Mass for the cleansing of those "once cleansed in the waters of Baptism" (Prayer over the Offerings II), that they may know "the fullness of eternal joy" (Prayer after Communion III).

Other Ideas

Display holy cards from funerals of loved ones, photographs, or other mementoes of family members or friends who have gone before you. Read the Beatitudes often this month, and think of your deceased loved ones who exemplified them. Clean up the area around the graves of deceased loved ones and place flowers on the graves if weather permits. Pray for the souls of all who have died, especially those who have no one to pray for them. Bake soul cakes, which are little spice cakes about the size of a biscuit (recipes can be found online). According to tradition, these cakes originated during the Middle Ages in Wales, Ireland, and England, and were given to children and the poor who went door to door as they prayed for the dead on All Souls' Day. Folklore held that each cake eaten represented a soul freed from purgatory. It is believed that our Halloween custom of trick-or-treat grew out of this tradition.

#153   green
☀ 3
Thirty-first Sunday in Ordinary Time

Orientation

One of the most poignant details in the story of Zaccheus is the moment his newfound joy at welcoming the Lord to his house is possibly jeopardized by the judgmental grumbling of the crowd. We can imagine his panic, fearing perhaps that when Jesus hears the grumbling he will change his mind. He fervently promises to amend his ways to convince the Lord, not realizing that Jesus Christ reaches out to us because of pure grace. We cannot earn a visit from Christ. Yet we can rest assured that he does come to us, even if we are as unworthy as Zaccheus. Negative comments will not change God's enduring love for us, a love that reaches out to us even in our darkest, lowest moments.

Lectionary for Mass

◆ FIRST READING: Our text from the Book of Wisdom focuses on God the creator, not in terms of his power, but in terms of his mercy and love for what he has created. What a tender God! Our loving and merciful God knows our sinfulness and failures, and takes the initiative in leading us back to himself.

◆ RESPONSORIAL PSALM 145: What response can we make to our God for his goodness and loving mercy other than praise and thanksgiving, as is voiced throughout today's Psalm. The Lord our God is faithful, and in his mercy, he lifts up all who fall.

◆ SECOND READING: Acknowledging God's power at work in them, Paul prays for the Thessalonians, that they may be worthy of the calling they have received. What a beautiful wish: that the Lord Jesus be glorified in them, and they in him. Would that it also be realized in us! We, like the Thessalonians, must be firmly grounded in our faith.

◆ GOSPEL: In Jesus's day, tax collectors were a despised lot. They worked for the Romans, the Gentile power who ruled their land. Tax collectors commonly supplemented their income with a surcharge. It was with this despised man who was so eager to see Jesus that he climbed a tree for a better look, and it was at this man's home that Jesus chose

to stay. What a change in Zaccheus as a result! How are we changed by Jesus's presence with us?

The Roman Missal

Even to praise God is God's gift. We pray that "we may hasten without stumbling" to the promises of God (Collect).

We pray that our "sacrificial offerings" to God may be pure and bring us "a holy outpouring" of God's mercy (Prayer over the Offerings).

We pray that God's power might be at work in us, so that the gift we receive in the Eucharist may prepare us to receive what it promises: eternal life (Prayer after Communion).

Other Ideas

What people or groups are victimized or ostracized by their reputation or others' prejudice? How does Jesus invite us to act differently, rather than going along with the crowd's perception and judgment? When have you had to personally break from the crowd?

What practice of caring for the environment could you add to your family's life or to your parish's routine? Could you recycle paper, grow native plants or trees, or install weather-stripping? The list is large and varied.

#485   white

M O N 4 Memorial of Saint Charles Borromeo, Bishop

Lectionary for Mass

◆ FIRST READING: Paul comes close to making the claim that the mission to the Gentiles resulted from the Jews' rejection of the Gospel. It is a point that serves his argument well. Only in the experience of our disobedience and sin can we know (personally experience) the mercy of God. God's plan, God's ways are mysterious—but in him, in them, we find life. "To God be glory forever!"

◆ RESPONSORIAL PSALM: The psalmist's prayer arises from an experience of distress and cries out for God's salvation. Is this not our experience when we are aware of our sinfulness? God is not deaf to the cries of those who are his own.

◆ GOSPEL: The theme of selfless love and concern for the needs of others is likewise heard in today's Gospel. We should reach out to the less fortunate who have no means to repay us rather than to those who can and do repay us.

The Roman Missal

The prayers for this memorial are found in the Proper of Saints. Saint Charles was a leading figure in the internal reforms of the Church following the Protestant Reformation. In the Collect, we pray that his reforming spirit may live on, that the "Church may be constantly renewed" and conform "herself to the likeness of Christ."

Today's Saint

Saint Charles Borromeo (1538–1584), a doctor of civil and canon law, was a great champion of the Church redefining itself in light of the Protestant Reformation. As Archbishop of Milan, he promulgated the reforms of the Council of Trent, giving special attention to liturgical and clerical renewal. Other significant contributions he made to the Church include the establishment of new seminaries for the education of the clergy, defining a code of moral conduct for clergy, and founding the Oblates of Saint Ambrose, a society of diocesan priests, to enforce the reforms of Trent. Saint Charles adopted a simple life in which he responded to the needs of the poor and sick by providing monetary and spiritual support.

TUE 5 #486 green
Weekday

Lectionary for Mass

◆ FIRST READING: Paul uses the analogy of a human body with its varied and interrelated parts to describe the Body of Christ, the Church, with its varied and interrelated—and necessary—gifts. Paul encourages all Christians to use the gifts they have received for service to others. The second part of the reading consists of a series of exhortations on the practicalities of living a Christian life, both in relation to the Lord and to one another.

◆ RESPONSORIAL PSALM 131: Today's response is the prayer of one who has emptied himself or herself in order to be filled with, and focused on, the Lord who alone is the source of our peace. The peaceful image of a child resting on its mother's breast describes the psalmist's experience of inner peace, rooted in the Lord.

◆ GOSPEL: Today's text is a continuation of Gospel passages heard over the past several days. It begins with a saying looking forward to the heavenly banquet. The parable illustrates the relationship between our responses to God's invitation and our participation in the banquet. Are we among those who find excuses not to come? The Master desires that his banquet be filled. Those present may be the very ones we least expect or perhaps even shun (the blind, the sick, the widowed, the outcast, etc.), but who nonetheless responded to God's call.

WED 6 #487 green
Weekday

Lectionary for Mass

◆ FIRST READING: Paul's practical exhortations continue, today focusing exclusively on our relationship with our neighbor. The whole law is fulfilled when the commandment to love one's neighbor as oneself is observed.

◆ RESPONSORIAL PSALM 112: The blessedness spoken of in today's antiphon is a deep happiness that is the Lord's blessing and the reward of the one who is faithful. The stanzas of the Psalm give the criteria by which one is deemed worthy to receive the Lord's blessing.

◆ GOSPEL: If we would embrace discipleship, we must first consider the cost; specifically, we must be truly willing to put our relationship with the Lord before all other relationships and possessions.

THU 7 #488 green
Weekday

Lectionary for Mass

◆ FIRST READING: Romans 14 is primarily concerned with the attitudes—and judgments—that members of the community have toward one another when there are differences of opinion about religious practices and customs (see Romans 14:1–5). Paul commands the honoring, not the judging, of the other's view. In Christian community we are brothers and sisters of one another. The various customs and practices are to be observed for the Lord, to whom we all belong, for whom we live, for whom we die. It is the Lord who judges.

◆ RESPONSORIAL PSALM 27: In its original context, the Psalm referred to the good things of the Lord in this life, despite threats from opponents. Juxtaposed with our reading from Romans, we easily think

of the heavenly land of the living. The psalmist's longing is for God's dwelling place in the temple in Jerusalem; for us, it is for God's heavenly dwelling place. For this we wait with confidence, courage, and longing.

◆ GOSPEL: To sit at table together and share a meal signified the acceptance and welcome of the other person(s). Such was Jesus's attitude toward sinners. The two parables he tells in today's Gospel convey the joy of the heavenly Father when a sinner, found by Jesus, finds salvation in him.

FRI 8 #489 green
Weekday

Lectionary for Mass

◆ FIRST READING: What powerful and consoling words Paul speaks to the Romans in the first line of today's reading! Could the same be said of our local community? As we draw near to the conclusion of the letter, we find Paul reiterating that his mission to the Gentiles is a grace given to him by God. His ministry is an offering to God. Anything he accomplished is the result of Christ working in him through the power of the Spirit.

◆ RESPONSORIAL PSALM 122: The Lord did indeed reveal his saving power to the nations (Gentiles) through his servant Paul. Like Paul, the psalmist acclaims the Lord as the one who has accomplished marvelous deeds, revealing his salvation to the Gentiles even as he is mindful of his covenant with Israel. We have seen the Lord's salvation and joyfully sing his praise.

◆ GOSPEL: Today's parable of the steward who squandered his master's property stands in stark contrast with the example of Paul who was such a faithful servant of the Gospel with which he was entrusted! Commentators on this parable point out the necessity of understanding Palestinian business practices of the time. The steward was the owner's representative in financial matters and would normally add on his own commission to the debt. Accordingly, by reducing the debts, the steward was foregoing his own commission. In this was the prudence for which he was commended.

SAT 9 #671 white
Feast of the Dedication of the Lateran Basilica

Orientation

The Lateran Basilica of Saint John is the cathedral church for the diocese of Rome and the seat of the Bishop of Rome, which is the ancient and official title of the pope. As with many other places in Rome, the site of the basilica has a long and impressive history. The first Christian basilica on the spot was originally a meeting hall (the meaning of the word "basilica") that belonged to the Laterani family who worked for the imperial court . It was given as a gift to the Bishop of Rome by the Roman emperor Constantine during the fourth century. Only a few decades before, Christians were still being persecuted and martyred throughout the empire. Now they had found favor with the most powerful man in the Roman Empire, who would become the first emperor to convert to Christianity at the end of his life. The Lateran Basilica is a symbol of this transition, from a marginal and persecuted faith community to the great Church almost synonymous with Rome today.

Lectionary for Mass

◆ FIRST READING: Today's First Reading is Ezekiel's vision of the life-giving waters that flow from the dwelling place of God. What a vision of hope this must have been for the people exiled from their homeland. All creatures flourish in these waters of life whose source is God. Their fruits provide nourishment and healing.

◆ RESPONSORIAL PSALM 46: Our antiphon and the second stanza of the Psalm echo the theme of the life-giving waters flowing from God's holy temple. This Psalm is one of confidence as it acknowledges God's presence and strength in times that shake us.

◆ SECOND READING: What a profound image is given us in this reading, especially in light of the First Reading and Responsorial Psalm. *We* are God's building. *We* are God's holy place. God's life-giving water flows in us (see John 7:38).

◆ GOSPEL: Jesus's body is the true dwelling place of God, the true temple. "Destroy it," he tells his adversaries, "and it will be raised" (author's paraphrasing). His actions, in driving out those who were making God's house a place for their own financial profit, challenge us to ask ourselves what is going on in our hearts, since through Baptism, God now dwells in us.

The Roman Missal

The prayers and Preface for this feast are found in the Proper of Saints. The Gloria is said or sung. The prayers are the same as those for the Dedication of a Church, outside the church building. They speak of the "living and chosen stones" of the Church, the people of God (Collect). The Church is not a building—but "the Church, the Bride of Christ, [is] foreshadowed in visible buildings" (Preface). The Prayer after Communion reminds us that by our sharing in the Eucharist, we are "the temple" of God's grace.

Other Ideas

As sacramental people, we care about concrete objects, and what's more concrete than a major church building constructed of marble and adorned with rich artwork? Paul tells us we, too, are God's building. That means we, too, are sacramental and speak through our very presence of the things of God. Make a point this week to let your physical presence speak of the goodness and glory of God. Perhaps that means more formal or more festive attire. Perhaps it means putting a smile or a bigger smile on your face. But it may also mean caring for the "temple" of your body with the level of care and attentiveness one would give to a grand basilica.

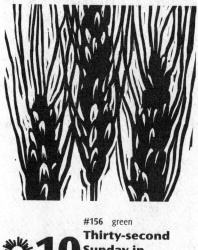

☀ 10 #156 green
Thirty-second Sunday in Ordinary Time

Orientation

The Sadducees were a Jewish philosophical sect, who among other things, did not believe in the afterlife, heaven, or the Resurrection. In today's Gospel passage, some Sadducees try to challenge Jesus on this point, inventing the far-fetched hypothetical example of the woman who marries seven brothers. Jesus cuts through the word-games and gets to the point: our God is the Source and Author of life, and God's gift of life is full and eternal. Believing in the afterlife grants our lives a whole different meaning-making lens. Looking to heaven fills us with joyful trust and hope in life, as well as comfort and healing about those who have gone before us. Like Abraham, Isaac and Jacob, we can hope to join the ranks of the saints in heaven, who surround the throne of God as a cloud of witnesses to the gift of eternal life.

Lectionary for Mass

◆ FIRST READING: This is the account of eight Jewish martyrs, a mother and her seven sons, who attest to their belief in the resurrection of the dead. Their martyrdom took place at the time of Greek rule over Palestine. These brave martyrs chose death rather than to disobey the law of the Lord. Encouraged by their mother, the brothers confessed their belief in being raised up by God after their death.

◆ RESPONSORIAL PSALM 17: One who is upright and faithful in keeping God's law cries out for deliverance in today's Psalm. Notice the reference to "waking" in the last line of the third stanza. Juxtaposed with today's First Reading, we can hear it as a reference to living in the presence of the Lord after the sleep of death.

◆ SECOND READING: The first part of this reading is actually a prayer for the Thessalonians to be strengthened in what they say and do. In the second, Paul asks the Thessalonians to pray for him and his companions in the ministry of evangelization (note the specific mention of deliverance which echoes today's Responsorial Psalm). The last part of the reading expresses confidence that the Lord will strengthen and protect the community.

◆ GOSPEL: Today's Gospel, like our First Reading, looks to the resurrection in the age to come. The Sadducees were a sect within Judaism who, unlike the Pharisees, did not believe in resurrection. The Sadducees held only to what was revealed in the Law of Moses, and resurrection was a later development in understanding. Our resurrected life will be completely other than what we know now in this life.

In the age to come, we will be gloriously transformed like the Risen Christ.

The Roman Missal

We ask God to "keep from us all adversity," not so that we may carry out our own plans, but so that "we may pursue in freedom of heart / the things that are" God's (Collect).

In the Mass, we celebrate "in mystery" the Passion of Christ. We pray that we may always honor this great mystery with "loving devotion" (Prayer over the Offerings).

We ask "the grace of integrity" for all those who have received God's "heavenly power" through sharing in the "sacred gift" of the Eucharist (Prayer after Communion).

Other Ideas

Name some images of God from the various readings or from Jesus's teachings to his disciples. You may need to look over the readings from the past few weeks to create your list. You might pay special attention to the images in the Psalms.

Often, we wait until someone we love dies to think about life after death. In a group, talk about what it means to be raised into new life by God. How do we keep that faith in the midst of pain and sorrow?

Name some people who have died for their beliefs. Your list might include martyrs and saints of the Church. Are there others who have died in the face of persecution? What do you think gave them courage?

#491 white

11 Memorial of Saint Martin of Tours, Bishop

M
O
N

Lectionary for Mass

◆ FIRST READING: The Book of Wisdom begins with an exhortation to seek the Lord in integrity of heart, in goodness and righteousness. We

are assured that he will manifest himself to us. However, the Spirit of the Lord shuns deceit and evil. The Spirit of God knows what is in the human heart. Let us never forget this.

◆ RESPONSORIAL PSALM: Our antiphon is a prayer for God's guidance. Psalm 139 acknowledges God as one who knows every aspect of human existence, our thoughts, our speech, our actions. We should be mindful of his all-knowing presence.

◆ GOSPEL: Today's Gospel reading includes: a warning against being a cause of scandal; an exhortation to forgiveness regardless of the number of times we are wronged; and a teaching on the power of faith. How do the images of the millstone and the mustard seed help us to understand Jesus's message?

The Roman Missal

The prayers for this memorial are found in the Proper of Saints. We pray that we may be united with Christ in life and in death (Collect), "in tribulation" and "in prosperity" (Prayer over the Offerings), as Saint Martin was.

Today's Saint

Saint Martin of Tours (316–397) was forced by his father, a pagan officer in the Roman army, to join the military. While serving in the military, he had a life-changing event in which he cut his cloak in half to clothe a freezing beggar. Following this encounter he had a vision of Christ wrapped in the cloak. As a result of this experience, Saint Martin chose to be baptized and declared himself a soldier of peace for Christ, refusing to participate in any act of violence. He took up the life of a hermit, thereby introducing monasticism into Gaul. Following his election as bishop of Tours he continued living as a monk, but made numerous trips to visit his people and establish new monasteries. The people of Gaul converted to Christianity due to his example.

#492   red

TUE 12 Memorial of Saint Josaphat, Bishop and Martyr

Lectionary for Mass

◆ FIRST READING: God created human beings in his own image (Genesis 1:26–27) to be immortal, but death came into the world through Satan—an allusion to the story of the sin of Adam and Eve in Genesis 3. God, however, does not abandon those whom he intended for immortality. The author of Wisdom speaks at length regarding the fate of the souls of the just who have died: they are in God's hand (3:1); they are in peace (3:3). Verse 7 speaks of their "visitation," that is, the time of divine judgment. They shall be gloriously transformed; they shall shine like sparks. The imagery is also used in other biblical and extra-biblical literature of the time to describe heavenly angelic beings. (Note: this same belief was expressed in last Sunday's Gospel!) The souls of the just are destined for a glorious heavenly reward with the Lord.

◆ RESPONSORIAL PSALM: Today's Psalm is a hymn of praise voiced by the just who cried out for deliverance from their distress and who experienced the Lord's salvation.

◆ GOSPEL: Does it seem like a lot is being asked of servants? We must do all that we have been commanded by the Lord, especially to love and serve one another.

The Roman Missal

The prayers for this memorial are found in the Proper of Saints. We pray that we may be "strengthened by the same Spirit" that gave Saint Josaphat the courage to lay down his life for the sheep (Collect). We

ask for "a spirit of fortitude and peace," so that we may work for Church unity as he did (Prayer after Communion).

Today's Saint

As a young man, Saint Josaphat (1580–1623) was excited about the possibility of the Orthodox metropolitan city of Kiev, comprising Belarussians and Ukrainians, reuniting with the Church of Rome. When he was elected Archbishop of Polotsk, Lithuania, he worked tirelessly to continue the efforts to bring the Orthodox communities of Kiev into full communion with the Catholic Church. Many people were strongly opposed to this reunion; therefore, they established a rival hierarchy and set up groups to defame his name. While preaching in a particularly hostile city, he was murdered. His commitment to ecumenical relations was eventually realized in the Byzantine Rite of Catholicism. Saint Josephat, the martyr, is the first Eastern saint to be formally canonized.

#493   white

WED 13 Memorial of Saint Frances Xavier Cabrini, Virgin

Lectionary for Mass

◆ FIRST READING: Wisdom voices a foreboding warning to the kings and rulers of the earth, reminding them that they are accountable to God the Most High for all of their judgments. What is more, they will be subject to a perhaps more rigorous scrutiny than the poor and lowly. Those in power should seek the Lord's instruction manifest in his words and in his law.

◆ RESPONSORIAL PSALM 82: Our responsorial antiphon, a prayer for God to come and judge the earth, is the last verse of Psalm 82. In the preceding verses, God addresses those

who judge unjustly and admonishes them about what they should be doing as people in power (first stanza today). They must remember that they, too, will be subject to death and judgment (second stanza).

◆ GOSPEL: Lepers were among the outcasts in Israel because of their physical defilement (see Leviticus 13) and the fear of contagion. Thus, they stand at a distance from Jesus. Jesus's healing acts are another example of the kindness and love of the Lord. Note that the leper was shunned both because of his physical affliction and ethnic origin (he was a Samaritan) is the one who returns to give thanks.

The Roman Missal

The Collect is found in the Proper of Saints, with the remaining prayers drawn from the Common of Virgins: For One Virgin or the Common of Holy Men and Women: For Those Who Practiced Works of Mercy. The Collect echoes the parable of the Last Judgment in Matthew 25. We pray that we may follow Saint Frances's example of "concern for the stranger, / the sick, and all those in need," so that, like her, we may "see Christ / in all the men and women we meet."

Today's Saint

Frances Xavier Cabrini was the first American citizen to be canonized. Born in Italy, she studied to be a teacher and wanted to join a religious community but was rejected because of ill health. When the orphanage she managed closed in 1880, Frances and six others took religious vows and founded the institute of the Missionary Sisters of the Sacred Heart of Jesus. Her work brought her to the attention of Leo XIII, who sent her to New York in 1889 to minister to Italian immigrants. Saint Frances founded institutions all over the United States of America, as well as in

South America and Europe. She died in Chicago in 1917.

THU 14 #494 green
Weekday

Lectionary for Mass

◆ FIRST READING: Today's reading offers a beautiful description of the attributes of divine wisdom. Note that the feminine pronoun is used for Wisdom as the word is feminine in gender in Greek (the book was written in Greek). Wisdom's work among humankind is timeless, "passing into holy souls from age to age she produces friends of God and prophets" (Wisdom 7:27). May we be found among them.

◆ RESPONSORIAL PSALM 119, the longest Psalm in Scripture, acclaims the wisdom and value of the Law of the Lord. With but one or two exceptions, each verse contains some reference to the Law, under a variety of different names. What attributes of God's word—God's Law, are named today? How does it affect our lives?

◆ GOSPEL: The coming of the kingdom cannot be observed. It is already present in the person of Jesus and in the lives of believers. We await the coming of the Son of Man at the end of time when God's kingdom will be fully manifest.

FRI 15 #495 green
Weekday

Optional Memorial of Saint Albert the Great, Bishop and Doctor of the Church / white

Lectionary for Mass

◆ FIRST READING: The greatness and beauty of creation bear witness to the existence of God, yet sadly, not all people have recognized it. Instead, they reckoned one or another creature as god. How could

they not find God in the marvelous things he has made? May we not be among those who fail to recognize the Creator in the work of his hands.

◆ RESPONSORIAL PSALM 19: In this hymn of praise, creation speaks the praises of God through its very existence. Its message extends throughout the world, indeed, throughout the universe.

◆ GOSPEL: Today's First Reading and Responsorial Psalm can be heard as a call to mindfulness. Today's Gospel, on the other hand, draws on the stories of Noah and Lot and their contemporaries to warn about inattentiveness and its consequences. Let us not take God's call, God's commands, and the judgment to come for granted.

Today's Saint

To the great disappointment of his father, Saint Albert the Great (1206–1280), known as "the universal doctor," entered the Dominican order where he was recognized for his acumen. Ahead of his time, he believed that learning did not take place in a vacuum; one must be an interdisciplinary learner. He loved the world of academia, studying everything from the natural sciences to the connection between reason and experience, and more. As a prestigious teacher, he had the privilege of instructing and mentoring Saint Thomas Aquinas, author of the *Summa Theologiae*. Toward the end of his life, he began to experience memory loss and dementia, which led to his gradual demise. He was declared a Doctor of the Church by Pope Pius XI.

SAT 16 #496 green
Weekday

Optional Memorial of Saint Margaret of Scotland / white; Saint Gertrude, Virgin / white; Blessed Virgin Mary / white

Lectionary for Mass

◆ FIRST READING: Wisdom's words speak of the night of the first Passover, when God's angel came down to the earth. The first-born of the Egyptians who had oppressed God's people died while the Israelites were spared and subsequently passed through the waters of the sea into freedom. The author of Wisdom describes the Israelites as frolicking with joy in praise of their Creator (see Exodus 15:1–21, note especially verses 20–21).

◆ RESPONSORIAL PSALM 105 recounts the history of Israel. The verses chosen for today fittingly pertain to the Passover-Exodus event. Note the joy and celebration in the last line of the last stanza!

◆ GOSPEL: Perseverance in prayer is the instruction Jesus's disciples receive in today's Gospel. The parable serves to illustrate the fact that if even a mortal judge yields to the persistent pleas of the widow, the immortal God will certainly respond to the pleas of his chosen ones.

Today's Saints

Saint Margaret of Scotland (1045–1093), the wife of King Malcolm III of Scotland, managed to raise eight children while promoting Church reform, especially in the area of liturgical practice. As a woman of great faith, she founded and restored monasteries, provided hospitality to pilgrims, spoke out on behalf of the falsely accused, and fed the poor from her own dining table. All of her charitable activity was grounded in a strong prayer life.

Saint Gertrude the Great (1256–1302) was a nun at the Benedictine monastery of Helfta, the abbey where two other great female spiritual writers lived: Mechtilde of Magdeburg and Saint Mechtilde (Matilda von Hackeborn-Wippra). Through prayer she was graced with many mystical and ecstatic experiences, which are recorded in the five-volume *Legatus divinae pietatis*, commonly called *The Life and Revelations of Saint Gertrude the Great*. Her spirituality focused on the humanity of Christ and was characterized by a strong devotion to the Sacred Heart of Jesus. According to many scholars, Saint Gertrude's writings easily compare with those of other influential mystics, such as Saint Teresa of Avila.

#159   green

☀ 17 Thirty-third Sunday in Ordinary Time

Orientation

The theme of suffering and redemption go hand in hand in Christian theology. Good Friday leads to Easter Sunday. Death to sinfulness leads to Christ's invitation to the fullness of life. In the same way, Christ describes the end times being preceded by turmoil and trials. Whatever we may face, our faith in Jesus Christ teaches us to trust that his redeeming love will always win out at the end. This is true for the end times and for the daily struggles and trials we face in our lives. Sustaining hope in our everyday ups and downs helps us to mature in

faith as we await the return of Christ at the end of time.

Lectionary for Mass

◆ FIRST READING: The day of the Lord will be a day of judgment and vindication: judgment against Israel's enemies and Israelites who were unfaithful, and vindication for all who were faithful. It will be a time of healing and wholeness. That day is coming soon, says the prophet Malachi.

◆ RESPONSORIAL PSALM 98: The coming of the Lord who brings justice and judgment is reason for all the earth to break forth into joy-filled songs of praise.

◆ SECOND READING: The Thessalonians are to imitate Paul's example in working for their livelihood to avoid being a burden on anyone. They are to be focused on the Lord Jesus and the work that is theirs, not dissipated in their thoughts and actions.

◆ GOSPEL: Speculation about the end-time has been around for a long time. When will it happen? What signs will precede it? People have always wanted certainty about it. In today's Gospel, Jesus warns his listeners against false prophets and mistaken signs. With foreboding words, he tells his disciples that before the end comes, they will suffer and be persecuted because of his name—even by members of their own families. He assures the disciples of his presence with them and promises that through perseverance they will save their lives.

The Roman Missal

We ask God for the grace of devoted service, for only in serving the "author of all that is good" is "full and lasting happiness" to be found (Collect).

The Prayer over the Offerings echoes the Collect: We ask for "the

grace of being devoted" to God, and "the prize of everlasting happiness."

We have done what Christ commanded us to do "in memory of him." We pray that this Eucharistic sharing "may bring us growth in charity" (Prayer after Communion).

Other Ideas

Decide what three things you would do differently in your life if you knew for sure you had only three months to live. Fully expecting that you will have 100 years to live, do those three things anyway.

#497   green

MON 18 Weekday

Optional Memorials of the Dedication of the Basilicas of Saints Peter and Paul, Apostles #679 / white; Saint Rose Philippine Duchesne, Virgin / white

Lectionary for Mass

◆ FIRST READING: We begin reading from the books of Maccabees which recount events during the time of the Greek rule of Palestine beginning in the fourth century before Christ. By the second century, it had become a time of "terrible affliction" for the Jews. The Greek influence was so strong that some of the Jewish people abandoned the ways of their ancestors and became more and more acculturated and sympathetic to the Gentile way of life. At one point, King Antiochus Epiphanes promulgated a decree that all the citizens should adopt his religious practices and even went so far as to erect an altar of Zeus (the chief god of the Greeks) in the temple precincts, an "abomination" of the holy place. Scrolls of the Law were destroyed; those who observed Jewish laws and customs were put to death. Many willingly chose death, rather than disobey God's Law.

◆ RESPONSORIAL PSALM: Psalm 119 acclaims the Law of the Lord as a way of—and to—life. The verses which are the stanzas of today's response focus on the oppression experienced by those who strive to be faithful.

◆ GOSPEL: The man in today's Gospel might have been blind, but he knew who Jesus was and what he could do. He relentlessly calls out for mercy. Jesus restores his sight not only on the physical level, but in the depth of his being. He then follows Jesus as a disciple.

Today's Optional Memorial

There are four major basilicas in Rome, and each of them has an observance on the Church's universal calendar: Saint Mary Major on August 5, Saint John Lateran on November 9, and now the Basilicas of Saint Peter and Saint Paul. It is not so much the church buildings we are honoring, of course, as the saints to whom they are dedicated. The proper readings for today's memorial focus our attention on the special grace God gave all believers through two imperfect, impetuous, but exceptional men: Peter and Paul.

Today's Saint

Beginning her life as a nun in the Order of the Visitation in France, Saint Rose Philippine Duchesne (1769–1852) eventually joined the Society of the Sacred Heart, founded by Saint Madeleine Sophie Barat. Due to her missionary zeal, she was sent, along with five other sisters, to St. Louis, Missouri, to care for the poor and educate Native Americans. Under her leadership, the sisters established numerous schools and orphanages. She is remembered for her remarkable work, including evangelization and catechesis with Native Americans, particularly the Potawatomi people. Recognizing her extraordinary ministry, amazing ability to navigate difficulties,

and profound spirituality, a contemporary said, "She was the Saint Francis of Assisi of the Society."

T U E **19** #498 green **Weekday**

Lectionary for Mass

◆ FIRST READING: Eleazar, a 90 year-old Jewish man, chooses death rather than dishonor and disobey the Law of the Lord. He was very much aware of the example that he could be for those who were young, showing them "how to die willingly and generously for the revered and holy laws." He was a martyr who suffered joyfully for the sake of God's covenant.

◆ RESPONSORIAL PSALM 3: As with yesterday's Psalm, the Lord is acclaimed as the source of strength and endurance for those who strive to be faithful to God's Law. The psalmist expresses confidence in God's deliverance despite the mockeries of his oppressors.

◆ GOSPEL: Zaccheus is certainly an enterprising man in more ways than one. Like Elezar, Zaccheus offers us an example of one who is firm in his convictions and acts on them. Zaccheus's behavior after his encounter with Jesus evokes the description of the just person in today's Psalm.

W E D **20** #499 green **Weekday**

Lectionary for Mass

◆ FIRST READING: This is the account of eight Jewish martyrs, a mother and her seven sons, who attest to their belief in the resurrection of the dead. Today's text focuses on the mother, her courage and fidelity in exhorting her sons to choose death—and thus life—rather than disobey the Law of the Lord.

◆ RESPONSORIAL PSALM 17: Today's Psalm is a prayer for deliverance. The psalmist asserts his fidelity and expresses confidence in God's vindication. Notice the word "waking" in the last line of the third stanza. Juxtaposed with today's First Reading, we can hear the reference to living in the presence of the Lord after the "sleep" of death.

◆ GOSPEL: Jesus makes his way to Jerusalem where death awaits him. He is the nobleman of the parable who is despised by his own people who face imminent destruction. Those servants who remain faithful will be rewarded abundantly. The negligent, idle, or fearful ones will lose what they have.

T H U **21** #500 white **Memorial of the Presentation of the Blessed Virgin Mary**

Orientation

According to tradition, Mary spent her life at the temple from the time she was a little girl. Her parents, Joachim and Anna, presented their young daughter to the temple for service and study, in thanksgiving for the great gift God had given them through her. Today's memorial celebrates this occasion. It also calls us to think about the ways we prepare and ready ourselves for Jesus Christ in our lives. Mary, conceived in grace, was prepared to carry the Son of God, but her time at the temple helped form her mind and heart. Likewise, intentionally nurturing our relationship with God builds on the grace God offers each of us. What are some ways you can ready yourself to encounter Jesus Christ today?

Lectionary for Mass

◆ FIRST READING: We meet Mattathias, a leader and respected man in the city of Modein, who refuses bribes from the king's officers. They want him to comply with the king's command and thus disobey the Law of the Lord. Mattathias and his sons, leaving all possessions behind, flee to the mountains, and his supporters to the desert, so they can live faithfully according to the Law of the Lord.

◆ RESPONSORIAL PSALM 50: Those who live righteously will experience the saving power of the Lord in their lives! Psalm 50 depicts God gathering all peoples for judgment. The verses chosen for today are addressed to those who are just and faithful, and exhort them to offer sacrifices of praise and to honor their vows to the Lord.

◆ GOSPEL: Jesus weeps for Jerusalem. The people have failed to recognize the presence of the one sent by God or accept his message. Destruction, not peace, awaits them. The Romans destroyed Jerusalem in the year 70 AD.

The Roman Missal

The Collect for the memorial is found in the Proper of Saints, with the remaining prayers drawn from the Common of the Blessed Virgin Mary.

F R I **22** #501 red
Memorial of Saint Cecilia, Virgin and Martyr

Lectionary for Mass

◆ FIRST READING: The Lectionary omits the account of the death of Mattathias and the succession of his son, Judas, called Maccabeus, as the leader of the people. Judas's victories in war against the Gentiles are also omitted. Following their victories, Judas and his followers turned their attention to the purification and rededication of the temple after its abomination by the Gentiles. Today's reading tells of the celebration of this event. We know it today as the Jewish Festival of Hanukkah.

◆ CANTICLE: Today's response is a hymn of praise from the first book of Chronicles, originally sung on the occasion of King David entrusting his son Solomon with the precious metals and stones to be used in the construction of God's temple. It is a fitting response to the account of the temple's rededication.

◆ GOSPEL: The first thing Jesus does upon entering Jerusalem, at least as Luke tells it, is to go to the temple, that most sacred site for Jews, the place where God is invisibly present among his people. Sacrifices are offered regularly. Accordingly, there are numerous sellers of animals for sacrifice and money-changers for the convenience of those traveling at a distance. Profit, however, has superseded service and Jesus drives them out. We also hear in today's text about the growing animosity of Jewish religious leaders toward Jesus.

The Roman Missal

The Collect for the Memorial of Saint Cecilia is found in the Proper of Saints, with the remaining prayers drawn from the Common of Martyrs or the Common of Virgins. We pray that the story of this Virgin Martyr, "devoutly handed down," may continue to inspire us (Collect).

Today's Saint

According to legend, Saint Cecilia (third century) was beheaded because she would not forsake her vow of virginity. She is the patron of musicians, singers, and poets. Her association with music is most likely related to a line from her Passio (the oldest historical account of her life), where she is said to have sung "in her heart to Christ" as the musicians played at her wedding. Upon its foundation in 1584, the Academy of Music in Rome declared her the patron of musicians. Saint Cecelia's popularity grew so much that several hymns were written in

her honor, and her life is referenced in Chaucer's *The Canterbury Tales*.

S A T **23** #502 green
Weekday

Optional Memorials of Saint Clement I, Pope and Martyr / red; Saint Columban, Abbot / white; Blessed Miguel Agustín Pro, Priest and Martyr / red; Blessed Virgin Mary / white

Lectionary for Mass

◆ FIRST READING: Today's reading recounts King Antiochus's reaction upon hearing of the defeat of his armies in Palestine and of the rebuilding of the temple in Jerusalem. Things were not going well for the king at this point. His attempt to capture the Persian city of Elymais to obtain its wealth as booty had failed as well. He became sick with grief, even to the point of death. According to the biblical author, Antiochus recognized that his failures were punishment for his actions in Jerusalem.

◆ RESPONSORIAL PSALM 9: Today's song of thanksgiving for victory in battle could well have been sung by God's people after the defeat of the Gentiles and the rebuilding of the temple. Note how the third stanza echoes what Antiochus realized about his armies in the First Reading: their own actions had brought destruction upon themselves. Nevertheless, God does not abandon those who are his own.

◆ GOSPEL: The Sadducees were a sect within Judaism who, unlike the Pharisees, did not believe in resurrection. The Sadducees held only to what was revealed in the law of Moses, and resurrection was a later development in understanding. What is most important in today's text is what is said about the nature of our resurrected life: we will be gloriously transformed like the angels.

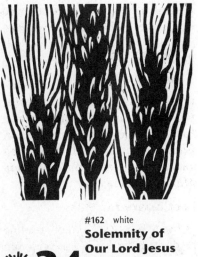

#162   white

☀ 24 Solemnity of Our Lord Jesus Christ, King of the Universe

Orientation

The Solemnity of Our Lord Jesus Christ, King of the Universe is the last Sunday of the liturgical year, bringing us full circle toward Advent hope. Christ reigns, enthroned in heaven, King of heaven and earth for all time. After listening to stories of his life and ministry through Ordinary Time, our parting image is that of majesty. Like a great rose window of a medieval cathedral, Christ the King reminds us that Jesus is the source and center of our lives, and his divine power extends over all of creation. As Saint Paul tells us, "Christ is before all things, and in him all things hold together. May the Holy Spirit help us today to open our hearts to Christ, and invite him to reign there now and forever."

Lectionary for Mass

◆ FIRST READING: In today's reading, all the tribes of Israel acclaim David as King, thus unifying the country. When God chooses David as king, he is shepherding his father Jesse's flocks. As king, he is to shepherd God's people. Mention is also made of David's military prowess during the reign of Saul.

◆ RESPONSORIAL PSALM 122: Today's Psalm acclaims Jerusalem as the home of all the Israelites and a sign of their unity. David and his house, or descendants, receive special mention in the last stanza. In its original context, Psalm 122 was a hymn sung by pilgrims as they made their way to the temple for worship.

◆ SECOND READING: Today's text is part of Paul's prayer for the Colossians in the first chapter of the letter. It is likewise an exhortation to them: they are to be thankful that as believers they belong to the kingdom of God's beloved Son, in whom and through whom they are redeemed and reconciled to God. Verses 15 to 20 are from an early Christian hymn which acclaims Jesus as the image of God and the one in and through whom all things were created. He is the firstborn from the dead in a new creation, and head of his Body the Church, to which the Colossians belong.

◆ GOSPEL: When he was crucified, Jesus was mocked as "King of the Jews" by those who failed to recognize him as the promised messiah, the Christ or "anointed" one. One of the criminals crucified with Jesus recognized his innocence and begged to be remembered when he entered his kingdom. His prayer was answered when Jesus assured him that he would be with him in Paradise that very day.

The Roman Missal

The Collect is a prayer for freedom. God's will is to restore all things in Christ. We pray that all of creation, "set free from slavery," may serve God and praise him forever

Through the sacrifice of reconciliation, we ask "the gifts of unity and peace" for all the nations (Prayer over the Offerings).

Jesus Christ was anointed "eternal Priest and King." As priest, he offered himself on the altar of the cross "to bring us peace"; as King, he subjected "all created things" to his rule, that he might offer to his Father "a kingdom of truth and life . . . / holiness and grace . . . / justice, love and peace" (Preface).

As we honor Christ as King of the universe, we pray that we may glory "in obedience" to him and come to live with him in the kingdom of heaven (Prayer after Communion).

Other Ideas

Because this solemnity marks the end of the liturgical year, in a sense today is New Year's Eve. Celebrate with friends the joy of being subjects of so great and so good a king. Even though it is traditionally associated with Epiphany and Mardi Gras, find a recipe and bake a "king's cake" in honor of Christ the King.

#503   green

M O N 25 Weekday / Thirty-fourth or Last Week in Ordinary Time

Optional Memorial of Saint Catherine of Alexandria, Virgin and Martyr / red

Lectionary for Mass

◆ FIRST READING: We begin the Book of Daniel, our readings for this last week of Ordinary Time. With the destruction of Jerusalem, many Israelites were taken to Babylon in captivity. Among them were the nobility who had professional training or special expertise in various crafts and skills. Today we are introduced to Daniel and his companions, four young Jewish men determined to remain faithful to the laws of Israel despite their privileged status as those destined for the king's service. God rewarded them for their fidelity with good health, knowledge of literature and science, and more wisdom than their peers. Daniel, in addition, had the gift of interpreting dreams.

◆ CANTICLE: Today's response, from the Book of Daniel, is the hymn of praise sung by the Daniel and his companions from the midst of the fiery furnace. Today's verses focus on God, enthroned in heavenly glory.

◆ GOSPEL: Today's Gospel is the beautiful story of the widow whose offering to the temple treasury came from the very little she had to live on. Needy herself, she freely gave of what she had to God.

The Roman Missal

Prayers for the ferial day are found in the Proper of Time for the Thirty-Fourth or Last Week in Ordinary Time.

Today's Saint

Saint Catherine of Alexandria: This fourth-century Christian woman lived in Alexandria, Egypt, during the reign of the Roman emperor Maxentius. Legend says that Catherine bravely confronted the emperor about his pagan beliefs. Maxentius gathered 50 pagan philosophers and challenged her to a debate. Her arguments were so convincing that many of the philosophers converted to Christianity. He then threatened to kill her unless she married him and renounced her faith. She refused and was condemned to death on a spiked wheel, but the wheel fell apart when she touched it. She was then beheaded, and legend says that angels carried her to Mount Sinai. She has been venerated since the tenth century.

**T
U 26 #504   green
E   Weekday**

Lectionary for Mass

◆ FIRST READING: The Babylonian King Nebuchadnezzar had a dream which greatly disturbed him. He sought an interpretation from the wise men of his kingdom, but was unwilling to tell them the dream first, lest they "make up" an interpretation. If they were truly men of wisdom, he thought, they would know what he had dreamt and he could be sure of the validity of their interpretation. He threatened them with death if they failed. None, of course, succeeded. When the king's death order was to be carried out, Daniel and his companions were to be among those killed. When Daniel found out why, he begged the king to give him time to interpret the dream. Daniel succeeded, with the help of the God of Israel. Today's reading recounts both the dream and Daniel's interpretation.

◆ CANTICLE: Our response is again from Daniel's hymn of praise. Today's stanzas call on various creatures and elements of nature to praise the Lord.

◆ GOSPEL: There are two foci in today's Gospel. The first is the destruction of the temple, which took place in the year 70 AD. The second is the terrifying signs that will precede the end time.

**W
E 27 #505   green
D   Weekday**

Lectionary for Mass

◆ FIRST READING: The account of Daniel's remarkable gift of interpretation continues, but during the reign of another king. This time the challenge for Daniel is to interpret a mysterious event that happened during a banquet when the sacred vessels from the temple in Jerusalem were being used by the Babylonians as ordinary drinking cups and thus profaned. As Daniel so wisely points out, the mysterious hand and the writing on the wall are God's judgment against the king.

◆ CANTICLE: More elements of creation are called upon to praise the Lord in these verses from the canticle of Daniel 3. This praise of God the Creator stands in stark contrast with the Babylonians' worship of their idols mentioned in the First Reading.

◆ GOSPEL: Today's Gospel speaks of afflictions Jesus's followers will endure, such as betrayal by family and friends and civil persecution, all because of their belief in Jesus's name. Jesus assures his followers of his continuing presence and protection.

**T
H 28 #506; #943–947   green
U   Weekday**

Optional proper Mass for Thanksgiving Day / white (U.S.A.)

Lectionary for Mass

◆ FIRST READING: Today's reading begins with Daniel 6:12, so a reading of the first 11 verses of this chapter would be most helpful in understanding the context. During the reign of King Darius, Daniel had attained a very high position in the kingdom, and his reputation for wisdom was unequalled. As a result, he was envied by his colleagues and subordinates who contrived a scheme to be rid of him. They had the king issue a decree prohibiting the petitioning of any god or any human being other than the king for a period of 30 days. Quite easily, they caught the pious Daniel at prayer—a clear violation of the king's decree—and here the reading begins. Despite the king's desire to save Daniel from the fate of the lions' den, he was bound to carry out the punishment. We hear today how God preserved Daniel's life. As a result, the king proclaimed that Daniel's God was to be reverenced.

◆ CANTICLE: Still more of creation is called upon to give praise to God in these verses from the canticle in Daniel 3.

◆ GOSPEL: In an apocalyptic tone, Luke describes the destruction of Jerusalem by the Romans. God's people must wait for the end time when cosmic signs will herald the coming of the Son of Man. Believers should not fear these signs, for they announce the time of their redemption. Victorious in their struggle, they have every reason to stand up straight (a posture of freedom) when facing the judgment at the end time.

The Roman Missal

There is a complete set of prayers for Thanksgiving Day, including a Preface, found at the end of November in the Proper of Saints. On this national holiday, we give thanks to God for his countless gifts of love and his infinite goodness, and we pray that our hearts may be open "to have concern / for every man, woman, and child" (Collect). With the gifts God has given comes a "responsibility and commitment" to advance the dignity of others (Preface), and to "share with them / the good things of time and eternity" (Prayer after Communion).

#507 green

Weekday

Lectionary for Mass

◆ FIRST READING: Today's reading from Daniel has special significance since it gives us important Old Testament background for the figure of the Son of Man, a title used in the Gospels with reference to Jesus. This section of Daniel belongs to a genre of writing known as "apocalyptic." (The word means "revelation.") Apocalyptic literature consists of highly symbolic revelations about the end of time. Today's text recounts a nighttime vision given to Daniel. The four beasts represent different kingdoms that are ultimately conquered when brought to judgment before the "Ancient

One" (God). Perhaps readers will recognize imagery evoking other descriptions of God's heavenly throne (see, for example, Isaiah 6:2.4; Ezekiel 1; Revelation 4:1–6). The one "like" a son of man, is one like a human being (see Psalm 8:5). In Daniel's vision, this Son of Man is exalted by God and given dominion, power, and glory. In New Testament traditions, this points to the exaltation of the risen and glorified Lord.

◆ CANTICLE: Still more verses from the canticle of praise in Daniel 3. The juxtaposition of verses with references to the sea and the animals which praise the Lord stand in stark contrast with the arrogant beasts of Daniel's vision!

◆ GOSPEL: Today's Gospel is a continuation of Jesus's discourse on the end time. He speaks of signs that will warn people that the end time, the coming of the kingdom of God in all its fullness, is near. Luke's audience, like other Christians of their day, believed that the end time would be within their lifetime.

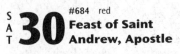

#684 red

Feast of Saint Andrew, Apostle

Lectionary for Mass

◆ FIRST READING: A twofold emphasis is heard in today's reading. The first is on the importance of professing faith in Jesus as Lord (God) and as raised from the dead, if one is to be saved. The second is on the necessity of someone preaching the Gospel so that others may hear and believe. Without hearing, there can be no faith. Today, we celebrate the feast of the Apostle Saint Andrew, one of the first to go out to all the earth to proclaim the Gospel.

◆ RESPONSORIAL PSALM 19: There is a choice for the antiphon: a verse from the Psalm, which celebrates the righteousness of God's judgments, particularly as made known in the law, which the body of the Psalm acclaims; or a verse from John's account of the Gospel which acclaims the word of the Lord as the source of life.

◆ GOSPEL: Today's Gospel is the call of Andrew, the fisherman, whose mission will be to make a catch for the Lord through the proclamation of the Gospel. Notice the immediacy of the response of Andrew and the others to Jesus's call.

The Roman Missal

The prayers for this feast are found in the Proper of Saints. The Gloria is said or sung today. One of the Prefaces of the Apostles is used. We pray that Andrew "may be for us a constant intercessor" (Collect). The Prayer after Communion alludes to the words of Saint Paul (2 Corinthians 4:10): we "carry in our body the Death of Christ," as the Apostle did, and therefore we hope "to live with him in glory."

Today's Saint

Saint Andrew was the first of the Twelve to meet Jesus. He was one of the two disciples of John the Baptist who saw John point out Jesus and say, "Behold the Lamb of God" (John 1:36). Andrew told his brother, Peter, "We have found the Messiah," and brought him to Jesus. Saint Andrew is venerated as the protoclete, or first-called, by the Eastern Churches. Tradition says that he may have preached in parts of Asia Minor and Greece before being crucified on an X-shaped cross. The Scots claim Andrew as their patron saint, and his cross is on their flag.

The Vigil Fire:
A Call to Encounter Christ

Kristopher Seaman

Fearful. Terrified. Scared. These describe feelings that I had—and probably a good many children have—toward the darkness. Fear of the darkness as the lights went out for sleep, scared as the lights went out during a terrible storm. Then, as many candles were lit during the storm or the night light slowly brightened, a glow began to push out the darkness, and a sense of relief and peace set in. In the Church, there is an annual celebration where darkness has a pretty significant role to play, and that is the Easter Vigil.

As night descends on the evening of Holy Saturday (though in liturgical time it marks the beginning of Sunday), people gather outside the worship space, as a large, roaring fire lights up the night: faces glow, the heat warms those in colder climates, and passersby look in wonder at what is going on. Then, the vigil officially begins with the *Lucernarium*, which basically means a vigil or service of light. The large, roaring fire evokes the "fire of [God's] glory" (*The Roman Missal*, 344). Fire is a natural symbol that conveys transformation. Fire provides heat in the cold and light in the darkness, and can bring destruction to houses and forests. Yet the fire of a flame atop a candle also can dispel the fear of the night for a child. Fire also purifies. The "fire" of a fever will try to "burn off" an infection and that used to boil water purifies baby bottles. While our human inclinations to fire might be both fear and terror, fire also can provide resources for life to survive, grow, and be transformed.

At the Easter Vigil, the people of God gather to "vigil," to stay awake while praying and waiting for God to "inflame us" with his transforming light and warmth. The prayer texts of the blessing of the fire from *The Roman Missal* pray that this "fire of [God's] glory, / sanctify + this new fire, we pray, / and grant that, / by these paschal celebrations, / we may be so inflamed with heavenly desires, / that with minds made pure / we may attain festivities of unending splendor. / Through Christ our Lord. Amen."

This fire is blessed, so that we might be blessed through the evening and grow in discipleship, that is, to be "inflamed with heavenly desires." As disciples not completely free from sin, we must continue to grow, as we encounter and participate in the Triune God who not only inflames us, but also works to purify us, and calls us to follow the pilgrimage of life led by the light of God's glory and splendor.

Next, the paschal candle is lit from the newly blessed fire. This candle represents Christ Jesus, who gave up his life so that life might triumph. Candles likewise "give up their life," or decrease, so that the flame may continue to provide light and warmth. Out of death, God raised Christ from death to newness of life. The candle that represents Christ shows forth the God who transforms death into newness of life.

The flame of the candle is shared among those gathered who hold candles/tapers. In Baptism, we were given the flame of Christ within us as we were immersed in the baptismal font and then we (or our sponsors/godparents on our behalf) accepted the baptismal candle lit from the Easter fire. As the flame is shared among those gathered, brightness grows, and it is as we hear proclaimed at the Vigil: "a fire into many flames divided, / yet never dimmed by sharing of its light." The sharing of Christ's light does not dim, but rather the opposite: it multiplies and grows and begins to push out the darkness, which is sin, evil, hurt, and pain. This same flame we received in Baptism is shared with others, when we tend to their pain, hurt, and fears, so that new life might emerge. In truth, this is Christ the Light working in, with, and through us to bring about his transforming grace to those around us.

The Easter Proclamation—the Exsultet—is chanted by the deacon (or in the absence of a deacon, a cantor or other minister). The proclamation praises and thanks God, who through Christ the Light, "dispels wickedness, washes faults away, / restores innocence to the fallen, and joy to mourners, drives out hatred, fosters concord, and brings down the mighty."

The fire of the Easter Vigil calls us to encounter Christ the Light. In Baptism, we received Christ's light and are called through our earthly pilgrimage to share Christ's light with one another so that life might flourish.

KRISTOPHER W. SEAMAN, DMIN, is the director of the Office of Worship for the Diocese of Gary.

Singing the Exsultet

John Mark Klaus

The Easter Proclamation, commonly called the Exsultet, "tells by means of a great poetic text the whole Easter mystery."[1] Ideally, it is to be sung by the deacon at the solemn beginning of the Easter Vigil. A priest or cantor may also sing the Exsultet if a deacon is not available. (If a cantor sings the Exsultet, in place of a deacon or priest, some parts are omitted.)

The composition of the Exsultet can be thought of as similar to that of a Preface to the Eucharistic Prayer.

In the third edition of *The Roman Missal* both the text and musical notation have changed slightly from the 1985 edition of *The Sacramentry*. The Exsultet has the same structure and character as previously, but the additional wording contains more biblical images.

HISTORY AND FORM ANALYSIS

In preparing to sing the Exsultet, it is important first to look at the structure. The composition can be thought of as similar to that of a Preface of the Eucharistic Prayer. A main difference, though, is that the Exsultet has five sections. It moves from the introduction to a greeting, to the "this is the night" section, "extolling the candle," and finally the conclusion. The structure is similar to the poetic sequences in the Lectionary, i.e., at Pentecost and others.

The words of the Exsultet in the third edition of the Missal differ slightly from the 1970 and 1985 editions. Returning in this edition is the sentence telling of the work of the bees that had been omitted in the 1985 edition. The most marked difference in the Exsultet occurs in the final part, with three changes. Two of the added parts are about the bees and another part, earlier in the text, has been moved down to the end section from its 1970 and 1985 Sacramentary location.

PRACTICAL SUGGESTIONS

Deacons learning the new version of the Exsultet will recognize similar wordings and chant melodies from the 1985 version, but with additions to both. Learning the Exsultet can be challenging but rewarding for the deacon, and a well-sung Exsultet brings great solemnity to the vigil. This chant is always unaccompanied and should not be sung at a slow tempo. Its proclamation requires confident singing.

Several recordings are available from publishers demonstrating the singing of the Exsultet for the deacon to listen to and practice. (*Learning the Chants of the Missal, Part II: Essential Presidential Prayers and Texts*, as chanted by J. Michael Joncas, published by LTP, includes the singing of the Exsultet.) Since the Exsultet is more complex than other proclamations deacons are familiar singing, I would suggest beginning practicing the setting the first week of Lent. Such early practice will help the deacon be comfortable with the setting by the Easter Vigil, making it less likely that he will revert to the more familiar previous chant and wording.

During practice, find a good pitch in the middle range of your voice. It would be a good idea to ask your parish music director to help you learn to sing this new proclamation. Many directors will be glad to assist you in practicing it. They can also help you find a comfortable range, which may not be the pitch written in *The Roman Missal*.

Since the Exsultet is in five parts, it may be wise to learn one section a week during Lent. Most, but not all, of the sections are dividing by double bars that show the end of a section. The first section ends with the words "this candle's perfect praises." The singing of the words "The Lord be with you" begins section two. Part three begins "This is the night," ending on "brings down the mighty." The fourth section begins "On this, your night of grace," and the fifth section starts with "Therefore O Lord, we pray."

The Exsultet may take time to learn, but it truly can be a spiritually memorable moment for our congregations to experience and cherish each year at the Easter Vigil of the Holy Night. ◆

Note

1. Congregation for Divine Worship. "Circular Letter Concerning the Preparation and Celebration of the Easter Feasts," 16 January 1988. Washington: United States Catholic Conference, 1988. Print.

REV. JOHN MARK KLAUS, TOR, the former director of the Office of Worship for the Diocese of Venice, is the province secretary for the Third Order Regular of St. Francis.

LITURGY TRAINING PUBLICATIONS

The text originally appeared in the March/April 2012 issue of Pastoral Liturgy®. If you like this article, please subscribe to Pastoral Liturgy®.

Singing the Exsultet ©2012 Archdiocese of Chicago, Liturgy Training Publications, 3949 South Racine Avenue, Chicago IL, 60609; 1-800-933-1800, website: www.LTP.org.

Proclaiming Our Story of Faith

Denise C. Thompson

As salvation history is recounted during the readings at the Easter Vigil, the assembly journeys through the millennia, hearing of the blessings God has promised, that our God is like no others, and "you shall be my people, and I will be your God."

Parishes will want to ensure that the proclaimers of these Scriptures approach the ambo ready to proclaim the spirit of these texts. The readers will have spent time prayerfully reflecting on and working with the texts. Anyone who speaks in public realizes the three components to successful presentation: content, preparation, and delivery. If any of these elements is missing, the speech, or in our case, proclamation, will fall short.

In Scripture, content has been provided through the divine inspiration of the Holy Spirit. The other elements are left to the proclaimers. We must prepare carefully and completely to reach the congregation.

Selecting the readers and assigning the readings three to four weeks before Holy Saturday provides ample opportunity for the proclaimers to study and practice. It also allows time for a group rehearsal with all readers present (the deacon as well, if possible). At this rehearsal, the proclaimers will read their readings as if they were at the Vigil. Each proclaimer must be well prepared before the group rehearsal as the group's leader, and other members of the Vigil reading team, will provide encouragement and feedback. The leader can be the lector coordinator, deacon, liturgy director, liturgy coordinator, an experienced lector trainer, or speaking coach familiar with liturgy. Discussing each reading as a group will deepen insights, confirm interpretation of the passages, and strengthen bonds among the readers.

The following practices will aid readers in proclaiming the Scriptures:

Study all nine readings. Just as on Sunday, the proclaimers should be familiar with all of the readings of the liturgy, as they are often connected in topic, theme, or meaning, so at the Easter Vigil should the proclaimers have read each reading. Studying all of the readings will put your reading in perspective in terms of our journey of faith.

Pay close attention to *Workbook for Lectors, Gospel Readers, and Proclaimers of the Word.* It provides excellent background on each of the readings, including geographical and historical commentary, remarks about the theological significance, reflections on how the passages relate to today's events, background on the people in the readings and their relationships to one another, and the author's intentions. It also supplies suggested punctuation considerations, emphasis tips, and pronunciation guidelines.

Consult the Bible and read the complete chapter. Our readings are excerpts from a larger story, letter, book, poem, or Psalm. Go to your Bible, locate the reading, and read all around it to appreciate more fully the bigger picture. This may color your interpretation and help you more easily decide upon the main point of the reading as well as the words or phrases you will emphasize.

Photo by Yvette M. Dostatni

Preparation for proclaiming a reading should include studying all of the Vigil readings.

Write down the reading in your own words. After you think you know what the reading is about, close the book, get out a piece of paper, and write down the reading in your own words as if you were the author. Do not try to memorize it; just understand it so you can meaningfully convey the reading to others. If you cannot do this, go back and find out more about the passage. If you do not understand the reading, you will not be able to proclaim it credibly. Ask for assistance from your lector coordinator, deacon, priest, or fellow lector. They will be happy to help you.

Practice aloud. Be sure to proclaim your reading aloud multiple times to hear how your proclamation sounds. Make sure you are striking the chords you intend. Get used to the sound of your voice and when it is at its best. Call yourself on the phone and proclaim your reading on voicemail, then dial into your voice mail and listen to your reading. Is this what you thought it would sound like? Adjust as necessary. Videotape yourself if you have the equipment. Proclaim aloud for a friend or family member for feedback and practice.

Use the Internet. The Internet has some excellent reading preparation websites. Especially good sites are *www.lectorprep. org, www.lectionary.com,* and the U.S Conference of Catholic Bishops site at *www.usccb.org.* Here you will find the complete *New American Bible* online. You can click on any book of the Bible and find the entire passage with footnotes that help explain the reading. ◆

DENISE C.THOMPSON provides training and formation for lectors, readers, and proclaimers of the Gospel at *www.greatlectors.com.*

LTP

LITURGY TRAINING PUBLICATIONS

The text originally appeared in the January/February 2012 issue of Pastoral Liturgy®. If you like this article, please subscribe to Pastoral Liturgy®.